THE ROUTLEDGE COMPANION TO CULTURAL HISTORY IN THE WESTERN WORLD

T0399783

The Routledge Companion to Cultural History in the Western World is a comprehensive examination of recent discussions and findings in the exciting field of cultural history.

A synthesis of how the new cultural history has transformed the study of history, the volume is divided into three parts – medieval, early modern and modern – that emphasize the way people made sense of the world around them. Contributions cover such themes as material cultures of living, mobility and transport, cultural exchange and transfer, power and conflict, emotion and communication, and the history of the senses. The focus is on the Western world, but the notion of the West is a flexible one. In bringing together 36 authors from 15 countries, the book takes a wide geographical coverage, devoting continuous attention to global connections and the emerging trend of globalization. It builds a panorama of the transformation of Western identities, and the critical ramifications of that evolution from the Middle Ages to the twenty-first century, that offers the reader a wide-ranging illustration of the potentials of cultural history as a way of studying the past in a variety of times, spaces and aspects of human experience.

Engaging with historiographical debate and covering a vast range of themes, periods and places, *The Routledge Companion to Cultural History in the Western World* is the ideal resource for cultural history students and scholars to understand and advance this dynamic field.

Alessandro Arcangeli is Associate Professor of Early Modern History at the University of Verona, Italy, the author of a reference book on cultural history and its methods and a scholar in Renaissance studies. He chaired the International Society for Cultural History from 2013 to 2017.

Jörg Rogge is Academic Director and Adjunct Professor of History, Middle Ages, at the University of Mainz, Germany, and specialized in the history of urban and noble societies. He is the current Chair of the International Society for Cultural History.

Hannu Salmi is Professor of Cultural History at the University of Turku, Finland, Academy Professor for the years 2017–2021 and a historian of the nineteenth and twentieth centuries. He was the first chair of the International Society for Cultural History from 2008 to 2013.

THE ROUTLEDGE COMPANION TO CULTURAL HISTORY IN THE WESTERN WORLD

Edited by Alessandro Arcangeli, Jörg Rogge and Hannu Salmi

Routledge
Taylor & Francis Group

LONDON AND NEW YORK

First published 2020
by Routledge
2 Park Square, Milton Park, Abingdon, Oxon OX14 4RN

and by Routledge
605 Third Avenue, New York, NY 10017

First issued in paperback 2022

Routledge is an imprint of the Taylor & Francis Group, an informa business

Publisher's Note
The publisher has gone to great lengths to ensure the quality of this
reprint but points out that some imperfections in the original copies may
be apparent.

British Library Cataloguing-in-Publication Data
A catalogue record for this book is available from the British Library

Library of Congress Cataloging-in-Publication Data
A catalog record has been requested for this book

ISBN 13: 978-0-367-53033-4 (pbk)
ISBN 13: 978-1-138-64946-0 (hbk)
ISBN 13: 978-1-00-308020-6 (ebk)

DOI: 10.4324/9781003080206

Typeset in Bembo
by Swales & Willis Ltd, Exeter, Devon, UK

CONTENTS

Contents

Contents

ILLUSTRATIONS

Figures

Table

CONTRIBUTORS

Alessandro Arcangeli teaches early modern and cultural history at the University of Verona. He is the author of a reference book on historiography and method (*Cultural History: A Concise Introduction*, 2012) and of specialist studies of attitudes towards dance (with particular emphasis on cultural exchange) and play (*Recreation in the Renaissance*, 2003). Passions and dreams offered some of his recent research topics. He chaired the International Society for Cultural History from 2013 to 2017. As well as the author of various contributions in the field, he is the editor of several forthcoming collective volumes of cultural history (of memory and sport, among other topics).

Franz-Josef Arlinghaus is Professor of History with a particular focus on high and late medieval history at Bielefeld University. Between 1991 and 1999, he worked in different positions at the 'Collaborative Research Centre (SFB) 231' in Münster on pragmatic literacy, where he wrote his PhD thesis on Italian bookkeeping (Datini Company). In 2007, he finished his habilitation on legal proceedings in late medieval Cologne at the University of Kassel. After a short stay as Assistant Professor at the Max Planck Institute for Legal History in Frankfurt, he became full professor at the University of Vechta and in 2009 at Bielefeld. During the academic year 2014/2015 he was Mercator-Fellow at the University of Duisburg-Essen. His current research interests are urban history, history of literacy and rituals as well as history of law and history of individuality.

Jackson W. Armstrong is a Senior Lecturer in History at the University of Aberdeen. He is co-editor (with Andrew Mackillop) of 'Communities, Courts and Scottish Towns', *Urban History*, special section, 44:3 (2017). His book *England's Northern Frontier: Conflict and Local Society in the Fifteenth-Century Marches towards Scotland* will be published by Cambridge University Press. He is principal investigator in the Law in the Aberdeen Council Registers project (Leverhulme Trust, 2016–2019).

Mita Banerjee is Professor of American Studies at the University of Mainz. In her research she has explored issues of citizenship and naturalization (*Color Me White:*

Naturalism/Naturalization in American Literature, 2013), as well as the role of indigenous communities in their quest for sovereignty. More recently, she has explored the promise of American democracy in its relevance not only for political participation, but also for medical care and health equity (*Medical Humanities in American Studies*, 2018). She is co-speaker of the research training group 'Life Sciences, Life Writing: Boundary Experiences of Human Life between Biomedical Explanation and Lived Experience', which is funded by the German Research Foundation.

Antonio Castillo Gómez is a Professor of the History of Written Culture at the University of Alcalá. He is a specialist in writing and reading practices in the early modern Hispanic world. He has published, among other books, *Entre la pluma y la pared. Una historia social de la escritura en los siglos de Oro* (2006); *Leer y oír leer. Ensayos sobre la lectura en los Siglos de Oro* (2016); and *El placer de los libros inútiles y otras lecturas en los Siglos de Oro* (2018). He has been a visiting professor and given invited lectures in many universities in Spain, Europe and Latin America. At present he is preparing a book on writings displayed in Hispanic cities during the sixteenth and seventeenth centuries.

Constance Classen is a cultural historian specializing in the history of the senses. She is the author of *The Museum of the Senses: Experiencing Art and Collections* (2017) and *The Deepest Sense: A Cultural History of Touch* (2012), along with numerous other works. She is also the general editor of the six-volume *Cultural History of the Senses* series (2016) and the editor of *The Book of Touch* (2005). She is a research associate on several international projects investigating the cultural life of the senses, and is currently undertaking research on cognition and perception.

Esther Cohen is Professor Emerita at the Hebrew University of Jerusalem, Israel. Her specialty is medieval European history, with an emphasis on the social and cultural history of the later Middle Ages. She has published on the economics of popular religion, on the history of law and crime and on the history of pain. She is a Fellow of the Netherlands Institute for Advanced Study (NIAS), a Life Member of Clare Hall, Cambridge University and a Fellow of the National Humanities Center.

Steven Conn teaches American history at Miami University in Oxford, Ohio where he is the W. E. Smith Professor. He is the author of six books, most recently *Nothing Succeeds Like Failure: The Sad History of American Business Schools*, numerous articles and many reviews. He has also taught and lectured widely including in Xi'an, China and Warsaw, Poland. Conn is the founding editor of the online magazine *Origins: Current Events in Historical Perspective* which reaches more than 150,000 readers each month.

Brendan Dooley is Professor of Renaissance Studies at University College Cork. He has previously taught at Harvard, Notre Dame and Jacobs University Bremen. He works on the histories of culture and knowledge with reference to Europe and especially to Italy and the Mediterranean world. Publications include *The Social History of Skepticism* (1999), *A Mattress Maker's Daughter: The Renaissance Romance of Don Giovanni de' Medici and Livia Vernazza* (2014), *Angelica's Book and the World of Reading in Late Renaissance Italy* (2016) and, as author/editor, *The Dissemination of News and the Emergence of Contemporaneity in Early Modern Culture* (2010).

James R. Farr is the Germaine Oesterle Professor of History at Purdue University. He is the author of several books and articles on early modern European history, including *Hands of Honor: Artisans and Their World in Dijon, 1550–1650* (1988), *Authority and Sexuality in Burgundy, 1550–1730* (1995), *Artisans in Europe, 1300–1914* (2000), *A Tale of Two Murders: Passion and Power in Seventeenth-Century France* (2005), *The Work of France: Labor and Culture in Early Modern Times* (2008) and *Who Was William Hickey? A Crafted Life in Georgian England and Imperial India* (2020).

Hjalmar Fors is a historian of science, first librarian at the Hagströmer medico-historical library, Karolinska Institutet and an associate researcher at the department of history of science and ideas, Uppsala University. His research is focused primarily on the circulation of knowledge and the spatiality and materiality of science during the early modern period, and in areas such as chemistry, mining, pharmacy and botany. His monograph *The Limits of Matter: Chemistry, Mining and Enlightenment* was published in 2015.

Jan Hirschbiegel studied Ancient, Medieval and Modern History as well as European Ethnology in Kiel. In 1998 he received his PhD in History. From 1995 to 2011 he worked as a research associate on the research project 'Hof und Residenz im spätmittelalterlichen Deutschen Reich (1200–1600)' of the Göttingen Academy of Sciences. His habilitation effected in 2011. His habilitation treatise is entitled 'Nahbeziehungen bei Hof – Manifestationen des Vertrauens. Karrieren in reichsfürstlichen Diensten am Ende des Mittelalters', published in 2015. Since 2012 he has been working as a research associate on the research project 'Residenzstädte im Alten Reich (1300–1800)' of the Göttingen Academy of Sciences. In 2016 he was appointed as Professor. His fields of interests cover medieval travel accounts, theory, cultural, economic and social history of courts, residences and residential cities.

David Howes is a cultural anthropologist based at Concordia University, Montreal. He has conducted field research on the cultural life of the senses in the Massim region of Papua New Guinea, Northwestern Argentina and the Southwestern United States. He is currently directing a project on 'Law and the Regulation of the Senses' and collaborating with new media artist Christopher Salter to produce a series of sense-based art installations. His latest publications include *Ways of Sensing: Understanding the Senses in Society* (co-authored with Constance Classen) and the four-volume *Senses and Sensation: Critical and Primary Sources* compendium.

Hermann Kamp teaches as Professor of Medieval History at the University of Paderborn. His work focuses on the history of late medieval Burgundy, the history of conflict management and conflict resolution and political rituals in the Middle Ages. He has written books about the pious foundations of the Burgundian chancellor Nicolas Rolin, and about peace-making and mediation in the Middle Ages. Most recently, he has dealt with the forms of conquest policy and resistance to foreign rule at that time. In this area he has edited with Martin Kroker a book of collected articles about violence and Christianization under the title sword mission.

Jared Poley is Professor of History at Georgia State University. He is the author of the books *Decolonization in Germany: Weimar Narratives of Colonial Loss and Foreign Occupation* (2005) and *The Devil's Riches: A Modern History of Greed* (2016) and a co-editor of the collections *Conversion and the Politics of Religion in Early Modern Germany* (2012), *Kinship, Community, and Self* (2015), *Migrations in the German Lands, 1500–2000* (2016) and *Money in the German-Speaking Lands* (2017). He is currently working on a history of gambling in nineteenth-century Europe.

Jörg Rogge is Academic Director and Adjunct Professor of History, Middle Ages, at the University of Mainz. His main research interests are the methods and theories of cultural history and the social, military and cultural history of urban and noble societies. He has published on German imperial cities, European high nobility and kings as well as on the methods of cultural history. His publications include the edited collections *Cultural History in Europe: Institutions – Themes – Perspectives* (2011) and *Killing and Being Killed: Bodies in Battle – Perspectives on Fighters in the Middle Ages* (2017). Since 2010 he has been a full member of the philosophical and cultural-historical class of the European Academy of Sciences and Arts (Salzburg). From March to June 2012 he was Fellow at the International Research Center for Cultural Studies (IFK) in Vienna. Currently he is the chair of the International Society for Cultural History.

Linnéa Rowlatt is the Research Coordinator for the International Network for Training, Education, and Research on Culture, based in Ottawa. Her work as an environmental historian focuses on climate history, cultural history and historical anthropology. She has written on the role of climate in early modern society and culture, including the cultural changes introduced by the Protestant Reform. Most recently, she is working with Indigenous communities to explore differences in matrilineal views of nature. In this area, she is currently editing with Marie-Françoise Guédon a book presenting 13 distinct matricultures from around the world.

Willemijn Ruberg is Associate Professor of Cultural History at Utrecht University. Her research interests include the modern history of gender, sexuality and the body as well as the history of forensic medicine and psychiatry in the nineteenth and twentieth centuries. In 2019 she published the book *History of the Body* as part of the Macmillan International/ Red Globe Press's series on Theory and History. In 2017 she received an ERC Consolidator grant for a research project that she is currently leading; the project (running from 2018 to 2023) studies the forensic cultures of four European countries (Russia, Spain, England, the Netherlands) in the period 1930–2000.

Hannu Salmi is Professor of Cultural History at the University of Turku, Finland, and was nominated Academy Professor for the years 2017–2021. His research interests focus on the cultural history of the nineteenth century, media and music history, the history of technology and the history of emotions and the senses. He is also the founding member of the Turku Group for Digital History. He is the author of many books, including *Nineteenth-Century Europe: A Cultural History* (2008), and the editor of *Catastrophe, Gender and Urban Experience, 1648–1920* (with Deborah Simonton, 2017) and *Travelling Notions of*

Culture in Early Nineteenth-Century Europe (with Asko Nivala and Jukka Sarjala, 2016). He was the first chair of the International Society for Cultural History from 2008 to 2013.

Raffaella Sarti teaches early modern history and gender history at the University of Urbino, Italy. She has also worked in Paris, Vienna, Bologna and Murcia. Her studies address the family and material culture; domestic service and care work; Mediterranean slavery; marriage and celibacy; gender and the nation; masculinity; and graffiti. She is the author of approximately 150 publications in nine languages, including *Europe at Home: Family and Material Culture 1500–1800* (2002) and *Servo e padrone, o della (in)dipendenza: un percorso da Aristotele ai nostri giorni* (2015). For more details see www.uniurb.it/it/cdocs/CVPROF/cv-docente_100580.pdf and www.uniurb.it/sarti.

Dominik Schuh finished his studies in history and German literature at the University of Mainz in 2011. From October 2011 to December 2012 he worked as a research assistant at the Research Unit Historical Cultural Sciences in Mainz and began working on his doctoral thesis on lay masculinities in the later Middle Ages. Since January 2013 he has worked at the University Library Mainz on the project 'Academic Integrity', funded by the German Federal Ministry of Education and Research (BMBF). Since October 2018 he has been assistant of the Vice-President for Learning and Teaching at the University of Mainz. His main topics of practice and research include: gender history (history of masculinities), history of chivalry, historical cultural sciences, information literacy, questions of academic integrity and scientific misconduct and teaching of fundamental methods of scientific working.

Pelle Snickars is Professor of Media and Communication Studies – a chair directed towards the digital humanities – at Umeå University, Sweden, where he is also affiliated with the digital humanities hub, Humlab. His research is situated at the intersection between media studies, media history and the digital humanities. Snickars is currently (since 2019) in charge of two major research projects: 'Welfare State Analytics: Text Mining and Modeling Swedish Politics, Media and Culture, 1945–1989' and 'Digital Models: Techno-Historical Collections, Digital Humanities and Narratives of Industrialisation'. At present Snickars is also finishing a book manuscript on the media history of the cultural heritage sector.

Peter N. Stearns is Professor of History at George Mason University. He has written widely in the field of world history, with books on themes such as childhood and globalization. His research has focused on modern social and cultural history in Europe and the United States, with a strong recent interest in emotional patterns. He has published widely in the growing field of emotions history, with books on the histories of emotions like grief and fear. He also works on the nature of history learning.

Marek Tamm is Professor of Cultural History at the School of Humanities at Tallinn University and Head of the Tallinn University Centre of Excellence in Intercultural Studies. His primary research fields are the cultural history of medieval Europe, the theory and history of historiography and cultural memory studies. He has recently published *Rethinking Historical Time: New Approaches to Presentism* (ed. with Laurent Olivier, 2019), *Debating New Approaches to History* (ed. with Peter Burke, 2018) and an edited volume, *Afterlife of Events: Perspectives on Mnemohistory* (2015).

Kirsi Tuohela is a cultural historian working as a university lecturer at the University of Turku. She has focused on the cultural history of the North and written about the history of women's writing, the cultural history of psychiatry, madness and melancholia. Her PhD research analysed women's autobiographical texts on melancholia in late nineteenth-century Scandinavia. Lately she has been involved in two research projects, one of them focusing on the written madness – mental illness in Finnish (and Nordic) autobiographies and novels. The other focuses on the 'inner child' in Finnish autobiographical literature, and how the psychic and its roots are narrated as part of one's inner life and subjectivity.

Gabriel Zeilinger studied History and Scandinavian Philology in Kiel and Oslo and was a research associate at Kiel and Greifswald Universities. After terms as Visiting Professor in Heidelberg and Hagen, he is currently Lecturer in Mediaeval Economic and Social History at the University of Kiel, and also a Fellow of the German Maritime Museum at Bremerhaven. His fields of research cover urban history, warfare and disasters in the Middle Ages. His most recent book is *Verhandelte Stadt. Herrschaft und Gemeinde in der frühen Urbanisierung des Oberelsass vom 12. bis 14. Jahrhundert* (2018).

Dhan Zunino Singh is a CONICET Associate Researcher at the National University of Quilmes, Argentina. He is associate editor of the *Journal of Transport History* and vice-president of the T2M (international association of mobility historians). He works on the history of culture, cities and mobilities, looking at the production of urban infrastructures as well as the daily experience of travelling. He has worked on urban mobility in Buenos Aires in the early twentieth century and the transnational history of the underground railways. He has recently edited a volume about keywords in mobilities studies in Latin America.

ACKNOWLEDGEMENTS

This volume has been in preparation for several years and is based on the cooperation of a large group of historians from 15 countries and three continents. The editors would like to thank all the authors for their valuable contributions and for their patience during the long editorial and publishing process. We would like to express our special gratitude to Kristina Müller–Bongard (Mainz), who has considerably helped in our editorial work. We would also like to thank Philippe Poirrier for his contribution to this volume at its early stage, as well as our home institutions, the Universities of Mainz, Turku and Verona, for their support. We also thank Eve Setch and Zoe Thomson at Routledge for their continuous encouragement and smooth cooperation.

Alessandro Arcangeli, Jörg Rogge, Hannu Salmi
October 2019

GENERAL INTRODUCTION

Alessandro Arcangeli, Jörg Rogge and Hannu Salmi

Cultural history is today established as a respected branch of history.[1] The perspective into the past afforded through the lens of culture has been enrooted in the hermeneutic toolbox of historians of all epochs. A large selection of publications of various types demonstrates this centrality: from collections of important articles[2] and edited volumes taking a specific perspective of cultures in general or those enquiring into specific aspects of culture[3] to case studies.[4] Meanwhile, the interested reader can approach the field of cultural history by accessing introductions, which concentrate more on the theories and methods of cultural history,[5] or by exploring regions and states or epochs.[6]

Aside from the subject matter and topics of research, cultural history has always reflected on its methodological and theoretical premises. Most cultural historians would subscribe to the idea that the choice of focus and method determines the outcome of the research. One of the features of cultural history is its claim to reflect on its own activity – the research concepts, topics and fields – and its track record of doing so. We have to take into consideration that we as historians are influenced by our current social and cultural circumstances.[7]

Therefore, it is part of the state of the art of cultural history today to discuss the history of cultural history and its theoretical and methodological influences as well as current themes and issues.[8] One consequence is that cultural historians consider themselves not just as distanced observers, who are able to write about the past 'as it was': they acknowledge their interest in bringing the past back into our own time, constructing the past with the eyes of our present age. We can hardly escape our norms, prejudices and personal attitudes, even if we try to do this by the use of methodological and theoretical tools.

Cultural history is in more than one respect an interdisciplinary and collaborative effort. On the one hand, a cultural historian has to equip him- or herself with knowledge from different disciplines in the humanities such as anthropology and ethnology. On the other hand, he or she has to rely on the work of colleagues with expertise in other fields and epochs of history. However, if cultural historians want to tackle overall themes or topics – for example, the shaping of Western identities from

1

the Middle Ages to modern times – then they have to cooperate with colleagues from a wide range of research areas. The editors of this volume are an example of the productivity of such an approach, because they have developed the book project in their additional capacity as members of the committee of the International Society for Cultural History (ISCH).[9]

The present book is an attempt to show how considerations of methods and theories have influenced current research in the field of cultural history. The authors of this volume emphasize that the experiences people have contribute to their behaviour and are the basis for their interpretation of the world. People are linked together and with their environment by social practices and various forms of communication. In the process, they generate interpretations and give their living world meaning.

Culture and cultural history are highly problematic terms to define. They have accompanied and marked very different ways of doing history over the past century and a half. Surely the so-called *new cultural history* that emerged in various academic contexts and linguistic domains from the 1970s and 1980s has departed sharply from a narrow understanding of culture typical of previous historical traditions and has adopted a broader meaning, significantly influenced by anthropology. In the present volume, we have rather followed a bottom-up approach to the question of definitions. The individual contributors were not given a prefabricated set of concepts, or a precise indication of the territory they were to map and the tools they were supposed to use on the task. The editors had described the expected contents in short abstracts of the planned chapters, in order to orientate the volume towards an effective and engaging coverage of a wide expanse of topics and problems. In the end, the plan underwent some adjustments, authors brought in their own expertise and tastes in re-shaping their assignment and the notion of culture and cultural history that emerges from the reading of the whole book is the product of interactions between a variety of academic habits and research paths.

What is the result of this polyphony, this flash-mob experience of writing? Some threads and leitmotifs are recognizable, thus offering that bottom-up approach to the definition of the field.

With this volume, we never intended to achieve the comprehensiveness characteristic of a textbook. It is certainly our hope that it may serve, among other purposes, as a wide-ranging illustration of the potentials of cultural history as a way of studying the past in a variety of times, spaces and aspects of human experience, for the use of students, as well as scholars and general readers. Nevertheless, such illustration could only aspire to offer a selection of potential – and actual – areas of research. Whenever desirable and possible, we identified some subject foci and followed their metamorphoses throughout the examined periods. In other cases, a theme emerged as being more relevant to a particular period. Throughout the volume, the reader will have the opportunity to follow some threads, and find aspects of past life structures and experiences that have been highlighted as particularly interesting and examined in their historical dynamics, in the customary dialectics between continuity and change: from the way people made sense of the world to material cultures of living, mobility, cultural exchange and transfer, power and conflict, emotion and communication.

In general, we aimed at striking a balance between the wider generalizations that may assist us in imagining key trends in the past, and the in-depth analysis allowed by the examining of case studies. However, this balance itself is one of the many characteristics that each chapter may to some extent develop in its own way – so the reader will find more theoretical reflection in some places, and more empirical work elsewhere. As a general rule, we avoided a concentration on one cultural area only in any one chapter. The chronological breadth of the contributions also varies: while some concentrate on narrower periods that appear to offer a significant opportunity to map key phenomena and major developments, others engage in overarching long-term views.

Historiography – the history of history writing – is always part of what historians do, and cultural historians may have additional reasons to pay attention to the ways in which their problems had been previously formulated and the answers they had obtained. Such a preoccupation notwithstanding, this book is not predominantly about what historians have already said; a historiographical survey and dialogue with past and current scholarship is likely to appear in most chapters, but it will not predominate.

Cultural history is not easily (or, for many, desirably) identifiable with a specific method or set of research tools. Some approaches have characterized particular phases and research orientations within the discipline: from historical anthropology, to the emphasis on representations, to the rise of constructivism – the idea that many aspects of reality, not only those obviously cultural but also those appearing as social or natural, are the result of some process of production.[10] The essays collected here exemplify a variety of methods: the subject matter, combined with the specific style and taste of the given author, will, each time, offer the reader the opportunity to explore an archive, to apply a comparative approach, to enter into textual analysis, or otherwise to concentrate on the material and sensual experience of the past.

Every history has temporal and spatial boundaries. The title of the book at hand, *The Routledge Companion to Cultural History in the Western World*, refers to both of these axes. Our presentation starts from the thirteenth century, which has been seen as the century of early urbanization in Europe, the infectious intellectual activity at the universities and the rise of vernacular languages and literatures. The dominance of the Christian Church was characterized by the rivalry between Roman Catholicism and Eastern Orthodoxy, on the one hand, but also by the birth of many religious communities and orders, and thus ways of life, on the other. Furthermore, the emergence of nation states can be traced down to this era, although the sense of belonging to particular regions had longer roots in the past and of course would become even more influential during the centuries to come.

In his article 'The Cultural Logic of Historical Periodization', Peter Toohey has pointed out the seductiveness of periodization. It is comforting to draw on periodization; in 'regularizing, packaging and calibrating the apparent disorder of historical record, positing chronological or intellectual blocks, it creates a type of order'.[11] Evidently, periodization can be deceptive, since it is not a neutral process. But simultaneously, as a counter-argument, its very nature as an act of interpretation is its strength. The historian's work involves the idea of interpreting the past and organizing it in temporal blocks. Once it has been organized, it can again be criticized and possibly rearranged to emphasize new perspectives. We have chosen a rather conventional composition for the book by dividing it into three chronological parts. The first part begins in the middle of the thirteenth century, on the grounds summarized above, and ends around 1500, where the second part commences. The early signs of modernity, including such features as the consolidation of the printing press as a proponent of culture, increasing movements of texts[12] and the changing of reading habits towards more extensive practices of adopting and digesting knowledge,[13] are usually associated with this era. The period also includes the encounter with the New World, and the significant cultural, social and biological exchange that commenced at the turn of the fifteenth and sixteenth centuries. Intellectually, the second part extends from the fifteenth-century humanism to the birth of the movement that became known as the Enlightenment in the eighteenth century. The third part of the book begins from the 1750s, at the time of emerging industrial production, scientific work and rising social turmoil, and extends to the present day. As the chapters will show, there are always multiple rhythms in history. This means that the chapters will move rather freely in time and encompass larger cultural developments.

This book, as its title suggests, also evokes spatial ramifications, since it concentrates on the cultural history of 'the Western world'. Our idea of 'Western' is more inclusive than exclusive. Already the very idea is defined by its outside, by what is 'non-Western', and goes beyond geographical boundaries. Therefore, all chapters in this book aim at wide geographical coverage, rather than concentrating on narrow and specialized topics. Our notion of the West is a flexible one, in full appreciation of the changing boundaries and connotations that have characterized such a cultural conception, and also of its continuous contacts and exchanges with other areas and cultures, near and far away, which contributed to its reshaping and redefinition through time. This book draws mainly on European and American examples, but it devotes continuous attention to global connections and to the emerging trend of globalization that occurred throughout the period under scrutiny. Many of the chapters in this volume deal with identities, emotions and forms of sociability. At the same time, we hope, it offers a panorama of the transformation of Western identities and the critical ramifications of that evolution from the Middle Ages to the twenty-first century.

Notes

1 For the debate between the protagonists of cultural history and social history in Germany, see J. Rogge, 'Narratologie interdisziplinär: Überlegungen zur Methode und Heuristik des historischen Erzählens', in M. Unseld and L. Oberhaus (eds), *Musikpädagogik der Musikgeschichte*, Münster: Waxmann Verlag, 2016, 15–27; for the development in other European countries, see, for example, J. Rogge (ed.), *Cultural History in Europe: Institutions – Themes – Perspectives*, Bielefeld: transcript, 2011.
2 P. McCaffery and B. Marsden (eds), *The Cultural History Reader*, London and New York: Routledge, 2014.
3 A. Classen (ed.), *Handbook of Medieval Culture*, 3 vols, New York: de Gruyter, 2015; H.-E. Lessing, *Das Fahrrad: Eine Kulturgeschichte*, Stuttgart: Klett-Cotta, 2017; P. Poirrier (ed.), *Histoire de la culture scientifique en France: Institutions et acteurs*, Dijon: Éditions universitaires de Dijon, 2016.

4 For example, memory studies and history of emotions are two very productive fields of research: B. Wagoner (ed.), *Handbook of Memory and Culture*, Oxford: Oxford University Press, 2018; H. Aali, A.-L. Perämäki and C. Sarti (eds), *Memory Boxes: An Experimental Approach to Cultural Transfer in History, 1500–2000*, Bielefeld: transcript, 2014; E. Brenner (ed.), *Memory and Commemoration in Medieval Culture*, Farnham: Ashgate, 2013; E. Sullivan and M. L. Herzfeld-Schild (eds), 'Emotions, History and the Arts', *Cultural History* 7, 2018, 117–238; S. Broomhall, J. Davidson and A. Lynch (eds), *A Cultural History of the Emotions*, 6 vols, London: Bloomsbury, 2019; L. Minou and T. Macsotay (eds), 'Suffering, Visuality, and Emotions', *Cultural History* 8, 2019, 1–119.

5 P. Burke, *What Is Cultural History?*, Cambridge: Polity, 2005; A. Green, *Cultural History*, Houndmills: Palgrave, 2008; P. Poirrier (ed.), *L'histoire culturelle: Un tournant mondial de l'historiographie?*, Dijon: Éditions universitaires de Dijon, 2008: P. Ory, *La culture comme aventure: Treize exercices d'histoire culturelle*, Paris: Complexe, 2008; A. Arcangeli, *Cultural History: A Concise Introduction*, London and New York: Routledge, 2012; A. Landwehr, *Kulturgeschichte*, Stuttgart: Ulmer, 2009; M. Maurer, *Kulturgeschichte: Eine Einführung*, Cologne: Böhlau, 2008.

6 H. Salmi, *Nineteenth-Century Europe: A Cultural History*, Cambridge: Polity, 2008; K. Brunner, *Kleine Kulturgeschichte des Mittelalters*, München: Beck, 2012; A. Grabner-Haider, K. Davidowicz and K. Prenner (eds), *Kulturgeschichte der Frühen Neuzeit, 1500 bis 1800*, Göttingen: VuR, 2018.

7 P. Burke, 'Strengths and Weaknesses of Cultural History', *Cultural History* 1, 2012, 1–13.

8 S. Handley, R. MacWilliam and L. Noakes (eds), *New Directions in Social and Cultural History*, London: Bloomsbury, 2018; C. von Braun, *Blutsbande: Verwandtschaft als Kulturgeschichte*, Berlin: Aufbau, 2018.

9 They have been or are the chairs of the ISCH: www.culthist.net.

10 Burke, *What Is Cultural History?*

11 P. Toohey, 'The Cultural Logic of Historical Periodization', in G. Delanty and E. F. Isin (eds), *Handbook of Historical Sociology*, London: Sage, 2003, 209.

12 K. Asdal and H. Jordheim, 'Texts on the Move: Textuality and Historicity Revisited', *History and Theory* 57, 1, 2018, 56–74.

13 The idea of extensive, in contrast to intensive, reading refers to Rolf Engelsing's studies on eighteenth-century literary culture: see R. Engelsing, *Bürger als Leser*, Stuttgart. Metzler, 1974. On Engelsing's ideas, see also G. Reuveni, *Reading Germany: Literature and Consumer Culture in Germany Before 1933*, New York: Berghahn, 2006, 6–7.

PART 1

Shaping Western identities, 1250–1500

INTRODUCTION

Jörg Rogge

In accordance with the general methodological development in cultural history, research on the Middle Ages also stresses the importance of narratives and narrative patterns in the written record. The focus is no longer on the question of whether a reported incident was true in a positivistic sense. Instead, the cultural historians of this period are more interested in how people wrote about their experiences.[1] The manner in which they recounted or recorded events and behaviour was a contribution to the process of world shaping and expressing of values and beliefs within a society. With the focus on the narrative strategies or dominant patterns of argumentation, we can get an insight into the value system and guiding concepts for proper behaviour in a given society.[2] Another fruitful perspective and attempt to understand the cultures of the Middle Ages better is the research on rituals and gestures; perhaps the most important form of communication in our period. Rituals not only reflect the norms and values of a culture, but are also used by contemporaries as a means to create meaning in social or political spaces.[3]

These research fields help to show that people in medieval Europe developed norms, ideas and values which contributed to the shaping of their identities. Some chapters in this part of the book describe and analyse what kind of influence political rituals, travelling and encounters with other cultures had on the shaping of a Western identity proper. Other chapters show how people expressed their emotions, and their understanding of themselves, their bodies and their world, as well as their experience of otherness. All this takes place – as the chapters demonstrate – in political settings, social spaces and material frames like courts, cities, villages, churches, monasteries and frontiers. Contemporaries tried to explain the world by creating a web of meanings that offered orientation in the world and helped them to develop and shape diverse forms of expression of Western identities. In sum, the chapters cover a wide range of recent and important research on the cultures from the High Middle Ages to 1500. In what follows, I will stress and highlight some aspects of the chapters in the first part of the Companion. All chapters argue that the Middle Ages, like our modern world, were characterized by different and sometimes contradictory voices or discourses; in other words, by different cultures.

Concerning politics, there has been a major change in resent research as the focus is more on the decipherment of the symbolic meaning of political actions; we have envisaged the establishment of a cultural history of politics. This is demonstrated in this section of the volume by the chapters (Arlinghaus, Kamp) that deal with the importance of rituals for the creation of (political) order, (social) status and hierarchies (honour). Rituals are considered to be part of the practices of communication in and between individuals and groups in medieval societies, like other forms of communication (writing, gestures).[4] It is argued here (Arlinghaus) that in pre-modern times the social aspect of communication was more important than the information itself, because the culture insists on the co-presence of actors. Valuing the written documents as materializations of immaterial interaction and communication has opened new perspectives for the understanding of medieval cultures (Hirschbiegel and Zeilinger). Even for the regulation of conflicts, communication played an important role, because in the late Middle Ages kings and other juridical authorities had to work with their nobles and/or subjects to enforce their laws and jurisdiction.[5] The research shows that in most European realms there was an amalgamation of 'private' power and 'public' authority (Armstrong).

Princely and noble courts were important centres for communication and networks of relations. Like the town halls in the cities, they were important for the functioning of face-to-face societies. However, they did not pre-exist but were socially constructed by the interaction of location, objects and actors (Hirschbiegel and Zeilinger). Courts and towns also functioned as catalysts for the development of identities or medieval personhood, which was not an innovation of the Renaissance (Lutter). Moreover, research on the concepts and categories used by medieval people to make sense of their subjectivity has shown that they have always expressed their personalism within different groups (Tamm). This is a form of identity that differs from our modern understanding of individualism. However, the chapters in this section highlight that there was even a medieval form of personality and understanding of oneself at all.

In current research the study of emotions starts with the assumption that we can see the performance of an emotion as a cultural construct (Cohen). The importance of emotions has been stressed and it has become clear that it is not only necessary but also possible to consider the manner in which emotions influenced the creation and stability of social groups of different kinds (couples, families, associations) and cultures as well.[6] Love, for example, was a core emotion, which could be an intimate emotion in the context of religious belief (compassion) as well as a public expression of juridical settlement (Cohen). Moreover, emotions were used as means of communication in the political public sphere if, for example, a queen begged with tears in her eyes for the pardon of trespassers in front of her king.

Closely linked with the research on emotions is the work on medieval bodies, which often includes gender and sex. The questions that have guided and are guiding the research in this field range from whether there was a medieval body at all to whether it was a result of human experience and environmental influences. Again, we are able to describe body concepts of common (peasant), noble (chivalric) and religious (ecclesiastic) people in this case, to illustrate the plurality of medieval cultures (Schuh). On the basis of medieval discourses on medicine and fertility, it becomes evident that during the Middle Ages much knowledge and scholarly opinion with regard to the human body and gender relations circulated in the towns, courts and universities, as well as in the quarters of soldiers and mercenaries.[7]

During the later Middle Ages people in Europe broadened their knowledge about other people and cultures by travelling. An important consequence of travelling was its potential to open up new perspectives on oneself and one's society and home culture (O'Doherty). Maps and travel accounts, used as gifts for high nobles, are also seen as being important objects for the representation of exclusive knowledge for the noble elite in Western Europe. Encounters with other cultures is shown to have been a frequent experience during the Middle Ages not only in Europe but in other parts of the world as well.[8] The research with regard to these cultural encounters has stimulated a debate about the terms, methods and heuristics that are most suitable for this kind of research. The consequences of the encounters as a form of cultural transfer or exchange are shown in this volume for Syria, Palestine and Egypt after the Muslim occupation (Pahlitzsch).

Notes

1 V. Nünning (ed.), *New Approaches to Narrative. Cognition – Culture – History*, Trier: Wissenschaftlicher Verlag, 2013.
2 J. Rogge (ed.), *Recounting Deviance. Forms and Practices of Presenting Divergent Behaviour in the Late Middle Ages and Early Modern Period*, Bielefeld: Transcript, 2016.
3 B. Stollberg-Rilinger, *Rituale*, Frankfurt, New York: Campus Verlag, 2013.
4 L. Ross, Communication in the Middle Ages, in: Albrecht Classen (ed.), *Handbook of Medieval Culture*, vol. 1, Berlin, Boston: De Gruyter, 2015, 203–31.
5 C. Valente, *The Theory and Practice of Revolt in Medieval England*, Aldershot: Ashgate, 2003; M. Kintzinger, F. Rexroth, J. Rogge (eds), *Gewalt und Widerstand in der politischen Kultur des späten Mittelalters* (Vorträge und Forschungen LXXX), Ostfildern: Schwabenverlag, 2015.
6 S. Broomhall (ed.), *Gender and Emotions in Medieval and Early Modern Europe: Destroying order, structuring disorder*, Aldershot: Ashgate 2015.
7 J.M. Bennett, R.M. Karras (eds), *The Oxford Handbook of Women and Gender in Medieval Europe*, Oxford: Oxford University Press 2013.
8 C. Holmes, N. Standen (eds), *Towards a Global Middle Ages* (Past and Present, vol. 238, Supplement 13), Oxford: Oxford University Press, 2018.

1

CULTURE OF POLITICS IN THE MIDDLE AGES

Rituals to create and confirm political order

Hermann Kamp

The people in the Middle Ages did not have a concept of rituals that corresponds to our modern understanding of the term. However, they had a sense for the extraordinary character of certain symbolic acts such as custom (*mos*), festivity (*solemnitas*) or rite (*ritus*). The belief of the binding character of what was demonstrated and said during such acts beyond the present time was inherent to rituals. The binding nature of these acts arose from the participants' claim to act as per tradition and thereby recreate it. Rituals were staged in public because this underlined the extraordinary and memorable character of the event and again increased the binding nature. The chapter shows how rituals stabilized and recreated the political order. Generally, rituals support the cohesion and self-assurance of societies and communities. Their primary function is to initiate and make visible a person or group of people transitioning into a new status. Certain recurring and combined symbolic acts indicate the change of status. At the same time, they display the religious, social and political order altered by this transition.[1] In cases where the intended alteration caused by these acts recedes into the background, and the acts themselves are performed to display the social order, symbolic acts become ceremonies.[2] This makes it difficult in specific cases to distinguish a ritual from a ceremony. In either case, a doubled power is inherent in rituals: they restore and confirm the social order and they provide a sense of meaning for it.[3]

To what degree rituals can develop their power highly depends on the structure of the respective society. Generally, rituals served to alter the social order in societies with a lack of institutions and literacy, and to make this alteration visible.[4] Nonetheless, rituals did not lose their importance as the literacy rate increased and the political order was more and more institutionalized. This is particularly evident in European medieval history. During this time, the importance of rituals did not decrease; although, from the twelfth century onwards, written records were on the rise, and offices came to be increasingly structured.[5]

However, not only is the degree to which rituals can restore and shape social order subject to change; the form, meaning and practice of rituals also alter and adapt to their circumstances. Rituals consist of a permanent and almost unchangeable set of symbolic acts which ensure the outcome, but because of alterations and additions of symbolic acts as well as substitutions of symbolic acts, the appearance of rituals was changed and meaning added to them.[6] Therefore, rituals are historic phenomena, although the possibility to re-enact them is vital to them. The potential of change depends on the type of ritual. Religious rituals are fixed to a higher degree than those that perform and make social and political changes visible.

However, during the Middle Ages, it is not possible to strictly separate between religious, social and political rituals because the Church supported and the Christian religion legitimized political power. Because of this, religious rituals received political meaning, while political rituals developed in dependence on religious rituals at the same time.[7] Furthermore, rituals that structured the daily routine were vital to political communication.[8] However, some rituals were especially crucial to transfer and exercise power and can therefore be referred to as political rituals.[9] These include enthronements, inaugurations of dukes, bishops or aldermen, entries and the ruler's *adventus*, encounters between rulers, surrender and other rituals of reconciliation, homage, symbolic service or solemn oaths.

Such transitions indicate that rituals contain a fixed meaning, but do not necessarily deliver precise messages. They make statements on various levels about the relationship between the participants, their future responsibilities as well as shared moral concepts. However, this is done without specifying the rights or obligations to meet the future. In the Middle Ages, this was left to customs or sometimes to additional written records, but the ritual did not show it.[10] In view of this tendency to ambiguity, the question whether the meaning of rituals in past societies can be decoded gains weight. To achieve this, older works regarding the inauguration of kings consulted the regalia and especially the ordines of coronation, which contained instructions for the bishops concerning the arrangement of the king's consecration.[11] Although it is uncertain whether these instructions were used in specific coronation acts, they not only describe ritual acts, but also enlist several speeches and prayers that shed light on how these symbolic acts were perceived, at least by the clergy. On the other hand, historiography contains numerous descriptions of rituals by means of which historians tried to decode the meaning of certain rituals during the last decades.[12] However, this method led to the discussion of how valid statements based on historiographic accounts can be. In some cases, it became evident that the medieval authors did not provide a faithful account of the events, but merely recorded one of many possible interpretations to construct a meaning which suited their intended representation of the event.[13] This is intended as a word of caution regarding the interpretation of individual rituals, especially in cases where there is only a single record. However, historiography provides so many descriptions of certain rituals that they may serve as a basis to develop a model of the form, meaning and functions of rituals,[14] the more so as the late Middle Ages offer additional material such as minutes, letters or illustrated accounts that contribute to understanding of the course of events as well as the perception of rituals.

Although the Middle Ages did not have a concept of rituals that corresponds to our modern understanding of the term, medieval people had a sense for the extraordinary character of certain symbolic acts such as custom (*mos*), festivity (*solemnitas*) or rite (*ritus*).[15] The belief of the binding character of what was demonstrated and said during such acts beyond the present time was inherent to rituals.[16] The binding nature of these acts arose from the participants' claim to act as per tradition and thereby recreate it. Rituals were staged in public because this underlined the extraordinary and memorable character of the event and again increased the binding nature. In this respect, the peculiar meaning of their symbolic acts was recognized by the people in these centuries. The ways in which their rituals stabilized and recreated the political order shall be demonstrated below.

To create an aura of sacredness and sanctity

Undoubtedly, one of the most important political rituals was the inaugurations of kings. They were the political highlights as every new king marked the beginning of a new era, since time was measured by the king's years in power. Inaugurations structured the political order and appeared as rituals of inauguration;[17] at the same time, they were rituals of transition, especially since the anointing had developed into a traditional part of the consecration from the eighth century onwards,[18] although it took until the end of the ninth century before the anointing was an inherent part of the ritual. This development started in the Western Kingdom of the Franks[19] and slowly spread to the other Latin Christian realms. During the tenth century, it became a fixed custom in East Francia as well as in Anglo-Saxon England. One century later, this also applied to Poland and Hungary and in the twelfth century, anointing was part of the consecration in the Scandinavian realms and in Sicily, while in Spain it appeared as a fixed tradition only since the thirteenth century.[20]

Consecration was able to spread mainly because of the belief that it could compensate for a lack of legitimation and protect the kingship or the kingship of the descendants from other families or pretenders to the throne.[21] This ritual transformed the ruler into someone anointed by God. It proved his closeness to God and vested the new king with parts of priesthood.[22] Based on this, he received a mediating role between the clergy and the common people and was declared inexorably as the divine right of kings. Because of the newly gained aura of sacredness, the king distinguished himself clearly from other magnates and princes. The anointing changed him into a new person, as it is written in the Old Testament, and as Conrad II's biographer Wipo claims.[23] It was a ritual of transition par excellence.

The importance of creating an aura of the king's sacredness is not least demonstrated by arranging the ritual of inauguration while introducing the anointment, because handing over the regalia and inaugurating the new king were now part of the ecclesiastical consecration and thereby underlined the divine right of kings.[24] Simultaneously, it marginalized the election as part of the inauguration, especially in hereditary kingdoms such as France or England. Since around 1200, no French king had been inaugurated without anointment;[25] in England, the election was pushed back and deleted from the *ordines*.[26]

At the same time, there are indications that the anointing and coronation gradually lost their significance until they merely had a confirming role, because it was already certain at the birth of the new king that he was chosen by God und would sit on the throne one day. From 1270 onwards, this idea led to the practice whereby the prince was considered king immediately after his father's death. Thus, Edward I was declared king after Henry II's death in 1272, but because he was participating in a crusade at that time, he was anointed and crowned two years later at Westminster.[27] The consecration ceased to be a ritual of inauguration. This was not only true for England, but also for France, where Philip II had already held office as king for one year before he was anointed.[28] In the Holy Roman Empire, the consecration lost its significance as well. The Church reform contributed to this development by questioning the king's sacred position and denying the anointing's sacramental character. Furthermore, the Holy Roman kingship developed towards an elected kingship since the thirteenth century and was legitimized by a rule-governed procedure including a majority voting system. This process was brought to a close with the Golden Bull of 1356. It laid down that the newly elected king and emperor could exercise his rights immediately after the election. Therefore, the consecration in Aachen also lost its significance as a ritual of inauguration.[29] Nevertheless, the consecration did not lose its sacred meaning in the mentioned kingdoms and continued to be an essential element of the king's inauguration as it still demonstrated God's grace. The king was recognized as God's representative on earth and was thereby raised above all other princes.[30] Initially, the emperor had also been anointed by the pope in Rome from the mid-ninth century in the context of his coronation, and by the cardinal bishop of Ostia in the tenth century.[31] However, this merely had a confirming function and did not add to the ruler's sacred position since the emperors had usually already been anointed as kings.

Practices were different when queens were anointed. This tradition started in the ninth century in West Francia and spread to the other Latin realms during the tenth and eleventh centuries. The queen's anointing was closely connected to the coronation, bestowed her with sacred authority and raising her above the laypersons.[32] This practice was especially distinct in France, where the queen along with the king had the right to celebrate the Holy Communion in both forms.[33] In addition, the prayers recorded in the *ordines* concerning the queen's or empress' inauguration suggested the idea of her share in the king's reign, which was sacredly legitimized by the anointing.[34] The fact that the queen and the empress in Italy could exercise power even more so because of their coronation reveals that an inauguration and its rituals could have an impact on the political order in another manner: it bestowed authority, rights and property.

Bestowing authority, rights and property

Consecration was only one ritual during the investiture of a king. As with many other rituals of investiture, consecration took its meaning from the fact that it vested the king with his intended regal rank and the associated rights.[35] This was symbolized especially by handing over the regalia by means of which he received his *potestas*, his right to rule his reign.[36] The most common regalia were the sceptre, the crosier, the sword, the crown, the coat and occasionally the orb.[37] The enthronement had the same function.[38] Although the ritual of handing over the regalia had lost its significance after the thirteenth century, obtaining them continued to be crucial for the assumption of power because they represented the right to rule, although it was not crucial for the regalia to be genuine.[39] For the new king, it was only important to obtain the central symbols to legitimize his future actions and to be able to execute power.[40]

Bishops, dukes or counts were vested with their authority with the help of symbolic actions as well. Since the Merovingian and Carolingian eras, handing over a crosier in return for an oath of loyalty was occasionally recorded in addition to the mere nomination of a candidate.[41] In the Holy Roman Empire, banners or lances with banners were used at rituals of inauguration of dukes and counts since the eleventh century. These objects primarily symbolized the offices' military character.[42] In places where dukes acted rather autonomously, such as in Bohemia or Carinthia, the inauguration usually contained additional elements symbolizing a close relation between the new duke and his land and subjects. In the High Middle Ages, the dukes of Bohemia were therefore seated on a throne during their inauguration in Prague.[43] In Carinthia, the duke acted in an elaborate ritual during which he had to wear peasants' clothes. He was received by a peasant at Kranburg Castle in front of the so-called *Fürstenstein*, which translates as 'stone of princes' and was an upside-down plinth. The duke would not be enthroned before promising the peasant that he would rule the land peacefully and according to the Christian spirit of justice.[44]

While bishops were appointed in writing in Late Antiquity, in the early Middle Ages the position was vested by the king handing over a staff (crosier) to the new bishop. This ritual is recorded since the ninth century, but was probably practised even before that time.[45] During the eleventh century, the Holy Roman kings started to hand over a ring in addition to the crosier and thereby equipped the bishop with the main insignia of their office.[46] Soon, the Church reformers condemned this practice as an inadmissible interference in the 'affairs' of the Church and disavowed it. This turned out to be one point at issue during the Investiture Controversy of the eleventh century. Once it was solved at the beginning of the twelfth century, the Holy Roman kings refrained from handing over the ring. The king's role in the investiture of bishops was restricted to handing over only the regalia, namely the sceptre, and receiving an oath of loyalty.[47] Sooner or later, rulers of other European kingdoms also relinquished symbolic acts that could be mistaken for a spiritual investiture.[48] Because of this, the consecration of a bishop being carried out by other bishops and allowing him to discharge his ecclesiastical duties regained its central meaning for the transmission of an episcopate, but lost its political significance.[49]

In the High Middle Ages, the emergence of the feudal system led to a solemn arrangement of the rituals for the investiture of counts or dukes because the offices developed an increasingly feudal character.[50] Therefore, the entrance into vassalage – which was performed by placing the hands into those of the lords and speaking an oath of fealty since the late Carolingian era – was connected to the investiture of the fief. For princely fiefs, it was common to use sceptres and lances with banners.[51] The latter, for example, applied when the duchy of Austria was granted to its first duke, who received the fief with two banners from Frederick Barbarossa.[52] This practice was firmly established during the thirteenth century, but changed its character. The focus of interest was no longer the office, but receiving a fief directly from the king. Such fiefs did not merely transform the new office-holder into a duke, but a prince whose rank and rights were confirmed in this manner. However, in such cases, the exercising of regal rights was bound to rituals as well.

Whether it concerned kings, bishops or dukes, all of them were vested with their offices' rights, especially the *potestas* that granted them authority, by performing rituals of investiture. By changing a person's rank and status, these rituals ensured that the political order could be reproduced. This was especially crucial because the offices were granted for a lifetime. This might have been one factor that determined the significance of rituals for an investiture. At least, this impression is evoked by examining the inaugurations of aldermen or mayors in the later Middle Ages, which were elected every year or every second year. There were elements that resemble older rituals of inauguration as, for example, taking the aldermen's chairs in the town hall or the town council's benches in certain churches. However, the rituals primarily sought to represent the election as an open procedure and to express its advantages for the community of the city.[53]

The significance of rituals of investiture for the political order is also reflected in the accounts of divestitures. Since the offices were granted for a lifetime and the inherent rights had become part of the person itself because of the rituals, it did not seem to suffice to merely divest someone of his title. The symbolic language of a ritual was necessary to divest the person in question of his rank, rights and authority.[54] However, only a few cases are recorded. To divest someone, it was first necessary to capture the person. This was rarely successful. In other cases, the persons that were to be divested submitted themselves voluntarily. In this case, they would hand out the insignia of their authority as, for example, Tassilo of Bavaria resituated the duchy of Bavaria by handing over a staff to Charlemagne.[55] Another possibility was that the person appeared before the king in a penitential garment, submitted himself and consciously forwent the symbols of his former position.[56] However, some accounts of divestiture are recorded. The most famous case is the divestiture of Pope Formosus. His dead body was taken from his grave, placed on the throne in full regalia and then stripped of all papal regalia. Furthermore, the finger by which he had sworn his oath of office was cut off. In the end, he was placed onto the back of a donkey facing backwards and led through the streets of Rome to revoke his entrance to the city.[57] However, divestitures could also happen to kings that were still alive. John Balliol, who became king of Scotland in 1292, had to learn this after he rebelled against the English king Edward I, whom he had previously accepted as an overlord. In 1292, King John was captured after losing the battle. Edward I publicly stripped the royal regalia from John's coat and took the kingdom of Scotland under his charge.[58]

Establishing ties

Many rituals were of special importance for the stability of the political order, establishing, revising and supporting the ties between individual persons and individuals and collectives of all types and shapes. Frequently, this strength was gained by an oath or a vow which was part of many political rituals. Since the eleventh century and in the context of his consecration, the Roman-German king had promised justice and peace for the Church and the people subordinated to him. Moreover, he pledged to give the bishops, abbots, counts and king's lieges the accounted honour.[59] The numerous oaths of fealty to be sworn when entering vassalage or later in a feudal relationship as part of the *Handgang*, or those that were vowed either to the king, a sovereign or a town lord within the framework of the act of a subject's homage, were more specifically related to single persons.[60] The bonding force of such oaths was frequently strengthened by the establishment of mutual obligations. Thus, the vassalistic oath of allegiance was associated with a promise of protection, the oath of fealty with the enfeoffment and, furthermore, the act of the homage of subject communities mostly took place after the respective rulers had formally accepted their privileges.[61] Essentially, these ties, which had been generated through more or less developed ritual acts, established the political order.

In addition, by participating in ritual acts, such ties were also created and renewed. At this point, the coronation can also serve as an illustrative example in several ways. On the one hand, the coronation tied all those present to the new king by means of the different forms of the acclamation. On the other, those who were also directly involved in the performance of the rituals were tied to the king. This applied to the archbishops, who carried out the anointing, as well as to the other ecclesiastical and secular magnates, who were involved in entrusting the insignia or the coronation, as was the case in England, France and Denmark.[62] Besides, it applied to those who attended the feast and who possibly took over specific ritual services there, like serving food and beverages.[63]

The indispensable ritual integration of all important political groups was carried out most clearly in the course of the so-called *adventus*, the late medieval entry of the kings, princes or bishops into their cities, which was, at least at their first encounter, accompanied by their homage.[64] The form of this political ritual had already been developed during Late Antiquity. By the time a ruler approached a city subordinated to him, the city's representatives came to meet him outside the city gates and were welcomed by him, surrounded by his entourage.[65] Thereafter, they would enter the city together in form of a procession, in which the most important groups of the city, including the clergy, participated also. Such entries, which had been carried out by the French and English kings since the High Middle Ages in Paris and London as part of their coronation and which, in terms of the imperial coronation in Rome, dated back to a much longer tradition,[66] played an important role in the late Middle Ages and took on a constitutive significance for the reign of the counts and dukes in the urbanized regions in Flanders and Brabant. Through the entries into the cities of their dominion at the beginning of their rule, said counts and dukes paid their respects to these cities. In doing so, they also confirmed the cities' rights and privileges.[67] The constitutive significance of these entries, legally as well as politically, can be seen with regard to the city government of Ghent, which asked the Duke of Burgundy, Philip the Good, after a failed uprising and a subjugation to him several times to re-establish and visualize the good understanding in the form of a public entry into the city, as the obvious dissent, the missing bond, entailed many disadvantages for the city.[68]

As the medieval political order was mainly kept together by personal relationships, the establishment or re-establishment of bonds was the pivot of rituals for conflict resolution. This applied particularly after military conflicts and became highly evident during submissions carried out by the magnates and princes who had rebelled against the king. These *deditiones*, which had received a specific, Christian-shaped appeal since the late Carolingian time, aimed at ending a conflict instead of fighting to the bitter end, and played an important part in conflicts involving the king.[69] The arrangement implied that the rebel or rebels should show repentance and that they could reckon with the ruler's leniency in return. Ultimately, the appeal of this arrangement caught on with those who negotiated such a submission. However, the ritual acts essentially resembled each other. The rebels had to be dressed in a simple robe. Occasionally, they also had to appear barefooted and fall on their knees or to the floor in front of the ruler. Thus, they surrendered to his power. Afterwards, the ruler either lifted them up or allowed them to stand up. Now, he had to decide on the extent of punishment for the person in question. However, after such submission, the king was no longer able to sentence the former adversary to death. As the town and territorial lords increasingly made use of the *deditio* in order to settle their conflicts with their cities, it was the representatives of the city who had to be humiliated in front of the ruler.[70] At all times, submissions served as a means of reopening the lines of communication with the ruling authorities. Because of the *deditio*, the rebels were then able to establish direct relations and interactions with the ruler and his entourage. In addition, these rituals were used to reconcile a secular magnate and a bishop, an aristocratic lord and a prince, or an old and a new town council.[71]

Depending on the relationship of the conflicting parties with each other, the forms and rituals of the conflict resolution varied. In the case of foreign and coequal adversaries, the sworn peace treaty, which had been negotiated by envoys, testified under oath and put in place by the respective ruler, was a common feature.[72] Frequently, a personal peace agreement was concluded between the adversaries, which called for a sophisticated arrangement of the rituals that had to have been negotiated beforehand. However, a fixed pattern had quickly been developed in the Middle Ages which was adapted to the particularities on a case-by-case basis. These included approaching by foot, horse or boat, the handshake with the right hand, the embrace, the kiss of peace, the mutual serving of gifts and the common banquet as well as the oath, which was meant to permanently support the peaceful and friendly relationship represented by the respective acts.[73] Whereas the mutual attendance of the mass presumably merely played a minor role during the early Middle Ages, in the later centuries the shared Eucharist came to be a constitutive act in the process of building peace, which was therefore vested with a stronger religious integration.[74] Yet, the mutual and reciprocal performance of the rituals by the protagonists that bound them together and reorganized their relationships was crucial to the ritual's role of restoring order. The importance of this process of the peace agreement becomes apparent in light of the fact that, until the fifteenth century, one consistently urged a face-to-face encounter of the quarrelling parties despite logistical difficulties, to establish or confirm a good and friendly relationship.[75]

Another factor emphasizes the fundamental significance of the ritual in the peace-making process. The development of peace treaties, which increasingly defined the relationships between kings and their realms since the twelfth century,[76] obviously did not result in breaking with the habit of personal encounters.[77] Naturally, this observation refers not only to peace treaties. Since the High Middle Ages, one had also proceeded in a number of other areas to fix the respective relationships in written form and in detail without abstaining from rituals, which therefore remained fundamental for the establishing of such a relationship. This can be seen in both the feudal relationships, which were frequently based on feudal contracts, and in the relationships between the princely lords and their cities, which were arranged by privileges, contracts of expiation and other statutes. Certainly, the rituals did not lose their importance in these areas, but were arranged even more lavishly than before.[78]

Even though performing rituals created new or renewed old bonds and visibly established consent, they themselves were the result of political, occasionally also military, conflicts and negotiations which made consensus possible. This consensus was then raised by ritual acts to become the normative guideline of future behaviour. With this, a further effect of the rituals has already been mentioned: they obliged those who were involved in them or who went through them to certain values through which not only their own role or position was justified but also the political order was legitimized.

The obligation to values and former role models

The force inherent in political rituals to oblige the protagonists to certain values arose primarily from the symbolic meaning of the objects and actions of which the rituals were composed. No less did the speeches, wordings, litanies and prayers delivered in the course of the ritual contribute to reveal the ethical meaning of the respective actions or symbols for the contemporaries.

The easiest way to identify this ethical dimension of the political ritual is to look at the king's inauguration act with its various ritual acts, and to take into account the abundance of *ordines* regarding the consecration of the ruler, which specified what the bishops had to say and to do during the rituals. Even ahead of the acclamation in the Church, the king had to promise to take a stand for the Church.[79] During the ritual of handing over the sword, the king declared to support the Church against its enemies. The new ruler was supposed to be a guarantor for Christendom who should, as recited during the handing over the sceptre and the staff, 'caress the devout and terrorize the impudent' and raise the supplicants.[80] At the same time, however, the new ruler had to pledge to reign justly and to look after the widows and orphans.[81] What was demanded from him at his inauguration was a full declaration of a Christian king's virtues, which had been renewed throughout the course of the Middle Ages at every inauguration of a new king. Consequently, the rulers opposed the Church and its representatives in individual cases, but could hardly flinch from the Christian ideas of reign. Yet, it is of course another question how far the kings acted strictly in accordance with these norms.

Other political rituals also referred to these virtues of a Christian king. Thus, the submission (*deditio*), which had developed since the ninth century, was an enactment of Christian clemency.[82] Since the submission did not lift the ruler's right to inflict punishment, it could also be used to display his sense of justice and penal power. This started to occur more frequently from the twelfth century onwards and could come to the fore regionally, as in the kingdom of Sicily.[83] Therefore, the virtues claimed while carrying out the rituals cannot be reliant on the Christian theory of reign alone. Generosity, voluntary submission and a readiness to fulfil duties were repeatedly represented as exemplary behaviour by means of various political rituals. This happened, for instance, by way of symbolic services of the electors towards the king at the Imperial Diet[84] as well as by the strator service demanded by the popes from the emperors as a sign of recognition since the High Middle Ages.[85] This also applies to the service of bearing the sword of the king. It was often willingly accepted by foreign princes to receive the king's recognition by this honourable service.[86] Furthermore, such symbolic services aimed at honouring the person who was served, and in this way they ensured that honour, as a central value of society, was repeatedly maintained and substantiated.[87] Last but not least, the ritual exchange of gifts performed, for example, during encounters of rulers contributed to the circulation of honour as well.[88]

These different rituals reflect and confirm the fundamental ideals of the medieval society. But some rituals open up new ideals and therefore support their implementation. Thus, the knightly ideal, which had spread in Europe since the eleventh century, found its way into the ritual of the ruler's consecration. In France, the order of the rituals was changed so that handing over the sword was performed before the anointing and the coronation. In this way, the French king, who was donned with spurs, received some sort of accolade at the beginning of his inauguration.[89] In England, a ritual purgatory bath was introduced before the ruler's consecration, which was clearly inspired by the accolade.[90] In the fifteenth century, the new king of the Holy Roman Empire presented himself as a knight by knighting more than 100 aristocrats after his enthronement.[91] However, such changes should not obscure the fact that the political rituals tended to promote awareness of traditional values. The values claimed in the context of a coronation, a submission or an encounter of rulers in the early Middle Ages did not differ from those referred to in the late Middle Ages.

The political rituals did not only tie the present to traditional values; they also linked the respective current political order to historical or biblical examples. Thus, they created traditions that became normative. For example, the story of the prodigal son represented an important reference in the context of earlier submissions and legitimized the actions of the ruler by tying to the biblical example.[92] In the same way, the anointing explicitly committed the new king in the tradition of the Israelite kings David and Saul, and the queen to the Old Testament's role model of Esther.[93] The rituals also connected the historical past to its present. In the Holy Roman Empire, the enthronement of a new king on the supposed throne of Charlemagne formed an important ritual act bound by tradition, which placed the Empire and its rulers in the succession of the King of the Franks.[94] Similarly, the anointing with oil from the Holy Ampulla in France established a link between the new king and the Merovingian dynasty, as it was Clovis who had been baptized with this oil brought by a dove from heaven.[95] This memory was then kept alive at every coronation of a new king. Finally, the importance of creating traditions in this manner manifests itself in the connection of the rituals to the site from where the traditions were believed to have come. Aachen did not without reason develop from a former residence of Charlemagne into a permanent site for the king's anointing and coronation, as Reims did from the place of

Clovis' baptism. Thereby, both sites became an important element of the respective political order.[96]

Performing rituals evoked certain values, recalled the past and thereby addressed traditions. Thus, rituals did not only establish future obligation for those participating in them but also justified the political order created during the ritual act. Therefore, rituals appeared as a sort of preamble. The mentioned and symbolically expressed values displayed this effect even more since the political order was simultaneously represented in the ritual or in connection with the ritual act. Thereby, however, a further manner in which rituals influenced the political order comes into view.

Representing order

Even though political rituals initially appeared as performative acts, their political impact arose from their ability to display the political order in the participants' and spectators' minds as well. The rank and power structures were mirrored in the participants' actions, which demonstrated their relationships to each other, e.g. proximity and detachment as well as precedence, subordination or equality by their spatial positioning and their appearance. The ceremonial dimensions of the ritual acts were accompanied by particular ceremonial acts which aimed to represent the social and political order. The seating arrangements during the banquets, the welcoming ceremony before encounters of rulers or processions of citizens during the *adventus* of the ruler or the princely lord of the town conveyed particularly well an image of the respective order of rank and class.[97]

The great significance attributed to this function of the rituals by contemporaries is revealed in the written records. Many detailed descriptions of rituals in historiography are as much an indication as the illustrations in manuscripts. Especially the great differences in descriptions of the very same ritual show to what extent the role an individual played in the context of a ritual could say something about the individual's political significance. An example of this is the Visegradian chronicler, which describes the events at the *Hoftag* in Magdeburg in 1135, when the Holy Roman Emperor Lothair III entered an alliance with the Polish duke Boleslaw III and appointed him as his sword bearer, as if the Pole was humiliated and degraded to a semi-free servant, who was supposed to keep the path clear for the emperor. Moreover, the Polish duke was depicted as a culprit who had to sit opposite the emperor, whereas the Bohemian duke, his own lord, was allowed to sit at the right-hand side of the emperor.[98] For the very reason that rituals represented the balance of power, one had to adjust the respective image, if necessary.

Accordingly, it comes as no surprise that conflicts arose repeatedly concerning the involvement in rituals. Thus, two bishops fighting over the right for the anointing and coronation can be seen in England, in the developing kingdom of France and in the Holy Roman Empire in the decades during which the anointing had gradually been established.[99] Especially such fighting for particular interests indicates to what extent the visible participation in rituals influenced one person's own standing. This is even more relevant as rituals tended to perpetuate all that had been shown by the use of repetition. Therefore, since the twelfth century, the English bearers of certain offices at court, the earls and the barons, as well as the great lords who were permitted to carry the insignia, let their rights be certified to be allowed to take part in the processions to Church.[100] This is similar to the way in which the electors in the Holy Roman Empire displayed their exclusive standing by having their so-called services of honour at the coronation feast defined by the Golden Bull. Such services of honour included saying grace, the services as a constable and the provision of a towel, a chalice and food.[101]

The events, which were rituals that served to change the existing balance of power, emphasize the fact that the image of the political order transported by rituals supported the order itself. In this respect, those acts representing hierarchies, such as occupying one's rightful seat and attending the procession, played a decisive role, since they frequently became the scene of usurpation attempts. If somebody had not been satisfied with his position within the hierarchy, he simply would have occupied his favoured seat to demonstrate his claims. This often led to violent conflicts as those who were deprived of their seat knew that relinquishing their former seat would result in a loss of honour and power.[102] Similarly, conflicts on the proper order arose repeatedly during municipal processions, because participating in the procession represented one's rank in the respective community.[103] Furthermore, processions in the cities were used to overthrow the old order by leading it away from the traditional course and by using new routes to demonstrate that the balance of power had shifted.[104]

Although the king's inauguration mirrors the political structures most sweepingly by representing the king as head, and the princes, councillors and office bearers who participated in the execution of power as limbs of the political order, other political rituals from the *adventus* and the grant of a fief to the submission also add to represent it. The fundamental relationship between the king and a magnate or a princely lord and his town was even represented by the sole granting of a fief or one public entry. Such acts conveyed how these relationships were supposed to be. Although arranged as exceptional as possible, the ritual act itself referred to all former granted fiefs or entries as well as to those that were still about to happen. Thereby, it provided the idea of the interdependencies established by such ritual acts.[105]

At both the *adventus* and the encounter of rulers, the ceremonial element played an important role from the very start. Even though the primary aim of these rituals was to establish new obligations between the protagonists, the participants used the various ritual acts to represent themselves in a good light and to express their own position either by the size of their entourage or by impressing their counterparts by means of gifts or feasts.[106] This tendency seemed to have become more important during the late Middle Ages. The entries, and especially the *Joyeuses Entrées* which had developed in Flanders and Brabant, aimed at involving all important political forces. This was true for both sides, as the princes would be accompanied by their court and the cities would not only be represented by their aldermen but also involve their brotherhoods, guilds and ecclesiastical communities to represent themselves as a whole.[107] At this point, the rituals elements which marked a transition overlapped with those ceremonial acts that primarily aimed at mirroring the political order as it should have been. In the late Middle Ages, this development affected almost all political rituals. Even the anointing and the coronation lost their status-altering character and were then predominantly used to display the divine order with the king as its secular head designated by God on one side, and the Church supporting the king and being supported by him in return on the other.[108] Extravagant banquets with seating arrangements, services of honour which were rendered by princes, barons and counts, as well as processions and parades left their mark on the character of the rituals. The lavish feasts at the Burgundian court with fanciful banquet tableaux, which accompanied a wedding as much as the encounters with other rulers, raised the stakes of a tendency, which could also be found in other countries and realms.[109] However, not every potentate had to adhere to the growing ceremonial arrangement. Thus, the French king Louis XI intentionally behaved like a ruler to whom ceremonies and representation meant little.[110] Looking at the overall situation, the increasing ceremonialization of political rituals may be based on the growing social differentiation in terms of estates and ranks in the late Middle Ages.

Although rituals were occasionally disrupted to protest against them, they were essentially aimed at demonstrating the consensus of the participants.[111] In most cases, these demonstrations were successful since those being dissatisfied expressed their discontent by staying away. At the same time, the consensus, which had been documented in the ritual, was supposed to deter these people from questioning the newly established order. The picture and message of this consensus was proclaimed by the fact that everyone had apparently participated in the rituals.

All things considered, rituals influenced the political order in a variety of ways. Most political rituals had an impact on all levels, allowed individuals or groups of people to achieve a new status and new rights, created binding obligations, evoked fundamental values regarding both the new relations and the political order as a whole and reflected the balance of power. Their force, which became apparent by the fact that rituals were considered to be necessary for all fundamental changes, emerged from the combination of these different effects. Their impact on the political order meant that they were frequently the result of negotiations.

Accordingly, their influence was at the same time limited since rituals eventually only represented changes and relationships that had been developed previously because of other factors.[112] A submission mainly occurred if one side had emerged victorious from a military conflict. However, the political circumstances did not only determine the potential effectiveness of a single ritual. It was due to the rise of the princes and electors that the rituals of granting a fief in the Holy Roman Empire were arranged more lavishly at the end of the Middle Ages. The changing significance of the anointing in the Holy Roman Empire was a result not only of theological and canonical developments, but also of the common efforts of the king and the princes to increase the value of the election and to repel the claims of the papacy.

At least, the rituals remained limited in their effect at first glance because many of them only took place sporadically. Occasionally, the time between the coronations in the individual kingdoms ranged from 30 to 40 years. The ceremonial entries of the princely lords into their cities remained the exception. Besides, the submissions received by the kings or other princes can mostly be counted on the fingers of one hand. The encounters of rulers in the Carolingian period took place rather frequently, yet they were only regarded as sparse highlights in the kings' daily events of government during the following centuries. Also, the granting of fiefs was not carried out daily. As a result, political rituals remained something special. In this way, their power was restricted, but at the same time, an extraordinary aura was bestowed on them due to which they gained a special impact, of which one frequently made use in the Middle Ages to renew, strengthen or change the political order.

Notes

1 Cf. G. Althoff, *Die Macht der Rituale. Symbolik und Herrschaft im Mittelalter*, Darmstadt: Primus-Verlag, 2003, 10–14; S. Patzold, 'Wirkreichweite, Geltungsbereich, Forschungsperspektive: Zu den Grenzen des Rituals', in A. Büttner, A. Schmidt, P. Töbelmann (ed.), *Grenzen des Rituals. Wirkreichweiten – Geltungsbereiche – Forschungsperspektiven*, Köln: Böhlau, 2014, 350–2. On the various options of definition and their use in modern historiography see B. Stollberg-Rilinger, *Rituale*, Frankfurt: Campus-Verl., 2013, 7.

2 See K. Leyser, 'Ritual, Zeremonie und Gestik. Das ottonische Reich', *Frühmittelalterliche Studien* 27, 1993, 1–26, 2f., and B. Stollberg-Rilinger, 'Symbolische Kommunikation in der Vormoderne. Begriffe – Forschungsperspektiven – Thesen', *Zeitschrift für Historische Forschung* 31, 2004, 489–527, 504. Regarding the development of political rituals in the late Middle Ages (see below, p. xx), it appears to be useful to differentiate more strongly between ritual and ceremony in terms of terminology.

3 See G. Althoff, 'Rituale als ordnungsstiftende Elemente', in W. Pohl (ed.), *Der Frühmittelalterliche Staat. Europäische Perspektiven*, Wien: Verl. der Österr. Akad. der Wiss., 2009, 391–8.

4 See Althoff, *Die Macht der Rituale*, 21 and 31.

5 See ibid., 20 and Stollberg-Rilinger, *Rituale*, 233f.

6 See Althoff, *Die Macht der Rituale*, 189ff. and more explicitly G. Althoff, 'Die Veränderbarkeit von Ritualen im Mittelalter', in ibid. (ed.), *Formen und Funktionen öffentlicher Kommunikation im Mittelalter*, Stuttgart: Thorbecke, 2001, 157–76.

7 See S. Weinfurter, 'Die Welt der Rituale: Eine Einleitung', in C. Ambos, S. Hotz, G. Schwedler, S. Weinfurter (eds), *Die Welt der Rituale. Von der Antike bis heute*, Darmstadt: Wiss. Buchges., 2006, 1f.

8 See H. Fuhrmann, '"Willkommen" und "Abschied". Über Begrüßungs- und Abschiedsrituale im Mittelalter', in W. Hartmann (ed.), *Mittelalter. Annäherungen an eine fremde Zeit*, Regensburg: Univ. Verl., 1993, 111–39; C. Garnier, *Die Kultur der Bitte. Herrschaft und Kommunikation im mittelalterlichen Reich*, Darmstadt: Wiss. Buchges., 2008; G. Koziol, *Begging Pardon and Favor: Ritual and Political Order in Early Medieval France*, Ithaca, NY, London: Cornell Univ. Press, 1992.

9 See J.L. Nelson, 'Rituals of Power: By Way of Conclusion', in J.L. Nelson, F. Theuws (eds), *Rituals of Power: From Late Antiquity to the Early Middle Ages*, Leiden: Brill, 2000, 477–86, here 478 and 480, and Althoff, *Die Macht der Rituale*, 199f.

10 See G. Althoff, 'Symbolic Communication and Medieval Order: Strength and Weakness of Ambiguous Signs', in W. Jezierski, L. Hermanson, H.J. Orning, T. Småberg (eds), *Rituals, Performatives, and Political Order in Northern Europe, c650–1300*, Turnhout: Brepols, 2015, 63–75, 68ff. and Koziol, *Begging Pardon and Favor*, 289f.

11 See esp. P.E. Schramm, *Geschichte des englischen Königtums im Lichte der Krönung*, Weimar: Böhlau, 1937; P.E. Schramm, *Der König von Frankreich. Das Wesen der Monarchie vom 9. zum 16. Jahrhundert*, 2 Bde., Darmstadt: Wiss. Buchges., 1960, and the various contributions in J. Bak (ed.), *Coronations. Medieval and Early Modern Monarchic Ritual*, Berkeley, Los Angeles, CA, Oxford: Univ. of California Press, 1990.

12 On the development of the historic research on rituals with lots of literature see most recently G. Schwedler, 'Ritual und Wissenschaft. Forschungsinteressen und

Methodenwandel in Mittelalter, Neuzeit und Zeitgeschichte', in A. Büttner, A. Schmidt, P. Töbelmann (eds), *Grenzen des Rituals. Wirkreichweiten – Geltungsbereiche – Forschungsperspektiven*, Köln, Wien: Böhlau, 2013, 229–68, esp. 253ff., and F. Rexroth, 'Rituale und Ritualismus in der historischen Mittelalterforschung. Eine Skizze', in H.W. Goetz, J. Jarnut (eds), *Mediävistik im 21. Jahrhundert, Stand und Perspektiven der internationalen und interdisziplinären Mittelalterforschung*, München: Fink, 2003, 391–406.

13 See P. Buc, *The Dangers of Ritual: Between Early Medieval Texts and Social Scientific Theory*, Princeton, NJ, Oxford: Princeton Univ. Press, 2001, 8–11, 21, 248. See also A. Büttner, 'Vom Text zum Ritual und zurück – Krönungsrituale in Quellen und Forschung', in A. Büttner, A. Schmidt, P. Töbelmann (eds), *Grenzen des Rituals. Wirkreichweiten – Geltungsbereiche – Forschungsperspektiven*, Köln, Weimar, Wien: Böhlau Verlag, 2014, 287–306, esp. 291ff. and Patzold, 'Wirkreichweite, Geltungsbereich, Forschungsperspektive', 353 and 355.

14 See Althoff, *Die Macht der Rituale*, 187f. Thereby, the analysis of literary texts, which frequently reflect upon themselves regarding their representation of rituals, can prove to be extremely helpful. On this see esp. C. Witthöft, *Ritual und Text. Formen symbolischer Kommunikation in der Historiographie und Literatur des Spätmittelalters*, Darmstadt: Wiss. Buchges., 2004.

15 See Buc, *The Dangers of Ritual*, 6, and Stollberg-Rilinger, *Rituale*, 15f. and 181.

16 See Althoff, *Die Macht der Rituale*, 23f.

17 See J.L. Nelson, 'Inauguration Rituals', in ibid., *Politics and Ritual in Early Medieval Europe*, London: Hambledon, 1986, 283–307, first in P. Sawyer, I. Wood (eds), *Early Medieval Kingship*, Leeds: Univ. of Leeds, 1977, 50–71 and R. Giesey, 'Inaugurial Aspects of French Royal Ceremonials', in J. Bak (ed.), *Coronations: Medieval and Early Modern Monarchic Ritual*, Berkeley, Los Angeles, CA, Oxford: Univ. of California Press, 1990, 35–45.

18 See J. Le Goff, 'A Coronation Program for the Age of Saint-Louis: The Ordo of 1250', in J. Bak (ed.), *Coronations. Medieval and Early Modern Monarchic Ritual*, Berkeley, Los Angeles, CA, Oxford: Univ. of California Press, 1990, 46–57, 47f. and 52.

19 On this and on the following see R. Schieffer, 'Die Ausbreitung der Königssalbung im hochmittelalterlichen Europa', in M. Becher (ed.), *Die mittelalterliche Thronfolge im europäischen Vergleich*, Ostfildern: Thorbecke, 2017, 43–79.

20 Most recently on Aragon see S. Péquignot, 'Die Krönung der aragonesischen Könige. Überlegungen zu Ergebnissen und Grenzen einer performanzorientierten Interpretation', in K. Oschema (ed.), *Die Performanz der Mächtigen: Rangordnung und Idoneität in höfischen Gesellschaften des späten Mittelalters*, Ostfildern: Thorbecke, 2015, 165–93.

21 See Schieffer, 'Die Ausbreitung der Königssalbung', 78f.

22 See F.R. Erkens, *Herrschersakralität im Mittelalter. Von den Anfängen bis zum Investiturstreit*, Stuttgart: Kohlhammer, 2006, and E. Boshof, *Königtum und Königsherrschaft im 10. und 11. Jahrhundert*, München: Oldenbourg, 1993, 78f, 112f.

23 See 1. Samuel, 10,6, and Wipo, Gesta Conradi (MGH SSrG 61), ch. 3, 23.

24 See Boshof, *Königtum und Königsherrschaft*, 77 and 112f.

25 See Schramm, *Der König von Frankreich*, 110.

26 See Schramm, *Geschichte des englischen Königtums*, 78 and 164.

27 See ibid., 166f.

28 See ibid.; J. Rogge, '"Tum quia regalis unctio in anima quicquam non imprimit …" Zur Bedeutung von Königskrönungen und Königssalbungen in England und im römisch–deutschen Reich während des Spätmittelalters', in L. Pelizäus (ed.), *Wahl und Krönung in Zeiten des Umbruchs*, Frankfurt a.M.: Lang, 2008, 41–64, 46f.

29 See J. Rogge, *Die deutschen Könige im Mittelalter. Wahl und Krönung*, Darmstadt: Wiss. Buchges., 2006, 109, and most recently F.R. Erkens, 'Thronfolge und Herrscher-sakralität in England, Frankreich und im Reich während des späteren Mittelalters: Aspekte einer Korrelation', in M. Becher (ed.), *Die mittelalterliche Thronfolge im europäischen Vergleich*, Ostfildern: Thorbecke, 2017, 349–448, 400.

30 See Erkens, 'Thronfolge und Herrschersakralität', 370f.

31 See Schieffer, 'Ausbreitung der Königssalbung', 45.

32 See A. Fößel, *Die Königin im mittelalterlichen Reich. Herrschaftsausübung, Herrschaftsrechte, Handlungsspielräume*, Stuttgart: Thorbecke, 2000, 48; A. Büttner, *Der Weg zur Krone. Rituale der Herrschererhebung im spätmittelalterlichen Reich*, 2 vols, Ostfildern: Thorbecke, 2012, 692, on the Holy Roman Empire; E. v. Houts, 'Queen in the Anglo-Norman/Angevin Realm (1066–1216)', in C. Zey (ed.), *Mächtige Frauen? Königinnen und Fürstinnen im europäischen Mittelalter (11.–14. Jahrhundert)*, Ostfildern: Thorbecke, 2015, 199–224, here 200, on England; Schramm, *Der König von Frankreich*, 127ff., on France; E. Hoffmann, 'Coronation and Coronation Ordines in Medieval Scandinavia', in J. Bak (ed.), *Coronations. Medieval and Early Modern Monarchic Ritual*, Berkeley, Los Angeles, CA, Oxford: Univ. of California Press, 1990, 125–51, here 132, and C. Rock, *Herrscherwechsel im spätmittelalterlichen Skandinavien. Handlungsmuster und Legitimationsstrategien*, Ostfildern: Thorbecke, 2016, 396f., on Scandinavia.

33 See Schramm, *Der König von Frankreich*, 203.

34 See Fößel, *Die Königin im mittelalterlichen Reich*, 47ff.; B. Kasten, 'Krönungsordnungen für und Papstbriefe an mächtige Frauen im Mittelalter', in C. Zey (ed.), *Mächtige Frauen? Königinnen und Fürstinnen im europäischen Mittelalter (11.–14. Jahrhundert)*, Ostfildern: Thorbecke, 2015, 249–306, here 270; Houts, 'Queen in the Anglo-Norman', 200ff.; Rock, *Herrscherwechsel*, 397. On the loss of significance of the coronation and the anointing for the status of the queen in the Holy Roman Empire in the late Middle Ages accompanied by a loss of political influence see S. Dick, 'Die römisch-deutsche Königin im spätmittelalterlichen Verfassungswandel', in M. Becher (ed.), *Die mittelalterliche Thronfolge im europäischen Vergleich*, Ostfildern: Thorbecke, 2017, 341–58, here 346.

35 On rituals concerning investiture and coronation see M. Steinecke, S. Weinfurter, *Investitur- und Krönungsrituale. Herrschaftseinsetzungen im kulturellen Vergleich*, Köln, Weimar, Wien: Böhlau, 2005, and G. Althoff, H. Basu (eds), *Rituale der Amtseinsetzung. Inaugurationen in verschiedenen Epochen, Kulturen, politischen Systemen und Religionen*, Würzburg: Ergon-Verlag, 2015.

36 See R. Schneider, *Königswahl und Königserhebung im Frühmittelalter. Untersuchungen zur Herrschaftsnachfolge bei den Langobarden und Merowingern*, Stuttgart: Hiersemann, 1972, 219; J. Petersohn, 'Über monarchische Insignien und deren Funktion im mittelalterlichen Reich', *Historische Zeitschrift* 266, 1998, 61–5; H. Keller, 'Die Investitur. Ein Beitrag zum Problem der "Staatssymbolik" im Hochmittelalter', *Frühmittelalterliche Studien* 27, 1993, 51–86, 56ff.

37 See on the Holy Roman Empire Peterson, 'Über monarchische Insignien'; on Scandinavia Hoffmann, 'Coronation and Coronation Ordines', 128, 132f., 139, on Poland A. Giesywztor, 'Gesture in Coronation Ceremonies of Medieval Poland', in J. Bak (ed.) *Coronations: Medieval and Early Modern Monarchic Ritual*, Berkeley, Los Angeles, CA, Oxford: Univ. of California Press, 1990, 152–64, 158f., on France Le Goff, 'A Coronation Program', 54f.

38 See on enthronements recorded in the Merovingian Frankish Empire and its succeeding kingdoms Schneider, *Königswahl und Königserhebung*, 213ff., Boshof, *Königtum und Königsherrschaft*, 118; on stone settings in Scotland and Sweden Hoffmann, 'Coronation

and Coronation Ordines', and Rock, *Herrscherwechsel*, 29 and 390. On the occasional raisings of shields in the early Frankish Empire see M. Hardt, 'Art: Schilderhebung', in *Reallexikon für Germanische Altertumskunde* 27, 2005, 106–8.

39 See Peterson, 'Über monarchische Insignien', 56.

40 See ibid., 54, 71.

41 See P. Depreux, 'Investitures et destitutions aux temps carolingiens', in W. Falkwoski, Y. Sassier, *Le monde carolingien. Bilan, perspectives, champs de recherche*, Turnhout: Brepols, 2009, 157–82, 167.

42 See V. Rödel, 'Lehnsgebräuche', in *Handwörterbuch zur deutschen Rechtsgeschichte*, vol. 3, Berlin: Erich Schmidt Verlag, 2016, 747–50; P. Depreux, 'Lehnsrechtliche Symbolhandlungen. Handgang und Investitur im Bericht Galberts von Brügge zur Anerkennung Wilhelm Clitos als Graf von Flandern', in J. Dendorfer, R. Deutinger (eds), *Das Lehnswesen im Hochmittelalter. Forschungskonstrukte – Quellenbefunde – Deutungsrelevanz*, Ostfildern: Thorbecke, 2010, 387–99, 389; Keller, 'Die Investitur',71.

43 See R. Schmidt, 'Die Einsetzung der böhmischen Herzöge auf den Thron zu Prag', in H. Beumann, W. Schröder (eds), *Aspekte der Nationenbildung im Mittelalter*, Sigmaringen: Thorbecke, 1978, 436–63.

44 See most recently Witthöft, 'Ritual und Text', 106–16.

45 See P. Töbelmann, *Stäbe der Macht. Stabsymbolik in Ritualen des Mittelalters*, Husum: Matthiesen, 2011, 119f.; Keller, 'Die Investitur'.

46 On this and on the following see C. Zey, *Der Investiturstreit*, München: C.H. Beck, 2017, 30f.

47 See ibid., 106.

48 See ibid., 88–91.

49 See K. Schreiner, 'Wahl, Amtsantritt und Amtsenthebung von Bischöfen: Rituelle Handlungsmuster, rechtlich normierte Verfahren, traditionsgestützte Gewohnheiten', in B. Stollberg-Rilinger (ed.), *Vormoderne politische Verfahren*, Berlin: Duncker & Humbolt, 2001, 73–117, who points out that the entry into the bishop's city emerged as a political ritual during the late Middle Ages.

50 On the rituals at the entrance of vassalage see J. Le Goff, 'Les gestes symboliques dans la vie sociale. Les gestes de la vassalité', in Centro italiano di studi (ed.), *Simboli e simbologia nell'alto medievo*, Spoleto: Presso di Sede del Centro, 1976, 679–779; K. Eickels, *Vom inszenierten Konsens zum systematisierten Konflikt. Die englisch-französischen Beziehungen und ihre Wahrnehmung an der Wende vom Hoch- zum Spätmittelalter*, Stuttgart: Thorbecke, 2002; Depreux, 'Lehnsrechtliche Symbolhandlungen'.

51 See Peterson, 'Über monarchische Insignien', 75.

52 On this and on the following see O. Auge, 'Lehnrecht, Lehnswesen', in: *Handwörterbuch zur deutschen Rechtsgeschichte,* vol. 3, Berlin: Erich Schmidt Verlag, 2016, 717–36, 729f.

53 See D.W. Poeck, *Rituale der Ratswahl. Zeichen und Zeremoniell der Ratssetzung in Europa*, Köln, Weimar, Wien: Böhlau, 2003, esp. 314ff.

54 See K. Schreiner, 'Gregor VIII., nackt auf einem Esel. Entehrende Entblößung und schandbares Reiten im Spiegel einer Miniatur der Sächsischen Weltchronik', in *Ecclesia et Regnum. Beiträge zur Geschichte von Kirche, Recht und Staat im Mittelalter. Festschrift für Franz-Josef Schmale zu seinem 65. Geburtstag*, Bochum: Verlag Dr. Dieter Winkler, 1989, 155–202; F. Rexroth, 'Tyrannen und Taugenichtse. Beobachtungen zur Ritualität europäischer Königsabsetzungen im späten Mittelalter', *Historische Zeitschrift* 278, 2004, 27–54.

55 See Althoff, *Die Macht der Rituale*, 53ff.; Depreux, 'Investitures et destitutions aux temps carolingiens', 165ff.

56 See below, p. 19.

57 See H. Zimmermann, *Papstabsetzungen des Mittelalters*, Graz, Wien, Köln: Böhlau, 1968, 47–76.

58 See H. Kamp, 'New Masters and Old Rituals: Edward I, Robert the Bruce, Philipp the Fair and the Role of Rituals with Conquest', in G. Schwedler, E. Tounta (eds), *State, Power and Violence*, vol. III, Wiesbaden: Harrassowitz, 2010, 485–503, 489ff.

59 See Büttner, *Der Weg zur Krone*, 111.

60 See Rödel, 'Lehnsgebräuche'; Depreux, 'Lehnsrechtliche Symbolhandlungen'; L. Kolmer, *Promissorische Eide im Mittelalter*, Kallmünz: Michael Lassleben, 1989, 89ff. On the homage see Althoff, *Die Macht der Rituale*, 171ff. and A. Holenstein, *Die Huldigung der Untertanen. Rechtskultur und Herrschaftsordnung (800–1800)*, Stuttgart: Fischer, 1991, 278ff. On the oaths of the aldermen and on the journeys for swearing the citizen oaths see Poeck, *Rituale der Ratswahl*, 65.

61 See Depreux, 'Lehnsrechtliche Symbolhandlungen', 399; Holenstein, *Die Huldigung der Untertanen*, 321ff.; Kolmer, *Promissorische Eide*, 95f.

62 See Schramm, *Geschichte des englischen Königtums*, 67ff. on England; Le Goff, 'A Coronation Program', 54, and M. Kintzinger, 'Sakrale Repräsentation bei der Thronsukzession der König von Frankreich im Spätmittelalter', in L. Pelizäus (ed.), *Wahl und Krönung in Zeiten des Umbruchs*, Frankfurt a.M.: Lang, 2008, 23–39, 35 on France; Hoffmann, 'Coronation and Coronation Ordines', 132f. on Denmark; and on Aragon Péquignot, 'Die Krönung der aragonesischen Könige', 184–6, where, because of the tradition of the self-coronation, the consecrated archbishops had to be unintentionally satisfied with touching the crown.

63 See G. Schwedler, 'Dienen muss man dürfen oder: Die Zeremonialvorschriften der Goldenen Bulle zum Krönungsmahl des römisch-deutschen Herrschers', in C. Ambos, S. Hotz, G. Schwedler, S. Weinfurter (eds), *Die Welt der Rituale. Von der Antike bis heute*, Darmstadt, 2005, 156–66, and Büttner, *Der Weg zur Krone*, 687f. who relativized the significance of the coronation feast and the services which were to be rendered in the Holy Roman Empire. In France the coronation meal did not play an important role either – Schramm, *Der König von Frankreich*, 203 – unlike in England – Schramm, *Geschichte des englischen Königtums*, 71.

64 See P. Johanek, A. Lampen (eds), *Adventus. Studien zum Herrscherlichen Einzug in die Stadt*, Köln, Weimar, Wien: Böhlau, 2009; G. Schenk, *Zeremoniell und Politik. Herrscheinzüge im spätmittelalterlichen Reich*, Köln, Weimar, Wien: Böhlau, 2003; G. Kipling, *Enter the King: Theatre, Liturgy, and Ritual in the Medieval Civic Triumph*, Oxford: Oxford University Press, 1998; P. Arnade, *Realms of Ritual: Burgundian Ceremony and Civic Life in Late Medieval Ghent*, Ithaca, NY, London: Cornell Univ. Press, 1996. On the *adventus* of the bishops see most recently A. Bihrer, 'Einzug, Weihe und erste Messe. Symbolische Interaktion zwischen Bischof, Hof und Stadt im spätmittelalterlichen Konstanz. Zugleich einige methodische Ergänzungen zu den Ergebnissen der aktuellen Adventusforschung', in G. Deutschländer (ed.), *Symbolische Interaktion in der Residenzstadt des Spätmittelalters und der Frühen Neuzeit*, Halle: Akad.-Verlag, 2013, 65–88.

65 For an ideal schema of the entry see Schenk, *Zeremoniell und Politik*, 238–42.

66 See L. Bryant, 'The Medieval Ceremony at Paris', in J. Bak (ed.), *Coronations. Medieval and Early Modern Monarchic Ritual*, Berkeley, Los Angeles, CA, Oxford: Univ. of California Press, 1990, 88–118 on France; Kipling, *Enter the King*, on England, and A. Hack, *Das Empfangszeremoniell bei mittelalterlichen Papst-Kaiser-Treffen*, Köln: Böhlau, 1999, on Rome.

67 W. Blockmans, E. Donckers, 'Self Representation of Court and City in Flanders and Brabant in the Fifteenth and Early Sixteenth Centuries', in W. Blockmans, A. Janse (eds), *Showing Status: Representation of Social Positions in the Late Middle Ages*, Turnhout: Brepols, 1999, 81–111.

68 See Arnade, *Realms of Ritual*, 127ff.

69 See on this and on the following Althoff, *Die Macht der Rituale*, 68–84.

70 See C. Garnier, 'Zeichen und Schrift. Symbolisches Handeln und literale Fixierung am Beispiel von Friedensschlüssen im 13. Jahrhundert', *Frühmittelalterliche Studien* 32, 1998, 263–87; J.M. Moeglin, 'Pénitence publique et amende honorable au Moyen Age', *Revue Historique* 298, 1997, 225–69 and J.M. Moeglin, 'Harmiscara – Harmschar – Hachée. Le dossier des rituels d'humiliation et de soumission au Moyen Age', *Archivium Latinitatis Medii Aevi* 54, 1996, 11–65.

71 See H. Kamp, *Friedensstifter und Vermittler im Mittelalter*, Darmstadt: Wiss. Buchges., 2001, 137f. and 252ff.

72 See J.M. Moeglin, S. Péquignot, *Diplomatie et « relations internationales » au Moyen Âge (IXe–XVe siècle)*, Paris: puf, 2017, 511ff; J. Benham, *Peacemaking in the Middle Ages: Principles and Practices*, Manchester: Cambridge Univ. Press, 2011, 145ff.; G. Schwedler, *Herrschertreffen des Spätmittelalters: Formen, Rituale, Wirkungen*, Ostfildern: Thorbecke, 2008, 275ff.

73 See Schwedler, *Herrschertreffen des Spätmittelalters*, esp. on the oath 125ff., and with an exemplary representation of the individual acts from 331. See for the early Middle Ages K. Schreiner, '"Gerechtigkeit und Frieden haben sich geküßt". Friedensstiftung durch symbolisches Handeln', in J. Fried (ed.), *Träger und Instrumentarien des Friedens im hohen und späten Mittelalter*, Sigmaringen: Thorbecke, 1996, 37–86; W. Kolb, *Herrscherbegegnungen im Mittelalter*, Bern: Lang, 1998 and I. Voss, *Herrschertreffen im frühen Mittelalter*, Köln, Wien: Böhlau, 1987.

74 See N. Offenstadt, *Faire la paix au Moyen Age. Discours et gestes de paix pendant la guerre de Cent ans*, Paris: Jacob, 2007, esp. 176.

75 See Schwedler, *Herrschertreffen des Spätmittelalters*, 412.

76 See Moeglin, Péquignot, *Diplomatie*, 498ff.

77 See Schwedler, *Herrschertreffen des Spätmittelalters*,134ff., 271ff., 292ff.

78 See on the feudal system S. Patzold, *Das Lehnswesen*, München: Beck, 2012, 117–19, and on the friendship alliances and the expiatory records Garnier, 'Zeichen und Schrift', 267.

79 See on this and on the following C. Vogel, R. Elze (eds), *Le Pontifical romano-germanique du dixième siècle*, vol. 1., Cittá del Vaticano: Bibl. Apostolica Vaticana, 1963, LXXII, c7–9, 248ff.

80 Ibid., c21, 256.

81 See ibid., c19, 256.

82 See Althoff, *Die Macht der Rituale*, 84.

83 See ibid., 151, and T. Broekmann, *Rigor iustitiae. Herrschaft, Recht und Terror im normannisch-staufischen Süden*, Darmstadt: Wiss. Buchges., 2005.

84 See B. Schneidmüller, 'Die Aufführung des Reichs. Zeremoniell, Ritual und Performanz in der Goldenen Bulle von 1356', in E. Brockhoff, M. Matthäus (eds), *Die Kaisermacher. Frankfurt am Main und die Goldene Bulle 1356–1806*, Frankfurt am Main: Societäts-Verlag, 2006, 76–92, 82ff.

85 See Althoff, *Die Macht der Rituale*, 138ff.; Hack, *Das Empfangszeremoniell*, 434ff. and 504ff.

86 Althoff, *Die Macht der Rituale*, 95, and G. Althoff, C. Witthöft, 'Les services symboliques entre dignité et contrainte', *Annales Histoire, Science Sociale* 58, 2003, 1293–318.

87 See K. Bourré, *Dienst, Verdienst und Distinktion. Fürstliche Selbstbehauptungsstrategien der Hohenzollern im 15. Jahrhundert*, Köln, Wien: Böhlau Verlag, 2014, 50f. On the relationship of ritual and honour K. Görich, *Die Ehre Barbarossas. Kommunikation, Konflikt und politisches Handeln im 12. Jahrhundert*, Darmstadt: Wiss. Buchges., 2001; G. Althoff, *Spielregeln der Politik im Mittelalter. Kommunikation in Frieden und Fehde*, Darmstadt: Wiss. Buchges., 1997, 252–7.

88 Schwedler, *Herrschertreffen des Spätmittelalters*, 380ff.; C. Garnier, 'Gabe, Macht und Ehre: Zu Formen und Funktionen des Gabentauschs in den Beziehungen zwischen Mongolen und Europäern im 13. Jahrhundert', *Jahrbücher für Geschichte Osteuropas* 63, 2015, 47–68.

89 See Le Goff, 'A Coronation Program', 54.

90 See Schramm, *Geschichte des englischen Königtums*, 77.

91 See Rogge, *Die deutschen Könige im Mittelalter*, 108.

92 See Althoff, *Spielregeln der Politik*, 119.

93 See Erkens, *Herrschersakralität im Mittelalter*, 28; Fößel, *Die Königin im mittelalterlichen Reich*, 49.

94 See Boshoff, *Königtum und Königsherrschaft*, 118; N. Gussone, 'Ritus, Recht und Geschichtsbewußtsein. Thron und Krone in der Tradition Karls des Großen', in M. Kramp (ed.), *Krönungen: Könige in Aachen – Geschichte und Mythos*, Mainz: Zabern, 2000, 35–47.

95 See J. Ehlers, *Die Kapetinger*, Stuttgart: Kohlhammer, 2000, 64, 191.

96 On Reims see J. Le Goff, *Reims: Krönungsstadt*, Berlin: Wagenbach, 1997; on Aachen Rogge, 'Die deutschen Könige im Mittelalter', 94.

97 See H.W. Goetz, 'Der "rechte" Sitz. Die Symbolik von Rang und Herrschaft im Hohen Mittelalter im Spiegel der Sitzordnung', in G. Blaschitz (ed.), *Symbole des Alltags – Alltag der Symbole. Festschrift Harry Kühnel*, Graz: Akad. Dr.- und Verl.-Anst., 1992, 11–47; Schwedler, *Herrschertreffen des Spätmittelalters*, 341ff.; and profoundly on the last point A. Löther, *Prozessionen in spätmittelalterlichen Städten. Politische Partizipation, obrigkeitliche Inszenierung, städtische Einheit*, Köln: Böhlau, 1999.

98 See Z. Dalewski, 'Lictor imperatoris. Kaiser Lothar III., Sobeslav I. von Böhmen und Boleslaw III. von Polen auf dem Hoftag in Merseburg im Jahre 1135', *Zeitschrift für Ostmitteleuropaforschung* 50, 2001, 317–36. Fundamentally on the problem also Buc, *The Dangers of Ritual*, esp. 15ff., and H. Kamp, 'Tugend, Macht und Ritual. Politisches Verhalten beim Saxo Grammaticus', in G. Althoff (ed.), *Zeichen – Rituale – Werte*, Münster: Rhema, 2004, 179–200.

99 This was done by the archbishops from Canterbury and York, cf. Schramm, *Geschichte des englischen Königtums*, 40f., as well as by those from Sens and Reims, cf. Le Goff; *Reims*, 22–31 and also by those from Mainz and Cologne, cf. Rogge, *Die deutschen Könige im Mittelalter*, 92.

100 See Schramm, *Geschichte des englischen Königtums*, 68ff.

101 See Schneidmüller, 'Die Aufführung des Reichs'.

102 See Goetz, 'Der "rechte" Sitz'.

103 See Löther, *Prozessionen in spätmittelalterlichen Städten*, 281ff; 334f.

104 See H. Skoda, *Medieval Violence: Physical Brutality in Northern France 1270–1330*, Oxford: Oxford Univ. Press, 2013, 173ff.

105 See Keller, 'Die Investitur', 56 and 72.

106 This has already been pointed out by Schramm, *Geschichte des englischen Königtums*, 90ff.

107 See Blockmans, 'Self Representation of Court and City', 84–7, 110.

108 See E.D. Hehl, 'Die Erzbischöfe von Mainz bei Erhebung, Salbung und Krönung des Königs (10.–14. Jahrhundert)', in M. Kramp (ed.), *Krönungen. Könige in Aachen,*

Geschichte und Mythos. Katalog der Ausstellung, vol. 1, Mainz: Zabern, 2000, 97–104, 101f.; Erkens, *Herrschersakralität im Mittelalter,* 26ff.; Erkens, 'Thronfolge und Herrscher-sakralität', 370f.

109 See W. Paravicini, 'The Court of the Dukes of Burgundy: A Model for Europe', in ibid., *Menschen am Hof der Herzöge von Burgund. Gesammelte Aufsätze,* Stuttgart: Thorbecke, 2002, 507–34, first in R. Asch, A. Birke (eds), *Princes, Patronage and the Nobility: The Court at the Beginning of the Modern Age,* Oxford: Oxford Univ. Press, 1991, 207–63, 512ff., 523f.

110 See W. Paravicini, 'Schlichtheit und Pracht: Über König Ludwig XI. von Frankreich und Herzog Karl den Kühnen von Burgund', in C. Nolte, K.H. Spieß, R.G. Werlich (eds), *Principes. Dynastien und Höfe im späten Mittelalter,* Stuttgart: Thorbecke, 2002, 235–76, 76ff.

111 See Althoff, *Die Macht der Rituale,* 201f.

112 See Patzold, 'Wirkreichweite, Geltungsbereich, Forschungsperspektive', 357, and Althoff, *Die Macht der Rituale,* 203.

2

CULTURES OF CONFLICT

Jackson W. Armstrong

The problem of conflict

Conflict encompasses at one extreme the great political clashes of kings, popes, and emperors, and at the other the quotidian minutiae of social relationships negotiated among the humblest peasants or townspeople. Along this broad spectrum of phenomena the sort of conflict to which this overview is primarily addressed is not strife and war of the high order that played out on battlefields such as Crécy or Tannenberg in the fourteenth and fifteenth centuries, but rather it is the 'several kinds of inter-personal or inter-group tension' which, as Brown and Górecki have summarized, might include 'threats, promises, negotiation, ritual, use of force', related emotions, and disputing.[1] And it is especially about the latter – disputing – a type of conflict that could very much be about politics, and could involve power-holding kings, magnates, bishops, town governments, or groups of nobles, clergy, or of townspeople or others of lower social status who gained a political voice by coordinating their actions. This sort of conflict has come to be much better understood in recent decades as a result of attention to cultural patterns, ideas, and norms, and as such it comprehends disputes originating among kinsmen, neighbours, or political or business relations which could expand in scope to include other more powerful parties, or to activate various social and jurisdictional frameworks.[2]

The problem of conflict, and in particular the ideas and expectations about how it should be pursued, managed, and resolved, is that it is intimately tied up with ideas and expectations of government, especially with regard to justice and law. In his magisterial synthesis on late medieval political life, Watts has convincingly argued that across the fourteenth century and up to about the middle of the fifteenth century the prevailing pattern in the growth of government was the increased provision and assertion of jurisdiction by kings, princes, towns, and other ruling authorities. This was part of a process of the articulation and defence of various rights which often led to clashes of jurisdiction and in many cases to war and unrest, but a process also partly in response to demand from subjects (of lesser and greater status) who saw in the assertion of jurisdiction by rulers a means to articulate and defend their own rights as well.[3] As Watts puts it, governmental growth was an uneven and 'ambivalent process' and, furthermore, it 'has been underestimated as a cause of conflict' in its own right.[4]

Another writer, on the related topic of violence in medieval Europe, has framed that matter in terms of an ebb and flow of competing norms, chiefly between norms that allowed rulers to claim an exclusive right and duty to regulate violence, and those that recognized the right of individuals or groups (especially among the nobility) to wield violence on their own behalf.[5] With this in mind, our focus of attention here is on approaches to the expected and accepted patterns of behaviour associated with disputing as a form of conflict, or in other words the norms by which conflict was managed. These norms might be expressed formally through laws and institutions, or informally through custom and usage, and be reflected in accompanying forms of social organization.[6]

Bound up as it is with expectations of governmental regulation of social tensions, conflict has often been understood as a symptom of disorder, the antithesis of good order.[7] Some initial examples will help to illustrate the problem. In 1435 Jehanne la Hardie, a 'receiver, counsellor and supporter of the Brigands' of Normandy, was seized and delivered to justice at Falaise. Condemned for her offences, she was put to execution by being placed in a gibbet, lowered into a pit, and buried alive. The 'Norman Brigands' whom la Hardie aided were peasant bands who self-organized in resistance to the English occupation and more particularly in response to the countryside raiding conducted by English soldiers and deserters in France.[8] The phenomenon of social groups whose members acted with violence contrary to governmental authority is also to be found elsewhere in Europe. For instance, the example of the Norman Brigands suggests comparison with the so-called 'Surnames' of the Anglo-Scottish borderlands. These 'surnames or clannes' (as they were described in a judicial bond of 1506) focused on identification of an extended kin group with a particular family name, such as Nixon, among several others.[9] They were implicated in an illicit culture of livestock raiding and 'feud' in the region known as the marches. The question of how to understand such phenomena – in this case of certain social structures and the conflict associated with them, sometimes in 'frontier' areas such as these – is usually answered by turning the question into one about the strength of governmental structures. A received interpretation is that if local people identified readily with groups like the Brigands or Surnames, they did so of necessity because governmental organization was impaired.[10] Claims like this have been made about local societies in the various English borderlands facing Scotland, Wales, and Gaelic Ireland, and as such they have been about forms of social organization as much as patterns of conflict.[11] But all the same, comparable illustrations of conflict may be found in other social and political contexts. For instance, in the Portuguese town of Evora, the killing of a Muslim man named Ahmad Caeiro in about 1440 precipitated a protracted sequence of reprisal killings which lasted until 1466. We know of these killings because of the documents of protection which those involved sought and secured over time, and one historian has shown these connected episodes to constitute a dispute between family groups in a struggle over office-holding.[12] This further illustration of self-directed activities by groups (in this case, groups also defined by apparent kinship solidarities) entailed violence not to subvert governmental authority but to compete over aspects of its control. The familiar conjecture is that if people acted in such ways, driven by motivation to seek vengeance to remedy wrong, they did so for mutual protection because government failed to offer them adequate security.[13] All this can lead quickly to questions of the role of authority, law, and the 'state', and from thence to the anthropological study of 'stateless' societies, and sociological conceptions of social and political power.[14] But if the state is now recognized by some to be a distorting concept when applied to the later Middle Ages,[15] still Evora, Normandy, and the Anglo-Scottish borderlands were hardly places devoid of the apparatus of government, even if their particular local circumstances presented complexities. The challenge is then how to understand the phenomenon of conflict as it occurred within medieval polities, and within the culture of medieval politics.

The phenomenon of conflict has been closely linked to the question of how to understand apparently disorderly behaviour within political society. In urban northern Europe, for instance, particularly with reference to Flanders, recent decades have seen significant attention directed at examining rebellion and challenges to civic authorities, particularly patterns of urban revolt and more generally the vocabularies of political subversion. This work has also noted the extent to which personal disputes, including claims to the right to vengeance, could be expressed in ways that challenged the authority of governing bodies, including, for instance, craft guilds.[16] The French kingdom after *c.* 1350 was a realm where monarchical power could seem tenuous, but historians have come to locate the assertion of royal power in the exercise of clemency, and recent work on violent seigneurial conflicts among the nobility of southern France argues for the 'accommodating authority' of the crown and royal officials in limiting or seeking to pacify these conflicts through 'collaborative practices', rather than by 'coercive compulsion'.[17] In England the topic of late medieval aristocratic 'lawlessness' generally has long occupied historians' attention. The present paradigm of understanding turns upon the view that English kings were successful in asserting their jurisdictional dominance when they recognized their own reliance upon the private power of landowners to execute and fulfil their commands. Historians of England have come to view political power as built as much and more upon compromise, consent, and consensus than upon coercion or force.[18] These few examples demonstrate the ways in which conflict has been integral to the interpretation of different political societies in western Europe.

Violence, crime, and war

Three subjects, violence, crime, and war, are intimately linked with some of the ideas about conflict just set out. Each has developed its own specialist literature, and deserves some specific comment in this context. As a universal human experience violence has been the subject of considerable scholarly attention, often through studies which privilege cultural interpretations.[19] Violence answers to a range of definitions, but the conventional understanding of physical force exercised against persons or property has been retained in a number of studies.[20] All the same, the scope for overt physical violence to act as a 'language of social order'[21] highlights violence's symbolic and 'ritual' potential, sometimes viewed as a mechanism for the constraint and canalization of aggressive behaviour. And it has been observed that formulaic ritual lends violent acts a measure of predictability, even where hot-blooded passion is mixed with rational calibration.[22] In no small part it is from attempts to legitimate, regulate, and categorize violence that the related notions of crime and war emerged over time. Early modernists have favoured crime and the records of criminal justice for the investigation of social order and discipline as negotiated through everyday life, and as achieved through the autonomy exercised by officials in the local administration of government.[23] Similar agendas have been applied to the later Middle Ages, although with varied emphasis on political considerations.[24] The terminology adopted for this second subject is telling. 'Crime', albeit an expression often wielded freely by many medievalists, is nevertheless a shorthand term, freighted with the unambiguous modern-day division between criminal and civil law. It is a notion widely accepted that public criminal justice, akin to our modern understanding of the idea as concerning offences against 'public order', was administered in an intensively governed realm such as late medieval England.[25] On the one hand, this is a helpful and constructive way to make sense of the copious legal records which survive from the period in that kingdom.[26] On the other, it projects deceptively finite categories onto an indefinite reality – categories that may be clearer to historians than to the medieval offenders, victims, and litigants. Altogether it seems preferable to avoid speaking of 'crime' wherever possible in favour of a less loaded terminology of offences, reflecting situations and allegations of fact that could and did enter the courts in a number of ways.[27] Circumvention of the word 'crime' altogether may be helpful to assist us in better understanding the nature of conflict and its official regulation. The English common law writ of trespass *vi et armis* was a popular means to bring cases into the court of King's Bench from the fourteenth century. It was useful because of its flexibility, being deployed to initiate litigation between private parties concerning a wide range of offences including violence to the person, threats, and damage to property and goods – all of which might fundamentally relate to disputes about title and possession of land.[28] To take an example from another jurisdiction, consider the Scottish offence of 'strublance' (Latin *perturbatio*) which certain urban courts in fifteenth-century Aberdeen were competent to hear and determine. This encompassed a wide range of possibility: including personal injury or harm to property, verbal assault, the deforcement of town officials, and more general peace-breaking misdeeds. Strublance's very breadth allowed the town courts to assert jurisdiction over a wide array of matters, for which a modern criminal–civil distinction was not relevant.[29]

The third subject, war, is perhaps even more multifarious. Whereas its anthropological definition turns on questions of organization and social sanction, its historiographical legacy is to be both cause and symptom of apparent disorder in the later Middle Ages.[30] For medievalists, the categorization of war (with its accompanying complexity of related legal and customary issues) is a problem that concerns both scale and authority.[31] Interpretations of war in late medieval France and Germany have come to avoid the familiar binary distinction between 'public' and 'private' war, encumbered with assumptions about modern nation-states.[32] Indeed, linking violence, crime, and war has been the modern expectation that sole legitimate authority over these matters is the ambition and test of the state.[33] Narratives of the 'rise' of the state in pursuit of this aspiration for sole legitimacy often rely on ideas about the transition from the primitive to the developed, from the archaism of medieval decline to the sophistication of modern progress.[34] The role of law and war in the development of the English 'state' in the thirteenth and fourteenth centuries (in terms of the crown's scope to assert itself through judicial intervention, or to yield such judicial responsibilities to landowners when faced with the pressures of military over-extension) has been the subject of significant attention in recent decades,[35] but any division between a 'law state' and a 'war state' has been shown to be misleading, not least in that war helped to integrate English political society and also served as a 'catalyst for government growth'.[36] Legislative efforts in different realms to 'criminalize' the use of violence in the form of 'private' (or seigneurial, or sub-princely) war – through restrictions enacted in France in the thirteenth and fourteenth centuries, in England through the Great Statute of Treasons of 1352, and in the German-speaking lands at the Imperial Diet of 1495 – may seem blunt measures but they were significant milestones achieved by maturing 'states'.[37] Still, what these French, English, and German enactments have in common is that they are attempts by late medieval rulers and assemblies to recognize and regulate aspects of a culture of conflict, to some extent a shared one, at the point where violence, crime, and war intersect.

Justice and redress

England, Germany, France, and Scotland provide illustrations of another important aspect of conflict: notions of justice, and the redress of injury. In England the monarch's duty was to guarantee his law and see justice dispensed according to it, but in order to achieve this the king required the consent and cooperation of landowners, because they implemented his authority and governed his subjects as the law's primary administrators. It was landowners also who, with a reliance on specialist common lawyers, shaped the growth and use of the law in pursuit and defence of their own rights, especially in property.[38] All the same, England's localities were self-policing, and while pressure from social peers and superiors could steer a disputant towards pursuing a claim in court, self-help involving the use of force remained not just an outside option but at times a necessity. No longer are violent disputing and extra-judicial peace-making understood simply to demonstrate governmental failure to preserve public order. Studies of conflict among English local elites have come to view 'private' power as amalgamated with 'public' authority. Landowners had the right and means to use violence but, while it was intended that force should be used to maintain authority, if violence was misused, the access and means to use it, and the undermining of authority from such abuse, were highly destabilizing.[39] In this regard the gentry and nobility of England shared an aversion to the use of inter-personal violence which risked undermining established authority as anything other than a last resort.[40] Redress was to be found particularly in 'private' processes of dispute resolution, typically through arbitrations conducted either under the auspices of a great lord, or by the cooperative networks of local gentry. This has come to be considered an adjunct to, not an aberration from, the system of royal justice. Most arbitrations can be shown to have happened in conjunction with the use of the legal system.[41]

Beyond England, other patterns emerge in relation to the ways that the powerful approached justice, and the redress of wrong. In the German-speaking lands the practice of 'feud' (see further below) among late medieval and early modern noblemen and princes is a well-attested phenomenon. What this entailed was a range of violent actions (small-scale raiding, burning, looting, cattle rustling, kidnapping) which were 'regulated by accepted rules of conduct and by a more or less fixed repertoire of sanctioned methods'.[42] One significant set of rules was introduced in 1356 by the Golden Bull of Emperor Charles IV, which required that attacks on opponents be preceded by formal announcement, publicly witnessed, in order to render them legitimate. Thus documents known as 'cartels of defiance' came to be accepted as formal declarations of hostilities, allowing time for enemies to prepare for an assault and warn their allies. Yet there was less clarity to all this than might at first be assumed. In the words of one authority on the subject, German feud 'was neither a generally undisputed legal institution, nor a legally prohibited practice'.[43] It involved as disputing parties not only noblemen – who might both offer 'protection and safeguard' to their inferiors and seek the same from their superiors – but also prelates and princes, and towns as corporate bodies. Even peasants might become engaged as principal parties in disputes. In all cases the practice of feuding was an important means for the 'activation of the law' in the jurisdictionally fragmented territory of the Holy Roman Empire.[44] The practice served as a framework through which to assert and defend rights.

France has furnished enriching studies touching on justice and redress which offer another point of comparison.[45] Recent work on late medieval Languedoc, already noted above, has examined the phenomenon of 'seigneurial warfare' among noblemen, and has found that this 'remained a vigorous local tradition' in the period at least up to 1380, involving sieges, raiding, burning, kidnapping, and other violent actions. Although offering a rather less fragmented jurisdictional landscape than did the Empire, the kingdom of France posed for its rulers the difficulty of asserting sovereignty against the claims of greater lords and prelates to their own jurisdictional rights. One way in which French royal officials sought to insert the power of the crown into conflicts arising between local parties was through the extension of royal letters of safeguard which promised protection and marked it out with public proclamation, the display of *fleur-de-lis* pennants, and the assignment of a *gardiator* to the safeguarded person. In this way the French crown asserted, albeit in an incomplete manner, its own claims to prohibit violence and protect its subjects.[46] A similar view of the extension of royal power has been taken in the study of royal grace. Mercy, in the form of royal pardons granted in response to petitions from parties, was a means by which the crown and its agents could affirm the supremacy of kingly jurisdiction.[47] It is helpful to note that the fluctuating scope of English political control over French territory in the period makes it difficult to draw clear 'national' boundaries around the experience of justice. References to the '*maxima inimicica*' noted in an English grant in favour of the lord of Garro in Gascony in 1378 suggest the relevance of the language of seigneurial warfare.[48] Similarly, the range of options considered by one party in a suit between Englishmen in northern France in 1426 is suggestive of the fluidity of ideas of the legitimacy of revenge. There the relevant court recorded that one litigant '*en fu mal content et pensa comment il s'en vengeroit, et mist x ou xij homes armes [...] pour le grever*'.[49]

A further comparative gesture may briefly be drawn with Scotland. Historians of Scotland have discarded an earlier emphasis on a purported antagonism between crown and nobility, and now appreciate the cooperation required between rulers and magnates for the successful governance of the kingdom.[50] Justice and legal development in the Scottish kingdom in the period have been understood to be bound up with the phenomenon of 'feud', as a form of dispute that could be destructively violent and also aimed at the construction of peace, but the focus and emphasis of that work has tended to be on the period after 1500. Scottish feuding has been understood to be both a legal phenomenon and one that underwent a transformation and challenge through the growth of 'public' justice and legal culture in the period and, eventually, through the rhetoric of the reformed church.[51] For the later Middle Ages, the emphasis has been on the degree to which feuding among landowners served to link local and national politics and shape crown–nobility relations. A major study of the topic relies heavily on the surviving evidence in the form of arbitration awards between parties, and emphasizes the degree to which contractual bonds between noblemen often served to recruit supporters in the course of disputes.[52] And examination of the itinerant court of the justice ayre has underscored the importance of mercy and pardon and points to a more than passing resemblance to the 'French' practices noted above. It also shows the extent to which mercy was interlinked with the payment of compensation (Scots 'assythement') in redress of wrong. In Scotland royal pardon frequently *preceded* the payment of compensation to the offended party, and upon the acceptance of this redress the offended party might issue a written receipt or an even more formal document, which was in effect a 'private' pardon mirroring that which was purchased from the crown.[53] Royal justice in Scotland was thus more compensatory than retributive in its emphasis.

'Feud'

'Feud' has unavoidably entered into the preceding discussion of conflict, particularly as it relates to ideas and practices of justice, and feud merits dedicated comment in its own right. This elusive concept and its processes of public, customary violence and peace-making are well explored by scholars across a range of fields. Just as conflict was once understood as destructive disorder, so feud has carried a negative reputation. The two seminal statements on the subject were to turn this reputation on its head. Familiar to historians working in the English language is Max Gluckman's anthropological treatment of feud as a functionalist mechanism for peaceful equilibrium in 'stateless' societies, first published in 1955.[54] For scholars working in German the major interpretative advance came from Otto Brunner in his 1939 study of the feud in late medieval Austria.[55] Brunner's understanding of feud emphasized its legal, political, and constitutional dimensions. In his conception it was a legitimate mechanism for the assertion and defence of noble rights, a modality of justice that had its own formulas and rules.[56] In the words of his translator, Brunner's feud had a 'constitutionally creative role', which has stood in stark contrast to the monarchist emphasis of French historiography, and the story of the advancing common law in the English tradition.[57] Feud is a sprawling and fascinating subject, and scarcely more can be done here than to highlight some aspects pertinent to cultures of conflict generally.[58] First, feud is as much a tool for peace and the binding of the social fabric as it is a pretext for violence. Second, in aiming to dispel the idea of feud as antithetical to the state, some have argued that feuding was integrated – however problematically and with mixed results – into processes of governmental growth in the Middle Ages and later. In Germany, this was through the assertion of rights and jurisdictions, even by princely 'state-builders'.[59] In France and Scotland, as noted already (and indeed also in the Burgundian Low Countries), this was through pardon as a mechanism of royal grace, whereby rulers aspired to harness and regulate peace-making processes.[60] Third, and perhaps most significantly in the context of cultural history, it should be observed that feud is a category of analysis which refers to a contested array of words describing behaviours recorded in historical sources.

Here is a prime example of the trouble identified by Susan Reynolds when scholars 'tend to confuse words, concepts and phenomena'.[61] Frequently blurring together words and concepts, writers have assigned various distinctions between feud words (the English term 'bloodfeud' is one such variant) to describe underlying phenomena of social behaviour. These distinctions have hinged on questions of social status, of individual or group action and liability, or of whether what is described in the record is a single hostile episode or an interminable chain of retaliatory acts.[62] Yet one durable view, first expressed by Brunner, has been of the essential difference between knightly feud (*Fehde*, as the prerogative of the nobility) and all the rest.[63] Even so, recent work on Germany, France, and Denmark has challenged this idea, breaking down the distinction between the knightly or noble feud and similar customary practices found among the lower orders, notably among townspeople and peasants.[64] The result of all this is a cacophony of interpretation, which leads to a fourth point: that a broadly agreed definition of feud continues to elude scholars.[65] Early medievalists have been the most severely sceptical, suggesting that feud was more fiction than fact, or that it should be dispensed with altogether in favour of more precise terminology.[66] With these challenges in mind, it is useful to think in terms of a descriptive concept of feud, rather than a restrictive definition.[67] Scholars working along these lines have tended to give feud a 'light' working definition, and from there identify and look for what may be termed feud-like elements in their sources.[68] What is still required is a clearer understanding of the differences (and overlaps) between words and concepts. Such an approach has recently aspired to think not

> about a concept as a single entity, but as a network of value-laden terms that constitute a conceptual field, a network that is constantly changing both in the composition of terms and in the meanings of some of those terms.[69]

In such a way medieval historians have, for instance, homed in on French *guerre*.[70] Other words that have drawn attention in a comparable lexicographical approach include 'enmity' or 'hatred', related words like 'malice' or 'anger' or *odium*, the Latin antonyms *amicus/inimicus* and *amicitia/inimicita* and their vernacular equivalents, and those to do with love and friendship.[71] A maturing history of emotions has assisted some of this work, putting the focus on the patterns of emotion shaping feud-like behaviours, including the seeking of vengeance to right a wrong. This comes with the recognition of emotion as an instrumental aspect of human social behaviour. Work on the late medieval Italian context has advanced the idea of a 'culture of vengeance', shaped significantly by the focus of analysis on the language of friendship and enmity.[72] In a comparable study, with the idea and language of vengeance as the focus of attention, one scholar has traced a vibrant 'enmity culture' in England up to the end of the thirteenth century.[73] The idea remains underdeveloped that such a culture of enmity might have existed also in late medieval England, involving the patterned behaviours that might be identified under the rubric of 'feud', although new work is addressing that question.[74]

Conflict and cities

Conflict has already been noted as a feature of urban life, and two further examples are illustrative of recent work that has led the subject forward here. The first of these is Smail's set of studies of the 'hatreds' which motivated claims brought in the courts of late medieval Marseille. This work demonstrates how a focus on the historical vocabulary of disputing can bear fruit. Smail shows how a particular emphasis on 'emotional' language used in the course of disputes can reveal a great deal about the relationships between parties in conflict, and also about the motivation behind particular confrontations. By the same token, emotional language used to signal a relationship, or to explain a motivation for action, may serve to legitimate those same relationships and behaviours. Smail's focus of attention has been on the language of 'social emotion', and here, on the scale of a townscape, he has shown publicly acknowledged enmities to have functioned as a social institution, whereby such 'hatreds' shaped the legal behaviours of parties seeking justice in and out of court.[75] Hatreds expressed publicly could also form the basis of political associations and shape 'factional warfare' between groups within the city itself.[76] A major claim of this work is that late medieval governing authorities (such as those of the Angevin crown in Marseille) harnessed private enmities and the desire for vengeance, and presented disputants with a useful opportunity to 'consume' justice by way of asserting and advertising their hostile relationships in courts of law. Relevant to all this is the related point that to an extent language provides the conceptual apparatus within which social activities take place. Thus the words used to describe particular disputes and relationships merit attention for what they express of the frameworks by which conflict was understood, and of the norms invoked to address it.[77]

Urban conflict has also been approached from a different direction. A second example concerns the recent effort by Lantschner to identify common patterns of conflict deployed in several cities of the southern Low Countries and northern Italy. This work is at pains to identify occurrences of 'political' conflict as its subject of study, concentrating on affairs which affected 'urban public organization' and so excluding disputes where there was 'no visible public dimension'.[78] In this exercise the author traces a 'logic' of conflict as a crucial part of political organization, its strategies of legitimation (such as by invoking justice), and its various 'modes' (by way of popular protest, constitutional bargaining, and urban warfare) and types of 'action groups' (including corporate and quasi-corporate, factions and parties, and coalitions). In this way Bologna and Liege are found by Lantschner to exhibit 'volatile' systems of conflict; Florence and Tournai, 'constitutional' systems of conflict; and Lille and Verona, 'contained' systems of conflict. These three distinct pairs of patterns underscore the polycentricity of urban politics in the case studies, and Lantschner argues that conflict was 'expressive and constitutive' of urban political organization.[79] If Smail's work on Marseille serves to illustrate the way in which the growth of 'state sovereignty' occurred in a consumer-driven way,[80] Lantschner's study undercuts any sense that cities in two of Europe's most urbanized belts were in any meaningful sense the cohesive and unitary entities they have been assumed to be in major accounts of state growth in the later Middle Ages. Rather, while tracing the pluralist and corporatist nature of urban public organization, it shows the extent to which conflict can be a useful framework through which to understand political forms and patterns.[81]

There are three brief points on which to conclude this overview. I began with the claim that conflict is best understood as encompassing a spectrum of phenomena from the everyday at one extreme to the highest affairs of state at the other, and that the idea of conflict has been a problematic one for historians because its treatment has been bound up with ideas and expectations of government and social order. If conflict is helpfully understood in this way, it seems difficult to find an advantage in attempting to mark any hard point of division between 'political' and 'non-political' conflict along this continuum. Much of the work reviewed here (Lantschner's approach aside) tells of how useful it can be to focus on dispute as a type of conflict with breadth of scope and ability to comprehend both the personal and the official, how 'private' confrontations could readily acquire 'public' dimensions, or be shaped by them, and how a focus on disputing at a range of social levels can reveal a great deal about politics and political behaviour. Second, while the historical understanding of conflict has come to be better understood through attention to cultural patterns, ideas, and norms in recent decades, it has been especially a vigorous focus on language, and emotional language in particular, that has driven this advancement and enabled the investigation of norms and expectations in a range of source materials. Finally, even as it remains a broad and problematic field of historical enquiry, conflict has ceased to be thought of solely in terms of social disorder and destruction. Historians of the later Middle Ages are to varying degrees moving towards an understanding of conflict and its cultural expressions as a socially and politically creative and constructive subject.

Notes

1 W.C. Brown and P. Górecki (eds), *Conflict in Medieval Europe: Changing Perspectives on Society and Culture*, Aldershot: Ashgate, 2003, 1.
2 Brown and Górecki construe disputing to be a 'phase of conflict which is articulated as a claim, between two or more parties, concerning some specific subject matter': ibid., 1–2.
3 J. Watts, *The Making of Polities: Europe, 1300–1500*, Cambridge: Cambridge Univ. Press, 2009, 203–4, 207, 213–18.
4 Ibid., 279, 280.
5 W.C. Brown, *Violence in Medieval Europe*, London, New York: Routledge, 2014, 292–3.
6 Brown and Górecki, *Conflict in Medieval Europe*, 1–2.
7 For comment see P. Lantschner, *The Logic of Political Conflict in Medieval Cities: Italy and the Southern Low Countries, 1370–1440*, Oxford: Oxford Univ. Press, 2015, 5.
8 V. Challet, 'Tuchins and "Brigands de Bois": Peasant Communities and Self-Defence Movements in Normandy during the Hundred Years War', in L. Clark (ed.), *The Fifteenth Century IX: English and Continental Perspectives*, Woodbridge: Boydell, 2010, 94, 99.
9 *A Descriptive Catalogue of Ancient Deeds in the Public Record Office*, 6 vols, London: H.M.S.O., 1890–1915, iii, 497 (D 790).
10 D.W. Sabean, S. Teuscher, and J. Mathieu (eds), *Kinship in Europe: Approaches to Long-Term Development (1300–1900)*, New York and Oxford: Berghahn Books, 2007, 1–3, 4, 12, 13, 15, 20, 24. A conventional statement is found in J. Heers, *Family Clans in the Middle Ages*, Amsterdam, New York, Oxford: North-Holland, 1977, 251–2.
11 J.A. Tuck, 'Richard II and the Border Magnates', *Northern History* 3, 1968, 27–30; J.A. Tuck, 'Northumbrian Society in the Fourteenth Century', *Northern History* 6, 1971,

26–8; R.R. Davies, 'The Survival of the Bloodfeud in Medieval Wales', *History* 54, 1969, 341, 350; C. Maginn, 'English Marcher Lineages in South Dublin in the Late Middle Ages', *Irish Historical Studies* 34, 2004, 114, 117.

12 F. Soyer, 'Living in Fear of Revenge: Religious Minorities and the Right to Bear Arms in Fifteenth-Century Portugal', in S.A. Throop and P.R. Hyams (eds), *Vengeance in the Middle Ages: Emotion, Religion and Feud*, Farnham: Ashgate, 2010, 93–6.

13 D.L. Smail, 'Faction and Feud in Fourteenth-Century Marseille', in J.B. Netterstrøm and B. Poulsen (eds), *Feud in Medieval and Early Modern Europe*, Aarhus: Aarhus Univ. Press, 2007, 114, discussing B. Guenée, *Tribunaux et Gens de Justice dans le Bailliage de Senlis à la fin du Moyen Âge*, Paris: Soc. Déd. Les belles Lettres, 1963, 293–5, on 'la justice impuissante'. See also S. Carroll (ed.), *Cultures of Violence: Interpersonal Violence in Historical Perspective*, Basingstoke: Palgrave Macmillan, 2007, 4, 16, 24, 76.

14 C. Tilly, 'War Making and State Making as Organized Crime', in P.B. Evans, D. Rueschmeyer, and T. Skocpol (eds), *Bringing the State Back In*, Cambridge: Cambridge Univ. Press, 1985, 169–91; D.L. Smail, 'Violence and Predation in Late Medieval Mediterranean Europe', *Comparative Studies in Society and History* 54, 2012, 7–34; H. Zmora, *The Feud in Early Modern Germany*, Cambridge: Cambridge Univ. Press, 2011, 13, 21, 80, 128; M. Mann, *The Sources of Social Power*, 3 vols, Cambridge: Cambridge Univ. Press, 1986–2012, i, Ch. 1, esp. 22–7.

15 R.R. Davies, 'The Medieval State: The Tyranny of a Concept?', *Journal of Historical Sociology* 16, 2003, 280–300; Watts, *Making of Polities*, 23–34.

16 J. Dumolyn and J. Haemers, '"A Bad Chicken was Brooding": Subversive Speech in Late Medieval Flanders', *Past & Present* 214, 2012, 79; J. Dumolyn, J. Haemers, H.R. Oliva Herrer, and V. Challet (eds), *The Voices of the People in Late Medieval Europe Communication and Popular Politics*, Turnhout: Brepols, 2014; J. Dumolyn and J. Haemers, 'Patterns of Urban Rebellion in Medieval Flanders', *Journal of Medieval History* 31, 2005, 369–93.

17 J. Firnhaber-Baker, *Violence and the State in Languedoc, 1250–1400*, Cambridge: Cambridge Univ. Press, 2014, 183.

18 M.C. Carpenter, *Locality and Polity: A Study in Warwickshire Landed Society, 1401–1499*, Cambridge: Cambridge Univ. Press, 1992, 283–4 (and literature cited there), 349, 354, 592, 628. Elsewhere see E. Powell, *Kingship, Law and Society: Criminal Justice in the Reign of Henry V*, Oxford: Clarendon Press, 1989, 271–2; G.L. Harriss, *Shaping the Nation: England 1360–1461*, Oxford: Clarendon Press, 2005, 163–4, 193, 206; P.C. Maddern, *Violence and Social Order: East Anglia 1422–1442*, Oxford: Clarendon Press, 1992, esp. 11–12, 66, 71, 110, 133, 218, on 'righteous' violence to reinforce the moral and social order.

19 These issues will be explored in my forthcoming book *England's Northern Frontier: Conflict and Local Society in the Fifteenth-Century Scottish Marches*, Cambridge: Cambridge Univ. Press. For instance, Carroll, *Cultures of Violence*, 1–43; S. Carroll, *Blood and Violence in Early Modern France*, Oxford: Oxford Univ. Press, 2006, 5; H. Skoda, *Medieval Violence: Physical Brutality in Northern France 1270–1330*, Oxford: Oxford Univ. Press, 2013, 1–8, 18–49; G. Halsall (ed.), *Violence and Society in the Early Medieval West*, Woodbridge: Boydell, 1998, 7–19.

20 As per Carroll, *Cultures of Violence*, 8. See also Martin Kinzinger, Franz Rexroth, and Jörg Rogge (eds), *Gewalt und Widerstand in der politischen Kultur des späten Mittelalters*, Ostfildern: Thorbecke, 2015, Introduction, which concentrates on physical and bodily violence; Brown, *Violence in Medieval Europe*, 6–7 discusses the concept of 'violence' (at its narrowest referring to the use of physical force to cause injury or harm).

21 Maddern, *Violence and Social Order*, 234 (quotation); S.D. Amussen, 'Punishment, Discipline and Power: The Social Meanings of Violence in Early Modern England', *Journal of British Studies* 34, 1995, 6–7; Skoda, *Medieval Violence*, 23.

22 See C. Phythian-Adams, 'Rituals of Personal Confrontation in Late Medieval England', *Bulletin of the John Rylands Library* 73, 1991, 72–3, 77, 90; D.J. Kagay, 'The Iberian *Diffidamentum*: From Vassalic Defiance to the *Code Duello*', in D.J. Kagay and L.J.A. Villalon (eds), *The Final Argument: The Imprint of Violence on Society in Medieval and Early Modern Europe*, Woodbridge: Boydell, 1998, 73–82; E. Cohen, *The Crossroads of Justice: Law and Culture in Late Medieval France*, Leiden: Brill, 1993. For predictability: Carroll, *Cultures of Violence*, 5, 12, 29, 21.

23 M. Weisser, *Crime and Punishment in Early Modern Europe*, Hassocks: Harvester Press, 1979; V.A.C. Gatrell, B. Lenman, and G. Parker (eds), *Crime and the Law: The Social History of Crime in Western Europe Since 1500*, London: Europa Publ., 1980; S. Hindle, *The State and Social Change in Early Modern England, 1550–1640*, Basingstoke: Palgrave, 2000; G. Walter, *Crime, Gender and Social Order in Early Modern England*, Cambridge: Cambridge Univ. Press, 2003; Z. Schneider, *The King's Bench: Bailiwick Magistrates and Local Governance in Normandy, 1670–1740*, Rochester: Boydell & Brewer, 2008.

24 For a European survey see X. Rousseau and R. Lévy (eds), *Le pénal dans tous ses états: justice, états et sociétés en Europe: XIIe–XXe siècles*, Brussels: Facultés Universitaires Saint-Louis, 1997. Politically attuned assessments of England include M.T. Clanchy, 'Law, Government and Society in Medieval England', *History* 59, 1974, 73–8; M.C. Carpenter, 'Law, Justice and Landowners in Late Medieval England', *Law and History Review* 1, 1983, 205–37; Powell, *Kingship, Law and Society*.

25 J.H. Baker, *An Introduction to English Legal History*, 3rd edn, London: Butterworth, 1990, 571.

26 'Crime' (*criminis, causis criminalibus*) is a term used by the medieval judge John Fortescue with reference to felony and treason, *The Governance of England*, ed. C. Plummer, Oxford: Clarendon Press, 1885, 141; John Fortescue, *De Laudibus Legum Angliae*, ed. S. Chrimes, Cambridge: Cambridge Univ. Press, 1942, 62–5.

27 See J.A. Sharpe, 'The History of Crime in Late Medieval and Early Modern England: A Review of the Field', *Social History* 7, 1982, 188–9; T. Dean, *Crime in Medieval Europe, 1200–1550*, London: Pearson Education, 2001, 96–108; A. Harding, *Medieval Law and the Foundations of the State*, Oxford: Oxford Univ. Press, 2002, 60, 240, 242–6; E.M. Peters, 'Introduction: The Reordering of Law and the Illicit', in R.M. Karras, J. Kaye, and E.A. Matter (eds), *Law and the Illicit in Medieval Europe*, Philadelphia, PA: University of Pennsylvania Press, 2008, 7. For Maddern, *Violence and Social Order*, 49, 'crime' is a label partly dependent on an offender's relative position in the social hierarchy. On the use of legal records see Carpenter, *Locality and Polity*, 705–9. See also P.R. Hyams, *Rancor and Reconciliation in Medieval England*, Ithaca, NY: Cornell Univ. Press, 2003, 80 (using 'downward justice' as an alternative).

28 Maddern, *Violence and Social Order*, 31.

29 See entry ARO-6-0825-01, in E. Frankot, A. Havinga, C. Hawes, W. Hepburn, W. Peters, J. Armstrong, P. Astley, A. Mackillop, A. Simpson, A. Wyner (eds), *Aberdeen Registers Online: 1398–1511*, Aberdeen: University of Aberdeen, 2019, www.abdn.ac.uk/aro (accessed 21 May 2020).

30 J. Haas (ed.), *The Anthropology of War*, Cambridge: Cambridge Univ. Press, 1990: 1–2. On the historiography of 'war and disorder' see Watts, *Making of Polities*, 19–23.

31 M.H. Keen, *The Laws of War in the Late Middle Ages*, London: Routledge & Kegan Paul, 1965, 104–5, 108–9.

32 G. Algazi, 'The Social Use of Private War: Some Late Medieval Views Reviewed', *Tel Aviver Jahrbuch für deutsche Geschichte* 22, 1993, 253–73; H. Kaminsky, 'The Noble Feud in the Later Middle Ages', *Past & Present* 177, 2002, 55–6, 74; Zmora, *The Feud*, 15, 47–9; J. Firnhaber-Baker, '*Jura in medio*: The Settlement of Seigneurial Disputes in Later Medieval Languedoc', *French History* 26, 2012, 445–7.

33 C. Tilly, 'Reflections on the History of European State-Making', in C. Tilly (ed.), *The Formation of National States in Western Europe*, Princeton, NJ: Princeton Univ. Press, 1975, 42; J.J. Sheehan, 'The Problem of Sovereignty in European History', *American Historical Review* 111, 2006, 3–4, 6; Carroll, *Cultures of Violence*, 6; Halsall, *Violence and Society*, 19–29; J. Firnhaber-Baker, 'Techniques of Seigneurial War in the Fourteenth Century', *Journal of Medieval History* 36, 2010, 91.

34 On narratives of transition see Watts, *Making of Polities*, 11–12, 25; Halsall, *Violence and Society*, 4.

35 R.W. Kaeuper, *War, Justice and Public Order: England and France in the Later Middle Ages*, Oxford: Clarendon Press, 1988, esp. 381–92. For critique see G.L. Harriss, 'Political Society and the Growth of Government in Late Medieval England', *Past & Present* 138, 1993, 28–57.

36 M.C. Carpenter, 'War, Government and Governance in England in the Later Middle Ages', in L. Clark (ed.), *The Fifteenth Century VII: Conflicts, Consequences and the Crown in the Late Middle Ages*, Woodbridge: Boydell & Brewer, 2007, 2 (quotation), 17–22.

37 G. Prosser, 'The Later Medieval French Noblesse', in D. Potter (ed.), *France in the Later Middle Ages*, Oxford: Oxford Univ. Press, 2002, 200; Harding, *Medieval Law*, 240; H. Zmora, *State and Nobility in Early Modern Germany: The Knightly Feud in Franconia, 1440–1567*, Cambridge: Cambridge Univ. Press, 1997, 129; Kaminsky, 'The Noble Feud', 66, 68, 75–6; J.G. Bellamy, *The Law of Treason in England in the Later Middle Ages*, Cambridge: Cambridge Univ. Press, 1970, 14, 62–3, 90–2, 201.

38 Baker, *Introduction*, 178–85, on the late medieval legal profession.

39 M.C. Carpenter, *The Wars of the Roses: Politics and the Constitution in England, c.1437–1509*, Cambridge: Cambridge Univ. Press, 1997, 60; Maddern, *Violence and Social Order*, 16, 18–20, 228–34; S.M. Wright, *The Derbyshire Gentry in the Fifteenth Century*, Chesterfield: Derbyshire Record Society, 1983, 119, 122.

40 Carpenter, *Locality and Polity*, 358–9, 397, 433, 561, 572, 581, 610, 612, 620–2; Harriss, 'Political Society', 51.

41 There is a large literature here, from which a leading example is E. Powell, 'Settlement of Disputes by Arbitration in Fifteenth-Century England', *Law and History Review* 2, 1984, 21–43.

42 Zmora, *The Feud*, 25, 44 (quotation), 53.

43 Ibid., 34, 41 (quotation), 61; O. Volckart, 'The Economics of Feuding in Late Medieval Germany', *Explorations in Economic History* 41, 2004, 287–91.

44 C. Reinle, 'Peasants' Feuds in Late Medieval Bavaria (Fourteenth-Fifteenth Century)', in Netterstrøm and Poulsen, *Feud*, 161–74; Zmora, *The Feud*, 9, 14–16, 125 (quotation).

45 S. Carroll, 'The Peace in the Feud in Sixteenth- and Seventeenth-Century France', *Past & Present* 178, 2003, 74–115; Carroll, *Blood and Violence*.

46 J. Firnhaber-Baker, 'Seigneurial War and Royal Power in Later Medieval Southern France', *Past & Present* 208, 2010, 41, 44, 46–7, 71–2, 75.

47 C. Gauvard, '*De Grace Especial*': *Crime, État et Société en France à la fin du Moyen Âge*, 2 vols, Paris: Publications de la Sorbonne, 1991, esp. Ch. 2, 20.

48 A. Curry, P. Morgan, P. Spence, et al. (eds), *The Gascon Rolls Project 1317–1468*, C 61/91 m 7, entry 64, www.gasconrolls.org/en/edition/images/C61_91/m7.html (accessed 1 January 2018).

49 *English Suits Before the Parlement of Paris, 1420–1436*, ed. C.T. Allmand and C.A.J. Armstrong, Cambridge: The Royal Historical Society, 1982, 117.

50 K. Stevenson, *Power and Propaganda: Scotland 1306–1488*, Edinburgh: Edinburgh Univ. Press, 2014, 88–97.

51 J.M. Wormald, 'Bloodfeud, Kindred and Government in Early Modern Scotland', *Past & Present* 87, 1980, 54–97; K.M. Brown, *Bloodfeud in Scotland 1573–1625: Violence, Justice and Politics in an Early Modern Society*, Glasgow: Donald, 1986; A.R.C. Simpson and A.L.M. Wilson, *Scottish Legal History: Volume One 1000–1707*, Edinburgh: Edinburgh Univ. Press, 2017, 163; A.M. Godfrey, *Civil Justice in Renaissance Scotland: The Origins of a Central Court*, Leiden: Brill, 2009, 55–440, 446–8.

52 S.I. Boardman, 'Politics and the Feud in Late Medieval Scotland', unpubl. Ph.D. thesis, Univ. of St Andrews, 1989.

53 J.W. Armstrong, 'The Justice Ayre in the Border Sheriffdoms, 1493–1498', *Scottish Historical Review* 92, 2013, 30–2.

54 M. Gluckman, 'The Peace in the Feud', *Past & Present* 7, 1955, 1–14; M. Gluckman, *Custom and Conflict in Africa*, Oxford: Blackwell, 1956, Ch. 1. Gluckman built upon the anthropological work of E.E. Evans-Pritchard, *The Nuer*, Oxford: Clarendon Press, 1940, and E. Colson, 'Social Control and Vengeance in Plateau Tonga Society', *Africa* 23, 1953, 199–212. In turn he inspired J.M. Wallace-Hadrill, 'The Bloodfeud of the Franks', *Bulletin of the John Rylands Library* 41, 1959, 459–87. See also J.B. Netterstrøm, 'Introduction: The Study of Feud in Medieval and Early Modern History', in Netterstrøm and Poulsen, *Feud*, 9–12.

55 O. Brunner, *Land and Lordship: Structures of governance in medieval Austria*, trans. H. Kaminsky and J.V.H. Melton, Philadelphia, PA: Univ. of Pennsylvania Press, 1992, esp. Ch. 1. C. Petit-Dutaillis, *Documents nouveaux sur les moeurs populaires et le droit de vengeance dans les Pays-Bas*, Paris: Champion, 1908, illustrated 'the right of vengeance' and '*guerres familiales*' in the Burgundian Low Countries, but here, as elsewhere in his work, the author remained firmly within a French monarchist historical tradition.

56 On Brunner see Algazi, 'The Social Use of Private War'; Zmora, *State and Nobility*, 4–8; Zmora, *The Feud*, 4–8, 47–9; Netterstrøm, 'Introduction: The Study of Feud', 20–3.

57 Kaminsky, 'The Noble Feud', 58. O. Fenger, *Fejde og mandebod. Studier over slægtsansvaret i germansk og gammeldansk ret*, Copenhagen: Juristforbundets Forl., 1971, was perhaps the first to combine inspiration from both Gluckman and Brunner in a major study of Danish feud: J.B. Netterstrøm, 'Feud in Late Medieval and Early Modern Denmark', in Netterstrøm and Poulsen, *Feud*, 175–6.

58 See Netterstrøm, 'Introduction: The Study of Feud', 9–67, and, more succinctly, Dean, *Crime in Medieval Europe*, 98–108. For the historiography of feud in Germany see Zmora, *The Feud*, 1–28.

59 Zmora, *The Feud*, 21, 80, 128, 137, 144, 164: Kaminsky, 'The Noble Feud', 58, 79, 82. See also M. Strickland, 'Treason, Feud and the Growth of State Violence: Edward I and the "War of the Earl of Carrick", 1306–7', in C. Given-Wilson, A. Kettle, and L. Scales (eds), *War, Government and Aristocracy in the British Isles, c.1150–1500*, Woodbridge: Boydell & Brewer, 2008, 103–5.

60 Carroll, 'The Peace in the Feud', 109–10, 115. On vengeance and pardon see Gauvard, 1991: Chs 2, 20; C. Gauvard, 'Justification and Theory of the Death Penalty at the *parlement* of Paris in the Late Middle Ages', in C. Allmand (ed.), *War, Government and Power in Late Medieval France*, Liverpool: Liverpool Univ. Press, 2000, 190–208. W. Prevenier, 'The Two Faces of Pardon Jurisdiction in the Burgundian Netherlands: A Royal Road to Social Cohesion and an Effectual Instrument of Princely Clientelism', in P. Hoppenbrouwers, A. Janse, and R. Stein (eds), *Power and Persuasion: Essays on the*

Art of State Building in Honour of W.P. Blockmans, Turnhout: Brepols, 2010, 177–95. For Scotland, see Armstrong, 'The Justice Ayre', 30–7.

61 S. Reynolds, *Fiefs and Vassals: The Medieval Evidence Reinterpreted*, Oxford: Oxford Uni. Press, 1994, 12.

62 A non-exhaustive list would include: in Latin, *faida, guerra, odium*, and *inimicitia* (sometimes *inimicitia mortalis* or *capitalis*); in French *guerre*; in Italian *vendetta* and *faide;* and in German *Fehde, Totschlagsfehde*, and *Blutrache*: Netterstrøm, 'Introduction: The Study of Feud', 21, 45, 39–40; E. Muir, *Mad Blood Stirring: Vendetta and Factions in Friuli during the Renaissance*, Baltimore, MD: Johns Hopkins Univ. Press, 1993, xxiv.

63 Kaminsky, 'The Noble Feud', 55–6.

64 T. Kuehn, *Law, Family, and Women: Toward a Legal Anthropology of Renaissance Italy*, Chicago, IL: Univ. of Chicago Press, 1991, esp. Ch. 2; T. Dean, 'Violence, Vendetta and Peacemaking in Late Medieval Bologna', *Criminal Justice History* 17, 2002, 1–17; Reinle, 'Peasants' Feuds'; J.B. Netterstrøm, 'Feud, Protection and Serfdom in Late Medieval and Early Modern Denmark (c. 1400–1600)', in P. Freedman and M. Bourin (eds), *Forms of Servitude in Northern and Central Europe: Decline, Resistance and Expansion*, Turnhout: Brepols, 2005, 369–84.

65 This is despite numerous attempts at an overall definition, including J. Black-Michaud, *Cohesive Force: Feud in the Mediterranean and the Middle East*, Oxford: Blackwell, 1975, 121–3, 126–8, 162–7, 191–204; C. Boehm, *Blood Revenge: The Anthropology of Feuding in Montenegro and Other Tribal Societies*, Lawrence, KS: Univ. Press of Kansas, 1984, 218–20.

66 P. Sawyer, 'The Bloodfeud in Fact and Fiction', *Acta Jutlandica* 63, 1987, 27–38; Halsall, *Violence and Society*, 19, 22, 24–5, proposes 'customary vengeance'. For scepticism about feud in late medieval Normandy: A.J. Finch, 'The Nature of Violence in the Middle Ages: An Alternative Perspective', *Historical Research* 70, 1997, 249–68.

67 On the trend towards description over definition see Netterstrøm, 'Introduction: The Study of Feud', 49–59. An astronomer points out the difference between concepts and definitions: M. Brown, *How I Killed Pluto and Why It Had It Coming*, New York: Spiegel & Grau, 2010, 272.

68 Brown, *Bloodfeud*, 4–5; Hyams, *Rancor*, xvi, 8–9, 12, 32–3, 210–15. On 'feud-like hostilities', which he excludes from his model, see Black-Michaud, *Cohesive Force*, 129.

69 M. Knights et al., 'Commonwealth: The Social, Cultural and Conceptual Contexts of an Early Modern Keyword', *Historical Journal* 54, 2011, 661.

70 Firnhaber-Baker, 'Techniques of Seigneurial War', 91, 97 (although distanced from notions of feud).

71 R.J. Bartlett, '"Mortal Enmities": The Legal Aspect of Hostility in the Middle Ages', in B.S. Tuten and T.L. Billado (eds), *Feud, Violence and Practice: Essays in Medieval Studies in Honor of Stephen D. White*, Farnham: Ashgate, 2010, 197–212; Hyams, *Rancor*, Ch. 2; M.T. Clanchy, 'Law and Love in the Middle Ages', in J. Bossy (ed.), *Disputes and Settlements: Law and Human Relations in the West*, Cambridge and Oxford: Cambridge Univ. Press, 1980, 47–67.

72 A. Zorzi, 'Conflits et pratiques infrajudiciaires dans les formations politiques italiennes du XIIIe au XVe siècle', in B. Garnot (ed.), *L'infrajudiciaire du Moyen Age à l'époque contemporaine*, Dijon: EUD, 1996, 19–36; T. Dean, 'Marriage and Mutilation: Vendetta in Late Medieval Italy', *Past & Present* 157, 1997, 3–36.

73 Hyams, *Rancor*, Ch. 8 (quotation); B.H. Rosenwein (ed.), *Anger's Past: The Social Uses of an Emotion in the Middle Ages*, Ithaca, NY: Cornell Univ. Press, 1998, 3; S.D. White, 'The Politics of Anger', in ibid., 127–52; L.A. Pollock, 'Anger and the Negotiation of Relationships in Early Modern England', *Historical Journal* 47, 2004, 567–90.

74 J.W. Armstrong (forthcoming), *England's Northern Frontier: Conflict and Local Society in the Fifteenth-Century Marches Towards Scotland*.

75 D.L. Smail, 'Hatred as a Social Institution in Medieval Society', *Speculum* 76, 2001, 90–126; Smail, *Consumption of Justice*, Ch. 2.

76 D.L. Smail, 'Faction and Feud in Fourteenth-Century Marseille', in Netterstrøm and Poulsen, *Feud*, 113–33.

77 For a related approach to a different topic see C. Fletcher, 'What Makes a Political Language? Key Terms, Profit and Damage in the Common Petition of the English Parliament, 1343–1422', in J. Dumolyn, J. Haemers, H.R. Oliva Herrer, and V. Challet (eds), *The Voices of the People in Late Medieval Europe: Communication and Popular Politics*, Turnhout: Brepols, 2014, 91–106.

78 Lantschner, *Logic of Political Conflict*, 9–10.

79 Ibid., 200.

80 Smail, 'Hatred as a Social Institution', 126.

81 Lantschner, *Logic of Political Conflict*, 200–1, 205.

3

MATERIAL CULTURES OF LIVING

Spatiality and everyday life[i]

Jan Hirschbiegel and Gabriel Zeilinger

Trust and confidence as fundamental preconditions for the establishment of social spaces

In any given moment of life, one proceeds into an unknown future. All efforts to persist in such a specific presence apply to care for further circumstances. Those precautions refer to diverse aspects, which undergo historical changes and are visible in varied institutions and instruments to secure survival not only of individuals but also of societies. Therefore, the human objective in general is to interact proactively and to thereby generate and ensure confidence and trust, because confidence and trust form a hypothesis for future behavior, yet strong enough to translate into practical actions.[1] The sociologist Niklas Luhmann pursued this notion of Georg Simmel and determines trust in the first instance as confidence in own expectations.[2] For that reason, it is in fact necessary to explain the world based on confidence as defined by the function to mediate between the unlimited complexity of future possibilities and the limited stock of past experiences. The fundamental aim is supposedly to be capable of acting in diverse present social environments.[3] To trust in distrust,[4] as the historian Ernst Schubert phrases, is one of the basic principles of human coexistence. The general objective in social relationships based on past experiences is to establish security in an ever-threatened present, because the present is burdened by a merely estimated and therefore incalculable option for the future.[5] Trust in its interpersonal variant can be described as intensified confidence.[6] It is a fundamental organizing principle of social exchange, always reciprocally geared,[7] indispensable as the basic element of social cohesion and therefore essential for communitization ('Vergemeinschaftung') and socialization ('Vergesellschaftung'),[8] especially in premodern face-to-face societies,[9] particularly visible in all forms of gift-giving. Finally, all institutions are built on trust often secured by (written) contracts.[10] After all, every form of communitization or socialization can be understood as a specific social context, defined by Martina Löw as a space socially constructed through human action.[11] This also applies to the contemporaries of the Middle Ages and their different sets of human experience and behavior. Thereby, they left material and immaterial traces of interaction, which allow us to study how they tried to create and to understand their world. Therefore, we will present exemplarily two social spaces in the following – the noble court and the urban commune – by means of an interactive triangle of location, objects and actors, because space is a relational order and collocation of bodies and social goods, as Löw argues, generated by the synthesis and placing of these elements.[12] According to this concept, court and city are institutions which can be characterized as social spaces with different functions due to specific patterns of interaction and established by specific shapes of trust.[13] This will here be demonstrated by two exemplary samples: gift-giving at court, and the production of written documents in town-halls.

Fields of analysis: court and city

Gift-giving at court: social networks as spaces of interaction decoded by their relicts

When talking about gift-giving at court, the focus is commonly directed only to the material court culture and especially on those objects which were produced for representative and consumptive purposes of the court society.[14] Nevertheless, the non-material aspects of court culture have to be mentioned as well: behavioral patterns, gestures and rituals.[15] Many traditions clearly combine material and non-material aspects of court culture: a common court scene shows a prince in a chamber while receiving the honors of his noblemen, proved by numerous illustrations of dedicated manuscripts.[16] Also, gift-giving implied the mutual existence of material and non-material court culture. It always meant both the context and the action of giving – along with receiving from others, of course – and the object that was given away as a present.[17] This interplay between material and non-material forms of court culture can be ideally observed by the gift exchange on New Year's Day at the French courts around 1400.[18]

Not only in this context, princely courts have to be considered as space-creating[19] social systems consisting of personal relationships between interacting individuals.[20] Within the numerous different social relationships, the set of personal bilateral relationships between a prince and his courtiers is of particular importance. As these specific relationships were based on the exchange of obedience against favor,[21] they were at the core of the whole system and formed its functional kernel. These court-internal relationships between a prince and his courtiers had to be affirmed and reassured on a regular basis. Affirmation and reassurance were not only attained by committing to joint social actions such as festivities, ceremonies or rituals in the rhythms of daily life at court;[22] the visibility of this commitment in public was of high importance, too.[23]

Manuscripts as gauges of social relationships assume a particular role in this system,[24] because they are almost without any material value, but of important validity in the frames of inevitable courtly representation for the spaces and horizons of politics, knowledge and interests at court.[25] As well as other gifts, books were of great functional significance for the interacting participants of the gift-giving circles with respect to the representational, perceptual, experiential and therefore socializing perspectives of those whose presence at court was laid down by the customs and ordinances in the late Middle Ages. The *Livre de la Paix* by Christine de Pizan (c. 1364–c. 1431), which the Duke of Berry received from the author in 1414,[26] was valued at only five *livres*,[27] whereas the Duke himself was once prepared to pay 200 *livres* for a collection of poems by the said Christine.[28] In contrast, the French translation by Laurent de Premierfait (c. 1350–1418)[29] of Boccaccio's[30] *De mulieribus claris*, a New Year's Day gift from Martin Gouge de Charpaignes (c. 1360–1444),[31] at this time Bishop of Chartres and the Duke's Chancellor, was valued at 100 *livres*.[32] The embellishments could well have played a decisive role here. For Boccaccio's work was 'bien enluminé, couvert de drap de damas noir' and fitted with two silver-gilt fastenings.[33] In Christine de Pizan's book the fastenings were made from brass.[34] Nevertheless, the limited capital value of the manuscripts raised their chances of survival exponentially. Contrary to countless objects created by the goldsmiths of the time, they could not be melted down and turned into money. After all, an ordinance of Charles VI (1368–1422), dating from 1416, determined that after the death of John of Berry in 1416 an 'assez grand quantité d'orfevrerie d'or et d'argent' from his collection should be sold 'pour payer les soldats qui luttaient contre les Anglais'.[35]

Except for Christine de Pizan and the Patriarch of Alexandria,[36] partners in the exchange of manuscripts were nearly exclusively members of the Duke of Berry's court. With the exception of Philip the Bold (1342–1404),[37] who was Duke of Burgundy, and the King's brother, Louis I, Duke of Orleans (1372–1407),[38] it is the Duke of Berry who is recorded mostly as the receiver of gifts.

Philip received a Chronicle of France in 1396.[39] The gift-giver was Gilles Malet (d. 1411), 'garde de la librairie' in the Royal Palace from 1369, thus virtually the founder of the Bibliothèque nationale de France.[40] The first inventory of the royal book collection in the year 1373 also comes from Malet.[41] In return, Gilles Malet had received silver cutlery worth a significant sum of 200 *livres*[42] from Philip. Furthermore, Gilles Malet was involved in other ways in the courtly giving of gifts. In 1402 it was the trader and moneylender Dino Rapondi (before 1350–c. 1414),[43] an Italian merchant, who presented the Duke of Burgundy with a manuscript. It was Livy's *Ab urbe condita*. Rapondi came from Lucca and was the manager of the commercial and financial affairs of the 'Societe des Raponde', whose business activities embraced especially Bruges, Paris, Avignon and Venice.[44] In return for this manuscript gift, Philip made a present to Dino of 500 *livres*.[45] Giacomo, brother of Dino, honored the Duke of Burgundy with a copy of Boccaccio's *De mulieribus claris*.[46] In return Philip spent Giacomo a gift of 300 *livres*.[47]

Louis of Orleans received a gift in 1400 which is only described as a 'grant livre en latin', but it was obviously of great material value, as the fastenings were made of gold and the front cover was decorated with a coat of arms in enamel.[48] The donor was Amaury d'Orgemont (d. 1400), a prominent royal councilor, chancellor to the Duke and at that time the master of the royal Audits Office.[49] A further manuscript, which Louis received in 1402, was an edition, translated into French with the title *Archiloge Sophie*,[50] of parts of the so-called *Sophilogium,* a moralistic and scholarly compilation in which love of wisdom and knowledge as well as love of the theological virtues is recommended.[51] The donor, author and translator was the erudite scholar Jacques Legrand (c. 1360–c. 1415), otherwise known as Jakobus Magni, an Augustinian teacher at the University of Paris.[52]

The *Chronique de France* and Boccaccio's *De mulieribus claris*, but even more so the work by Livy or the 'grant livre en latin', reveal the early humanistic cultural interests of this period and make clear the role and significance of the courts as open-minded centers for the transmission of knowledge.[53] The heads of the courts also played an active part with respect to the transfer of scientific knowledge by the court and the transmission of cultural awareness. For instance, there is a translation of Boccaccio's work now preserved in the library at Wolfenbüttel,[54] and the dedication by Laurent de Premierfait to the Duke of Berry suggests that the Duke has assisted him in the translation of this work.[55]

Another example is Simon Aligret, the personal physician of the Duke of Berry. He was one of those who most frequently gave gifts to the Duke.[56] From him Berry received, rather appropriately, a 'livre d'Abvinscene',[57] a 'livre de Medicine, appelé Galien',[58] another 'livre de medicine, qui traicte de la vertu des herbes et des bestes'[59] and for his spiritual well-being a Book of Psalms.[60] We may assume that Berry and Aligret shared an interest in medical themes.

Top-ranking clerics took also place in the circles of the exchange of manuscripts as gifts around the Duke of Berry. Gérard du Puy, Bishop of Saint Flour (d. 1420),[61] gave the Duke an edition of the *Orationes sive Meditationes*[62] of Anselm of Canterbury (1033–1109). In 1406 he had already honored the Duke with a small manuscript with the title *Lamentations de la mort du roy Charlemaigne*,[63] by Aymeric de Peyrac (c. 1340–1406), the Abbot of St-Pierre de Moissac.[64] From Martin Gouge de Charpaigne (c. 1360–1444),[65] Bishop of Chartres and the Duke's Chancellor, who was later to become Chancellor of France, Berry received an edition of Terence's comedies[66] in 1408 as well as the expensively produced translation of Boccaccio[67] in 1411. Another clerical participant was Guillaume de Boisratier (1365–1421), who occupied the posts of master of the court, councilor and – as Martin Gouge's successor – chancellor to the Duke. In 1409 he became archbishop of Bourges, and later, like Gouge, one of the councilors of Charles VII.[68] In 1404 Berry received the *Livre de Sidrac*[69] from Boisratier, an encyclopedic work which brought together knowledge of religious, ethical, medical and scientific nature.[70] Earlier, in 1403, Boisratier had given him a 'tres bel Pontiffical'[71] and in 1405 he presented Berry with a 'mappamonde de toute la Terre sainte'.[72] At least Pierre Trousseau, a canon of the cathedral of Bourges,[73] gave to the Duke a manuscript of the *Epitres saint Pol.*[74]

Also the Secretaries of the Duke of Berry, Erard Moriset, Jean de Cande, Michelle Beuf and Pierre de Gynes, appeared as donors.[75] They gave him the *Livre des Propriétés des choses.*[76] Guillaume Beaumaître, the Duke's almoner,[77] gave the Duke a missal,[78] and Gieffroi Robin the *Trésor de Sapience*[79] by Jean Gerson.[80]

The New Year's Days of 1410, 1413 and 1414 were the occasions on which Christine de Pizan emerged as a giver of gifts. In 1410 Berry received a Book of Psalms[81] from Christine, in 1413 the *Livre des Faiz d'armes et de chevalerie*[82] and in 1414 the *Livre de la paix.*[83] In 1405 the Duke had received the *Faiz et bonnes meurs du saige Roy Charles* from her.[84] Philip the Bold had apparently also received the *Livre de la mutacion de fortune* from Christine for New Year's Day in 1404;[85] she mentions this in her book on King Charles V of France.[86]

Only the Dukes of Burgundy appear as representatives of other courts as donors of manuscripts to the Duke of Berry. Philip the Bold had made a gift of a copy of

Anglicus' 'De proprietatibus rerum' in 1402,[87] quoted in a Burgundian record of accounts, with the value of the manuscript given as 400 *ecus d'or*.[88] John the Fearless made a gift to Berry in 1413 of the *Livre des Merveilles*, a French translation of the travel account of Marco Polo.[89] The Duke reciprocated the Fearless's gift with another a few months later, giving him the French translation of the *Speculum historiale*, translated as *Mirouer historical*, from the four-part work by Vincent de Beauvais (before 1200–64) entitled *Speculum quadruplex*.[90] This was one of the first encyclopedic works dating from the thirteenth century, which gives an overview of the state of theology and philosophy of the time.[91]

As pointed out, manuscripts were an ideal medium of representation at court that could express the contemporary and enduring significance of princely largesse, specialist knowledge and patronage. Furthermore, the manuscripts given as gifts in the years around 1400 and their contents are related to current events and highlight a specific discursive space of learned and artistic communication and interaction among those partaking.[92] Accordingly, Paris was, around 1400, a literary, artistic and intellectual center,[93] influenced by early humanists like Jean de Montreuil, the Col brothers and Nicolas de Clamanges (c. 1362–1437), theologians such as Jean Gerson, Pierre d'Ailly (c. 1350–1420) and Jacques Legrand, and erudite translators like Laurent de Premierfait. Paris was the arena of the first literary debate about a vernacular text, the *Roman de la Rose*,[94] and courtly society engaged in it through Christine de Pizan.[95] The manuscripts given as gifts testify a vivid and active participation in the theological, political, cultural, scientific and artistic interests and debates of the time. They reveal an open, wide-reaching and manifold network of relationships (which, naturally, can only be outlined here) comprising the political and artistic elite of the time, a space of communication, that was certainly not only limited to the partners in the exchange of gifts.

As documented by the empirical indications, the theoretically stated efforts are due to confirm persisting social relations. In the given frame this attitude is nothing other than the attempt to generate trust. Moreover, the observation of gift-giving at court reveals that hierarchical structures could be burst: Guy de La Trémoille appears in the exclusive circle of gift-giving dominated by the princes as one of the few non-princely persons, therefore marked as one of the closest confidants of the Burgundian duke.[96] As demonstrated, the space-building function of the interaction of humans in this social system with its confidence-building implications could be clearly carved out in its material and non-material aspects, which constitutes a suitable methodological approach for the examination and interpretation of all fields of communication and interaction.

Written documents in town-halls: materialized expression of immaterial interaction

Most European towns in the Middle Ages were not 'founded' on 'greenfield' sites. The formation and further development of towns usually took place at locations with some pre-existing central functions for the surroundings – be it economic, religious, administrative, legal or others.[97] A surplus of such services is one possible definition for urban settlements in general and had a particular material and cultural manifestation in the urban practices of writing and preserving of records – as we shall outline in the following.

Most European towns of the High and Late Middle Ages also reveal – not solely in their early development toward urbanity – a distinct seigneurial character. It is striking that in many places of eventually developed towns there were several lords with substantiated rights and consistent representations on site. Thus, the importance of 'mediators between lordship and commune',[98] i.e. among others sheriffs, judges and city councilmen, for the formation and development of urban settlements and their communes can hardly be overstated. Several and occasionally even competing lords in one place sometimes but not automatically meant more agency and thereby more liberty for these mediators and/or the communes that were no monolithic blocs in themselves. This is impressively shown not least by the pervasive intra-urban power struggles in medieval Europe. Also, the communicative, political or even familial networks of seigneurial representatives and early urban elites have to be taken into account. These aspects figure as one important basis for (the need for) urban interaction, its increasing scriptualization and filing.[99]

Another one is of a spatial nature: local communes mostly had two starting points and continuous reference points for their communalization and their public life: the parish church and churchyard as well as the common land and their power of control over it. Many of the early written documents of active communal actions refer to at least one of these two places, notably regarding the cooperative appropriation (especially of the churchyard) and the cooperatively transacted disposal (especially of the commons). While particularly the earliest of such transactions can hardly be perceived as entirely cooperative operations of equals, communities, confraternities, guilds and the neighborhood of people adhering to different jurisdictions, yet belonging to the same parish, have to be interpreted as fundaments of the commune. The interactions between lordships and evolving communes (and the written records thereof) show that the processes of negotiation and their scriptualization are often essentially richer in content for an understanding of a settlement's development toward urbanity than the mere central-space factors comprised in such documents. Hence, the processes of communication – with their chronological sequence, their spatial transitions and their changing forms and subjects of negotiation – can, at least in some respects, portray and explain the process of medieval urbanization more comprehensively than the albeit indispensable question of central spaces alone.[100]

The cultural, social and political logic of scribality, notably the preceding interaction for and the production of written documents in town-halls and their use,[101] reveals both a specific urban space of communication[102] and the contractual protection of trust which is essential for the future existence of urban communities. The town-hall itself – not least as a building – is the emblem of the urban commune both within the city walls as well as for the perception from the outside (relations to the hinterland).[103] The culture of writing and of preserving the written documents – formerly situated at court[104] and in ecclesiastical institutions[105] – was subsequently taken over by urban elites[106] with the arising town-halls serving as localities for magistrates or, for instance, municipal courts. This process not only included the development of municipal institutions but in turn increased the amenity of cities in the eyes of the contemporaries.[107] When, in the High Middle Ages, parish localities or mercantile parlors had often served as places for congregation of the magistrates, separate build-ings were later on re-dedicated or newly erected to function as town-halls in the following centuries – often in splendid style and in ensembles with other communal buildings (parish churches, market- and guildhalls) on the (central) marketplace.[108] These ensembles were in a way the showcases of cities where everyday life took place, but also where assemblies or festivities (even tournaments) were held – 'the city as theatre'.[109]

Scribality also meant 'order' in a wider sense, i.e. trust protected by contracts, as the function of magistrates as notaries public even for the extra-mural vicinity indicates: in thirteenth-century Alsace, countrymen and -women would stream into even the (relatively young) small- or medium-sized towns to have their wills or other business certified and enshrined.[110] In effect, written documents by urban institutions repre-sent the materialization of (partially) immaterial interaction – which again could take place around objects such as the magistrate's bench or the clerks' desks.[111] The way from intent to interaction to inscription can be followed literally and topographically in many town-halls preserved in their late medieval/early modern form, exception-ally so in the Northern German city of Lüneburg.[112] From entering the segmented complex to ascending the winding staircases to approaching the inner hall and its magistrate's bench – to interact or be judged by the council or to see the scribe in order to get matters taken care of by the official scribe – any actor (rich or poor) was all the way confronted with emblems and insignia of the city as well of the Empire and Duchy. Thus, there was no way around the political representation and manifes-tation of the urban elites even in everyday dealings.[113]

In consideration of the above-mentioned fact that premodern cities were mostly not autonomous entities, because most of them adhered to particular sovereignties, interrelated interaction in these towns between the authority and/or the urban elites obeyed an explicitly or implicitly expressed specific logic.[114] This can be observed at its best in the example of the so-called 'Residenzstädte',[115] a unique phenomenon of the premodern Holy Roman Empire.[116] Nevertheless, the research on 'urbanism as a network of integrative and competing relationships between seigneurial rulership and civic community' by focusing on residential cities in the Holy Roman Empire is quite a recent topic in historical sciences.[117]

In these cities, specific conditions, shapes and processes of mediation and nego-tiation can be observed that are reflected by various records of courtly, ecclesiasti-cal and communal origins.[118] In contrast, the so-called 'Stadtbuch' – *liber civitatis* or *Statpuech* – offers a specifically urban form of documentation[119] with the general function of establishing legal certainty. Since the thirteenth century, 'Stadtbücher' had been emerging as collections of legally binding documents with various contents of different functions, in the beginning as mixed compilations, later as thematically in-dependent volumes:[120] collections of privileges served to protect urban communities against the claims of different rulers and statute books combined specific urban laws. While so-called 'Gerichtsbücher' collocated transcripts or sentences and some books examined urban tax collection or important urban services, other books listed trans-actions of the citizens among themselves (business dealings or testaments) or assem-bled the official correspondence.[121] Notably in the last two categories, we even find townspeople not usually practicing scribality in everyday life themselves – not least the economically weaker or even marginalized social groups who still might seek the benefit of public record for their meagre wills, rents or purchases.[122] Therefore 'Stadtbücher' are a future-oriented hedge and a contractual protection of trust in one of its purest forms. They not only visualize intra- and extra-urban communication and interaction, but also former urban self-conception as a central point of reference for intra-urban social relations.[123]

All spaces of courtly and urban communication and interaction – be it social spheres or actual buildings – were established by different representatives of authority, in particular the nobility, the clergy, the urban council or the guilds' leaders; they were also sustained by and connected with these and even more urban groups, thereby configuring the spatial and social frame for everyday life.[124]

Notes

i   We thank Lisa Leiber, Kiel, for support in preparing the English text. Abbreviations: ACO, Archives départementales de la Côte-d'Or, Dijon; AN, Archives nationales, Paris; BNF, Bibliothèque nationale de France, Paris; ms.fr., manuscrits français; ms.lat., manuscrits latins; n.a.fr., nouvelles acquisitions françaises.

1   G. Simmel, *Soziologie. Untersuchungen über die Formen der Vergesellschaftung*, Leipzig: Duncker & Humblot, 1908, 393. Simmel interprets trust in particular as a kind of creditworthiness, cf. B. Accarino, 'Vertrauen und Versprechen. Kredit, Öffentlichkeit und individuelle Entscheidung bei Simmel', in H.J. Dahme, O. Rammstedt (eds), *Georg Simmel und die Moderne*, Frankfurt am Main: Suhrkamp, 1984, 115–46; M. Endreß, *Vertrauen*, Bielefeld: transcript Verlag, 2002, 12–16; C. Muldrew, 'Zur Anthropologie des Kapitalismus. Kredit, Vertrauen, Tausch und die Geschichte des Marktes in England 1500–1750', *Historische Anthropologie* 6, 1998, 67–199.

2   Cf. N. Luhmann, *Vertrauen. Ein Mechanismus zur Reduktion sozialer Komplexität*, Stuttgart: Lucius und Lucius, 2000, 1. Therefore, Luhmann differentiates trust ['Vertrauen'] from confidence ['Zuversicht'] as a preliminary decision to trust somebody, cf. C. Mencke, *Vertrauen in sozialen Systemen und in der Unternehmensberatung. Eine Grundlagenanalyse und Hinweise für eine vertrauenssensible Beratungspraxis am Beispiel größerer mittelständischer Unternehmen*, Wiesbaden: Deutscher Universitätsverlag, 2005, 133seq.; J.P. Reemtsma, *Vertrauen und Gewalt. Versuch über eine besondere Konstellation der Moderne*, Hamburg: Hamburger Ed., 2008, 37–9.

3   Cf. Luhmann, *Vertrauen*, esp. 13seq., 27–38; essential as well is N. Luhmann, *Soziale Systeme. Grundriß einer allgemeinen Theorie*, Frankfurt am Main: Suhrkamp, 1991, 179–82; critical is H. Bleumer, 'Das Vertrauen und die Vertraute. Aspekte der Emotionalisierung von gesellschaftlichen Bindungen im höfischen Roman', *Frühmittelalterliche Studien* 39, 2005, 253–70, esp. 254–6 with notes 3–6, cf. Reemtsma, 'Vertrauen', 30seq., 37. Cf. M. Endreß, 'Vertrauen und Vertrautheit – Phänomenologisch-anthropologische Grundlegung', in M. Hartmann, C. Offe (eds), *Vertrauen. Grundlage Die Grundlage des sozialen Zusammenhalts*, Frankfurt am Main: Campus-Verl., 2001, 161–203. Regarding the functionality of trust in Luhmann's approach see M. Schweer, B. Thies, *Vertrauen als Organisationsprinzip. Perspektiven für komplexe soziale Systeme*, Bern: Huber, 2003, 12seq.

4   E. Schubert, *Alltag im Mittelalter. Natürliches Lebensumfeld und menschliches Miteinander*, Darmstadt: Primus-Verl., 2002, 202–11, cit. 211.

5 See e.g. M. Müller, *Besiegelte Freundschaft Die brandenburgischen Erbeinungen und Erbver-brüderungen im späten Mittelalter*, Göttingen: V&R Unipress, 2010, 192seq. for a discussion of the phenomenon of calculated trust.

6 'Nahvertrauen', see Reemtsma, *Vertrauen*, 35. Cf. the corresponding sociological concept of very close communication in familiar social environments named 'Nahweltkommunikation', N. Luhmann, *Liebe als Passion. Zur Codierung von Intimität*, Frankfurt am Main: Suhrkamp, 1982, 157. A confidant could not be a stranger, cf. also R. Schnell, 'Kommunikation unter Freunden vs. Kommunikation mit Fremden. Eine Studie zum Privaten und Öffentlichen im Mittelalter', in G. Krieger (ed.), *Verwandtschaft, Freundschaft, Bruderschaft. Soziale Lebens- und Kommunikationsformen im Mittelalter*, Berlin: Akad.-Verl., 2009, 127–50, treating the stranger among others as a member of a table fellowship of familiar persons.

7 See for a fundamental study T. Ripperger, *Ökonomik des Vertrauens. Analyse eines Organisationsprinzips*, Tübingen: Mohr Siebeck, 1998, esp. 152–8, cf. A. Picot, R. Reichwald, R.T. Wigand, *Die grenzenlose Unternehmung. Information, Organisation und Management. Lehrbuch zur Unternehmensführung im Informationszeitalter*, Wiesbaden: Gabler, 2001, 123seq. An economical explanation of social exchange on the basis of a definition of court given by the concept of institutional economics is offered by U.C. Ewert, 'Sozialer Tausch bei Hofe. Eine Skizze des Erklärungspotentials der Neuen Institutionenökonomik', in R. Butz, J. Hirschbiegel, D. Willoweit (eds), *Hof und Theorie. Annäherungen an ein historisches Phänomen*, Köln: Böhlau, 2004, 55–75. The relations between social exchange and trust are explained by P.M. Blau, *Exchange and Power in Social Life*, New York: Wiley, 1964, 91–7; cf. Frank Hillebrandt, *Praktiken des Tauschens. Zur Soziologie symbolischer Formen der Reziprozität*, Wiesbaden: VS, 2009, 180–206. For more information on reciprocity see A.W. Gouldner, *Reziprozität und Autonomie. Ausgewählte Aufsätze*, Frankfurt am Main: Suhrkamp, 1984, cf. M. Schenk, *Soziale Netzwerke und Kommunikation*, Tübingen: Mohr, 1984, 129seq. Such an understanding of alternating effective relations of trust is correlated to an interpretation of communication as a reciprocally determined process of sending and recognizing, cf. B. Stollberg-Rilinger, 'Die Welt als Symboluniversum. Überlegungen zur symbolischen Kommunikation in Vormoderne und Moderne', in G. Andenna (ed.), *Religiosità e civiltà Le comunicazioni simboliche (secoli IX–XIII)*, Mailand: V&P, 2009, 23–46, here 26.

8 Cf. Reemtsma, *Vertrauen*, 32.

9 Cf. R. Schlögl, 'Kommunikation und Vergesellschaftung unter Anwesenden. Formen des Sozialen und ihre Transformation in der Frühen Neuzeit', *Geschichte und Gesellschaft. Zeitschrift für historische Sozialwissenschaft* 34,2, 2008, 155–224; R. Schlögl, 'Vergesellschaftung unter Anwesenden. Zur kommunikativen Form des Politischen in der vormodernen Stadt', in ibid. (ed.), *Interaktion und Herrschaft. Die Politik der frühneuzeitlichen Stadt*, Konstanz: UVK, 2004, 9–60.

10 Cf. U. Frevert, 'Vertrauen in historischer Perspektive', in R. Schmalz-Bruns, R. Zintl (eds), *Politisches Vertrauen. Soziale Grundlagen reflexiver Kooperation*, Baden-Baden: Nomos-Verl., 2002, 54seq.

11 Martina Löw, *Raumsoziologie*, Frankfurt am Main: Suhrkamp, 2001.

12 Ibid., e.g. 158. Cf. J. Hirschbiegel, G. Zeilinger, 'Urban Space Divided? The Encounter of Civic and Courtly Spheres in Late-Medieval Towns', in A. Classen (ed.), *Urban Space in the Middle Ages and Early Modern Age*, Berlin: de Gruyter, 2009, 481–503.

13 Hirschbiegel attempted to show this by investigating the relations established by trust between rulers and their main servants, J. Hirschbiegel, *Nahbeziehungen bei Hof – Manifestationen des Vertrauens. Karrieren in reichsfürstlichen Diensten am Ende des Mittelalters*, Köln: Böhlau, 2015.

14 Cf. U.C. Ewert, J. Hirschbiegel, 'Nur Verschwendung? Zur sozialen Funktion der demonstrativen Zurschaustellung höfischen Güterverbrauchs', in W. Paravicini (ed.), *Luxus und Integration. Materielle Hofkultur in Westeuropa, 1200–1800*, München: Oldenburg, 2010, 105–21; U.C. Ewert, J. Hirschbiegel, 'Mehr als nur der schöne Schein: Zu einer Theorie der Funktion von Luxusgegenständen im zwischenhöfischen Gabentausch des späten Mittelalters', in M. Häberlein, C. Jeggle (eds), *Materielle Grundlagen der Diplomatie. Schenken, Sammeln und Verhandeln in Spätmittelalter und Früher Neuzeit*, Konstanz: UVK-Verlag, 2013, 33–58.

15 See e.g. J. Hirschbiegel, 'Hof. Zur Überzeitlichkeit eines zeitgebundenen Phänomens', in B. Jacobs, R. Rollinger (eds), *Der Achämenidenhof. The Achaemenid Court*, Wiesbaden: Harrassowitz, 2010, 13–37. Instead of quoting specific references see in particular the corresponding articles given in the handbook W. Paravincini, J. Hirschbiegel, J. Wettlaufer (eds), *Höfe und Residenzen im spätmittelalterlichen Reich. Hof und Schrift*, Ostfildern: Thorbecke, 2007.

16 Cf. E. Benesch, *Dedikations- und Präsentationsminiaturen in der Pariser Buchmalerei vom späten dreizehnten bis zum frühen fünfzehnten Jahrhundert*, University of Wien: unpublished dissertation manuscript, 1987; C. Stroo, *De celebratie van de macht: Presentatieminiaturen en aanverwante voorstellingen in handschriften van Filips de Goede (1419–1467) en Karel de Stoute (1467–1477)*, Brussels: De celebratie van de macht, 2002.

17 A theoretical approach is given by J. Hirschbiegel, *Étrennes. Untersuchungen zum höfischen Geschenkverkehr im spätmittelalterlichen Frankreich der Zeit König Karls VI. (1380–1422)*, München: Oldenburg, 2003, 123–31.

18 Hirschbiegel, *Étrennes*. Primarily records have been analyzed, in the first place financial accounts and inventories; see 70–110. The material forms are especially visible in valuable courtly gifts: precious stones, goldsmiths works, jewelries, tapestries, gold- and silverware, manuscripts – all these were very exclusive and visible gifts that were used for deeply impressing the public court and were usually circulating within the higher positions of the social hierarchy only. Those gifts were for instance a *bel et gros balay longuet* up to 18,000 *livres*, received by John, Duke of Berry, from Charles VI as a New Year's gift for the years 1402, 1403 and 1404, 446, no. 1292. The year before, in 1401, the king himself gave a *coffre* up to 4,000 *livres* to Berry, 420, no. 1071. In 1388 John of Berry received from Philip the Bold, Duke of Burgundy, a splendid clip up to 5,500 *livres*, 341, no. 268, in 1389 *un grant tableau de la Trinité, garny de plusieurs gros balais, gros saphirs et plusieurs grosses perles* up to 6,000 *livres*, 347, no. 311, and again in 1399 a golden cross, which was up to 7,400 *livres*, 414, no. 1009. The duke Philip the Bold of Burgundy also used the common gift-exchange ceremonies on New Year's Day in 1403 for acquiring a tableship up to 12,000 *livres* for himself, 443, no. 1275. Numerous other examples could be given.

19 In the sense of Löw, *Raumsoziologie*. Cf. W. Paravicini, 'Höfischer Raum', in G. Melville, M. Staub (eds), *Enzyklopädie des Mittelalters*, vol. 2, Darmstadt: Wiss. Buchges., 2008, 285–92.

20 Cf. J. Hirschbiegel, 'Der Hof als soziales System. Das Angebot der Systemtheorie nach Niklas Luhmann für eine Theorie des Hofes', in R. Butz, J. Hirschbiegel, D. Willoweit (eds), *Hof und Theorie. Annäherung an ein historisches Phänomen*, Köln: Böhlau, 2004, 43–54; J. Hirschbiegel, 'Gabentausch als soziales System? Einige theoretische Überlegungen', in U.C. Ewer, S. Selzer (eds), *Ordnungsformen des Hofes. Ergebnisse eines Forschungskolloquiums der Studienstiftung des deutschen Volkes*, Kiel: Residenzen-Komm. der Akad. der Wiss. zu Göttingen, 1997, 44–55; J. Hirschbiegel, 'Zeichen der Gunst. Neujahrsgeschenke am burgundischen Hof der Zeit König Karls VI. von Frankreich (1380–1422)', in S. Selzer, U.C. Ewert (eds), *Menschenbilder – Menschenbildner. Individuum und Gruppe im Blick des Historikers*, Berlin: Akad. Verl., 2002, 213–40; Hirschbiegel,

Étrennes, 111–20; J. Hirschbiegel, 'Zur theoretischen Konstruktion der Figur des Günstlings', in J. Hirschbiegel, W. Paravicini (eds), *Der Fall des Günstlings. Hofparteien in Europa vom 13. bis zum 17. Jahrhundert*, Ostfildern: Thorbecke, 2004, 23–39.

21 Hirschbiegel, 'Zeichen der Gunst', 227seq.; Hirschbiegel, 'Konstruktion', 32–4; Ewert, 'Sozialer Tausch', 57seq. and 60.

22 By the term 'public' the set of all actors who were relevant to the social system is circumscribed. Public communication usually was not only a verbal discourse; it was mainly done by the representation and the exhibition of objects. Cf. W. Paravicini (ed.), *Alltag bei Hof*, Sigmaringen: Thorbecke, 1995, in particular the introduction given by Werner Paravicini, 9–30. Cf. A. Ranft, 'Feste des deutschen Adels am Ausgang des Mittelalters, Form und Funktion', in S. Cavaciocchi (ed.), *Il tempo libero. Economia e società (Loisirs, Leisure, Tiempo Libre, Freizeit) secc. XIII–XVIII*, Prato: Le Monnier, 1995, 245–56, here 252–6.

23 Cf. W. Paravicini, 'Zeremoniell und Raum', in W. Paravicini (ed.), *Zeremoniell und Raum*, Sigmaringen: Thorbecke, 1997, 11–36, here 15; U. Daniel, 'Überlegungen zum höfischen Fest der Barockzeit', *Niedersächsisches Jahrbuch für Landesgeschichte* 72, 2000, 45–66, here 49.

24 Cf. B. Buettner, 'Past Presents: New Year's Gifts at the Valois Court, ca. 1400', *The Art Bulletin* 83, 2001, 598–624; J. Hirschbiegel, 'Gift Exchange at the French Courts around 1400: Manuscripts as Gauges of Social Relations?', in G. Müller-Oberhäuser (ed.), *Book Gifts and Cultural Networks from the 14th to the 16th Century: Symbolische Kommunikation und gesellschaftliche Wertesysteme. Schriftenreihe des Sonderforschungsbereichs 496, 41*, Münster: Rhema, 2019, 89–115.

25 See for instance the detailed indications given in the inventories of the treasure of the Duke John of Berry, J. Guiffrey, *Inventaires de Jean, duc de Berry (1401–1416)*, vol. 1, Paris: Leroux, 1894–96, 223–71, 328–36.

26 A. Hiver de Beauvoir, *La librairie de Jean, duc de Berry, au château de Melun-sur-Yèvre, 1416, publiée en entier pour la première fois d'après les inventaires, avec des notes*, Paris: Aubry, 1860. AN KK 258, fol. 214r, *Inventaires de Jean, duc de Berry*, vol. 1, 332, no. 1239. Cf. L. Delisle, *Le Cabinet des Manuscrits de la Bibliothèque Impériale. Étude sur la formation de ce dépôt comprenant les éléments d'une histoire de la calligraphie de la miniature, de la reliure, et du commerce des livres à Paris avant l'invention de l'imprimerie*, 3 vols., Paris: Imprimerie Impériale, 1868–81, 61; L. Delisle, *Recherches sur la librairie de Charles V, Roi de France, 1337–1380*, 2 vol., Paris: Champion, 1907, 269, no. 288. For the edition see W.C. Cannon (ed.), *Christine Pisan, Le Livre de la Paix. Of Christine de Pisan*, La Haye: Mouton, 1958.

27 J. Guiffrey, *Inventaires de Jean, duc de Berry*, 332, no. 1239; Delisle, *Cabinet*, vol. 3, 193, no. 288.

28 AN KK 258, fol. 152vf., *Inventaires de Jean, duc de Berry*, vol. 1, 252–3, no. 959, cf. cxliv.

29 For Laurent de Premierfait, see R.C. Famiglietti, 'Laurent de Premierfait: The Career of a Humanist in Early Fifteenth Century Paris', *Journal of Medieval History* 9, 1983, 25–42; C. Bozzolo (ed.), *Un traducteur et un humaniste de l'époque de Charles VI, Laurent de Premierfait*, Paris: Publ. de la Sorbonne, 2004.

30 AN KK 258, fol. 162v, *Inventaires de Jean, duc de Berry*, vol. 1, 265, no. 993. Cf. J. Lebeuf, *Recueil du divers écrits pour servir d'éclaircissemens à l'histoire de France, et de supplement à la notice de Gaules*, Paris: Babel, 1738, 259; L.C.D. d'Arcq, 'Notice sur la bibliothèque de Jean, duc de Berry, en 1416', *Revue Archéologique* 7, 1850, 152seq., no. 21; Delisle, *Recherches*, 256, no. 208. See also G. Di Stefano, *Decameron: Traduction (1411–1414) de Laurent de Pemierfait*, Montreal: CERES, 1999; P.M. Gathercole (ed.), *Laurent de Premierfait's 'Des cas des nobles hommes et femmes'*, Chapel Hill, NC: Univ. of North Carolina Press, 1968; A.D. Hedeman, *Translating the Past: Laurent de Premierfait and Boccacaio's 'De casibus'*, Los Angeles, CA: J. Paul Getty Museum, 2008. See also n. 46.

31 For Martin Gouge see A. Hiver de Beauvoir, 'Les Hommes d'État du Berry depuis le Duc
   Jean jusqu'a Henry IV', in Société des Antiquairs de l'Ouest (ed.), *Mémoires de la Société des
   Antiquitiares du Centre 2*, Bourges: Imprimeur de la Société des Antiuaires, 1868, 267–89.
32 Delisle, *Cabinet*, vol. 3, 187, no. 208.
33 See above n. 30.
34 See above n. 26.
35 BNF ms.fr. 6747 (Comptes du duc de Berry, fols 25r–34v: Compte de Lomer le Bez,
   1418 [List of purchases 'pour le fait de nostre guerre [...] et non pour autre cause']; for
   the ordinance of November 24, 1417 see esp. fols 31r–34v), *Inventaires de Jean, due de
   Berry*, vol. 2, 339–44, cf. esp. vol. 1, XIII.
36 For Hugues de Robertis or rather Ugo Roberti, Bishop of Adria 1386–92, Bishop of
   Padua 1392–6, Titular Patriarch of Jerusalem 1396–1409 and Titular Patriarch of Alexandria 1402–9, see E. Peverada, 'Ugo Roberti patriarca di Gerusalemme e un tentative
   di riforma giustiniana dell'abbazia di S. Spirito di Caltanissetta', in F.G. Trolese (ed.),
   Monastica et humanistica: Scritti in onore di Gregmio Penco 0. S. B., 2 vols, Cesena: Badia di
   Santa Maria del Monte, 2003, here vol. 1, 227–44. Hugues de Robertis gave as a gift
   'un bel messel, au commencement;duquel est le kalendrier', BNF ms.lat. 17173, fol. 228,
   no. 10, *Inventaires de Jean, duc de Berry*, vol. 2, 174, no. 145. Cf. Delisle, *Cabinet*, vol. 1,
   176, no. 67; Delisle, *Recherches*, vol. 2, 233seq., no. 67. Cf. BNF n.a.fr. 1363, no. 145.
37 For Philipp, see R. Vaughan, *Philip the Bold: The Formation of the Burgundian State*, Cambridge, MA et al.: Harvard Univ. Press 1962; Woodbridge: Boydell & Brewer, 2002.
38 For Louis, see E. Jarry, *La vie politique de Louis de France, duc d'Orléans 1372–1407*,
   Genève: Slatkine-Megariotis Repr., 1976.
39 This may well be the Inventory of Margarete of Flanders of 1405, recorded as a Chronicle, ACOB 302, fols 34, 35, see W.P.M. de Winter, *La bibliothèque de Philippe le Hardi,
   duc de Bouourgogne (1364–1404): Étude sur les manuscrits à peintures d'une collection princière
   à l'époque du 'style gothique international'*, Paris: Ed. du Centre National de la Recherche
   Scientifique, 1985, 166seq., no. 175, 171, no. 196. This may well be the same work as
   the *Inventoire des livres Roumans de feu Monseigneur Philippe le Hardi, que maistre Richart
   Conte, son barbier, a euz en garde à Paris 1404*, see J. Barrois, *Bibliothèque protypographique,
   ou Librairies des fils du roi Jean, Charles V, Jean de Beni, Philippe de Bourgogne et les siens*,
   Paris: Treuttel & Würtz, 1830, 105, no. 605, recorded as a Chronicle, cf. ACO B 301,
   fol. 36, cf. Winter, *Bibliotheque*, 130, no. 33. Of the many research reports on the book
   collections of the Dukes of Burgundy, esp., Philip the Bold, one should particularly
   consult M.J. Hughes, 'The Library of Philip the Bold and Margaret of Flanders, First
   Valois Duke and Duchess of Burgundy', *Journal of Medieval History* 4, 1978, 145–88.
   There is also information about Gilles Malet's gift, esp. 168seq., no. 10, 185, no. 5.
   Cf. G. Doutrepont (ed.), *Inventaire de 'Librairie' de Philippe le Bon (1420),* Bruxelles:
   Kiessling, 1906, 37seq., no. 75, as well as G. Peignot, *Catalogue d'une partie des livres
   composant la bibliothèque des ducs de Bourgogne, au XVe siècle*, Dijon: Lagier, 1841, 41seq.,
   73, 75. Winter, *Bibliothèque*, 59, 167, which is, in my opinion, wrongly dated to 1397.
40 For Gilles Malet, see J.B. de Vaivre, 'Monuments et ob jets d'art commande par Gilles
   Mal et, garde de la librairie de Charles VI', *Journal des Savants* 4.4, 1978, 217–39; Delisle, *Recherches*, vol. 1, 10–20.
41 G. Malet, *Inventaire ou catalogue des livres de l'ancienne Bibliothèque de Louvre fait en l'annnée
   1373*, ed. by Joseph van Praet, Paris: Chez de Bure Fréres, 1836; cf. Delisle, *Recherches*,
   vol. 1, 23–5, 337–64, 387seq.
42 ACO B 1508, fol.109r; BNF Coll. de Bourgogne, vol. LIII, fol.166. Cf. E. Petit (ed.),
   *Itinéraires de Philippe le Hardi et de Jean sans Peur, ducs de Bourgogne (1363–1419): D'après
   les comptes de dépenses de leur Hotel*, Paris: Imprimerie Nationale, 1888, 553.

43 For Dino Rapondi, see V. Fris, 'Dino Rapondi', in A. Van Hasselt (ed.), *Biographie Nationale: Vie des hommes et des femmes illustres de la Belgique, depuis les temps les plus* reculés jusqu'à *nos jours XVIII*, Bruxelles: Jamar, 1905, 735–9.

44 See B. Lambert, M. Bonne, *The City, the Duke and Their Banker: The Rapondi Family and the Formation of the Burgundian State (1384–1430)*, Turnhout: Brepols, 2006. Cf. L. Mirot, *Études lucquoises,* Paris: Daupeley-Gouverneur in Nogent-le-Rotrou, 1930, 79–86.

45 Hughes, 'Library', 169, no. 12, 181, no. 6.

46 Ibid., no. 13, 181, no. 8. Cf. B. Buettner, *Boccaccio's 'Des cleres et nobles femmes': Systems of Signification in an Illuminated Manuscript*, Seattle, WA: College Art Ass., 1996, 7–15.

47 Hughes, 'Library', 169, no. 13, 181, no. 8.

48 L.E.S.J. de Laborde, *Les Ducs de Bourgogne: Études sur les lettres, les arts et l'industrie pendant le XVe siècle et plus particulièrement dans les Pays-Bas et le Duché de Bourgogne*, Paris: Plon, 1849–51, 201seq., no. 5946.

49 For Arnaury d'Orgemont see F.A.A. de La Chenaye des Bois, *Dictionnaire de la noblesse, contenant les généalogiques, l'histoire et la chronologie des familles nobles de France*, 15 vols, Paris: Kraus, 1770–86, here vol. 2, 92; J.B. Hennemann, 'Who Were the Marmousets?', *Medieval Prosopography* 5, 1984, 19–63, esp. 60seq. See also L. Mirot, *Les d'Orgemont: Leur origine, leur fortune, le boiteux d'Orgemont*, Paris: Champion, 1912.

50 J.H. Wylie, *History of England under Henry the Fourth,* 2 vols, London: Longmans, Green and Co., 1884–98, vol. 2, 66, n. 1. Cf. A.P. Paris, *Les manuscrits françois de la Bibliothèque de roi, leur l'histoire et celle des textes allemands, anglois, hollandois, italiens, espagnols de la même collection*, 7 vols, Paris: Imprimerie de Bethune et Plon, 1836–47, vol. 1, 284. Extant in four copies, including BNF ms.fr. 143. Cf. Paris, *Manuscrits*, vol. 1, 284.

51 For information on this edition see J. Legrand, *Archiloge Sophie*, ed. Evenico Beltran, Genève: Slatkine, 1986.

52 For Jacques Legrand, see S. Lefevre, 'Jacques Le grand', in G. Greme (ed.), *Dictionnaire des lettres françaises: Le Moyen Age,* Paris: Fayard, 1996, 773seq.; R.E. Rahner, '19. J. Magni', *Lexikon des Mittelalters*, vol. 5, München: Artemis & Winkler, 1991, 259.

53 Cf. e.g. C. Arcelli (ed.), *I saperi nelle corti: Knowledge at the Courts*, Florence: SISMEL, 2008; G. Grebner, 'Zur Einleitung: Interkulturalität und Verwissenschaftlichung am Fürstenhof des Mittelalters', in G. Grebner, J. Fried (eds), *Kulturtransfer und Hofgesellschaft im Mittelalter: Wissenskultur am sizilianischen und kastilischen Hof im 13. Jahrhundert,* Berlin: Akademie Verl., 2008, 1–11. Cf. A. Buck (ed.), *Höfischer Humanismus*, Weinheim: Acta Humaniora, 1989. See also C. Bozzolo, E. Ornato (eds), *Préludes à la Renaissance: Aspects de la vie intellectuelle en France au XVe siècle*, Paris: Ed. du Centre National de la Recherche Scientifique, 1992.

54 Herzog August Bibliothek Wolfenbüttel, Codex Guelferbytanus A.3 Augusteus 2: Giovanni Boccaccio, *Des cas des Nobles Hommes et Femmes*, parchment, 362 leaves, 43,2 x 32,5 cm, fifteenth century, northern France, fol. 169r, see also O. von Heinemann, *Die Handschriften der Herzoglichen Bibliothek zu Wolfenbüttel: Die Augusteischen Handschriften*, vol. 1, Wolfenbüttel: Hansebooks, 1890, 12.

55 H. Bergen (ed.), *Lydgate's 'Fall of Princes'*, 4 vols, Washington, DC: Oxford Univ. Press, 1923–27, LXIV seq.

56 For Simon Aligret, see J.L. Romelot, *Description historique et monumentale de l'eglise patriarcale, primatiale et métropolitaine de Bourges*, Bourges: Imprimeur de la Cour royale, 1824, 212seq.

57 BNF ms.lat. 17173, fol. 228, no. 23; n.a. fr. 1363, no. 145, *Inventaires de Jean, duc de Berry*, vol. 2, 174, no. 145, cf., 176, no. 173. Cf. Delisle, *Cabinet*, vol. 3, 186, no. 183; Delisle, *Recherches*, vol. 2, 253, no. 183.

58 BNF ms.lat. 17173, fol. 228, no. 34, *Inventaires de Jean, duc de Berry*, vol. 2, 313seq. Cf. L. Delisle, 'Notes sur la bibliothèque de la Sainte-Chapelle de Bourges', *Bibliothèque de l'École des Chartes* 17, 1856, 142–59, esp. 143; Delisle, *Cabinet*, vol. 3, 185, no. 182; Delisle, *Recherches*, vol. 2, 252seq., no. 182.

59 AN KK 258, fol. 164v, *Inventaires de Jean, duc de Berry*, vol. 1, p. 269, no. 1003. Cf. Delisle, *Cabinet*, vol. 3, 186, no. 185.

60 AN KK 258, fol. 215V, *Inventaires de Jean, duc de Berry*, vol. 1, 334, no. 1243. Cf. Delisle, *Cabinet*, vol. 3, 173, no. 26; Delisle, *Recherches*, vol. 2, 227, no. 26.

61 For Gerard du Puy see V.J. Vigier, *Sainte-Croix de La Volte, Lavoûte-Croix, Haute-Loire: Un prieuré du réseau clunisien*, Nonette: Edité par CREER, 2000.

62 See F.S. Schmitt, *S. Anselmi Cantuarensis Archiepiscopi Opera Omnia: Orationes sive meditationes necnon epistolarum*, vol. 3, Edinburgh: Nelson, 1946.

63 AN KK 258, fol. 149v, *Inventaires de Jean, duc de Berry*, vol. 1, 249seq., no. 950. Cf. Lebeuf, *Recueil*, vol. 2, 259seq.; Barrois, *Bibliothèque*, 91, no. 523; Douët d'Arcq, 'Notice', 158, no. 46; Delisle, *Cabinet*, vol. 1, 59seq., vol. 3, 190, no. 245; Delisle, *Recherches*, vol. 2, 262seq., no. 245. There are two copies of this work in the BNF ms.lat. 5944 and 5946, but neither of them appears to be the one belonging to the Duke of Berry.

64 Or more precisely, Aimeri du Peyrat, the learned Abbot of St-Pierre de Moissac, see J. Dufour, 'Moissac', *Lexikon des Mittelalters*, vol. 6, München: Artemis & Winkler-Verlag, 1993, 719seq.

65 For Martin Gouge see Hiver de Beauvoir, 'Les Hommes d'État du Berry'.

66 See Lebeuf, *Recueil*, vol. 2, 260; Delisle, *Recherches*, vol. 2, 265, no. 261; Guiffrey, *Inventaires de Jean, duc de Berry*, vol. 1, 257, no. 969, vol. 2, 277, no. 1122. See M. Meiss, *French Painting in the Time of Jean de Berry: The Late Fourteenth Century and the Patronage of the Duke,* 2 vols, London: Thames and Hudson, 1967, vol. 2, 315seq. The Duke's copy is now in the BNF ms.lat. 7907A.

67 See above n. 30.

68 For Guillaume de Boisratier see Hiver de Beauvoir, 'Les Hommes d'État du Berry'. See also P.R. Gaussin, 'Les conseillers de Charles VII (1418–1461): Essai de politologie historique', *Francia* 10, 1982, 67–130, in particular 108 (Gouge), 116seq. (Boisratier).

69 AN KK 258, fol. 146vseq., *Inventaires de Jean, duc de Berry*, vol. 1, 245seq., no. 938. Cf. Lebeuf, *Recueil*, vol. 2, 259; Delisle, *Cabinet*, vol. 3, 183, no. 149; Delisle, *Recherches*, vol. 2, 248, no. 149. See also Meiss, *French Painting*, vol. 2, 49 with n. 170, 372.

70 Cf. O.S.H. Lie, M. Banda (eds), *Het boek van* Sidrac. *Een honderdtal vragen uit een middeleeuwse encyclopedie,* Hilversum: Verloren, 2006.

71 BNF n.a.fr. 1363, no. 143, *Inventaires de Jean, duc de Berry*, vol. 2, 174, no. 143. Cf. Delisle, *Cabinet*, vol. 3, 177seq., no. 88; Delisle, *Recherches*, vol. 2, 236, no. 88. It is not possible to establish the New Year's Day on which Philip the Bold received from his Chancellor Jean Canard '[…] ung bon Messel, à l'usaige de Paris', ACO B 301, fol. 17, cf. C.C.A. Dehaisnes, *Documents et extraits* divers *concernant l'histoire de l'art dans la Flandre, l'Artois et le Hainaut avant le XVe siècle,* 2 vols., Lille: Danel, 1886, vol. 2, 839; Doutrepont, *Inventaire de 'Librairie' de Philippe le Bon,* 2seq., no. 2. On the question of dating see Winter, *Bibliotheque*, 59, 122, no. 2.

72 BNF ms.lat. 17173, fol. 228, no. 36, *Inventaires de Jean, duc de Berry*, vol. 2, 317, no. 195. Cf. Delisle, 'Notes', 143; Delisle, *Cabinet*, vol. 3, 186, no. 195; Delisle, *Recherches*, vol. 2, 254, no. 195. On the Duke's gift to the cathedral of Bourges, see Meiss, *French Painting*, vol. 2, 50.

73 After Guiffrey, Pierre Trousseau 1405 became archdeacon of Paris, see Guiffrey, *Inventaires de Jean, duc de Berry*, vol. 2, 313, n. 3. In 1409 Trousseau appears as bishop of Poitiers, in 1413 as archbishop of Reims, see P. Kurmann, B. Kurmann-Schwarz,

'Französische Bischöfe als Auftraggeber und Stifter von Glasmalereien: Das Kunst-werk als Geschichtsquelle', *Zeitschrift für Kunstgeschichte* 60, 1997, 429–50, esp. 446–8.

74 BNF ms.lat. 17173, fol. 228, no. 35, *Inventaires de Jean, duc de Berry*, vol. 2, 313. Cf. Delisle, *Cabinet*, vol. 3, 174, no. 36; Delisle, *Recherches*, vol. 2, 229, no. 36.

75 Cf. Guiffrey, *Inventaires de Jean, duc de Berry*, vol. 2, 40, no. 2.

76 AN KK 258, fol. 147r, *Inventaires de Jean, duc de Berry*, vol. 1, 246, no. 939. Cf. Lebeuf, *Recueil*, vol. 2, 258seq.; Delisle, *Cabinet*, vol. 3, 183, no. 145; Delisle, *Recherches*, vol. 2, 247, no. 145. This manuscript was based on Bartholomaeus Anglicus' thirteenth-century encyclopedia *De proprietatibus rerum*. The aim of the work was to provide a deeper un-derstanding of concepts and facts referred to in the Bible, cf. H. Meyer, *Die Enzyklopädie des Bartholomäus Anglicus: Untersuchungen zur Überlieferungs- und Rezeptionsgeschichte von 'De proprietatibus rerum'*, München: Fink, 2000; C. Hünemörder, M. Mückshoff, '2. B. Angli-cus', *Lexikon des Mittelalters*, vol. 1, München: Artemis & Winkler, 1980, 1492seq.

77 It is possible that Beaumaître was a Canon of the cathedral of Chartres, see J.B. Souchet, *Histoire du diocèse et de la ville de Chartres, publ. d'après le manuscrit original de la bibliothèque communale de Chartres*, 3 vols, Chartres: Imprimerie de Garnier, 1866–73, vol. 3, 308.

78 BNF n.a.fr. 1363, no. 146, *Inventaires de Jean, duc de Berry*, vol. 2, 175, no. 146. Cf. Delisle, *Cabinet*, vol. 3, 176, no. 70; Delisle, *Recherches*, vol. 2, 234, no. 70.

79 AN KK 258, fol. 150v, *Inventaires de Jean, duc de Berry*, vol. 1, 250, no. 951. Cf. Lebeuf, *Recueil*, vol. 2, 260; Delisle, *Cabinet*, vol. 3, 185, no. 170. The 'Trésor de Sapience' – which is edited in extracts in J. Gerson, *Œuvres completes: L'œuvre polémique (492–530). Suppléments, documents, tables*, Paris: Desclée, 1973, no. 534, 345–65 – is a reflection on the proper way to live and to die and is influenced by the *Horologium Sapientiae* by Heinrich Seuse, for which see Herb en Backes, 'Seuse', *Lexikon des Mittelalters*, vol. 7, München: Artemis & Winkler-Verlag, 1995, 1801–3.

80 On Gerson, consult F.W. Bautz, 'Gerson, Johannes', *Biographisch-Bibliographisches Kirch-enlexikon*, F.W. Bautz, T. Bautz (eds), vol. 2, Hamm: Bautz, 1990, cols 229seq; R. Baumer, '79. J. Carlerius de Gerson', *Lexikon des Mittelalters*, vol. 5, München: Artemis & Winkler-Verlag, 1991, 561seq.

81 AN KK 258, fol. 158v, *Inventaires de Jean, duc de Berry*, vol. 1, 260, no. 977. Cf. Lebeuf, *Recuei*, vol. 2, 260seq.; Delisle, *Cabinet*, vol. 3, 181seq., no. 129; Delisle, *Recherches*, vol. 2, 245, no. 129. For information on the edition itself, see R.R.R. Rains (ed.), *Les sept psaumes allégorisés of Christine de Pisan*, Washington, DC: Cath. Univ. of Amer P., 1965.

82 AN KK 258, fol. 163r, *Inventaires de Jean, duc de Berry*, vol. 1, 270, no. 1004. Cf. Delisle, *Cabinet*, vol. 3, 193, no. 289; Delisle, *Recherches*, vol. 2, 269, no. 289. For information on the edition itself see A.T.P. Byles (ed.), *Christine de Pisan, The Book of Fayttes of Armes and of Chyvalye*, London: Oxford Univ. Press, 1937.

83 See above notes 26, 27.

84 AN KK 258, fol. 148r, *Inventaires de Jean, duc de Berry*, vol. I, 247, no. 943. Cf. Lebeuf, *Recueil*, vol. 2, 259; Barrois, *Bibliothèque*, 90, no. 518; Douët d'Arcq, 'Notice', 231: Delisle, *Cabinet*, vol. 3, 190, no. 246; Delisle, *Recherches*, vol. 2, 263, no. 246.

85 Guiffrey, *Inventaire de 'Librairie' de Philippe le Bon*, 57seq., nr 98.

86 S. Solente (ed.), *Christine de Pisan, Le livre des fais et bonnes meurs du sage roy Charles V.*, 2 vols., Paris: Champion, 1936–40, vol 1, 6seq. Incidentally, the Duke of Berry received a copy of this work as a gift from Christine in March 1404, *Inventaires de Jean, duc de Berry*, vol. 1, p. clxxvi; no. 70, vol 2, 250, no. 952. Cf. Meiss, *French Painting*, vol. 2, 372, no. 175, 300; 405, notes 109 and 310.

87 See above, n. 76.

88 ACO B 1526, fol. 298. Cf. H. David, *Philippe le Hardi au début du XVe siècle: Extraits somptuaires,* Dijon: Bernigaud et Privat, 1945, 46.

89 AN KK 258, fol. 165r, *Inventaires de Jean, duc de Berry,* vol. 2, 270, no. 1005 (cf., p. 242, no. 558 and vol. 1, clxxii, no. 49), but it cannot be identified as *étrennes.* Cf. Delisle, *Cabinet,* vol. 3, 186, no. 196; Delisle, *Recherches,* vol. 2, 254, no. 196. The Duke of Burgundy received a copy of this manuscript from Johan Hayton in person, see Buettner, 'Past Presents', 603, fig. 3.

90 AN KK 258, fol. 157v, no. 972, *Inventaires de Jean, duc de Berry,* vol. 2, 174, no. 972. First Berry gave this work to Jean de Montaigu, a prominent member of French courtly society and Chancellor to the Duke until 1406 – see R.C. Famiglietti, 'Montaigu', in W.W. Kibler, G.A. Zinn (eds), *Medieval France: An Encyclopedia,* New York: Garland, 1995, 632 – and got it back after Montaigu's death, cf. Meiss, *French Painting,* vol. 2, 49, 291, 404, n. 45.

91 Cf. J.B. Voorbij, *Het 'Speculum Historiale' van Vincent van Beauvais: Een studie van zijn ontstaansgeschiedenis,* Rijksuniversiteit Groningen: Univ. Diss, 1991.

92 Cf. Buettner, 'Past Presents', 609–13 with fig. 10.

93 Cf. E. Tauburet-Delahaye, *La création artistique en France autour de 1400. Actes du colloque. École du Louvre – Musée des Beaux-Arts de Dijon – Université de Bourgogne. École du Louvre, 7 et 8 juillet 2004, Musée des Beaux-Arts de Dijon – Université de Bourgogne, 9 et 10 juillet 2004,* Paris: Ecole du Louvre, 2006.

94 A gift Berry received in 1414 from Louis the Bearded, later sold by him to Bernard of Armagnac, his son-in-law, AN KK 258, fol. 214r, *Inventaires de Jean, duc de Berry,* vol. 1, p. clxxii–clxxiii, no. 51, 332, no. 1238. Cf. Douët d'Arcq, 'Notice', 164, no. 65; Delisle, *Cabinet,* vol. 1, 183, nr 148; Delisle, *Recherches,* vol. 2, 247, no. 148. Presumably it is now in the BNF ms.fr. 568. For the *Roman de la Rose* see G. de Lorris, J. de Meung, *Le roman de la rose,* ed. by Eugène Langlois, 5 vols., Paris: Firmin-Dido, 1914–24. Edition with German translation: G. de Lorris, J. de Meun, *Der Rosenroman,* ed. by K.A. Ott, 3 vols., München: Wiss. Buchges., 1976–9.

95 For later times cf. in particular N.Z. Davies, *The Gift in Sixteenth-Century France,* Madison, WI: Univ. of Wisconsin Press, 2000.

96 Cf. Hirschbiegel, 'Zeichen der Gunst', in particular 215. See also Hirschbiegel, 'Konstruktion'; cf. J. Hirschbiegel, A. Caliebe, 'Philipp der Kühne, Johann Ohnefurcht und der höfische Geschenkverkehr zum neuen Jahr um 1400', in W. Paravicini, B. Schnerb (eds), *Paris, capitale des ducs de Bourgogne,* Ostfildern: Thorbecke, 2007, 219–62.

97 As excellent overviews cf. D. Nicholas, *The Growth of the Medieval City. From Late Antiquity to the Early Fourteenth Century,* London, New York: Longman, 1997; D. Nicholas, *Urban Europe, 1100–1700,* Basingstoke, New York: Palgrave Macmillan, 2003; E. Isenmann, *Die deutsche Stadt im Mittelalter 1150–1550. Stadtgestalt, Recht, Stadtregiment, Kirche, Gesellschaft, Wirtschaft,* Wien, Köln, Weimar: Böhlau, 2012.

98 Cf. E. Gruber, S.C. Pils, S. Rabeler, H. Weigl, G. Zeilinger (eds), *Mittler zwischen Herrschaft und Gemeinde: Die Rolle von Funktions- und Führungsgruppen in der mittelalterlichen Urbanisierung Zentraleuropas,* Innsbruck: Studien-Verlag, 2013.

99 As more recent programmatic as well as exemplary works cf. among others M.F. Kluge, *Die Macht des Gedächtnisses. Entstehung und Wandel kommunaler Schriftkultur im spätmittelalterlichen Augsburg,* Leiden: Brill, 2014; P. Chastang, *La ville, le gouvernement et l'écrit à Montpellier (XIIe–XIVe siècle). Essai d'histoire sociale,* Paris: Publ. de la Sorbonne, 2013.

100 Cf. the latest case study for Upper Alsace: G. Zeilinger, *Verhandelte Stadt. Herrschaft und Gemeinde in der frühen Urbanisierung des Oberelsass vom 12. bis 14. Jahrhundert,* Ostfildern: Thorbecke, 2018, 78–80, 198.

101 Scribality understood here as 'pragmatische Schriftlichkeit', cf. K. Andermann, 'Pragmatische Schriftlichkeit', in W. Paravicini (ed.), *Höfe und Residenzen im spätmittelalterlichen Reich. Hof und Schrift*, Ostfildern: Thorbecke, 2007, 37–60.

102 Cf. J.M. Sawilla, R. Schlögl (eds), *Medien der Macht und des Entscheidens. Schrift und Druck im politischen Raum der europäischen Vormoderne (14.–17. Jahrhundert)*, Hannover: Wehrhahn, 2014; M. Pauly, M. Scheutz (eds), *Cities and their spaces. Concepts and their use in Europe*, Köln: Böhlau, 2014.

103 Cf. S.C. Pils, M. Scheutz, C. Sonnleucher, S. Speak (eds), *Rathäuser als multifunktionale Räume der Repräsentation, der Parteiungen und des Geheimnisses*, Innsbruck: Studien-Verl., 2012; S. Albrecht, *Mittelalterliche Rathäuser in Deutschland. Architektur und Funktion*, Darmstadt: Wiss. Buchges., 2004.

104 See W. Paravicini (ed.), *Höfe und Residenzen im spätmittelalterlichen Reich. Hof und Schrift*, Ostfildern: Thorbecke, 2007.

105 Cf. H. Keller, F. Neiske (eds), *Vom Kloster zum Klosterverband. Das Werkzeug der Schriftlichkeit. Akten des Internationalen Kolloquiums des Projekts L 2 im SFB 231 (22.–23. Februar 1996)*, München: Fink, 1997; H. Keller, C. Meier, T. Scharff (eds), *Schriftlichkeit und Lebenspraxis im Mittelalter. Erfassen, Bewahren, Verändern*, München: Fink, 1999.

106 P. Monnet, 'Zwischen Reproduktion und Repräsentation. Formierungsprozesse von Eliten in westeuropäischen Städten des Spätmittelalters: Terminologie, Typologie, Dynamik', in E. Gruber, M. St. Popovic, M. Scheutz, H. Weigl (eds), *Städte im lateinischen Westen und im griechischen Osten zwischen Spätantike und Früher Neuzeit. Topographie – Recht – Religion*, Wien: Böhlau, 2016, 177–93.

107 Cf. G. Fouquet, 'Die "schöne Stadt" – Bauen als öffentliche Aufgabe deutscher Städte (14. bis 16. Jahrhundert)', in S. Schweizer, J. Stabenow (eds), *Bauen als Kunst und historische Praxis. Architektur und Stadtraum im Gespräch zwischen Kunstgeschichte und Geschichtswissenschaft*, Göttingen: Wallstein, 2006, 123–57; Nicholas, *Urban Europe*, 154–74.

108 Cf. Nicholas, *Growth*, 193–6; C. Arnaud, *Topographien des Alltags. Bologna und Straßburg um 1400*, Berlin, Boston: De Gruyter, 2018, 288–90 *et passim*.

109 Nicholas, *Urban Europe*, 167.

110 Cf. Zeilinger, *Stadt*, 118, 134, 158.

111 Cf. A. Rüther, 'Predigtstuhl, Zunftstube, Ratsbank: Orte politischer Kommunikation im spätmittelalterlichen Breslau', in S. Klapp, S. Schmitt (eds), *Städtische Gesellschaft und Kirche im Spätmittelalter. Arbeitstagung auf Schloss Dhaun 2004*, Stuttgart: Steiner, 2008, 141–66.

112 Cf. J. Ganzert (ed.), *Das Lüneburger Rathaus. Ergebnisse der Untersuchungen 2008 bis 2011*, 3 vol., Petersberg: Imhof, 2014–15.

113 Cf. e.g. Kluge, *Macht*.

114 Cf. Gruber, *Mittler zwischen Herrschaft und Gemeinde*.

115 Cf. G. Deutschländer, M. on der Höh, A. Ranft (eds), *Symbolische Interaktion in der Residenzstadt des Spätmittelalters und der Frühen Neuzeit*, Berlin: Akad.-Verl., 2013; W. Paravicini, J. Hirschbiegel, J. Wettlaufer (eds), *Städtisches Bürgertum und Hofgesellschaft: Kulturen integrativer und konkurrierender Beziehungen in Residenz- und Hauptstädten vom 14. bis ins 19. Jahrhundert*, Ostfildern: Thorbecke, 2007; W. Paravicini, J. Wettlaufer (ed.), *Der Hof und die Stadt. Konfrontation, Koexistenz und Integration in Spätmittelalter und Früher Neuzeit*, Ostfildern: Thorbecke, 2009; T. Zotz, ,Informelle Zusammenhänge zwischen Hof und Stadt', in R. Butz, J. Hirschbiegel (eds), *Informelle Strukturen bei Hof*, Münster: LIT-Verl., 2009, 157–68.

116 Cf. J. Hirschbiegel, 'Hof, Residenz, Residenzstadt – alte und neue Forschungsfelder. Das Forschungsvorhaben "Residenzstädte im Alten Reich (1300–1800)"', in S. Tauss, J. Herrmann (eds), *Urbanität im integrativen und konkurrierenden Beziehungsgefüge von Herrschaft und Gemeinde. Herrschen – Leben – Repräsentieren. Residenzen im Fürstbistum*

Osnabrück 1600–1800, Regensburg: Schnell + Steiner, 2014, 303–13; J. Hirschbiegel, S. Rabeler, 'Residential Cities in the Holy Roman Empire (1300–1800). Urbanism as a Network of Integrative and Competing Relationships between Seignorial Rulership and Civic Community (A New Research Project of the Göttingen Academy of Sciences)', in L. Courbon, D. Menjot (eds), *La Cour et la ville dans l'Europe du Moyen Âge et des Temps Modernes,* Turnhout: Brepols, 2015, 91–100.

117 Further information about the current research project of the Göttingen Academie of Sciences is given at www.adw-goe.de/forschung/forschungsprojekte-akademienprogramm/residenzstaedte (accessed September 23, 2016). Cf. G. Fouquet, J. Hirschbiegel, S. Rabeler (eds), *Residenzstädte der Vormoderne. Umrisse eines europäischen Phänomens,* Ostfildern: Thorbecke, 2016, esp. Rabeler, 'Stadt und Residenz in der Vormoderne', and the summary given by Gabriel Zeilinger, 'Umrissene Residenzstädte. Beobachtungen zum Schluss', in ibid., 389–495.

118 For the history and written tradition of medieval cities in particular and in general B.U. Hergemöller (ed.), *Quellen zur Verfassungsgeschichte der deutschen Stadt im Mittelalter,* Darmstadt: Wiss. Buchges., 2000; H. Stoob (ed.), *Urkunden zur Geschichte des Städtewesens in Mittel- und Niederdeutschland,* vol. 1: *Bis 1350,* Köln: Böhlau, 1985, vol. 2: *1351–1475,* Köln: Böhlau, 1992; G. Möncke (ed.), *Quellen zur Wirtschafts- und Sozialgeschichte mittel- und oberdeutscher Städte im Spätmittelalter,* Darmstadt: Wiss. Buchges., 1982.

119 M. Kintzinger, ‚Stadtbücher', *Lexikon des Mittelalters,* vol. 8, München: Artemis & Winkler, 1997, 12seq. See esp. C. Speer, 'Der Index Librorum Civitatum als Instrument der historischen Grundlagenforschung', in W. Reininghaus, M. Stumpf (eds), *Amtsbücher als Quellen der landesgeschichtlichen Forschung,* Münster: Landschaftsverb. Westfalen-Lippe, 2012, 107–24; C. Speer, 'Der Index Librorum Civitatum (Verzeichnis der Stadtbücher des Mittelalters und der Frühen Neuzeit) als Instrument der historischen Grundlagenforschung', *Mitteilungen der Residenzen-Kommission der Akademie der Wissenschaften zu Göttingen. Neue Folge: Stadt und Hof* 1, 2012, 45–50; C. Speer, 'Stand und Perspektiven der Stadtbuchforschung – ein Überblick', *Documenta Pragensia* 32,2, 2013, 367–94; C. Speer, 'Account and Town Records as Mirrors of Social Change and Control in the 15th and 16th Century', in A. Wirth-Jaillard, A. Musin, N. Demaret, E. Bodart, X. Rousseaux (eds), *Monuments ou documents? Les comptabilités, sources pour l'histoire du contrôle social,* Bruxelles: Archives générales du Royaume, 2015, 269–78.

120 Cf. Isenmann, *Stadt,* 434–41; K. Beyerle, 'Die deutschen Stadtbücher', *Deutsche Geschichtsblätter. Monatsschrift zur Förderung der landesgeschichtlichen Forschung* 11, 1910, 145–200.

121 An overview is given by Speer, 'Der Index Librorum Civitatum', 47. See 'Index Librorum Civitatum': www.stadtbuecher.de (accessed November 23, 2017).

122 Cf. Isenmann, *Stadt,* 437–40; H. von Seggern, 'Die Behandlung von Nachlaßangelegenheiten vor dem Lübecker Rat', in H. Brand, S. Rabeler, H. on Seggern (eds), *Gelebte Normen im urbanen Raum? Zur sozial- und kulturgeschichtlichen Analyse rechtlicher Quellen in Städten des Hanseraums (13. bis 16. Jahrhundert),* Hilversum: Uitg. Verloren, 2014, 83–100.

123 Speer, 'Der Index Librorum Civitatum', 46.

124 Cf. e.g. J. Rogge, *Für den Gemeinen Nutzen. Politisches Handeln und Politikvorstellungen von Rat und Bürgerschaft in Augsburg im Spätmittelalter,* Tübingen: Niemeyer, 1996; M. Meinhardt, *Dresden im Wandel. Raum und Bevölkerung der Stadt im Residenzbildungsprozess des 15. und 16. Jahrhunderts,* Berlin: Akad.-Verl., 2009.

4
TRAVEL, MOBILITY, AND CULTURE IN EUROPE

Marianne O'Doherty

Introduction

The period between 1250 and 1500 was a remarkable one in the European history of travel, cultural contact, and exploration. In the 1240s and 1250s in response to the perceived threat of Mongol expansion, King Louis IX of France and Pope Innocent IV separately sent missionaries and diplomats on journeys of several thousand miles to treat with the Mongol Khans, initiating a period of contact that would last for more than a century and have profound effects.[1] Towards the end of the period, Portuguese navigators rounded the Cape of Good Hope and eventually crossed the Indian Ocean to make landfall in Calicut. Christopher Columbus and Amerigo Vespucci reached the shores of a new world, just as approximately 80,000 Jews were expelled from Spain, eventually reaching destinations from Portugal to Navarre to Italy, and North Africa.[2] Throughout this same period, ordinary people incorporated travel into their everyday lives as they visited pilgrimage sites from the small and local to the large and international.[3] Documents from the period also leave us a picture of mercantile communities in different countries whose prosperity is founded in a culture of mobility.[4] The period was also significant in the history of the founding of universities, and saw the inception of the international culture of humanism. Both developments mobilized people within their countries and beyond: scholars to masters; masters to schools; poets and scholars to patrons.[5] It was also a period in which conflicts displaced people in all sorts of ways: from the mass movement of soldiers from England and Wales to the continent during the Hundred Years' War to the capture and transit of hostages to the creation of exiles.[6] Professed religious, often thought less mobile by reason of the vow of *stabilitas loci* taken by most monks, travelled more than one might be inclined to think. Indeed, the early thirteenth century saw the foundation of the Franciscan and Dominican mendicant orders, whose mobility was put to the service of the papacy in matters of diplomacy and mission.[7] Largely founded in the twelfth century, the military orders – the Knights Templar, Knights Hospitaller, and Teutonic Knights – often required their members to travel to areas of need, and continued to grow throughout at least part of our period.[8] But ordinary clerics and monks could find also themselves propelled into movement by the great councils and synods of the church. It is a period in which women as well as men travelled; records tell of itinerant queens ruling territories, women undertaking pilgrimage in substantial numbers, and noble or royal women moving to marry.[9]

A chapter of this length cannot, of course, attempt a history of all such movements; the notes to this section should provide ample initial orientation for the curious.[10] Rather, its brief is to sketch out some of the more significant and widespread cultural dimensions and impacts of mobility and travel for Latin Europe in the later Middle Ages.[11] Focusing on Christian traditions in Europe, the first two sections explore two linked paradigms that framed medieval Christian Europeans' concepts of and approaches to travel and mobility.[12] Firstly, I trace the relationship of the journey to faith in a religious culture in which mobility and journeying is inextricably bound up with the post-lapsarian human condition. Secondly, I consider travel, the traveller, and mobility as sources of danger, whether to the traveller or to society. The third and final section surveys some of the impacts of later medieval patterns of travel and mobility on the formation of cultural identities, and on European writers' capacities and strategies for social and cultural critique and self-reflection.

Journeys of faith

Later medieval European Christians inherited from their early medieval, early Christian, and Jewish forebears a paradigm that encouraged believers to think of life as a form of journey and of the journey as signifying life, a paradigm that helped to create later medieval thinking and practice about journeying, and particularly pilgrimage. As Dee Dyas has shown, this model of exile as a punishment for human misdeeds or simply a test of faith can be traced back to the Hebrew Bible. Adam and Eve wander in the world as a punishment for their sin; Abraham was commanded to leave his land and travel as a stranger in the lands his successors would one day colonize; the Israelites live in slavery and in exile until called by God to the promised land, 'flowing with milk and honey', a land 'promised on oath to Abraham, Isaac, and Jacob' (*Exodus*, 3.17; 33.1).[13] These biblical stories of exile and wandering followed by the promise of return or arrival at one's new or promised homeland were of course richly allegorical, and this allegorization begins even in the New Testament, which, according to Dyas, set 'earthly exile against heavenly citizenship, temporary suffering against eternal joy'.[14]

In this model, the journey, or period of exile from friends, family, and home, with its hardships and temptations, becomes a figure for Christian life, and the homecoming a figure for the Christian's eventual welcome to the Father's heavenly home.[15] These notions fed into some of the influential myths of journeying inherited and created by the later Middle Ages. The eighth- or ninth-century *Voyage of St Brendan* was translated and recast multiple times in the period, popularizing the notion of the journey as a period of hardship, faith-testing, and spiritual learning and growth, thus a necessary prelude to obtaining the promised land.[16] Popular devotional reading such as the St Patrick's Purgatory narratives and the *Visio Tnugdali* tradition, in which a traveller or dreamer journeys through the various regions of the afterlife, emphasized similar connections and culminated in early fourteenth-century Dante's *Divine Comedy*. In the case of St Patrick's Purgatory, the textual tradition also had a hand in the promotion of place-pilgrimage to its supposed site at Lough Derg.[17] The powerful potential of the journey as a religious figure to sublimate mundane human experience is fully realized in works such as Guillaume de Deguileville's powerful and influential fourteenth-century allegorical work the *Pèlerinage de la vie humaine*.[18] Indeed, Dyas has suggested that in the Middle Ages 'it is in fact the process of journeying through life, rather than travelling to holy places, which constitutes the primary meaning of pilgrimage'.[19]

Late medieval European culture, then, both drew upon and fed into a powerful and emotionally charged matrix of thought about the relationship between the earthly life, journeying, and the afterlife. This leads to an important question: how did this way of conceptualizing journeying bear upon travel as practice and experience?

Place-pilgrimage in the later Middle Ages was shaped by the notion of visiting a site – a 'holy place', sometimes termed a sacred centre – sanctified in some way by the touch of God.[20] This was often the relic-sanctioned shrine of a holy person whose sanctity has been demonstrated through miracles.[21] For some, that might mean a journey to the land that was, in the words of the immensely popular pilgrimage narrative, *The Book of Sir John Mandeville*, 'blessed and hallowed and consecrated by the precious blood of Our Lord Jesus Christ'.[22] But ideas of place-pilgrimage also continued to be shaped by the Old Testament notions, alluded to above, of the journey itself as arduous and thus penitential.[23] The great preacher Jacques de Vitry (d. 1270), in a sermon intended for ordinary men and women, drew a direct connection between the journey of the pilgrim and the wanderings of Abraham in exile, as well as assuring would-be pilgrims that, through suffering on their journey as Christ suffered on his, they could ensure their presence at the Resurrection.[24] In the later Middle Ages, under the influence of increasing devotion to the person of Christ, place-pilgrimage increasingly entailed travelling to the scenes of Christ's suffering and, ideally, experiencing a vivid connection to event and place that involves the pilgrim in the suffering Christ's pain.[25] Even the Dominican preacher and pilgrim Riccoldo da Montecroce, travelling just before the fall of Acre in 1291, berates himself for insufficient devoutness, because he does not immediately 'die of sorrow or joy' from seeing the site of the crucifixion of Christ, and nor does he 'truly see with the eyes of my body my Lord hanging from the cross', but only 'with the eyes of faith'.[26] Just over a century later, the English mystic Margery Kempe not only fell into bouts of uncontrollable weeping that seized control of her entire body at the sites of Christ's suffering, but also seemed to revel in the exclusion and abuse she received at the hands of her fellow-pilgrims. Both experiences served to underscore her connection to and imitation of Christ.[27] In Margery's text in particular, the notion that the sufferings she experiences in her earthly pilgrimage will merit subsequent reward surfaces regularly.[28]

The important medieval paradigm of journeying for faith, and of the journey as a liveable, performable figure of the Christian's journey towards the heavenly home, had significant cultural effects. Travelling to the Holy Land on pilgrimage became for many a mass transit phenomenon and a collective experience, particularly after the Franciscans were granted occupancy and access privileges to the holy sites by the Egyptian Sultan in 1333 and the title of official custodians of the Holy Places for the Catholic Church by Clement IV in 1342.[29] Under Franciscan guidance, pilgrims' tours and thus experiences were closely controlled and curated.[30] Anthropologists and medievalists alike have in recent decades queried and nuanced earlier theories of pilgrimage as a liminal phenomenon, and the extent to which medieval pilgrimage created a kind of 'communitas' and 'social antistructure' in which normal social hierarchies were inverted or disrupted.[31] Yet it is important to recognize that medieval pilgrims' reports of their journeys do often emphasize the community of pilgrims in different, context-dependent ways. At times it is compared to a family or a monastery; at times it is more like a congregation.[32] Dominican Riccoldo da Montecroce's describes leading and participating in activities designed to bring the community of faithful pilgrims together as one as they evoke and indeed recreate New Testament events, including Christ's entry into Jerusalem and the women's discovery of the empty tomb after the Resurrection.[33] Scholars have also recently begun to consider how this creation of community around the experience of pilgrimage extends beyond the experience itself and permeates European culture, involving people mentally in pilgrimage, and bringing them into a community of pilgrims even if they did not undertake the journey themselves.[34] The creation of Holy Sepulchre copies and 'mini-calvaries' across Europe enabled communities to participate in, and make their own, the culture of Holy Land pilgrimage near their own homes.[35] Religious and secular pilgrims and non-pilgrims alike shared accounts of journeys to the Holy Land or Rome that allowed them to relive journeys, or experience them for the first time, creating an image of the Holy Land that was, as Anthony Bale has put it, more of a meme – shared cultural property – than an individually experienced and described reality.[36] Pre-humanist scholar Petrarch was so confident in his knowledge of this shared cultural property that he produced a guide to the Holy Land for his friend Giovanni Mandelli without having travelled there, reasoning that 'we generally know many things we have not seen and do not understand many things we have seen'.[37] The compelling resonance of pilgrimage as a shared cultural experience – an experience familiar, paradoxically, even to those who have *not* experienced it – explains something of the power of Chaucer's *Canterbury Tales*, which ultimately uses its depiction of a fractious but nonetheless cohesive 'companye' of pilgrims to draw readers into a broader fellowship: that of Christians on the pilgrimage of life.[38]

Travel dangers

The idea of the journey as a test of faith or endurance, and thus as a figure for the 'real' pilgrimage that is the journey of life, brings us to a second key cultural paradigm: the conceptualization of travel, or its consequences, as dangerous. This conceptualization of travel was of course founded in very real dangers. Long-distance and, for some groups in particular, even short-distance journeys could pose serious risks. Pilgrims' guides and narratives of their journeys to the Eastern Mediterranean record dangers ranging from the sinking of crowded galleys to attacks by bandits to fleecings by untrustworthy guides.[39] The *Book of Margery Kempe*'s third-person account of the English mystic's travels and pilgrimages in Northern Europe records her fears of shipwreck, of robbery, and of physical and sexual attack.[40] For those travelling further afield, political instability, sickness, and expropriation may be added to the list of potential dangers and, for missionaries, that of persecution by the authorities of the lands they were sent to convert.[41] As well as being very real, however, the physical dangers and discomforts of travel clearly form part of its mythology in cultural production, a point that Shayne Legassie makes when he underscores the deep links between the medieval concepts of travel and 'travail'.[42] These links are particularly visible in imaginative literature. Under the guidance of their abbot, the monks of the *Navigatio sancti Brendani*, with two exemplary exceptions, are preserved or rescued from the terrifying dangers of oceanic travel: the island of the smiths; the giant fish Jasconius; hunger, thirst, and dangerous indulgence in foreign food and drink; being driven hither and thither by wind; and being becalmed.[43] The escape of Custance, heroine of Chaucer's Man of Law's Tale, from the terrible physical and sexual dangers that her enforced journeys impose upon her is heralded as proof of divine intervention on her behalf.[44]

Ideas about the dangers of travel and what it meant to risk one's physical or spiritual safety worked differently among different communities. Among the Franciscan and Dominican orders, charged with the longest-distance journeys in the service of ecclesiastical diplomacy and conversion in the later Middle Ages, the risks run by missionary friars in pursuit of a harvest of souls become important to their individual and collective identity. Emotive letters and compilations outlining how bands of intrepid friars had attained the palm of martyrdom circulated around Franciscan and Dominican houses in Europe; such stories were sometimes incorporated into their orders' chronicles, and even painted onto the walls of their European convents.[45] Such promotional efforts were no doubt intended to underpin a sense of shared, universal mission between European friars and their brethren in *partes infidelium* (the lands of the infidels). These retellings of stories of the success of intrepid missionaries among the *gentes* (unconverted tribes), triumphantly spreading the faith even as they were martyred, were called upon to support orders' claims to authority. An Italian interpolated version of the *Chronicle* of Nicholaus Minorita features a report of a papal consistory meeting in the 1320s in which a Franciscan bishop traded fierce words with Pope John XXII and a Dominican over the extent and longevity of each order's activities in the East, and the amount of blood each order has shed in pursuit of their dangerous missions.[46] Both orders' commitments to distant, dangerous missions were intertwined with their authority. For pilgrims and missionaries alike, then, the physical dangers and hardships experienced in travel were proofs of merit and played a crucial role in the formation of individual and shared identities. But there is evidence, too, that inventive writers saw the comic potential of the trope of the intrepid traveller facing spiritual and moral dangers on a journey into distant, wild regions. A set of reminiscences, certainly inauthentic, added anonymously to Italian manuscripts of Franciscan missionary Odorico da Pordenone's account of his travels through the Indies to China relate the friar's comical attempts to escape a father's imprecations to the friar to have sex with his daughter, apparently in accordance with local custom. Pope Pius II, in his autobiography, reminisces, tongue-in-cheek, on how fear of physical dangers of his 1435 journey as a young cleric through the 'uncultivated, savage' Scottish borderlands prevented him from taking advantage of such an offer from two young local women.[47]

Travel and mobility in the later Middle Ages were, however, sometimes seen as having the potential to generate dangers with more troubling social, political, religious, and cultural resonances.[48] In theology, political theory and poetry alike, travel and mobility were in some quarters seen as potentially destabilizing to social body and the individual soul. Many scholars have pointed out that notions of the potential spiritual dangers of pilgrimage formed part of a contradictory attitude to the phenomenon that dates back to late antiquity.[49] Debra Birch cites a series of twelfth-century criticisms pertaining to the waste of money spent by pilgrims that would be better spent alleviating suffering, and of the spiritual usefulness of pilgrimage at all, if pilgrims simply take their vices with them.[50] Giles Constable has shown how criticism of monks and nuns from enclosed orders who have eschewed their vow of stability to undertake pilgrimage or crusade focused on how these put at risk both their own spiritual health and that of their monastic houses.[51] Critics of place-pilgrimage also highlighted what they perceived as a fundamentally misguided substitution of temporal, earthly goals for spiritual, eternal ones in the veneration of Jerusalem. 'Christ gave the price of His blood not to acquire the land of Jerusalem but rather to acquire and save souls', wrote the Cistercian abbot Adam of Perseigne (d. 1221).[52] Such criticism grew during the course of the later Middle Ages. Condemnations of pilgrims' motives and practices are to be found in the writings of orthodox theologians and advocates of movements dubbed heretical alike, and can be as explicit as Thomas à Kempis's warning that '[t]hose who make many pilgrimages rarely find salvation', or as implicit as Geoffrey Chaucer's backhanded, innuendo-laden praise for the well-travelled Wife of Bath's exceptional knowledge of 'wandrynge by the weye'.[53]

The effects of spiritual and societal dangers thought to be associated with mobility were not confined to pilgrims, of course. It is often remarked upon that, following the Black death of 1348–50, monarchies and city states across Europe responded to actual or potential labour shortages and the threat of economic instability arising from these with, among other measures, restrictions on freedom of movement for specific classes (often, but not always or exclusively, agricultural labourers).[54] But the social and cultural dangers identified in many sources are sometimes more subtle and intangible than this. The thirteenth-century political treatise known as *De regimine principum*, the first part of which is normally attributed to Thomas Aquinas, sets out some of the perceived problems of allowing foreign travellers to one's city:

> A city that needs a multitude of mercantile transactions for its own sustenance must endure continual interaction with foreigners. According to the doctrine of Aristotle, this commonly corrupts the customs of citizens because foreigners, nourished on other laws and usages, necessarily act in many ways that differ from the customs of the citizens. When their example provokes the citizens to act in similar ways, civil intercourse is disturbed.[55]

The *De regimine*'s phrasing here gestures towards a thread of concern that surfaces in unexpected places across the literature of the Middle Ages: that of the capacity of mobility, and the interaction between cultures and communities that it requires, to somehow weaken or destabilize the self or the self's community. In his *Topographia Hiberniae*, written and revised in the late twelfth and early thirteenth centuries in justification of English conquests in Ireland, but recopied and read throughout the later Middle Ages, Gerald of Wales expresses concern about the corrupting influence on the English of communications with the native Irish.[56] The deracination of a people for the purposes of conquest elsewhere is presented as a double-edged sword even by Marco Polo, in his otherwise laudatory account of the origins of the Tartars (Mongols) and the Empire of the Great Khan (1298). Those Tartars who have moved to conquered regions are no longer 'true tartars', but 'greatly debased', having adopted 'the habits, manners and customs' of the conquered.[57] Climates and environments as well as the manners and customs are also blamed for certain places' corrupting influence on travellers. Petrarch warns the dedicatee of his *Itinerarium*, Giovanni Mandelli, to stay away from Cyprus, where it is 'as though people's temperaments have conformed to physical environment' and 'French arrogance, Syrian luxury, and Greek flattery and deceit all meet'.[58]

Finally, the associations between travel, mobility, cultural contact, and danger often extended to perceptions of travellers and those whose professions required mobility. Throughout the later Middle Ages, popes made repeated attempts to prevent or minimize trade between Christians and 'infidels'. Merchants (and indeed cities) who, without special licence, failed to comply with the papacy's total or partial embargoes were seen as not only potentially aiding the enemy militarily (particularly if they traded in militarily useful materials), but also as endangering their own souls.[59] It has been noted above that monastic pilgrimage was a cause of suspicion in the period, but even the mendicant orders, whose rules were designed to permit the mobility their missions required, found themselves attracting suspicions on this account. Members of the Dominican *Societas peregrinantium propter Christum*, the section of the order to which overseas missionaries were attached, were accused even within their own order of failing to carry out their duties in the East and instead evading discipline by their wanderings. Other accusations included abusing their privileges by investing in mercantile activity and treating with the merchants of Alexandria in contravention of papal prohibition.[60] Mendicant practices of travelling locally to beg for their orders and preach aroused opprobrium too.[61] From such criticisms emerged the familiar images of the unscrupulous, wandering friar, breaking vows with impunity or defrauding the credulous with travellers' tall tales that we find in the works of Chaucer, Boccaccio, and contemporaries.[62] Stories of wandering, dangerous friars, of course, formed part of a wider tradition concerning the dangers to the 'host' community or family of the attractive but untrustworthy stranger temporarily resident in their midst: stories exemplified in the *Canterbury Tales* by the Miller's and Reeve's Tales' accounts of the tricks of wandering students and the Shipman's Tale's distinctly unstable, roving monk, Don John.

New cultures of mobility and travel

The changing pattern of medieval Europeans' mobility had important cultural impacts. As Robert Bartlett showed in his ground-breaking work, *The Making of Europe: Conquest, Colonization, and Cultural Change 800–1350*, internal and external expansion – and the modes of mobility from all levels of society that these required – were critical to the profound cultural change, towards an 'expansive and increasingly homogeneous society' that took place during this period.[63] According to Bartlett, the age saw the 'Europeanization' of forms of cultural expression from personal names, to iconography, to religious cult, to coinage, and in many other areas, all facilitated through increased mobility, at a range of social levels, between the lands forming part of this emerging meta-geographical conceptual unit.[64] Medieval western European literary culture before 1350 was profoundly shaped, for example, by what Bartlett has termed the 'aristocratic diaspora' that helped spread shared stories, world views, ideals, and knowledge along with Latin and vernacular languages from the former Carolingian Empire across a region that stretched from the British Isles to the Holy Land.[65] During the period 1250–1500, the distances travelled increased, and, due in part to increased numbers of travellers and in part increasing literacy levels, so did the numbers of travellers' accounts of their movements in circulation. What, then, were the cultural effects of these later medieval trends? In the final section of this chapter, I look briefly at three significant, interconnected areas: the perceived value of travel and of the new forms of knowledge it generated; the roles of this new travel knowledge in shaping individual and shared cultural identities; and travel's potential to open up new perspectives on oneself and one's society.

The capacity of travel and mobility to impact upon the social and cultural status of the traveller in various contexts in the later Middle Ages has been well recognized. Legassie has investigated the relationship between the enhancement of traveller's reputations and status and the development of a 'prestige economy of long distance knowledge'; Marco Polo's status is enhanced, for instance, through the process of travel, the opportunities it affords him to demonstrate his abilities, and the curation of the story in his *Book*.[66] Legassie has also put the case that Castilian Pero Tafur's early fifteenth-century travels served to prove his knightly virtues, and thus his claim to aristocratic status at home.[67] Similarly, Mary Fischer has argued that the Northern Crusades in Prussia and Lithuania became a proving-ground for knights travelling from all over Europe in the fourteenth century, cementing the link between journeying, masculine, military prowess, and membership of a social and cultural elite.[68]

But changing patterns in long-distance travel and mobility also shaped the shared cultural identities of non-travellers and their communities. As medieval travellers and their amanuenses boasted of undertaking journeys to places more distant than ever before, interest and excitement in their discoveries grew. Access to the knowledge that these travellers brought back became, in some quarters, not just – or not even – an end in itself or a means subordinated to a clear external purpose, but a marker of social, cultural, or intellectual prestige. As Marco Polo's *Book* and other accounts of the Empire of the Great Khan began to circulate in literate circles in the late thirteenth and early fourteenth centuries, these inspired a fashion for all things exotic and oriental, and, more specifically, Tartar (Mongol). In Italy, scholars have identified vogues for Tartar forenames and styles in circles from Genoese merchants to the scions of noble families, while in England, Edward III in 1331 held a Tartar-themed pageant at Cheapside.[69] Over the course of the fourteenth century, the new geographical, ethnographic knowledge generated through long-distance travel appears to have gained a certain cultural cachet among the ruling classes. Objects associated with the further reaches of the expanded world become objects both of display – showing the vast reach of one's knowledge – and exchange, sealing diplomatic ties between powerful nobles. The Aragonese Infante, Don Juan, son of Pedro IV, seems to have been particularly partial to making diplomatic gifts with a veneer of exoticism. In the 1380s, the prince had two copies made of Juan Fernández de Heredia's translation of Marco Polo to give to the Count of Foix and the Duke of Berry.[70] He also appears to have been instrumental in the Aragonese Crown's ordering of Mallorcan world maps from the most experienced mapmakers of the day, furnished with recent information gathered directly or indirectly from long-distance travellers about the furthest reaches of the known world. The most famous surviving example, thought to have been gifted by the Aragonese crown to the young French King Charles VI sometime after its creation in 1375, is the Catalan Atlas now in the Bibliothèque nationale, Paris. It features information derived from Marco Polo, among a range of other anonymous, but certainly often eyewitness, sources. Something of the cultural significance of such a gift can be gathered from Don Juan's instructions concerning it. He required his agent to find the map's maker, 'Cresques lo juheu' (Cresques the Jew), and learn about the map in order to pass that knowledge, along with the artefact itself, to the thirteen-year-old King.[71] Through his gift, the Aragonese Infante was able to intimate to the young king his superior knowledge of the world and his generosity in sharing it, and at the same time confirm their shared membership of an exclusive noble elite, set apart in part by their access to such exclusive knowledge.

Moving into the early fifteenth century, we find similar examples of prestigious artefacts of travel knowledge being deployed to signal shared membership of an exclusive nobility. John the Fearless, Duke of Burgundy, in 1413 presented his uncle, the Duke of Berry, with the magnificent *Livre des Merveilles* (Paris, Bibliothèque nationale, MS fr. 2810), a collection of exquisitely written and lavishly illuminated exotic travel texts. No doubt the nephew, attempting to shore up his relationship with his uncle following a period of hostility, was mindful in choosing this diplomatic gift of Berry's known taste for exotica and tales of eastern wonders, as manifest in his ownership of six tapestries featuring scenes of the Great Khan.[72] To share, in exquisitely written and decorated codices, knowledge of the furthest reaches of the world brought back by recent travellers was to signal one's participation in the shared cultural values and prestigious, exclusive knowledge of the highest rank of western European nobility and royalty.

From at least the early fifteenth century, however, these changed patterns in travel and mobility and the knowledge exchange they generated shaped not just secular and noble but learned and clerical communities too. Whether at the papal court, councils of the Church, or general chapters, gatherings of clerics, monks, and friars had often provided venues for the exchange of knowledge generated through religious travel, such as the exchange of information about missions and martyrdom discussed in the last section. However, with the ecumenical councils of the early fifteenth century, we see a change in this trend. The Councils of Constance, Basel, and Ferrara-Florence generated a series of encounters and opportunities for exchange of knowledge concerning faraway places between delegates, their entourages, visitors, and petitioners from near and far. News of Gadifer de la Sale and Jean de Béthencourt's 1402 conquests in the Canaries, exchanged at the Council of Constance (1415–18), swiftly reached France through the offices of French Cardinal Guillaume Filliastre, while, at the same council, a monk from the far North West of the known world, Vadstena in Sweden, took the opportunity to copy the Lombard Franciscan Odorico da Pordenone's account of its furthest eastern and southern reaches to take back to his home monastery.[73] At the time of the Council of Florence (1437–45), which aspired to heal the divisions between the Eastern and Western Churches, the city was, as John Larner puts it, 'filled with delegates from the whole Christian World, from Constantinople, Russia, and many parts of the east'.[74] It is during this Council that papal secretary Poggio Bracciolini met Chioggian merchant Niccolò de' Conti, just returned from twenty-five years in Asia, come to seek absolution from the pope. He also records more doubtful information from the Christian Patriarch of an unidentified Central Asian region, and from a group of Ethiopians, all drawn to Italy by the council.[75] As well as travellers from such far-flung regions, the council brought together delegates from across Europe and helped foster the development of a shared international, humanist geographical culture, with interests in both classical geography and medieval long-distance travellers' accounts of their discoveries.[76]

The late medieval travel cultures outlined in this chapter had one final very important impact that should be highlighted here: they provided new frameworks and tools for self-examination and reflection and for critical consideration of one's home culture and society. It is no exaggeration to suggest that these new frameworks helped to transform medieval people's sense of the possible. Travellers use their own accounts in this way from early on in the period. Dominican pilgrim and diplomat Burchard of Mont Sion returned from his journeys to the Eastern Mediterranean to produce not just a detailed verbal map of the Holy Land (1283–85), but also with information about the social organization, religious practices, and hierarchy of the Kingdom of Armenia. After recounting such wonders as the King and his nobles' humble reverence before the Catholicus, the increased authority of monks compared to the reduced authority of priests and clerics, the harshness of criminal punishments, and the piety of the laity, Burchard notes, 'I saw many other highly commendable things in that land, both among the laity and among the clerics and monks, which in our land would scarcely be thought possible'.[77] Just a few years later, Marco Polo's *Book* (1298) famously brought back tales of the marvellous social organization, political administration, and urban planning of the Empire of the Great Khan and its constituent parts, commending the wisdom and effectiveness of administrative practices from the Emperor's postal system to the medieval southern Chinese equivalent of the modern hotel register.[78]

The notion that long-distance travel has the capacity to inspire useful critical reflection on social, political, and religious organization, on administration, on governance, and on the self becomes increasingly important in the later Middle Ages, and filters through into genres beyond the eyewitness travel narrative. The immensely influential travel fiction, *The Book of Sir John Mandeville*, famously sees its protagonist's complacency concerning his own Christian society punctured by the sharp criticisms of a well-informed Egyptian Sultan who offers his perspective, shaped by the stories of his many well-travelled spies, on the many ways in which it falls short of Christian ideals.[79] If only one could learn lessons in faith and behaviour from the Muslims, the *Book* implies, the Holy Land could easily be retaken for Christendom. Indeed, the idea that through travelling, in body or mind, one can truly know one's own country, society, or self becomes a trope that is revisited with increasing sophistication throughout the period. Petrarch, famously, uses his *Itinerarium* to Jerusalem to write a laudatory account the coastline of the Italian peninsula and its islands, whilst neglecting much of the Holy Land proper. As Bale notes, for Petrarch, 'to travel to Jerusalem, it appears, was to appraise one's homeland'.[80] We see a different deployment of a fundamentally similar idea underlying the organizing principle of Chaucer's *Canterbury Tales*. Chaucer's unfinished collection attempts to set out a comprehensive and critical vision of society through the frame of a journey that places its members, temporarily, at a tangent to its norms. A little earlier in the fourteenth century, Giovanni Boccaccio had drawn upon then destabilized the trope to comic effect in *Decameron* I.II, in which a Jewish traveller's exposure to corruption in Rome triggers a set of reflections on Latin Christendom's social and religious order that have an unexpected outcome. In Boccaccio's story, a Parisian Christian urges his friend Abraham the Jew to agree to baptism, but Abraham refuses to do so until he has seen the behaviours of the head of the church, the pope, and his entourage in Rome. Knowing that his friend will witness the corrupt and dissolute lives of the Roman clergy, the Christian gives up any hope that his friend will convert. Abraham does indeed find the clergy of Rome 'steeped in lust, greed, avarice, fraud, envy, pride, and other like sins and worse'. However, observing that, irrespective of such evident corruption, 'your religion continues to grow in popularity, and become more splendid and illustrious', he concludes that it must be 'a more holy and genuine religion than any of the others' and promptly requests baptism into the faith.[81] Here, as in so many late medieval uses of the cultural trope of travel, we can trace a relationship between the journey, a resulting change of perspective (shared with listener or reader), and presentation of an alternative – the possibility of transformation – for oneself or one's society. We can ultimately trace the influence of this trend on Thomas More's *Utopia* of 1516. At the close of his account of an imagined journey to a remarkably sophisticated alternative commonwealth, the book's fictionalized narrator, Morus, seems almost to evoke the spirit of Burchard of Mount Sion when he remarks wistfully that this society contains 'many features [...] which I might more truly wish for than expect to see in our own cities'.[82] By the time we reach the early sixteenth century, then, changes in medieval patterns of mobility and travel have brought about significant cultural change, including the development of new frameworks for envisioning achievable social alternatives and for considering how oneself and one's society might fall short of these.

Notes

1 See P. Jackson, *The Mongols and the West*, London: Longman, 2005.

2 F. Fernandez-Armesto, 'Exploration and Discovery', in C. Allmand (ed.), *The New Cambridge Medieval History*, vol. VII, c.1415–c.1500, Cambridge: Cambridge University Press, 1998, 175–201. J. Ray, *After Expulsion: 1492 and the Making of the Sephardic Jewry*, New York: New York University Press, 2012, 39.

3 See for instance the documentary sources gathered and translated in *Pilgrims and Pilgrimage in the Medieval West*, ed. and trans. by Diana Webb, London: Tauris, 2001.

4 The literature on mercantile mobility in the Middle Ages is vast. For a general orientation, see P.B. Newman, *Travel and Trade in the Middle Ages*, Jefferson, NC: McFarland, 2011 and J.B. Friedman et al. (eds), *Trade, Travel, and Exploration in the Middle Ages: An Encyclopedia*, New York, London: Garland, 2000. For the English situation, see in particular T.H. Lloyd, *Alien Merchants in England in the High Middle Ages*, New York: St. Martin's, 1982, and several essays (notably Childs, Jenks, Bolland) in C.M. Barron and A.F. Sutton (eds), *The Medieval Merchant*, Donington: Shaun Tyas, 2014. On the long-distance travels of European merchants, see a series of articles by R.S. Lopez, including 'European Merchants in the Medieval Indies: The Evidence of Commercial Documents', *Journal of Economic History* 3, 1943, 164–84.

5 On the mobility of scholars, see several essays in W.J. Courtenay and J. Miethke (eds), *Universities and Schooling in Medieval Society*, Leiden, Boston, MA: Brill, 2000. On mobility and humanism see R. Black, 'Humanism', in Allmand (ed.), *The New Cambridge Medieval History*, vol. VII, 269–72 and a questioning account in D. Rundle, 'Beyond the Classroom: International Interest in the *studia humanitatis* in the University Towns of Quattrocento Italy', *Renaissance Studies* 27, 2013, 533–48.

6 On soldiers from Britain on the continent, see 'The Soldier in Later Medieval England Project': www.medievalsoldier.org (accessed 18 August 2017); on hostages, see M. Bennett and K. Weikert (eds), *Medieval Hostageship c.700–c.1500: Hostage, Captive, Prisoner of War, Guarantee, Peacemaker*, London: Routledge, 2017.

7 On *Stabilitas loci* see C.H. Lawrence, *Medieval Monasticism: Forms of Religious Life in Western Europe in the Middle Ages*, 2nd edn, London: Longman, 1989, 27. On the mobility of the mendicant orders, see C.H. Lawrence, *The Friars: The Impact of the Early Mendicant Movement on Western Society*, rev. paperback edn, London: Tauris, 2013, 181–217.

8 R. Lützelschwab, 'Western Monasticism' in A. Classen (ed.), A *Handbook of Medieval Culture*, Berlin: De Gruyter, 2015, 1126–32.

9 A.E. Bailey, 'Wives, Mothers and Widows on Pilgrimage: Categories of "Woman" Recorded at English Healing Shrines in the High Middle Ages', *Journal of Medieval History* 39, 2013, 197–219; T. Earenfight, *Queenship and Power in Medieval Europe*, Basingstoke: Palgrave Macmillan, 2013, *passim* but esp. 13–40; Z. Rohr, 'On the Road Again: The Semi-Nomadic Career of Yolande of Aragon (1400–1439)', in M. O'Doherty and F. Schmieder (eds), *Travels and Mobilities in the Middle Ages: From the Atlantic to the Black Sea*, Turnhout: Brepols, 2015, 215–24.

10 In addition to works cited in notes above and below, see also: M.W. Labarge, *Medieval Travellers: The Rich and the Restless*, London: Phoenix, 1982; N. Ohler, *Reisen im Mittelalter*, Munich, Zurich: Artemis, 1986, translated as N. Ohler, *The Medieval Traveller*, trans. by C. Hillier, Woodbridge, Suffolk, 1995; J. Verdon, *Travel in the Middle Ages*, trans. by G. Holoch, Notre Dame, IN: University of Notre Dame Press, 2003; P. Horden (ed.), *Freedom of Movement in the Middle Ages*, Donington: Shaun Tyas, 2007.

11 This conceptual territory is less well trodden. See for example C.K. Zacher, *Curiosity and Pilgrimage: The Literature of Discovery in Fourteenth-Century England*, Baltimore, MD: Johns Hopkins, 1976, and an important recent intervention by S.A. Legassie: *The Medieval Invention of Travel*, Chicago, IL: University Press, 2017.

12 Inevitably, this results in problematic exclusions. Mobility in Islamic culture, including Al-Andalus, cannot be considered here for reasons of space, nor can the cultural practice and significance of mobility in medieval Judaism and the cultural impact of Jewish travels. Both are large topics and rightfully the subjects of dedicated articles and monographs in their own right. For initial English-language orientation see S.M. Toorawa, 'Thinking about Travel in the Medieval Islamic World', *al-'Uṣūr al-Wusṭā: The Journal of Middle East Medievalists* 20.2, 2008, 46–55; M. Jacobs, *Reorienting the East: Jewish Travelers to the Medieval Muslim World*, Philadelphia, PA: University of Pennsylvania Press, 2014, and E.N. Adler (ed.), *Jewish Travellers in the Middle Ages: 19 Firsthand Accounts*, New York: Dover, 1987.

13 D. Dyas, *Pilgrimage in Medieval English Literature, 700–1500*, Woodbridge: Boydell and Brewer, 2001, 12–20. Elsner and Rubiés also trace it to classical roots: J. Elsner and J.P. Rubiés, 'Introduction', in Elsner and Rubiés (eds), *Voyages and Visions*, Cambridge: Reaktion, 1999, 8–20.

14 Dyas, *Pilgrimage in Medieval English Literature*, 25.

15 See for example two sermons on pilgrimage discussed in D.J. Birch, 'Jacques de Vitry and the Ideology of Pilgrimage', in J. Stopford (ed.), *Pilgrimage Explored*, Woodbridge: Boydell and Brewer, 1999, 79–93.

16 W.R.J. Barron and G.S. Burgess (eds), *The Voyage of St Brendan: Representative Versions of the Legend in English Translation*, Exeter: Exeter University Press, 2005.

17 C.G. Zaleski, 'Saint Patrick's Purgatory: Pilgrimage Motifs in a Medieval Otherworld Vision', *Journal of the History of Ideas* 46.4, 1985, 467–85; For an instance of these visions as inspiring place-pilgrimage, see M. Purcell, 'St. Patrick's Purgatory: Francesco Chiericati's Letter to Isabella d'Este', *Seanchas Ardmhacha: Journal of the Armagh Diocesan Historical Society* 12:2, 1987, 1–10.

18 On the two versions of this work within the context of Guillaume's other pilgrimage allegories, and its influence, see the essays collected in M. Nievergelt and S.A. Viereck Gibbs Kamath (eds), *The Pèlerinage Allegories of Guillaume de Deguileville: Tradition, Authority, and Influence*, Cambridge: Brewer, 2013. On the longer history of the paradigm see M. Nievergelt, *Allegorical Quests from Deguileville to Spenser*, Cambridge: Brewer, 2012.

19 Dyas, 'Chaucer and the Communities of Pilgrimage', in *Chaucer and Religion*, ed. by H. Phillips, Cambridge: Brewer, 2010, 134.

20 For an anthropological discussion of what is a 'holy place', including a critique of Mircea Eliade's notion of the 'sacred centre', see J. Eade and M.J. Sallnow, 'Introduction' in Ibid. (eds), *Contesting the Sacred: The Anthropology of Christian Pilgrimage*, London: Routledge, 1991, 1–29.

21 On this practice of 'join[ing] Heaven and Earth at the grave of a dead human being', see most influentially P. Brown, *The Cult of Saints: Its Rise and Function in Latin Christianity*, Chicago, IL: University of Chicago Press, 1981, 1.

22 *The Travels of Sir John Mandeville*, trans. by C.R. Moseley, Harmondsworth: Penguin, 1983, 43.

23 D. Webb, *Medieval European Pilgrimage, c.700–c.1500*, Basingstoke: Palgrave Macmillan, 2002, 49–52.

24 D.J. Birch, 'Jacques de Vitry', 83, 87.

25 See C. Morris, *The Sepulchre of Christ and the Medieval West: From Beginning to 1600*, Oxford: OUP, 2005, 328–36.

26 Riccoldo da Montecroce, 'Itinerary', in *Pilgrimage to Jerusalem and the Holy Land, 1187–1291*, trans. by D. Pringle, Farnham: Ashgate, 2012, p. 373.

27 B. Windeatt (ed.), *The Book of Margery Kempe*, Longman: Harlow, 2000. On Margery's *imitatio Christi* see S. Beckwith, *Christ's Body*, London: Routledge, 1993, 80–3.

28 See for example Windeatt (ed.), *Book of Margery Kempe*, 170–2, where Margery's visit is 'for meryte and for mede' according to Christ.

29 See P. Moukarzel, 'Les franciscains dans le sultanat mamelouk des années 1330 jusqu'a 1516', *Le Moyen Âge* 120, 2014, 135–49; Morris, *The Sepulchre of Christ*, 302–3.

30 N. Chareyron, *Pilgrims to Jerusalem in the Middle Ages*, trans. by W. Donald Wilson, New York: Columbia University Press, 2005, 82–4.

31 The notions of 'communitas' and 'social antistructure' were famously raised by V. and E. Turner in *Image and Pilgrimage in Christian Culture: Anthropological Perspectives*, New York: Columbia University Press, 1978. Among critiques, see in particular Eade and Sallnow, 'Introduction', in *Contesting the Sacred*, 1–29 and, more briefly, Dyas, 'Chaucer and the Communities of Pilgrimage', 133.

32 N. Chareyron quotes Felix Fabri on pilgrims as akin to a family or monastery in *Pilgrims to Jerusalem in the Middle Ages*, 49. On the social and national divisions between pilgrims, see 50, 82.

33 Riccoldo da Montecroce, 'Itinerary', 369; 373–4. On pilgrims' re-enactments at the sepulchre, described as 'guerrilla theatre', see R. Ousterhout, '"Sweetly Refreshed in Imagination": Remembering Jerusalem in Words and Images', *Gesta* 48:2, 2009, 159.

34 See in particular K.M. Rudy, *Virtual Pilgrimages in the Convent*, Turnhout: Brepols, 2011, and K. Beebe, *Pilgrim and Preacher: The Audiences and Observant Spirituality of Friar Felix Fabri (1437/8–1502)*, Oxford: Oxford University Press, 2014.

35 See Morris, *The Sepulchre of Christ*, 230–45 (on Crusade-era Holy Sepulchre copies) and 369 (on local calvaries and sepulchres in the later Middle Ages).

36 A. Bale, '"ut legi": Sir John Mandeville's Audience and Three Late Medieval English Travelers to Italy and Jerusalem', *Studies in the Age of Chaucer* 38, 2016, 208–10.

37 F. Petrarca, *Itinerarium: A Proposed Route for a Pilgrimage from Genoa to the Holy Land*, ed. and trans. by H. James Shey, Binghamton, NY: Global Academic Publishing, 2004, 157.

38 For the relationship between the community in the *Canterbury Tales* (and pilgrim fellowships generally) and the wider Christian community, see Dyas, 'Chaucer and the Communities of Pilgrimage', 132–42.

39 On reports of storms, shipwrecks, and pirates in the Mediterranean, see Chareyron, *Pilgrimage to Jerusalem in the Middle Ages*, 64–7. See 127–45 for reports of the rarer additional journey to St Catherine of Sinai that discuss brigand attacks.

40 B. Windeatt (ed.), *The Book of Margery Kempe*, London: Longman, 2000, e.g. II, chs 3–7, 396, 401, 402, 412.

41 J.R.S. Phillips, *The Medieval Expansion of Europe*, Oxford: Clarendon Press, 1998, 92–3 and C. Dawson, 'Introduction', in C. Dawson (ed.), *The Mongol Mission*, London: Sheed and Ward: 1955, vii–xxxv (p. xxxiv). For friars' descriptions of dangers and persecutions, see in particular the first letter of Franciscan missionaries to China John of Montecorvino (224–27) and Andrew of Perugia (235–7) in the same volume.

42 Legassie, *The Medieval Invention of Travel*, 2.

43 J.J. O'Meara and J.M. Wooding, 'The Latin Version', in *The Voyage of Saint Brendan: Representative Versions of the Legend in English*, trans. by G.S. Burgess, Exeter: University of Exeter Press, 2005, 35 (Jasconius); xii, 39 (wind, exhaustion, prayer).

44 L.D. Benson et al. (eds), *The Riverside Chaucer*, Oxford: Oxford University Press, 1988, 87–104.

45 On the incorporation of records and letters concerning missionary activities and martyrdoms into chronicles, see M. O'Doherty, *The Indies and the Medieval West*, Turnhout: Brepols, 2013, 80. Ambrogio Lorenzetti's Martyrdom of the Franciscans was painted in the Chapterhouse in Church of San Francisco, Siena, while a now lost painting of the execution of the Franciscans at Tana was in the cloister: A. McClanan, 'The Strange Lands of Ambrogio Lorenzetti', in R. Bork (ed.), *The Art, Science, and Technology of Medieval Travel*, Aldershot: Ashgate, 2008, 89–92.

46 F. Zambrini (ed.), *Storia di fra Michele Minorita come fu arso in Firenze nel 1389 con documenti riguardanti i fraticelli della povera vita: Testi inediti del buon secolo*, Bologna: Romagnoli, 1864, 69–70. The episode is appropriated by Umberto Eco, *The Name of the Rose*, trans. by W. Weaver, London: Picador, 1983, 343–4. I am indebted to Dr Melanie Brunner for this reference.

47 Odorico da Pordenone, *Le libro delle nuove e strane e meravigliose cose*, ed. by Alvise Andreose, Padova: Centro studi Antoniani, 2000, 182; Pius II, *Commentaries,* vol. I, Books I–II, ed. by M. Meserve and M. Simonetta, Cambridge, MA: Harvard University Press, 2003, Ch. 6, 10–15.

48 See for instance D. Dyas, 'Chaucer and the Communities of Pilgrimage', 138.

49 G. Constable, 'Opposition to Pilgrimage in the Middle Ages', in *Religious Life and Thought (11–12 Centuries)*, London: Variorum, 1979, IV, 125–46. Dyas, *Pilgrimage in*

Medieval English Literature, 10; Dyas, 'Chaucer and the Communities of Pilgrimage', 134–5.

50 Birch, 'Jacques de Vitry', 85.

51 Constable, 'Opposition to Pilgrimage', 140–1.

52 Quoted in Constable, 'Opposition to Pilgrimage', 143.

53 Thomas à Kempis quoted in Constable, 'Opposition to Pilgrimage', 145; G. Chaucer, 'General Prologue', in Benson (ed.), *Riverside Chaucer*, 21–36 (l. 467).

54 Measures are comparatively surveyed in S. Cohn, 'After the Black Death: Labour Legislation and Attitudes Towards Labour in Late-Medieval Western Europe', *The Economic History Review*, N. S., 60.3, 2007, 457–85.

55 Ptolemy of Lucca and Thomas Aquinas, *On the Government of Rulers*, trans. by J.M. Blythe, Philadelphia, PA: University of Pennsylvania Press, 2005, 109.

56 On the recensions, see Nóirín Ní Bheaglaoi, 'Two Topographies of Gerald of Wales? A Study of the Manuscript Tradition', *Scriptorium* 67:2, 2013, 377–93. Gerald of Wales, *The Topography of Ireland*, in *The Historical Works of Giraldus Cambrensis*, trans. by T.W. Forrester, London: Bell, 1881, III, Ch. 24, 137–8.

57 Marco Polo, *The Travels*, trans. by N. Cliff, London: Penguin, 2016, 74–5.

58 Petrarch, *Itinerarium*, 171.

59 S. Stantchev, *Spiritual Rationality: Papal Embargo as Cultural Practice,* Oxford: Oxford University Press, 2014, 88. On the licensing of exemptions, see M. Carr, 'Crossing Boundaries in the Mediterranean: Papal Trade Licences from the Registra supplicationum of Pope Clement VI (1342–52)', *Journal of Medieval History* 41:1, 2015, 107–29.

60 J. Richard, *La Papauté et les missions d'orient au moyen âge (XIII–XV siècles)*, Rome: École française de Rome, 1977, 138, and n. 64.

61 For an overview of work on mendicant *terminario* and discussion of it in Scandinavian context, see J.G.G. Jakobsen, '"Them Friars Dash About": Mendicant *Terminario* in Medieval Scandinavia', in O'Doherty and Schmieder (eds), *Travels and Mobilities in the Middle Ages*, 3–29.

62 Chaucer, 'General Prologue', in *The Riverside Chaucer*, ll. 208–69; Giovanni Boccaccio, *Decameron*, trans. by G.H. McWilliam, Harmondsworth: Penguin, 1972, 505–14.

63 R. Bartlett, *The Making of Europe: Conquest, Colonization, and Cultural Change 950–1350*, London: Penguin, 1994, *passim*; quotation at 3.

64 Ibid., 269–91.

65 Ibid., 24–59.

66 Legassie, *The Medieval Invention of Travel*, 22; 39–47.

67 Ibid., 203–11.

68 M. Fischer, 'The Perfect, Gentle Knight: Fourteenth-Century Crusaders in Prussia', in O'Doherty and Schmieder (eds), *Travels and Mobilities in the Middle Ages*, 163–88.

69 On these and other oriental, including Mongol, fashions of the period, see F. Reichert, *Begegnungen mit China: Die Entdeckung Ostasiens im Mittelalter*, Thorbecke: Sigmaringen, 1992, 236–40.

70 J.J. Nitti (ed.), *Juan Fernández de Heredia's Aragonese version of the Libro de Marco Polo*, Madison, WI: The Hispanic seminary of medieval studies, 1980, x.

71 On the problems of securely identifying the Catalan Atlas with Don Juan's intended gift see G. Grosjean (ed.), *Mapamundi: The Catalan Atlas of the Year 1375*, Zurich: Dietikon, 1978, 12.

72 See D.H. Strickland, 'Text, Image and Contradiction in the *Devisement dou monde*', in S.C. Akbari and A.A. Iannucci (eds), *Marco Polo and the Encounter of East and West*, Toronto: University of Toronto Press, 2008, 25; F. Avril, 'Le livre des merveilles, manuscript 2810 de la Bibliothèque Nationale de France', in Marie-Hélène Tesnière, François

Avril, and Marie-Thérèse Gousset (eds), *Marco Polo. Le livre des Merveilles*, Tournai: Renaissance du Livre, 1999, 291–324.

73 P.G. Dalché, 'L'oevre geographique du cardinal fillastre (d. 1428). Representation du monde et perception de la carte à l'aube des découvertes', in D. Marcotte (ed.), *Humanisme et Culture Géographique à l'époque du Concile de Constance autour de Guillaume Fillastre*, Turnhout: Brepols, 2002, 305; O'Doherty, *The Indies and the Medieval West*, 170.

74 J. Larner, 'The Church and the Quattrocento Renaissance in Geography', *Renaissance Studies* 12.1, 1998, 33.

75 Poggio Bracciolini, De *L'Inde: Les voyages en Asie de Niccolò de' Conti*, ed. and trans. by M. Gueret-Laferté, Turnhout: Brepols, 2004, 165–7.

76 J. Larner, *Marco Polo and the Discovery of the World*, New Haven, CT: Yale University Press, 1999, 141–2. On the influence of the Council on the circulation of geographical and travel literature, see O'Doherty, *The Indies*, 170–1.

77 Burchard of Mont Sion 'Description of the Holy Land', in *Pilgrimage to Jerusalem and the Holy Land, 1187–1291*, trans. by D. Pringle, Farnham: Ashgate, 2012, 317–19.

78 For the Mongol postal system, see Polo, *The Travels*, 128–9; for the 'fine custom' of recording the names and dates of guests in lodging-houses in Manzi, 211.

79 *The Travels of Sir John Mandeville*, 107–8.

80 Petrarch, *Itinerarium*, 158–69. A. Bale, 'European Travel Writing in the Middle Ages', in C. Thompson (ed.), *The Routledge Companion to Travel Writing*, London: Routledge, 2016, II, 603–37 (para. 26.24).

81 Boccaccio, *Decameron*, I.II, 85.

82 Thomas More, *Utopia* trans. by D. Baker-Smith, London: Penguin, 2012, 122.

5

CULTURAL ENCOUNTERS AND TRANSFER

The case of pious foundations in the Islamicate world

Johannes Pahlitzsch

Cultural encounters and transfer: some theoretical reflections

The concept of cultural transfer is based on the idea of a cultural encounter that has taken place, leading to communication between members of different cultural areas. In this sense, this model presupposes the existence of distinct 'cultures' and thus seems to contradict more recent ideas of transculturality that proclaim an 'interweaving of different cultural traditions in the social space', and thus lead to the assumption that cultures are not homogenous units but themselves in constant development processes.[1]

Without doubt, this concept of transculturality has contributed to a more nuanced view of contact and exchange in the historical cultural sciences. However, it should be remembered that social groups always construct their own identities in contrast to other groups by postulating certain cultural differences. These constructed cultures, as 'collective imaginations', are part of historical practice and thus shape the cultural and social world.[2] For example, the lists of errors of the Latins, which were written by Greek Orthodox clergymen from the eleventh century, increasingly include the external characteristics of the others, such as clothing or hairstyle, in addition to dogmatic, ecclesiastic or ritual issues; the more intense the contact – and inevitably the exchange – between Latin and Orthodox cultures since the First Crusade, the greater, sharper and more detailed these lists were in their demarcation.[3] This raises the question of how viable the concept of transculturality, whereby all cultures are hybrid, entangled, shared or fluid, to use some of the current buzzwords, is in practical use.

In particular, the applicability of this concept – initially developed for modern societies – to premodern cultures needs to be further critically developed.[4] Michael Borgolte has pointed out that in the Middle Ages, when connections and communication over long distances were more limited, the assumption of the existence of a fundamental hybridity of cultures must not necessarily have to apply to the same degree. Borgolte calls for differentiation, so as not to succumb to tautology and fall into heuristic dead ends. He argues that it is far more a task for historians to better define supposedly universal phenomena and processes as epoch-specific.[5] The task of historical research is not only to determine 'how it actually happened' (*'wie es eigentlich gewesen'*),[6] but also to identify the ideas and concepts that can be grasped in the sources and to question their constructedness. In this sense, the idea of different 'cultures' or 'cultural systems' becomes more relevant. The study of cultural contact, exchange and transfer must therefore involve the concepts of transculturality and interculturality, the latter of which is based on the existence of demarcated cultures, equally and simultaneously. Current cultural transfer research is thus not only multi-linear (instead of applying linear teleologically concepts), but also multi-perspectival.[7]

Against this background, cultural encounter and cultural transfer are to be understood as models whereby 'culture' represents, on the one hand, a heuristically necessary construct that should not be confused with what actually exists,[8] and on the other a specific 'culture', as the construct of social groups could become an actual historical reality. As far as cultural encounters are concerned, the anthropologist Urs Bitterli developed four gradually differing categories; namely, *cultural contact (Kulturb-erührung)*, *cultural collision (Kulturzusammenstoß)*, *cultural relationship (Kulturbeziehung)* and *cultural entanglement (Kulturverflechtung)*. According to Bitterli, *cultural contact* is a temporary, usually friendly encounter between a small group of travellers and representatives of a closed population group,[9] as opposed to *cultural collision*, which often results in the displacement, prolonged subjugation or annihilation of the losing group.[10] However, contact can also lead to a positive *cultural relationship*, co-existence with peaceful exchange,[11] and in the longer term, it may result in *cultural entanglement*.[12] According to Jürgen Osterhammel, the consequences of the cultural encounter can be gradiated into six categories: *inclusion*, *accommodation*, *assimilation*, *exclusion*, *segregation* and *extermination*.[13]

A weakness of these categories, however, is that they are based largely on the assumption of the encounter of coherent units, as Ulrich Gotter has shown. In contrast to this, Gotter emphasizes that they are rather groups of identities that understand each other in opposition to others as belonging together and constantly construct themselves anew in the perception and discourse about themselves and the others.[14] On the basis of Gotter's work, there are four aspects to consider in the study of cultural encounter and cultural exchange: (1) the determination of the respective groups according to their self-definition; (2) the determination of 'foreignness' and differences in sub-areas, such as political organization, economic structure, religion, etc.; (3) the dynamics and context of reception, by which is meant a precise differentiation of the contact situation, for example of the power relations, which in turn allow statements about the freedom of action and interests of the groups involved; and (4) the change of the 'original patterns' in the cultural sub-areas that Gotter calls 'comparative categories', whereby self-perception is again decisive. For example, assimilation takes place if a group itself no longer recognizes differences between itself and the others, regardless of whether any differences actually still exist.[15]

In order to be able to examine cultural contact and transfer, it seems to be sensible to construct a test case that allows us to analyse these phenomena. Firstly, in the analysis of reception processes it can be assumed that the 'foreign' must already be recognizable to the potential recipient on the basis of his knowledge, to such an extent that a perception of 'otherness' becomes possible at all.[16] Hence, the premise is that different human societies have developed over the course of history various similar structures and institutions. These are discernible as what should be called *cultural domains* and can be roughly divided into their respective social and political organization, economy, law, ideology and religion, sciences and learning, language or art.

It is assumed that these *cultural domains*, formed among various cultural groups in a similar manner, are comparable, even when they differ from group to group and place to place in form and content.[17] The example of language, which is created by every human society, makes this quite clear. Regardless of this *cultural domain* being shared by human civilization, individual languages developed independently of each other and in many cases display only marginal similarities. The pre-existence of language only then enables exchange in cross-cultural contact, quite independently of how close or distant the languages in question are. Only because cultures have access to languages can translations be made, translators trained, learning transmitted and similar phenomena.

Furthermore, it can generally be assumed that *cultural domains*, such as law, religion or politics, were not understood as separate areas in premodern societies; however, for a differentiated analysis of historical processes with regard to cultural contact and cultural exchange, it seems justifiable for pragmatic reasons alone to single out individual *cultural domains*.[18] Thus when two similar *cultural domains* that are comparable in their function could be found in groups that are in communication or contact, then it seems reasonable to describe this comparability, which enables or at least eases cultural exchange, as the *compatibility of cultural domains*. The respective individual organization of *cultural domains* leads to the question of how far and in what way a certain *cultural domain* is actually accessible to encounters or exchange, for instance in the case of religion, which, perhaps even more so than language, sets apart the identity of a specific group from another, at least where monotheistic religions are concerned.

Cultural encounters principally occur in contact zones: temporally and locally definable spaces of interaction between different groups. These meeting spaces can be border regions between different cultural areas (areas dominated by a group with a specific cultural identity),[19] or within a cultural area, in very different places and different situations, such as trade, court or places of worship; that is, especially public spaces. Jens Oliver Schmitt, in his study of the so-called Levantines as cultural mediators in the Ottoman Empire, accordingly emphasizes the importance of space for intercultural communication, differentiating between professional and private contact and between individual and community contact. This leads to the important and methodologically relevant observation that co-existence strategies in public space could be contrasted with strict segregation in the private sphere, which was particularly maintained by community leaders.[20]

The folklorist Klaus Roth has shown in this connection that cultural exchange between the groups and the development of social strategies of cohabitation were a vital necessity for the establishment of a group-wide *modus vivendi* in the multi-ethnic Ottoman state. This required specific cultural knowledge as well as social and communicative skills; that is, intercultural competence acquired over a longer period of time. On the basis of this knowledge, difference and foreignness were transformed into familiar otherness that could be dealt with in everyday life with the help of formalized rules of social behaviour.[21] These rules now served to maintain their own group identity, preserving fixed cultural boundaries despite open and often familiar association with each other. Roth speaks here of 'glass walls'; John Cole and Eric Wolf use the term 'hidden frontier'.[22]

Stamatios Gerogiorgakis, Roland Scheel and Dittmar Schorkowitz have systematically examined the transfer as a process, but with a very narrow definition of cultural transfer. According to this, cultural transfer is a special case of general exchange relations and cannot be equated with cultural exchange. While exchange takes place accidentally and repeatedly, but ultimately remains diffuse, cultural transfer refers in this sense to a deliberate, intentional and rational action that serves to transfer certain goods in a unilinear way from a sender to a recipient. According to Gerogiorgakis, Scheel and Schorkowitz, the research into transfers must develop in steps. The process-oriented analysis of the transfer action – that is, of removing, transferring and inserting foreign cultural elements – should be followed by an impact analysis to determine the qualitative innovation and the impact and dynamics of cultural import. Cultural assets and practices, such as information, discourses, texts, images, institutions and behaviours, material cultural goods and social and political institutions, are transferred. According to Johannes Paulmann, the inner motive for the transfer of cultural assets, in general, is their usefulness, which is a prerequisite for the reception of concrete cultural goods.[23] While the proposed methodology of Gerogiorgakis, Scheel and Schorkowitz provides a very helpful basis for future research, no differentiation between transfer and exchange will be made in the following.

Case study: pious foundations in the Islamicate world

A most important aspect of cultural transfer is that acquired cultural assets are never adopted unaltered, but are always reinterpreted.[24] For example, this is clearly seen in the transition from Byzantine to Islamic rule in Syria and Palestine in the seventh and eighth centuries. While the Muslim sources for the founding of Islam and the establishment of the Arab empire, written in most cases only in the ninth century, depict the transition from Byzantine to Islamic rule in Syria in the seventh century as a significant break,[25] archaeological research has revealed a general continuity of social and economic conditions.[26] When the Umayyads began to establish new cities in Syria at the beginning of the eighth century, such as ar-Ramla and ʿAnjar, they adopted Hellenistic ideas of the layout of a city, following the classical, rectangular building plan.[27] At the same time, however, the Hellenistic city layout was redesigned according to Muslim requirements. Thus, the central assembly mosque and the governor's palace were placed in the centre of the city at the intersection of *cardo* and *decumanus*. The Islamic character of the city was thus clearly expressed. But even at the residential level, the Arabian *bayt* system prevailed in the sense of interconnected rooms grouped around a courtyard. In this way, according to Robert Hillenbrand, the classic model was transformed from the inside out.[28]

This example illustrates an essential characteristic of the early Islamic period, which was characterized by both continuity and change. Old identities and institutions were maintained at the local level, especially; at the same time, however, Islamic culture also represented something new. Foreign elements were indeed adopted, yet they were adapted in a translation process to the newly created structures and concepts and transformed accordingly. Referring to early Islamic culture, Garth Fowden concludes in his book on the Umayyad desert castle of Quṣayr ʿAmra, 'But what is borrowed is put together in novel ways and to thoroughly contemporary ends'.[29] Charles Halperin interprets the discrepancy between the takeover of the culture of the subjugated population and the total concealment of this fact in the Muslim sources as the result of a consciously applied strategy. Their goal was to uphold the claim of cultural superiority advocated by the conquerors in contrast to their actual behaviour. Halperin calls this method the 'ideology of silence'. Otherwise, the conquerors would have been forced to ideologically justify the acceptance of the traditions and institutions of the subjugated population.[30]

Based on these more general considerations, various stages of the cultural encounter and the cultural transfer between Christians and Muslims will be dealt with in more detail in the example of the formation of the Islamic pious foundation (*waqf*) and the subsequent adoption of this institution of Islamic law by Christians living under Muslim rule.[31] The first question to ask is whether, in the *cultural domain* of law, there has occurred a veiled adoption of Christian traditions by Muslims. As for the beginnings of Islamic law as such, Patricia Crone has tried to prove the dependence of Islamic law on Roman and Hellenistic provincial law in her work on Islamic patronage. According to Crone, it cannot be assumed that Roman law had a direct influence on the *šarīʿa*. Rather, provincial legal traditions that included Roman elements alongside ancient Near Eastern, Jewish and Sasanian law influenced the development of Islamic law.[32] Irene Schneider confirmed this finding in her monograph on child slavery and debt bondage, in which there is not a straight adoption, but rather Islamic jurists have critically debated late Antique law.[33] Wael Hallaq and Norman Calder have argued against the thesis of a direct adoption of foreign legal traditions because the evidence for such cannot be drawn from the existing sources as they are known now and in consideration of the cultural synthesis that had taken place in the eighth and ninth centuries AD. Hallaq and Calder have thus drawn attention to a fundamental problem in the research into cultural exchange that runs the risk of not going beyond a list of similarities in law.[34]

The *waqf* as an institution of Islamic law became tangible only from the ninth century onwards. Following Crone, Peter Hennigan explains the emergence of the *waqf* as evolving out of various local traditions, which in turn could be influenced by Byzantine, Jewish, Sasanian or pre-Islamic Arab models.[35] While Maria Macuch has worked on the relevant sources for possible Sasanian models,[36] Claude Cahen and, more recently, Norbert Oberauer have elaborated the Arabic-Islamic origins of the *waqf*.[37] Accordingly, there was also a legal tradition on the part of the Muslim conquerors who encountered different legal traditions in the newly conquered lands that could be compared with Byzantine and Sasanian pious foundations. This appears to have provided the *compatibility of cultural domains* which is here assumed as a prerequisite for cultural exchange.

The next questions should be how and to what extent Muslims between the seventh and ninth centuries came into contact with Christian charitable foundations. As far as Christian foundations in the early Islamic period are concerned, the Vita of the Syriac Orthodox Saint Symeon of the Olives (d. 734) describes in unusual detail the foundation of various Syriac Orthodox monasteries by the saint.[38] Symeon won especial fame as the administrator of the Monastery of Qarṭmīn in the Ṭūr ʿAbdīn mountains in northern Mesopotamia by planting two thousand olive trees that he had brought specially from 'distant lands'. After just five years, the trees would have borne fruit, which was obviously a great success, as the region was not actually suitable for planting olive trees. It is for this reason that Symeon is called 'of the Olives'.[39]

The economic activities of the saint are also emphasized in the course of the Vita. After giving up his life as a stylite at the Qarṭmīn Monastery, Symeon went to Nisibis and, with the permission of the Muslim authorities,[40] founded a large and richly decorated monastery with a high pillar for stylites outside the eastern city gate. He added a guest house to the monastery as a lodging for travellers and merchants, and also acquired five millstones and three gardens. Symeon also renewed the Monastery of the Nativity, as well as the Monastery of St Febronia,[41] and acquired many fields within the city at the eastern gate for this monastery.[42] He settled nuns in the Monastery of St Febronia, also giving them a religious rule. He bought shops, farms and houses for rent to supply these monasteries. Outside the city wall, Symeon had a mill constructed, which was connected by a wall and a tower to the city wall. He also opened a gate for access to this mill, named after him as 'Symeon's Mill', and donated the mill to the monastery of Qarṭmīn. Furthermore, he also bought baths, which he donated to the Mār Elishā Monastery (also founded by Symeon), which was possibly the aforementioned monastery with the pillar.[43]

Symeon's new foundations seem to have been independent foundations equipped with the types of revenue-generating property that are typical of such institutions: agricultural land, shops, houses intended to provide rental income, baths that also generated revenue and courtyards, which may have been *ḥān*-type buildings where traders could spend the night and store and sell their goods. Endowing these types of property became a very common means of financing Islamic foundations.

We do not have comparable narrative sources for Syria. However, the numerous inscribed mosaics of Greek Orthodox churches and monasteries in Jordan dated from the fifth to eighth centuries show that foundations or donations for the financing of building measures were an important part of the social and religious life of the Christian population in the early Islamic period.[44] St Stephen's Church in Umm ar-Raṣāṣ (Kastron Mefaa) is particularly rich in inscriptions from the Umayyad period.[45]

In Egypt we can gain a better insight into the foundation activity of the Copts because of the relatively numerous preserved Coptic papyri. As under Byzantine rule, the Copts maintained their own legal institutions under Islamic rule in the countryside in the seventh and eighth centuries, and tried to resolve their legal affairs among themselves.[46] Indeed, recognition of the respective right of various non-Muslim communities and their legal autonomy by the Muslim authorities constituted the basis for their special status as a protected minority (*dhimmīs*).[47] In this respect, it is not surprising that Coptic deeds of donation (*dōreastikon*) of the eighth century hardly differed from those of pre-Islamic times. For example, a 735 Coptic papyrus records the donation or rather supplemental endowment (Zustiftung) of a house from a certain Anna of Jeme to the monastery of Paulos of Kulol. As in later *waqf* documents, it is emphasized that the donation is permanent and that none of the donor's heirs or relatives could reclaim the property. The boundaries of the property are given by the four cardinal directions, as is also customary in Islamic foundation charters. The monastery could freely dispose of the property it had been given, sell it, give it away or destroy it. In addition, Anna expressed her desire to preserve her memory before God through this donation.[48] Finally, the document stated that no secular or spiritual institution could ever change or reverse this gift.[49] Thus, this Coptic donation is very similar to a *waqf* as regards its irrevocability, but differs from the *waqf* in respect of the right of the beneficiary to dispose of it freely. Under Islamic law, not even the original founder was allowed to change his own foundation once it had been arranged.

On the one hand, it can be seen from the examples given that from Egypt to Iraq in the seventh and eighth centuries, Christian foundations remained unaffected by Islamic conquest. On the other hand, striking similarities to Islamic foundations, as they are known to us from the ninth century, can be found. Yet, these correspondences do not provide any evidence that Christian foundation practices actually influenced the formation of the *waqf*. However, various examples in the sources of the support of prominent Muslim figures and caliphs for financing Christian monasteries that were apparently established as foundations prove direct contact of Muslims with Christian foundations.[50] An extraordinary case of continuity from Christian to Muslim patronage is the public bath of Ḥammat Gader in Gadara. This bath was founded in the second century AD and was restored several times in the Byzantine period by various donors. This tradition continued under the Umayyads, as a Greek inscription of 661 shows, according to which the regional Umayyad governor commissioned a Christian official, John of Gadara, to restore the bath for the healing of the sick.[51] The new rulers adopted not only the Greek language and the style of Byzantine inscriptions in accordance with the aforementioned inscriptions from Jordanian churches, but also the concept of a benevolent gift for the public good, as seen with the restoration of the bath by clearly pursuing a charitable purpose, that of healing the sick.

The direct transformation of a Christian charitable institution into an Islamic one cannot yet be proven, although there are examples of the transformation of Zoroastrian foundations into Christian ones.[52] However, the inscription of Ḥammat Gader comes very close to being the establishment of a foundation based on a Christian model by Muslims, even if it is not a permanent endowment, but rather a one-time donation. But here the transition between a donation and a foundation is fluid. On this basis, there is a high probability that the Christian tradition of religious foundations and donations has influenced the Muslim practice of charity in general and the emergence of the *waqf* in particular.

That is not the end of the history of Christian-Islamic cultural transfer in the area of pious foundations. While the Muslim conquerors adopted the cultural traditions of the various conquered groups in the early Islamic period, the direction of the transfer changes, at the latest from the ninth century, once the *waqf* as an institution of Islamic law had been established and the Islamization of the subjugated population increased.

It was a protracted process. A close examination of various deeds written by Christians in Arabic and other sources from the ninth to the thirteenth centuries, documenting foundations or supplemental endowments to existing Christian institutions, has shown that the legal form and the terminology used in the process conformed increasingly to the established Islamic form of endowment deeds and the usage of Islamic *waqf* law, but a complete assimilation was averted until the thirteenth century.[53]

Until then, Christian endowments were certainly also recorded in Islamic courts, but understood neither by the Christians nor the Qadis as *waqf* according to Islamic law. For example, a series of deeds from St Catherine's Monastery, Mount Sinai deals with an endowment from a Melkite Christian to the monastery in 1197. In the endowment deed as in the deed of confirmation from the same year, which was issued by the court of the Melkite bishop of Sinai, describing the endowment as a *waqf* is explicitly avoided. In 1276, the endowment was confirmed twice, both in a deed issued by the Qāḍī and in a deed issued by the episcopal court. In both documents, the standard formulations of Islamic law are found by which a *waqf* is designated and defined. The adoption of the institution of the *waqf* by the Christians had thus been finally completed.[54]

In addition, the documentation of the history of this donation illustrates how Christians simultaneously accessed both legal systems, the internal Christian and the Muslim, by issuing confirmations from both the episcopal tribunal and the Qāḍī. The fact that turning regularly to the Qāḍī court had to influence the form of the Christian legal documents is also shown by this example, since the Christian confirmation of 1197 corresponds entirely to the form of Islamic confirmation (*iqrār*), even if describing the endowment as *waqf* is still avoided.[55] Christian family foundations dating from the fourteenth century, where the beneficiaries were restricted to family members, represent yet another step in the assimilation of Christians to Islamic law, since pure family foundations were not previously known in Byzantium or by Oriental Christians.[56]

Using the example of the practice of pious foundations, it was possible to show how a particular institution or more abstractly a particular cultural asset,[57] in a more or less uniform political space, covering Iraq, Syria and Egypt, over a long period of time and between strongly differentiated groups that repeatedly emphasized their own identities, especially in the field of law,[58] is exchanged in multiple directions and thereby changes. In this sense, cultural transfer is a multilateral, ongoing process whose direction depends crucially on the given social and political conditions.

At the same time, it can be seen here how groups that can be called social minorities sought to preserve their group identity and maintain cultural boundaries – that had to be continuously reconstructed – between acculturation, accommodation and segregation. The fact that members of a church on their own initiative turned to Islamic law instead of their own ecclesiastical jurisdiction to establish legal certainty posed a problem for the Eastern churches from the early Islamic period onward. Without doubt, this damaged the autonomy of *dhimmī* communities because this practice had to lead to the gradual adoption of Islamic legal forms.[59] The leaders of various minority communities tried to preserve the special status of their community, upon which their own social position ultimately depended, by pronouncing strict prohibitions against turning to Islamic courts, continuing until the fourteenth century, although probably of limited effectiveness.[60] By contrast, parishioners were accustomed to constantly transgressing the boundaries of their own community in their daily lives through exchange with the Muslim majority (in the sense of the dominant social group). As a consequence, rather unconsciously the cultural reality of their own group changed through this cultural contact and exchange.[61]

In the area of law, therefore, conflicting influences seem to have affected Christian communities. This situation may be considered typical, for the hybridity of the culture of the Eastern Christians may perhaps be considered one of their most characteristic traits. The example of the pious foundation shows particularly clearly how the different groups, which defined themselves by their own 'culture', were shaped by cultural transfer from all sides and constantly changed. The fact that the practice of foundations can be regarded as a universal concept[62] – that is, that there was a high degree of compatibility – certainly contributed significantly to this intensive mutual exchange.

Notes

1 This chapter is based on research that has been conducted at the Institute for Advanced Study in Princeton. G. Christ, S. Dönitz, D. König, Ş. Küçükhüseyin, M. Mersch, B. Müller-Schauenburg, U. Ritzerfeld, C. Vogel and J. Zimmermann, *Transkulturelle Verflechtungen. Mediävistische Perspektiven*, Göttingen: Universitätsverlag, 2016, 72–1. This idea of transculturality was developed by W. Welsch, 'Was ist eigentlich Transkulturalität?', in: L. Darowska, T. Lüttenberg and C. Machold (eds), *Hochschule als transkultureller Raum? Kultur, Bildung und Differenz in der Universität*, Bielefeld: transcript, 2010, 39–66; idem, 'Transculturality: The Puzzling Form of Cultures Today', in: M. Featherstone and S. Lash (eds), *Spaces of Culture: City, Nation, World*, London: Sage, 1999, 194–213; for the modern age, but then also transferred to the premodern, according to which already spatially adjacent premodern 'peoples' had lived in a transcultural and thus culturally closely interrelated world (Welsch, 'Transculturality', 55–6). This idea takes as its premise that there was (and is) a diverging Euro-Mediterranean culture in which the cultural characteristics would have been harmonized so far that 'none were really foreign and none were really separate' (ibid., 52; for a contrary argument, see e.g. N. Blum-Barth, 'Transkulturalität, Hybridität, Mehrsprachigkeit: von der Vision zur Revision einiger Forschungstrends', *German as a Foreign Language* 1, 2016, 114–30).
2 M. Mersch, 'Transkulturalität, Verflechtung, Hybridisierung – "Neue" epistemologische Modelle in der Mittelalterforschung', in: W. Drews and C. Scholl (eds), *Transkulturelle Verflechtungsprozesse in der Vormoderne*, Berlin: de Gruyter, 2016, 239–51, here 247; Christ, Dönitz, König et al., *Transkulturelle Verflechtungen*, 76, where the question is also raised whether a world without cultural identities and thus also without cultural otherness would even be imaginable.
3 For the Lists, see T.M. Kolbaba, *The Byzantine Lists: Errors of the Latins* (Illinois Medieval Studies), Urbana, IL: Illinois University Press, 2000.
4 Mersch, 'Transkulturalität', 245–6.
5 M. Borgolte, 'Mittelalter in der größeren Welt: eine europäische Kultur in globaler Perspektive', *Historische Zeitschrift* 295, 2012, 35–61, here 43.
6 L. Ranke, *Geschichten der romanischen und germanischen Völker von 1494 bis 1535*, vol. 1, Leipzig, Berlin: Reimer, 1824, VI.
7 For a broader understanding of cultural transfer, see also Christ, Dönitz, König et al., *Transkulturelle Verflechtungen*, 60.
8 Borgolte, 'Mittelalter in der größeren Welt', 41–3.
9 U. Bitterli, *Die "Wilden" und die "Zivilisierten", Grundzüge einer Geistes- und Kulturgeschichte der europäisch-überseeischen Begegnung*, München: Beck, 1976, 81; idem, *Alte Welt – Neue Welt. Formen des europäisch-überseeischen Kulturkontakts vom 15. bis zum 18. Jahrhundert*, München: Beck, 1986, 17–21.

10 Bitterli, *Alte Welt*, 34–42.

11 Bitterli, *Alte Welt*, 27.

12 Bitterli, *Die "Wilden"*, 161.

13 Cf. J. Osterhammel, 'Kulturelle Grenzen in der Expansion Europas', *Saeculum* 46, 1995, 101–38, here 121–2. If there is a complete and peaceful reception of the other – that is, a cultural pluralism with protection of the respective legal spheres – then this is classed as *inclusion*. In a slightly weakened form, *accommodation* means the formation of a *modus vivendi*, which still allows the groups an independent and distinct existence. Active approximation of a cultural group on its own accord to its environment can be termed *acculturation*, while *assimilation* is a more or less forced loss of cultural identity. *Exclusion* refers to the separation of the own group through the rejection of the foreign; *segregation*, in turn, within one society is the exclusion or isolation of the other from one group's own environment. The extreme end of the scale is *extermination*; that is, the complete annihilation of the other culture, understood as such, as a result of physical violence or by forced assimilation.

14 U. Gotter, '"Akkulturation" als Methodenproblem der historischen Wissenschaften', in: W. Eßbach (ed.) *Wir – ihr – sie. Identität und Alterität in Theorie und Methode* (Identitäten und Alteritäten, Bd. 2), Würzburg: Ergon, 2000, 373–406, 391–5.

15 Gotter, '"Akkulturation"', 396–9.

16 S. Gerogiorgakis, R. Scheel and D. Schorkowitz, 'Kulturtransfer vergleichend betrachtet', in: M. Borgolte, J. Dücker, M. Müllerburg and B. Schneidmüller (eds), *Integration und Desintegration der Kulturen im europäischen Mittelalter* (Europa im Mittelalter 18), Berlin: Akademie-Verlag, 2011, 385–466, here 417, after H.-R. Jauß, 'Einleitung', in idem (ed.), *Alterität und Modernität der mittelalterlichen Literatur. Gesammelte Aufsätze 1956–1976*, München: Fink, 1977, 9–47.

17 The foregoing is derived from the ideas of R. Barzen, V. Bulgakova, L. Güntzel, F. Musall, J. Pahlitzsch and D. Schorkowitz, 'Kontakt und Austausch zwischen Kulturen im europäischen Mittelalter: theoretische Grundlagen und methodisches Vorgehen', in: M. Borgolte, J. Schiel, B. Schneidmüller and A. Seitz (eds), *Mittelalter im Labor: die Mediävistik testet Wege zu einer transkulturellen Europawissenschaft* (Europa im Mittelalter 10), Berlin: Akademie-Verlag, 2008, 195–209, here 196–9.

18 Also Gotter, '"Akkulturation"', 396, who talks of 'kulturellen Teilbereichen'. A similar idea is also found in Christ, Dönitz, König et al., *Transkulturelle Verflechtungen*, 294: 'The "cultural" elements that meet in the framework of transcultural entanglements are not to be viewed as representative, monolithic cultural blocks, but originate only from different milieus that can be defined ethnically, politically, economically, religiously, literarily, stylistically, etc., and are only encompassed under the generic term "cultural."'

19 Cf. Osterhammel, 'Kulturelle Grenzen'.

20 O.J. Schmitt, *Levantiner. Lebenswelten und Identitäten einer ethnokonfessionellen Gruppe im Osmanischen Reich im "langen 19. Jahrhundert"* (Südosteuropäische Arbeiten 122), München: Oldenbourg, 2005, 452–7.

21 K. Roth, 'Zu einer „Politik der ethnischen Koexistenz". Kann Europa von den historischen Vielvölkerstaaten lernen?', *Südosteuropa Mitteilungen* 40, 2000, 3–21, here 9.

22 Roth, 'Zu einer "Politik der ethnischen Koexistenz"', 7–10; J.W. Cole and E. Wolf, *Die unsichtbare Grenze. Ethnizität und Ökologie in einem Alpental*, Vienna, Bozen: Folio, 1987, 348.

23 Gerogiorgakis, Scheel and Schorkowitz, 'Kulturtransfer', 391–5; J. Paulmann, 'Internationaler Vergleich und interkultureller Transfer. Zwei Forschungsansätze zur europäischen Geschichte des 18. bis 20. Jahrhunderts', *Historische Zeitschrift* 267, 1998, 649–85, here 675.

24 After P. Burke, 'Kultureller Austausch', in idem (ed.), *Kultureller Austausch* (Erbschaft unserer Zeit 8), Frankfurt a. M.: Suhrkamp, 2000, 9–40; initially, a decontextualization takes place, whereupon a recontextualization takes place during reception. Gerogiorga-kis, Scheel and Schorkowitz, 'Kulturtransfer', 418.

25 The transition from late Antiquity to Islamic civilization is thus reduced to 'a simple change of actors: exeunt the Byzantines, taking classical culture with them; enter the Arabs, bringing theirs', P. Crone, *Roman, Provincial and Islamic Law: The Origins of the Islamic Patronate* (Cambridge Studies in Islamic Civilization), Cambridge: Cambridge University Press, 1987, 17.

26 For the general development, see C. Foss, 'Syria in Transition, A.D. 550–750: An Archaeological Approach', *Dumbarton Oaks Papers* 51, 1997, 189–269; A. Walmsley, 'Production, Exchange and Regional Trade in the Islamic East Mediterranean: Old Structures, New Systems?', in: I. Lysen Hansen and C. Wickham (eds), *The Long Eighth Century* (The Transformation of the Roman World 11), Leiden, Boston, MA and Co-logne: Brill, 2000, 265–343; H.C. Evans (ed.), *Byzantium and Islam: Age of Transition (7th–ninth century)*, in conjunction with the exhibition 'Byzantium and Islam' organized by The Metropolitan Museum of Art, New York, 14 March to 8 July 2012, New Ha-ven, CT: Yale University Press 2012.

27 N. Luz, 'The Construction of an Islamic City in Palestine: The Case of Umayyad al-Ramla', *Journal of the Royal Asiatic Society*, series 3, 7, 1997, 27–54; R. Hillenbrand, ''Anjar and Early Islamic Urbanism', in: G. Brogiolo and B. Ward-Perkins (eds), *The Idea and Ideal of the Town between Late Antiquity and the Early Middle Ages* (The Trans-formation of the Roman World 4), Leiden, Boston, MA, Cologne: Brill, 1999, 59–98; Walmsley, 'Production', 283, 296 (zu Ayla/Aqaba); A. Walmsley, 'The "Islamic City". The Archaeological Experience in Jordan', *Mediterranean Archaeology* 13, 2000, 1–9; R.M. Foote, 'Commerce, Industrial Expansion, and Orthogonal Planning. Mutually Compatible Terms in Settlements of Bilad al-Sham during the Umayyad Period', *Med-iterranean Archaeology* 13, 2000, 25–38.

28 Hillenbrand, ''Anjar and Early Islamic Urbanism', 76–5.

29 G. Fowden, *Quṣayr ʿAmra. Art and the Umayyad Elite in Late Antique Syria* (The Trans-formation of the Classical Heritage 36), Berkeley, Los Angeles, CA, London: Univ. of California Press, 2004, XXIII.

30 C. Halperin, 'The Ideology of Silence: Prejudice and Pragmatism on the Medieval Frontier', *Comparative Studies in Society and History* 26, 1984, 442–66.

31 Or the origin of the *waqf* see in general I. Sánchez, s.v. 'Periodisierungen, 4.3. Muslime', in: M. Borgolte (ed.), *Enzyklopädie des Stiftungswesens in mittelalterlichen Gesellschaften*, vol. 1: Grundlagen, Berlin: de Gruyter, 2014, 275–93, here 278–82; as well as J. Pahlitzsch, 'Christian Pious Foundations as an Element of Continuity Between Late Antiquity and Islam', in: M. Frenkel and Y. Lev (eds), *Charity and Giving in Monotheistic Religions* (Studien zur Geschichte und Kultur des islamischen Orients 22), Berlin, New York: De Gruyter, 2009, 125–51.

32 Crone, *Roman, Provincial and Islamic Law*.

33 I. Schneider, *Kinderverkauf und Schuldknechtschaft. Untersuchungen zur frühen Phase des islamischen Rechts* (Abhandlungen für die Kunde des Morgenlandes 52,1), Stuttgart: Steiner, 1999.

34 W. Hallaq, 'The Use and Abuse of Evidence: The Question of Provincial and Roman Influences on Early Islamic Law', *Journal of the American Oriental Society* 110, 1990, 79–91; N. Calder, *Studies in Early Muslim Jurisprudence*, Oxford: Clarendon Press, 1993, 209–14.

35 P.C. Hennigan, *The Birth of a Legal Institution: The Formation of the Waqf in Third-Century A.H. Ḥanafī Legal Discourse* (Studies in Islamic Law and Society 18), Leiden: Brill, 2004, 50–70.

36 M. Macuch, 'Die sasanidische fromme Stiftung und der islamische *waqf*: eine Ge-genüberstellung', in: A. Meier, J. Pahlitzsch and L. Reinfand (eds), *Islamische Stiftungen zwischen juristischer Norm und sozialer Praxis*, Berlin: Akad.-Verlag, 2009, 19–38.

37 C. Cahen, 'Réflexions sur le waqf ancien', *Studia Islamica* 14, 1961, 37–56; N. Oberauer, 'Early Doctrines on Waqf Revisited: The Evolution of Islamic Endowment Law in the Second Century AH', *Islamic Law and Society* 20, 2013, 1–47.

38 For a more detailed discussion of Symeon of the Olives and his founding activities, see Pahlitzsch, 'Christian Pious Foundations'. On the Vita, see A. Palmer, *Monk and Mason on the Tigris Frontier: The Early History of Ṭūr ʿAbdīn* (University of Cambridge Oriental Publications 39), Cambridge: Cambridge Univ. Press, 1990, 159–65. S. Brock, 'The Fenqitho of the Monastery of Mar Gabriel in Tur 'Abdin', *Ostkirchliche Studien* 28, 1979, 168–82, here 174–9, offers a paraphrase of the text after an abridged and linguistically revised version. The text of the Vita has not been edited yet. In what follows, I refer to the nineteenth-century manuscript Paris, syr. 375. I would like to thank Richard Payne for providing his translation of the Syriac text of this manuscript. Although the Vita has obviously been revised and supplemented several times and contains numerous anachronisms, an historical core is recognizable; see Brock, 'The Fenqitho', 174; and Palmer, *Monks and Mason*, 161f.

39 Vita of Symeon of the Olives, ms. Paris, syr. 375, fol. 161–3; Brock, 'The Fenqitho', 175f.

40 Cf. R.G. Hoyland, *Seeing Islam as Others Saw It: A Survey and Evaluation of Christian, Jewish and Zoroastrian Writings on Early Islam* (Studies in Late Antiquity and Early Islam 13), Princeton, NJ: Darwin Press, 1997, 170f.

41 Vita of Symeon of the Olives, ms. Paris, syr. 375, fol. 170.

42 Vita of Symeon of the Olives, ms. Paris, syr. 375, fol. 166.

43 Vita of Symeon of the Olives, ms. Paris, syr. 375, fol. 177f.

44 The inscriptions make no distinction between endowments in the true sense, which provide long-term income, and one-off donations. The latter was most probably the case to a large extent, while, according to Baumann, the preservation of the build-ings was financed from a community-owned fund; see P. Baumann, *Spätantike Stifter im Heiligen Land. Darstellungen und Inschriften auf Bodenmosaiken in Kirchen, Synagogen und Privathäusern* (Spätantike – frühes Christentum – Byzanz, Reihe B, Studien und Perspektiven, Bd. 5.), Wiesbaden: Reichert, 1999, 302f. J.-P. Caillet, 'L'évergétisme monumental chrétien dans la Jordanie de la fin de l'Antiquité', in: N. Duval (ed.), *Les églises de Jordanie*, 297–302; on the founders, so far as they are identifiable, see Baumann, *Spätantike Stifter*, 298–309.

45 Baumann, *Spätantike Stifter*, 179.

46 T.G. Wilfong, 'The Non-Muslim Communities: Christian Communities', in: C.F. Petry (ed.), *Cambridge History of Egypt, vol. 1: Islamic Egypt, 640–1517*, Cambridge: Cambridge Univ. Press, 1998, 175–97, here 181f.; P.M. Sijpesteijn, 'Arabic Papyri and Islamic Egypt', in: R.S. Bagnall (ed.), *Oxford Handbook of Papyrology*, Oxford: Oxford Univ. Press, 2009, 452–72, here 459–63; M. Tillier, 'Du pagarque au cadi: ruptures et continuités dans l'administration judiciaire de la Haute-Égypte (Ier–IIIe/VIIe–IXe siè-cle)', *Médiévales* 64, 2013, 19–36.

47 J. Pahlitzsch, *Der arabische Procheiros Nomos. Untersuchung und Edition der arabischen Üb-ersetzung eines byzantinischen Rechtstextes* (Forschungen zur Byzantinischen Rechtsges-chichte 31), Frankfurt am Main: Löwenklau- Gesell., 2014, 37★–41★.

48 The foundation is referred to here as *prosphora*.

49 W.E. Crum, *Koptische Rechtsurkunden des achten Jahrhunderts aus Djême (Theben)*, Leipzig: Zentralantiquariat d. Dt. Demokrat. Republik, 1912 (reprint in Subsidia Byzantina lucis ope iterata 18, with an introduction by A.A. Schiller. Leipzig 1973) (= KRU 106);

German translation in W.C. Till, *Erbrechtliche Untersuchungen auf Grund der koptischen Urkunden* (Österreichische Akademie der Wissenschaften, Philosophisch-historische Klasse, Sitzungsberichte, 229. Band, 2. Abhandlung), Wien: Rohrer, 1954, 205–12. On this document, see also J. Pahlitzsch, 'Christian *Waqf* in the Early and Classical Islamic Period (Seventh to Twelfth Centuries)', in: S. Mohasseb Saliba (ed.), *Les fondations pieuses Waqfs chez les Chrétiens et les Juifs du Moyen Âge à nos jours*, Paris: Geuthner, 2016, 33–56.

50 See Pahlitzsch, 'Christian Pious Foundations', 145–9.

51 For the Greek text with English translation and detailed discussion of the various readings, see L. Di Segni, 'The Greek Inscriptions of Hammat Gader', in: Y. Hirschfeld (ed.), *The Roman Baths of Hammat Gader: Final Report*, Jerusalem: Israel Exploration Soc., 1997, 185–266, here 237–40.

52 Indeed, from the pre-Islamic period as well as the eighth century, see Pahlitzsch, 'Christian Pious Foundations', 143f.

53 Pahlitzsch, 'Christian *Waqf*', 33–56.

54 See D.S. Richards, 'Some Muslim and Christian Documents from Sinai Concerning Christian Property', in: U. Vermeulen and J.M.F. van Reeth (eds), *Law, Christianity and Modernism in Islamic Society. Proceedings of the Eighteenth Congress of the Union Européenne des Arabisants et Islamisants* (Orientalia Lovaniensia Analecta 86), Leuven: Peeters, 1998, vol. 1, 161–70.

55 Richards, 'Some Muslim and Christian Documents', 170.

56 The earliest known evidence of Christian family foundations under Islamic law (*waqf ahlī*) is, to my knowledge, documented in D.S. Richards, 'Documents from Sinai Concerning Mainly Cairene Property', *Journal of the Economic and Social History of the Orient* 28, 3, 1985, 225–93, here 229f. and 240, referring to documents of 1393 and 1481.

57 On this terminology, see Gerogiorgakis, Scheel und Schorkowitz, 'Kulturtransfer', 391f., after H.-J. Lüsebrink, *Interkulturelle Kommunikation. Interaktion, Fremdwahrnehmung, Kulturtransfer*, Stuttgart: Metzler, 2005, 129.

58 In general, see Pahlitzsch, *Der arabische Procheiros Nomos*, 34★–49★.

59 Similarly, Jonathan Ray points out that the communal autonomy of thirteenth-century Jewish communities in Spain was undermined, especially by the Jews themselves, by turning to Christian judges, J. Ray, *The Sephardic Frontier: The Reconquista and the Jewish Community in Medieval Iberia*, Ithaca, NY: Cornell Univ. Press, 2006, 136. The example of the documents of the Jewish community of Cairo from the Geniza makes it clear that Islamic law exerted a strong influence on the legal forms of other-faith minorities. In legal transactions with Muslims, the use of Islamic forms was a matter of course. In addition, in legal transactions between two Jews, the Islamic form was also used, G. Khan, *Arabic Legal and Administrative Documents in the Cambridge Genizah Collections* (Cambridge University Library, Genizah Series 10), Cambridge: Archaeopress, 1993, 1. The Syrian Orthodox Church, especially in the matter of inheritance, was strongly influenced by Islamic law; see H. Kaufhold, 'Islamisches Erbrecht in christlich-syrischer Überlieferung', *Oriens Christianus* 59, 1975, 18–35; idem, 'Über die Entstehung der syrischen Texte zum islamischen Recht', *Oriens Christianus* 69, 1985, 54–72.

60 See N. Edelby, 'L'origine des jurisdictions confessionnelles en terre d'Islam', *Proche-Orient Chrétien* 1, 1951, 192–208, here 203 n. 50.

61 Pahlitzsch, *Der arabische Procheiros Nomos*, 46★.

62 M. Borgolte, *Weltgeschichte als Stiftungsgeschichte. Von 3000 v.u.Z. bis 1500 u.Z.*, Darmstadt: Wissenschaftliche Buchgesellschaft, 2017.

6

PRACTICES OF COMMUNICATION

Literacy, gestures and words: research on late medieval communication

Franz-Josef Arlinghaus

Introduction

It goes without saying that understanding communication is a key element of understanding society. However, at a time when the internet and telephone were not invented and even writing was less common than today, would a chapter on 'practices of communication' be a little short? As it turns out, during the centuries we focus on here, people communicated in very refined and highly differentiated ways. The following text not only tries to focus on literacy, orality, messengers and rituals, but also attempts to shed light on how a combination of these elements worked in a given situation.

Rituals are irrational and literacy means rationalization. For a long time, historians have written about how 'the Middle Ages were already quite literate/rational' or looked at the trajectory 'from rituals to rationalization' and the like. In the meantime, the picture has become much more complex. Rituals are increasingly seen as an expression of clever political moves, and charters, books and the reading of texts portrayed as ritualized performances. While dichotomies seem to vanish and teleological narrative is discredited, despite long and intense research efforts, the relationship between rituals, literacy and medieval society is still a story ending with 'to be continued'. However, historical research today knows a lot more about these phenomena than, say, 20 or 30 years ago and, what is more, today we are able to ask very refined questions that, thanks to inquiries during the recent decades, are able to avoid many of the pitfalls and mistakes of the past.

Medieval History, with the auxiliary sciences Diplomatics and Paleography, always took a special interest in writing. However, with McLuhan's *The Gutenberg Galaxy* of 1962 which, with reference to television, saw 'the end of the age of books' coming (*Das Ende des Buchzeitalters* was the subtitle of the German edition),[1] the humanities in general became more and more interested in the phenomenon of literacy. Jack Goody and Walter Ong pushed this even further when arguing that the use of writing would, to make a complex argument very short, change the minds of those who use it.[2] The same holds true for rituals. As far back as Jacob Grimm's *Deutsche Rechtsalterthümer* of 1828,[3] Medieval History, especially Medieval Legal History, looked at gestures and performances. However, John L. Austin's *How to Do Things with Words* (1963) and the studies of Erving Goffman on interaction in everyday life,[4] to name but two authors, opened up a new approach in terms of rituals.

Nonetheless, it seems that it was not until the 1980s and 1990s that a shift in the perspective on literacy and ritual took place in Medieval History. Whereas at first, historical research proclaimed a strong dichotomy between literacy and ritual, roughly around and after the year 2000, writing in premodern times was increasingly seen as part of (oral) performances and gestures, and sitting orders and the like are now looked at as having their own 'rationality'.

Framing premodern times: new theoretical approaches

Interestingly enough, the sources upon which the new approach draws are often very well known, but parts of the texts have either been ignored so far or interpreted in quite a different way. For example, a great part of the text of the 'Golden Bull' of 1356, which outlines the election of the German king, describes gestures as well as sitting orders. Older research tended to neglect these paragraphs of the (often called) first German constitution, while precisely these elements are considered most useful in order to understand the way premodern societies function today.[5] Why is that?

The central issue here is a change of paradigms, which altered the view on this and other well-known texts:

(1) First, gestures, rituals and sitting orders are no longer considered as 'plays' that demonstrate reality to a wider (and illiterate) public. Rather, they themselves are seen as ways of creating reality. In this view, sitting orders, for instance, *establish* and *manifest* a hierarchy and an order between those seated, and that is why positions are sometimes defended violently. In other words: rituals do not demonstrate, but create order.

(2) Second, this paradigm is linked to a new way of looking at premodern society as such. Different from today, medieval and early modern society is considered to be a society built on the co-presence of the actors ('Vergesellschaftung unter Anwesenden', 'Präsenzgesellschaft').[6] This paradigm places a question mark on the notion of premodern institutions having the same shape as modern and, for instance, emphasizes that the Holy Roman Empire exists mainly in the form of diets and other 'come-together'.[7] Interestingly enough, this concept was mainly developed by historians specializing in the sixteenth and seventeenth centuries. At this point, one may rightly ask why or how, after the enormous spread of literacy during the High and Late Middle Ages and especially after the invention of the printing press, charters, books and writing as such fit into this picture.

(3) What 'status' do media (in the broadest sense of the word) have in premodern times? Since the 1990s especially, scholars emphasize that, in the Middle Ages, words and pictures had the capacity to make those who are absent – whether

because they are in another place or because they lived in another century – appear to be present.[8] This is due to an almost ontic understanding of signs, a legally binding concept of representation and a perception of pictures as cult images.[9] This even holds true if one takes into account that the identity of words and objects was questioned, for instance, in the context of the universal controversy of the eleventh and twelfth centuries, and as early as in the ninth and again in the eleventh century, the real presence of Christ in the Eucharist was a matter of debate.[10]

These paradigms, although developed mainly from different points of view on the Middle Ages (historical and sociological approaches for points one and two, literature and cultural theories for point three), do match insofar as they clearly indicate a warning against interpreting medieval forms of communication without taking into account the different cultural and societal 'environment' in which they take place, and to be careful when attributing today's aims and functions to gestures and texts that were performed and written 20 or 30 generations ago. On the other hand, one could ask whether recent research in medieval and literary history does not overstretch this approach, and whether there is a tendency to certain 'medievalism' that portrays the epoch as just the opposite of modernity. And is it not true that medieval empires and cities developed modern forms of administrative techniques, such as written laws, protocols and the like since the early days?

Performing literacy

Since the inspiring, already-mentioned works of Jack Goody and Walter Ong, literacy was looked at as *the* technology that paved the way to Western modernity for a long time. Writing seems not only useful in terms of administration, economy and law. More than that, the use of the pen and reading seemed to alter the way people think and look at the world. Since writing with letters instead of pictograms (as in Egypt or China) is considered to lead to a more abstract view on the world,[11] it is essentially a story of the rise of the West. Elizabeth L. Eisenstein's book about the printing revolution seemed to be designed to complete this picture,[12] since Ong has already emphasized the importance of that invention, although more occupied with ancient Mesopotamia.[13]

This short sketch is merely designed to illustrate the type of intellectual background medievalists consulted to examine literacy and writing in their epoch of research. With its long-standing tradition of auxiliary sciences, such as Palaeography, Diplomatics and Sigillography, to name but a few, medieval research seemed to be well prepared for a new look at literacy. Michael Clanchy's *From Memory to Written Record*, first published in 1979 and thoroughly revised for the second edition of 1993, can be considered *the* ground-breaking study on the effects of literacy in the Middle Ages. The book's table of contents almost reads like a programme or summary of the international medieval research on literacy undertaken during the 1980s and 1990s: the analysis of 'Technology of Writing' (including wax, parchment, rolls and books), 'Preservation and Use of Documents', 'Types' and 'Language of Record', as well as 'Literate and Illiterate', was on the agenda. While at least part of these themes can be considered 'classics' of medieval auxiliary sciences, it was (a) the new perspective on these 'classics' and (b) their combination with new themes such as 'Proliferation of Documents', 'Spoken versus the Written Word' and 'Trust in Writing' that framed a new understanding of writing in the Middle Ages.

A number of individuals and research groups (namely in Münster, Freiburg, Utrecht and Zürich) devoted themselves to the theme,[14] often without being directly inspired by the named book, but quite often with a similar agenda. The overall question in most research projects was how the spread of literacy, especially during the High Middle Ages,[15] changed the way people organized their everyday lives and how it changed the way people conceptualized the world. With Rosamond McKitterick's book on the use of writing during the eighth and ninth centuries, the approach was tested also for the early Middle Ages.[16] Practical literacy was considered an everyday tool that helped to organize the political sphere of the rising Italian city communes of the eleventh and twelfth centuries as well as the economic organization of cloisters or late medieval noble households. The consequences of this 'help' went far beyond better administration. If I may simplify: what was once mostly memorized or decided anew in assemblies more and more could be looked up in charters or statutes. Cloisters as well as merchants started to write down their economic transactions, legal contracts, etc. Along with this, groups such as notaries and city scribes played a new and increasingly important role in society.[17] It seems that, in summary, a new way of communicating gained ground that centred on written records. Writing now played a prominent role in all spheres of everyday life, and this life and even the approach of the people to this life, and thus the idea, changed dramatically.[18]

While Goody, Ong and others[19] took on a very broad view, suggesting that the use of writing, especially the alphabetic writing of the near east and Europe in contrast to the pictographic writing of China, changed the *way of thinking* since its invention a few thousand years ago, medievalists of the 1980s and 1990s discussed how the *use* of the already implemented writing and its *application* beyond the religious field changed between the eighth and fifteenth centuries. Research, with all differences in details, seemed to agree that writing now used for the political and legal organization of cities, the administration of property or in commerce – the use of feather and parchment or paper – took on a different meaning. With literacy spreading to these mundane purposes, society seemed to turn to more rational ways of dealing with life, shifting 'from sacred script to practical literacy'.[20] In the same way, Hagen Keller emphasized that Western medieval society with its book religion was more book- and scripture-centred than antiquity. Nevertheless, it was only from the eleventh and twelfth centuries onward that city-dwellers as well as monks and noblemen organized their everyday life with writing, now increasingly using charters and registers and 'inventing' new types of account books and notarial documents.[21] Without being prominent in the debates, the arguments somewhat echo Max Weber's claim of rational bureaucracy as a hallmark of the modern state and modernity in general; anyway, the overall perspective was certainly to detect the roots of our time in an epoch before the printing press.

It is far too easy to simply denounce this as a teleological or functional approach, because the great efforts and achievements made by this research cannot be questioned. The information gathered and presented provides a view on a (mostly) High and Late medieval society, in which in every field writing played an important role, even though movable types were not yet in use and even though most people were still illiterate. Therefore, if one were not to agree that we can see modernity in the making with the spread of the use of writing in the eleventh and twelfth centuries, the question is whether the use of writing might have served different purposes during the High and Late Middle Ages as presumed.

A great part of the articles and books on medieval literacy feed from the presumption of a divide between the oral and the written word, and that this would hold true for all epochs. Even if one looks at the simple act of reading silently or aloud, differences between the epochs are greater than the similarities. In contrast to today, practical literature, be it 'commercial' letters, charters or even account books, were read aloud most of the time[22] until the sixteenth or seventeenth centuries. Even in fifteenth-century central Europe, despite a long tradition of written statutes, legal norms were more often deduced from (ad-hoc-invented) oral traditions than from written statutes.[23]

These findings coincide with the second paradigm which portrays premodern society as one that relies on the co-presence of actors. Writing, when applied by such society and embedded in such culture, adopts a different meaning and is assigned a different place in communication. Rather than being considered as an 'institution',[24] highly independent from the given situation it is employed for, and even from the people that use it (as today generally is the case), writing in premodern times can be seen as an intrinsic part of the gatherings and meetings it is applied to. Writing may have been a tool for rationalization; it is also true that many texts were closely revised and commented on with marginal notes or glosses. However, more than that, it was an instrument to shape and enhance communication as such. Just one example: when administrators in fifteenth-century Switzerland, as Simon Teuscher explored, recorded what the people of a village told them about the (presumably) old rights of their lords, the scribes increasingly tended to use pseudo-archaic, presumably peasant-like language to describe 'old' rituals that would accompany the pay of duties. The purpose of the document is to look at both the way the text came to be as well as the content part of communication that takes place in assembly-like situations. This goes hand in hand with the observation that the materiality of a charter and its presentation was often more interesting (and convincing) than the content of the document.[25]

Waiting for the postman: orality, literacy and messengers

Messengers in the Middle Ages, similar to today, carried letters from sender to recipient. But, unlike today, the letter often worked more like a passport to identify and authorize the messenger, who then delivered the decisive information orally. Sometimes, on the other hand, the messenger's status underlined the importance of the written text and contributed to its interpretation. All three, the spoken word of the messenger, the messenger as a person and the writing, seem to feed from each other, and seemed to be engaged in a flexible but nevertheless unresolvable relationship, and sender and recipient had to be aware of this.[26] The postman as someone who simply delivers a letter and does not influence the way the text of the letter is to be understood was yet to come.

One example of Late Medieval Cologne may illustrate how these more abstract considerations may help to understand what sources describe. When dealing with a defiant citizen in the fourteenth century, the Cologne city council would ask a number of councilmen (called 'Schickung') – generally two – to visit the insubordinate and urge him to behave properly. If these returned without success, the council would send out a second 'Schickung' and increase the number of councilmen, sometimes decisively. After all, in a pars-pro-toto situation, in the premodern sense of the word *in nuce*, the 'Schickung' represents the council as a whole.[27] During the fifteenth century, the way in which the council communicated with its citizens changed: in 1469, the Cologne council ordered two of its members to urge Lenart Engelbrecht to stop suing a fellow citizen at an ecclesiastical court. If he would not obey, the order demanded that the two men should read out the respective law to Lenart aloud. The next (and last) step was to revoke his citizenship.[28] While the text read aloud probably did not provide new information to someone who, like Lenart, knew how to manoeuvre between the different courts of fifteenth-century Cologne, reading meant that the 'speech' of the councilmen would become more impersonal. At the same time, the text read aloud *represented* the city council better than an increased number of councilmen, thus making the absent present.[29]

The scene may seem a slightly atypical, since it is a group of councilmen 'transforming' into messengers. Nevertheless, it proves to be very typical because, to understand what the 'message' is really about, the situation as a whole and the 'relationship' between all 'players' (orality, written text, persons, the location where all this took place) has to be taken into account. The hidden question behind these efforts was how to communicate even difficult matters by minimizing the risk of (violent) escalation and harming the parties involved.

Writing down rituals

Today, journalists and the public are trained to observe not only what political leaders and CEOs of important companies say, but also the gestures that accompany their statements. Did the presidents of two given nations shake hands, and how intense was that handshake? Did they smile, put on a grim face or not even look at each other? The public, being excluded from intimate conversations between world leaders and having a distrust in the all-too-well-known wording of press conferences, try to learn what is really going on by interpreting gestures – and politicians, being well aware of this, play that instrument quite well.

At first glance, gestures seem to be a timeless phenomenon, but the difference between their modern and premodern significance could not be greater. Today, gestures are looked at as signs that need to be read and interpreted to understand their meaning, a meaning the sign points to but is distinct from. In contrast to this, a premodern sitting order or who is given precedence to whom when entering a church not only displays who is closest to a duke or king or who knows how to behave properly.[30] Rather, such 'moves' do not demonstrate, but *create* and *define*, the positions of the given person in the order of society as such, thus holding almost constitutional status.[31] In this respect, it is no surprise that the Golden Bull of 1356, as mentioned above, dedicated a considerable number of its pages to how the prince-electors are seated and who would have to give the first vote.[32] Gestures are written down because they themselves carry the meaning,[33] and because they themselves create order. Rituals and gestures that produce meaning are, of course, not absent in modern society (as Austin and Searl already pointed out[34]). However, premodern society seems to be built almost entirely on performances, because (a) as mentioned above, it favours the co-presence of the actors and conceptualized signs and media in a different way; and (b) as a society that clearly distinguishes between different groups and statuses[35] (instead of roles and classes), the changes of membership or status are accompanied by rituals.

But what are rituals anyhow? It seems worthwhile to remember some classical definitions, because they are still relevant as underlying presumptions for the analysis of sources and their meaning (although not always made explicit). There are at least four important perspectives on rituals that can be named:

(1) A descriptive approach portrays rituals as solemn ostentatious acts, which are often combined with certain gestures and special clothing.

The three other approaches are more functionalistic:

(2) Rituals demonstrate and emphasize a fact to a (mostly illiterate) public that otherwise would be difficult to bring across. In this respect, rituals are somewhat like a play, and the spread of writing and schooling would work against rituals.[36]
(3) With the (at least intended) participation of all people of a given entity (like city-dwellers who participate in a procession), rituals may foster or establish the identity of a given community.[37]
(4) Rituals are capable of changing the status of a person – which often goes hand in hand with a change of clothes (see definition 1).[38] Needless to say, speech acts, as described above, suit this image well and can be considered part of such rituals.

It goes without saying that the different approaches named here rarely appear in their pure forms (for instance, the coronation of a king is a solemn act that changes the status of the person and increases the identity of the nobility and society as such). However, it is worthwhile to bear in mind the differences in order to see upon which a certain ritual (or better, the report of a certain ritual) lays its emphasis.

Since the early nineteenth century, historical and especially legal history[39] took an interest in medieval rituals and their meanings. In 1990, Jean-Claude Schmitt clarified the importance of gestures and ritualized acts during the Middle Ages in his book *La raison des gestes dans l'Occident medieval*.[40] His influential study covered the time from late antiquity until the thirteenth century. What is more, Jean-Claude Schmitt looked at reflections on gestures in medieval texts as well as 'practical' implementations of ritual acts. On the one hand, his main thread was to 'read' the gestures as a language of their own that has to be deciphered, and, combined with this, to see them as theatre-like performances that try to emphasize certain things. While *La raison des gestes* addresses specific movements of the body and with that rituals, focusing strongly on the religious sphere, Geoffrey Koziol's *Begging Pardon and Favor* (1992), in contrast, sees rituals as a general basis of political order, but limits his findings to northern France in the tenth and eleventh centuries.[41] Nevertheless, his study already pointed the way to a new understanding of these acts.

During the late 1990s and the early years of the new millennium, premodern research on rituals and symbolic communication, as it was now often called, flourished especially in the German-speaking countries. In Konstanz (speaker: Rudolf Schlögl), Heidelberg (speakers: Axel Michaels, Bernd Schneidmüller) and Münster (speakers: Gerd Althoff, Barbara Stollberg-Rilinger), a great number of researchers worked together in these three different 'Collaborative Research Units', who dealt with that problem. Probably the most prominent has been the Münster Unit, named 'Symbolic Communication and Social Value Systems from the Middle Ages to the French Revolution', and the theoretical frame given at the beginning is not by accident inspired by the research done here.[42] Besides a great number of interesting studies on specific phenomena, two main ideas guided the research especially of the Münster group:

(1) Rituals cannot be attributed to extra-rational behaviour and they do not document a premodern mentality. Rather, the persons involved negotiated (in a quite rational way) how in a given situation a ritual should be performed, and what it should mean and express.
(2) Rituals do not just show what has been agreed upon (i.e. written down in charters). Rather, they create and put into place new relationships and new orders. They are, in other words, the cornerstones of the 'constitution' medieval society is built on.[43]

This research dissolved the once strong dichotomy between *literacy* as rational, and with it the growing literacy as a sign that a society is on the way to modernity on the one hand, and *orality*, and with it rituals as a sign of a premodern mentality, on the other. What is more: since the 1990s, some doubts concerning the link between administrative 'rationality' and 'writing' emerged,[44] because literacy now was increasingly seen as part of symbolic and ritualistic performances, and precisely this 'togetherness' of writing and ritual was considered a hallmark of premodern societies.[45]

Communities, identity and performances

The lack of centralized administration in the Middle Ages, a professional army or even a police force that deserves the name invites us to look for the famous 'glue' that would hold society together. Even modern states make use of ritualized acts, be it the inauguration ceremony of a president or a military parade, to foster identity. Medieval sources, legal texts included, every now and then describe gatherings and processions, the entry of a bishop in his city or the advent of a king as acts that meet similar requirements. More importantly, they seem to follow sometimes strange, although readable 'scripts' that provide identity for the communities involved; these acts also inform us about power relations between the protagonists.

Since the works of Simon Teuscher, we see a 'handle with care' stamp on at least some of these sources. Teuscher discovered that presumably very old legal rituals described in fifteenth-century sources are more a kind of late medieval 'invention of tradition' instead of native peasant (or Germanic) ways of doing justice.[46] Nevertheless, there is no question that the above-mentioned performances were very prominent in medieval society. This holds true for processions and the cult of city saints, the adventus as well as imperial diets. While the aspects of performing a kind of 'constitution' through rituals has already been discussed (establishing hierarchies and power relations), building 'identity' is another major viewpoint.

As far as can be seen, urban historians are those who have most intensively looked at different features that fostered the identification of city-dwellers with the town in which they live.[47] Especially processions, which required the (sometimes forced) participation of all or most of its inhabitants, as well as – often combined with processions – the cult of city saints, are seen as public gatherings that aim to establish unity. But performances go far beyond religious festivities in the narrow sense of the word. Collective swearing of citizens' oath, elections or even legal proceedings – when 'designed' in a performative way – are considered as means of creating an urban identity. Such gatherings – with great differences – can be observed in most western European cities during the Late Middle Ages, be it Nurnberg, London, Paris, Milan or Florence.[48]

To determine the problem and the 'solution' offered by performances, the 'unity' of a medieval city was nothing one could expect in the first place. 'The task for the late medieval and early modern cities was to transubstantiate these disparate characteristics of a community into a mystic body, a mystified city', as Edward Muir highlights in his classic study.[49] Even more important, the walls of medieval cities regularly embraced a number of more or less independent communities (be these groups organized in city quarters or rather 'subtowns' or guilds), with Prague, Luzern but also Paris the most important examples, among many others.[50]

One of the most striking examples is the northern medium-sized German city of Braunschweig, whose five quarters had their own councils and even town halls. Each year, several processions took place in the northern German city of Braunschweig (an important member of the Hanseatic League). During one of such events, 12 members of the councils carried the remains of the Braunschweig city Saint, the holy Auctor, in his silver and golden shrine through the streets of the town, followed by all the citizens. With such processions, the otherwise socially and administratively strongly divided city presumably gained unity and identity.[51] The core features of these performances are that (a) through the participation of all in these ritualized acts, individuals regarded themselves as part of a community. This is not by accident combined with (b) a religious dimension of these performances, especially when a saint (meaning the real Lord of the city) is addressed, who (c) through these performances is requested to support the city in various ways.[52]

However, one should not overlook that 'community' is, in the end, a very modern concept that obtained its contours mostly during the nineteenth century in opposite to 'society'.[53] A closer look at urban rituals may well conclude that these processions and gatherings do not so much foster 'community'. Rather, they establish a hierarchical order between independent groups by especially emphasizing precisely this: the independence of these groups.[54] In this respect, urban performances would be more closely related to the establishment of premodern forms of constitution, as Barbara Stollberg-Rilinger clearly showed in respect of late medieval and early modern imperial diets.[55] Either way, research agrees on the importance of performances as well as their specific otherness in the context of premodern society.

Summary

One of the fundamental insights offered to us by Reinhard Koselleck was that words and concepts, although they may look the same, changed their meanings completely between modern and premodern times. The same seems to be true for gestures, rituals and even literacy. In this other societal environment, the texts, gestures and performances occupy other places of meaning. Sometimes together – in different combinations – sometimes separately, the relationship of the named elements to the co-presence of persons is as essential as the idea that all people present participated in these acts, instead of just watching them. This does not mean that everybody present understood a certain ritual or a certain text, read out in public. But what members of this culture certainly share is a concept of communication that does not distinguish between (quasi-meaningless) ceremonies and 'real' written-down agreements as the only basis of court cases.

To take this observation a step further: as theory suggests, communication has (at least) two sides: an informational and a social (or, in other words, one can distinguish between information and utterance).[56] It seems that greater emphasis is placed on the social aspect of communication in premodern times. One reason is probably that this culture largely insists on the co-presence of actors; another that the hierarchical order of society can hardly be ignored in any space or placed in the second row. The striking sensitivity of premodern societies in terms of ritualized acts, or of the way texts are read aloud, and with it the possibility that meetings and gatherings may suddenly lead to (even violent) escalations, is thus not so much rooted in a certain mentality, but in a certain culture of communication.

Notes

1 M. McLuhan, *The Gutenberg Galaxy: The Making of Typographic Man*, Toronto: University of Toronto Press, 1962; Ibid., *Die Gutenberg-Galaxis: das Ende des Buchzeitalters*, Bonn u.a.: Addison-Wesley, 1995.

2 J. Goody, *The Domestication of the Savage Mind*, Cambridge: Cambridge University Press, 1977; J.-W. Goody, I. Watt, 'The Consequences of Literacy', *Comparative Studies in Society and History* 5, 1963, 304–45; W.J. Ong, *Orality and Literacy: The Technologizing of the Word*, London: Methuen, 1982.

3 J. Grimm, *Deutsche Rechtsalterthümer*, 2 vols, Leipzig: Mayer & Müller, 1922.

4 J.L. Austin, *How to Do Things with Words*, Oxford: Clarendon Press, 1963, based on a lecture delivered in 1955; E. Goffman, *Behavior in Public Places: Notes on the Social Organization of Gatherings*, New York: Free Press of Glencoe, 1963.

5 B. Schneidmüller, 'Inszenierungen und Rituale des spätmittelalterlichen Reichs. Die Goldene Bulle von 1356 in westeuropäischen Vergleichen', in U. Hohensee et al. (eds), *Die Goldene Bulle Kaiser Karls IV. Politik – Wahrnehmung – Rezeption,* Berlin: Akad.-Verl., 2009, 269ff.; G. Schwedler, 'Dienen muss man dürfen oder: Die Zeremonialvorschriften der Goldenen Bulle zum Krönungsmahl des römisch-deutschen Herrschers', in C. Ambos et al. (eds), *Die Welt der Rituale. Von der Antike bis heute,* Darmstadt: Wissenschaftliche Buchgesellschaft, 2005, 159ff.

6 The terms are coined by Rudolf Schlögl (Vergesellschaftung unter Anwesenden) and Barbara Stollberg-Rilinger (Präsenzgesellschaft). While there are differences between the two concepts, they are both based on the systems theory of Niklas Luhmann, and they both point in the same direction – and that is of interest here; R. Schlögl, 'Kommunikation und Vergesellschaftung unter Anwesenden. Formen des Sozialen und ihre Transformation in der Frühen Neuzeit', *Geschichte und Gesellschaft* 34, 2, 2008, 171ff.; B. Stollberg-Rilinger, *Des Kaisers alte Kleider. Verfassungsgeschichte und Symbolsprache des Alten Reiches,* München: C. H. Beck, 2008, 299ff and 310f.

7 Ibid., *Des Kaisers alte Kleider.*

8 'Wort und Bild sind Medien der Repräsentation, des Gegenwärtig-Werden-Lassens, In-die-Gegenwart-Rufens von etwas, das abwesend ist (lokaler Aspekt) oder vergangen (temporaler Aspekt)'; H. Wenzel, *Hören und Sehen, Schrift und Bild. Kultur und Gedächtnis im Mittelalter,* München: Beck, 1995, 306.

9 C. Kiening, 'Mediale Gegenwärtigkeit. Paradigmen – Semantiken – Effekte', in Ibid. (ed.), *Mediale Gegenwärtigkeit,* Zürich: Chronos, 2007, 19f.: 'Premodern times add an ontological understanding of the sign, a juridically binding of representation, an iconic of the image, and an auratic understanding of writing etc. Recent medieval research has taught us: gestures, rituals, ostentations, documents, seals and objects, images, sculptures and buildings did not only serve as means to transmit or store information or as means of communication. They also, and even more than that, served to make the absentee present, to establish aura, to transmit salvation … This in turn can mean: With the Middle Ages, a certain "culture of presence" comes into view, which would allow us to observe what was before the modern "culture of sense" and which, for this modern one, is hard to describe and to categorize' (author's translation).

10 Ibid., 20.

11 W.J. Ong, *Orality and Literacy*; J. Goody, *Domestication*; J.-W. Goody, I. Watt, 'The Consequences of Literacy', 344f.

12 E.L. Eisenstein, *The Printing Revolution in Early Modern Europe,* Cambridge et al.: Cambridge University Press, 1983.

13 Both Ong and Eisenstein highlight the importance of tables and lists; Ibid., 63; W.J. Ong, *Oralität und Literalität. Die Technologisierung des Wortes,* Opladen: Westdeutscher Verlag, 1987, 102.

14 In Münster, an interdisciplinary Collaborative Research Center (Sonderforschungsbereiche), led by Hagen Keller and Christel Meier, worked for more than 12 years on literacy in the Middle Ages; C. Meier et al. (eds), *Pragmatische Dimensionen mittelalterlicher Schriftkultur. Akten des Internationalen Kolloquiums des Sonderforschungsbereichs 231 26.–29. Mai 1999,* München: Wilhelm Fink, 2002; C. Meier, 'Vierzehn Jahre Münsteraner Forschung zur Schriftlichkeit im Mittelalter. Die Arbeit des Sonderforschungsbereichs 231, Träger, Felder, Formen pragmatischer Schriftlichkeit im Mittelalter', in F.-J. Arlinghaus et al. (eds), *Beitrag auf der CD-ROM Schrift im Wandel – Wandel durch Schrift,* Turnhout: Brepols 2004. The Collaborative Research Center of Freiburg im Breisgau, led by Wolfgang Raible, was not limited to the Middle Ages; see H. Günther and O. Ludwig (eds), *Schrift und Schriftlichkeit/Writing and Its Use. Ein interdisziplinäres Handbuch*

internationaler Forschung/An Interdisciplinary Handbook of International Research 1, Berlin, New York: De Gruyter 1994, and the various books published in the 'ScirptOralia', Gunter Narr Publisher, Tübingen. Rogier Sablonier and Simon Teuscher and their team worked in Zürich on that theme; R. Sablonier and S. Teuscher, *Schriftlichkeit, Kommunikationskultur und Herrschaftspraktiken im Spätmittelalter. Forschungsprojekt am Historischen Seminar der Universität Zürich*, Zürich: no publisher, 1996. Marco Mostert and his team worked in Utrecht, the Netherlands, on literacy in the Middle Ages. See the series 'Utrecht Studies in Medieval Literacy', Brepols publishers, Turnhout. For Zürich see R. Sablonier, 'Verschriftlichung und Herrschaftspraxis. Urbariales Schriftgut im spätmittelalterlichen Gebrauch', in C. Meier et al. (eds), *Pragmatische Dimensionen mittelalterlicher Schriftkultur. Akten des Internationalen Kolloquiums des Sonderforschungsbereichs 231, 26.–29. Mai 1999*, München: Wilhelm Fink 2002, 91ff., and S. Teuscher, 'Notiz, Weisung, Glosse. Zur Entstehung "mündlicher Rechtstexte" im spätmittelalterlichen Lausanne', in U. Kleine and L. Kuchenbuch (eds), *Textus?*, Göttingen: Vandenhoeck & Ruprecht, 2006, 253ff.

15 The inspiring study of R. McKitterick, *The Carolingians and the Written Word*, Cambridge, UK: Cambridge University Press, 1989, argues that one should not overlook the prominence of writing already during the eighth and ninth centuries. But as far as one can see, for major and profound changes, historical research looks more at the High Middle Ages than at the Carolingian period.

16 Ibid.

17 On Italian notaries see P. Schulte, *Scripturae publicae creditur. Das Vertrauen in Notariatsurkunden im kommunalen Italien des 12. und 13. Jahrhunderts*, Tübingen: Niemeyer, 2003.

18 H. Keller, 'Über den Zusammenhang von Verschriftlichung, kognitiver Orientierung und Individualisierung. Zum Verhalten italienischer Stadtbürger im Duecento', in C. Meier et al. (eds), *Pragmatische Dimensionen mittelalterlicher Schriftkultur. Akten des Internationalen Kolloquiums des Sonderforschungsbereichs 231, 26.–29. Mai 1999*, München: Wilhelm Fink, 2002, 1ff.

19 For instance, E.A. Havelock, *The Literate Revolution in Greece and Its Cultural Consequences*, Princeton NJ: University Press, 1982.

20 M.T. Clanchy, *From Memory to Written Record: England 1066–1307*, Oxford: Blackwell Publishing, 1993, 333.

21 H. Keller, 'Vom "heiligen Buch" zur "Buchführung" – Lebensfunktionen der Schrift im Mittelalter', *Frühmittelalterliche Studien* 26, 1992, 1–31.

22 R. Schlögl, 'Kommunikation unter Anwesenden', 194; already M.T. Clanchy, *From Memory to Written Record*, 195, 271, 278. P.H. Saenger, *Space Between Words: The Origins of Silent Reading*, Stanford, CA: Stanford University Press, 1997, makes clear that silent reading was a novelty in High and Late Medieval Europe.

23 S. Teuscher, *Erzähltes Recht. Lokale Herrschaft, Verschriftlichung und Traditionsbildung im Spätmittelalter*, Frankfurt/M., New York: Campus Verlag, 2007, 313.

24 I owe this term to a discussion with Rudolf Schlögl.

25 S. Teuscher, *Erzähltes Recht*, 312 and 260ff.

26 See the classical study of H. Wenzel, *Hören und Sehen*, 253ff.; R. Köhn, 'Latein und Volkssprache, Schriftlichkeit und Mündlichkeit in der Korrespondenz des lateinischen Mittelalters', in G.O. Fichte (ed.), *Zusammenhänge, Einflüsse, Wirkungen. Kongreßakten zum ersten Symposion des Mediävistenverbandens in Tübingen*, Berlin: De Gruyter, 1986, 340; M. Jucker, *Gesandte, Schreiber, Akten. Politische Kommunikation auf eidgenössischen Tagsatzungen im Spätmittelalter*, Zürich: Chronos, 2004, 80f.; in regard to the investiture controversy: T. Wetzstein, 'Von der Unmöglichkeit zu kommunizieren. Briefe, Boten

und Kommunikation im Investiturstreit', in F. Hartmann (ed.), *Brief und Kommunikation im Wandel*, Köln, Weimar, Wien: Böhlau, 2016, 43ff.

27 M. Groten, 'Im glückseligen Regiment. Beobachtungen zum Verhältnis Obrigkeit – Bürger am Beispiel Kölns im 15. Jahrhundert', *Historisches Jahrbuch* 116, 1996, 307. On premodern representation as pars-pro-toto see H. Hofmann, *Repräsentation: Studien zur Wort- und Begriffsgeschichte von der Antike bis ins 19. Jahrhundert*, Berlin: Duncker & Humblot, 2003.

28 HAStK, Rm 10–2, fol. 122r, 05.07.1469; a regesta gives *Beschlüsse des Rates der Stadt Köln 1320–1550*, vol. 1: Die Ratsmemoriale und ergänzende Überlieferung 1320–1543 (Publikationen der Gesellschaft für Rheinische Geschichtskunde 65), ed. by Manfred Huiskes, Düsseldorf: Droste, 1990, no. 1469/26, 366f.; see F.-J. Arlinghaus, *Inklusion – Exklusion. Funktion und Formen des Rechts in der spätmittelalterlichen Stadt. Das Beispiel Köln*, Wien, Köln, Weimar: Böhlau, 2018, 298ff.

29 Ibid., 298ff.

30 K.-H. Spieß, 'Rangdenken und Rangstreit im Mittelalter', in W. Paravicini (ed.), *Zeremoniell und Raum,* Sigmaringen: Jan Thorbecke, 1997, 39ff.

31 B. Stollberg-Rilinger, 'Zeremoniell, Ritual, Symbol. Neuere Forschungen zur symbolischen Kommunikation in Spätmittelalter und Früher Neuzeit', *Zeitschrift für historische Forschung* 27, 2000, 389.

32 J. Rogge, *Die deutschen Könige im Mittelalter. Wahl und Krönung*, Darmstadt: Wiss. Buchges., 2006.

33 One of the first studies to pave the way on looking at gestures and rituals was Jean-Claude Schmitt: J.-C. Schmitt, *La raison des gestes dans l'Occident médiéval*, Paris: Gallimard, 1990.

34 J.L. Austin, *How to Do Things with Words*, Oxford: Harvard University Press, 1977; U. Wirth, 'Der Performanzbegriff im Spannungsfeld von Illokution, Iteration und Indexikalität', in ibid. (ed), *Performanz. Zwischen Sprachphilosophie und Kulturwissenschaften,* Frankfurt/M.: Suhrkamp, 2002, 9ff.

35 See K. v. Greyerz, *Passagen und Stationen. Lebensstufen zwischen Mittelalter und Moderne*, Göttingen: Vandenhoeck & Ruprecht, 2010.

36 See J.-C. Schmitt, *La raison des gestes.*

37 The central concept goes back to Émile Durkheim: 'Voilâ donc tout un ensemble de cérémonies qui se proposent uniquement de réveiller certaines idées et certains sentiments, de rattacher le present au passé, l'individu à la collectivité'; É. Durkheim, *Les formes élémentaires de la vie religieuse. Le système totémique en Australie*, Paris: Félix Alcan, 1912, 541.

38 The classical study is that of A. van Gennep, *Les rites de passage*, Paris: Editions A. Et J. Picard, 1981, 2nd edn. K. v. Greyerz, *Passagen und Stationen*, seems to lean on this.

39 See for instance J. Grimm, *Deutsche Rechtsalterthümer.*

40 J.-C. Schmitt, *La raison des gestes.*

41 G. Koziol, *Begging Pardon and Favor: Ritual and Political Order in Early Medieval France*, Ithaca, NY, London: Cornell University Press 1992.

42 Konstanz: https://cms.uni-konstanz.de/fileadmin/archive/sfb485/index.html (last visited August 2018); see: R. Schlögl, B. Giesen and J. Osterhammel (eds), *Die Wirklichkeit der Symbole. Grundlagen der Kommunikation in historischen und gegenwärtigen Gesellschaften*, Konstanz: UVK Verl.-Ges., 2004; Heidelberg: www.ritualdynamik.de/index. php?id=1&L=1 (last visited August 2018); see M. Steinicke and S. Weinfurter (eds), *Investitur- und Krönungsrituale. Herrschaftseinsetzungen im kulturellen Vergleich*, Köln et al.: Böhlau, 2005.

43 Münster: www.uni-muenster.de/SFB496/Welcome-e.html (last visited August 2018); see G. Althoff, *Die Macht der Rituale. Symbolik und Herrschaft im Mittelalter*, Darmstadt: Primus, 2003; B. Stollberg-Rilinger, 'Symbolische Kommunikation in der Vormoderne. Begriffe – Thesen – Forschungsperspektiven', *Zeitschrift für Historische Forschung* 31, 2004, 489ff.

44 A concrete example gives S. Teuscher, *Erzähltes Recht*, 265f. See in respect of double-entry bookkeeping F.-J. Arlinghaus, *Zwischen Notiz und Bilanz. Zur Eigendynamik des Schriftgebrauchs in der kaufmännischen Buchführung am Beispiel der Datini/di Berto-Handelsgesellschaft in Avignon (1367–1373)*, Frankfurt/M.: Peter Lang, 2000.

45 H. Keller and C. Dartmann, 'Inszenierungen von Ordnung und Konsens. Privileg und Statutenbuch in der symbolischen Kommunikation mittelalterlicher Rechtsgemeinschaften', in G. Althoff (ed.), *Zeichen – Rituale – Werte. Internationales Kolloquium des Sonderforschungsbereichs 496 an der Westfälischen Wilhelms-Universität Münster*, Münster: Rhema, 2004, 201ff., see R. Schlögl, *Anwesende und Abwesende. Grundriss für eine Gesellschaftsgeschichte der Frühen Neuzeit*, Konstanz: Konstanz University Press, 2014, 160f.

46 S. Teuscher, *Erzähltes Recht*.

47 See the excellent study of B.A. Hanawalt (ed.), *City and Spectacle in Medieval Europe*, Minneapolis, MN et al.: Univ. of Minnesota Press, 1994, who put ceremonies and rituals in a broader context.

48 The path-breaking study is still R.C. Trexler, *Public Life in Renaissance Florence*, New York: Cornell Univ. Press, 1980; A. Löther, *Prozessionen in spätmittelalterlichen Städten. Politische Partizipation, obrigkeitliche Inszenierung, städtische Einheit*, Köln, Weimar, Wien: Böhlau, 1999; Recently B.A. Hanawalt, *Ceremony and Civility. Civic Culture in Late Medieval London*, Oxford: Oxford Univ. Press, 2017 (with literature); E.A.R. Brown and N. Freeman Regalado, 'Universitas et communitas: The Parade of the Parisians at the Pentecost Feast of 1313', in K. Ashley and W. Hüsken (eds), *Moving Subjects: Processional Performance in the Middle Ages and the Renaissance*, Amsterdam, Atlanta: Rodopi, 2001; C. Dartmann, *Politische Interaktion in der italienischen Stadtkommune. 11.–14. Jahrhundert*, Ostfildern: Jan Thorbecke, 2012.

49 E. Muir, *Ritual in Early Modern Europe*, Cambridge: Cambridge Univ. Press, 1997, 233.

50 For a general discussion see J. Rogge, 'Viertel, Bauer, Nachbarschaften. Bemerkungen zu Gliederung und Funktion des Stadtraumes im 15. Jahrhundert (am Beispiel von Braunschweig, Halberstadt, Halle und Hildesheim)', in M. Puhle (ed.), *Hanse – Städte – Bünde. Die sächsischen Städte zwischen Elbe und Weser um 1500. Ausstellungskatalog*, Magdeburg: Kulturhistorisches Museum Magdeburg, 1996, 231ff. For Prague L. Belzyt, '"Sondergemeinden" in Städten Ostmitteleuropas im 15. und 16. Jahrhundert am Beispiel von Prag, Krakau und Lemberg', in P. Johanek (ed.), *Sondergemeinden und Sonderbezirke in der Stadt der Vormoderne*, Köln, Weimar: Böhlau, 2004, 165ff.; Lucerne: C. Thévenaz-Modestin, *Un mariage contesté. L'union de la Cité et la Ville inférieure de Lausanne (1481)*, Lausanne: Université de Lausanne, 2006; J. Oberste, *Die Geburt der Metropole. Städtische Räume und soziale Praktiken im mittelalterlichen Paris*, Regensburg: Schnell + Steiner, 2018.

51 U. Israel, 'Die Stadt und ihr Patron. Konstituierung und Stabilisierung sozialer Ordnung im europäischen Mittelalter am Beispiel Braunschweigs', *Zeitschrift für Kirchengeschichte* 122, no. 4, 60, 2011, 173ff. (with an abstract in English and further literature).

52 'Ein sakrales Ritual besteht im Kern darin, dass die Handelnden durch den Vollzug normierter, symbolisch aufgeladener Formen das Eingreifen einer transzendenten

Macht provozieren und auf diese Weise eine gewünschte Wirkung herbeiführen'; B. Stollberg-Rilinger, *Des Kaisers alte Kleider*, 95.

53 L. Gertenbach et al. (eds), *Theorien der Gemeinschaft zur Einführung*, Hamburg: Junius, 2010.

54 F.-J. Arlinghaus, 'The Myth of Urban Unity: Religion and Social Performance in Late Medieval Braunschweig', in C. Goodson, A. E. Lester and C. Symes (eds), *Cities, Texts, and Social Networks, 400–1500: Experiences and Perceptions of Medieval Urban Space,* Farnham, Burlington, VT: Ashgate, 2010, 215ff.

55 B. Stollberg-Rilinger, *Des Kaisers alte Kleider*, 17f.

56 Communication as a process distinguishes between 'information and utterance and [has] to indicate which side of the distinction is supposed to serve as the base for further communication'; N. Luhmann, 'The Autopoiesis of Social Systems', in F. Geyer and J. von der Zouwen (eds), *Socicybernetic Paradoxes. Observation, Control and Evolution of Self-Steering Systems,* London: SAGE Publications, 1986, 4; Ibid., *Social Systems, Translated by John Bednarz, Jr., with Dirk Baecker,* Stanford, CA: Stanford Univ. Press, 1995, 139ff.

7

MAKING SENSE OF ONE'S LIFE AND THE WORLD

Marek Tamm

Sense, or meaning, is the fundamental capacity of the human mind to make sense of the world in which we live. This mental procedure – making sense – can be considered as an anthropological universal in the cultural orientation of human life. Sense is the primary criterion by which humans structure the relationships with themselves and with other human or non-human beings, and that shapes their intentions and the direction of their will. 'Sense makes orientation possible. It places human life in an interpretative context. It makes it possible to understand the world and the people in it'.[1] In this perspective, culture can be understood as a toolbox for making sense of what was going on in the past, how to interpret the present, what to expect from the future and how to relate to oneself and to others.

Like all people since time immemorial, also medieval people tried to make sense of their world and used diverse cultural concepts and categories for the purpose. However, it is important to keep in mind that our contemporary cultural toolbox differs significantly from that available to the medieval. As historians, we use concepts unknown to medieval culture, such as society, politics, religion and economy.[2] Neither, it must be emphasized, did the *outillage mentale* of medieval persons include the term 'culture' in its modern sense. Even though Sebastien Morlet has recently shown that the foundations of the modern term 'culture' were laid in the first Christian centuries, when the notion of culture as a broad pluralistic phenomenon began to take shape, the word 'culture' (*cultura* in Latin) was only used in connection with agriculture up to the early modern period.[3]

It is of course risky to present medieval European culture as one integral system, since its temporal boundaries are so arbitrarily drawn and the period itself internally highly heterogeneous. Nevertheless, the medieval world was basically holistic – a type of culture that valued order and lacked the conceptual distinctions articulating our modern world. The main guarantor of the internal cohesion of medieval culture was Christianity, yet a Christianity not reducible to mere religion in the modern sense of the term, but comprehending as an ideology all the layers and nooks of society. At the same time, Christianity secured the spatial integration of medieval European culture, as recently reiterated by Miri Rubin:

European cohesion was facilitated […] by the increasingly pervasive culture of Christianity. Its presence affected the landscape – cathedrals seen by travellers from afar, especially in northern Europe, once the lofty Gothic prevailed; the presence of individuals in habits or in penitential chains on European roads, the soundscape with processional chants and the ringing of bells; and even the smell of cities (during Lent, the smell of roasting meat was absent from city streets).[4]

Thus, granting the internal diversity and internal tensions of medieval culture, in the following, I shall be primarily interested in what late medieval European culture held in common, even if it may require great simplifications and generalizations. More specifically, my intention is to outline some of the most fundamental forms on meaning making in medieval society, from making sense of time and space to making sense of the subject, the Other and the afterlife.[5]

Making sense of time

Time plays a key role in the social organization of all cultures: it marks boundaries and transitions, the life stages and rhythms of both individuals and collectives. Although in itself time is a continuum, each culture divides its steady flow into certain sections, creating thereby its own cultural time, an orderly time reckoning, and social rhythms and relations with the past. The way time is understood in a culture says much about how the people constituting it think and offers a key for understanding the cultural foundations of a society.

Notions of time

The abstract and limitless time characteristic of the modern era was unknown in the Middle Ages: the medieval notion of time was complex and fragmented; the measuring, articulation and control of time evolved only slowly. In the first centuries of the Christian era, there was no unified system of time reckoning, with different regions and authors using different traditions. The situation began to stabilize only in the sixth century, when the monk Dionysius Exiguus (d.560) fixed the birth of Christ on December 25, in the year 753 after the foundation of Rome. The new system was adopted and further developed by Venerable Bede (d.735), who became the first author to use the new system of time reckoning in history writing. More broadly, however, the new reckoning began to take root only from the eleventh century onwards.

Medieval Europe retained the Roman calendar. At first, the Julian calendar was adopted, with the year divided into seven months of 31 days each, four months of 30 days each and one month with 28 days except on leap years, when one day was added to make it 29. Later, in 1582, most of Europe adopted the Gregorian calendar, instead. The Christian calendar is essentially a liturgical calendar, articulated by feasts associated with Christ or the saints. Broadly speaking, the calendar is divided into two great liturgical cycles: those of Christmas (from Advent to Epiphany) and Easter (from Lent to Pentecost).

Although the division of the year into 12 months was a Roman device taken over by the Christian calendar, the internal division of months into weeks constitutes a significant Christian innovation: while in Rome, months were divided into decades, in the Christian calendar these are replaced by the seven-day week, following the example of the Biblical creation legend. Sunday was designated as the day of rest and prayer – the Lord's day. Although the common Roman 24-hour system was known in the Middle Ages, in real life it played a secondary role; the division of the day into eight parts corresponding to the liturgical hours was dominant. These hours moved according to the movement of the Sun and were thus, as it were, liquid. Although liturgical hours primarily regulated the life of the clerics, they clearly influenced the laymen's sense of time, too.

Until the end of the thirteenth century, shorter units of time were usually measured with sundials, sandglasses and clepsydrae, with another important measuring device being the candle. The transition to mechanical clocks, initiated in the last decades of the thirteenth century, became revolutionary in European time reckoning. In France, the first public mechanical clocks were installed on the clergy's initiative in late thirteenth century; in the first half of the fourteenth century their example was followed by secular potentates in major cities all over Europe. The new mechanical mode of time reckoning, although initially often imprecise and unreliable, signifies the triumph of a new urban notion of time, even if for a long time mainly it concerned only a relatively small urban population. This needn't necessarily be regarded as a conflict between 'the time of the church' and 'the time of the merchants'[6] since the clergy were eager to use mechanical clocks in cathedrals, yet it clearly points to the tendency of 'secularization' of time.

Social rhythms

Considering the flexibility of the medieval modes of time reckoning, it is important to understand the general appreciation of time of that period: how people made sense of the passage of time and its rhythms. Jean-Claude Schmitt aptly notes that in the Middle Ages, time was 'essentially Christian time', clearly distinguishable from the pagan time of Antiquity, from old Judaist and modern Western times.[7] Medieval culture 'Christianized time', provided it with new values, subjected it to liturgical needs and articulated it with new rhythms.

A peculiar feature of the medieval Christian conception of time was that it combined two different, occasionally rivalrous concepts of time. On the one hand, the linear and irreversible historical time that began with the creation of the world and would end with the Last Judgement; on the other, the cyclical and periodical liturgical time, with the same feasts repeated from year to year. While the latter articulated primarily the year, the former helped to make sense of longer stretches of time; thus, in a sense, they complemented each other.

Within the framework of a general Christian notion of time, different social groups lived according to different temporal rhythms. Agricultural time, essentially cyclical and based on the rhythms of nature – the alternations of light and darkness, warmth and cold – significantly affected the greatest number of people. However, it was not only the rhythms of nature, but also the peasant's labour that created time in the medieval peasant society. Within a general rural time, a separate seigneurial time can be discerned. Although subjected largely to the same natural rhythms as the peasants, with whom it occasionally intertwined – like, for instance, during the collection of taxes – the seigneurial time was enriched by the rhythms of war.

Urbanization laid the foundations for a new mechanical conception of time in medieval culture that rose to ever greater significance from the fourteenth century onwards. Although urban time remained largely dependent on rural time, the effect of natural rhythms on urban life decreased. A characteristically urban organization of work, the emergence of wage labourers and the importance of trade and craftsmanship and of monetary relations laid the foundations of new social rhythms, supported by the spread of mechanical clocks over the last medieval centuries. However, the regimes of day and night, often governed by different legal orders, remained clearly distinct in towns, too.[8]

Yet it is liturgical time that can be considered dominant in the Middle Ages. In spite of their comparatively small numbers, clerics were the most important shapers of the notion of time – in a sense, the professional guardians of time. It was in the church's competence to compose a liturgical calendar whose rhythms were observed by the whole society; a very flexible calendar, with new feasts added over time and various peculiarities introduced locally. The liturgical calendar regulated the most common and intimate activities of people: what could be eaten and when (days and periods of fasting), when they were allowed to work or wage war, when sexual acts were permissible (thus, sex was forbidden during Lent, major feasts of the church, etc.). The church dictated the public sense of time by means of church bells that came into use beginning in the seventh century and established the rhythm of liturgical hours and ecclesiastical feasts. A widely observed custom in the country as well as in the town was to organize one's daily labours according to liturgical time.[9] In the village of Montaillou in southern France, written to fame by Emmanuel Le Roy Ladurie, the inhabitants' sense of time hinged on the church calendar:

> While the division of the day and of the night remained largely lay, the division of the year was largely ecclesiastical. All Saints, Christmas, Carnival and Lent, Palm Sunday, Easter, Whitsun, Ascension Day, the Assumption, the Nativity of the Virgin and the Holy Cross made up a universally known cycle.[10]

Time as history

Each culture elaborates its own relationship with the past, and the ways it is interpreted, represented and used. A great interest in and distinctive conception of the past emerged during the Middle Ages, expressed most clearly by various forms of history writing. The past enjoyed an authoritative status; a study of the genealogies of the world and its regions, peoples, institutions, families and individuals was considered one of the most important intellectual activities already in the early Middle Ages but rose to particular prominence over the last centuries of the period.

Medieval historical culture in general is characterized by presentism – past events were not recorded or interpreted for their intrinsic value but in order to teach lessons and provide reasons for current activities.[11] Instead of factuality, the actuality of history was appreciated. The study of history thus satisfied the medieval society's great curiosity for its (glorious) origins, on the one hand, while on the other providing the society with models of behaviour and instructions for action.

The florescence of the medieval historical culture was supported by the linear Christian time, the example of the historical books of the Bible and the need to compute the liturgical calendar. Bernard Guenée has succinctly said that 'the great achievement of medieval erudition was the conquest of time'.[12] This was expressed by the emergence of new genres of history writing and ever more thorough and accurate chronological systems. At the same time it must be noted that 'history' had a significantly broader meaning in the Middle Ages than today:

> the use of the word *historia* was not restricted to historiography [...], it could refer to narrative works of art, saints' lives, parts of the Bible, the literal sense of scriptural texts, liturgical offices, epic poems, and other texts and objects.[13]

The modern way of dividing the past into successive periods was alien to medieval culture; instead, the idea of dividing time into cycles to emulate the different stages of human life was widespread. The most popular periodization of history into six ages, based on the six days of creation and six phases of human life, originates with St Augustine. According to this doctrine, world history is divided into periods from Adam to Noah (corresponding to infancy), Noah to Abraham (childhood), Abraham to David (the teens), David to Babylonian captivity (youth), Babylonian captivity to the birth of Christ (adulthood) and finally from the birth of Christ to the end of the world, followed by eternal unchangeability, just as the seventh day of rest followed the six of creation.

Making sense of the world

Although a new original conception of time was elaborated in the Middle Ages, the cultural type of this era is better considered space-centred. Jerôme Baschet has exemplified this from penal policies: while in modern Europe, the highest degree of punishment is imprisonment for life, limiting the prisoner's space, in medieval times it was exile, casting him out of space, turning him into an outlaw.[14] Yet medieval space was understood quite differently from how we customarily understand it: the various parts of space were variously valued and arranged in hierarchical relations, with everything in the world, far from being accidental, being reflected a divine order. Alain Guerreau justly says: 'Medieval civilization had a truly original system for the representation of space, on which probably hinged the society's whole system of representations'.[15]

Notions of space and place

Just as the Middle Ages lacked the notion of abstract and vacuous time, so space, too, was 'neither abstract nor homogenous, but individual and qualitatively heterogeneous'.[16] In fact, the term 'space' in its modern sense was unknown; the Latin *spatium*, signifying mostly 'duration' or 'a stretch of time', thus constituted rather a temporal concept. Instead of space, the Middle Ages spoke of place (*locus*). Unlike space, place does not precede the objects but is formed by and around them. Thus, place presumes a presence, an active relationship; 'it is not so much perceived as lived'.[17] Harald

Kleinschmidt succinctly writes: 'Theoretically speaking, one might say that space was perceived as the aggregate sum of qualitatively different places occupied by persons, groups or objects and not as the space in between persons, groups and objects'.[18]

The medieval sense of space is closely connected to religious and moral judgements: different places have different meanings and some are valued more than others. Space is arranged hierarchically, on the social as well as ideological plane. All spatial relationships are constructed vertically, with all creatures placed on different grades of perfection according to their nearness to God. More generally it can be said that the medieval conception of space had a strong symbolic nature: the concepts of life and death, good and evil, sacred and secular were related to those of high and low, of distinct countries and parts of the world space – they acquired topographical coordinates.

Similarly to other traditional societies, the medieval sense of space was characterized by anthropocentrism – the space was primarily an anthropomorphic space where distances were measured according to the immediate human experience or the human body: the foot, the step, the cubit, the span, the digit, etc.[19] One expression of the anthropomorphic perception of space was the notion, widespread in medieval scholarly circles, of man as a microcosm that corresponds to the universe – the macrocosm. Like the universe, so the human being consists of four elements: earth (flesh), water (blood), air (breath) and fire (warmth).

But scholars were the only persons in the medieval world to engage in abstract discussions of the world or universe as a whole. For the large majority of medieval people, the sense of space was limited to particular places and the distances between them. The radius of a peasant's inhabited space was generally limited to one day's journey; that is, about 15 kilometres. The social space of a merchant, clergyman or nobleman was somewhat larger, stretching to the radius of at least one day's horseman's journey, but could on some occasions (a trade journey, pilgrimage, clerical visitation, etc.) reach as far as several hundred kilometres or more.

Cultural geography of the world

Geography lacked clear disciplinary status in the Middle Ages; elements of geographical knowledge can be found in theological as well as historical, encyclopaedic and other texts.[20] Discussions of the structure of universe or geographical articulation of the world involved but a small number of scholars; only in the fifteenth century did they begin to acquire a more practical nature and broader influence. Mostly, the cosmological and geographical knowledge relied on the authority of the Bible and the works of a few classical authors. In the Middle Ages, geographical description was primarily a textual exercise within an authoritative canon of theological doctrine.

According to the medieval view, the universe consisted of various concentric spheres with the Earth in the middle. That is, the cosmos was geo-, not heliocentric. The number of spheres varied in different authors' works: some counted seven (air, ether, Olympus, fire, stars, the heaven of angels and that of the Trinity), others three spheres, while some late medieval scholastics, referring to Aristotle, reckoned they numbered 56. As for the shape of the Earth – flat versus spherical – there was no consensus, although beginning with the high Middle Ages, at the latest, the view prevailed that it was spherical.[21] Yet the shape of the Earth was not the most urgent issue for medieval scholars who gave primacy to the internal articulation of the Earth – topography.

Most commonly, the Earth was divided into five climatic zones: very cold in the north and very hot in the south, with a temperate zone in the middle. The northern temperate zone was inhabited by humankind; concerning the inhabitants of the southern temperate regions, opinions differed, with many thinking them inhabited by the so-called antipodes. The northern habitable lands were in turn divided by the Mediterranean (or Great) Sea into three continents: Asia, Africa and Europe, surrounded by the great sea or ocean. The three continents were associated with Noah's sons: Asia the land of Sem, Europe of Japhet and Africa of Ham.

In the Middle Ages, little was known about Africa, the size of which was estimated to be roughly equal to that of Europe, with the scarcity of knowledge compensated for by imaginative thinking: it was mainly associated with natural bounty and believed to be inhabited by savages. Relations with Asia, deemed twice the size of Europe, underwent several developments over the centuries. The original fantastic view of the region began to become more lifelike from the late thirteenth century onward, with an increasing number of missionaries and merchants travelling there, primarily to China and India. The Mongol conquest cast a pall over Asia's positive exotic reputation, turning it from a very promising missionary region into a hostile Muslim country.

The European scholars' changing ideas about Asia are best represented by India. In the thirteenth century, India was still 'the place that most completely represents the exotic in the medieval imagination'.[22] This is eloquently demonstrated by the English author Gervase of Tilbury's *Otia Imperialia* (c.1214):

> There are other peoples in India who eat raw fish, and drink salt-water from the sea. There are also various kinds of monstrous creatures there, some of which are regarded as human, others as animals. There are some, for instance, whose feet point backwards, and they have eight toes on each foot. Others have a dog's head and hooked claws; their skin is like the hide of cattle, their voice like the barking of dogs.[23]

Less than a century later, the Italian Franciscan missionary, John of Monte Corvino, wrote a new survey of India, observing:

> As regards men of a marvellous kind, to wit, men of a different make from the rest of us, and as regards animals of like description, and as regards the Terrestrial Paradise, much have I asked and sought, but nothing have I been able to discover.[24]

Europe must be understood primarily as Christendom (Latin *Christianitas*), i.e. a region dominated by Latin Christianity in medieval cultural geography. Although the first large-scale expansion of the European Christendom falls into the early Middle Ages, its boundaries took shape between the years 950 and 1350, a period Robert Bartlett called 'the making of Europe'.[25] Within three centuries, Christendom increased its territory nearly twofold, managing to implement a unified cultural model over a large territory from Ireland to Livonia. As a consequence of this expansion and colonization, the newly occupied regions needed to be translated into the cultural geography of Latin Europe. Because of the great importance of written models, this translation work can be called 'intertextual integration', meaning a method of interpreting new geographical information in the light of old authoritative texts.[26]

Mapping the world

As noted above, we cannot speak about geography or cartography in the modern sense in a medieval context. Geographical knowledge aimed not so much at learning to know distant lands as at ordering the universe and providing a visual narrative of Christian history cast in a geographical framework. Although map-making began to spread as early as the twelfth century, for a long time – up to the early fifteenth century – maps remained predominantly symbolic in content and not well suited for practical use.

One of the most popular medieval devices for mapping the world were the so-called *mappae mundi*. Regardless of the name, these were not maps of the world in the contemporary sense of the word, but abstract and symbolic drawings. However, the symbolic character of the *mappae mundi* does not exclude their 'practical' use, as Patrick Gautier Dalché has recently emphasized. 'Through their topographical juxtaposition of regions, corresponding to textual descriptions inherited from Antiquity, the *mappae mundi* helped situate the points of departure and arrival for a journey and to think out its stages'.[27] *Mappae mundi* could be of different structures: tripartite, zonal, quadripartite or transitional. The oldest and best known was the first disk-shaped representation of the inhabited world, displaying an East-oriented tripartite schema (T) with Asia occupying the upper half of the circle, Europe the lower left and Africa the lower-right quarter. The parts of the T represent the three major hydrographic features known to separate the three parts of the Earth: the Tanais (Don) River between Europe and Asia, the Nile between Africa and Asia and the Mediterranean between Europe and Asia as well as Asia and Africa.

Beginning with the thirteenth century, other more practical maps emerged alongside the *mappae mundi*, primarily portulan charts – coastal navigational maps based on the observation and evaluation of distances. During the last medieval centuries, the world came to be mapped ever more accurately, even though the Christian ideological filter never quite lost its importance. Space came to be perceived more and more as continuous and homogeneous, enabling Kleinschmidt to generalize: 'Around 1500, the medieval universal world picture gave way to a category of space that comprised the world as a globe'.[28]

Making sense of the subject

In studying how medieval people made sense of themselves, a medievalist faces far greater problems than merely analysing how the world was understood. For decades, historians have debated the meaning and importance of the concept of the 'individual', with some stating that the idea was non-existent in the Middle Ages and only began to emerge during the Renaissance, whereas others claim it was precisely the Middle Ages that brought forth the idea of the individual. Recent studies, however, have made it possible to define the terms of this argument more precisely and cast clearer light on how the human condition was made sense of in the Middle Ages.[29]

Notions of the human person

While human subjectivity can be considered a psychological universal, it is a universal expressed and developed in different cultural categories during different eras. The Middle Ages provide an important and distinctive example of the various forms of subjectivity; that is, of the cultural means of individuation.

Chronologically, the period 1050–1200 can be regarded as key for the development of medieval individuation, with first the 'anthroponymic revolution'[30] taking place – ever more people beginning to have two names instead of one: an individual baptism name (*nomen proprium*) and a surname (*cognomen*) demonstrating their belonging to a particular family. Secondly, the creation of various status symbols (heraldic signs, seals, etc.) became popular in the higher ranks of the society. Thirdly, more and more autobiographical texts were written while in lyrics, the fictional 'I' gained importance. Last but not least, the issue of self-cognition rose to significance in scholastic debates, in the course of which several original definitions of human nature were developed. This process further intensified during the last medieval centuries, where we encounter ever more forms of expressing one's subjectivity, including the celebration of personal anniversaries, visual self-representations and deeply individual mystic visions.

In the interests of clarity, this medieval individuation might be called 'personalism' as distinct from the modern 'individualism'. Medieval subjectivity never quite acquired autonomous forms, such as we know from modernity; instead, personal identity was always expressed within different social groups (family, community, congregation, etc.). Thus, the dynamics of individuation was significantly favoured by the emergence of new social roles, groups and networks in the late Middle Ages.

In the medieval view, personality is formed in the union of body and soul. While the former ties a person to matter and temporality, the latter secures his connection with spirituality and eternity. This dual dimension of the personality should not, however, be seen as antagonistic, but complementary. Baschet has convincingly warned of a simplified juxtaposition of the body and soul in medieval contexts: 'the dominant concepts of the human being in the Middle Ages can be defined as *dual but not dualistic*'.[31] In the medieval view, body and soul form a single whole serving as a model for the structure of the entire society, including the institution of the church that also consists of two facets – an earthly and a spiritual.

Autobiographical writing

One of the more original medieval forms of making sense of oneself is self-writing. After St Augustine's *Confessions*, autobiographical writing fell into neglect for several centuries, displaying fresh signs of life only on the threshold of the twelfth century. The first and most important achievements are the French Benedictine Guibert of

Nogent's (d. c.1125) *De vita sua* and Pierre Abélard's *Historia calamitatum* (c.1133). Guibert's book, although rather unnoticed in the Middle Ages, includes an original theory of human psychology that has, in more recent times, inspired several psychohistorians and psychoanalysts. The more widely renowned *Historia calamitatum* follows the classical model of a consolatory letter to a friend. Although a consolation by genre, it rather sounds like a justification – the author's attempt to present his life as a long series of harassments and misunderstandings.

A later noteworthy work is the autobiographical narrative of Herman, a former Jew of Cologne turned Christian, *Opusculum de conversione sua* (c.1150) – a relatively rare example of the autobiography of a convert.[32] A highly original instance of a 'cartographic autobiography' is presented by the two manuscripts of the Italian cleric Opicinus de Canistris (d. c.1354), composed in the 1330s. These extremely inventive manuscripts, discovered only in the early twentieth century – a mixture of autobiographical notes, anthropomorphic maps, biblical quotations, diagrams, symbols and mystical visions – still provide scholars with material for new interpretations.[33]

But the revival of the autobiographical narrative was accompanied in late medieval times by other important developments in the practices of self-writing, among them the rise of the vernacular lyric tradition culminating in Dante's *Vita nuova* (1295), and the proliferation of visionary literature, particularly by female mystics. In the fourteenth century, the first self-analysing prose texts emerged, harbingers of a new individualistic manner of thought, foremost among them Petrarch's *Secretum* – a trilogy of imaginary dialogues written sometime between 1347 and 1353.

Confession and subjection

While written self-fashioning remained the privilege of a few literate or holy persons, confession became the most important late medieval technology of the self at the grass-root level. In the history of penance, the Fourth Lateran Council of 1215 marks an important turning point, establishing yearly confession mandatory for all Christians. Previously, regular confession had been encouraged, but not required; it was often made only publicly, not in privacy. Now, confession became an annual obligatory dialogue with the priest, introspection guided by specific questions.[34] Since interrogation during confession was new for the clergy, too, a motley supply of pastoral literature came into being from the thirteenth century onward, including general confession manuals as well as specific treatises on 'how to hear confessions', or 'how to examine one's conscience'.[35] All of them encouraged the confessors to be 'diligent inquisitors' in interrogating the sinner and ferreting out hidden details and intentions.

Confession generally consisted of two parts: first, the penitent would recite a ritual formula of confession or confess spontaneously the sins that came to his or her mind. Next, after this self-generated confession, the priest was to conduct his own interrogation based on the interrogatory of the confessor's manual. The most common framework of self-examination offered by the manuals was the seven deadly sins. As noticed by John Bossy, an important shift in confessional culture occurred in the fifteenth century, when the scheme of the seven sins was exchanged for that of the Ten Commandments. According to Bossy, with this exchange, the Christians acquired a moral code stronger on obligations to God, somewhat narrower on obligations to the neighbour, and in both directions more precise, more penetrative and more binding.[36]

The new confessional culture can be considered a good example of a phenomenon described by Michel Foucault as 'subjection' (French *assujettissement*): it is a dual process simultaneously subjecting people to power and creating a new subjectivity. During confession, a person subjected himself to the demands and rules of the church; at the same time, regular verbal introspection surely contributed to persons' self-fashioning and to acquiring better knowledge of oneself. The confession can be considered the technology that enabled the individual to translate his acts and thoughts into words, even if the vocabulary was largely prescribed by the clergy.

Making sense of the Other

Medieval society held order, clear ideological boundaries and well-defined social roles in high esteem. This attitude is well capitulated by regular canon Philip of Harvengt in his treatise *On the Institution of Clerics* (c.1150):

> It is good for a man to know the order in which he is constituted and its limit or boundary so that he may neither insolently exceed the clear boundaries nor weakly shrink from them by retiring to the side.[37]

The ideologized nature and comparatively strict internal articulation of the society meant that outcasts and marginals were a remarkably numerous and motley crew. In the interests of clarity, the entire multifarious contingent of 'others' can be reduced to two main types: those repulsed because of their origins and/or religion, and those marginalized because of their activities.

Religious minorities and enemies

All religious 'others' were, in the medieval view, reduced to 'infidels' without hope of redemption. Yet, they were not perceived in a monolithic and unchanging manner. Particular attention must be paid to temporal dynamics; beginning from the twelfth century onward, the attitudes to religious minorities grew increasingly more negative.

Jews could be regarded as the outcasts *par excellence* of the medieval society. On the one hand, they inhabited the margins of society because of their ethnical identity and religion; on the other, they mostly (often under external pressure) pursued such trades (usurer, doctor, etc.) as were either religiously spurned or at least ambivalent. Yet, for a long time, Jews were also the only religious minority allowed to exist within Christian society; only in the twelfth century did the heretofore-tolerant attitude undergo a greater change. As a result, as summed up by Ora Limor, 'whereas in the early thirteenth century Jews lived throughout Europe, by the end of the Middle Ages (1500), Jews were to be found in Western Europe only in Italy and in a few regions of the German Reich'.[38] The mainsprings of persecution were diverse and related to the centralization of church power, the crusading movement, developments in theological thought, urbanization and a rapid demographic growth.

Marginalization mainly resulted from antagonism with the church, with it usually impossible subsequently to determine whether the church had reacted to various dissident trends or rather provoked them into existence while consolidating its power. The twelfth century saw an increase of negative attention not just to the Jews, but also heretics. The church set out to 'ideologize the heretics', placing them on a highly symbolic level insofar as they presented a threat for the collective peace on Earth and welfare in the after-world of the faithful.[39] We must remember that 'heretic' was not an autonym, but a term applied by the church to those who deviated from the official doctrine, a fact that has enabled scholars to justly speak of 'the invention of heresy' in the Middle Ages.[40]

If Jews and heretics constituted the 'internal others' of medieval society, Muslims and pagans played the role of the 'external other', although the importance of Muslim communities in the various parts of Europe, primarily in the Mediterranean basin and Central and Eastern Europe, should not be underestimated, either.[41] Attitudes to Muslims are clearly linked to the dynamics of the expansion of Christendom. Up to the eleventh century, the church paid relatively little attention to Islam. As the bounds of Christian Europe expanded, however, and as its confidence and strength grew and missionary ideology gained momentum, the church and state engaged even more in defining Muslims and their faith. As early as in the eleventh century, the main anti-Islamic stereotypes took shape, as succinctly recapitulated by David Nirenberg: 'First, Islam was a false religion. Second, it was a carnal one, glorying in violence and sexuality'.[42]

The term 'pagan' has no single obvious referent in medieval culture. As Sara Lipton reminds us, the word was applied to a wide and heterogeneous range of peoples: the Old Testament gentiles, ancient Greeks and Romans, unconverted Celts, Germans, Magyars, Scandinavians and Slavs, 'Tartars' (Mongols), Asian Buddhists and Hindus, etc.[43] On many occasions, the term 'pagan' was used to indicate a political, not religious adversary. For instance, relying on the sources from the Baltic Sea area, Henrik Janson has shown that many Christian rulers were depicted as pagans because they had renounced one or another of their political allegiances.[44] In other words, 'pagan' functioned mostly as a flexible metaphor for a broad variety of negative values and behaviours.

Social outcasts

The number of social 'others', however, exceeded that of religious ones throughout the medieval period, particularly in the late Middle Ages when their emergence was favoured by the process of urbanization. At first, town-engendered paupers and beggars were viewed with ambivalent feelings at the time: although poverty itself was not shameful, it could lead to immoral behaviour and breach of social rules. Medieval scholars distinguished two types of the poor: some had fallen into poverty through no fault of their own, like the biblical Lazarus (*pauperes cum Lazaro*); others deliberately led a life of poverty to emulate the apostles (*pauperes cum Petro*).[45] A step further from the poor were the sick, particularly the lepers, who again were regarded ambivalently: on the one hand, the leper was a sufferer, a kind of 'Christ's pauper', and helping him could be seen as helping Christ himself. On the other hand, leprosy was regarded as bodily proof of sin; the fall of the body reflected the soiledness of the soul. The segregation of lepers was carried out parallel with charitable activities: from the twelfth century on, leproseries were established all over Europe, intended simultaneously for taking care of the diseased and for isolating them from society.

The so-called dishonourable trades, whose list was rather long and diverse, provide an interesting example of the social others: executioners, butchers (both having to do with blood), jugglers, fools, doctors, usurers, prostitutes and many others. Another informative example regarding the contradictory manner in which to make sense of the 'Other' is provided by prostitutes: from a moral vantage point, they were marginalized because condemned by the church, while from a social vantage point, they were well integrated into urban life, having their own professional pride and legal rights. Official attitudes could undergo major revolutions over time: thus, in 1254, Saint Louis, king of France, decided to cast all depraved women out of his kingdom and confiscate their property; yet, before long, prostitution flourished again. Jacques Rossiaud estimates that prostitution consolidated in the towns of France in 1350–1450.[46]

An instructive example of the integration of the social other is provided by the fate of a medieval usurer. Usurers were condemned by the church mainly for two reasons. First, they kept committing the cardinal sin of greed; secondly, they traded what belonged not to them but to God, namely time. Contemporary attitude is well captured in an *exemplum* from the anonymous thirteenth-century manuscript *Tabula exemplorum*:

> Usurers are thieves, for they sell time that does not belong to them, and selling someone else's property, despite its owner, is theft. In addition, since they sell nothing but the expectation of money, that is to say, time, they sell days and nights. But the day is the time of clarity, and the night is the time for repose. Consequently they sell light and repose. It is, therefore, not just for them to receive eternal light and eternal rest.[47]

But developing trade relations and increasing demand for monetary credit forced the church to revise its attitude, and from the fourteenth century on, we see merchants and usurers winning ever broader respect.

Formation of a persecuting society

The above-mentioned survey delineated a certain pattern in the attitude to the 'Other' that took increasingly radical forms from the twelfth century onward. R. I. Moore has called this pattern 'the formation of a persecuting society' and discerns two mutually connected underlying reasons for this.[48] First, the growth of nascent state bureaucracies capable of institutionalizing repression, and second, the rise of a self-conscious class of educated churchmen and administrators who rhetorically demonized those they deemed 'others', as a means of reinforcing their own elite legitimacy. This naturally does not mean that the persecuting society arose as a result of conscious planning; rather, it constituted one of the consequences of the internal dynamics of state and church power.

An original expression of the persecuting mentality was what could be called 'semiotic segregation'.[49] The beginnings of the practice can be dated to the Fourth Lateran Council in 1215, which ruled that in order to keep Muslims and Jews from merging with Christians, they must wear specific clothes. The council's lead was followed by diverse authorities in several parts of Europe. Thus, King Henry III of England decreed in 1218 that all Jews must wear a badge in the form of two white tablets, on their outer garments. In 1227, the synod of Narbonne, France ruled in the same spirit that Jews must wear a circular sign, the size of half a palm, on the breast of their clothes. Analogous decisions were adopted in many other places, and it is worth noting how the original demand for distinctive clothing quickly metamorphosed into a command to wear distinctive signs on their clothes.[50]

However, Jews were not the only ones to be set apart from the others with semiotic means; similar devices were used to mark out several social minorities, too. Thus, beginning with the thirteenth century, lepers were forced to wear special clothes and a white or red distinguishing sign, frequently complemented by the duty to carry a rattle or bell to warn others of their approach. At the end of the thirteenth and beginning of the fourteenth centuries, the obligation to set themselves apart from the others, either by a special belt, sleeves of different colours, a certain ornament on the clothes, a striped hood or other such means, was in many places extended to prostitutes. In some late medieval Italian towns, prostitutes were made to wear earrings – an obligation extended also to Jewish women.[51] Confessed heretics came to be customarily punished by publicly wearing shaming signs, such as a mitre, the letter H (signifying *hereticus*) or, most frequently, a yellow cross to be worn both on the breast and the back.[52]

On the one hand, this kind of semiotic segregation naturally constituted an expression of the persecuting society, as pointed out by Bronislaw Geremek: 'These objective signs of marginal condition were thus instruments of infamy, exclusion, or repression more often than they were natural symptoms'.[53] On the other hand, however, we must keep in mind the highly semiotic nature of the medieval society, at least in two senses: first, symbols and symbolic behaviour were held in high esteem at the time; and second, semiotic thinking was one of the cornerstones of theological thought – scholasticism is, in essence, theoretical semiotics. Beginning with the twelfth century, we can also observe that practical sign creation – the adoption of diverse material signs of status and identity – becomes more and more important.[54] Thus, it is not surprising that high medieval society resorted to semiotic means in its bid to control and organize society.

Making sense of the afterlife

In medieval times, life on Earth was regarded as preparation for a life after death. *Dies natalis*, birthday, in the Middle Ages meant the day of death; that is, birth to eternal life. In view of the great importance of everything related to death, which furthermore concerned all age groups to an almost equal degree, it is not surprising that an original and elaborate system of ideas and rules related to death and the afterlife was created in the Middle Ages.

Art of dying

Dying was a ritualized event in the Middle Ages, participated in by the entire community. The sacrament of extreme unction, instituted by the church throughout the twelfth century, formed the core of that corporate ritual. Dying thus presumed time and preparations; it became if not an art, then at least a craft – *ars moriendi*. This notion, *ars moriendi*, became popular especially in the late Middle Ages, referring to the body of Christian art and literature that provided practical guidance for the dying and those attending them. Unprepared, unexpected death, on the contrary, was considered bad death. Therefore, before a longer journey, pilgrimage or crusade, all arrangements were made for facilitating a departure into eternity.

The Christian era marks an important shift in the treatment of the dead. While in the Roman society, the living and the dead, the sites of worship and of burial, were kept strictly apart, Christianity, as it were, domesticated the dead, and buried them in a focal part of the living area – inside or around the church; they sacralized the burial place. The process was, of course, lengthy – the extension of the sacral space of the church to the burial ground dragged on into the tenth century. Thus, the Middle Ages 'invented the cemetery';[55] the burial place of the dead became sacral, equal with the church and closely connected to it. In the late Middle Ages, the cemetery became a highly important social space, one of the major theatres for preaching the new, fear-tempered culture of death. At the same time, the cemetery was an important field of power – only those approved of by the church were deemed worthy of a burial in sacred ground, while many social outcasts, from heretics to the pliers of dishonourable trades, were excluded.

The relations between the living and the dead underwent an important change in the late Middle Ages whose reasons can be found in the exodus of people from villages and the expansion of urbanization, in the consolidation of a written legal order and in a rise of mortality caused by epidemics and famines. A tangible result of the new relationship was the last will and testament, the origins of which go back to the late twelfth century, but florescence falls into the last centuries of the Middle Ages. The exquisite late medieval testaments document what has been called 'accounting for the hereafter'[56] or 'arithmetic of salvation'.[57] The testaments vividly show a deepening worry for the welfare of one's soul and the resultant interest in exchanging one's earthly treasure for intercessory prayers. Other symptoms of the new fear of death include the flourishing of macabre themes in the visual culture, the *artes moriendi* mentioned above, and the rapid increase in the numbers of urban clergymen who profited handsomely from the new culture of death.

Culture of memoria

Commemoration of the dead forms part of a very important and multifaceted phenomenon of medieval culture that could be described as the culture of *memoria*. The Latin word *memoria* is one of the most important concepts of the Middle Ages; 'there are few words in medieval vocabulary in possession of so large a range of meanings as *memoria*'.[58] Although originally referring to the commemoration of the dead in all its conceivable forms, as well as the objects and buildings connected with commemoration, *memoria* was also used in the secular sphere, primarily in the field of law, where it referred to the historical legitimacy of institutions. Finally, *memoria* played an important role in medieval philosophy, where it was often considered one of the three components of human intelligence.

Naturally, the main impresarios of the medieval culture of *memoria* were the clergy. They elaborated the rules and rituals of commemoration and decided what and who were *memoranda* – worth commemorating. An important innovation in this field was the introduction of a new feast of commemoration of the dead, the All Souls' Day, celebrated on November 2 and initiated by Abbot Odilo of Cluny (d.1049) which, with the support of the pope, rapidly spread over the entire Christendom in the eleventh century and became highly popular in the late Middle Ages.

Liturgical *memoria* was the main mode of communication between the living and the dead; thanks to regular commemoration, the dead never left the community of the living but contributed to its cohesion or, as observed by David D'Avray, '*memoria* is the creation of community by making the absent present in a non-physical way'.[59] But the liturgical *memoria* interacted – and was intertwined – with a diversity of other social practices. *Memoria*, as Gustavs Strenga has shown in the example of late medieval Livonia, was a 'total social phenomenon' that impacted every aspect of medieval life. It played an integral role in creating the fabric of Livonian society and was essential for maintaining the continuity of its institutions: the guilds and brotherhoods, the Teutonic Order, episcopal sees and cathedral chapters.[60]

Geography of the other world

Belief in bodily resurrection and life in the hereafter is one of the most original features of Christianity.[61] Life on Earth was a struggle for achieving eternal life; real life was not lived here, but hereafter. In the Middle Ages, this conviction gave rise to rich iconography and literature, but it also forced the theologians to elaborate on very detailed explanations of how the soul fares in the other world, particularly because the Scripture offered very little on this matter. Yet, it must at once be said that the term 'the other world' was unknown in medieval Latin. Various terms circulated to designate specific locations in the hereafter, but there was no common denominator.

A general conception of the hereafter was offered by St Augustine and was slowly elaborated by later authors. It was a fourfold scheme: the completely good would go to Heaven and the completely evil to Hell; in between, the not-entirely-good would be in Paradise with complete confidence in their future access to Heaven, and the not-entirely-evil would be subject to temporary torment in a place of purification. While the general dual conception of the hereafter remained unchanged throughout the Middle Ages, the geography of the other world underwent several important changes. The most important of them was the evolution and consolidation of the concept of Purgatory – a place between Hell and Paradise – in the twelfth to thirteenth centuries.[62] Baschet has justly noted that in a sense, it was not merely a rearrangement, but truly the 'birth of a geography of the other world'.[63] Only Purgatory made it possible to depict the hereafter in spatial terms, as the soul's journey between its various locations, which the visionary literature immediately began to illustrate with specific examples.

Not only texts but images, too, were used to make sense of the hereafter. The iconography of Hell achieved truly diverse and magnificent forms, particularly in late medieval Italy.[64] Images of Paradise were significantly paler and rarer; for a long time, the lap of Abraham remained the dominant iconographic symbol of Paradise, replaced in the late Middle Ages by the court of heaven, with saints gathered around the godhead.[65] The iconography of Purgatory remained largely neglected during the Middle Ages, although the last centuries of the period saw an increasing number of visual representations, mainly in the illustrated books of piety meant for the nobility.[66] The medieval modes of making sense of the other world were crowned by Dante's (d.1321) *Divine Comedy* and its numerous illustrations in late medieval and early modern times. In a sense, Dante's tripartite *magnum opus* can, however, be regarded as a summary of all of the main attitudes and values of the medieval culture in general.

Notes

1 J. Rüsen, *Evidence and Meaning: A Theory of Historical Studies*, New York: Berghahn, 2017, 17. My understanding of the 'sense' or 'meaning' is largely based on the work of Rüsen. For a cultural-historical perspective, see J. Rogge (ed.), *Making Sense as a Cultural Practice: Historical Perspectives*, Bielefeld: transcript Verlag, 2013. The work on this chapter was supported by the Estonian Research Council grant IUT 18–8.

2 In connection with the latter two macro concepts that emerged in the eighteenth century, Alain Guerreau has spoken about a 'conceptual double fracture' (*double fracture conceptuelle*) separating the medieval from the modern world. See A. Guerreau, *L'Avenir d'un passé incertain. Quelle histoire du Moyen Âge au XXIe siècle?*, Paris: Seuil, 2001.

3 S. Morlet, *Les Chrétiens et la culture. Conversion d'un concept (Ier–VIe siècle)*, Paris: Les Belles Lettres, 2016.

4 M. Rubin, *The Middle Ages: A Very Short Introduction*, Oxford: Oxford University Press, 2014, 110.

5 The topics covered in this chapter are too wide to be presented with an overview of the latest research. However, some most important recent works are pointed out in the Notes.

6 J. Le Goff, 'Merchant's Time and Church's Time in the Middle Ages', in J. Le Goff, *Time, Work and Culture in the Middle Ages*, Chicago, IL, London: University of Chicago Press, 1980, 29–42.

7 J.-C. Schmitt, *Les rythmes au Moyen Âge*, Paris: Gallimard, 2016, 254.

8 Claude Gauvard has demonstrated that in the letters of remission issued during the reign of King Charles VI (1380–1422), the time of perpetration of the crime is far more frequently given according to the position of the sun (in almost 60% of the cases) than according to liturgical time (11%) or the time of mechanical clocks (14%). See C. Gauvard, *'De grace especial'. Crime, État et société en France à la fin du Moyen Age*, 2 vols, Paris: Publications de la Sorbonne, 1991.

9 Thus, for instance, the statutes of the stonemasons' guild of late medieval Tallinn ruled that work must begin right after the Dominicans' morning mass and continue until the bells of the abbey mark the time of evening prayers. See Tallinn City Archives, f. 230, n. 1, s. Ac 5, fol. 21v.

10 E. Le Roy Ladurie, *Montaillou: Cathars and Catholics in a French Village 1294–1324*, Harmondsworth: Penguin Books, 1980, 279.

11 See H.-W. Goetz, *Geschichtsschreibung und Geschichtsbewusstsein im hohen Mittelalter*, 2nd rev. edn, Berlin: Akademie Verlag, 2008.

12 B. Guenée, *Histoire et culture historique dans l'Occident médiéval*, 2nd rev. edn, Paris: Aubier, 1991, 165.

13 D.M. Deliyannis, 'Introduction', in ibid (ed.), *Historiography in the Middle Ages*, Leyden: Brill, 2003, 2–3.

14 J. Baschet, *La civilisation féodale. De l'an mil à la colonisation de l'Amérique*, Paris: Aubier, 2004, 353.

15 A. Guerreau, 'Il significato dei luoghi nell'Occidente medievale: struttura e dinamica di uno "spazio" specifico', in E. Castelnuovo and S. Giuseppe (eds.), *Arti e Storia nel Medioevo*, vol. 1, Turin: Einaudi, 2002, 201.

16 A.J. Gurevich, *Categories of Medieval Culture*, London: Routledge & Kegan Paul, 1985, 90.

17 P. Zumthor, *La mesure du monde*, Paris: Seuil, 1993, 36.

18 H. Kleinschmidt, *Understanding the Middle Ages: The Transformation of Ideas and Attitudes in the Medieval World*, Woodbridge: Boydell & Brewer, 2000, 37.

19 This is confirmed, for instance, by Le Roy Ladurie's research of the village of Montaillou: 'Space, whether immediate, geographical, sociological or cultural, was basically linked to physical perception, especially that of the hand and the arm. [...] Longer distances are measured in terms of a league, a stage of a journey or a stage of the migration. In the mountain village of Montaillou, people did not go simply from point A to point B; they went up or down'. See Le Roy Ladurie, *Montaillou*, 282.

20 See P. Gautier Dalché (ed.), *La Terre. Connaissance, représentations, mesure au Moyen Âge*, Turnhout: Brepols, 2013.

21 See J.B. Russell, *Inventing the Flat Earth: Columbus and Modern Historians*, New York: Praeger, 1991.

22 P. Freedman, 'Locating the Exotic', in J. Weiss and S. Salih (eds), *Locating the Middle Ages: The Space and Places of Medieval Culture*, London: King's College London, Centre for Late Antique and Medieval Studies, 2012, 23.

23 Gervase of Tilbury, *Otia Imperialia: Recreation for an Emperor*, ed. and transl. by S.E. Banks and J.W. Binns, Oxford: Clarendon Press, 2002, 187–9.

24 Quoted in J.R.S. Phillips, *The Medieval Expansion of Europe*, 2nd edn, Oxford: Clarendon Press, 1998, 184.

25 R. Bartlett, *The Making of Europe: Conquest, Colonization and Cultural Change, 950–1350*, London, New York: Allen Lane, 1993.

26 M. Tamm, 'A New World into Old Words: Eastern Baltic Region and the Cultural Geography of Medieval Europe', in A.V. Murray (ed.), *The Clash of Cultures on the Medieval Baltic Frontier*, Farnham: Ashgate, 2009, 11–35.

27 P. Gautier Dalché, 'Maps, Travel and Exploration in the Middle Ages: Some Reflections about Anachronism', *The Historical Review/La Revue Historique* 12, 2015, 148.

28 Kleinschmidt, *Understanding the Middle Ages*, 61.

29 See, e.g., B.M. Bedos-Rezak and D. Iogna-Prat (eds), *L'individu au Moyen Âge. Individuation et individualisation avant la modernité*, Paris: Aubier, 2005. See also Christina Lutter's chapter in this volume.

30 M. Bourin (ed.), *Genèse médiévale de l'anthroponymie moderne: études d'anthroponymie médiévale*, Tours: Université François Rabelais, 1989.

31 J. Baschet, *Corps et âmes. Une histoire de la personne au Moyen Age*, Paris: Flammarion, 2016, 22.

32 J.-C. Schmitt, *The Conversion of Herman the Jew. Autobiography, History, and Fiction in the Twelfth Century*, Philadelphia, PA: University of Pennsylvania Press, 2010.

33 K. Whittington, *Body-Worlds: Opicinus de Canistris and the Medieval Cartographic Imagi-nation*, Toronto: Pontifical Institute of Mediaeval Studies, 2014; S. Piron, *Dialectique du monstre. Enquête sur Opicino de Canistris*, Brussels: Zones sensibles, 2015.

34 See P. Biller and A.J. Minnis (eds), *Handling Sin: Confession in the Middle Ages*, Suffolk: York Medieval Press, 1998; A. Firey (ed.), *A New History of Penance*, Leyden: Brill, 2008.

35 See P. Michaud-Quantin, *Sommes casuistique et manuels de confessions du XIIe au XIVe siècle*, Louvain: Lauwelaerts, 1961; L. Boyle, '*Summa confessorum*', in *Les genres littéraires dans les sources théologiques et philosophiques médiévales*, Louvain-la-Neuve: Publications de l'Institut d'Etudes médiévales, 1982, 227–37.

36 J. Bossy, 'Moral Arithmetic: Seven Sins into Ten Commandments', in E. Leites (ed.), *Conscience and Casuistry in Early Modern Europe*, Cambridge: Cambridge University Press, 1988, 214–34.

37 Quoted in G. Constable, *Three Studies in Medieval Religious and Social Thought*, Cambridge: Cambridge University Press, 1995, 326.

38 O. Limor, 'Christians and Jews', in M. Rubin and W. Simons (eds), *The Cambridge History of Christianity*, vol. 4, Cambridge: Cambridge University Press, 2009, 137.

39 G.G. Merlo, 'Christian Experiences of Religious Non-Conformism', in J. Arnold (ed.), *The Oxford Handbook of Medieval Christianity*, Oxford: Oxford University Press, 2014, 440.

40 M. Zerner (ed.), *Inventer l'hérésie? Discours polémiques et pouvoirs avant l'Inquisition*, Nice: Z'editions, 1998.

41 B.A. Catlos, *Muslims of Medieval Latin Christendom, c.1050–1614*, Cambridge: Cambridge University Press, 2015.

42 D. Nirenberg, 'Christendom and Islam', in *The Cambridge History of Christianity*, vol. 4, 151.

43 S. Lipton, 'Christianity and Its Others: Jews, Muslims, and Pagans', in *The Oxford Handbook of Medieval Christianity*, 424.

44 H. Janson, 'What Made the Pagans Pagans', in R. Simek and J. Meurer (eds), *Scandinavia and Christian Europe in the Middle Ages*, Bonn: Handdruckerei der Universität Bonn, 2003, 250–6.

45 M. Mollat, *The Poor in the Middle Ages: An Essay in Social History*, New Haven, CT: Yale University Press, 1986.

46 J. Rossiaud, *Medieval Prostitution*, Oxford and New York: Blackwell, 1988.

47 Quoted in J. Le Goff, *Your Money or Your Life: Economy and Religion in the Middle Ages*, New York: Zone Books, 1988, 40–1.

48 R.I. Moore, *The Formation of a Persecuting Society: Power and Deviance in Western Europe, 950–1250*, Oxford and New York: Blackwell, 1987.

49 See M. Tamm, 'Naissance de la persécution sémiotique: la création des signes distinctifs des minorités sociales et religieuses dans l'Occident médiéval (XIIIe–XIVe siècles)', in J. Albuquerque Carreiras, G. Rossi Vairo, K. Toomaspoeg (eds), *Através do olhar do Outro: Reflexões acerca da sociedade medieval europeia (séculos XII–XV)*, Tomar: Instituto Politécnico de Tomar, 2018, 57–78.

50 See, e.g., D. Sansy, 'Marquer la différence: L'imposition de la rouelle aux XIIIe et XIVe siècles', *Médiévales* 41, 2001, 15–36; I.M. Resnick, *Marks of Distinction: Christian Perceptions of Jews in the High Middle Ages*, Washington DC: The Catholic University of America Press, 2012; J. Tolan, 'The First Imposition of a Badge on European Jews: The English Royal Mandate of 1218', in D. Pratt, J. Hoover, J. Davies, J. Chesworth (eds), *The Character of Christian-Muslim Encounter: Essays in Honour of David Thomas*, Leyden: Brill, 2015, 145–66.

51 D.O. Hughes, 'Distinguishing Signs: Ear-Rings, Jews, and Franciscan Rhetoric in the Italian Renaissance City', *Past and Present* 112, 1986, 3–59.

52 See J.H. Arnold, *Inquisition and Power: Catharism and the Confessing Subject in Medieval Languedoc*, Philadelphia, PA: University of Pennsylvania Press, 2001, 66–71; T. Scharff, 'Die Inquisitoren und die Macht der Zeichen: Symbolische Kommunikation in der Praxis der mittelalterlichen dominikanischen Inquisition', in *Praedicatores, Inquisitores I: The Dominicans and the Mediaeval Inquisition*, Rome: Istituto Storico Domenicano, 2004, 111–43.

53 B. Geremek, 'The Marginal Man', in J. Le Goff (ed.), *The Medieval World*, London: Parkgate Books, 1997, 378.

54 B.M. Bedos-Rezak, 'Semiotic Anthropology: The Twelfth-Century Approach', in T.F.X. Noble and J. Van Engen (eds), *European Transformations: The Long Twelfth Century*, Notre Dame, IN: University of Notre Dame Press, 2012, 426–67.

55 M. Lauwers, *La naissance du cimetière. Lieux sacrés et terre des morts dans l'Occident médiéval*, Paris: Aubier, 2005.

56 J. Chiffoleau, *La comptabilité de l'au-delà. Les hommes, la mort et la religion dans la région d'Avignon à la fin du Moyen Age*, Rome: Ecole française de Rome, 1980.

57 T. Lentes, 'Counting Piety in the Late Middle Ages', in B. Jussen (ed.), *Ordering Medieval Society: Perspectives on Intellectual and Practical Modes of Shaping Social Relations*, Philadelphia, PA: University of Pennsylvania Press, 2001, 55–91.

58 P. Geary, 'Mémoire', in J. Le Goff and J.-C. Schmitt (eds), *Dictionnaire raisonné de l'Occident médiéval*, Paris: Fayard, 1999, 684–98.

59 D.L. D'Avray, *Medieval Religious Rationalities: A Weberian Analysis*, Cambridge: Cambridge University Press, 2010, 35.

60 G. Strenga, 'Remembering the Dead: Collective *Memoria* in Late Medieval Livonia', PhD dissertation, Queen Mary, University of London, 2013.

61 C.W. Bynum, *The Resurrection of the Body in Western Christianity, 200–1336*, New York: Columbia University Press, 1995.

62 J. Le Goff, *The Birth of Purgatory*, Chicago, IL and London: University of Chicago Press, 1984. See also G. Cuchet (ed.), *Le Purgatoire. Fortune historique et historiographique d'un dogme*, Paris: Éditions de l'EHESS, 2012.

63 Baschet, *Corps et âmes*, 176.

64 See J. Baschet, *Les justices de l'au-delà. Les représentations de l'enfer en France et en Italie (XIIe–XVe siècle)*, Rome: École française de Rome, 1993.

65 See J. Baschet, *Le Sein du père. Abraham et la paternité dans l'Occident médiéval*, Paris: Gallimard, 2000.

66 See L. Marshall, 'Purgatory in the Medieval Imagination: The Earliest Images', in G. Kratzmann, *Imagination, Books and Community in Medieval Europe*, South Yarra: MacMillan Art Publishing, 2009, 213–19.

8

CONCEIVING OF MEDIEVAL IDENTITIES

Christina Lutter

'Identity/Identities', used in the singular or plural, has over the last decades developed into a key concept in many fields of the humanities, social sciences, and cultural studies. In the wake of the cultural turn it has also become successful in the academic discipline of history. By now, inquiries into the ways people perceive of themselves and are seen by others, into their forms of attachment to and identification with a wide range of social groups, have become abundant in interdisciplinary medieval and early modern studies committed to the paradigm of cultural history.[1]

Key categories for discussing present-day identities are, among others, gender, class, ethnicity, and religion. Historians working on pre-modern times have adopted and adapted these categories for their specific inquiries into the past. Yet, they have also complemented them with further categories referring to identity markers conveyed by source material of the specific times and geographical areas under scrutiny. Hence, religious and urban identities, ethnic, regional, and territorial identities, and noble identities and their various figurations (such as family, dynasty, and genealogy) have been discussed in a large number of case studies. More recently, this trend has spread to comparative studies, originally concentrating on Europe, but increasingly also moving beyond it. What is more, cultural and social historians have also critically reflected upon the category itself and refined their methodological approaches to identity formations.

In this chapter I will sketch out some of the thematic fields in medieval history that have been, since the 1990s, increasingly used as important frames for exploring identities. They shall be introduced against the background of recent theoretical and methodological debates in cultural history and their interdisciplinary legacies (e.g. from cultural anthropology, sociology, or cultural studies). Identity and related concepts such as community, otherness, and diversity, in turn, are closely connected to thematic and conceptual issues discussed in other chapters of this volume, for instance those on symbolic communication, cultural encounters, and translations. Significant links will thus be highlighted.

A strategic concept

Identities in the past and present can be understood as articulating relations between persons and social groups. It is helpful to understand identities less in terms of something that people 'have' than as relational modes of being in the world and making sense of it. Identities result from complex and open-ended interactions between personal and social forces.[2] They are constantly constructed within a variety of cognitive and cultural processes through which individuals identify with others and with specific ideas, or oppose them. Such series of identifications and distinctions work by means of cultural representations.[3] They are culturally produced to make sense of complex worlds. Belonging and 'otherness' are symbolically marked and classified. Symbolic markers in turn have concrete effects on social life. Classifications define inclusion and exclusion. They provide frames for identification and strategies of distinction. Culturally produced ideas of belonging and 'otherness' are deeply embedded in power relations and interact with social hierarchies. Whatever different components identities are made up from, they are not fixed, but often ambivalent and contested, as I will show in the following sections.

Identity is also a theoretically contested term. Already in the 1990s Stuart Hall diagnosed a 'discursive explosion' around the concept in the wake of a series of global crises around the millennium.[4] Many critics have addressed the vague and unsystematic uses of the term. Others, by contrast, have pointed to the tendency of the concept of identity to convey an essentialist understanding of a 'core' of the self or a specific group. If the term identity as such seems to lend itself to perceptions of what has been called 'bounded groupness', and if this, in turn, conveys the image of clear-cut oppositions in terms of a binary logic (identity vs. difference; individual vs. collective; in-group vs. out-group; inclusion vs. exclusion), should we perhaps give up on concept altogether to avoid running into the dangers of reifying exactly those master-narratives we want to overcome?[5] Or should we strive for terminological alternatives to conceive of the complex and contingent nature of human life, of which all constructions of identity try to make sense? However, others argue that just abolishing the term completely would not solve but only shift the problem; nor would it help to answer the question 'Who am I?' that after all addresses one of the key dimensions of human being.[6]

Constant debate has led to re-thinking the potential and the limits of the 'loaded' concept identity and to the development of a more differentiated set of 'lower-threshold' terms (such as identification, belonging, togetherness) to approach the multidimensional quality of identities. They are part of a terminological toolbox designed to address 'identity' and its dimensions in more nuanced ways and also to strategically bridge traditional binaries. In addition, scholars in the field of cultural anthropology and cultural studies have developed and refined relational concepts such as 'alterity', 'otherness', or 'diversity' to highlight the plurality of identity dimensions both in individual persons and in their social environments. In these conceptions, 'identity' always addresses both personal and social aspects, locates the self in a complex web of social relations, and at the same time includes belonging and not-belonging. Importantly, all these approaches stress the contextual specificity of identities.[7]

Many historical studies have substantiated these epistemological claims with evidence from a large variety of time periods and geographical regions. Perhaps even more importantly, these studies have shown that the contextual specificity of identity constructions also implies their historicity: identities are constructed within historical processes and thus change over time. Although some constructions have become so successful that they may seem almost immutable (e.g. gender roles), they have constantly been produced, negotiated, sometimes affirmed or adapted, and sometimes challenged, changed, or dismissed.[8]

When was 'the individual' born?

After what has been laid out so far, this section's heading may seem odd at first glance. Is it possible to imagine any historical setting where human beings would have lived without a sense of themselves?[9] However, a considerable part of earlier historiography that addressed processes of identity formation was influenced by the idea of a rather linear 'history of the individual', whose birth the nineteenth-century historian Jacob Burckhardt famously located in the Renaissance. It was subsequently defined as a cornerstone of modernity and developed into a long-lasting master narrative of the origins and progressive development of a 'modern' rational and independent 'individual' set against its allegedly 'archaic' medieval counterpart. Renaissance utterances of self-assessment and self-reflection were read as a novel state of mind opposed to medieval mentalities characterized rather in terms of group membership within hierarchically organized social strata. Hence, communal and personal interests were often conceived of along a timeline from medieval to modern, either positively in terms of 'emancipation' towards conscious individuality, or negatively in terms of 'alienation' from community life as two poles of a spectrum rather than as interrelated frames of reference.[10]

Subsequently, historians have critically reflected upon those master-narratives, pushing the date of the 'discovery' of human individuality ever further back into the past, most often to the eleventh and twelfth centuries.[11] But also early medieval texts, though fewer in number, show no lack in addressing the self. Christian theological reasoning, based on the Bible as an outstanding 'repertoire of identification', provides a wide range of powerful narratives and imagery as resources for religious, but also ethnic or gendered identity formation. Ancient traditions served medieval authors throughout the centuries as models for introspection and reflection on the self.[12] Moreover, the reciprocity of the personal and the communal is deeply embedded in Christian theology. On the one hand, people expected to stand before the last judgement on their own and not as part of a community. On the other hand, paradise was conceived of as the community of all saints; coenobitic community life – ideally secluded from the world outside – served as its prefiguration, while numerous individual saints were used as exemplary role models and addressed as intercessors for each individual soul.[13]

The work of St Augustine (d. 430) and Gregory the Great (d. 604) immensely influenced further understanding of the individual conscience as the site of moral choice, along with confession and penance as key conditions of salvation.[14] Early medieval monastic regulations both highlighted community-based aspects of love and fraternity (most prominently St Augustine's *praecepta*) and stressed personal growth in virtue by means of obedience and discipline (above all the rule of St Benedict, d. 547). Hence, techniques of self-scrutiny and self-control became central dimensions of religious life. They addressed the self as a mind–body unit and were developed in a framework of regular spiritual, above all liturgical, practice and in personal interactions that were simultaneously directed at social control.[15]

More recently, historians critically 'revisiting the individual' have challenged the concept of 'the individual' as such on a more fundamental level and have taken alternative routes to learn more about historical perceptions of the self in pre-modern as well as modern times.[16] Today, there is a broad consensus that, throughout the Middle Ages, a large number of articulations of personhood, including conscious self-reflections, can be found in a wide range of sources. They make clear that medieval people's sense of their selves was not opposed to a sense of belonging to their social environment, but rather shaped through and within it. Thus, it seems more helpful to think of all – including medieval – personhood as an open-ended process constructed in historically specific contexts and embedded within a web of various socio-cultural bonds that are subject to change.

Times of reform – rise of sources

This said, there were certainly times of more fundamental change and more tangible social differentiation than others, accompanied by a heightened awareness of and reflection on such processes. This in turn resulted in a rise of source material that provides us with deeper and more diversified insights into how contemporaries conceived of themselves and of their relations to others. Research on medieval personhood recognized quite early that monastic space was a key site to locate processes of identity construction, above all in times of religious reform that mostly answered to wider societal challenges. The decisive conflicts over supremacy between the Papacy and the German emperors (the so-called 'Investiture Controversy', 1075–1122) triggered ecclesiastical reform, but also a large variety of broader reform movements. Across the continent, they resulted in novel forms of spiritual life and the establishment of new religious orders that made a point of being differentiated against each other, for instance by the colour of their habit, their styles of devotion, more or less strict separation from the world, and various adaptations of existing monastic rules.[17]

Religious houses were centres of teaching and learning. Throughout the Christian Middle Ages monks and nuns practised literacy on a variety of levels and expanded on religious models that were conveyed, for instance, in biblical exegesis or saints' lives. Didactic and edifying literature served the production of 'inward' images for spiritual exercise. Illuminated liturgical books played an important role as visualizing tools for prayer. Collections of examples provided templates for identification with role models; textual 'mirrors' offered complementary devices for introspection. From the twelfth and thirteenth centuries onwards this type of material was produced and copied in increasingly large amounts.[18] Theological treatises originating from reform orders such as Regular Canons and Cistercians, if in distinctive ways, stressed the importance of biblical love for one's neighbour and developed an affective language aimed at personal identification.[19]

Mixed spiritual and secular education

Moreover, pastoral care started to reach out more systematically beyond the monasteries' walls, promoted especially by the Franciscans and Dominicans. Sermons aimed at wider audiences; penance books were designed to implement the precept of the Fourth Lateran Council (1215) to establish confession as a regular spiritual exercise for the laity. This crucial practice for individual self-scrutiny quickly became embedded in the basic forms of community life most medieval people shared.[20] It was anchored on the level of parishes, which formed an organizational network, which, in turn, covered rural and urban space and thus was closely linked to villages and urban structures. Hence, for most people early education and identity formation were situated in the overlapping space between the household they grew up in and the village/parish community that provided for their most basic material and spiritual needs.

Penitential manuals like the one put together by Robert of Flamborough (Yorkshire) as a canon at the royal abbey and school of St Victor near Paris (d. ca 1219–33) conveyed theory-based instruction for the confessor and the formula for confession.[21] Books of hours with prayers for each canonical hour of the day testify to religious instruction in private households. Those belonging to the noble or urban elites were often richly illuminated like the famous 'Beautiful Hours' (*Belles Heures*) commissioned by the French prince John, duke of Berry, in the early fifteenth century. These books were often in the possession of women and used for personal devotion to specific saints – often the Virgin Mary, but also male and female saintly intercessors symbolically related to the owner's family or to her place of birth. The books' illustrations highlight various dimensions of self-representation, for instance clothing and heraldry as status-markers, and thus provide insight into entangled spiritual and secular dimensions of personal identity. The *Belles Heures* include a set of illustrations with typical scenes of everyday life occupations, each representing one of the twelve months and conveying an ethnographically framed albeit idealized image of identity formation.[22]

By the same token, an important part of the new spiritual literature that flourished from the thirteenth century onwards addressed personal as well as community concerns, and it did so in both conceptual and pragmatic ways, integrating monastic education with the pastoral care of lay audiences. Some of these works became very popular and were passed on and adapted over generations in dozens, at times even hundreds of manuscripts. A prominent example is the *Legenda aurea*, the largest collection of saints' lives for pastoral use put together around 1264 by the Italian Dominican and later archbishop of Genoa, Jacobus de Voragine. Another one, the learned allegorical treatise modelled on the example of bees' community life (*Bonum universale de apibus*), was written around the same time by another prolific Dominican, Thomas of Cantimpré in Brabant. Thomas uses a wide range of examples not only to sketch out his vision of both the communal and hierarchical aspects of religious life; he also stretches his allegory to embrace the secular dimensions of social order and typologically define the place of each individual within it.[23]

The work of the Cistercian monk Caesarius of Heisterbach (d. after 1240) near Cologne on the Rhine is an earlier testimony of interactions between spiritual and secular, elite and popular knowledge. His widely spread *Dialogus Miraculorum* ('Dialogue on Miracles') illustrates available patterns of religious and social identification.[24] Working in the first decades of the thirteenth century, this experienced preacher collected a large number of exemplary miracle stories and used them both in his sermons and for his spiritual guide, which is organized as a dialogue between a monastic teacher and a pupil. Caesarius introduces complex issues of moral doctrine and theological anthropology in an explicitly didactic manner. His tales address lived practice and aim at reaching his audience through narrations for affective identification.

Virtues and vices are personified, temptation and salvation presented by means of dramatic scenery:[25] demons lull poor monks to slumber during common prayer and cruelly mock them once they have fallen asleep. Hence, individual temptation is often represented in terms of social interaction in communal space.[26] Likewise, both the Virgin Mary and Christ himself are repeatedly represented in personal interactions with monks and nuns. A monk who used to fall asleep while singing the psalms is woken by Christ Crucified with a punch on the chin so hard that he dies within three days. On another occasion, the Virgin Mary heals a nun from her sinful love towards a cleric with a slap on her face so forceful that she falls unconscious for a while, but is then relieved from temptation. In each of his interpretations, personal motifs are linked to the grade of punishment. Once, when the Virgin relieves a knight with a kiss from longing for his mistress, Caesarius adds a more general comment: 'By this', he explains, 'she simply shows us that she does not abhor us men, but loves us just as dearly as the women'.[27]

Challenging and re-affirming social order

If Caesarius' exemplary tales focus on monastic space, they simultaneously reflect a broad spectrum of medieval life in convergent social spheres – his presentation of the gendered nature of social order that the Virgin easily overcomes is a case in point. Religious reform movements were deeply entangled with societal renewal that challenged traditional models of social order.[28] After all, one of the central goals of reform was a true apostolic life regardless of social distinction. St Paul's famous letter to the Galatians provided reformers with a powerful community model embracing key dimensions of identity, when he says: 'There is neither Jew nor Gentile, neither slave nor free, nor is there male and female, for you are all one in Christ Jesus' (Gal 3:28). Consequently, women and men, though mostly from affluent families, chose a religious community life and understood themselves as 'partners in spirit', even if separated from each other by enclosure.[29]

Such claims seem at odds with other basic conceptions of society explicitly governed by the principle of inequality that were likewise deeply built into medieval Christian thought. The triple model of social estates divided humans into different orders (*ordines*): clerics, knights, and peasants represented the model's main pillars, defined by the basic tasks that they reciprocally had to fulfil for society at large.[30] Novel forms of social organization clearly cut across classical typologies. They included the rise of urban communities, which in turn consisted of a variety of social groups such as merchants or craftspeople organized in new corporate bodies (e.g. confraternities, guilds) or subject to distinct legal regulations, like Jewish communities. The institutional differentiation of places for religious teaching and learning – new orders, but also cathedral schools – was complemented by the emergence of distinct social institutions, above all universities; their members' mobility in turn contributed to the emergence of wider communities of learning.[31]

Generally, an increasing geographical mobility and permeability of social elites was a distinctive feature already of the eleventh and twelfth centuries and resulted in differentiations of and within the nobility. Still, all of the new affiliations were tightly entangled with traditional axes of belonging. Kinship, friendship, and gender continued to play key roles in the organization of individual and institutional community life, but changed within processes of diversification.[32] These changes presented interrelated challenges both to individual persons and to social groups. Consequently, narrative offers for identification increased, as diversified groups achieved their share of economic and political power: historiography and courtly epic conveyed ancient myth and foundational stories; poetry, exemplary tales, and didactic literature addressed new and old, urban and noble elites who competed over meaning among each other. Texts and pictures not only made the past memorable; they also produced and negotiated new visions of it that answered to present and future needs.[33]

Many of these texts were increasingly (sometimes exclusively) written in the regional vernacular instead of Latin, the universal language of elite education to this point. Often, the uses of language overlap in interesting ways that reveal their conscious deployment according to specific needs. For instance, at the early thirteenth-century court of the counts of Toulouse in Southern France, two languages were in practice for different tasks. Comital scribes issued official charters in Latin, while troubadours used Old Occitan for their love lyrics. Yet, as different as the two genres and their uses may seem, they also shared important aspects. Both employed a highly affective vocabulary. The official language of the charters that addressed nobles and high clergy was an 'emotional language of power'.[34]

Love, friendship, and fidelity on the one hand, as well as deceit, enmity, and treason on the other, are key terms in these documents – a common feature of comparable cartulary material in many European regions. They articulate central values of a noble society rooted in landed property and warrior culture, whose members were fundamentally linked by their personal bonds, which were established in complex relations that tied material components (fiefs) to personal aspects (vassalage) of allegiance.[35] The use of this vocabulary in charters and other records contributed to maintaining and affirming these bonds by means of a powerful discourse of politically charged fidelity.

The troubadours of Toulouse, by contrast, drew on the same vocabulary to talk about chivalry and courtly love, to entertain the court and make a living there. Yet, a main message owed to the logic of the genre is that love is bound to fail. As the troubadours in their poems shifted their focus from love and fidelity between the count of Toulouse and his male followers to love between the poets themselves and their lady, this gendered strategy simultaneously empowered them to criticize the counts' reliance on love as a political instrument. Drawing on different registers of interrelated discourses of power and courtly love, poets were thus able to entertain the duke and his courtly entourage while simultaneously questioning the social institution of fidelity as a general frame for noble identity.[36]

Shaping noble identities

A mix of education and entertainment is characteristic of a significant portion of didactic literature, originating both from the ecclesiastic and from the secular sphere. Instruction books, such as 'mirrors' for princes, which were also intended for the lay elites more generally, were increasingly written in the vernaculars and, like courtly epic, performed at many European courts. Like their religious equivalents, these pragmatic guides provided moral instruction that was tightly linked to shaping proper noble behaviour. Training ethically defined courtly virtues aimed at forging and affirming elite identities.[37] An important example is the first epic-length didactic poem in the German vernacular written in 1215/16 by the Italian cleric Thomasin of Zerclaere. Already the personification conveyed in the book's title, *Der Welsche Gast* ('The Italian Guest'), hints at the work's dialogical structure.[38]

Thomasin's personal identity is located in overlapping ecclesiastical, courtly, and urban milieus: his family name (Zerclaere/Cerchiari/Cerclara) points to Cividale in the bilingual North-Italian province of Friuli, with notaries and merchants among his relatives. Besides his proficiency in courtly literature, the work displays broad theological and historical knowledge, which suggests a good education probably at a cathedral school. He most likely wrote his poem at the court of Wolfger (d. 1218), the powerful patriarch of the region's ecclesiastical centre Aquileia. Wolfger had previously been bishop of Bavarian Passau, where his governance was famous for its splendid courtly life and generous patronage. The eminent troubadour Walther von der Vogelweide worked there, as did the unknown author of the *Nibelungenlied*, one of the outstanding European epics, which was probably written in Passau around 1200. Thomasin's elite audience – ladies, clerics, and children, as *Der Welsche Gast* puts it – probably can be found among upwardly mobile *ministeriales*. Particularly in the German-speaking lands, these once legally dependent princely followers had during the twelfth and early thirteenth century risen to become a powerful land-owning nobility. Thomasin's poem can be read as a handbook for this new nobility.[39]

Thomasin constructs an ideal vision of courtly culture governed by noble virtues and courtly behaviour. The guide itself thus contributed to the ministeriales' identity formation as part of an 'imagined community' of courtly nobility distinguished from those lower-status groups from which they themselves originated.[40] Central didactic devices of the poem are its many illustrations, which obviously contributed to its popularity. Text and images are related to mutually support each other's message.[41] However, while the text itself remained rather stable, the many surviving manuscripts also show important transformations of the visual programme over 300 years of reception that convey a shift from symbolic to narrative preferences. Changing images answered to novel needs of changing audiences, above all of mixed elites in urban space.[42]

Negotiating distinction

Dynamics of social mobility and strategies of distinction were constantly responding to each other. Rising complexity was answered with attempts to re-affirm knowledgeable order. The thirteenth to fifteenth centuries saw a great variety of attempts to balance these forces. Many vernacular works composed across the continent, both in prose and in verse, criticized a decline of morals linked to ambition in general and aspirations by lower-status groups in particular. William Langland's (d. ca 1386) *Piers Plowman* is a case in point for English society, as is the sharp wit in the thirteenth-century German songs of the thirteenth-century Neidhart (of Reuenthal), or the story of the exemplary fall of the over-ambitious peasant's son Helmbrecht by Werner the Gardener, which was widely read in Bavaria and Austria.[43] Key visual examples of a 'call to order' include the many representations of the late medieval allegory of the 'Dance of Death' (*Dance Macabre*). Originating from illustrated sermons, early wall paintings of Death personified leading people from all social strata to the grave, irrespective of their standing, have survived from the early fifteenth century onwards, in cities like Paris and Basel as well as in, for instance, the little village church of Hrstovlje in today's Slovenia.[44]

Texts and pictures, material culture, and performative acts can be understood as media that reveal the multiple forms of belonging. Various types of written and pictorial narratives, their symbols, and their modes of communication have become key subjects of interdisciplinary medieval studies when approaching identity constructions.[45] Outstanding literary examples include Giovanni Boccaccio's (d. 1375) 'Decameron', which embraces 100 tales told by individual members of a group of female and male Florentine youth at a time when Black Death struck the city. Comparably, Geoffrey Chaucer (d. 1400) introduced the personal accounts of a group of pilgrims on their way from London to Canterbury as a narrative frame to structure his 'Canterbury Tales'. Both works draw on a large number of sources, ancient and contemporary, theological and secular, stemming from many European traditions. Critically making use of traditional typology, both comment sharply on social differentiation and conflicts between the increasingly heterogeneous and conflicting social groups in their respective environments and, thus, contribute to forging and questioning identities; both also employ the regional vernacular, which together with the tales' anecdotal structure made them enormously popular and contributed to their wide and sustained reception.[46]

The multitude of urban identities

The first century of the period under investigation in this volume was marked by ongoing demographic growth that in turn, notwithstanding substantial regional differences, fuelled urban development across the continent. Although major capitals certainly stand out in population – such as Paris, and later London, the city of Rome with its ancient imperial past, or eminent Italian city-states like Venice, Genoa, and Florence, and their Northern European counterparts in medieval Flanders like Bruges or Ghent – the sheer size of European urban growth between ca. 1050 and ca. 1300 is impressive everywhere. Even a comparatively small region like the Austrian lands saw the emergence of around seventy cities by 1300, with only a handful of additional foundations in the following first 100 years of Habsburg rule. Importantly, however, the largest number of urban dwellers by far lived in small towns with 2,000–5,000 inhabitants, especially outside the Mediterranean area.[47] Market functions and the resulting regional and long-distance business and trade relations were a central feature of urban settlements. Depending on their geographical location, for instance as port cities or located at the crossroads of central land or river routes, migration both from the countryside and from distant places was a distinctive feature of medieval urbanity.[48]

Hence, because diversity was a defining element for towns and cities across the continent, a key common trait of urban milieus was a high degree of internal social heterogeneity, which lends itself particularly well to analysing processes of urban identity-building.[49] Ways of belonging to and in medieval towns and cities were multiple and varied from region to region. Cities were political communities, their actions based on consensus within socio-political and legal elites; yet, urban space embraced various groups related to each other both in hierarchical ways and in terms of more egalitarian cohabitation. Urban development often originated in special privileges bestowed on settlements by rulers (royal, manorial, or episcopal) in return for economic benefits; yet, cities gained various degrees of independence from their lords (relatively high, for instance, in Italy and the German-speaking lands, relatively low in Central Europe). They developed specific forms and symbols of corporate agency and, thus, identities as political bodies.[50]

However, within and beyond urban space, economic, legal, kinship, and religious affiliations overlapped in such complex ways that interdisciplinary urban history has critically revisited the older influential model of urban development that highlighted 'autonomy' and 'unity' as general defining features of urban life in Europe. By contrast, recent studies have collected evidence from legal and economic sources, from documents of practice, as well as from visual and material culture, to portray towns and cities as 'composite units'.[51] By the same token, they underline the variety of bonds between urban communities, for instance confederations like the Hanseatic League, and to their respective hinterlands, as well as between individual actors ranging from merchants with wide-reaching commercial networks to ordinary craftspeople. Thus, both corporate and individual urban identity formations can be conceived of as placed within a matrix of plural encounters and interrelated axes of belonging: family and business networks, place of origin and legal status, personal property, education and occupation, and linguistic and religious affiliations formed the web of bonds providing for the making of situated identities together with forms of inclusion and exclusion.[52]

This complexity notwithstanding, urban space was marked in characteristic ways that show social distinction as well as interaction. Urban topography reveals both physical and social structures represented in a wide range of sources: street and family names – such as Tailor or Smith – explicitly address local or occupational identities; archaeological discoveries and documentary records convey a nuanced picture of medieval forms of living together and articulating belonging. Specifically, urban architecture (city halls, open loggias as meeting places for the urban elite) and religious buildings (churches, chapels, monasteries) were defining markers in cityscapes. They also figured prominently in chronicles and visual representations, for instance as the background of biblical scenes on altarpieces.[53] Neighbourhoods had their distinctive features according to occupational groups, e.g. merchants' houses were located at waterfronts in port cities; wealthy craftspeople like clothiers and goldsmiths had their workshops in affluent quarters; butchers or bakers operated near public marketplaces.

In a detailed description of late medieval Vienna, the humanist writer and later pope Enea Silvio Piccolomini (d. 1464) – his personal career was exemplary for the integration of many aspects of identity typical for the profile of a European clerical intellectual of his time – commented in detail on the city's social topography.[54] On the one hand, he explicitly underlined the multitude of distinctive social spaces – for burghers and nobility, the ducal court and its courtiers, clerics, monks and nuns, the university with its faculties and students from diverse regions, craftspeople, and the lower classes. On the other hand, he also showed how individual representatives of these categories constantly interacted across their boundaries, which resulted not least in various conflicts between burghers, craftspeople, courtiers, and students.

Comparably, the strategically built environment of the Hungarian royal cities Buda and Visegrád shows distinct royal, urban, and ecclesiastic spheres of influence, but also conveys a sense of their interplay. Against the background of his pragmatic urban policies, King Sigismund (d. 1437) used the royal foundation of Franciscan friaries in these two residences in the immediate vicinity of the palace, to establish 'transitional zones'; appropriate in size to assemble larger urban crowds, they served as communication points between Sigismund and the burghers, as places where the king's public representation, for instance during specifically designed liturgies, played a significant role.[55] Such public performances of political power, negotiation, and decision-making as well as religious processions convey an idea of how identities could be created through repeated acts of identification and differentiation. Descriptions of prescribed rituals, but also of the many conflicts that could arise on such occasions, show the multiplicity of groups (e.g. guilds and confraternities, university members and clerics) addressed by and collectively participating in these complex performances. They also underline who was excluded from public representation, for instance Jewish communities and women's religious communities, both of which in other respects played important roles in urban life.[56]

For instance, women's as well as men's monasteries were frequent addressees of documents of practice,[57] such as last wills, that reflect on the range of individual persons' social and affective attachments. Sources from many European regions show women and men in legal transactions that underline the reciprocal nature of an economy that had to both fulfil earthly purposes and meet contemporaries' concerns for their afterlives. Hence, charitable donations show both individual decisions and general mechanisms of negotiating social bonds by exchanging property – among individuals and institutions, spouses and next of kin, but also in-laws and servants of both genders – within urban space and beyond it.[58]

Religious diversity

Yet, religion was not only a central factor of integration but also a crucial dimension of diversity and a key category of exclusion. Recent comparative research has underlined that religious life in Europe was generally much more heterogeneous, both in terms of intra-religious differentiation and in terms of inter-religious encounters, than it would seem at first sight. Diversity within Christianity colluded with the presence of several religious groups in Europe.[59] The variety of intra-Christian and inter-religious differentiation is particularly visible in urban environments, where cohabitation between Christians and Jewish minorities was common across the continent, as well as in borderland regions like the Baltic shore lands, South-Eastern Europe, and the Mediterranean.[60] *Intra*-religious diversification *and* 'othering' (for instance, between Latin Catholic and Greek Orthodox Christianity, which led to the schism of 1054) was deeply entangled with *inter*-religious contact *and* demarcation.

In the European North and East, such contacts included the indigenous religions of Danes, Lithuanians, and Slavs.[61] In the Mediterranean, Jewish, Muslim, and Christian communities lived together in various constellations resulting in a wide range of multiple identity formations. Times of religious coexistence and prosperity for individual people and groups alternated with periods of structural coercion by authorities and conflict between the religious majority and minority groups. In the wake of the Arabo-Islamic conquests, from the seventh century onwards, Jewish and Christian communities under Muslim rule developed distinctive features. Religious minorities had to pay taxes but could otherwise enjoy relative autonomy, as rulers profited from their locally established economic and political weight.[62] In early medieval Iberia, Jewish and Mozarab (as Catholic Christians were called) communities had to adapt to Muslim rule, as did the Greek Orthodox and Catholic populations on the lower Danube and in the Balkans during the late medieval Ottoman conquest.[63] But also other regions, such as medieval Hungary, were for a long time characterized by a high degree of religious diversity: Jewish, Cuman, and Muslim minorities cohabitated with the Christian majority, while from the fourteenth century onwards powerful alliances between the kings, nobility, and Christian religious orders increasingly constructed the country as a 'gate of Christendom'.[64]

Merchant activity was a central dimension of Jewish identity all over Europe. Already in the early tenth century, a singular surviving toll legislation documents the presence of 'Jews and other merchants' in the eastern borderlands of Bavaria; a late tenth-century Byzantine trading privilege to Venice forbade Jewish, Lombard, and Amalfitan tradespeople to travel on Venetian ships. The Cairo Geniza, a huge collection of primarily Jewish manuscript fragments from the Ben Ezra synagogue, includes more than 15,000 records from the eleventh and twelfth century that document the business correspondence of multi-lingual Jewish, Christian, and Muslim merchants, demonstrating their complex regional and trans-regional relations and interactions in the Eastern Mediterranean.[65]

However, the military, political, and economic expansion of Latin Christendom that characterized the period between the eleventh and thirteenth centuries caused major changes. Military expansion brought Iberian al-Andalus and Southern Italy under Latin Christian rule, and after the Crusaders' expeditions to the Holy Land and eventually the conquest of Constantinople in 1204, substantial Muslim, Jewish, and Orthodox Christian populations were dominated by Latin Christian forces.[66] Conceived of as 'Holy Wars', the Crusades were ideologically directed against 'heathens' – the 'other' conceptualized as opposing Christianity. Simultaneously, the papal Catholic Church answered to the increasing variety of intra-Christian religious life with centralizing and homogenizing measures. Categorically defining normative religious behaviour, clerical authorities constructed 'heretics' according to their deviance from these norms. They not only programmatically restricted religious diversity but also systematically persecuted inner-Christian 'heresies' by means of new inquisitional practices, which in turn resulted in the construction of heretical identities that could be sought out and eliminated. By the same token, the Fourth Lateran Council (1215) issued unprecedented legislation aiming at the Jewish population's social segregation.[67]

However, those measures only became effective in specific contextual interplays of political, religious, and social forces. In Southern France, fierce ecclesiastical prosecution of regional Cathar heretical communities joined forces with the French kings' efforts to eventually incorporate the powerful region of Languedoc into the French realm.[68] As elsewhere, religious identity politics were deeply entangled with popular anxieties and political struggles over hegemony and were often supported by local competition between rival elites. In thirteenth-century England, theological and legal measures against the Jewish population were taken up in acts of active hostility against Jewish individuals and extended by narrative constructions, such as tales of ritual murder that were even enacted in popular drama. In the 'Baron's War' of 1264, the raid of the Jewish quarter in London and comparable assaults in other towns were staged as an English victory against foreigners, before King Edward I eventually expelled all Jewish communities from the country in 1290.[69]

In Iberia, Christian rulers tended to offer security and concede a certain degree of religious and communal autonomy to both Jewish and Muslim communities in exchange for economic benefits. Although minorities suffered from the stronger trend towards segregation, were affected by popular violence, and were converted to Christianity as happened elsewhere in Europe, some communities continued to prosper even after the pogroms of 1391, when many Jews were killed or forced to convert.[70] It was only in the framework of the concerted efforts of the 'Catholic Monarchs' (Isabella I of Castile and Ferdinand II of Aragon) to establish royal power on the Iberian Peninsula that the conquest of Muslim Granada and the expulsion of all Iberian Jews and Muslims in 1492 caused a tremendous emigration of these ethno-religious minorities, mostly to Italy, North Africa, and the Ottoman Empire.[71]

Forging political identities in conflict and consensus

The Iberian example shows just how much late medieval political contests over hegemony, centralization, and state building, which operated on a variety of levels, were related to equally complex forms of religious identity politics that evolved around definitions of orthodoxy and heresy. In the course of the fifteenth century, power struggles across the continent were characterized by a wide spectrum of potentially overlapping axes of conflict: religious belief and status differences, language and occupation, origin of birth, and ethnicity were all categories of identification that could become salient in political conflicts.

In England, the religious movement of Lollardy initiated by the Catholic, Oxford University scholar John Wyclif (d. 1384) challenged the Roman Catholic church's authority, especially the privileged status of clerics. Accordingly, Wyclif also advocated the translation of the Bible into the Middle English vernacular.[72] Many representatives of noble and literate elites followed the movement that, although condemned by church authorities, was at first not prosecuted by King Richard II. However, when the Lancasters took over power and needed to make up for their ambiguous dynastic legitimation, religious orthodoxy and loyalty to the crown were integrated into a grand narrative promoted by a powerful alliance between ecclesiastic and royal authority. This reciprocal construction of devotion to church and crown deeply affected people's personal religious and political identities; being a good Christian was equated with being a loyal subject, while religious deviance was interpreted as political infidelity.[73]

In Bohemia, where religious reform circles at the Prague University around Jan Hus (d. 1415) also built upon Wyclif's ideas, the situation was even more complex. Although a kingdom since the twelfth century, Bohemia was also part of the Holy Roman Empire. From the mid-fourteenth century onwards, kings from the Bohemian dynasty of Luxembourg recurrently held the position of German emperors. In addition, earlier rulers had already fostered German migration to Bohemia, resulting in a linguistically mixed and socially differentiated population, especially in Bohemian cities. When Jan Hus and his followers made their claims for a reform based on the Bible and opposed to clerical structures, and like the Lollards advocated a translation of the foundational text into the Czech vernacular as the language accessible to all, including common people, several latent conflicts broke out.[74] They convey a picture of the many dimensions of identity potentially at stake in late medieval conflicts. The Bohemian king and German emperor Sigismund joined forces with the ecclesiastical authorities represented by the Council of Constance (1414–18), who invited Hus to defend his theses. However, despite being given guarantees for safe-conduct, he was eventually convicted of heresy and burnt at the stake. The subsequent upheavals in Bohemia were supported by broad alliances of Czech-speaking landed nobility and common people. The emperor's side framed the following military expeditions in terms of crusades; Hussite factions, who in the course of events turned against each other, conceived of them in terms of holy war.[75] The decade-long religious wars politically affected the neighbouring territories of Saxony, Brandenburg, Poland, Hungary, and the Austrian lands. Internal alliances cut across noble, urban, and rural milieus.

Importantly, alongside religious claims, language and social distinction emerged as crucial elements that warfare then transformed into a divide between Bohemia's Czech- and German-speaking populations. However, some of the tropes drawn upon in these identity constructions were considerably older. Already at the beginning of the fourteenth century, while German flourished at the royal court in Prague, Czech vernacular literature like the so-called Dalimil chronicle advanced anti-German resentment together with the promotion of a Czech identity.[76] But it was only the specific conjunction with religiously motivated zeal and violence during the Hussite wars that made these elements so salient that they were able to temporarily amalgamate into a constellation that historical research interpreted as an early example of 'national' sentiment.[77]

In a broader European perspective, loaded 'national' interpretations remained, during the fifteenth century, the exception rather than the rule. Even the eminent example of Joan of Arc cannot easily be narrowed down to a 'national' movement. It is rather an instance of how complex dynastic and territorial conflicts like those fought out in the Hundred Years' War, interwoven with religious reform and crusade ideology, shaped a powerful role model of a holy warrior that bundled a whole range of identity dimensions (gender, social status and upward mobility, secular and spiritual virtues). It thus had enormous popular response, but only gradually was it transformed into a national myth.[78] Late medieval power struggles clearly show how the dynamics of conflict and violence, threat and anxiety raised awareness of specific aspects of belonging and contributed to forging new, highly concentrated identity formations. Simultaneously, they forged an equally large sensitivity to those 'others' who did not match the criteria of identification that power holders and parties in conflict were able to construct as meaningful in the course of events.

However, during the same period, on both the local and regional levels (villages, towns) as well as on the level of larger political entities (kingdoms, countries), negotiation and the distribution of power continued to follow entangled hierarchical *and* consensual principles, while new formal mechanisms of decision-making were established and institutionally moulded.[79] On all political levels councils, assemblies, and election procedures that originated in personal bonds between peers, or between rulers and their close entourage, became increasingly formalized means to balance political participation. The groups that were qualified to take part in these processes, and therefore also contributed to the making of political identities, varied widely across the continent according to legal, social, and economic structures. In Poland and Hungary all nobles, irrespective of their individual background, at least theoretically enjoyed the same legal status within the politically active community that together with the king represented those countries. In many European regions, urban communities were part of the assemblies of the estate representatives that met regularly. Even peasants might enjoy important political representation, as they did in late medieval Dalmatia or in the valleys of the Swiss confederation.

Techniques of shared decision-making included a wide range of symbolic strategies of inclusion and exclusion that had gradually been developed over centuries. Some of them drew on ancient laws and customs; others on the mythical origins of the 'communities under construction', adapting ancient narratives and symbols to specific contemporary needs. When, after the Habsburg King Albrecht's death (1439), two powerful dynastic parties (Habsburg, Jagiełło) competed over succession in Hungary, a long controversy ensued over the coronation ritual and the question of which of the candidates held possession of the valid royal insignia and thus qualified as the legitimate king. The struggle involved the spectacular theft of the Holy Crown from the treasury vault in the royal castle of Visegrád, a theft which the widowed queen Elisabeth orchestrated for the coronation of her then as-yet-unborn son Ladislaus. Her court lady and confidant Helene Kottanner not only managed to carry out this amazing task, and participated prominently in the new-born baby's coronation, but also wrote an equally impressive report about her adventure.[80]

Eventually, the majority of the Hungarian magnates decided for the Polish candidate Władisław, who was crowned a short time later with another part of the insignia. However, political necessity ultimately ruled out considerations of both dynastic and symbolic politics: as Hungary was seriously threatened by Ottoman forces, they chose the candidate who was more promising as a military leader. The magnates argued, 'the crowning of kings is always dependent on the will of the kingdom's inhabitants, in whose consent both the effectiveness and the force of the crown reside'.[81] Although a strong argument for community-based action, the decision in the end had the opposite effect. It divided the politically relevant forces and led to long and devastating military conflicts between the two factions in the face of the Ottoman menace, during which both Queen Elisabeth and Władisław Jagiełło died. Hence, neither dynastic, tradition-oriented, nobility-based, nor 'proto-national' identity factors played out alone. In the long run, mixed strategies of symbolic identification and pragmatically oriented agency, drawing on a wide repertoire of political, religious, ethnic, and social arguments, had to converge to create successful political communities.

This often-precarious ratio between symbolic identity politics and the pragmatism necessary to do justice to the multiplicity of interests and affiliations was not just a matter of 'grand politics'. Helene Kottaner's 'ego-document' not least opens another window to better understand how medieval mechanisms of political identity-building and personal forms of identification could converge. Her testimony is an excellent case in point to show how individual interests and concern for larger societal causes interacted. Her loyalties were split between the royal family and her own next of kin. Her sorrows and anxieties, deeply embedded in her personal faith, addressed the common political good and the future of the Habsburg dynasty as well as her own material and immaterial rewards, both for her earthly and her eternal life. Not least, the memory of her active participation in crucial political decisions is a key motif of the text: Helene articulates her personal merits using an explicit 'I'. There is no doubt that she had a pronounced sense of herself as a member of a social elite, as a loyal servant to her mistress and to the crown, as a responsible caregiver for both her own and the Queen's children, and as a resolutely acting woman embedded in the specific circumstances of her social background and the political exigencies of the day.

This final example is representative for the dynamics and complexity that characterized the period under scrutiny in this volume. As with many other more or less well-documented cases, it helps us to understand some crucial aspects of the uses of a *strategic concept* of identity for medieval studies, as introduced at the beginning of this chapter: whenever medieval sources allow for insights into identity formations, they emerge as *relational, multidimensional,* and *contextually specific.* They are *relational* in conveying a sense of personhood and people's individual selves as not opposed to a sense of belonging to communities, but as deeply influenced by visions and practices of community. They are *multidimensional* because contemporary sources reveal a large variety of aspects of identification and distinction that include dimensions of both belonging and not-belonging which are not fixed, but fluid and often contested. They are *contextually specific* as their formations are embedded in power relations and constructed by means of social hierarchies, which, in turn, are culturally produced within historical processes and subject to change. During the period presented in this volume ever-growing bodies of sources provide insight into mixed strategies of symbolic identification and distinction and the variety of their media and modes of communication. Late medieval identity formations are located within a dense matrix of interrelated axes of belonging and conflict. Across the continent explicit identity politics and social pragmatics become visible as two sides of the same coin, resulting in shifting patterns of inclusion and exclusion. If 'identity' remains a 'loaded concept', a term to handle with care, its cautious use with an eye on this historical multidimensionality and specificity can help to contribute to better understanding the many ways of belonging in past societies and their changes over time.

Notes

1 Cf. editors' Introduction on cultural history as a paradigmatic way to conceive of the past and on the volume's broader conception of 'identity' embraced by the title of Part 1, 'Shaping Western identities'. This contribution is based on considerations developed within the Special Research Programme (SFB) 42 VISCOM *Visions of Community: Comparative Approaches to Ethnicity, Region and Empire in Christianity, Islam and Buddhism (400–1600 ce)*, Project 4206 *Social and Cultural Communities in High and Late Medieval Central Europe* (PI: Ch. Lutter), 2011–19, funded by the Austrian Science Fund (FWF). Special thanks for feedback and comments to Philippe Buc, Julia Burkhardt, Andre Gingrich, Jonathan Lyon, Walter Pohl, and Barbara Rosenwein.

2 Recent conceptual work includes G. Baumann and A. Gingrich (eds), *Grammars of Identity, Alterity: A Structural Approach*, Oxford/New York: Berghahn, 2004, for a socio-anthropological approach; R. Jenkins, *Social Identity*, New York: Routledge, 2008, for a sociological conceptualization; W. Pohl, 'Introduction – Strategies of Identification: A Methodological Profile', in W. Pohl and G. Heydemann, *Strategies of Identification. Ethnicity and Religion in Early Medieval Europe*, Turnhout: Brepols, 2013, for a medieval historian's perspective; E. Hovden, Ch. Lutter, and W. Pohl (eds), *Meanings of Community across Eurasia* (Visions of Community, vol. 1), Leiden: Brill, 2016, for a comparative approach.

3 S. Hall, *Representation: Cultural Representations and Signifying Practices*, London: Sage, 1997; L. Hunt, *New Cultural History*, Oakland, CA: University of California Press, 1989; R. Chartier, *Cultural History between Practices and Representations*, Cambridge: Cambridge University Press, 1993.

4 S. Hall, 'Who Needs Identity', in S. Hall and P. Du Gay (eds), *Questions of Cultural Identity*, London/Thousand Oaks, CA: Sage, 1996, 1–17.

5 The phrase 'bounded groupness' was coined by R. Brubaker and F. Cooper, 'Beyond Identity', *Theory and Society* 29, 2000, 1–47, who want to give up on the concept of 'identity'. For a critique of binary logic, but holding on to a – yet more nuanced – notion of identity, cf. L. Grossberg, 'Identity and Cultural Studies: Is That All There Is?', in Hall and Du Gay, *Questions of Cultural Identity*, 87–107.

6 Hall, 'Who Needs Identity'; A. Gingrich, 'Identity', in F. Keff, E.-M. Knoll and Id., *Lexikon der Globalisierung*, Bielefeld: transcript, 2009, 144.

7 Overview in Baumann and Gingrich, *Grammars of Identity*.

8 Pohl, 'Strategies of Identification', 4f.

9 B. Rosenwein, 'Y'avait-il un moi au moyen-age?', *Revue historique* 633, 2005,1, 31–52.

10 Discussions of the topic are abundant; methodologically oriented overviews include W. Pohl, 'Introduction. Ego Trouble?', in R. Corradini et al. (eds), *Ego Trouble: Authors and Their Identities in the Early Middle Ages*, Vienna: Verlag der ÖAW, 2010, 9–22, B.-M. Bedos-Rezak and D. Iogna-Prat (eds), *L'individu au moyen âge. Individuation et individualisation avant la modernité*, Paris: Aubier-Flammarion, 2005; F.-J. Arlinghaus (ed.), *Forms of Individuality and Literacy in the Medieval and Early Modern Periods*, Turnhout: Brepols, 2015.

11 The classic study is C. Morris, *The Discovery of Individual, 1050–1200*, Toronto: University of Toronto Press, 1972; for a systematic bibliography see Pohl, 'Ego Trouble?'.

12 Pohl, 'Ego Trouble?', esp. at 17f; Ibid., 'Strategies of Identification', the quote at 32.

13 G. Klaniczay, 'Using Saints: Intercession, Healing, Sanctity', *The Oxford Handbook of Medieval Christianity,* 2014, c. 13, 217–37; A. Vauchez, *Sainthood in the Later Middle Ages,* trans. J. Birrell, Cambridge: Cambridge University Press, 1997, 4; K. Schreiner, *Gemeinsam leben: Spiritualität, Lebens- und Verfassungsformen klösterlicher Gemeinschaften in Kirche und Gesellschaft des Mittelalters,* ed. by M. Breitenstein and G. Melville, Berlin: LIT, 2013.

14 B. Stock, *After Augustine: The Meditative Reader and the Text,* Philadelphia, PA: University of Pennsylvania Press, 2010; C. Straw, *Gregory the Great: Perfection in Imperfection,* Oakland, CA: University of California Press, 1991; M. Breitenstein, 'Die Verfügbarkeit der Transzendenz: Das Gewissen der Mönche als Heilsgarant', in: G. Melville, B. Schneidmüller, and St. Weinfurter (eds), *Innovation durch Deuten und Gestalten. Klöster im Mittelalter zwischen Jenseits und Welt,* Regensburg: Schnell + Steiner, 2014, 37–56.

15 G. Melville, *World of Medieval Monasticism: Its History and Form of Life,* Collegeville, PA: Cistercian Publications, 2016; on the self as a mind–body unit cf. C.W. Bynum, *Christian Materiality: An Essay on Religion in Late Medieval Europe,* New York: Zone Books, 2011; D. Iogna-Prat, 'Édification personelle et construction ecclésiale', in Ibid. and Bedos-Rezak, *L'individu au Moyen Age,* 247–70.

16 C.W. Bynum, 'Did the Twelfth Century Discover the Individual?', in Ead., *Jesus as Mother: Studies in the Spirituality of the High Middle Ages,* Berkeley, CA: University of California Press, 1982, 82–109; Ead. and S.R. Kramer, 'Revisiting the Twelfth-Century Individual: The Inner Self and the Christian Community', in G. Melville and M. Schürer (eds), *Das Eigene und das Ganze. Zum Individuellen im mittelalterlichen Religiosentum* (Vita regularis 16), Münster: LIT, 2002; R. Fulton and B.W. Holsinger (eds), *History in the Comic Mode: Medieval Communities and the Matter of Person,* New York: Columbia University Press, 2007.

17 G. Constable, 'Religious Communities, 1024–1215', in D. Luscombe and J. Riley-Smith (eds), *The New Cambridge Medieval History,* Cambridge et al.: Cambridge University Press, 2004, 335–67; S. Vanderputten (ed.), *Reform, Conflict, and the Shaping of Corporate Identities: Collected Studies on Benedictine Monasticism, 1050–1150* (Vita regularis 12), Vienna: LIT, 2013.

18 C. Bremond et al., *L'"Exemplum"* (Typologie des sources du moyen âge occidental 40), Turnhout: Brepols, 1996; N. Largier: 'The Art of Prayer: Conversions of Interiority and Exteriority in Medieval Contemplative Practice', in R. Campe and J. Weber (eds), *Rethinking Emotion: Interiority and Exteriority in Premodern, Modern, and Contemporary Thought,* Berlin/Boston, MA: De Gruyter, 2014, 58–71; J. Mews (ed.), *Listen, Daughter: The Speculum Virginum and the Formation of Religious Women in the Middle Ages,* New York: Palgrave, 2001, 159–79.

19 C. Bynum, *Jesus as Mother: Studies in the Spirituality of the High Middle Ages,* Oakland, CA: University of California Press, 1984; D. Boquet, *L'ordre de l'affect au Moyen Âge. Autour de l'anthropolgie affective d'Aelred de Rievaulx,* Caen: Brepols, 2005; B.P. McGuire, *Friendship and Community. The Monastic Experience, 350–1250,* Ithaca, NY: Cornell University Press, 2nd edn, 2010.

20 C. Muessig (ed.), *Preacher, Sermon and Audience in the Middle Ages,* Leiden: Brill, 2002; A. Filey (ed.), *A New History of Penance,* Leiden: Brill, 2008.

21 Cf. M. Rubin, 'Identities', in R. Horrox and W.M. Ormrod (eds), *A Social History of England: 1200–1500,* Cambridge: Cambridge University Press, 2006, 383–412, at 385.

22 M. Camille, 'The *"Très Riches Heures"*. An Illuminated Manuscript in the Age of Mechanical Reproduction', *Critical Inquiry* 17, 1990, 72–107; K.M. Ashley, 'Creating Family Identity in Books of Hours', *Journal of Medieval and Early Modern Studies* 1, 2002, 145–65.

23 J. de Voragine, *The Golden Legend: Readings on the Saints*, trans. by W.G. Ryan, with an introduction by E. Duffy, Princeton, NJ: Princeton University Press, 2012; J. Burkhardt, 'Predigerbrüder im Bienenstock des Herrn. Dominikanische Identitäten im "Bienenbuch" des Thomas von Cantimpré', in S. von Heusinger et al. (eds), *Die deutschen Dominikaner und Dominikanerinnen im Mittelalter* (Quellen und Forschungen zur Geschichte des Dominikanerordens 21), Berlin, Boston, MA: De Gruyter, 2016, 183–206.

24 *Caesarius of Heisterbach, Dialogus miraculorum/Dialog über die Wunder*, ed. and transl. N. Nösges and H. Schneider (Fontes Christiani 86/1–5), Turnhout: Brepols, 2009; V. Smirnova et al. (eds), *The Art of Cistercian Persuasion in the Middle Ages and Beyond: Caesarius of Heisterbach's Dialogue on Miracles and Its Reception*, Leiden: Brill 2015; S. Vanderputten (ed.), *Understanding Monastic Practices of Oral Communication (Western Europe, Tenth–Thirteenth Centuries)*, Turnhout: Brepols, 2011.

25 R. Newhauser, *The Treatise on Vices and Virtues in Latin and the Vernacular* (Typologie des sources du moyen âge occidental 68), Turnhout: Brepols, 1993; Ch. Flüeler and M. Rode, *Laster im Mittelalter/Vices in the Middle Ages* (Scrinium Friburgense 23), Berlin et al.: De Gruyter 2009.

26 Ch. Lutter, 'Social Groups, Personal Relations, and the Making of Communities in Medieval vita monastica', in J. Rogge (ed.), *Making Sense as a Cultural Practice: Historical Perspectives*, Bielefeld: Transcript, 2013, 45–61.

27 *Dialogus miraculorum*, vol. II, c. 4, 32–8, 756–65; the quote in vol. III, c. 7,33, 1393–7.

28 T.F.X. Noble and J. Van Engen (eds), *European Transformations: The Long Twelfth Century*, Indianapolis, IN: University of Notre Dame Press, 2012; B. Schneidmüller and St. Weinfurter (eds), *Ordnungskonfigurationen im Hohen Mittelalter* (Vorträge und Forschungen 64), Sigmaringen: Thorbecke, 2006.

29 F.J. Griffiths and J. Hotchin (eds), *Partners in Spirit: Women, Men, and Religious Life in Germany, 1100–1500* (Medieval Women: Texts and Contexts 24), Turnhout: Brepols, 2014.

30 Classic studies include G. Duby, *Les trois ordres ou l'imaginaire du féodalisme*, Paris: nrf, 1978; O.G. Oexle, 'Deutungsschemata der sozialen Wirklichkeit im Mittelalter', in F. Graus (ed.), *Mentalitäten im Mittelalter. Methodische und inhaltliche Probleme* (Vorträge und Forschungen 35), Sigmaringen: Thorbecke, 1987, 65–117.

31 C. Mews and J. Crossley, *Communities of Learning: Networks and the Shaping of Intellectual Identity in Europe, 1100–1500*, Turnhout: Brepols, 2011; S. Steckel, N. Gaul and M. Grünbart (eds), *Networks of Learning: Perspectives on Scholars in Byzantine East and Latin West, c. 1000–1200*, Zürich, Berlin: LIT, 2014.

32 G. Althoff, *Family, Friends and Followers: Political and Social Bonds in Early Medieval Europe*, Cambridge et al.: Cambridge University Press, 2004; D.W. Sabean, S. Teuscher and J. Mathieu (eds), *Kinship in Europe: Approaches to Long-Term Development (1300–1900)*, New York: Berghahn, 2007; J.M. Bennett and R.M. Karras, *The Oxford Handbook of Women and Gender in Medieval Europe*, Oxford: Oxford University Press, 2013.

33 D. Mauskopf Deliyannis, *Historiography in the Middle Ages*, Leiden: Brill, 2003; G.M. Spiegel, 'Historical Thought in Medieval Europe', in L. Kramer et al. (eds), *A Companion to Western Historical Thought*, Oxford: Blackwell, 2006, 78–98; G. Dunphy, *History as Literature: German World Chronicles of the Thirteenth Century in Verse*, Kalamazoo, MI: Medieval Institute Publications, Western Michigan University, 2003.

34 B. Rosenwein, 'Poetic Dissent', in F. Titone, *Disciplined Dissent, Strategies of Non-Confrontational Protest in Europe from the Twelfth to the Early Sixteenth Century*, Rome: Viella, 2016, 23–39, quote at 30; cf. Chapter 10 in this volume.

35 These elements were for a long time categorically linked by another master-narrative subsumed under the term 'feudal society'. For essential critique and debate cf. S. Reynolds, *Fiefs and Vassals*, Oxford: Oxford University Press, 1996; T. Bisson, 'The "Feudal" Revolution', *Past and Present* 142, 1994, 6–42.

36 I follow the argument of Rosenwein, 'Poetic Dissent'.

37 Classic studies are J. Bumke, *Courtly Culture: Literature and Society in the High Middle Ages*, New York: The Overlook Press, 2000, and C.S. Jaeger, *The Origins of Courtliness: Civilizing Trends and the Formation of Courtly Ideals, 939–1210*, Philadelphia, PA: University of Philadelphia Press, 1985.

38 K. Starkey, *A Courtier's Mirror: Cultivating Elite Identity in Thomasin von Zerclaere's Welscher Gast*, Notre Dame, IN: University of Notre Dame Press, 2013.

39 Ibid., 22–5.

40 The term 'imagined community' was famously coined by B. Anderson, *Imagined Communities: Reflections on the Origin and Spread of Nationalism*, London: Verso, 2006.

41 K. Starkey and H. Wenzel (eds), *Visual Culture and the German Middle Ages*, New York: Palgrave, 2005. The classic study is H. Wenzel, *Hören und Sehen, Schrift und Bild: Kultur und Gedächtnis im Mittelalter*, München: C.H. Beck, 1995.

42 Starkey, *A Courtier's Mirror*, esp. Chapters 4 and 5.

43 A. Cole and A. Galloway, *The Cambridge Companion to Piers Plowman*, Cambridge: Cambridge University Press, 2014.

44 E. Gertsman, *The Dance of Death in the Middle Ages: Image, Text, Performance* (Studies in the Visual Cultures of the Middle Ages 3), Turnhout: Brepols, 2010.

45 Cf. Chapters 1 and 6 in this volume.

46 N.S. Thompson, *Chaucer, Boccaccio, and the Debate of Love: A Comparative Study of the Decameron and the Canterbury Tales*, Oxford: Oxford University Press, 1996.

47 P. Clark, *European Cities and Towns: 400–2000*, Oxford: Oxford University Press, 2009; A. Simms and H.C. Clarke, *Lords and Towns in Medieval Europe: The European Historic Towns Atlas Project*, Farnham: Ashgate, 2015.

48 D. Keene et al. (eds), *Segregation–Integration–Assimilation: Religious and Ethnic Groups in the Medieval Towns of Central and Eastern Europe*, Farnham: Ashgate, 2009.

49 G. Chittolini and P. Johanek (eds), *Aspetti e componenti dell'identità urbana in Italia e in Germania (secoli XIV–XVI/Aspekte und Komponenten der städtischen Identität in Italien und Deutschland (14.–16. Jahrhundert)*, Bologna et al.: Duncker & Humblot, 2003; Colson, J./van Steensel, A., eds. (2017), *Cities and Solidarities: Urban Communities in Pre-Modern Europe*, London/New York: Routledge, 2017.

50 For instance E. Muir, 'The Idea of Community in Renaissance Italy', *Renaissance Quarterly* 55, 2002, 1–18; W. Blockmans, 'Constructing a Sense of Community in Rapidly Growing European Cities in the Eleventh to Thirteenth centuries', *Historical Research* 83/222, 2010, 575–87. For a recent overview, see e.g. E. Gruber, 'The City as Commune', in E. Hovden et al., *Meanings of Community*, 99–124.

51 For instance M. Boone, 'Cities in Late Medieval Europe: The Promise and the Curse of Modernity', *Urban History* 39, 2012, 329–49; C. Goodson et al. (eds), *Cities, Texts and Social Networks, 400–1500: Experiences and Perceptions of Medieval Urban Space*, Farnham: Ashgate, 2010, the quote at p. 16 of the editors' introduction; Lantschner, P., ed., *The Logic of Political Conflict in Medieval Cities: Italy and the Southern Low Countries, 1370–1440*, Oxford: Oxford University Press, 2015.

52 E.g. K.A. Lynch, *Individuals, Families, and Communities in Europe 1200–1800: The Urban Foundations of Western Society*, Cambridge: Cambridge University Press, 2003; Morsel, J., ed., *Communautés d'habitants au Moyen Âge (XIe–XVe siècles)*, Paris: Editions de la Sorbonne, 2018.

53 J.-L. Fray et al., eds. *Urban Spaces and the Complexity of Cities*, Cologne/Weimar/Vienna: Böhlau Verlag, 2018; S. Cardarelli et al. (eds), *Art and Identity: Visual Culture, Politics and Religion in the Middle Ages and the Renaissance*, Cambridge: Cambridge University Press, 2012.

54 C. Lutter, 'Ways of Belonging to Medieval Vienna', in E. Gruber and S. Zapke (eds), *Companion to Medieval Vienna* (Brill's Companions to European History 11), Leiden: Brill, 2020.

55 J. Laszlovszky, 'Crown, Gown and Town: Zones of Royal, Ecclesiastical and Civic Interaction in Medieval Buda and Visegrád', in D. Keene et al., *Segregation–Integration–Assimilation*, 179–203, quote at 200. Cf. B. Nagy et al. (eds), *Medieval Buda in Context* (Brill's Companions to European History 10), Leiden: Brill, 2016.

56 M. Kintzinger and B. Schneidmüller (eds), *Politische Öffentlichkeit im Spätmittelalter* (Vorträge und Forschungen 75), Sigmaringen: Thorbecke, 2011; M. Rubin, *Corpus Christi: The Eucharist in Late Medieval Culture*, Cambridge: Cambridge University Press, 1991; K. Goda, 'The Medieval Cult and Processional Veneration of the Eucharist in Central Europe: The Royal Cities of Cracow and Buda in a Comparative Perspective', *Mediaevalia Historica Bohemica* 18, 1, 2015, 101–84.

57 M. Mostert and A. Adamska (eds), *Medieval Urban Literacy*, vol. 1: *Writing and the Administration of Medieval Towns*; vol. 2: *Uses of the Written Word in Medieval Towns* (Utrecht Studies in Medieval Literacy 27 and 28), Turnhout: Brepols, 2014.

58 Classic studies include J. Chiffoleau, *La comptabilité de l'au-dela: les hommes, la mort et la religion dans la région d'Avignon a la fin du Moyen Âge (vers 1320–vers 1480)*, Paris: Albin Michel, 2nd edn, 2011; and M. Rubin, *Charity and Community in Medieval Cambridge*, Cambridge: Cambridge University Press, 1987. Most recently: M. Borgolte et al. (eds), *Enzyklopädie des Stiftungswesens in mittelalterlichen Gesellschaften*, vols 1–3, Berlin: De Gruyter, 2014, 2015, 2017.

59 For a general nuanced assessment cf. N. Jaspert, 'Communicating Vessels, Ecclesiastic Centralisation, Religious Diversity and Knowledge in Medieval Latin Europe', *The Medieval History Journal* 16, 2, 2013, 389–424; A. Pietsch/S. Steckel, 'Religious Movements before Modernity? Considerations from a Historical Perspective', *Nova Religio: The Journal of Emergent and Alternative Religions* 21/4, 2018, 13–37.

60 D. Abulafia and N. Berend, *Medieval Frontiers: Concepts and Practices*, New York: Routledge, 2002.

61 N. Berend, *Expansion of Central Europe in the Middle Ages, 1000–1500*, New York: Routledge, 2013.

62 B. Catlos, 'Ethno-Religious Minorities', in P. Horden and S. Kinoshita (eds), *A Companion to Mediterranean History*, London: Wiley-Blackwell, 2014, 361–77.

63 O. Schmitt (ed.), *The Ottoman Conquest of the Balkans: Interpretations and Research Debates*, Vienna: ÖAW Verlag, 2016.

64 N. Berend, *At the Gate of Christendom: Jews, Muslims and 'Pagans' in Medieval History, c. 1000–c.1300*, Cambridge: Cambridge University Press, 2006.

65 F. Astren, 'Jews', in P. Horden and S. Kinoshita, *A Companion to Mediterranean History*, 392–408; J.L. Goldberg, 'Choosing and Enforcing Business Relationships in the Eleventh-Century Mediterranean: Reassessing the "Maghribī Traders"', *Past & Present* 216, 1, 2012, 3–40.

66 Jaspert, 'Communicative Vessels'; Catlos, 'Ethno-Religious Minorities' provide recent overviews with a focus on the interdependencies of these events.

67 B. Moore, *The Formation of a Persecuting Society: Authority and Deviance in Western Europe 950–1250*, London: Wiley-Blackwell, 2nd edn, 2006.

68 J.B. Given, *Inquisition and Medieval Society: Power, Discipline, and Resistance in Languedoc*, Ithaca, NY: Cornell University Press, 2001.

69 Rubin, 'Identities', 407–8.

70 Catlos, 'Ethno-Religious Minorities', 371f; P. Tartakoff, 'Testing Boundaries: Jewish Conversion and Cultural Fluidity in Medieval Europe, c. 1200–1391', *Speculum* 90/3, July 2015, 728–62, for a nuanced comparative assessment of Iberian and Northern European Jewish history.

71 Astren, 'Jews', 402f.; H. Kamen, *Spain: 1469–1714—A Society of Conflict*, New York/London: Routledge, 2014. For a comparative perspective cf. J. Tolan (ed.), *Expulsion and Diaspora Formation: Religious and Ethnic Identities in Flux from Antiquity to the Seventeenth Century*, Turnhout: Brepols, 2015.

72 R. Lutton, *Lollardy and Orthodox Religion in Pre-Reformation England. Reconstructing Piety*, Woodbridge: Boydell Press, 2006.

73 Rubin, 'Identities', 409–10.

74 F. Šmahel, *Die Hussitische Revolution* (Monumenta Germaniae Historica 43), 3 vols, Hannover: Hahnsche Buchhandlung, 2002; F. Machilek (ed.), *Die hussitische Revolution. Religiöse, politische und regionale Aspekte*, Vienna et al: Böhlau, 2012; P. Soukup, 'Religion and Violence in the Hussite Wars', in W. Palaver et al., eds., *The European Wars of Religion: An Interdisciplinary Reassessment of Sources, Interpretations, and Myths*, Farnham, Burlington, VT: Ashgate, 2016, 19–44.

75 On the different motivations and differentiations between moderate and radical Hussite groups see N. Housley, *Religious Warfare in Europe, 1400–1536*, New York: Oxford University Press, 2002, Ch. 2, 33–61.

76 P. Rychterová, 'The Chronicle of the So-Called Dalimil and Its Concept of Czech Identity', in Ead. et al. (ed.), *Narrating Communities: Historiographies in Central and Eastern Europe c. 13th–16th*, Turnhout: Brepols, 2020.

77 F. Šmahel, 'The Idea of "Nation" in Hussite Bohemia', *Historica* 16, 1969, 143–247, *Historica* 17, 1969, 93–197.

78 Cf. Ph. Buc, *Holy War, Martyrdom, and Terror: Christianity, Violence and the West*, Philadelphia, PA: University of Pennsylvania Press, 2015, 187–95 for a comparative approach to Joan of Arc and the Hussite movement. S. Reynolds, 'Nations, Tribes, Peoples, and States', *Medieval Worlds* 1, 2, 2015, 79–88 provides a recent overview of medievalists' debates around the concept of 'nation'.

79 B. Schneidmüller, 'Rule by Consensus: Forms and Concepts of Political Order in the European Middle Ages', *The Medieval History Journal* 16, 2, 2013, 449–71; J. Burkhardt, 'Frictions and Fictions of Community, Structures and Representations of Power in Central Europe, c. 1350–1500', *The Medieval History Journal* 19, 2, 2016, 191–228.

80 G. Dunphy, 'Perspicax ingenium mihi collatum est: Strategies of Authority in Chronicles Written by Women', in J. Dresvina and N. Sparks (eds), *Authority and Gender in Medieval and Renaissance Chronicles*, Cambridge: Cambridge University Press, 2012, 166–201, at 190–6.

81 P. Engel, *The Realm of St Stephen: A History of Medieval Hungary 895–1526*, London/New York: L.B. Tauris, 2005, the quote at 281.

9

BODY, SEXUALITY, AND HEALTH

Dominik Schuh

'Why all the fuss about the body?'[1]

'In a sense, of course, "the body" is the wrong topic. It is no topic or, perhaps, almost all topics',[2] as Caroline Bynum stated more than twenty years ago in her – by now – classic article *Why All the Fuss about the Body?* Bynum gives a brief but intriguing overview of the research and the questions treated until the mid-1990s, linking those to contemporary thoughts on the body and identity discourses. She reminds her readers that 'the past is seldom usefully examined by assuming that its specific questions or their settings are the same as those of the present',[3] although 'the only past we can know is one we shape by the questions we ask; yet these questions are also shaped by the context we come from, and our context includes the past'.[4] For the issues discussed here, these considerations are of critical importance, keeping in mind that most of the questions asked and the theories involved in research of 'medieval bodies' are the outcome of twentieth- and twenty-first-centuries struggles with contemporary bodies and their production, variability, and cultural meaning.[5]

In this chapter, I would like to open up some perspectives on bodies in 'the' Middle Ages; always bearing in mind that 'Like the modern world, the Middle Ages was characterized by a cacophony of discourses'.[6]

Objects and objectives of research

As solid as the object seems to an everyday understanding and as fundamental as it is often described, it becomes fluid and fleeting if it is made the subject of research. That it could become such a subject nevertheless can only be explained by its relevance for different research interests and approaches of the twentieth century. Research has to deal with the question of whether the bodies examined are the product or the raw material of cultural practice.

Although such questions are commonly brought to issue in some way, actual research often abstains from taking a definite position – a generally accepted view can hardly be found in the field. One may wonder why the chapter at hand starts with quotes from a twenty-year-old article. The answer to this question is that many of Bynum's observations remain true: 'There is no clear set of structures, behaviors, events, objects, experiences, words, and moments to which *body* currently refers', so that one can hardly say current 'discussions of the body' have become less 'incommensurate across the disciplines'.[7] It can be said that although there has been substantial research on a medieval history of bodies, it still consists of a vast number of insights only loosely bound by this label – without giving a distinct definition of the 'body'.

Two examples for attempts at an overview of medieval body history shall be outlined: In *Une histoire du corps au Moyen Âge*,[8] Jacques Le Goff and Nicolas Truong aim at closing a 'research gap', claiming that historians 'have just forgotten' the human body in the Middle Ages.[9] They provide a brief overview of what they call 'the history of a research gap', correcting their before-mentioned statement by presenting exceptions from an overall ignorance of the history of the body.[10] Many of them belong to the field of sociology and anthropology – namely: Norbert Elias, Marcel Mauss, Claude Lévi-Strauss, and Michel Foucault.[11] What could be seen as one of the main motivators for contemporary body history, the history of sexualities, is rated as 'disguising the history of the body rather than enlightening it' because of its engagement with the concerns of its own contemporary situation.[12] Le Goff/Truong make clear which body shall be the object of their interest: 'The manner of dressing oneself, of dying, of eating, of working, of handling one's body, of wishing, of dreaming, of laughing and crying, was not elevated to the dignity of an object worthy of the historian's view'.[13] They aim at showing the body as an object of everyday practice and the location of passions. The book itself is structured in four greater parts, reaching from the fundamental tension between 'Lent and Carnival' to a more or less classical history of ideas treating 'the body as a metaphor'. The diversity of topics discussed and the shifting character of the 'medieval body' constructed in the book can be seen as an instance for the way the issue is treated in research. Putting aside such heuristic difficulties, Le Goff/Truong bring to mind what it could have meant to medieval people – or at least to medieval writers – to 'have' a body.

While the work of Le Goff and Truong stands in the tradition of the Annales, sidelining much of the theoretical input brought to issue from the 1970s to the 1990s, Linda Kalof's anthology *A Cultural History of the Human Body in the Middle Ages*,[14] published in 2010 in the series *A Cultural History of the Human Body*, can be seen as an approach to bring together the results of those inputs. The conception of the series raises the question of whether it makes sense to speak of a 'medieval body' as distinguished from an ancient or an early modern one.[15] The 'body' in question seems thereby to have a very wide definition: serving as 'a lively forum for dialogue across the disciplines'[16] from the modern scholar's perspective, and seen as an object for which 'no one area of medieval culture held a monopoly',[17] resulting in every discipline and source holding potential contributions to the topic. Although no direct attempt on a restricted understanding is made, the introduction gives a hint: 'The body serves as both a lens and filter through which pass all the stimulants and stresses of the surrounding world, absorbing the shocks, relishing the pleasures, and nursing the blows'.[18] The resulting body seems to be an instrument of human experience and an object for environmental influences – implicitly distinguished from something or someone 'looking through that lens'.

The volume as a whole consists of an introduction and ten thematically structured chapters, built around 'major aspects of the human body':[19] the basics of carnal existence (beliefs regarding the endpoints of life, 'Birth and Death'), nutrition and its impact on health, 'The Sexual Body', the body in medical theory and popular belief, and the social significance of the body – by means of ascribing beauty, difference, and identity to certain bodies. Most of the contributions rely heavily on scholarly sources or on examples from fine arts and literature.

Influential thoughts and theories

In *What Is Cultural History?* Peter Burke sums up: 'The history of the body developed out of the history of medicine, but historians of art and literature as well as anthropologists and sociologists have become involved in what might be called this "bodily turn"'.[20] Certainly, the history of medicine can be seen as the first historical approach to the body, complemented by the insights of archeology. The school of Annales, starting in the early twentieth century (followed by the history of mentalities), showed a certain interest in questions of body history too, following the 'scent of human flesh' wherever it could be found, demonstrating for instance the miraculous power of royal bodies.[21] Following up the history of daily life, the German *Alltagsgeschichte* and the historical approaches from cultural anthropology are to be seen as efforts to reveal bodies in history.[22] Besides these attempts to show 'the body as worker, consumer and producer',[23] the works of ethnologists like Arnold van Gennep and Mary Douglas have inspired medievalists to research the history of rituals, observing the meanings of bodies in motion. Closely connected to this field, the history of gesture has produced remarkable insights into the medieval use of the body.[24]

Many works engaged with the history of the body follow influences from other fields of discourse: women studies developed a critical perspective on existing body images, norms, and the meanings ascribed to bodily differences of the sexes, thereby challenging the justification of patriarchy. As a related field, gay and lesbian and later queer studies evolved especially in the 1980s, leading to intensified research on human sexuality besides the more psychological and medical-oriented sexuality studies, which originated in the late nineteenth century. Michel Foucault and Judith Butler could be seen as the most prominent and influential thinkers associated with the field of gender and sexuality studies. At last, the concept of habitus by Pierre Bourdieu, 'designed to bridge the gap or to avoid the simple opposition between minds and bodies',[25] is applied in the field.

Exemplary medieval bodies

To provide an introduction to medieval body history, three exemplary body concepts shall be discussed. The concepts are chosen with regard to the idea of the 'three orders'.[26] Certainly, this idea is far from a realistic representation of any medieval society. Its reduction to three functional estates emerged under specific historical circumstances – like attempts for peace in medieval France – and served as a legitimation of aristocratic rule over the majority of population. It furthermore leaves aside all those people that were not part of one of the three groups (noble fighters or *bellatores*, clerics or *oratores*, and peasants or *laboratores*). The number of people outside this system could be very high. To name some of them: women,[27] artisans, merchants, common soldiers, or religious minorities like Jews have no place in this system.

The following presentation of the body concepts of common, noble, and religious people follows five key questions: which sources can provide insights into the group's body history? What could be core issues of the group's body concept? What conditions of living shaped their bodies? What bodily practices did they engage in? What do we know about their bodily appearance?

'In the sweat of thy face shalt thou eat bread'[28] – common bodies

The majority of bodies in the Middle Ages remain largely untold. What can we know about the life of common people and their understanding of bodily existence? Because of a lack of valid data for accurate statistics of medieval societies, one can hardly say how many people lived as peasants in the Middle Ages. At least it can be assumed that up to 90% of the population worked in agricultural production.[29] Since peasants were regularly illiterate, they have left little for posterity. So, how can we get a concept of their life, their bodily practices, and their body concepts? We can use the writs and depictions made by other social groups, artifacts, and sources of comparable social groups of later times – assuming that the particular circumstances of the life of peasants did not change fundamentally until the French Revolution and industrialization. All named resources bear substantial problems for research and have to be used carefully. To gain an idea of how common people represented their life in their own voice, trial records can be of high value. Written down, for instance, in the course of an inquisition trial, they provide us with a glimpse of the thoughts of otherwise voiceless individuals.[30] It seems questionable to assume such a big group would share a uniform understanding of their existence; in some dimensions the members of the so-called third estate differed more from each other than from members of other estates (e.g. a wealthy free-holder would have more in common with a relatively poor nobleman than with a day laborer).

As mentioned before, most circumstances defining common people's lives were already relevant before the medieval period and held true long after. Leaving aside genetic dispositions, nutrition is the basis of shaping a body. The availability of different kinds of food distinguished the peasant from the noble,[31] the poor from the rich. Famines were an ever-recurring threat to medieval people – as in all agricultural societies – often followed by diseases. Many of the descriptions of such occurrences are linked with apocalyptic visions of clerical writers, portraying the desperate search for eatables and the production of different kinds of 'famine bread'.[32] Nevertheless, the High Middle Ages saw a substantial growth of population in Western Europe relying on the spreading and intensified use of agricultural techniques. Clerical influences and social changes led to the dissemination of crops and fruits and changed especially the food sources north of the Alps.[33] Typical dishes for common people consisted of bread, porridge, pottage, water, and beer. More prosperous freemen could complement these food sources with salted, dried, or smoked fish – whereby fish was defined in a much wider sense than today, reaching from real fish to fetal animals and beavers.

Furthermore, a body is shaped by the practices applied to it and the practices it is used to perform. The most significant activity of common people's body was work. Life was defined by natural conditions: daytime, season, climate, and soil. The last determined what agricultural products could be cultivated. Despite these differences, agricultural work was hard and demanding, beginning with the dawn of day and ending with sunset. There were elements of a gendered division of labor, so that spinning and weaving were marked as female activities while those kinds of labor seen as 'especially physical demanding' were usually ascribed to men (ploughing, threshing, or forestry works). People lived close to each other's bodies, sharing working and sleeping places alike. As sources for food, resources, and labor, animal bodies accompanied the rural population, often living in the same housings. Book illuminations provide us with insights into the practices of agricultural work of common people, illustrating seasonal activities or biblical motives. Certainly, peasants' bodily existence was not restricted to being consumers and workers. Although often depicted to make fun of them, late medieval literature shows members of the rural population engaging in various cultural practices and festivities. Dances, 'sporting' competitions, and carnivalesque plays, which often made use of a very corporal humor, were part of popular culture and provided the common people with a welcome distraction from labor.[34]

What did common people look like? The pictures usually available to us give us much information about their appearance. They show either working bodies (in order to illustrate an estate or a season) or they depict bodies in a rather poor condition – perhaps to trigger the viewer's compassion or to mark the depicted as crude beings. In courtly literature, the bodies of rural farmers and workers often served as a foil to emphasize the 'refined' quality of noble bodies. The population apart from the courtly centers was therefore described as uncivilized and unattractive. The Austrian knight Oswald von Wolkenstein (d. 1445) depicts commoners as 'bulky folk, black, ugly, [and] very snotty when winter comes',[35] while living in a remote valley. But rural sceneries could also be of some attraction to courtly writers. Literary genres like the pastourelle use especially 'common' women as objects of sexual fantasies of the nobility, telling stories of (masculine) pleasure in sharp contrast to the restrictions of courtly love.[36]

Regarding their own concepts, there is evidence that common people did work on their appearance, trying to adapt themselves to some kind of bodily ideal. Late medieval dress regulations give strong proof for the opportunity to transgress the social expected limits of self-representation and a widely shared concept of a good look – closely associated with attributes of a certain social position.[37]

'Too great a desire to cosset the body is against all good'[38] – noble bodies

The most prominent body of the Middle Ages was wrapped in iron. The typical appearance of knights was determined by armor, weapons, and horses, making them seem like supernatural or monstrous beings to some contemporary observers.[39] Nobility's life conditions and ideals are well researched compared with other social groups.[40] While the history of the early Middle Ages is accessible only through the narrations of clerical writers, the High Middle Ages (from the eleventh or twelfth century onwards) saw the rise of noble vernacular culture. With its center in France, the concept of chivalry (chevalerie) as a refined lifestyle and code of behavior for higher-ranking fighters spread all over Europe, accompanied by a rich literary production of courtly literature, tending from the love poetry of troubadours to epic narrations of bloody adventures (*chansons de geste*, or stories about King Arthur and his knights). Aside from courtly literature, chronicles, didactic literature, and guidebooks (mirrors or *specula*), depictions, buildings, and artifacts provide us with information about medieval nobility. The emergence of regional and all-European festivities of this new culture – especially tourneys – strengthened the connection between fighting nobles of different local origins. The rise of the crusades applied a holy mission to this forming social group.

With regard to gender relations, noble bodies are the most frequent object of research. While common people often could not afford a strict gender distinction of labor and lifestyle, and clerical bodies of both genders were subject to similar restrictions of asceticism, noble life differed eminently according to sexual assignment. Even though both genders had to represent their family, a nobleman's body was mostly thought of as an instrument of war, while a noblewoman's body was commonly seen as an instrument of reproduction and delight.

The life of a poor knight, a second-born son without hope of any heritage, equated much more to the life of a wealthy peasant than to that of an earl's son or even of a man with royal origins. Certainly, to fight side by side with kings and to share at least some elements of chivalrous lifestyle with them could foster strong relationships between men. The household-knights of a ruler built a strong community and provided career opportunities for its members. Medieval nobility was less exclusive than later aristocratic systems. A man could make his fortune by proving himself a capable knight, and he did so by using his body to fulfill noteworthy deeds.[41]

The mediocre noble had access to sufficient food and could enjoy manifold dishes. In contrast to the peasants working to supply him and his lord, noblemen ate larger amounts of meat – from pork to different kinds of game up to more exotic-sounding dishes like swan, or heron,[42] which were served at festivities to show noble splendor. Nobles would prefer white bread, had wine and beer at their disposal, and had access to local or even exotic spices – the use of spices was an important way to make one's wealth apparent. Despite catastrophe, a badly planned war campaign, or a siege, nobles surely did not have to starve. What did these supply conditions mean for their bodily appearance? Should we imagine knights and ladies as sturdy or even corpulent? Certainly, medieval body ideals cannot be compared to the imaginations of Greek athletes or modern lankiness, and some noblemen probably ate more than a physician would advise them to. The knight Geoffroi de Charny gives some clear hints at the behavior expected of a knight. He advises young men to flee excessive consumption and comfort as it would lead to a weakening of their body, resulting in softness unfit for battle-action. Instead of peace and pleasure, a young man of worth should use every hour possible to train his abilities, to seek challenges, and to hear stories of the profession of arms. Such advice can be found in different books of chivalry and courtly literature; we can therefore assume it to have had widespread acceptance. Narrations of knightly life give proof of their realization – e.g. those of William Marshal (d. 1219), Jean II Le Maingre, called Boucicaut (d. 1421), or Thomas Gray (d. 1369).[43] Remarkably, one of these, William Marshal, was said to be such a hungry young man that he earned himself the nickname 'greedy guts', which seems to be far from Charny's ideal of modesty.[44]

The core issues of a chivalric body concept could be formulated as follows: (1) The body is a means of gaining honor. It is a knight's first and most valuable tool to do 'noble' deeds and – on the other hand – it is the stake in the game of chivalry. One has to risk his body or at least his physical integrity to win honor. (2) To be a useful tool, a knight's body has to be trained early and steadily. Bad habits jeopardize a body's fitness as they may 'infect' it with softness and vulnerability. Popular exercises can be tracked back to antiquity and were passed on through Vegetius' *Epitoma rei militaris*; others are likely to have originated from knightly culture itself. Common were: riding, throwing stones or javelins, shooting with a bow or a crossbow, wrestling, fighting with a sword, axe, or lance, running, swimming, and climbing a ladder – which could prove very useful in case of a siege, especially if one were able to climb in full armor. Marshall Boucicaut was said to be capable of climbing a ladder fully armored on the 'wrong' side. Although skills like reading, writing, and playing music appear also, the focus lies on martial arts. There is little doubt that Charny meant anything other than military achievements when he stated that 'he who does more is worth more'.[45] A knight's value was rated with regard to his deeds in combat. (3) A knight's body is hard and tough, being able to resist hardships and violence. It is capable of suffering and enduring pain. The passion of Christ and the stories of martyrs provided medieval culture with positive connoted images of suffering, connecting pain and physical harm to holiness and redemption. (4) A noble person is to be recognized by a noble body. The nobility of a body depends on its noble origin, which depends on the nobility of its ancestors, building up a line of succession of noble bodies. As mentioned before, the state and rank of a person were signified primarily by their physical appearance. The main means to do so were posture, gesture, and clothing. The first time of 'reading' one's body was a person's birth, giving information about the gender and health of the new-born. In literature this foreshadows one's noble deeds, taking physical appearance as an indicator of innate abilities, as in the case of Perceval:

> When the queen came back to her senses and recovered her child, she and the other ladies began to look all over his little penis between his legs. He had to be much fondled since he had a man's member. Since then he became a smith with swords, so much fire did he beat out of helmets, and his heart showed a man's courage.[46]

The description of bodily appearance is a means to show someone's qualities. The Scottish military leader William Wallace (d. 1305) was depicted by the chronicler Walter Bower (d. 1449) as:

> a tall man with the body of a giant, cheerful in appearance with agreeable features, broad-shouldered and big-boned with belly in proportion and lengthy flanks, pleasing in appearance but with a wild look, broad in the hips, with strong arms and legs, a most spirited fighting-man, with all his limbs very strong and firm.[47]

For modern readers, the description of a man with 'broad hips' may seem strange. Probably, this feature is thought to be an advantage for horseback-warriors.[48] Most descriptions of knights – and nobility at all – share a certain positive valuation of the descripted, depicting them as rather attractive – often without mentioning what features would make them attractive to whom. However, we should not mistake modern perceptions of physical attraction as being timeless. Although some descriptions may remind us of contemporary ideals, they often do so by means of using a vocabulary open to different imaginations. Ideals of bodily appearance were already contested among the contemporaries regarding regional preferences, fashion, or even moral standards as, for instance, Bernhard's of Clairvaux critical view of knightly appearance shows. In order to promote the order of the Knights Templar, Bernhard accuses the 'worldly knighthood' of being vain and womanlike: 'Then why do you blind yourselves with effeminate locks and trip yourselves up with long and full tunics, burying your tender, delicate hands in big cumbersome sleeves?'[49] The question of what kind of appearance was appropriate for a man was disputed especially between members of the vernacular nobility and the clergy – combined with the question of which of these estates should have the highest reputation.

'The greatest enemy I have is my body'[50] – religious bodies

While knights were supposed to protect the physical bodies of Christianity, clerics had to secure the soul's salvation. Ecclesiastic life has left the greatest amount of source material. Clergymen wrote historiographic as well as hagiographic accounts, providing insights into their concepts of (spiritual) life and the circumstances of their living. Bishops, abbesses, abbots, nuns, and monks commented on political and social events with letters, treatises, and sermons. Monastic rules of different orders show their ideas of the 'right' order for Christian lifestyle and document the changes of cultural attitudes. Pictures, artifacts (like ritual objects), and architectural remains bear testimony to ecclesiastical practices.

As the clergy consisted of many learned people containing a major part of the educated elite of medieval societies, the sources show manifold opinions and perspectives on the 'proper' way of dealing with bodies. Simply put, the Christian perspective on human physicality was split into two main traditions – one following the biblical statement that God created humans in his image,[51] emphasizing the divine quality of bodily existence, and one focusing on the relation of body and soul, identifying the (transient) first as the source of sins and the last as the immortal part of humans, which could be either redeemed or condemned. The resurrection of the dead was thought of as a very physical event, leading to the scholastic discussion of what this resurrection would look like in detail and in which manner the bodily members would be reunited with the soul. As the vehicle of the soul and a part of God's creation, the body could not be despised outright. Although such an ambivalent attitude toward the body can be found in sources from all (Christian) groups, its consequences are most evident in ecclesiastic life. Combined with the ancient belief in cultic purity, restrictions of bodily practices played a major part in the daily life of religious men and women.[52] The following could therefore be seen as core issues of ecclesiastic body concepts: (1) The body has to be disciplined through asceticism in order to serve the Lord. Distractions from one's spiritual mission (like physical delights) have to be avoided. (2) In the following of Christ, one should show humility through his (or her) bodily practices and abstain from luxury. (3) The body of a Christian is to be kept pure and free from sin as any pollution would endanger the eternal soul of its owner. The bodies of those administering the holy mass (ordained priests, bishops) are to be kept especially pure, because any pollution of such a body could jeopardize the purity of the sacraments touched by it. (4) The bodies of clergy are instruments of salvation when ordained; God may act through their physical presence. (5) Divine grace is a physical, perceptible phenomenon appearing, for example, in the shape of stigmata. It can also prevent those bodies from decomposing, who served God, making their corpse fragrant and unaltered. Such bodily parts establish an efficacious link to the divine. In this belief, a saint's bones are connected to their (former) owner, enabling the living to make contact with him or her and ask them to intercede before God. In some cases, the physical presence of the holy was even attributed to objects touched by a Saint during his or her lifetime ('contact relics').

While the lifestyle of higher officials of the church – like the pope, cardinals, prelates, (prince-)bishops, and (prince-)abbots of wealthier monasteries – was very similar to the life of higher nobility, conditions for the mass of the clergy depended on their particular place in the structure of the church. Accommodation, diet, and restrictions varied substantially between the canon of a large cathedral and a simple friar in a remote monastery. Overall, life in monastic communities was regulated more strictly than life in a chapter or as a priest in a parish. Following the guiding principle 'omnia sunt communia' (everything belongs to everybody), nuns and monks had to abstain from private property, and in accordance with the principle 'ora et labora' (pray and work), life in a monastery was structured by (manual) work, mass, and spiritual exercise. The course of the year was determined by the Christian feast calendar, binding the inhabitants to fasting periods, but the diet of monks and nuns was also prescribed aside from the times of lent for ascetical purposes. To prevent the risk of sin and the resulting pollution, men and women were strictly separated (to share a bed with another brother was often prohibited, too). Rules discuss the threat of self-defilement and the question of guilt in case of unintentional emissions (for instance, caused by the wrong diet).[53] The purity of the ordained bodies of priests was safeguarded through celibacy – the roots of which reach back to late antiquity, although enforced through reform efforts of the eleventh and twelfth centuries.

Ecclesiastical bodies were engaged in manifold practices, depending on status and function – ranging from manual (fieldwork, crafts, paperwork) to social (pastoral work, nursing) to intellectual and spiritual work (teaching, preaching, and praying). The bodies of clergymen were ritual instruments and therefore means for salvation, administering sacraments, blessing people, places, and objects, and praying for the living as well as for the dead. With the emergence of the Knights Templar in the twelfth century (followed by a number of other religious orders of knights), the sharp distinction between *bellatores* and *oratores*, between fighting and praying men, diminished, adding another bodily practice to ecclesiastic life.

Their physical appearance should represent their way of life, their faith, and the institution they were obliged to. Originating from the vestments of roman officials, the appearance of Catholic priests and bishops was meant to show the church's dignity and power. Every part of their equipment (like the crook or the mitre) is bound to a symbolic tradition, often reflected and discussed by the clergymen themselves. Depending on the ecclesiastic fraction to which someone belonged, the particular compilation differed relating to their goal in representation – e.g. while high representatives of the institutional church might openly display wealth and rely on representative practices of the ruling elite, mendicant friars emphasized their ideal of the 'poverty of the church'. Many monastic orders used techniques of mild bodily mutilation in the form of the 'tonsure' to mark their members, showing openly their permanent division from secular life.

Harmed bodies

Because of economic limitations, not everyone had access to doctors and physicians with academic education and their expensive treatments. Besides these medical professionals, a large number of practitioners (like midwives, barbers, or trained surgeons) worked for their patients' physical health. The widespread picture that medieval medicine was a primitive hotchpotch is far from reality. Although bloodletting and amputations were common medical techniques, medieval practitioners had to offer a wide range of treatments.[54] Medical knowledge was not restricted to the experts, but spread through a growing number of popular writings, especially after the invention of printing.[55]

The understanding of bodily health was influenced mainly by three theories, explaining negative effects on human bodies: the miasma theory, humoralism, and the theological interpretation of diseases. The first two go back to antiquity and are connected to the Greek physicians Hippocrates of Kos and Galen. Their works were primarily brought to the medieval West through the mediation of the Persian scholar Ibn Sina (or Avicenna, 980–1037).[56] (As those theories developed in pre-medieval times, their impact lasts deep into the nineteenth century.)

Miasmatic theory explains diseases as the effects of air pollution. Perceptible as 'bad odors', miasmatic particles were thought to infiltrate human bodies through the nostrils, the mouth, or even the skin, infecting the 'pneuma' ('breath', the source of vitality) and causing sicknesses. Based on the idea of 'bad odors', fragrant substances such as perfumes or even flowers were used as countermeasures.[57] Being of especially high impact after its application during the great plague in the late 1340s, miasmatic theory was integrated in the system of humoralism 'as a model of understanding the emergence of epidemics'.[58]

Humoralism is based on the thought that every human body contains a complexion (balance of humors) of four bodily fluids, called humors (blood, yellow bile, black bile, and phlegm). The particular ratio of a person's humors establishes her or his temperament (sanguine, choleric, melancholic, or phlegmatic). Humors and temperaments are connected to several qualities (warm, dry, cold, and moist) and to the four elements (air, fire, earth, and water). While the equilibrium of humors was thought to be the ideal condition, mortal humans were not thought to be capable of reaching this state of being. Nonetheless, medical treatments based on humoralism aimed at (re)balancing a patient's bodily fluids, as illnesses were seen as the result of an excessive amount of one humor or the lack of another.

In the context of Christian religion and its strong link to healing narrations, the significance of religious explanations is unsurprising. The interpretation of illnesses as divine punishments (of an individual or a group of 'sinners') was widespread and occurred especially in the event of greater diseases combined with manifold efforts to win back God's grace. The boundaries between different models of explanation were surely not as strict as a modern observer may assume. '[A] medieval magistrate', as Carole Rawcliffe put it, 'inhabited a world in which personal vices such as gluttony, sexual promiscuity and the reluctance to work seemed to threaten the wellbeing of entire communities like a toxic miasma, weakening their resistance to disease and even inviting divine retribution'.[59]

A sharp distinction between injuries and illnesses in the modern sense was uncommon to medieval physicians. Both were treated as disruptions of bodily integrity. Nevertheless, I shall highlight the occurrence and treatment of bodily harms with regard to this distinction (illnesses/injuries), because of the different meanings ascribed to those varieties.

Treatment of the ill

Although popular as perspectives on the period tend to paint a dark picture of medieval health provision, attempts at the preservation of bodily well-being could be quite sophisticated. As in modern times, access to medical care depended much on economic opportunities and place of residence. Because of urban administrative sources, historians have a thorough knowledge of medieval towns' healthcare. Having the economic and infrastructural opportunities to do so, densely populated areas also had greater need of sanitary measures regarding the environmental risks of urban life. A greater population needs larger amounts of potable water, food supply, and arrangements for handling waste and sewage. Urban communities therefore undertook measures to monitor food production (especially for bakeries, butcheries, and breweries), regulated livestock farming within the towns, where many kept pigs or fowl for provision, supervised water supply, and promoted their inhabitants' hygiene. Baths and bathhouses were important places of urban life, serving social encounters, amusement, and healthcare alike – although sometimes criticized as spots of sinful pleasures, warm baths especially were recognized as a health-promoting activity.[60] At least in some parts of Europe (e.g. Aragon, Italy, and France), cities engaged salaried physicians to maintain public health and to take care of poor patients.[61]

In respect to care-institutions, these were not strictly distinguished between different 'types' of people in need – the ill, the poor, and the old were commonly treated in the same places, provided they could not afford to stay at their original homes or did not want to do so. As lodgings for pilgrims, other guests, or travelers, monasteries often had hospitals,[62] which could also serve as accommodation for those seeking medical help. The monastery inhabitants themselves were treated in an infirmary (infirmarium). Monastic orders, like the Hospital Brothers of Saint Anthony (founded to take care of those fallen ill to Saint Anthony's fire), bishops, and secular rulers built hospitals all over Europe, which mostly were controlled by the church and organized in the style of monastic life. In the later Middle Ages, hospitals became important institutions for towns and cities, not only contributing to efforts for public healthcare but serving also as retirement residences for city dwellers and as guesthouses for less wealthy travelers. The question of their organization and especially of the selection and separation (e.g. between male and female) of their potential inhabitants could lead to heated debates. Wealthier citizens made endowments to hospitals to enjoy a carefree evening of life. Associations like parishes, fraternities, or guilds could sometimes maintain their own hospitals or almshouses for members and their families, but most of these institutions had to rely on donations or the begging of their inmates.

The diseases most commonly connected to the Middle Ages are leprosy and the 'Black Death'. The importance of leprosy is often overemphasized in historical accounts. Because of 'complex responses in both ecclesiastical and secular society [...] historians have tended to focus upon it to the exclusion of more common but less well documented diseases'.[63] Illnesses like malaria, tuberculosis, dysentery, typhus, or diphtheria were far more fatal to medieval communities – especially in swampy regions, in cases of food shortages, and in overcrowded towns. The term 'Black Death' refers commonly to the great outbreak of the plague in Europe after the year 1348, causing the death of a large part of the European population. The biblical significance of leprosy made it a well-known phenomenon of 'public' interest, ensuring a widespread system of leprosaria or leper houses. First, leper houses were founded by members of the royal family, the aristocracy, and the church; later on there were also bourgeois foundations. Like hospitals, leper houses were funded by endowments, alms, and donations from nearby residents and travelers. Lepers themselves were obliged to wear special clothing and make their presence perceptible – for example, through the use of little bells. Like other groups of 'needy' people, they were integrated into the daily life of communities, although spatially excluded at the same time. A system of exclusion and quarantine was also applied after the outbreak of the plague besides spiritual efforts like processions and medical attempts such as the use of good odors and various kinds of medicine.[64]

Injury by means of battle

Apart from pain and the enduring consequences of injuries, damages to the human body could be seen as a risk for the eternal life of a person: 'A wounded body, especially one that was tortured or dismembered, may sever the connection with the soul or tear it apart'.[65] But there were at least two perspectives on the meaning of such harms, depending much on the context of their emergence – while (lawful) punishments could be compromising, martyrs and fighters for a just cause could hope to be rewarded for their suffering. Death and injuries were common results of armed conflicts; military practitioners often paid for their 'glory' with their bodily parts. What injuries a fighter suffered and how severe they were depended on his equipment and on the kind of battle he participated in. A rider had to expect attacks on his legs if he fought against foot-soldiers, who themselves would risk (lethal) hits on their head or shoulders – regarding chronical evidence and treatises on surgery, some typical injuries and their lethality can be identified.[66] In many sources, historians have found 'specific narrative patterns, which are the performance of Deeds of Arms, physical toughness or resilience, the ability to recuperate after injuries and the description of horse and fighter as a common fighting body'.[67] There are numerous descriptions of fighters left for dead after a battle, recovering from their severe injuries afterwards. Those narrations emphasize the importance of the ability to resist physical assaults and to recover from the damage dealt. The history of William Marshal, for example, tells the story of William's father, John Marshal, who was trapped in a burning church that was set on fire by enemy troops. Left for dead by his opponents, John survived the incident heavily wounded and was able to fight as a knight later on, although he lost an eye.[68] Many sources report of such injuries in the face or the loss of limbs on the battlefield, which could bring an end to a fighter's career, pressuring him to live on as a beggar if he was not part of a noble family. But if injuries were minor enough that he could fight again after a time of recovery, scars and other signs of former wounds could serve as proof of a fighter's experience and boldness. Such a visible manifestation of combative performance could make a fighter even more attractive to potential 'employers' like the leaders of mercenary companies, or secure him certain renown among his noble peers.[69]

Reproductive bodies

As a question of anatomy, a way to influence the equilibrium of bodily fluids (humoralism), and a vital activity for the continuation of a social group, the topic of bodily reproduction was often discussed by medical scholars and natural philosophers. From a medical perspective, the interest in sexual acts focused on the questions of fertility – although some scholars also looked for physical explanations for deviant behavior. Overall, our knowledge of sexual topics and their treatment in medieval times is based on sources from four main directions: a theological (or at least moral) one, a scholarly (medicine or natural philosophy) one, one from love literature, and one with more or less humorous intentions. The discourses that take place in these sources are not clearly divided; they share several characteristics and presuppositions, of which the central one is the idea of a given (natural/divine) order of the sexes and their interactions. As the vast majority of these sources were written by men (and many by men who had to abstain from sexual practice), they clearly privilege a male perspective on the topic; a perspective that was probably dominant in the patriarchal societies of the Middle Ages.[70]

Distinguishing between female and male bodies

Although the idea of male pregnancy was acted out in some narrations,[71] bisexual reproduction was the undoubted standard of reproduction. The differentiation between male and female is connected to the 'reproductive arena',[72] even though its impact reaches far beyond this part of human life. Notwithstanding the question of the 'nature' of human sexual differences, it is relatively undoubted that the physical traits considered as typical depend on cultural variable perspectives. How were female and male bodies distinguished in the Middle Ages? The afore-cited description of the birth of Perceval already gave proof of the meaning of genitalia – not only for the recognition of a person's sex but also as an omen for his (or her) future life, based on gender- and class-related expectations. Primary sex characteristics – to use the modern term – were surely the safest means to verify one's 'sex'. Although – following

Thomas Laqueur[73] – there is some evidence for the existence of a genital-oriented 'one-sex model' in scholarly writs, the significance of such a model has to be treated with caution: First, this view was probably restricted to a relatively small group of educated writers; second, it is somehow contrary to the biblical statement that God created humans as men and women (Genesis 1); third, it was most likely just one scholarly opinion among others.

As in modern times, one may assume that verification via genital inspection would be a seldom-used way to distinguish female and male persons in everyday interaction. It also was not the only bodily difference medieval writers saw between the sexes: the famous early medieval scholar Isidore of Seville discerned 'soft' (and 'weak') women from 'hard' (and 'strong') men, following his understanding of their names.[74] As an attribution this was shared by many other writers, even though the reasons for this distinction were rarely repeated. The next most common anatomical difference was seen in the growing of facial hair.[75] Other secondary sex characteristics – like the so-called Adam's apple, the breasts, or the vocal pitch – appear only seldom, while humoral approaches to sexual differences are more present. A detailed model of humoral differences is found in the works of the nun Hildegard of Bingen, who distinguished between several gendered variations – as was common, the ('adequate') male tended to be more 'dry' and 'hot', while the females were more 'moist' and 'cold'.[76] The temperaments ascribed to these humoral types connect bodily dispositions to the conception of typical gendered behavior (or gender performance).

A promising approach to shed light on gender performances and their meanings is the treatment of sources referring to gender role changes and cross-dresses. Besides some literary examples – like the French romance 'Silence' – a number of hagiographical sources can be found, while the most prominent medieval cross-dresser, Jeanne d'Arc, has to be seen as exceptional.[77] In most cases the stories told are concerned with women presenting themselves as men, especially as a means of protection against sexual violence or marriage against will. Examples of men presenting themselves as women are found seldom, being restricted to literary stories of lovers trying to approach their beloved in disguise and a few legal sources on male prostitutes performing as females.

What can be said about the concept of gender performance? A widespread understanding of gender division was based on the attribution of certain functions or responsibilities of the genders – beginning with the biblical punishment that men should work the field while women had to suffer from pregnancy and childbirth. Although there were certain voices arguing for a basic equality of men and women (like the scholastic Albert the Great),[78] the common opinion on gender relations was ruled by a very hierarchical understanding, envisioning the male father as the head of the family and the master of his wife. In general, the conceptions of gender depended much on the specific context in which they were applied, resulting in a diversity of ideas of 'masculinity' and 'femininity'. Although they regularly share a patriarchal gender hierarchy and a common understanding of reproduction, they differ so much that every abstraction to one 'medieval concept' holds the risk of misrepresentation – or, in the words of Joan Cadden:

just as we would be betraying the evidence if we took Eve to be the paradigm of women in the Middle Ages, so we would be unjustified in representing the Aristotelian opposition between male and female natures as a scientific model of sex difference. Indeed, we would be doing only a little better if we asserted that medieval concepts of women were contained within the conflict between the idea of Eve and the idea of the Virgin Mary or that the concepts of sex were contained within the conflict between Aristotelian duality and a Galenic system of sex parallels.[79]

'Doing unto others'[80] – sexual acts

As Ruth Mazo Karras stated, 'Medieval people, for the most part, understood sex acts as something that someone did to someone else'.[81] Sexual intercourse was seen as an act of penetration, defining the position of the penetrator as male, and the opposite position as passive, suffering, and female. Despite this distribution of roles, women were often conceived as more lustful than men, leading to the belief that female desire fosters sinfulness – at the same time, wives were seen as useful mediators to influence their husbands toward a virtuous and chaste lifestyle.[82] Late medieval literature provides us with a vast amount of more or less humorous narrations of voluptuous and cunning women, who seek sexual pleasure by all available means. Especially stories of passionate nuns seem to have been of certain popularity, ranging to strange examples like the late medieval tale of a tourney of nuns over a speaking male genital living separately from its former owner.[83]

Although there are examples to show sexual preferences as being somehow stable and bound to a 'natural' bodily condition in the Middle Ages,[84] in most sources another conception of sexuality is found: The majority of medieval writers conceptualized sexual desire as a pursuit of pleasure, relatively indifferent to the 'object used' for this purpose. That such an understanding would by no means include a moral indifference to different ways of satisfying desire surely remains true. Intercourse was equated with an act of (vaginal) penetration – leaving most other sexual possibilities aside. Common metaphors for sexual intercourse highlighted this understanding, speaking, for example, of a hammer hitting an anvil.[85] Besides the distinction of active and passive, a key to many of those metaphors lies in the emphasis on the act's possible result: reproduction. Fertility and reproduction were – not surprisingly – of vital social interest. Therefore, not only the main 'protagonists' were involved in reproductive decisions but also their families, local communities, and (dependent on their social status) their lords.[86] Successful reproduction was especially important for a dynasty's continued existence and the birth of a new heir was a certain social event. On the other hand, chastity was a somehow characteristic feature of medieval sexuality. The choice to refrain voluntarily from any sort of sexual performance was highly praised – leading to ideals like the chaste marriage. While the demand for chastity was applied likewise to women and men of an ecclesiastical lifestyle, laity tended to enforce female observance of chastity (and the preservation of virginity) more than male.[87]

Although it seems likely that most medieval people did not link sexual performance to a certain way of feeling or identity as contemporary Western people would,[88] personality and sexual behavior were often thought to be connected in a different way. Once regarded as 'unnatural' and sinful by means of being unproductive, certain sexual practices – often summarized under the term of 'sodomy' – could be ascribed to socially excluded groups like 'heretics' to present them as incorrigible sinners. The attribution of sexual practices was an effective tool to delegitimize and criminalize political opponents – the process against the Knights Templar is probably the most famous example of this strategy.[89]

Closing remarks: fuzzy bodies

What sense can be made of these perspectives on medieval bodies? Can they be summarized as something more than the diagnosis of a 'cacophony of discourses'? One could name the extremes – as did, for instance, Le Goff/Truong – defining the body as either an instrument of salvation or the source of sins. Such binary opposition may be helpful for the understanding of religious discourses, but many of the sources giving proof of the ways bodies were seen, used, and dealt with do not show much interest in these opposites, or just position themselves in the middle. It often seems more promising to look for the meaning a distinct body had for its 'owner' or a certain observer – whether a peasant or a fighter in need of his or her body as an instrument of survival or a medical practitioner looking at a body in order to heal. The understanding of a period can be enriched by the comparison of bodily practices in different social groups – e.g. distinguishing between the focus on vital practices in peasantry, a martial and representative focus in nobility, and a focus on purity and discipline in clergy. As the physical structure of human beings, the body should be present in most historical representations, making it possible to show the basic conditions and consequences of human practice, connecting them to the 'big trends' of history.[90]

The novelty of a history of the body is not only to make the body a part of history as a whole, but, perhaps, to make it the protagonist of a history of its own. It could only arise from a theoretical (and cultural) perspective that has dismissed the concept of a universal human body, making visible its variability and transformability. One problem remaining is that the body is firmly resistant against being turned into a story's protagonist: 'The result is not the history of *the* human body in Europe, merely a history'.[91] Such a history focused on the bodily dimensions of cultural practice can be restricted to a certain period of time for practical reasons, resulting in something like a history of bodily practice in the Middle Ages – the question of whether 'bodies had a medieval period'[92] remains unresolved.

So why make a fuss about bodies and history? The current approaches to the history of the body are far from a positivist interest in the body 'as it happened to be'. They rather focus on the question of how people of the past thought of their bodies, experienced their bodiliness, and dealt with the challenges of their carnal existence. In a time in which humanity could be about to leave behind many of the boundaries of this way of being,[93] a historicization of the body can provide us with an opportunity to reflect on the meaning and possibilities of bodily existence. Perhaps that is a good reason to make a fuss about it.

Notes

1 C. Bynum, 'Why All the Fuss about the Body? A Medievalist's Perspective', *Critical Inquiry* 22, no. 1, Autumn 1995, 1–33.

2 Ibid., 2.

3 Ibid., 29.

4 Ibid., 30.

5 Bynum refers to movies dealing with personal continuity (p. 8ff), stating their stories 'tend to erase the kind of line between mind and body' (p. 9). Today (2020) this line has perhaps grown stronger as a result of digitization. Movie-examples could be Spike Jonze's *Her* (2013), telling the story of a man who loves an artificial intelligence, or the episode *Silence in the Library* of *Doctor Who* (New Series, Series 4, Episodes 08 and 09, 2008), where the protagonists enter a library of digitalized individuals.

6 Ibid., 7.

7 Ibid., 5.

8 J. Le Goff and N. Truong, *Une histoire du corps au Moyen Âge*, Paris: Liana Levi, 2003. I refer to the German translation, *Die Geschichte des Körpers im Mittelalter*, trans. by R. Warttmann, Stuttgart: Klett-Cotta, 2007.

9 Ibid., *Die Geschichte des Körpers im Mittelalter*, 9 (translations from the German DS).

10 Ibid., 17ff.

11 Supplemented by Annales-historians Marc Bloch and Georges Duby, among others.

12 Le Goff and Truong, *Geschichte des Körpers im Mittelalter*, 18.

13 Ibid., 18.

14 L. Kalof (ed.), *A Cultural History of the Human Body in the Middle Ages* (A Cultural History of the Human Body vol. 2), Oxford, New York: Bloomsbury Academic, 2010.

15 Compare: J. Kelly, 'Did Women Have a Renaissance?', in ead., *Women, History, and Theory: The Essays of Joan Kelly*, Chicago, IL: Univ. of Chicago Press, 1984, 19–49 (first published in 1977).

16 M. Green, 'Introduction', in Kalof, *A Cultural History of the Human Body*, 1.

17 Ibid., 11.

18 Ibid., 1.

19 According to the series preface: 'under seven [sic!] key headings: birth/death, health/disease, sex, medical knowledge/technology, popular beliefs, beauty/concepts of the ideal, marked bodies of gender/race/class, marked bodies of the bestial/divine, cultural representations and self and society'.

20 P. Burke, *What Is Cultural History?*, Cambridge: Polity, 2nd edn, 2008, 73, the overview 72–4. Attesting a 'body turn' to his discipline: R. Gugutzer, 'Der body turn in der Soziologie. Eine programmatische Einführung', in ibid., *Body turn. Perspektiven der Soziologie des Körpers und des Sports*, Bielefeld: transcript, 2006, 9–53.

21 M. Bloch, *The Historian's Craft*, trans. by P. Putnam, published by P. Burke, Manchester: Manchester Univ. Press, 1992, 22. See also Bloch in his *Les rois thaumaturges*, translated to the English as *The Royal Touch: Monarchy and Miracles in France and England*.

22 See M. Rubin, 'Medieval Bodies: Why Now, and How?', in ead., *The Work of Jacques Le Goff and the Challenges of Medieval History*, Woodbridge: Boydell Press, 1997, 209–22. See also: J. Tanner, *Historische Anthropologie zur Einführung*, Hamburg: Junius Hamburg, 2nd edn, 2008, or A. Nitschke, *Historische Verhaltensforschung. Analysen gesellschaftlicher Verhaltensweisen – ein Arbeitsbuch*, Stuttgart: Ulmer, 1981.

23 Rubin, 'Medieval Bodies', 211.

24 E.g.: J.-C. Schmitt, *La Raison de gestes dans l'Occident médiéval*, Paris: Editions Gallimard, 1990.

25 Burke, *What Is Cultural History?*, 74.

26 See G. Duby, *The Three Orders: Feudal Society Imagined*, trans. by A. Goldhammer, Chicago, IL, London: Univ. of Chicago Press, 1980.

27 S. Shahar, *The Fourth Estate: A History of Women in the Middle Ages*, London, New York: Routledge, 2003 (first published in 1983).

28 Genesis 3:19, quoted from King James Version.

29 See: A.G. Carmichael, 'Disease, and the Medieval Body', in Kalof, *A Cultural History of the Human Body*, 39–57, here 39. Deeper reading: C. Dyer, *Standards of Living in the Later Middle Ages: Social Change in England c. 1200–1520*. Cambridge, New York, Melbourne: Cambridge Univ. Press, 4th rev. edn, 1998.

30 E.g.: E. Le Roy Ladurie, *Montaillou, village occitan*, Paris: Folio, 1975, and C. Ginzburg, *The Cheese and the Worms: The Cosmos of a Sixteenth Century Miller*, Baltimore, MD: Johns Hopkins Univ. Press, 1980, first published in Italian as *Il formaggio e i vermi*, 1976.

31 Carmichael, 'Disease, and the Medieval Body', 43–4. For archeological insights: A. Ervynck, 'Orant, pugnant, laborant: The diet of the Three Orders in the Feudal Society of Medieval North-Western Europe', in S. O'Day et al., *Behaviour Behind Bones: The Zooarchaeology of Ritual, Religion, Status and Identity. Proceedings of the 9th Conference of the International Council of Archaeozoology, Durham, August 2002*, Oxford: Oxbow Books, 2004, 215–23.

32 Example: Carmichael, 'Disease, and the Medieval Body', 44–5.

33 Ibid., 40–2. See also: W. Rösener, *Agrarwirtschaft, Agrarverfassung und ländliche Gesellschaft im Mittelalter* (Enzyklopädie Deutscher Geschichte 13), München: Oldenbourg Verlag, 1992, 21.

34 Sixteenth-century artist Pieter Bruegel the Elder (d. 1569) made famous depictions of rural life. Examples of popular culture: N. Zemon Davis, *Society and Culture in Early Modern France: Eight Essays*, Stanford, CA: Stanford Univ. Press, 1965 (Chapters 4, 5).

35 'und knospot leut, swarz, hässeleich, vast rüssig gen dem winder', Oswald von Wolkenstein, 'Durch Barbarei, Arabia', in ibid., *Die Lieder Oswalds von Wolkenstein*, ed. by K.K. Klein, Berlin: Walter de Gruyter, 2015, (Klein 44) II, v. 17–18. (translation DS).

36 'Common woman' was sexually connoted, see: R.M. Karras, *Common Women: Prostitution and Sexuality in Medieval England*, Oxford: Oxford Univ. Press, 1996. Oswald von Wolkenstein wrote several poems of such content, e.g. 'Ain graserin' ('a [female] reaper').

37 See J. Schneider, 'Kleiderordnungen' [clothing – regulations], in *Lexikon des Mittelalters* (Brepolis Medieval Encyclopaedias – Lexikon des Mittelalters Online), 10 vols, Stuttgart: Metzler, [1977]–1999, vol. 5, cols 1197–8.

38 G. de Charny, *The Book of Chivalry. Le Livre de chevalerie, Text, context, and translation*, ed. by R. Kaeuper, trans. by E. Kennedy, Philadelphia, PA: Univ. of Pennsylvania Press, 1996, 123, paragraph 21, lines 6–7.

39 Parzival, the protagonist of the romance of the same name, mistakes the first knight he meets for god.

40 'Introduction', in M.H. Keen, *Chivalry*, New Haven, CT: Yale Univ. Press, 1984; R.W. Kaeuper, *Chivalry and Violence in Medieval Europe*, Oxford: Oxford Univ. Press, 1999; M. Prestwich, *Knight: The Medieval Warrior's (Unofficial) Manual*, London: Thames & Hudson, 2010.

41 See the example of William Marshal: T. Asbridge, *The Greatest Knight: The Remarkable Life of William Marshal, Power Behind Five English Thrones*, London: Simon & Schuster Ltd, 2015; G. Duby, *William Marshal, the Flower of Chivalry*, trans. from the French by R. Howard, New York: Pantheon books, 1985 (French original: *Guillaume le Maréchal ou le meilleur chevalier du monde*, Paris: Edition Fayard, 1984).

42 See Ervynck, 'Orant', 216.

43 For William Marshal see Asbridge, *The Greatest Knight*; for Boucicaut: *Le livre des faits du maréchal de B.* (Nouv. Coll. des mémoires pour servir à l'hist. de France II, 1836), ed. by Michaud-Poujoulat; for Thomas Gray: A. King, *Sir Thomas Gray's Scalacronica, 1272–1363*, Woodbridge: Boydell & Brewer, 2005.

44 Asbridge, *The Greatest Knight*, 43.

45 Charny, *The Book of Chivalry*, 33.

46 W. von Eschenbach, *Parzival*, verses 112, 21–30, English translation quoted from A. Lefevere (ed.), *Wolfram von Eschenbach. Parzival*, New York: Continuum, 1991, 26. Discussion of nobility in C.B. Bouchard, *Strong of Body, Brave and Noble: Chivalry and Society in Medieval France*, Ithaca, NY: Cornell University Press, 1998, 3–4.

47 W. Bower, *Scotichronicon: In Latin and English, with notes and indexes*, General ed. D.E.R. Watt, part 5, Books IX and X, Aberdeen: Aberdeen University Press, 1990, Book IX, 28, translation 83.

48 For the description: Asbridge, *The Greatest Knight*, 32.

49 *The Works of Bernard of Clairvaux* (The Cistercian Fathers Series, no. 19), trans. by C. Greenia, Kalamazoo, MI: Cistercian Publications, 1977, vol. 7, Treatises III.

50 'Speculum Perfectionis', 59, in *Francis of Assisi: Early Documents*, ed. by R.J. Armstrong et al., New York: New City Press, 2001, vol. 3, 304.

51 See Genesis 1; see also St Paul's advice in 1. Corinthians 6:20.

52 See for thoughts on pollution especially connected to sexuality: D. Elliott, *Fallen Bodies: Pollution, Sexuality, and Demonology in the Middle Ages*, Philadelphia, PA: Univ. of Pennsylvania Press, 1999.

53 A. Diem, *Organisierte Keuschheit. Sexualprävention im Mönchtum der Spätantike und des frühen Mittelalters* (Invertito – Jahrbuch für die Geschichte der Homosexualitäten 3), 2001, 8–37.

54 See M. McVaugh, *The Rational Surgery of the Middle Ages* (Micrologus Library 15), Firenze: Sismel, 2006, especially Chapter III (p. 89) for examples for wound treatments and Chapter VI (p. 229) for the development of a 'scientific' mentality in the field.

55 E.g.: German physician and publisher Hans Folz (died 1513) wrote on 'bathing' or 'on pestilence and its signs'. Encyclopaedic medicine books (e.g. *hortus sanitatis*, printed 1491) were translated into various languages.

56 C. Rawcliffe, *Urban Bodies: Communal Health in Late Medieval English Towns and Cities*, Woodbridge: Boydell Press, 2013, 120.

57 Ibid., 120ff.

58 G. Keil, 'Miasma', in *Lexikon des Mittelalters* (Brepolis Medieval Encyclopaedias – Lexikon des Mittelalters Online), 10 vols, Stuttgart: Metzler, [1977]–1999, vol. 6, col. 593 (translation DS). See also Rawcliffe, *Urban Bodies*, 121, on miasmatic theory in the thirteenth century.

59 Rawcliffe, *Urban Bodies*, 5–6; 'Spiritual prophylaxis', 89ff.

60 Ibid., 50ff.

61 Ibid., 291f.

62 'Hospital', in *Lexikon des Mittelalters* (Brepolis Medieval Encyclopaedias – Lexikon des Mittelalters Online), 10 vols, Stuttgart: Metzler, [1977]–1999, vol. 5, cols 133–7.

63 Rawcliffe, *Urban Bodies*, 63.

64 C. Schott-Volm, 'Aussatz, V. Rechts- und Sozialgeschichte', in *Lexikon des Mittelalters* (Brepolis Medieval Encyclopaedias – Lexikon des Mittelalters Online), 10 vols, Stuttgart: Metzler, [1977]–1999, vol. 1, cols 1251–3, und Rawcliffe, *Urban Bodies*, 324.

65 L. Tracy and K. DeVries, 'Introduction: Penetrating Medieval Wounds', in ibid. (eds), *Wounds and Wound Repair in Medieval Culture* (Explorations in Medieval Culture 1), Leiden: Brill, 2015, 1–21, here 2.

66 Also I.A. MacInnes, 'Heads, Shoulders, Knees and Toes: Injury and Death in Anglo-Scottish Combat, c. 1296–c. 1403', in, Tracy and DeVries (eds), *Wounds and Wound Repair*, 102–27.

67 J. Rogge, 'Killed and Being Killed. Perspectives on Bodies in Battle in the Middle Ages – An Introduction', in ibid., *Killing and Being Killed: Bodies in Battle Perspectives on Fighters in the Middle Ages*, Bielefeld: transcript, 2017, 9–14, 11.

68 See Asbridge, *The Greatest Knight*, 16.

69 G. Morosini, 'The Body of the *Condottiero*: A Link Between Physical Pain and Military Virtue as It Was Interpreted in Renaissance Italy', in Rogge, *Killing and Being Killed*, 165–98; I. MacInnes, '"One man slashes, one slays, one warns, one wounds". Injury and Death in Anglo-Scottish Combat, c.1296–c.1403', in Rogge, *Killing and Being Killed*, 61–78.

70 One should be cautious not to overemphasize the restrictions of female life in medieval times – especially if compared to strictly organized gender orders in the early modern era or antiquity.

71 Especially the story of Nero, forcing a physician to impregnate him, was popular.

72 R. Connell, *Gender*, Cambridge: Polity Press, 2009, 68.

73 T. Laqueur, *Making Sex: Body and Gender from the Greeks to Freud*, Cambridge, MA: Harvard Univ. Press, 1992.

74 Isidore of Seville, *Etymologiae*, book XI,ii,17–18.

75 Ibid., book XI,i,45.

76 A. Moshövel, '"Der hât ainen weibischen muot". Männlichkeitskonstruktionen bei Konrad von Megenberg und Hildegard von Bingen', in M. Dinges, *Männer – Macht – Körper. Hegemoniale Männlichkeiten vom Mittelalter bis heute* (Geschichte und Geschlechter 49), Frankfurt, New York: Campus, 2005, 52–65.

77 See for a detailed treatment of the topic: V. Hotchkiss, *Clothes Make the Man: Female Cross Dressing in Medieval Europe*, New York: Routledge, 2012 (first published in 1991). A shorter overview is found in: V.L. Bullough, 'Cross Dressing and Gender Role Change in the Middle Ages', in Bullough and Brundage, *Handbook*, 223–42.

78 Regarding the creation of Eve out of Adam's rib, Albert considers it a sign of equality of the sexes, stating God would have taken a part of Adam's feet if he wanted to make her subordinate to him, and a part of his head if he should have been subject to her. Albertus Magnus, *Über den Menschen: lateinisch-deutsch = De homine*, Hamburg: Meiner, 2004, 152–5; in other questions he followed misogynic traditions, A.L. Jones, *The Gender Vendors: Sex and Lies from Abraham to Freud*, Lanham, MD, London: Lexington Books, 2014, 118.

79 J. Cadden, 'Introduction', in ibid., *Meanings of Sex Difference in the Middle Ages: Medicine, Science and Culture*, Cambridge: Cambridge Univ. Press, 1993, 1–10, 3.

80 R.M. Karras, *Sexuality in Medieval Europe: Doing Unto Others*, New York: Routledge, 2005. A helpful review: V.L. Bullough, Review of *Sexuality in Medieval Europe: Doing Unto Others* (review no. 497). www.history.ac.uk/reviews/review/497 (accessed 3 April 2017).

81 Ibid., 3.

82 E.g.: S. Farmer, 'Persuasive Voices: Clerical Images of Medieval Wives', *Speculum* 61, 3, 1986, 517–43.

83 See A. Classen, 'Sexual Desire and Pornography: Literary Imagination in a Satirical Context – Gender Conflict, Sexual Identity, and Misogyny in "Das Nonnenturnier"', in ibid. (ed.), *Sexuality in the Middle Ages and Early Modern Times: New Approaches to a Fundamental Cultural-Historical and Literary-Anthropological Theme* (Fundamentals of medieval and early modern culture 3), Berlin: Walter de Gruyter, 2008.

84 See: J. Cadden, 'Sciences/Silences: The Natures and Languages of "Sodomy" in Peter of Abano's *Problemata* Commentary', in K. Lochrie, P. McCracken, and J.A. Schultz, *Constructing Medieval Sexuality* (Medieval Cultures 11), Minneapolis, MN, London: University of Minnesota Press, 1997, 40–57.

85 E.g. Alanus ab Insulis, *De planctu naturae Metre 1*, see Alain of Lille, *The Complaint of Nature*, transl. by D.M. Moffat, New Haven, CT, 1908, translation at https://source-books.fordham.edu/basis/alain-deplanctu.asp (accessed 25 February 2019).

86 C. Dyer, *Making a Living in the Middle Ages: The People of Britain 850–1520*, New Haven, CT: Yale Univ. Press, 2002, 157.

87 Literary thematization of virginity: K. Coyne Kelly, *Performing Virginity and Testing Chastity in the Middle Ages* (Routledge Research in Medieval Studies 2), London, New York: Routledge, 2000. See also J. Wogan-Browne, 'Chaste Bodies: Frames and Experiences', in M. Rubin and S. Kay, *Framing Medieval Bodies*, Manchester: Manchester Univ. Press, 1994, 24–41, showing a perspective on the female body as a 'vessel for balsam' (the soul), always endangered by being broken through sexual activity (25–6).

88 Discussion on sexual dispositions: J. Cadden, *Nothing Natural Is Shameful: Sodomy and Science in Late Medieval Europe*, Philadelphia, PA: University of Pennsylvania Press, 2013.

89 See: M.D. Barbezat, 'Bodies of Spirit and Bodies of Flesh: The Significance of the Sexual Practices Attributed to Heretics from the Eleventh to the Fourteenth Century', *Journal of the History of Sexuality* 25, 3, 2016, 387–419.

90 See the conception in: G. Pomata, 'Close-Ups and Long Shots: Combining Particular and General in Writing the Histories of Women and Men', in H. Medick, *Geschlechtergeschichte und Allgemeine Geschichte: Herausforderungen und Perspektiven*, Göttingen: Wallstein Verlag, 1998, 99–124.

91 J. Robb and O.J.T. Harris, 'Preface', in ibid., *The Body in History: Europe from the Palaeolithic to the Future*, New York: Cambridge University Press, 2013, 1–6, here 4–5.

92 Compare Kelly, 'Did Women Have a Renaissance?'.

93 Especially limits of individual memory and perception by means of technical support, limits of 'given' bodies' organic appearances by means of cosmetic chirurgy, prostheses, and genetic engineering, and limitations to a single location and perspective by means of virtualization of different bodies as one's own.

10

CONTEXTUALIZING LATE MEDIEVAL EMOTIONS

Esther Cohen

Introduction

The study of emotions is not the preserve of historians. To the contrary, it is a topic studied in many humanities and social science disciplines. To quote the cover page of *Passions in Context*: 'In recent years, the emotions have gained increased attention in a wide variety of disciplines including anthropology, history, sociology, political science, legal theory, criminology, economics, cultural and media studies as well as literature.'[1] To this list, we might add psychology, brain studies, and medicine that have mapped in recent years the brain areas affected by different emotions.

Historians, interdisciplinary by the very nature of their discipline, cannot but be affected by the study of emotions in contiguous fields, especially sociology and anthropology.[2] Unfortunately, historians are handicapped by their very sources. They cannot interrogate their subjects or elicit hidden meanings from them. They are dependent upon the declared word or image of the sources, and cannot therefore reach the raw emotion behind the social construct of emotion. All they can do is study the performance of emotions as a cultural construct, while aware of the distance between performance and underlying reality. Hence, this chapter will examine emotions in the social, not psychological context. The inner emotional world of the past is closed to us. Those who believe that emotions are hardwired in the human brain and universal can simply extrapolate from modern emotions to the past.[3] However, those who believe that all emotions are culturally bound and constructed are not free to do so. We are constrained by the expressions of people in the past, and cannot reach any putative raw emotion that underlies the evidence. The two important syntheses that have appeared in the last few years support the temporal character of emotions.[4]

Given the nature of our evidence, it is no wonder that the emotions we encounter are manifest social mechanisms that control interaction between people. Intimate and introspective emotions, characteristic of modernity, are hard to find in our sources.[5] When they do appear, as they do indeed in poetry and philosophy, they are also constructed according to the rules of the genre. It is with those emotions that I shall deal.

Given these constraints, is our inquiry legitimate? I believe so. What we have is a treasury of emotion words, which sound familiar, but are in fact different. Words matter, for they represent the writer's perception of reality. In this, I follow the work of Barbara Rosenwein, who analyses emotional communities through the emotion words that they use.[6] Words and images are a code, but it is possible to decipher this code and grasp the meaning. If the meaning has social imports, it is still relevant; after all, emotions are part of our cultural world as well.

In the following, I examine four key emotions: love, fear, anger (including revenge), and shame. In these, I have identified two emotional levels: there is the basic emotion word, denoting a widely recognized emotion, amenable to comparative and diachronic examination. Nevertheless, each emotion term is in reality a box hiding within it a cluster of emotions that may differ from culture to culture. As we have seen, these clusters contain some emotions that we would not expect in a modern cluster under the name of love, fear, anger, or shame. In modern culture, for example, the concept of 'good shame' as imitation of Christ is practically unintelligible, though shame alone is a transcultural emotional concept.[7]

This hierarchy of emotions makes the argument between the supporters of the social context as a matrix of the emotions and those who believe in their universality regardless of culture irrelevant. It is perfectly possible, and indeed realistic, to view emotions as both universal and innate on the one hand and culture-specific on the other. The keyword labels are definitely transcultural, but beneath the labels lie culture-specific emotions that cannot be transposed to other cultures without losing all meanings. Emotions embedded in a specific cultural matrix can also be time-specific. Thus, the emotions discussed are not only specific to Christian culture; they are also temporally bound to the period of roughly 1200 to 1600 in the Catholic countries of Europe. Concepts such as holy zeal and anger lose their meaning in the modern world, and compassion is a completely different concept from what the word denoted in the Middle Ages.

The meanings of these emotion words can only be unpacked through familiarity with the societal and mental matrix in which they are encoded. One cannot discuss medieval compassion or medieval shame without considering the suffering Christ and the suffering Virgin, an emotional focus irrelevant to modern compassion and shame.

Once we have gone beyond universal labels to examine emotions *in situ* and *in tempore*, we can discover in the later Middle Ages a complex weave of contrasting emotions. The attrition over time of historical reality has erased all but the most exuberant and violent emotions, those having left their mark in the records. The resultant picture is of a 'Violent tenor of life,' as Huizinga put it, time having eroded the more mundane emotions. While we are aware of the bias of records towards the picturesque and the extravagant, the picture we have is indeed of intensely felt and vigorously acted-out emotions.

Love

Love (lat. *Amor*) is the umbrella covering a host of emotions, and therefore very hard to define. According to the Oxford English Dictionary, it is

A feeling or disposition of deep affection or fondness for someone, typically arising from a recognition of attractive qualities, from natural affinity, or from sympathy and manifesting itself in concern for the other's welfare and pleasure in his or her presence; great liking, strong emotional attachment; (similarly) a feeling or disposition of benevolent attachment experienced towards a group or category of people, and (by extension) towards one's country or another impersonal object of affection.[8]

As we shall see, this definition is geared towards modern sensibilities more than universal or medieval ones.

Love is also a highly time-specific emotion. 'The educated culture of the twelfth century was profoundly shaped by the trope of love, a phenomenon that touched court – both lay and ecclesiastical – and cloister and resulted from a singular conjunction of cultural, political, economic, and religious factors.'[9] Indeed, Damien Boquet is right, but the love of the twelfth century is decidedly not the love of the fourteenth century. Hence, I will specify the precise period we speak of in each type of love that we examine.

Medieval loves were probably the most central and pervasive emotions of the high and later Middle Ages. Spiritual and secular, they captured the senses, the imagination, and the experiences of clergy and laity alike. They also dictated practices of devotion and literary writings. Closely tied to compassion and pain, love in its imagined form constituted a cohesive psychological/emotive and social force, linking humans with God and with each other. In fact, love was not a single emotion; it was a cluster of emotions under one polysemic umbrella. For example, in medical parlance, love-sickness was a recognized malady requiring treatment and cure.[10]

Love and its impact could appear in the most unexpected of contexts. Among other manifestations, it appeared in the field of dispute settlement as early as the eleventh century. Disputes could be settled according to law, and then one side would win and the other lose. Conversely, a love settlement would award each side something, thus saving face and avoiding a continuation of hatred and rancour.[11] Indeed, in thirteenth- and fourteenth-century England days in which settlements rather than sentences were reached were called Lovedays.[12] In late medieval Rome, disputants stopped short of violence 'for love of' the peacemakers.[13] Judicial love was the opposite of judicial hatred, which pursued revenge either through legal proceedings or through direct violence.[14] A public declaration of love in such circumstances was not the avowal of an emotion, but a speech act. It could put an end to a cycle of revenge and counter-revenge by making all disputants members in a circle of mutual consent. It was thus the glue holding together society in the face of internecine feuds and vendettas. Like many categories of love, it was explicitly gendered male, for women were rarely part of a feuding and peace-making community. It was a basic constitutive element in the coalescence and survival of emotional communities.

Emotional communities are 'groups in which people adhere to the same norms of emotional expression and value – or devalue – the same or related emotions.'[15] Their existence has been formulated by Barbara H. Rosenwein, who has studied several such communities during the Middle Ages and early modern period.[16] Such groups, notes Rosenwein, may overlap, so that one may belong to several groups simultaneously, depending upon the specific social context. For example, a late medieval city dweller may well have belonged to a community that considered a judicial settlement an expression of love, and at the same time be a member of a religious confraternity devoted to the love and worship of a certain saint. It is indeed easy to find communities centred on love as the cohesive emotional element of their culture. Rosenwein herself has noted that the term 'love' begins appearing in charters of Cluny towards the end of the ninth century.[17] The new usage, promoted by Cluniac scribes, fostered the creation of an emotional community of donors and monks united in love for the foundation. Verdon has argued that the relationship of lord and vassal in thirteenth-century Provence was one of love, due by the lord's men to the lord, and articulated through rituals of fidelity, the mutual exchange of gifts, and shared festive meals.[18] These expressions of public love, enacted in the public sphere, are very different from the intimate emotion envisaged by modern observers of affective emotions. One might argue that such formal expressions were simply a genre, not an emotion, but that would constitute defining the emotion to begin with as an affective individual inclination. I would argue that such was not the case in the Middle Ages.

Yet, the distance is not so very great. The relationship between lord and men, abbot and monks, replicates the familial nuclear relationship of parent and child. The vocabulary employed in the former sphere is drawn from the private world of domestic relationships. The love of fathers for their children is documented in autobiographical writings of Italian merchants and humanists who mourned the loss of their beloved sons.[19] Love within the nuclear family – parents' love of children and children's love of parents – was most often depicted through paintings and descriptions of the Holy Family. The late medieval biographies of Christ and his family contain many expressions of love and devotion within the family.[20] Late medieval preachers also extolled the virtues of domestic love in their sermons.[21] The Holy Family became an iconographic and didactic motif and a model for the ideal pure and sexless marriage.[22] This ideal of familial love is far distant from the modern one, and it is very different from the public, legal, declarative love of medieval peacemakers. However, it was also labelled love and used as a model of familial cohesiveness.

Parallel to the ideal holy marriage, the motif of unmarried sexual love grew in secular circles during the very same centuries. Originating in ideas of courtly love that flourished already in the tenth-century Ottonian court and, two centuries later, in the courts of Aquitaine and Champagne, courtly love was a completely different social emotion.[23] From France, the ideal of heterosexual extra-marital love spread throughout western and central Europe in the following centuries. The love, supposedly involving a married lady and a knight of somewhat lower social standing, provided a great deal of the subject matter of troubadours' songs and the *romances* of the twelfth and thirteenth centuries. It was supposed to be more than a socializing instrument for the civilizing of young men in a courtly context. It was the social construct of an ennobling emotion promoting spiritual growth and a higher achievement as a lover and a courtier and even, in some cases, as a man of God. The archetypal lover was the romance hero Perceval who, from a gauche, illiterate Welshman who nearly rapes a strange noblewoman, becomes first a noted knight and in the end a contemplative hermit. In its ideal form, then, courtly love could function as an uplifting, improving mechanism that would eventually divert the lover from earthly attractions to higher ones. In most of the literature and the poetry, however, courtly love remained an earthly, albeit theoretically unfulfilled, attraction between man and woman.

The literature of courtly love was not wholly idealistic. It made a clear distinction between different social classes of women, and how one was to go about wooing women of the nobility, the middle classes, and even a peasant, whom one (who belonged to the right social class) could simply rape.[24] It is important to note that courtly love was gendered, in the sense that it dealt with two very different expressions of love. Men's trajectories in the world of love led to a search for fulfilment and transformation in love, while the women stood as the objects and recipients of emotion. In courtly love literature, they too loved and suffered for their love, but they were not transformed by it.[25]

How far did this set of ideals impinge upon reality? European nobility was familiar with the concept of courtly love but certainly did not allow it, for example, to affect marriage strategies. The ultimate pair of medieval lovers, Abelard and Heloïse, paid a frightful price for their love and had a lifetime to repent it at leisure. Abelard did repent; Heloïse did not, but still spent her life as an abbess rather than a lover.[26] Nevertheless, ideals do shape behaviour, and if one is to accept Johan Huizinga's view, love was a central factor also in the culture of the fifteenth-century European courts.[27]

But back in the twelfth century, love flourished also in other environments. Given that the greatest contribution to the literate culture arose from monasteries and convents, it is hardly surprising that monastic love should have loomed so large in the time's sensitivities. The feeling, usually labelled *affectus* by the monks, had a respectable classical background, being highly praised by Cicero, who identified it with intellectual friendship (male, of course): 'a benevolent and loving consensus of human and divine things.'[28] Though in earlier times monastic institutions feared that dyadic relationships among monks might lead to homosexuality, the twelfth-century new monastic orders actually encouraged dyadic friendships. The wealth of correspondence from the time shows that intellectual monks took to the affect of friendship with great enthusiasm. Was there also a hidden element of homoeroticism in those relationships? John Boswell had claimed so, and been thoroughly criticized for his interpretation.[29] Specific studies of the great monastic intellectuals whose emotional writing on friendship and love had had them labelled homosexuals have usually claimed that this was a misinterpretation. Nevertheless, the allusions to same-sex love in the original writings are clear manifestations of such a love, albeit asexual.[30] The incontrovertible fact remains that monastic intellectuals of the twelfth century spoke of spiritual friendship as love, as *affectus*, as the greatest of pleasures.[31]

The high point of spiritual friendships as love also gave birth to the introspective, devotional love that flourished as of the thirteenth century. While devotional religious love may appear as a very different emotion from courtly or monastic love, many motifs of both permeated mystical love literature. In Mechthild of Magdeburg's (c. 1207–c. 1282/1294) *Flowing light of the Godhead*,[32] sentences like 'I would gladly die of love,' describing the relationship between soul and divinity, frequently recur. Both the *Song of Songs* and the troubadour love poetry echo in her visions.[33] Love holds a central place in the writings and revelations of all mystics. In its ardent, overtly erotic form, it appears especially in ecstatic visions of women mystics from ca. 1200 onwards.

> Women regularly speak of tasting God, of kissing him deeply, of going into his heart or entrails … The thirteenth-century poet and mystic Hadewijch spoke of Christ penetrating her until she lost herself in the ecstasy of love.[34]

It was often a visceral, embodied sensation, physical love sensed through the emotion.[35]

Mystical love had other manifestations as well. One nun spent hours communing with a doll of Baby Jesus, discussing his life experiences. Others revelled in meditations on Christ's blood. For women mystics, all senses were involved in the love of God.[36] Though the phenomenon was present also in some male mystics, it is far rarer among men than among women. 'But those men (such as Bernard of Clairvaux, Francis of Assisi, Suso, Ruysbroeck or Richard Rolle) whose religiosity was most experiential and visionary often understood themselves in feminine images and learned their pious practices from women.'[37] Remarkably, mystical love of God is often described as overwhelming the mystic, beyond any choice or decision. It is not an emotion embraced following a decision, but an influx of irresistible feeling coming from God to the believer. As such, it is also very feminine. It is very different from social love, often pursued by the choice of the lover. On a scale of voluntary disposition, I would place the completely willing and aware choice of the disputant at one end, with the secular lover – part choosing, part swept by emotion – in the middle, and the mystic, totally open and overwhelmed by love of God, at the other end of the scale.

This laconic overview of different loves is no more than a selection of the best-documented types. Love of nature, for example, must remain unexplored for lack of space. However, the remarkable fact remains that people in the later Middle Ages used the same word for settling a dispute rather than taking vengeance and for unification with God. Does this usage indicate a shared perception of the emotion? I would argue that indeed, love as a binding, unifying force was a shared emotion for mystics and disputants alike. It was more than a haphazard cluster of emotions lumped together under one term; it was indeed a core emotion embracing various fields of interaction among humans and between humans and the divine.

Compassion

Compassion, in its specific medieval sense, was closely tied to love, and part of the same emotional cluster. Born of affective meditation meant to induce total sensory and emotional identification with the suffering Christ and with his pain-wracked mother, it was largely a gendered emotion, practised and performed primarily by women religious.[38] While the origins lie in the writings of eleventh- and twelfth-century mystics, such as John of Fécamp and Anselm of Canterbury,[39] by the thirteenth century it became a meditative practice adopted by religious women from England to Italy and Germany.[40] Compassion carried a strong somatic element, expressed in stigmata and other corporeal markings of the passion engraved upon the body of compassionate religious women. By the thirteenth century, it was adopted and carried on largely through Franciscan spirituality, where men joined too in contemplative compassion.[41]

It is hard to overestimate the importance of the compassionate affective revolution of the thirteenth century.[42] It dominated the art produced in late medieval German convents, where pictures of the crucifixion of Christ and the bleeding body of Christ proliferated.[43] By the fourteenth and fifteenth centuries, it percolated from individual meditations of practising religious women and men to the laity, through Lenten sermons and vernacular tracts and enacted in urban spaces in processions of flagellants and Corpus Christi plays. From an intimate devotional practice of recluses and nuns, it grew into a social emotion that defined new emotional communities.

Fear

Other emotions, however, could equally foster the coalescence of an emotional community. A group of people facing a Viking invader or the onslaught of an epidemic could form an emotional community of fear, trying to deal with the approaching menaces.

Like love, fear is not a culture-specific emotion. It is prevalent, to a greater or lesser degree, in all human cultures, both as an individual phenomenon and as a group emotion. Medieval medicine viewed it as one of the accidents of the soul, or passions – one that made the blood retreat from the heart.[44] Yet, certain periods and cultures in history have merited the label of periods and areas of prevalent fear. W.J. Bouwsma has characterized the sixteenth century as an age of fear, and Jean Delumeau delineated fears that dominated European cultures from the fourteenth to the eighteenth century.[45] Fear, then, is the first place where we encounter communal emotions, which function differently from individual ones.[46] I would argue that indeed the later Middle Ages were afflicted with many communal fears, not all of them deriving from natural and man-made catastrophes. True, there were plagues and wars, but there were also preachers who instilled the fear of hell and its fires in audiences of the time and public rituals of execution and punishments to arouse fear of temporal justice in the viewers.[47] We also have a rich documentation, lacking in earlier periods, from the thirteenth century onwards testifying to waves of fear. We have evidence of insecurity and fear in twelfth-century society,[48] but the evidence for the effects of fear on contemporary populations is thin. This does not mean that there were no communal fears, but merely that they were not chronicled. Earlier chronicles do record other communal emotions, mainly shared by the elite: anger in popular uprisings, waves of devotional penitence, enthusiasm for the crusades, and so forth. Thus, the paucity of records of mass fears in earlier times is indicative of fear's importance in the later Middle Ages. While individual fears may have remained roughly similar, the discourse fostering communal fear became a far more dominant emotion from the fourteenth century onwards. These fears come forth also in the propitiatory rituals undertaken, under church aegis, in order to achieve release from the evils of the times. In 1412, the denizens of Paris went out day after day in planned processions around specific parishes and around the entire city to allay the fears of siege and war.[49] Such processions were also organized in many cities in the face of plagues and other dangers. Other than combatting fear, they served to foster communal unity and stability.

Nevertheless, late medieval society was plagued also with fears that no procession could assuage: peasant and workers' revolts – described by chroniclers in terms of great cruelty and savagery – and the prevalence of crime. These fears were socially linked to the bourgeoisie and the aristocracy, who stood most to lose from the success of revolutionaries and thieves, but the fear was widespread: 'The population believed that crimes such as murder, arson, rape, highway robbery, incest, and sodomy struck at the very heart of society and threatened to tear apart the social fabric.'[50] These fears remained unaddressed to a considerable degree. True, in France and England, the state judicial system developed its criminal prosecution in order to control crime, but there is no evidence that crime control actually reduced crime. The evidence is misleading, for with the rise of judicial institutions came registration and bureaucratization, resulting in ever-increasing masses of documentation that create the illusion of unrestrained growth of crime. By the sixteenth century, the criminalization of hitherto non-criminal activities such as prostitution and witchcraft did serve to increase the criminal statistics.[51] Punishment therefore only heightened crime rates and the concomitant social anxiety about crime.

Sermons served the opposite purpose: to deter sinners by heightening the fear of hell. Such sermons described in minute detail all the nine pains of hell. The exact nature and order of the pains varied from author to author, but the descriptions were eloquent. Let us look at Jacobus de Voragine's (c. 1230–1298) description of hunger:

> perpetual hunger, so much so that from hunger their flesh [i.e. the souls in hell] is consumed; so much so that the hunger is enclosed between their ribs, and it is perpetual, so that it can never exit from their ribs … so much so that they eat their own tongues; so much so that they devour their own and others' arms … so much so that from the intolerable hunger they curse both devil and God …[52]

The description of hellfire, as preached by Johannes Herolt (d. 1468), is no less persuasive:

> Present fire is comparable, in its heat, to the heat of hellfire as a picture of fire on the wall is comparable to real fire … If one keeps a finger in the fire for an hour, it is a great pain. Imagine what pain it is for those whose entire body burns for all eternity![53]

While fear of present catastrophes may have been more imminent than fears of a distant future, it is impossible to underestimate the impact of medieval sermons upon listeners. In extreme cases (such as Savonarola in Florence), daily sermons could alter the behaviour and consumption patterns of a whole city because of the fear of hell.[54] This use of fear stemmed to a great extent from Thomas Aquinas' view of at least one kind of fear as a way to God.[55]

Fear was recorded and remembered as a communal emotion with social functions and handicaps. In a noble masculine culture, individual fear was coupled with shame and perceived as the opposite of courage and honour. In the prevalent devotional climate of the time, however, fear was a powerful tool of repentance and purification of sins. Indeed, the later Middle Ages were a period of increased mass fears. Government institutions and the church did not allay these fears. To the contrary, they exploited fear as a deterrent. It mattered little whether fears were to deter from sins or from crimes; they worked in a similar manner in both fields. Communal fears, then, had their own function in serving the authorities. Fear, however, was closely linked to anger in certain situations that were not conducive to communal stability. When one group, familial or political (or both), opposed another in a vendetta, fear and anger were intertwined.

Fears, however, could lead to an unexpected reaction. Instead of deterring people from committing certain actions, they could lead to an explosion of anger. Though medieval authors considered the sin of anger (*ira*) to be descended from envy, it can trace its pedigree also to fear.

Anger

Anger in the Middle Ages was more than an emotion. It was a cluster of emotions including hatred, desire for vengeance, enmity, shame, and honour. In addition, it was a theological and pastoral concept of a capital sin, and a medical condition of humoral imbalance. Given the prevalence of the concept and its common application to social situations, it is not surprising that anger recurs in the sources with a frequency equalled only by love.

Like other emotions, anger merited philosophical discussions going back to Aristotle. The Aristotelic tradition defined anger as a boiling of blood in the heart, which then goes outward to seek vengeance.[56] This definition, repeated throughout the centuries, embedded anger (and all other emotions) solidly within the human body and its humoral complexion. Most twelfth-century scholastics dealing with anger condemned it as destructive for the individual and the human polity.[57] Nevertheless, they acknowledged the existence of just anger. Already Lactantius in the fourth century pointed out that God could be angry, and that this anger was justified and good.[58] In fact, Christ had also manifested ire on rare occasions, such as the time he evicted the money-changers from the Temple.[59] Thomas Aquinas' definition of anger as 'the desire to hurt another for the purpose of just retribution, motivated by some injury inflicted by the other and perceived as unjust by the angry man'[60] is a vindication of just anger. Nevertheless, all scholastics include the concept of vengeance, for better or worse, in their definitions. The angry man (and I use the gendered form advisedly, for they speak of men's anger) is angry with someone, and will seek retribution in the form of revenge. While Thomas is aware that *ira* is an irascible passion of the soul and thus ineradicable, he does discuss both good and bad anger and their consequences. Anger can be, under justifiable circumstances, a venial rather than capital sin, and just anger in God's service, or zeal, can be laudable.[61]

For medical authorities, anger was an individual's problem, the result of a plethora of choler (yellow bile) in the humoral makeup of the body, leading to a boiling of blood around the heart. Since choler was dry and hot, the cures included cold treatments, such as baths and avoidance of irritation. In fact, some doctors recommended anger as an antidote to an overly cold and moist complexion. The heat of anger would then restore the balance of the body.[62] Like fear, it was a recognized passion, or accident of the soul.[63]

The traditional view of anger, aptly named by Barbara H. Rosenwein as the 'hydraulic' model of historical emotions, is of an uncontrollable, unwilling, and primitive eruption of violent feeling.[64] This view, though long discredited, has re-surfaced in the study of somatic gestures with a linking of body language and emotion.[65]

Nevertheless, the majority of medievalists agree that in many cases, anger was a calculated strategy of conflict management, based on a conscious decision to enact anger.

In the realm of social interaction attitudes resembled the scholastic rather than the medical approach. Thus, during the crusades, anger was zeal for the conquest of Jerusalem and for revenge against the Moslems. It was more than justified; it was holy zeal.[66] Zeal justified not only crusades against unbelievers, but also the workings of inquisitors driven to eradicate heresies. However, for lay society anger *tout simple* was neither good nor bad. It could be a useful social mechanism in many situations. Thus, kings were expected to manifest royal anger, *ira regis*, a public display of anger, in specific situations. On the evidence of chronicles, this display was not a purely ritual gesture, but often a manifestation of inner rage. Some kings, notably the Angevin kings of England, were notoriously given to angry explosions, a character trait that was slowly brought under control during the thirteenth century with the rise of a new model of kingship. This new model exalted patience rather than overt anger,[67] so that Henry III did not follow the behaviour and emotional patterns of his father, uncles, and grandfather. Anger was restored to its place among the capital sins and removed from the list of mandatory royal manifestations of emotion.

If anger was part of the royal *persona*, for European nobility it was a social and political strategy. Any knight or nobleman who felt his just rights infringed could become angry and seek retribution. Failure to do so brought shame; successful anger brought honour. Twelfth-century chronicles and *chansons* are full of angry and vengeful nobles who do not attempt to restrain their anger, but almost explode with it, swearing retribution and insults.[68] Thus, White notes that 'Anger … has a well-defined place in political scripts in which other emotions figure as well.' In addition, 'Joy … is a public marker of honor for *sires*.' Finally, he sums up:

> displays of anger are essential elements in a 'technology of power' that each lord must have used in a slightly different way and that cannot be reduced to the usual categories of political history and cannot be neatly classified as either overt or symbolic violence.[69]

Anger was thus a tool of social interaction commonly employed by the fighting classes – nobles and knights – among themselves. Did this 'technology of power' percolate also to other social classes?

The endless vendettas among urban factions in late medieval Italy show that urban elites adopted the code of honour and concomitant anger from the nobility.[70] Attempts to control anger and feuding during the later Middle Ages did not have long-term success, and feuds were still common during the sixteenth century.[71]

Below the level of patrician anger, the emotion was present in mass form in urban and peasant revolts. While nobility-oriented chroniclers presented those revolts as either ludicrous or monstrous, what information we possess of more sympathetic sources shows that the rebels saw themselves as justly angry and claiming justifiable redress for their wrongs.[72] In this sense, their anger fitted White's model as well. Though anger was supposed to be a noble preserve, urban proletariats and peasants saw themselves entitled to the same emotion and resultant actions.

'[A]nger was regarded as a significant danger for the well-being of society, and without proper anger management, violence could erupt, embroiling everyone involved.'[73] Thus wrote Albrecht Classen, relying upon philosophical and literary sources. His words imply a societal shrinking and fear of anger. Social historians, however, even when drawing upon narrative sources, consider anger a political strategy, often employed without plans for a long-term feud or a gory revenge. Even preachers who whipped up the crowd's anger at Christ's crucifixion, sending their audiences to the nearest Jewish neighbourhood for a pogrom, acted out of zeal.[74] True, they sought revenge, but they did not intend to rip social structures apart. Even the peasants who rebelled in 1381 England and the Swiss ones in the following century had an alternative vision of the future, rather than blind destruction in mind. True, anger needed management, but not obliteration. If physicians could use anger constructively to heal patients, so could city authorities, kings, and noblemen. Properly managed and channelled, anger was a social construct embedded in existing social structures.

Shame

Closely linked with anger was the feeling of shame when one was dishonoured. The loss of status brought with it one type at least of shame. The anthropological distinction of societies of shame as opposed to societies of guilt is problematic in the historical context of the Middle Ages. It is next to impossible to disentangle shame from guilt in a society that prized confession, awareness of sin, shame in sin, and repentance – the latter often public and shaming. Guilt and shame were tied closely together, and cannot be separated. Nevertheless, for the sake of order, I shall concentrate upon shame alone.

But first, one must distinguish shame as an inflicted punishment and the internal feeling of shame. I take as my example a little-known shaming ritual, the *harmiscara* (also known in German as Harmscharr and in French as Hachée). It was a ritual of punishment, inflicted mostly on people[75] who had rebelled against their lords and had merited the death penalty. Though rare, it was employed (especially in the Empire) from the ninth century to the fifteenth. According to the description in various legislative and condemnatory texts, the culprit was to make a specific journey, usually barefoot and wearing only breeches, carrying on his neck an identifying and shaming object – a sword (for noblemen), a saddle, a wheel (for serfs), or even (for a woman) a heavy stone or a distaff. The degree of nudity, the nature of the carried object, the trajectory of the culprit in public space – all these defined the culprit and shamed him publicly.[76] In these cases, the inner state of the culprit was immaterial. He was shamed and disgraced by society. The best definition in such cases is infamy rather than shame. Like honour, which could be either something imposed by society or an internal quality, shame was both.

The chivalric ethos of the higher Middle Ages placed a strong emphasis upon honour and shame. One could achieve honour in battle, but one could also become attainted with disgrace and shame when fleeing from battle.[77] The code of shame was a social mechanism that functioned also outside chivalric culture. In cities, honour and shame could lie in the order of a hierarchical procession, or in the defamatory punishments inflicted upon criminals in the pillory and the gallows.[78] Shame could even lie in demeaning costumes of castrated animals worn in a carnival.[79]

Nevertheless, in all those cases shame was an external force, an objective mechanism that labelled the shamed person, but did not necessarily induce the emotion of shame. The confusion of objective/external shaming with subjective/internal shame creates the false dichotomy of shame and guilt. Unlike Latin, which has a rich variety of terms for shame of all sorts, English has no useful synonyms to demarcate the various semantic fields and nuances of shame.[80]

The later Middle Ages recognized various distinctions of internal shame, both negative and positive. Preachers distinguished between 'bad' shame that prevented confession and 'good' shame following confession and repentance – shame of the sin.[81] Some named the bad shame *verecundia* and the good *erubescentia*, but the semantic distinction was not universal. The important point was the role of shame in the psychological dynamics of confession. Fear of public disgrace and shame could prevent or postpone confession, for despite the seal of secrecy, the penalties carried out after confession were public, and could lead to dissemination of the sinful facts. In the internal forum of the conscience, however, shame encouraged penitence and confession.

The early thirteenth century saw the appearance of another type of shame – *pudicitia*, to use the patristic terminology. The holy women of the period – beguines, tertiaries, laywomen, and nuns – practised, as part of their ascetic regime, shame that was meant to imitate Christ's shaming during the passion. Here, in a combination unique to the Middle Ages, external and internal shame combined. The external shame was Christ's; the internal was that of his followers. The source of this humility came from St Francis, who encouraged his followers to assume nudity, marginality, extreme poverty, and begging as a form of evangelical life. Several living saints of the period adopted extreme humility and sought humiliation as their hallmark.[82] Voluntary shame was a new category that was liable to encounter opposition and mistrust from surrounding society.

Shame, in short, was a whole complex of emotions as well as a social mechanism. Scholastics saw it as a laudable emotion, close to a virtue.[83] The contrast between the shame of the chivalric code, which was close to infamy and of negative social valence, and the Franciscan humility, or the penitent's voluntary humiliation, created a wide spectrum of emotions, all denoting negative social standing, but possibly also spiritual growth and merit.

Conclusion

The landscape of emotions is not an internal, psychological one. Emotions have a social role and a social life. Love, fear, anger, and shame are all widely disseminated emotions, universally recognized and utilized. They could be cohesive or disruptive of communal structures, but they could all form the focus of emotional communities. A close look, however, shows that each one of these emotions is actually a cluster of often-contradictory feelings, some of them very distant indeed from the meanings modern society attributes to them. Compassion for the crucified Christ, salvific fear, holy anger, and devout shame are incomprehensible outside the temporal context of the later Middle Ages. Are medieval emotions totally incomprehensible to modern viewers, then? By no means. Emotion words may have changed their nuanced meanings, but enough of the core feeling has remained for us to identify both similarity and difference. The very fact that we can pinpoint the differences is indicative of our capacity to understand the foreign language of the Middle Ages.

Notes

1 Cover page of *Passions in Context: International Journal for the History and Theory of Emotions*, www.passionsincontext.de/index.php?id=483 (accessed 21 January 2016).

2 For a concise review of social science literature on the subject and its impact on historians, see Barbara H. Rosenwein, 'Problems and Methods in the History of Emotions,' *Passions in Context* 1, no. 1, 2010, 1–32, and 'Theories of Change in Medieval Emotions,' in J. Lilienquist (ed.), *A History of Emotions, 1200–1800*, London: Pickering and Chatto, 2012, 7–20, 207–10.

3 This theory has come under a great deal of criticism recently. See A. Touroutoglou et al., 'Intrinsic Connectivity in the Human Brain Does Not Reveal Networks for "Basic" Emotions,' *Social Cognitive and Affective Neuroscience* 10, no. 9, 2015, 1257–65; S. Koelsch et al., 'The Quartet Theory of Human Emotions: An Integrative and Neurofunctional Model,' *Physics of Life Reviews* 13, 2015, 1–27; K. Hoemann et al., 'Mixed Emotions in the Predictive Brain,' *Current Opinion in Behavioral Sciences* 15, 2017, 51–7; E. Clark-Polner et al., 'Multivoxel Pattern Analysis Does Not Provide Evidence to Support the Existence of Basic Emotions,' *Cerebral Cortex* 27, March 2017, 1944–1948. Brain researchers are questioning the 'fact' that specific emotions are set in specific places in the brain, or that there are universal emotions.

4 J. Plamper, *The History of Emotions: An Introduction*, trans. K. Tribe, Oxford: Oxford University Press, 2015; R. Boddice, *The History of Emotions*, Manchester: Manchester University Press, 2018.

5 B.H. Rosenwein, 'Y avait-il un "moi" au haut Moyen âge ?,' *Revue Historique* 307, no. 1, 2005, 40.

6 Ead., *Generations of Feeling: A History of Emotions, 600–1700*, Cambridge: Cambridge University Press, 2015; Ead., *Emotional Communities in the Early Middle Ages*, Ithaca, NY: Cornell University Press, 2006.

7 F. Morenzoni, 'La bonne et la mauvaise honte,' in *Shame Between Punishment and Penance: The Social Usages of Shame in the Middle Ages and Early Modern Times*, ed. B. Sère and J. Wettlaufer, Florence: SISMEL, 2013, 177–93; D. Boquet, 'Rougir pour le Christ. La honte admirable de saintes femmes au XIII siècle,' ibid., 139–55.

8 www.oedcom/view/Entry/110566?rskey=cv5whX&result=1#eid (accessed 3 November 2018).

9 D. Boquet, 'Affectivity in the Spiritual Writings of Aelred of Rievaulx,' in M.L. Dutton (ed.), *A Companion to Aelred of Rievaulx 1110–1167*, Leiden: Brill, 2017, 167.

10 M.F. Wack, *Lovesickness in the Middle Ages: The Viaticum and Its Commentaries*, Philadelphia, PA: University of Pennsylvania Press, 1990.

11 F. Cheyette, 'Suum Cuique Tribuere,' *French Historical Studies* 6, 1970, 287–99; M. Clanchy, 'Law and Love in the Middle Ages,' in J. Bossy (ed.), *Disputes and Settlements: Law and Human Relations in the West*, Cambridge: Cambridge University Press, 1983, 47–67. S.D. White, '*Pactum … legem vincit et amor judicium*: The Settlement of Disputes by Compromise in Eleventh-Century Western France,' *American Journal of Legal History* 22, 1978, 281–308; W.I. Miller, *Bloodtaking and Peacemaking: Feud, Law*

and Society in Saga Iceland, Chicago, IL: Chicago University Press, 1990, 257–300. J.A. Palmer, 'Piety and Social Distinction in Late Medieval Roman Peacemaking,' *Speculum* 89, 2014, 974–1004; R.L. Keyser, '"Agreement Supersedes Law, and Love Judgment": Legal Flexibility and Amicable Settlement in Anglo-Norman England,' *Law and History Review* 30, no. 1, 2012, 37–88.

12 Clanchy, 'Law and Love in the Middle Ages.'

13 Palmer, 'Piety and Social Distinction,' 975.

14 D.L. Smail, 'Hatred as a Social Institution in Late-Medieval Society,' *Speculum* 76, 2001, 90–126; Ibid., *The Consumption of Justice: Emotions, Publicity, and Legal Culture in Marseille, 1264–1423*, Ithaca, NY: Cornell University Press, 2003; R. Bartlett, '"Mortal Enmities": The Legal Aspect of Hostility in the Middle Ages,' in B.S. Tuten and T.L. Billado (eds.), *Feud, Violence and Practice: Essays in Medieval Studies in Honor of Stephen D. White*, Farnham: Ashgate, 2010, 196–212. In fact, emotions in legal situations are not particular to the Middle Ages. They were undoubtedly raging when Socrates was tried for corrupting the mores of the young in classical Athens, and are present in legal proceedings to this day. See S.A. Bandes (ed.), *The Passions of Law*, New York: New York University Press, 2000.

15 Rosenwein, *Emotional Communities*, 2.

16 Ead., *Generations of Feeling*, 3–10.

17 Ead., 'The Political Uses of an Emotional Community: Cluny and Its Neighbors, 833–965,' in D. Boquet and P. Nagy, *Politiques des émotions au moyen âge*, Florence: SISMEL, 2010, 205–24.

18 L. Verdon, 'Expressions et usages de comportements affectifs dans le cadre de la seigneurie Provence, XIII siècle. L'example de l'amour dû au seigneur,' in D. Boquet and P. Nagy, *Politiques des émotions au moyen âge*, 255–74. One has only to compare the meaning of the kiss on the mouth between a twelfth-century rite of vassalage and a twentieth-century Hollywood film to see the widely different meanings.

19 J.R. Banker, 'Mourning a Son: Childhood and Paternal Love in the Consolateria of Gianozzo Manetti,' *History of Childhood Quarterly* 3, 1976, 351–62; G.W. McClure, 'The Art of Mourning: Autobiographical Writings on the Loss of a Son in Italian Humanist Thought 1400–1461,' *Renaissance Quarterly* 39, no. 3, 1986, 440–75.

20 P. Payan, *Joseph. Une image de la paternité dans l'Occident médiéval*, Paris: Aubier, 2006.

21 Y. Mazour-Matusevich, 'Late Medieval "Counselling": Jean Gerson 1363–1419 as a Family Pastor,' *Journal of Family History* 29, no. 2, 2004, 153–67; R. Rusconi, 'St. Bernardino of Siena, the Wife, and Possessions,' in R. Rusconi and D. Bornstein (eds), *Women and Religion in Medieval and Renaissance* Italy, Chicago, IL: Chicago University Press, 1996, 182–96.

22 Payan, *Joseph*, 301–12.

23 C.S. Jaeger, *The Origins of Courtliness: Civilizing Trends and the Formation of Courtly Ideals, 939–1210*, Philadelphia, PA: University of Pennsylvania Press, 1985, 19–49.

24 T. Adams, 'Performing the Medieval Art of Love: Medieval Theories of the Emotions and the Social Logic of the *Roman de la Rose* of Guillaume de Lorris,' *Viator* 38, no. 2, 2007, 55–74; John Scattergood, '"The Unequal Scales of Love": Love and Social Class in Andreas Capellanus's *De amore* and Some Later Texts,' in H. Coony (ed.), *Writing on Love in the English Middle Ages*, Basingstoke: Palgrave, 2006, 63–79.

25 E.J. Burns, 'Courtly Love: Who Needs It? Recent Feminist Work in the Medieval French Tradition,' *Signs* 27, no. 1, 2001, 23–57.

26 P. Abelard, 'Abelard's Letter of Consolation to a Friend,' *Medieval Studies* 12, 1950, 195–202; *The Letters of Abelard and Heloïse*, Penguin Classics Harmondsworth: Penguin, 1974.

27 J. Huizinga, *The Autumn of the Middle Ages*, trans R.J. Payton and U. Mammitzsch, Chicago, IL: University of Chicago Press, 1996, Chapter 5.

28 A. of Rievaulx, 'De spiritali amicitia,' in C.H. Talbot (ed.), *Aelredi Rievallensis Opera Omnia*, CCCM 1, Turnhout: Brepols, 1971, 292.

29 J. Boswell, *Christianity, Social Tolerance, and Homosexuality: Gay People in Western Europe from the Beginning of the Christian Era to the Fourteenth Century*, Chicago, IL: Chicago University Press, 1980; reprint 2015, 221–43. For the criticism, see M. Kuefler (ed.), *The Boswell Thesis: Essays on Christianity, Social Tolerance and Homosexuality*, Chicago, IL: Chicago University Press, 2006.

30 D. Boquet, *L'ordre de l'affect au moyen âge. Autour de l'anthropologie affective d'Aelred de Rievaulx*, Caen: CRAHM, 2005, 308–23; Idem, 'Affectivity in the Spiritual Writings of Aelred of Rievaulx'; B.P. McGuire, 'The Cistercians and the Transformation of Monastic Friendships,' *Analecta Cisterciensia* 37, 1981, 1–63; Ibid., 'Love, Friendship and Sex in the Eleventh Century: The Experience of Anselm,' *Studia Theologica* 28, 1974, 111–52.

31 E. Cohen, 'Reflections on High Medieval Monastic Pleasures,' in N. Cohen-Hanegbi and P. Nagy (ed.), *Pleasure in the Middle Ages*, Turnhout: Brepols, 2018, 21–33.

32 Mechthild von Magdeburg, *Das fliessende Licht der Gottheit: nach der Einsiedler Handschrift in kritischem Vergleich mit der gesamten Überlieferung*, ed. by H. Neumann and G. Vollmann-Profe, 2 vols (Münchener Texte und Untersuchungen zur deutschen Literatur des Mittelalters 100–101), Munich: Artemis, 1990–1993. English translation, F.J. Tobin, New York: Paulist Press, 1998.

33 A. Classen, 'The Literary Treatment of the Ineffable: Mechthild von Magdeburg, Margaret Ebner, Agnes Blannbekin,' *Studies in Spirituality* 8, 1998, 162–87.

34 C.W. Bynum, 'The Female Body and Religious Practice in the Later Middle Ages,' in ead. (ed.), *Fragmentation and Redemption: Essays on Gender and the Human Body in Medieval Religion*, New York: Zone Books, 1992, 190–1.

35 Ibid., 186–95.

36 R.D. Hale, 'Rocking the Cradle: Margetha Ebner Beholds the Divine,' in M.A. Suydam and J.E. Ziegler (eds), *Performance and Transformation: New Approaches to Late Medieval Spirituality*, London: Macmillan, 1999, 211–35; Ead.; '"Taste and See, for God is Sweet": Sensory Perception and Memory in Medieval Christian Mystical Experience,' in *Vox Mystica: Essays on Medieval Mysticism in Honor of Professor Valerie M. Lagorio*, ed Anne Clark Bartlett et al., Martlesham: D.S. Brewer, 1995, 3–14; C.W. Bynum, *Wonderful Blood: Theology and Practice in Late Medieval Northern Germany and Beyond*, Philadelphia, PA: University of Pennsylvania Press, 2007; Ead., 'The Blood of Christ in the Later Middle Ages,' *Church History* 71, 2002, 685–714.

37 C.W. Bynum, 'The Female Body and Religious Practice,' 191.

38 S. McNamer, *Affective Meditation and the Invention of Medieval Compassion*, Philadelphia, PA: University of Pennsylvania Press, 2010, 13–14.

39 R. Fulton, *From Judgment to Passion: Devotion to Christ and the Virgin Mary, 800–1200*, New York: Columbia University Press, 2002, 142–92.

40 S. McNamer, 'The Origins of the *Meditationes vitae Christi*,' *Speculum* 84, 2009, 905–56; P. Tóth and D. Falvay, 'New Light on the Date and Authorship of the Meditationes vitae Christi,' in S. Kelly and R. Perry (eds), *Devotional Culture in Late Medieval England and Europe: Diverse Imaginations of Christ's Life*, Turnhout: Brepols, 2014, 17–104; M. Weinhandl (ed.), *Deutsches Nonnenleben: Das Leben der Schwestern zu Töss und der Nonne von Engeltal Büchlein von der gnaden Überlast*, Munich: O.C. Recht Verlag, 1921; A. Blannbekin, *Leben und Offenbarungen der Wiener Begine Agnes Blannbekin d. 1315*, ed P. Dinzelbacher and R. Vogeler, Göppinger Arbeiten zur Germanistik 419, Göppingen: Kümmerle Verlag, 1994.

41 D. Boquet and P. Nagy, *Sensible moyen âge. Une histoire des émotions dans l'Occident médiéval*, Paris: Seuil, 2015, 274–84.

42 McNamer, *Affective Meditation*, 17.

43 J.F. Hamburger, *Nuns as Artists: The Visual Culture of a Medieval Convent*, Berkeley, CA: University of California Press, 1997.

44 S. Knuuttila, *Emotions in Ancient and Medieval Philosophy*, Oxford: Clarendon Press, 2004, 215.

45 W.J. Bouwsma, 'Anxiety and the Formation of Early Modern Culture,' in ibid., *A Usable Past: Essays in European Cultural History*, Berkeley, CA: University of California Press, 1990, 157–89; J. Delumeau, *La peur en Occident, XIVe–XVIIIe siècles. Une cité assiégée*, Paris: Fayard, 1978.

46 P. Nagy, 'Collective Emotions, History Writing and Change: The Case of the *Pataria* Milan, Eleventh Century,' *Emotions: History, Culture, Society* 2, no. 1, 2018, 132–52. This case is copiously documented by several chroniclers and analyzed in depth by B. Stock, *The Implications of Literacy: Written Language and Models of Interpretation in the Eleventh and Twelfth Centuries*, Princeton, NJ: Princeton University Press, 1983, 151–241. Its dating makes it highly unusual. As a rule, it is hard to find collective emotions so early.

47 See, for example, F. Mormando, *The Preacher's Demons: Bernardino of Siena and the Social Underworld of Early Renaissance Italy*, Chicago, IL: University of Chicago Press, 1999; E. Cohen, *The Crossroads of Justice: Law and Culture in Late Medieval France*, Leiden: Brill, 1993, 181–201.

48 T.N. Bisson, 'Hallucinations of Power, Climates of Fright in the Early Twelfth Century,' *Haskins Society Journal: Studies in Medieval History* 16, 2006, 1–11.

49 J. Chiffoleau, 'Les processions parisiennes de 1412. Analyse d'un rituel flamboyant,' *Revue Historique* 285, 1990, 37–76.

50 C. Gauvard, 'Fear of Crime in Late Medieval France,' in B.A. Hanawalt and D. Wallace (eds), *Medieval Crime and Social Control*, Minneapolis, MN: University of Minnesota Press, 1999, 1; P. Boglioni et al. (eds), *Le petit peuple dans l'Occident médiéval: Terminologies, perceptions, réalités* Paris: Publications de la Sorbonne, 2002; J. Haemers, 'A Moody Community? Emotion and Ritual in Late Medieval Urban Revolts,' in E. Lecuppre-Desjardin and A.-L. Van Bruaene (eds), *Emotions in the Heart of the City*, Turnhout: Brepols, 2005, 63–81.

51 L. Behrisch, 'Social Control and Urban Government: The Case of Goerlitz, Fifteenth and Sixteenth Centuries,' *Urban History* 34, no. 1, 2007, 39–50; S. R. Blanshei, 'Crime and Law Enforcement in Medieval Bologna,' *Journal of Social History* 16, 1982, 121–38; T. Dean, *Crime and Justice in Late Medieval Italy*, Cambridge: Cambridge University Press, 2007; T. Dean and K.J.P. Lowe, 'Writing the History of Crime in the Italian Renaissance,' in Ibid. (eds), *Crime, Society and the Law in Renaissance Italy*, Cambridge: Cambridge University Press, 1994, 1–15; A. Musson and E. Powell (eds), *Crime, Law and Society in the Later Middle Ages*, Manchester: Manchester University Press, 2009; M.K. Schüssler, 'German Crime in the Later Middle Ages: A Statistical Analysis of the Nuremberg Outlawry Books, 1285–1400,' *Criminal Justice History* 13, 1992, 1–60; J. Ángel Solórzano Telechea, '*Fama publica*, Infamy and Defamation: Judicial Violence and Social Control of Crimes against Sexual Morals in Medieval Castile,' *Journal of Medieval History* 33, 2007, 398–413.

52 Jacobus de Voragine, *Registrum in sermones de tempore*, Lyon15, sermo 125 n.p.; R.E. Pepin, 'Nouem species poenae: The Doctrine of Nine Torments in Honorius Augustodunensis, Alain de Lille, Pastoralia and Bernard de Morlas al. Morval,' *Latomus: Revue d'études latines* 47, 1988, 668–74.

53 J. Herolt, *Sermones discipuli de tempore et de sanctis una cum exemplorum promptuario ac miraculis B. Virginis*, Venice: Petrus Maria Bertano, 1603, sermon 125, n.p.

54 R. Rusconi, 'Public Purity and Discipline: States and Religious Renewal,' in M. Rubin and W. Simons (eds), *The Cambridge History of Christianity 4*, Cambridge: Cambridge University Press, 2009, 451–78.

55 R. Miner, 'Thomas Aquinas's Hopeful Transformation of Peter Lombard's Four Fears,' *Speculum* 92, no. 4, 2017, 963–75.

56 E. Carrera, 'Anger and the Mind-Body Connection in Medieval and Early Modern Medicine,' in ead. (ed.), *Emotions and Health, 1200–1700*, Leiden, Boston, MA: Brill, 2013, 128; M.B. Cels, 'Interrogating Anger in the New Penitential Literature of the Thirteenth Century,' *Viator* 45, no. 1, 2014, 203–19; R. Miner, *Thomas Aquinas on the Passions*, Cambridge: Cambridge University Press, 2009, 268–87; M. McCarthy, 'Divine Wrath and Human Anger: Embarrassment Ancient and New,' *Theological Studies* 70, no. 4, 2009, 845–74. I have not devoted a special section to revenge, largely because the latter is seen as an acting out of a variety of emotions: anger, hatred, jealousy, sorrow, mourning. See B.H. Rosenwein, 'Les émotions de la vengeance,' in D. Barthélemy et al. (eds), *La vengeance, 400–1200*, Rome: École française de Rome, 2006, 237–57; Ead., *Emotional Communities*.

57 A. Classen, 'Anger and Anger-Management in the Middle Ages: Mental-Historical Perspectives,' *Mediaevistik: Internationale Zeitschrift für interdisziplinäre Mittelalterforschung* 19, 2006, 21–50.

58 C. Casagrande and S. Vecchio, *Histoire des péchés capitaux au moyen âge*, trans. P.-E. Dauzat, Paris: Aubier, 2003, 97.

59 Ibid., 96.

60 M. Rota, 'The Moral Status of Anger: Thomas Aquinas and John Cassian,' *American Catholic Philosophical Quarterly* 81, no. 3, 2007, 403.

61 Thomas Aquinas, *Quaestio disputata de malo*, quaestio 12 in *Corpus Thomisticum*, ed. R. Busa, www.corpusthomisticum.org/qdm08.html (accessed 1 November 2018).

62 Carrera, 'Anger and the Mind-Body Connection,' 137–41.

63 Knuuttila, *Emotions in Ancient and Medieval Philosophy*, 215.

64 B.H. Rosenwein, 'Worrying about Emotions in History,' *The American Historical Review* 107, 2002, 834.

65 D.L. Smail, 'Emotions and Somatic Gestures in Medieval Narratives: The Case of Raoul de Cambrai,' *Zeitschrift für Literaturwissenschaft und Linguistik* 138, 2005, 34–48. See also P.R. Hyams, 'Was There Really Such a Thing as Feud in the High Middle Ages?,' in S.A. Throop and P.R. Hyams (eds), *Vengeance in the Middle Ages: Emotion, Religion and Feud*, Aldershot: Ashgate, 2010, 151–75. For a rebuttal of this approach, see M.L. Bailey and K.-J. Knight, 'Writing Histories of Law and Emotion,' *The Journal of Legal History* 38, no. 2, 2017, 117–29; S.D. White, 'The Feelings in the Feud: The Emotional Turn in the Study of Medieval Vengeance,' in K. Esmark et al. (eds), *Disputing Strategies in Medieval Scandinavia*, Leiden: Brill, 2013, 281–312.

66 S.A. Throop, 'Zeal, Anger and Vengeance: The Emotional Rhetoric of Crusading,' in S.A. Throop and P.R. Hyams (eds), *Vengeance in the Middle Ages: Emotion, Religion and Feud*, Aldershot: Ashgate, 2010, 177–201.

67 G. Althoff, '*Ira Regis*: Prolegomena to a History of Royal Anger,' in B.H. Rosenwein (ed.), *Anger's Past: The Social Uses of an Emotion in the Middle Ages*, Ithaca, NY, London: Cornell University Press, 1998, 59–74; P.R. Hyams, 'What Did Henry III of England Think in Bed and in French about Kingship and Anger?,' in Ibid., 92–124; S.R. Doubleday, 'Anger in the Crónica de Alfonso X,' *Al-Masāq* 27, no. 1, 2015, 61–76.

68 S.D. White, 'The Politics of Anger,' in B.H. Rosenwein (ed.), *Anger's Past: The Social Uses of an Emotion in the Middle Ages*, Ithaca, NY, London: Cornell University Press, 1998, 127–52; Boquet and Nagy, *Sensible moyen âge*, 240–4.

69 White, 'The Politics of Anger,' 142–3, 51.

70 See, for example, T. Dean, 'Marriage and Mutilation: Vendetta in Late Medieval Italy,' *Past and Present* 157, November 1997, 3–36; E. Muir, *Mad Blood Stirring: Vendetta and Factions in Friuli during the Renaissance*, Baltimore, MD: Johns Hopkins University Press, 1993; for feuds outside Italy, see Smail, 'Hatred as a Social Institution'; O. Volckart, 'The Economics of Feuding in Late Medieval Germany,' *Explorations in Economic History* 41, no. 3, 2004, 282–99; S. Pohl-Zucker, 'Hot Anger and Just Indignation: Justificatory Strategies in Early Modern German Homicide Trials,' in K. Gilbert and S.D. White (eds), *Emotion, Violence, Vengeance and Law in the Middle Ages: Essays in Honour of William Ian Miller*, Leiden: Brill, 2018, 25–48; Bartlett, 'Mortal Enmities.'

71 S. Carroll, 'The Peace in the Feud in Sixteenth- and Seventeenth-Century France,' *Past and Present* 178, February 2003, 74–115.

72 J. Rollo-Koster and A. Holstein, 'Anger and Spectacle in Late Medieval Rome: Gauging Emotion in Urban Topography,' in C. Goodson et al. (eds), *Cities, Texts and Social Networks, 400–1500*, Farnham: Ashgate, 2010, 149–74; P. Freedman, 'Peasant Anger in the Late Middle Ages,' in B.H. Rosenwein (ed.), *Anger's Past: The Social Uses of an Emotion in the Middle Ages*, Ithaca, NY, London: Cornell University Press, 1998, 171–88; Nagy, 'Collective Emotions, History Writing and Change.'

73 Classen, 'Anger and Anger-Management,' 50.

74 D. Nirenberg, *Communities of Violence: Persecution of Minorities in the Middle Ages*, Princeton, NJ: Princeton University Press, 1996.

75 J.-M. Moeglin, 'Harmiscara – Harmschar – hachee: Le dossier des rituels d'humiliation et de soumission au Moyen Age,' *Archivum Latinitatis Medii Aevi* 54, 1996, 11–65. Moeglin has found very few mentions of women undergoing this punishment.

76 Ibid., 15–16, 25–6.

77 B. Sère, 'Le roi peut-il avoir honte? Quelques réflexions à partir des Chroniques de France et d'Angleterre XIIe–XIIIe siècles,' in D. Boquet and P. Nagy (eds), *Politiques des émotions au Moyen Âge*, Florence: SISMEL, 2010, 56–63; Boquet and Nagy, *Sensible moyen âge*, 183–86, 244–8.

78 J. Wettlaufer and Y. Nishimura, 'The History of Shaming Punishments and Public Exposure in Penal Law 1200–1800: A Comparative Perspective Western Europe and East Asia,' in B. Sère and J. Wettlaufer (eds), *Shame Between Punishment and Penance*, Florence: SISMEL, 2013, 203–09; C. Gauvard, *Condamner à mort au moyen âge: pratiques de la peine capitale en France, XIIIᵉ–XVᵉ siècles*, Paris: PUF, 2018, 99–105.

79 E. Le Roy Ladurie, *Le Carnaval de Romans*, Paris: Gallimard, 1979.

80 Verecundia, pudor/pudicitia, confusio, erubescentia, rubor. See Boquet, 'Rougir pour le Christ,' 143–4.

81 F. Morenzoni, 'La bonne et la mauvaise honte,' ibid., 177–93; C. Vincent, 'Pastorale de la honte et pastorale de la Grâce en Occident entre le XIIe et le XV siècle,' Ibid., 157–76.

82 D. Boquet, 'Rougir pour le Christ'; Ibid., 'Christus dilexit Verecundiam. La honte admirable d'Angèle de Foligno et la cause des Franciscains spirituels,' *Rives Méditerranéennes* 31, 2008, 73–88.

83 S. Vecchio, 'La honte et la faute. La réflexion sur la *verecundia* dans la littérature théologique des XIIe et XIIIe siècles,' in B. Sère and J. Wettlaufer (eds), *Shame Between Punishment and Penance: The Social Usages of Shame in the Middle Ages and Early Modern Times*, Florence: SISMEL, 2013, 105–22.

PART 2

Europe meets the globe

Western identities in question, 1500–1750

INTRODUCTION

Alessandro Arcangeli

'Early modern period' is a relatively poor or at least not unproblematic historical category. While it has gained noticeable academic acceptance, partly to substitute more ethnocentric and value-charged terms, like Renaissance, it ultimately seems no less culturally biased, considering that the very notion of modernity is an intrinsically 'Whiggish' one and to look retrospectively for early signs of modernity is a methodologically faulty way to approach our knowledge and understanding of the past.[1] In the end, some prefer to go by centuries, which present the advantage of being undoubtedly cultural constructions (nothing changes astronomically, or from any other meaningful respect, at the turn of one century to the next). There are, however, definite events and phenomena that help mark the historical flow of time by splitting a continuum into segments that present some kind of coherence: many contemporaries were convinced, for instance, of a revolutionary role played by the advent of gunpowder, the compass and the printing press. Inevitably, their perception was shaped by their intellectual background and their experience, so in a way it was primarily cultural transformation that guided the early stages of historical periodization, from the work of fifteenth-century humanists onwards. In a sense, taking the second half of that century and, at the other end, the changes that took place in the late eighteenth as marking points appears to have a special justification in the context of *cultural* history.

What is, then, characteristic of those three centuries in cultural history? How have recent generations of cultural historians contributed to our understanding of the past between, roughly, those dates, perhaps departing from previous historical narratives?

The level of 'modernity' attributed to the era, as well as being dubious as retrospective diagnosis, is in the eyes of the beholder, and has undergone significant change in the transition between different generations of historians and their socio-cultural surroundings. Until, say, World War I, it was standard to emphasize the role of the (re-) discovery of America, the Renaissance and Reformation – just to mention a selection of developments and factors – not just as turning points somewhere in the past, but as marks of the beginning of the world we are in. This is no longer tenable in the post-modern and post-industrial society. In conjunction with an increasing awareness of profound changes that were taking place in the twentieth century, the adoption of ways of interpreting the past partly borrowed by – or re-elaborated from – cultural anthropology prompted a large portion of the historical profession to consider even the comparatively recent past as a foreign country. This significant hermeneutic shift required the abandonment of some characteristic tenets which, on the whole, generations of historians had shared.

Jacob Burckhardt's 1860 classic *The Civilization of the Renaissance in Italy*, with its emphasis on the discovery of the world and of man, and the idea of the emergence of the individual out of collective networks and identities, offers a typical example of a victim of such a shift: it is difficult today to think of the 'Renaissance man' as so different from the medieval one, or so close to ourselves. James R. Farr discusses this crucial point in Chapter 15, where, in a way distinctive of cultural history as it has been theorized and implemented over the past few generations, the early modern self is examined under the two interconnected lenses of practices and representations. Cultural identities are not the only field in which historiographical paradigms have changed. For instance, the fading of the influence of Marxist social theory over the practice of history during the last quarter of the twentieth century has watered down the ubiquitous presence and protagonism of the bourgeoisie as key agent in the historical imagination.

What we have aimed to offer in the following chapters is a representative selection of topics and approaches capable of depicting a portrait of the period that combines – as every type of history does – the identification of elements of continuity and change through those centuries, and does so with a culturalist aftertaste. Let us suggest a few ways in which this has been pursued (and hopefully achieved), as well as threads a reader may find when approaching this second Part, in whatever order.

If 'history of mentalities' is a phrase that has lost much of its appeal since the 1980s, as it appeared to assume too static and homogeneous attitudes towards the world throughout society, mental maps of various sorts and forms of understanding the human experience and its surroundings are still very much, in renewed ways, a key object of cultural history – in fact, they help mark its distinction from forms of historical enquiry more concerned with events. Thus, in Brendan Dooley's chapter what is offered is a sample of the contemporary experience of time, in its multiple dimensions: local, historical and cosmographical. The experience of space is surely not missing either, for instance as spaces of domesticity (Raffaella Sarti), or communication (Antonio Castillo Gómez).

Some areas and angles have emerged around the turn of the millennium. When Peter Burke published, ten years after its original 1991 release, his successful edited *New Perspectives on Historical Writing*, the one chapter that was added addressed 'Environmental History'.[2] We open with a chapter, by Linnéa Rowlatt, that concerns the interactions between humans and the environment. The variety of their forms is investigated in many human activities that have to do with the animal world and the rest of nature, as well as in the impact of climate and climate change on the human life and experience. The focus, however, is on ways of understanding that world, so Rowlatt, before surveying the cultural shifts the period witnessed, defines primarily, in the received tradition, the earth as a divine gift. This starting point may therefore offer us the opportunity to signal that faith and religious experience and practices emerge variously throughout this book even if they have not been assigned a special place. Our aim in this has been to avoid dividing the subject area into too standardized compartments, and revisit the everyday life of the past from less habitual perspectives. The religious component of the life of people of different creeds, and its contribution to determining who they thought they were and what they did, are given due consideration throughout the volume – for instance, when Jonas Liliequist discusses the impact of reformed Christian moral doctrine on the regulation of the behaviour of the faithful (including such unintended consequences as an epidemic of suicidal murders). Manners of understanding the natural world play a significant role later on in Hjalmar Fors's contribution, where late Renaissance botanical scholarship is offered as an example of ways in which contemporaries made sense of the world, by creating and transferring knowledge.

Gender, the body and health are also major themes of historical research on which cultural history has given strategic contribution to the historical knowledge of the past couple of generations; in this Part of the volume, for the early modern period the reader will find them disseminated and entangled with the other topics and perspectives.

Two interconnected approaches that have marked the most recent research in a distinguished way are the attention to the visual and material culture of the past, signalling the search for a wider range of sources rather than the more traditional verbal texts.[3] Images appear here and there in this section to testify how historians nowadays can hardly work without evoking them to their readers. In the case of Farr's chapter, they also provide the specific object of a section of his analysis (portraits and self-portraits). As for material culture, it is a main theme in Raffaella Sarti's contribution, which explores contemporary habits of food consumption, clothing and dwelling; it also appears, as resulting from cultural encounters, in Giuseppe Marcocci's chapter, where attention is paid to the specific forms of cultural practice that accompanied the production, circulation and consumption of goods, such as the gift; or, in the one by Castillo Gómez, in the artefacts and materiality of the forms of communication.

The affective and sensual turn has provided another distinctive flair of the international historiography of the past fifteen years, so in this section too the reader will be confronted with an exercise in the history of emotions (Liliequist), where the choice has been to select a limited number of items in the affective palette – reverence, shame and guilt – and monitor the way their experience has interacted with such factors as authority, religion, gender, age group and class.

The emphasis on forms of historical practice, which we have already mentioned for the case of the experience of the self (Farr), is also clear when we revisit, with Castillo Gómez, the early modern communication system. Learning from anthropological understandings of human agency and its cultural conditions, the exploration of the way individuals and groups interplay, decision-making is made in specific cases and facts are subjectively interpreted is a thread that runs through much of the historical enquiry; but the history of the book and reading has offered a special opportunity for the past half-century, responding to Marshall McLuhan's emphasis on the revolutionary role of the printing press, by rediscovering orality and aurality and the survival of the manuscript, and assigning a significant role to appropriation, the active reception and transformation of texts and messages that reshapes their meanings.

Communication therefore turns into the terrain of a conflict (a topic that is also thematized by Marcocci in relationship with cultural encounters). And conflict is inevitably a key category when we come, with Tomás A. Mantecón, to explore the cultural history of politics, in the form of manifestations and dynamics of power, from interpersonal violence to social unrest and war. The fact that the author of that contribution adopts, among others, quantitative methods, should act as a helpful reminder that there are a multiplicity of historical approaches, and it is the variety of their use and mix that can ensure a richer heuristic harvest.

That earlier trio – gunpowder, the compass and the printing press – shares another peculiar characteristic (although they share it with many other technological inventions): while they were used to advance the position and redefine the relation of the West with the rest of the world, they all ultimately came from China.[4] The global dimension history took from then onwards has offered material for many research areas and stimulated a variety of approaches. 'Overseas history' is a paradigm that emerged from the dismissal of old imperialist ways of seeing the rest of the world.[5] More recently, global, connected and entangled history paradigms have competed to show how rich – and, to some extent, unacknowledged – the interactions between events occurring in different parts of the world were already many centuries ago.[6] Marcocci's contribution below addresses mobility (voluntary or otherwise), global interaction and cultural transfers in the Age of Discoveries. In the aftermath of recent migrations and new levels of globalization, historians have looked at the past and made mobility a specific field of enquiry, as well as the process of cultural hybridization that derives from encounters and transfers.[7] This has also suggested a self-reflection of cultural history on ways to stand up to the challenges posed by today's phenomena and learn from them adequate and renewed ways also to question the past.[8]

The Columbian Exchange is considered also by Rowlatt, for instance, inasmuch as it provided Europeans with tobacco, a new plant that opened up a variety of cultural practices; or in Fors's chapter, where the curiosity for exotic botanicals is examined as a case study in the history of knowledge. This is even more systematically the case with Sarti, for whom the European acquisition of natural products and artefacts originating from different parts of the world (the East as well as the newly encountered Americas) is the subject of such consideration that, to sum up the whole experience of material cultures of living, she selects attitudes to novelties as a meaningful thread to be monitored in its historical evolution. Once again, a rich spectrum of human experience is under scrutiny with an eye for mental maps and cultural orientation, and a question of paramount importance is faced, if we are to test the degree of 'modernity' of our past.

Notes

1 H. Butterfield, *The Whig Interpretation of History*, London: G. Bell, 1931.

2 P. Burke (ed.), *New Perspectives on Historical Writing*, Cambridge: Polity, 1991 and 2001.

3 A guide of admirable clarity is offered by a fellow cultural historian in L. Jordanova, *The Look of the Past: Visual and Material Evidence in Historical Practice*, Cambridge: Cambridge University Press, 2012.

4 That the length of such primacy is ordinarily overstated is argued convincingly in F. Fernández Armesto, *Millennium: A History of Our Last Thousand Years*, London: Bantam, 1995.
5 H. Wesseling, 'Overseas History', in P. Burke (ed.), *New Perspectives on Historical Writing*, 67–92 (2nd edn 2001).
6 S. Gruzinski, *Les quatre parties du monde: Histoire d'une mondialisation*, Paris: La Martinière, 2004. See also Chapter 18 in this volume for references to the work of Sanjay Subrahmanyam.
7 For thought-provoking syntheses see S. Greenblatt, *Cultural Mobility: A Manifesto*, Cambridge: Cambridge University Press, 2010; P. Burke, *Cultural Hybridity*, Cambridge: Polity, 2009. Also, Chapter 25 below, by Dhan Zunino Singh.
8 L. Hunt, *Writing History in the Global Era*, New York: W.W. Norton and Company, 2015.

11

GOD'S GREEN GARDEN

Interactions between humans and the environment

Linnéa Rowlatt

Nature continued to challenge human communities in a variety of ways, including the general worsening of weather conditions during the Little Ice Age, whose effects are examined here in a selection of climate zones. Logging, farming, fishing, and mining in the early sixteenth century provide case studies of the interaction between nature and human culture, at a time when the range of animals and plants that were vital to the life of human communities underwent a dramatic globalization. The natural environment was understood by contemporaries largely from the perspective of theology, although the outset of natural science may be found, and the Protestant Reform affected European mental maps on this front as well. Discussing interactions between humans and the environment in a meaningful way asks for a reliable theoretical context by which to identify causation, discuss relationships, and follow transformations over time. A useful frame to discuss the cultural history of human relations with the environment is the hybrid and interactive model of socio-economic metabolism, which recognizes a dynamic, recursive, and reciprocal interrelationship between nature and culture (Figure 11.1).[1] The theory recognizes causative action from both the cultural and natural spheres as exerting an impact on human and social biophysical structures, as well as each other. Hence, it allows a mutually interactive relationship between human culture and nature.

The hybrid and interactive model of socio-economic metabolism is based on the recognition that our human bodies are simultaneously qualitatively constructed through culture and organic beings which function within the laws of nature, affected – although not determined – by the natural world where we exist. The model establishes the materials of human society, including artefacts and human bodies, as hybrids of the symbolic sphere and the material sphere. That is, material society is rendered intelligible by symbolic culture while at the same time each item, living and non-living, takes part in flows of energy and materials with the natural environment. Changes in either the natural world or the cultural sphere, or sometimes both, may have an effect on the material conditions of human societies.

An essential element of this model is the colonization of natural ecosystems, where certain natural processes, forces, or events are used for humans to reach their

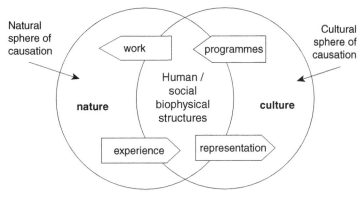

Figure 11.1   Humans and the natural environment, autonomous and interrelated. ©Richard C. Hoffmann, *An Environmental History of Medieval Europe*, Cambridge: Cambridge University Press, 2014, 9; Hoffmann in turn acknowledges his debt to M. Fischer-Kowalski and H. Weisz, 'Society as Hybrid Between Material and Symbolic Realms: Toward a Theoretical Framework of Society-Nature Interaction', *Advances in Human Ecology* 8, 1999.

goals – which are established by cultural preferences and priorities. Clearing woods to create pasture or arable fields, for example, may have intended consequences for the biosphere, such as the introduction of livestock or cereals, and unintended consequences, such as increased rates of erosion, subsequent loss of topsoil, and, eventually, infertile soils.

In the early sixteenth century, Western culture was limited to the continent of Europe and this chapter indeed explores interactions between humans and nature in Europe during the first half of the sixteenth century. But are the limits of a geographic region and period of study justly defined so swiftly? Consider the continent, whose winds sometimes arrive from the Sahara Desert or from Siberia, whose fish may have migrated across oceans before landing on a Christian plate for Friday supper, or whose invaders face no natural barriers to the east, as discovered by the Huns during the thirteenth century and by the Ottoman Empire on several occasions. The European natural environment is seamlessly integrated into global systems which contribute to conditions in the innumerable distinct bioregions that make up the continent, creating unique combinations of regional terrain, watersheds, soils, and native plants and animals. Further emphasizing the artifice of delimiting the natural environment of Europe once and for all, this period saw the beginnings of the Columbian Exchange where organisms and objects arrived in Europe from the Americas and slowly transformed the biotic foundations of European society.[2] Temporal limits are also chosen for our convenience, because the interactions we shall be discussing did not begin in 1500 or end in 1550. For example, climatic trends began centuries earlier and would end centuries later; basic methods of early sixteenth-century agriculture, logging, fishing, and mining had developed before this time, with only slow techno-logical improvements that would not leap forward until the onset of industrialization.

These technologies serve as important avenues for inquiring about the effect the work of Europeans had on their environment. Unlike today, during the early six-teenth century most European adults were directly involved in primary resource extraction, but the diverse qualities in bioregions mentioned earlier mean that a wide variety of methods were used to produce adequate caloric intake and the raw materials for a material infrastructure. Even accounting for regional differences, con-ditions in Europe's natural environment deteriorated unevenly during the course of the Little Ice Age to reach a nadir in the late sixteenth century and then slowly im-proved. Specific forms of stress experienced from the natural world depended upon the needs of each region, as the same volume of rain falling to flood the Zuiderzee in the Netherlands could bring a successful harvest to farms on the Iberian Peninsula.

The Roman Catholic Church held interpretative authority over events, forces, and processes in nature in 1500, with results that ranged from annual festivities across Christendom held during the late summer petitioning God for successful harvests to the wearing of amulets and talismans by some individual Christians to protect against storms. Wide distances between Christians meant local rituals, regional saints, and personal prayers based on Catholic dogma vied with official doctrine as spiritual shield against natural disaster or for other petitions to divinity with respect to the environment. Despite all efforts, long-term instability based on unreliable weather conditions typical of the Little Ice Age contributed to sporadic outbreaks of social turmoil and, following ritual failure to address natural challenges, is suspected of having shared in founding receptive conditions for cultural reforms. The reforms initiated by Martin Luther in 1517 included a new representation of nature, one that continues to influence humans' programmes in nature today.

This chapter explores the above themes, provides case studies sketching represen-tative areas and approaches of research, and emphasizes recent research showing a complex image of European interactions with nature in the early sixteenth century. To support the establishment of at least a single comprehensive image, most case studies will be drawn from the Upper Rhine Valley, a single bioregion in which, during the early sixteenth century, there were common expectations of the natural environment.

Inherited views of nature in 1500 CE

Questions about the fact and behaviour of the natural environment are a concern of theology as well as natural science. During the many seasons when the two were a single intellectual pursuit, Scriptural-based explanations for the existence and struc-ture of the natural world exerted wide-ranging implications for faith and practice. In this devoutly Christian worldview, the natural environment was created by God as a *scala naturae* with God's wisdom placed in every creature. This 'Great Chain of Being' was an intricate hierarchy of natural and supernatural beings and an important vehi-cle for God to deliver instruction, inspiration, and chastisement to humanity. Those who understood God's messages were considered to be reading the Book of Nature, a second source of revelation alongside the Book of Scripture.[3]

The *scala naturae* and the Book of Nature were two influential organizing concepts representing the natural environment held by late medieval Europeans. The first in particular was central to many Catholic rituals begging God for success or protection as, similar to an appeal to one's feudal overlord for assistance in re-establishing the social order after suffering from a military invasion, Christians appealed to God for assistance in re-establishing the Creator's natural order after disturbances. Some of these rituals took the form of priests leading rogations around cities and towns to erect walls of divine protection from disaster, natural and otherwise;[4] some involved the blessing of oncoming storm clouds to dissolve demon-caused hailstorms,[5] blessing water to be sprinkled over kitchen gardens, or blessing fishing boats. Other priests, such as Strasbourg's cathedral preacher Johann Geiler von Kaysersberg, preached obedience to God as the way of bringing good weather – rather than making a deal with the devil to bring rain.

Case study one: Johann Geiler von Kaysersberg and the natural environment

The first official preacher of the *Liebfrauenmünster zu Straßburg*, orthodox Catholic priest Johann Geiler von Kaysersberg, held forth every Sunday, every day from Advent to Lent, and for certain feasts and processions from 1478 to 1510. For 1509 Lent, Geiler found inspiration from the Biblical verse *Vade ad formicam o piger et considera vias*; his sermons were published in 1516 under the title *Die Emeis*. They contain a comprehensive description of several elements of the natural environment, including details of the *scala naturae*, the creation of inclement weather by demons, and suggestions for addressing problems.

> As well, all animals approach to the wisdom of men, as much as they can (To a certain extent, they touch the horizon of human reason, as do men of the angels or intelligences.) The creatures are like a chain, one ring grips the other ring, the second, the third, etc. In the same way all creatures are fastened together. The trees go towards the reason of man as much as they can, consequently the animals even more so, and one animal more than the other gets closer to the reason of man reaching towards the reason of angels and one angel to the next. In such a way that all creatures hang together like rings in a chain.[6]
>
> So the devil can make snow, rain, and wind, hail, and thunder, because he can bring the humours together in a short time, when he sees the signs of the witches. For which reason the witches can make a hailstorm in a heated room. But there must always be water there (Material must have a subject).[7]
>
> From that it is taken that one rings the bells against the storm, that one chases away the bad spirits with the ringing, when they hear the trumpets of God, the bells. For in the Old Testament, they used the trumpets as we now use the bells. Again: one rings to exhort the world, that they should pray and call upon God, those are our weapons against the evil spirit. It is also taken from that that someone in Gaul and also in Alsace, too, they work against the storm with the sacrament. In Swabia, the priest must go forth outside the village, and must speak the Gospel of John, 'In the beginning was the word', etc., against the storm and he must exorcize the storm. The Emperor, as well, in imperial law praises those who punish and execute the female storm-makers …[8]

In a context of inherited views of nature similar to these, growing knowledge of the so-called New World challenged Scriptural assumptions about the earth by introducing people unmentioned in the Bible and by existing on a scale so large as to be unimagined. Along with corruption in the church hierarchy, such challenges contributed to increasing degrees of doubt about the value and efficacy of Catholic practice and explicit anti-clericalism.[9] Political and religious hierarchies which ordered European communities had developed during the medieval period, but by 1500 rudimentary capitalism was exerting an effect on social relationships as well. While feudal vows of personal loyalty between a land-owning class of nobility and peasants ensured a stable workforce, land ownership was the primary source of wealth.[10] Communities, however, were not helpless in the face of noble landowners, with most village councils regulating themselves with respect to field crops, animal pasturage, and other land management requirements. Far from being a 'tragedy of the commons', such self-management was sustainable over centuries and the foundation of long-term social stability.[11] Wilderness areas slowly transformed from open access to private lands, usually owned and managed for the benefit of noble landowners, which included as hunting grounds, as woodlots, and as areas to pasture one's pigs and other domestic animals.[12] Depending on the region, communities had greater or lesser success in negotiating with overlords for reliable access to land and, arguably, success itself may have been a motivating force for the 1525 German Peasants' War – largely a non-violent event until lords united to militarily repress peasants and reject their demands.[13]

Logging, farming, fishing, and mining in the early sixteenth century

Prior to the flood of raw materials which would later arrive from the Americas, early sixteenth-century Europeans relied on medieval technological, legal, and social systems to produce and distribute resources for consumption, construction, and luxury goods. The diverse methods of farming, fishing, mining, and logging were fundamental to the experience of nature by most Europeans. Varieties of resource extraction will be described and illustrated here, along with two brief case studies exploring consequent dietary regimes.

Silviculture

Four types of resources were extracted from woodlands: fuel, forage, raw materials, and timber. A low-energy civilization, wood and charcoal (wood from which water and other volatile elements have been baked off in a kiln) were the primary sources of energy for heating in Europe before the introduction of fossil fuels. This meant that access to woodlands or wood fuel was necessary for cooking, heating, making pottery, and other necessities of life. A household of four or five people would burn on average almost 5 tons of wood fuel per year, with regional variations from 1.5 tons in Italy to 10 or more tonnes in Scandinavia and other northeastern areas.[14] Forage, or 'wood pasture', fed domestic livestock both *in situ*, where the beasts were released into the woods and later recaptured, and through the cutting of leafy green branches by humans then carried to animals outside the woods.

Early sixteenth-century humans foraged in the woods as well. Plant uses included dyeing, medicines, and food; small branches have been found woven into baskets, wicker, fences, or wattle walls, while wood was worked into objects both utilitarian and decorative, from spoons to tapestry frames. Sticks, used for such things as kindling or to support grapevines, were bundled into short or long faggots (2 feet in circumference and either shorter or longer than 3 feet) for easy transportation by both women and men. Timber, distinguished by its larger size, was the basis of construction for houses, castles, churches and cathedrals, ships, city walls and gates, and water- and windmills; it is challenging to identify construction which did not require beams from mature trees. Timber had to be hauled, though, from its point of origin to construction sites. As Hoffmann notes, the oak post for a windmill could be approximately 0.6 metres square and 13 metres long, with a weight near 4 tons; the mast for a ship could weigh up to 500 kg if made of spruce. An oak mast could weigh as much as 750 kg after drying for a year, thereby losing 20% of its mass.[15] Such giants were ideally floated by river to their destinations, although dragging them with draught animals was also common.

In 1500, most European woodlands were carefully and sustainably managed through coppicing, pollarding, or shredding. Coppicing means to cut a broad-leaf tree back to near-ground level, manage the new growth of shoots, and then cut again when the shoots have reached a desired size. Pollarding follows the same methods but the tree is cut higher from the ground, usually above the reach of a grazing animal. Cutting only wide branches while allowing the trunk to continue growing upwards was known as shredding the tree. Although pollarding and shredding are more dangerous to the woodcutter than coppicing, using these methods allowed multiple uses for the woods and contributed to replenishing soils with fertilizers. These methods of woodland management are not without ecological consequences, however; regular human passage compacted some soils and the inability of some tree species to endure repeated cutting back created woodlands with few tree species outside of the selected varieties.

The extent of woodlands in Europe has had an inverse relationship with the European population: increasing numbers of people during the first centuries of the second millennium caused the great clearances of the twelfth and thirteenth centuries, where, for example, by 1340 only 6% of England was covered in woods.[16] The mid-fourteenth-century demographic disaster of the Black Plague, however, where up to two-thirds of the European human population died over a few years, created a context of diminished human exploitation that allowed woodlands to regrow. Nevertheless, by the early sixteenth century when human population levels were finally returning to pre-plague levels, deforestation in several regions led once again to high prices for all types of forest products, as well as tightening legislation aimed at controlling access. For example, saws were frequently banned from woodlands, as saws allowed poachers to take wood silently; axes, on the other hand, were and are noisy indicators of illegal activity that are more likely to lead to apprehension and arrest by authorities.

Agriculture

Different climate zones in northern and Mediterranean Europe required different principles and methods of agriculture to provide enough calories for human survival, particularly where cultural preferences selected cereal production as a priority. North of the Alps and the Pyrenees, western Europe has characteristically maritime or semi-continental climates featuring high levels of precipitation and moderate temperatures, while the eponymous climates of Mediterranean Europe feature a drier climate and warmer average temperatures (climate is discussed in greater detail below).

Agriculture in Mediterranean Europe centred upon three primary crops – olives, grapes, and cereals – cultivated alongside the practice of transhumance for domestic livestock. Rainy cool winters, hot dry summers, generally light sandy soils, and a broken, mountainous relief led to an annual cycle where grains were planted in the autumn and received enough moisture over winter to harvest in May or June, before the onset of the following summer's drought. Wheat and barley were the most important cereals, although rice was also grown in humid areas such as the Po River valley on the Italian Peninsula. In an effort to maintain soil fertility, a bare fallow system was followed where fields rested one year in two. Ploughing under the weeds and cereal plant remnants after a spring harvest enriched the soil and captured precious water underground, as did leaving the field bare to precipitation during the fallow year. However, arable soils were regularly lost through erosion from wind and water throughout the Mediterranean bioregion.

As well as serving to hold soil in place, olive trees are tolerant of the region's characteristically thin and dry soils. After growing for a dozen or so years to reach maturity, the popular olive tree will bear fruit for many decades. Native to the Mediterranean, the grapevine sends down deep roots and will also provide fruit for many years once mature. The two staples share other qualities: both may be grown in mixed gardens or alongside cereal crops, as well as in orchards or vineyards, and both grapevines and olive trees go dormant during the summer heat, an adaption common to many other trees and plants of the bioregion.

With respect to livestock, sheep and goats outnumbered cattle or pigs in early modern Mediterranean Europe. A significant challenge to rearing livestock was the difficulty of obtaining summer forage in areas subject to summer drought; the solution frequently lay in vertical transhumance, where livestock and their minders moved to summer pastures in the mountains. This practice, though, deprived cultivated fields of manure and, combined with soil erosion, rendered soil fertility management an ongoing concern.

Cereal cultivation north of the Alps and Pyrenees took advantage of heavier, richer soils and a maritime or continental climate to increase yields through following a short fallow cycle. This approach to soil fertility management saw each field planted in a three-year cycle of winter grain (wheat or rye) followed by spring grain (barley or oats), with the third year fallow and, often, pasturing livestock.[17] Fields themselves were organized either as the 'Champion' system (also known as *champagne* system, from the French) – great expanses of fields with a few groves of trees, separated by hedgerows, centred on a village – or the 'ancient countryside' or 'woodland' system, known as *bocage* on the continent, where fields were irregular in layout, with smaller, more numerous villages. According to Richard Hoffmann, the ancient countryside system of field organization was 'less communal' than the Champion system, which was organized to facilitate gangs of peasant labourers whether engaged communally in ploughing, harvesting, or pasturing livestock, or working on behalf of a lord.[18]

Since higher levels of precipitation meant that livestock did not need to go to higher elevations in search of forage, northern European livestock was generally pastured on fallow fields and thereby contributed to the fertility of heavy clay soils. By the early sixteenth century, there was widespread use of the heavy mouldboard plough, which picks up the soil and turns it over. This, too, contributed to soil fertility, as nutrients were lifted to the surface and made available for crops. Animals needed to pull the plough, though, had their own needs, whether in the shape of fodder for oxen or as fodder and grain for horses. A balance between having enough land to sustain the workers, both human and bestial, and the right number of workers to cultivate the land available was essential but elusive.

Case study two: early modern food culture of western Europe 1 – grains

In early sixteenth-century western Europe, regional culinary variety based upon geographic and climatic differences comfortably co-existed alongside broader, culturally based food preferences which transcended local agricultural production. Consumption patterns generally followed socio-economic status; the regular diet of the nobility and other aristocracy was similar across the continent but unavailable to peasants, who relied on local produce to a much greater extent. No matter how exalted or how humble, though, cereal products were a reliable element of every meal and, for common people, provided up to 90% of their daily nutritional needs.

Grains were ground and boiled to various consistencies as porridge, gruel, and flour soup. The soup was served to the elite when flour was added to sweetened water, beef stock, or soft curds, with mature cheese, spices, sugar, or rose water sprinkled on top. Porridge for the gently bred was usually a thick meal made from groats, hulled seeds, or coarsely ground grains cooked in beef stock or milk, or, during the late medieval religious year's one hundred and forty fast days, almond milk. Demonstrating its widespread popularity among those who could afford it, a dish of hulled wheat berries boiled in milk and seasoned with cinnamon and sugar was known as *frumenty* in England, *fourmentée* in France, and *fromentiera* in Italy. For common folk, porridge, gruel, and soups made from water and coarsely ground flour supplemented with vegetables were daily fare. *Pepu*, where rye flour was stirred into cold water or fish stock, was particularly popular in Finland, along with *mutti*, where flour was boiled in the liquid.

Baked bread, though, reigned over tables high and low and was usually cooked in communal ovens staffed by professional bakers, used even by the wealthy. For the prosperous, serving bread assisted in declaring social status: the host would expect a freshly cooked loaf, guests of honour received day-old bread, and older bread was given to others. Bread served at elite tables would be pure white wheat bread, while dark bread made from rye, barley, oat, millet, or mixed flours was the purview of the lower classes. As well as foodstuff, bread also acted as a trencher, particularly in the north when sliced from loaves a few days old, as a spoon, or, in the end, as a finger wipe. Diners could anticipate regular replacement of their trencher during meals and, if not consumed, trenchers were given to animals or to the poor as alms.[19]

Pisciculture

For wealthier Europeans, fish were a solution to the regular Catholic ritual demands for abstinence from meat and dairy products (see case study three, below), but the availability of aquatic wildlife for consumption depended on one's location as well as personal financial resources. By the early sixteenth century, maritime coastal areas such as those bordering the North Sea, Baltic Sea, western Mediterranean Sea, and the nearby North Atlantic Ocean had developed commercial fisheries focused on both fish and marine mammals. Their catch of fish was mainly herring and cod in the north and sardine, hake, and tuna in southern Europe, and was available to consumers fresh-caught; mammals such as seals, whales, or walruses were prized for oil, hides, and flesh, but rare and costly. Inland dwellers were not so fortunate in their supply and relied on dried, salted, smoked, or pickled marine fish as well as fresh-water fish.

Fresh-water fish, however, were mostly seasonal delicacies and to remedy this, many landowners dammed creeks, exerted control (private or public) over entire bodies of water, or built and stocked artificial fishponds, mostly with carp. For example, the Perugian government established regulatory control over Lago Trasimeno in Umbria with several thirteenth-century ordinances and statutes which regulated fishing until 1568. Rules included size limitations on netting, complete bans on netting specific species at particular times, and restrictions on the use of enclosure traps. Every third October lakeside residents were required to put bundles of reeds and branches in the shallows to shelter and protect spawning and overwintering fish. In 1490, an armed patrol vessel was introduced to the lake, with officers of the special communal fisheries overseer ready to penalize infractions with fines of up to 500 *lire*.

Case study three: early modern food culture of western Europe 2 – fish

Fish held an important place in a food culture regulated by regular and seasonally extensive periods of religiously inspired fasting, as from the eighth century onwards, Christians were encouraged to practise abstinence from meat and dairy products as a personal exercise in repentance. Specific dates for fasting varied throughout the centuries, but in 1500, lay people were confronted with demands for abstaining every Friday, in commemoration of the crucifixion, and for Lent, the forty days immediately before Easter. Members of religious orders were expected to only eat meat when ill or aged. For the poor, expense led to regular abstinence from meat and dairy products; salted fish was consumed most regularly by them, and fresh fish with the same frequency as meat itself (maybe once per week).

For those who could bear the cost, fish was prepared in a multitude of fashions including poached, fried in oil, baked by itself or inside a pie or pastry shell, or grilled. Cold and moist, medical experts recommended that to maintain a healthy internal balance, any fresh fish should be served warm and with a savoury or spicy sauce. Dishes such as trout simmered in ginger broth, boiled eel with pepper, grilled Baltic herring with mustard, or fish in an acidic sauce might grace the table of early modern diners. Salted fish was much less expensive than fresh and required soaking or boiling for consumption.

Mining

Late medieval Europeans conceptualized metals as having a first existence deep in the fiery bowels of the earth. There, it was thought, a mixture of vapours precipitated out purer metals which slowly ripened into silver and gold – a process alchemists strove to duplicate. The act of bringing raw metals to the surface, however, was based on strenuous digging to pursue a vein of ore until it ran out or went into areas too deep or too filled with water for miners to safely work. Mines were owned by overlords (often royalty and sometimes territorial princes), who granted access to individual miners in return for a fee or a royalty on what they took out of the ground. Typically beginning as individual entrepreneurs, miners regularly formed self-governing but short-lived communities under the authority of an officer of the overlord (Figure 11.2).[20]

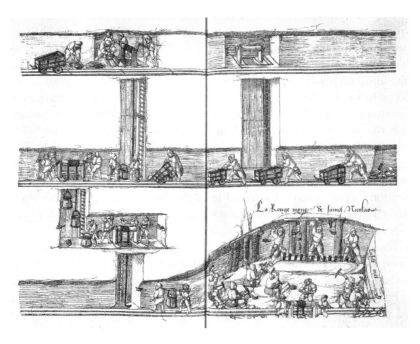

Figure 11.2   Drawing by Heinrich Gross for the Duke of Lorraine (sixteenth century). This cross-cut shows three levels of the sixteenth-century mine at the Saint-Nicolas mine at La-Croix-aux-Mine in the Vosges Mountains of France. A mine was generally composed of three main elements: the gallery, the well, and the area where pit-props have been removed. The entrance is at the upper gallery, the main level of exploitation is at the second level, and the third shows the deepest, leading edge of the operation. A dozen miners are occupied at the bottom right. Some are seated on their leather skirts and work with pointer and hammer. Others break apart a large rock by striking it with iron weights. Lamps rest on the ground or hang suspended from wooden supports. Two workers tote some ore to the well in a pail, which will be carried up by winch. In the middle gallery, where digging is located some distance away from the well, raw ore is carried to the winch by carts. Paris, Bibliothèque nationale de France. Public domain.

By 1500, blast furnaces were in use throughout western Europe as the primary means of extracting iron and other metals from ore. Based on regular blasts of air supplied from bellows operated by windmills or water wheels, furnaces reached 1,500°C and melted a mixture of iron and carbon into an ingot called a 'pig'. Pig iron may more easily be re-melted and cast into another mould. A single operational cycle of a blast furnace could take several weeks and yielded between 3 and 9 tons of cast iron, all requiring vast amounts of wood to burn as fuel. The average family in late medieval Europe might own somewhere between 20 and 100 kg of metal objects.

Natural events, forces, and processes

Where the previous section explored human exploitation of the natural environment, this section looks at those elements of the natural world outside of human control, focusing particularly on the climate. According to the Köppen-Geiger climate classification system, Europe – which is located in the northern temperate zone – has three major climate zones: marine, continental, and Mediterranean. Northwestern Europe's coastal areas from Portugal to Denmark have a marine climate, which is heavily mediated by the moist, warm air carried from the equator by the Gulf Stream; precipitation is high while temperatures infrequently dip below freezing. Seasons of hot, dry weather are also the exception for marine climates; temperatures generally hover between 0° and 23°C. Continental climate, found primarily in eastern Europe, has the greatest annual variation with generally hot summers and cold, sub-zero winters. Sandwiched between coastal areas and eastern Europe, much of central western Europe has a semi-continental climate: milder than continental because of open waters in the North and Baltic Seas, but colder than coastal areas and with more precipitation falling as snow. Protected from the Atlantic by the Iberian Peninsula, the Mediterranean climate found around that sea has only two seasons: warm, dry summers and mild, wet winters.

The five decades between 1500 and 1550 occurred at the conclusion of the Spörer Minimum, the second coldest trough of the Little Ice Age, itself several centuries of cooler-than-mid-twentieth-century averages.[21] Also characteristic of non-anthropogenic climate change, extreme weather events increased in frequency and intensity and led to long-term material instability created in part by erratic and unreliable weather conditions throughout the continent. Since thirty years of weather observations are required before confident statements may be made about climate in any particular area, isolated incidences cannot 'demonstrate' the effects of climate change, anthropogenic or non-anthropogenic. However, the following three case studies which briefly describe the impact of weather on three early sixteenth-century European communities provide an example of challenging conditions which increased in incidence and severity during the Little Ice Age.

Case study four: the Little Ice Age and marine climate zones – England

Following weather-related English harvest failures in 1518, 1519, 1520, and 1521, daily rain in 1527 from 12 April to 3 June caused that year's harvest to fail once more.[22] The price of grain rose dramatically; dearth followed, with famine in East

Anglia, and by 1528, real wages declined over 25%, implying a surfeit of unemployed. Henry VIII's Lord Chancellor, Cardinal Thomas Wolsey, introduced social policy that was intended to re-distribute basic foodstuffs (primarily grain) in times of dearth in order to prevent famine. Similar to Wolsey's policy regarding plague, which was to be kept away by quarantine, dearth policy was intended to keep grain in England by prohibiting exports when prices were high and to share regional surpluses with areas experiencing scarcity supplemented by purchases from abroad when necessary. Included in the policy were surveys of grain supplies and searches through 'barns, garners, ricks, and stacks' for stored grain, undertaken by the authorities with the aim of ensuring a regular and orderly provisioning of local markets.[23]

Wolsey's dearth policies are considered the beginnings of responsibility by the English state for social welfare. At the same time, though, the surveys and searches extended state knowledge and control over national resources and also served to inhibit popular unrest, while providing an opportunity for corruption and graft, as well as disguising the vulnerability of the state to forces outside its influence.

Case study five: the Little Ice Age and semi-continental climate zones – Alsace

From 1490 to 1550, consecutive harvest failures in the Upper Rhine Valley were followed by dearth or famine six times: 1491 and 1492 (famine), 1500 and 1501 (famine), 1510 and 1511 (dearth), 1515 and 1516 (famine), 1534 and 1535 (dearth), and 1540 and 1541 (famine). Collectively known as the *Bundschuh* movement, strident demands for a redistribution of grain supplies were accompanied by plans for insurgency in the springs of 1493 and 1502 but discovered and foiled. Open rebellions with the same goals took place in the springs of 1513 and 1517, but were militarily suppressed by landowners and the governing elite. Following this last, in August 1518 there was an outbreak of the Dancing Plague in Strasbourg, where sufferers shook and 'danced' until exhausted, only to resume upon awakening; several dozen died. Medical historians now understand this as a communal hysterical response to extreme stress.[24]

After a disastrous harvest in 1524, the German Peasants' War erupted throughout the southwestern Holy Roman Empire in spring 1525. Military suppression of the peasants was accompanied by heavy fines of individuals and communities, with controls placed on peasant culture and society. There were no further rebellions, despite consecutive harvest failures in 1534 and 1535 (famine) and 1540 and 1541 (dearth). The opportunity space for rebellion had passed and other means of addressing suffering caused by weather-related harvest failures were created.[25]

Weather conditions were clearly not the only factor involved, as institutionalized and deepening social inequality played its part in ensuring that the economic repercussions of harvest failure were felt most keenly by the poor. Nevertheless, social inequality on its own did not inspire rebellion; this is demonstrated by the years of good weather and successful harvests in the region, during which social inequality was unrelieved. Plans or outbreaks of armed rebellion followed poor weather conditions, as their economic consequences imposed unbearable stress on the more vulnerable people in society.

Case study six: the Little Ice Age and Mediterranean climate zones – Venice

The Venice lagoon has a surface area of about 550 km^2 and a freezing temperature of about -2°C, due to its salty marine water composition. In 1549, the lagoon froze for three days to a depth of 20 cm, meaning that the cold was intense enough to counteract the warmer waters arriving from the sea with each tide. Water in all the springs and wells froze as well. Some boats were drawn around on the ice by men with hawsers, but mostly pedestrians walked across canals and even ventured into the 'hinterlands'. There, they found vineyards, olive orchards, and other fruit-bearing trees perished of the cold. Six people trapped on a sea-going vessel at anchor also died, despite rescue attempts by two Greek men.

This uncharacteristic cold was shared by contemporaries from Modena to Ravenna, the first inland and the second another coastal city southwest of Venice.[26] Weather-related harvest failure contributed to famine and dearth in the region.

Cultural responses to environmental stress

Catholic responses to environmental stresses such as those described in the previous section included rogations, exorcisms, sacred architecture, and ascription of destructive events to witchcraft, with ensuing legislative and theological condemnation of same. Communal processions pleading with God are known as rogations and, while they may be inspired for a variety of motives, were specifically conducted by early modern European Catholics to pray for a successful harvest and security from bad weather annually on 25 April and the three days of Ascension Thursday. In a worldview where the supernatural might intervene in God's will for Creation, exorcisms invoked God's power to restore order in the natural world by removing diabolic forces. By 1500, exorcisms followed recognized templates, such as those offered to priests as a method to drive demons from storm clouds.[27]

Although witchcraft was dismissed by orthodox theologians, popular credence in the power of witches over weather revived in the late fifteenth and early sixteenth centuries. The *Malleus Maleficarum*, first published in 1487, both reflected and catalysed a tidal wave of belief which would crest after the focus period of this chapter, but whose growing momentum can be found in sermons, legislation, and other public denunciations. During the last decades of the fifteenth century, trials of individuals or small groups are known to have occurred in six towns of western Switzerland,[28] but diminished in number even in those areas where they had sprung up most quickly. Trials petered out by 1507, only to return in the second half of the century. Legislation, however, remained active, like that of Holy Roman Emperor Maximilian I or of the Bishop of Bamberg, whose new laws issued in 1507 justified the use of torture and execution for the crime of using magic. These laws from the early sixteenth century were frequently invoked during the second and greater wave of accusations and executions in the latter part of the sixteenth and during the seventeenth century.[29] Wolfgang Behringer noticed a correlation between extreme weather events and scapegoating activities such as witch trials and burnings.[30]

New views of nature after 1517

The pervasive changes introduced to Christendom with Luther's religious insights included new views of Creation and the appropriate human relationship to it. Theologically, Luther asserted a direct relationship with God for Christians, removing both the Catholic Church hierarchy and many supernatural beings (saints, martyrs, angels, devils, demons, etc.) from consideration. This new worldview also meant the disappearance of supernatural intermediaries from the relationship between humanity and the natural environment, as events, forces, and processes found in nature, even nature itself, became interpreted as directly intended by God for humans.

Wolfgang Capito, a leading theologian of the early reform, made this new understanding of humanity's relationship with nature explicit in his 1538 publication *Hexameron Opus dei*, where a central part of his exegesis of Genesis 1:11 was based on an elaborate representation of the natural environment as God's created vehicle for human salvation. This view included assertions that the appropriate human relationship with the environment should be one of enthusiastic exploitation of its natural resources, as Capito concluded that God was pleased with human use of nature for survival and economic benefit. Moreover, by removing spiritual agents as mediators between humanity and the natural environment, God's will was presented as directly responsible for all events, forces, and processes in nature. Capito left little room for succour except prayers to God for mercy, and human compassion.[31]

Other Evangelicals such as Philip Melanchthon would later moderate this uncompromising view, instead offering the perspective that nature is 'a theatre for human minds which God wished us to view'.[32] Melanchthon's approach allowed for the study of nature for its own sake alongside the interpretation of God's will through Creation. Natural philosophy as practised by both Protestants and Catholics increasingly adopted this perspective, which likely contributed to the development of the Age of Enlightenment.[33]

An extensive hunger for social reform as well as religious reform among European peasantry inspired the development of a worldview based upon Luther's insights but parallel to Evangelical theology. Initially referred to as radical, adherents eventually became recognized as Anabaptists. In their descriptions of the Kingdom of God on earth, many radical theologians described an orderly, egalitarian, and, above all, agricultural society. Humanity's responsibility to create a farm or garden from the wilderness was central to their view of nature, understood as re-creating the Garden of Eden.[34] Meanwhile, Jean Calvin, the humanist lawyer from France turned theologian, published the first Latin edition of *Institutio Christianae religionis* in 1536 and revised it for the first French edition in 1541. Its focus was almost entirely on God and humans, with little attention given to the earth, the natural environment, or a suitable Christian relationship with it. With this absence, Calvin revealed his attitude to nature by representing it as outside of proper Christian concern.

Introduction of the New World into European culture

Implications of the existence of the American continents trickled through both intangible and material European culture (see, for example, Chapter 14 in this volume).

For example, Petrus Apianus's 1524 *Cosmographicus Liber* included the New World, as it was called, as did Sebastian Münster's best-selling *Cosmographia* of 1544. Western culture was forced to integrate new lands and new people into a Biblical worldview which had not mentioned them, leading, among other things, to papal bulls *Intra Arcana* (1529) and *Sublimus Dei* (1537).

Materially, the Columbian Exchange brought fauna, flora, and bacteria from the Americas to Europe as well as the reverse. Syphilis, cacao, and Indigenous people arrived in Europe as early as 1493, the last kidnapped by Columbus to prove the truth of his accounts. Future imports, such as tomatoes, potatoes, and gold, would completely transform European diets as well as fattening their purses, destabilizing the Iberian economy, and introducing new diseases.[35]

Case study seven: the Columbian Exchange – tobacco

Tobacco has been cultivated by Indigenous people of the Americas for at least 3,000 years and likely even longer. Indeed, their long practice may have altered several tobacco species genetically and phenotypically, perhaps even leading to the generation of unique varieties or species. Smokers experience a range of physiological effects, including euphoria, increased heart rate and alertness, and the suppression of hunger and thirst; very high doses can induce hallucinations, out-of-body experiences, and colour blindness, effects valued by shamans, traditional healers, and others as related to vision quests, healing, and other spiritual practices.[36]

Bestowed upon Columbus at his arrival, tobacco was among the first treasures carried to Europe by explorers and it gained rapidly in popularity, such that by 1533 a tobacco merchant was firmly established in Lisbon. Europeans initially accepted the plant as a medicinal treatment for ailments ranging from the common cold to, ironically, cancer.

Conclusions

In the turbulent – albeit subtly so – environmental context of the Little Ice Age and the Columbian Exchange, Western culture also demonstrated dramatic transformations, including religious reforms which introduced new attitudes and approaches to the natural environment. While Roman Catholic doctrine represented the natural world as a hierarchy of beings where God's relationship was with each creature from angels to ants, early Reformers reinterpreted Scripture to represent God's relationship as primarily with human beings, and the earth provided as a vehicle for human survival until salvation.

While contemporary technologies employed for resource exploitation were adequate in a supportive environment, climatic stress on European society contributed to open conflict and social turmoil, which are likely to have been conducive to an eagerness for new interpretations of central Christian concepts of humanity's place in the universe. At the same time, encounters with the people, plants, and animals of the Americas expanded horizons both tangible and intangible, as Europeans (poorly) integrated Indigenous people of the Americas into their understanding of God's Creation and increasingly enjoyed the benefits of new resources.

During the fifteenth and sixteenth centuries, western European experience of the natural world could be characterized as one of instability due to unreliable climatic conditions identified as the later Spörer Minimum of the Little Ice Age. While selecting fifty years to assess the effect of these experiences is an artificial construct introduced by the author, the hybrid and interactive model of socio-economic metabolism invites historians to seek new culturally acceptable representations of the natural environment as older representations lose interpretative authority. Such new representations were included in the early Reform movement and may have contributed to the role of Protestantism in the history of science.[37]

Notes

1 The hybrid and interactive model of socio-economic metabolism was initially developed in 1999 by Marina Fischer-Kowalski and Helga Weisz in the department of social ecology at the Institute for Interdisciplinary Studies of Austrian Universities (IFF), and modified by Verena Weniweter and Richard Hoffmann. See M. Fischer-Kowalski and H. Weisz, 'Society as Hybrid Between Material and Symbolic Realms: Toward a Theoretical Framework of Society-Nature Interaction', *Advances in Human Ecology* 8, 1999, 215–51, and R. Hoffmann, *An Environmental History of Medieval Europe*, Cambridge: Cambridge University Press, 2014, 6–13.

2 A.W. Crosby, *The Columbian Exchange: Biological and Cultural Consequences of 1492*, Westport, CT: Greenwood, 2003 (1st edn 1972).

3 P. Harrison, *The Bible, Protestantism and the Rise of Natural Science*, Cambridge: Cambridge University Press, 1998.

4 J. Hanska, *Strategies of Sanity and Survival: Religious Responses to Natural Disasters in the Middle Ages*, Studia Finnica Historica 2, Helsinki: Finnish Literature Society, 2002.

5 M. Parayre-Kuntzel, *L'Église et la vie quotidienne du paysan d'Alsace au Moyen Age*, Strasbourg: Librairie Istra, 1975.

6 J. Geiler von Kaysersberg, *Die Emeis*, ed. J. Pauli, Strasbourg: J. Grüninger, 1516 (1517), fols XVIII^v–XIX^r. Jointly translated with Rose Fuhrmann.

7 Ibid., fol. LV^v. Jointly translated with Rose Fuhrmann.

8 Ibid., fols LV$^{r–v}$. Jointly translated with Rose Fuhrmann.

9 A suitable source to begin exploring anticlericalism is the following: P.A. Dykema and H.A. Oberman (eds), *Anticlericalism in Late Medieval and Early Modern Europe*, Leiden: Brill, 1994.

10 European society in the early sixteenth century has been the subject of much scholarship. For information about direct relationships between landowners and peasants, one could begin with G. Algazi, 'Lords Ask, Peasants Answer: Making Traditions in Late Medieval Village Assemblies', in G. Sider and G. Smith (eds), *Between History and Histories: The Making of Silences and Commemorations*, Toronto: University of Toronto Press, Anthropological Horizons Series, 1997, 199–229.

11 Lands managed in common were the subject of a 1968 article 'The Tragedy of the Commons'. Taken up by neoliberal ideologues as justification for privatization of public spaces in the late twentieth century, further research provides a more nuanced view of late medieval land management strategies, including the awareness that most European commons were sustainably managed by villages. For both sides of the debate, see G. Hardin, 'The Tragedy of the Commons', *Science* 162, 1968, 1243–8, and D. Feeny *et al.*, 'The Tragedy of the Commons: Twenty-Two Years Later', *Human Ecology* 18.1,

1990, 1–19. See also E. Ostrom, *Governing the Commons: The Evolution of Institutions for Collective Action*, Cambridge: Cambridge University Press, 1990.

12 R. Bechmann, *Trees and Man: The Forest in the Middle Ages*, trans. K. Dunham, New York: Paragon House, 1990.

13 Religious, political, economic, and climatic factors assembled to inspire widespread peasant rebellion in the southern German-speaking lands from 1524 to 1526. For a range of views on the event, see P. Blickle, *The Revolution of 1525: The German Peasants' War from a New Perspective*, trans. T.A. Brady Jr and H.C.E. Midelfort, Baltimore, MD, London: The Johns Hopkins University Press, 1981; T. Scott, *Freiburg and the Breisgau: Town-Country Relations in the Age of Reformation and Peasants' War*, Oxford: Clarendon Press, 1986; J.M. Stayer, *The German Peasants' War and Anabaptist Community of Goods*, Montreal, Kingston: McGill-Queen's University Press, 1991.

14 O. Rackham, 'Woodland and Wood Pasture', in I.D. Rotherham (ed.), *Trees, Forested Landscapes and Grazing Animals: A European Perspective on Woodlands and Grazed Trees-capes*, Abingdon, New York: Routledge, 2013, 11–22. See also I. Rotherham, *Ancient Woodland: History, Industry and Crafts*, London: Bloomsbury, 2013.

15 R.C. Hoffmann, *An Environmental History of Medieval Europe*, Cambridge: Cambridge University Press, 2014, 184.

16 Ibid., 181. For more information about England's woodlands, see the expanded edition of Oliver Rackham's classic volume, *Ancient Woodland: Its History, Vegetation and Uses in England*, London: E. Arnold, 2003.

17 Hoffmann, 160.

18 Hoffmann, 127 and 129.

19 H. Klemettilä, *The Medieval Kitchen: A Social History with Recipes*, London: Reaktion Books, 2012, Ch. 2. See also F. Ravoire and A. Dietrich (eds), *La cuisine et la table dans la France de la fin du Moyen Âge. Contenus et contenants du XIVe au XVIe siècle*, Caen: Publications du CRAHM, 2009; T. Scully, *The Art of Cookery in the Middle Ages*, Martlesham: Boydell Press, 1995.

20 Hoffmann, 218.

21 Climate historians and historical climatologists have established a large body of knowledge about pre-Industrial climate in Europe. Those primarily interested in the climate could begin with *Climate Change* 101.1–2, 2010, particularly R. Brázdil *et al.*, 'European Climate of the Past 500 Years: New Challenges for Historical Climatology', *Climate Change* 101, 2010, 7–40, or R. Glaser, *Klimageschichte Mitteleuropas: 1000 Jahre Wetter, Klima, Katastrophen*, Darmstadt: Wissenschaftliche Buchgesellschaft, 2001. As an example of regional studies: O. Wetter and C. Pfister, 'Spring-Summer Temperatures Reconstructed for Northern Switzerland and Southwestern Germany from Winter Rye Harvest Dates, 1454–1970', *Climate of the Past* 7, 2011, 1307–26. Works by climate historians, those who research the role of climate in human history, include E. Le Roy Ladurie, *Histoire humaine et comparée du climat*, 3 vols, Paris: Fayard, 2004, and *Naissance de l'histoire du climat*, Paris: Fayard, 2013, or W. Behringer, *Kulturgeschichte des Klimas*, Munich: C.H. Beck, 2007, trans. as *A Cultural History of Climate*, Cambridge: Polity Press, 2010.

22 B. Sharp, *Famine and Scarcity in Late Medieval and Early Modern England: The Regulation of Grain Marketing, 1256–1631*, Cambridge: Cambridge University Press, 2016, 153–4.

23 P. Slack, 'Dearth and Social Policy in Early Modern England', *Social History of Medicine* 5.1, 1992, 1–2.

24 J. Waller, *The Dancing Plague: The Strange, True Story of an Extraordinary Illness*, Naperville, IL: Source Books, 2009.

25 Linnéa Rowlatt, 'A Godly Environment: Religious Views of Nature in Early Sixteenth-Century Strasbourg', unpublished doctoral thesis, Free University of Berlin and University of Kent, 2016, Ch. 1 and p. 263.

26 D. Camuffo *et al.*, 'When the Lagoon Was Frozen Over in Venice from A.D. 604 to 2012: Evidence from Written Documentary Sources, Visual Arts and Instrumental Readings', *Méditerranée* [Online], Varia, online since 7 February 2017, connection on 9 February 2017. URL: http://mediterranee.revues.org/7983.

27 Strassburg, Stadtarchiv, Serie V 136, 2. Papierhandschrift des 15. Jahrhunderts; see also A. Pfleger, 'Wettersegen und Wetterschutz im Elsass', *Archiv für Elsässische Kirchengeschichte* 16, 1943, 259–72 (266).

28 Valais, Lausanne, Vevey, Neuchâtel, Bern, Frieburg im Breisgau, and Basel. E. Peters, 'Superstition, Magic and Witchcraft on the Eve of the Reformation', in K. Jolly, C. Raudvere, and E. Peters (eds), *Witchcraft and Magic in Europe: The Middle Ages*, London: The Athlone Press, 2002, 173–245 (238).

29 Ibid., 238–45.

30 W. Behringer, 'Climate Change and Witch-Hunting: The Impact of the Little Ice Age on Mentalities', *Climate Change* 43, 1999, 335–51.

31 Rowlatt, Ch. 4.

32 P. Melanchton, *Initia doctrinae physicae*, in C.B. Bretschneider and H.E. Bundseil (eds), *Corpus reformatorum Philippi Melanthonis opera quae supersunt omnia*, 13, Halle, 1834–1852; Brunswick, 1853–1860, 187.

33 S. Kusukawa, *The Transformation of Natural Philosophy: The Case of Philip Melanchthon*, Cambridge: Cambridge University Press, 1995.

34 See J.M. Stayer, *The German Peasants' War and the Anabaptist Community of Goods*, Montreal and Kingston: McGill-Queen's University Press, 1994; T. Scott, *The Early Reformation in Germany: Between Secular Impact and Radical Vision*, Farnham: Ashgate, 2013; and M.G. Baylor (ed. and trans.), *The Radical Reformation*, Cambridge: Cambridge University Press, 1991.

35 Crosby.

36 S. Tushingham and J.W. Eerkens, 'Hunter-Gatherer Tobacco Smoking in Ancient North America: Current Chemical Evidence and a Framework for Future Studies', in E.A. Bollwerk and S. Tushingham (eds), *Perspectives on the Archaeology of Pipes, Tobacco and Other Smoke Plants in the Ancient Americas*, Interdisciplinary Contributions to Archaeology, Cham, New York: Springer, 2016, 211–30 (211–12).

37 Speculation about the role of Protestantism in the history of science is abundant and contentious. A small sample includes P. Harrison, *The Bible, Protestantism and the Rise of Natural Science*, Cambridge: Cambridge University Press, 1998; R. Stark, *For the Glory of God: How Monotheism Led to Reformations, Science, Witch-Hunts, and the End of Slavery*, Princeton, NJ: Princeton University Press, 2015; and the classic M. Weber, *The Protestant Ethic and the Spirit of Capitalism*, trans. S. Kalberg, Chicago, IL, London: Fitzroy Dearborn, 2001.

12

MATERIAL CULTURES OF LIVING

European attitudes to novelties

Raffaella Sarti

On a summer's day, I am sitting on a terrace in shorts, working on my laptop. On the table, there are my phone and books, papers, pens and pencils. Each of these objects has its own history, both as a single item and as part of a category. Before me, there is a courtyard with a rubbish bin in a corner, and a garden with trees and flowers belonging both to nature and culture, being largely species created by gardeners or brought from distant places. Around me, there are houses whose styles disclose that they were built in different periods, revealing different housing cultures. On the street, there are people and goods moving from one place to another: pedestrians, bicycles, motorcycles, cars, coaches and some lorries. It is 12.30 and, to cook lunch, I will use vegetables from my garden as well as ingredients bought in the market and brought from more or less distant regions. All these goods, artefacts, objects – working tools, technological devices, media, furniture, houses, rubbish, gardens, food, meals, clothes, means of transport – and numerous related activities can be considered as pertaining, as many others, to the material cultures of living.

The concepts of 'culture' and 'material' are rather blurred and controversial, but the breadth of the topics is in any case enormous. The challenge is to deal with them within 8,000 words.[1] Therefore, I will try to illustrate, in a cultural-historical perspective,[2] *some* features and trends of the European material cultures of living between the sixteenth and eighteenth centuries, mainly focusing on the encounters between Europeans and goods from other parts of the world.

As a period characterized by booming connections between Europe and the other continents, early modern history is interesting not only because of its intrinsic value, but also to understand the origins of globalization. Today, human material artefacts are radically changing the environment, while dematerialization is affecting many items that used to be material. Focusing on centuries when the material configuration of the world was rapidly changing, but remained radically different from our present one, is therefore especially inspiring.

Books on material goods in an age of growing de-materialization

In the last decades, while books have increasingly become dematerialized, those on material goods have experienced a real boom, enriching an already quite rich land-scape. A 'material turn' has taken place, although one that tends to overcome the traditional divide between material and immaterial.[3]

In the 1990s, when I started to work on material culture,[4] as many other scholars I was influenced by Fernand Braudel's works (1967, 1979). Braudel had addressed material culture within his awesome programme of *histoire totale*. His approach to the material world was rather materialistic.[5] The works by another French historian, Daniel Roche (1981, 1997), were less encompassing but more attentive to the mean-ings of objects for people, and to the ways people 'appropriate' material goods.[6] The objects' meanings were also the focus of Arjun Appadurai, who in 1986 edited an influential collection on the 'social life' of things and their 'biographies'.[7]

During the 1980s–90s, a debate arose on the periodization of change in con-sumption. In 1982, Neil McKendrick, John Brewer and J.H. Plumb suggested that in eighteenth-century England a 'consumer revolution' had taken place.[8] On the contrary, many other authors believe(d) that the growth in consumption was not peculiar to eighteenth-century England.[9] Richard Goldthwaite, without refusing the idea of such a revolution, stressed the important changes that had taken place in Renaissance Italy,[10] while Chandra Mukerji and Lisa Jardine placed the origin of modern consumerism in the Renaissance.[11] They all highlighted people's changing attitudes towards material goods, increasingly seen as a desirable source of satisfac-tion rather than corruption and sin. This was also crucial to Simon Schama, who studied the ambiguous mix of desire and discomfort felt by the Dutch towards their booming affluence during the seventeenth-century Dutch 'Golden Age',[12] and to Jan de Vries, who argued that, around 1650, European North-Western households started to work harder, supporting an expansion of production, to afford to buy new and more consumer goods: an 'industrious revolution' that preceded and then flanked the Industrial Revolution.[13] Joan Thisks had already stressed the simulta-neous development of by-activities in rural households and growth in demand. Yet she had also argued that poverty had pushed many families to work harder,[14] a view shared by many scholars. Growing consumption in a period of falling real wages is, however, an intriguing puzzle.[15] Moreover, as suggested by Donald Quataert, the seventeenth century may have witnessed a 'worldwide pattern of increasing con-sumption in Western Europe'.[16]

Braudel had already broadened his gaze to the 'games of exchange' in a mar-ket that, between the fifteenth and eighteenth centuries, grew to involve the entire world.[17] Later, Immanuel Wallerstein developed Braudel's concept of world economy, focusing on the asymmetric unification of the markets in circuits of centres and pe-ripheries.[18] The increased consumption of 'exotic' (often colonial) goods such as cof-fee, tea, sugar, tobacco, china and cotton fabrics has become a crucial issue in world and global history, and the history of globalization.[19] Moreover, the 'global turn' and the 'material turn' have implied an intermingling of global history and the history of material culture and consumption. Today, some scholars try to understand how certain things became/become global by investigating the plural meanings taken on by transported things during their trajectories, and the transformative impact of these trajectories on the goods themselves.[20]

Importantly, 'the human imprint on the global environment has now become so large and active that it rivals some of the great forces of Nature in its impact on the functioning of the Earth system'.[21] In a sense, the whole planet could be included in a cultural history of material culture. This chapter will inevitably have a much more limited scope, focusing (because of my expertise) on food, the domestic environment and clothing.

Enjoy your meal! Food as culture

I am wondering what to cook for lunch. There are ripe tomatoes in the garden: I will prepare pasta with tomato sauce, a dish that is an icon of Italian cuisine.[22] Eating and drinking are certainly natural needs. Yet the ways to satisfy them differ according to places, periods, groups, etc.: they are genuinely cultural practices.[23] 'Tell me *what* you eat and I'll tell you who you are': this statement by French politician and gourmet Savarin (1755–1826)[24] has not become a proverb by chance, in addition to the similar version, 'Tell me *how* you eat and I'll tell you who you are'.[25]

Today we are experiencing an unprecedented global standardization of some eating and drinking stuffs and styles, from Italian pizza to McDonald's hamburgers, from kebabs to Coca Cola, from take-away to self-service. Yet we are also witnessing the refashioning of 'typical' local cuisine, for contrasting reasons: the reaction to the standardization brought about by globalization but also growing tourism – a component of the increasing interconnectedness. Additionally, new cultural choices and/or health reasons are leading to 'alternative' cooking and eating, such as Vegan cuisine or wheat-free products, while growing concern for the environment leads us to refuse GMOs and prefer organic food and locally grown produce.[26]

The progress in agricultural techniques and in processing, preserving and distributing food and drink seems to make the ancient dream of eliminating thirst and hunger achievable. Yet climate change, desertification, pollution and booming population growth (which has reached 7.6 billion people, of whom more than 800 million are undernourished[27]) are creating new concerns about how to feed the present and future generations, to the extent that several experiments with (relatively) new food ranging from GMOs to insects are being conducted.[28]

Different food cultures have a different impact on the environment. It has been calculated that the Earth, with the current techniques, could feed 10 billion people eating as Indians, 5 billion eating as Italians and barely 2.5 billion eating as US Americans.[29] While the data used for such calculations are controversial,[30] there is no doubt that eating large quantities of meat, as many Americans do, implies the exploitation of more resources than following a vegetarian diet as many Indians do.

What did our European ancestors eat in early modern times? What were their ideas on food? And how did their foodways change through exchanges with other cultures? While most people ate locally produced food, plants, animals and techniques had actually travelled from one place to another since the beginning of agriculture and breeding. Humans, while using them, altered the species, the environment and their own lifestyles:[31] forms of standardization and differentiation have existed for millennia.

At the beginning of early modern times, the food culture of a large part of Europe resulted from the encounter/clash between the Mediterranean diet, based on bread, wine and olive oil but also milk, cheese, vegetables and meat, brought about by the Romans and then Christianity, a religion founded in the Mediterranean for which bread, wine and olive oil were/are crucial; and the diet of the people whom the Romans considered 'barbarians', based on meat, dairy products, beer, cider, oat porridge and flat barley bread, popularized by the migrations of mainly German tribes.[32]

Through this mix, bread had become the food *par excellence*. Yet many different preparations were labelled as such. The seventeenth-century author Vincenzo Tanara explained that bread could be prepared with any dried and milled seeds, herbs, roots, meats and fish.[33] However, he believed the best was soft, fresh bread made from wheat flour. Stale black bread made with oats, rye, chestnuts, lupins, etc. was considered the worst. Black bread was for lower people.[34] 'Their Diet among the Peasants is very miserable, who feed on black Bread', confirmed Richard Wolley in his book on France (1691).[35] In the cities, where bread was bought from bakeries, the authorities generally tried to guarantee the supply of white bread, whereas countryside people usually baked bread at home but infrequently, to save fuel and eat less. Despite the success of bread, however, porridges remained popular in Central and Northern Europe.[36]

While frugality and sobriety were considered virtues in the Mediterranean tradition, eating and drinking abundantly were seen as values by the German tribes: thanks to their success in late antiquity and the Middle Ages, for centuries being well-off implied eating a lot. The banquets of the ruling classes were a real display of wealth and power.[37] For instance, the lunch offered in April 1536 by Cardinal Lorenzo Campeggi in Rome to Emperor Charles V featured twelve courses with about 190 different dishes, including several marzipan statues. And it was Lent![38]

People were not distinguished by the abundance of their food alone. In the late Middle Ages, the idea that the food's quality should be appropriate to the people's 'quality' (to their gender, age, health and, above all, social position) reached new complexity. While an abundance of meat distinguished the elites, certain types of meat, such as birds, fowls and wild game, were considered particularly suitable to them, whereas others, such as pork, suited the lower classes. In later times, the more certain the food supply became, and the more the quantity of food gulped by the elites approached the human limits, the more quality became necessary to stand out. From the mid-eighteenth century, the elites began to shift their preferences towards a more refined, but less abundant cuisine.[39]

In the seventeenth to eighteenth centuries, growing criticism was addressed at meat-eating. Revolutionaries attacked the bloodthirsty luxury of mainstream culture; demographers accused the meat industry of wasting resources which could otherwise be used to feed people; anatomists claimed that human intestines were not equipped to digest meat; and travellers to the East presented India as a peaceful alternative to the rapacity of the West. Well-known philosophers provided arguments supporting vegetarianism: though not a vegetarian, Rousseau argued that originally humans were peaceful and did not eat meat; Voltaire extolled the Indus' respect for animals and the Brahmins' vegetarianism, and others, too, spoke against meat-eating.[40]

In European cultures, vegetarianism had actually been advocated at least since Socrates and Pythagoras.[41] Furthermore, in later times, the abstention from meat had developed as an ascetic practice followed by many devout men and women and imposed on all Christians on particular days such as Friday and Lent – among Orthodox Christians, abstinence days were particularly numerous and monks were forbidden to eat meat.[42]

While the spread of Christianity had contributed to a growing homogeneity of European eating cultures, the Protestant Reform halted this trend. Protestants, believing that good deeds are not a means or prerequisite for salvation, reject(ed) any religious rule about eating and drinking: a real revolution. On the contrary, Catholics and Orthodox Christians, as well as Jews and Muslims, continue(d) to have rules about food.[43]

'They made me live like a Turk and always eat meat, at any time, on Fridays and Saturdays as well', Mario Speri – a Christian who, after being captured by the Turks, had converted to Islam – declared to the inquisitor in the 1630s.[44] Islam forbade/ forbids pork, animals killed for sacrifice, animals that were not slaughtered according to Islamic rules and fermented beverage (permitted food is *ḥalāl*, banned food *ḥarām*). Furthermore, it imposed/imposes a month of fasting during *ramadan*, from sunrise to sunset.[45]

As for Jews, their complex rules prevent(ed) them from eating carnivores, pigs, horses, camels, hares, apes; birds of prey, scavengers, birds living in contact with water (gulls, cormorants, swans, pelicans, herons) as well as those that do not fly (such as ostriches); 'fish' without fins and scales (such as crustaceans); and reptiles and insects (apart from certain locusts). To be edible, animals must not have been castrated and not show anomalies. They must be slaughtered according to precise rules and the blood must not be consumed, while meat cannot be consumed with milk. Considering that norms about *kosher* food did/do include further requirements, we can imagine what a difficult reorganization of eating habits conversion might imply.[46]

Making new products from the (West and East) Indies, the Middle East and China their own

A few years before Luther started the Protestant Reformation (1517), Columbus' accidental 'discovery' of the Americas (1492) had started new food exchanges between the two shores of the Atlantic that would radically change the vegetables grown, livestock bred and foodstuff eaten in both continents. Their history reveals, among other things, not only the colonizers' curiosity and rapacity towards the products of the New Continent but also the Europeans' prejudices and difficulty to 'appropriate' them, mentally and practically. Furthermore, it shows that adoption implied adaptation: transferring items, including plants, created not only standardization but also new differences.

Interestingly, for instance, the Catholics debated whether drinking chocolate, a beverage from America, broke their fasting or not. The Dominicans generally argued that it did, while the Jesuits that it did not, and the dispute continued for a couple of centuries, showing the difficulty of integrating the new product in the old taxonomies.[47]

Among the plants from the New Continent, there were also the ancestors of the tomatoes in my garden. In Spain, Languedoc, Provence and Italy the tomato was already known in the sixteenth century.[48] Yet botanist Pietro Antonio Michiel (1510–76) argued that it was harmful;[49] and a century later Giuseppe Donzelli claimed that it gave 'little, and bad nourishment'.[50] In fact, tomatoes became a staple of the Italian cuisine very slowly. Tomato sauce was added to pasta (produced since the twelfth century, initially in Sicily) only from the 1830s onwards.[51] At that time, some German and North-European people were still convinced that tomatoes were toxic.[52] The fact that they 'quickly found a place in preexisting plant classifications', as part of the nightshade family (*Solanum genus*), contributed to distrust, because this family, besides aubergines, includes poisonous and/or hallucinatory plants (henbane, belladonna and mandrake).[53]

Potatoes, possibly known by Spanish conquistadors in the 1530s, and first described in books in the 1550s, were also classified into the *Solanum genus* (by the Swiss botanist Gaspard Bauhin in 1597[54]) and they, too, aroused suspicion. Moreover, a medieval tradition associated the sky with the nobles and the earth with the plebs and animals.[55] This contributed to many people considering potatoes suitable for pigs and toxic for humans.[56] In Italy, however, they were also associated with (edible) truffles and initially called *tartuffoli* (hence the German name *Kartoffel*). In Spain their use as food is first documented in 1573; in Germany and Britain, they were attested from the end of the sixteenth century.[57] Nonetheless, they remained uncommon. As late as 1771, the Faculty of Medicine in Paris was consulted by the French authorities about diseases possibly caused by them. Ah! if it were possible to eliminate all prejudice against potatoes, sobbed in 1789 their French promoter, the agronomist Parmentier. He, however, suggested using them to make bread, which proved a failure.[58] In fact, the Andean *Indios* bake(d) bread from the flour of *chuño*, i.e. frozen and dried potatoes, yet their foodways were not adopted in Europe (maybe also for environmental constraints).[59] For these reasons, potatoes did not spread quickly; their popularity dates from the eighteenth century, a period of growing population pressure. Destined to become a staple food in Central and Northern Europe more than in Southern Europe, they would contribute to reshape the differences within European eating cultures, as did maize.[60]

Maize was brought to Spain by Columbus as early as 1493. It was easily introduced into the European taxonomies. As with *tartuffoli*, several names employed to define it reveal the effort to become acquainted with novelties by associating them with known items, for instance the French definition of *millet*, and the Italian ones of *miglio grosso* (coarse millet) or *grano grosso* (coarse wheat). They also reveal the geographical imagery of the time that associated exotic novelties with the East rather than the West: other names for maize were corn of Rhodes, corn of Egypt, corn of India, Arab corn and Turkish corn.[61] A similar process involved the new edible bird brought from America, called turkey in English, i.e. from Turkey, and *dinde*, i.e. 'd'Inde', 'from India', in French,[62] as well as chocolate, sometimes called 'Indian broth'.[63]

Europeans, considering American native societies inferior, imported maize but not the American ways of preparing it, despite early information.[64] Before making tortillas, the *Indios* put maize in lime water, which allows the vitamin PP (or B3, i.e. niacin) to be metabolized by humans. Europeans didn't soak it and didn't prepare tortillas either; they prepared 'polenta', a porridge-like meal according to their traditions. This caused the spreading of pellagra, a deadly disease caused by vitamin PP deficiency, to those regions in Spain, Southern France, Northern Italy and the Balkans where maize became a staple food. In fact, for a long time, maize was grown in small quantities in vegetable gardens or used as fodder. It spread in the eighteenth century, when the population grew rapidly and the landowners, aware of the high yields of maize, pushed peasants to use it as a staple food. Although the link between pellagra and a maize-based diet was discovered as late as the twentieth century, peasants knew that maize was less healthy than other cereals and often tried to resist as long as possible.[65]

At the time when the new American products were spreading throughout Europe, the flow of novelties from the East had not stopped.[66] One was coffee. The first Westerner to describe it after a trip to the Middle East (1573–5) was probably the German doctor Leonhard Rauwolf.[67] Within a few decades, coffee was traded in Venice and then in the whole continent, and coffee houses (common in Istanbul and the Middle East) spread in Europe too, the first probably opening in Venice.[68] In 1686, a witness maintained (perhaps rather hyperbolically) that there were countless ones in Livorno, Paris and London.[69] In contrast with maize, potatoes, tomatoes, beans, peppers and other American plants that were acclimatized to Europe, coffee became a colonial product.[70] The Dutch started to grow it in their colonies of Java and Ceylon between the end of the seventeenth and the beginning of the eighteenth centuries; in the 1720s, the French introduced it to Martinique and then to other French colonies; the British to Jamaica and the Portuguese to Brazil, which would become the world's largest coffee producer. If in 1726 the Yemen exported about 2,500 tonnes, in 1835 the world production, largely colonial, had reached 100,000 tonnes (today it fluctuates between 5 and 6 million tonnes annually).[71]

Unlike other products, coffee was believed to have medicinal properties.[72] Doctors and travellers such as Prospero Alpini (1591) and Pietro Della Valle reported that Egyptians and Turks 'say that it very much contributes to health'.[73] Europeans largely trusted them.[74] Because of its stimulating effect, coffee became a symbol of bourgeois rationality and efficiency, but its consumption soon spread to other classes, too. The need for social distinction that for centuries had supported the trade in exotic products now clashed with the needs of the colonial economy, interested in expanding the market.[75]

Like coffee, tea, another drink of Asian origins (Chinese), conquered Europe in the seventeenth and eighteenth centuries. Thanks to the Portuguese expeditions to the East, it was probably first introduced to Lisbon. A Portuguese princess, Catherine of Braganza, wife of Charles II Stuart (1662), seems to have brought it to England. In Holland it had already arrived at the beginning of the century, in France possibly a short time later. In Britain, it spread to all social classes, whereas on the European continent it was successful only in Russia, imported directly from China. For centuries, tea was actually produced only in China. But, in 1827, the Dutch introduced it to Java. In 1834, the British started large plantations in Assam and in 1842 in Ceylon. They also promoted tea in North Africa, where during the nineteenth century it partly replaced coffee (Figure 12.1).[76]

Figure 12.1   Philippe Sylvestre Dufour, *Traitez nouveaux & curieux du café, du thé et du chocolate. Ouvrage également nécessaire aux Medecins, & à tous ceux qui aiment leur santé,* Lyon: Jean Girin, & B. Riviere, 1685. Title page showing a Turk drinking coffee, a Chinese man drinking tea and a Native American drinking chocolate. Open access.

Tea and coffee are and were consumed with sugar, another product of oriental origin transferred to the colonies. The sweet and pleasant product was obtained with the exhausting work of the slaves brought to America from Africa: a deadly machine that crushed lives to supply the growing demand of sugar, an Indian product introduced to Europe by the Arabs in the Middle Ages; significantly, all European words echo the Arab term *sukkar*. If in medieval times in the Mediterranean islands there were sugar-cane plantations grown by slaves, after the colonization of America such plantations were introduced into the New World. The sweetness of sugar was obtained through the bitter work of slaves to supply the European demand.[77] The consumption by the

English, for example, went from a yearly average of 2 kg per person at the beginning of the eighteenth century to 9 kg around 1800. Europe imported 75,000 tonnes of sugar yearly in 1730, and as much as 250,000 at the end of the century.[78]

In the eighteenth century, colonial sugar and coffee also invaded the Islamic markets, although colonial coffee was of lower quality than the Yemeni one. Significantly, Voltaire wrote that the good Turk offered Candide and his friends 'Mocha coffee unadulterated with the bad coffee of Batavia or the American islands'.[79] For centuries, exotic products had arrived in Europe *from* the East. Now colonial sugar and coffee, as many other products, were *exported to* North Africa and the East, with a crucial change in the commercial circuits and power balance.

The domestic environment

In Europe, the popularity of coffee and tea was accompanied by that of the crockery suitable for sipping them. In 1675, no English family owned cups or other utensils for hot drinks, while in 1725 15% of families did.[80] As the name testifies, china was initially imported from China (Figure 12.2). Europeans, however, appreciating it, tried to produce their own Chinese-style hard porcelain. Germans succeeded at the beginning of the eighteenth century. Meissen became the home of successful production, soon followed by other locations, such as Sevres.[81] Imported and, later,

Figure 12.2   Giovanna Garzoni, *Chinese porcelain vase with flowers* (ca. 1622–70). Poggio a Caiano (Prato, Italy), Museo della Natura Morta. Courtesy of the Italian Ministry of Cultural Heritage and Activities/Alinari Archives, Florence (SEA-F-000230-0000).

226

European-made porcelain spread, contributing to the growth and change in the European households' endowment of crockery, tablecloths and cutlery in early modern times. Pottery and stoneware, glass and china replaced wood, tin and copper vessels.[82] There was both a proliferation of refined objects and a spread of cheap ones (between the seventeenth and eighteenth centuries, 'populuxe goods', i.e. cheap imitations of refined objects, also began to spread).[83]

In Europe, good manners at the table were a means of distinction. The fork played an important role. Probably 'invented' in Byzantium, it appeared in Venice in the tenth century but was condemned by the Catholic clergy after the schism between the Orthodox Church and the Church of Rome (1054) as a kind of devil's instrument. Nonetheless, it slowly spread in Italy and then to the rest of Europe. In France it was perhaps introduced by Catherine de' Medici, who in 1533 married King Henri II; in England by Thomas Coryat (1577–1617) who had come across it in Italy. In 1725, however, only 10% of English households owned them, but towards the end of the eighteenth century their use was well established among the European upper-middle classes, distinguishing them from the lower classes. Interestingly, today – after a century-long popularity of cutlery in all social classes – the custom of fast food, eaten with one's hands, is spreading even among the well-off.[84]

In early modern Europe, cooking did not take place in every house: the poor, especially in the cities, might not be able to afford a dwelling equipped with a fireplace, and might eat food obtained as alms or bought in inns, in shops or from street sellers.[85] In certain regions, however (particularly, it seems, in Mediterranean Europe), eating on the streets, in taverns or in open-air working places was widespread and not necessarily a sign of poverty.[86]

Furthermore, up to the sixteenth century, tables with fixed legs existed in convents' refectories, but elsewhere those with trestles (assembled where and when needed) prevailed. Fixed tables spread from the sixteenth century,[87] contributing to defining the purpose of the rooms where they were placed. The early modern times in fact witnessed not only processes that made houses more stable and durable, the domestic interior more clearly separated from the outside, more protected from wind, rain and snow, and better heated thanks to chimneys, glass windows etc.; they also witnessed the increasing specialization of rooms: sleeping, cooking, eating, working all in the same room became less common. New cultures of comfort, privacy and intimacy developed, as well as new notions of a hygienic and healthy environment.[88]

Furniture greatly contributed to many such trends. Comparing 'Christians' (West-Europeans) and 'Turks' (people living in East-Mediterranean and North-African countries), an author argued that 'in his house, a Christian keeps bed bases, mattresses, straw beds, sheets, chairs, seats, sideboards, tables, andirons, etc. A Turk has only one rug, with three or four cushions on some wooden boards'.[89] While such opposition was not completely wrong, in fact for a long time furniture in the houses and huts of the European poor, especially in the countryside, remained rather scant, and sitting on the ground was not uncommon.[90] Even though, in West-European homes, furniture was mainly wooden, this does not mean that carpets were absent. In Venice, the import of Middle-Eastern and North-African fabrics was established from the thirteenth century.[91] In Italy, carpets were particularly appreciated, to the extent they were considered suitable for churches, despite coming from the world of 'infidels', as also shown by paintings such as Andrea del Verrocchio's *Madonna and Child with the Saints John the Baptist and Donatus* (ca. 1475–83) in the Cathedral of Pistoia[92] and Lorenzo Lotto's *Madonna and Child with the Saints Peter, Christine, Liberale and James* (ca. 1505) in St Cristina's Church in Treviso (Figure 12.3). Interestingly, however, in Europe, until the eighteenth century, carpets were often used not only on the floor and as wall hangings, but also as table covers (Figures 12.4 and 12.5), differently from the Islamic world. Oriental producers sometimes adapted their products to their European customers' needs by producing cross-shaped carpets suitable for use as table covers.[93] On the other hand, Europeans tried to produce oriental-like carpets themselves. 'Persian and Turkey carpets are those most esteemed', *The Complete Dictionary of Arts and Sciences* explained,

> though in Paris there is a manufactory after the manner of Persia, where they make them little inferior, not to say finer, than the true Persian carpets. They are velvety, and perfectly imitate the carpets which come from the Levant.[94]

East–West exchanges could be even more complex. In the Renaissance, there were silver or gold-plated metal vases decorated in black, Islamic in style and design (sometimes signed by Muslim craftsmen), but with Western coats of arms: they were produced for the European market. There were pitchers and other metal objects

Figure 12.3　Lorenzo Lotto, *Madonna and Child with the Saints Peter, Christine, Liberale and James* (ca. 1505). Quinto di Treviso, Italy, Church of Santa Cristina. Public domain.

Figure 12.4 Lorenzo Lotto, *Husband and Wife* (1523). Saint Petersburg, Hermitage. Public domain.

Figure 12.5 Johannes Vermeer, *A Lady at the Virginals with a Gentleman* (1662–5). London, Royal Collection. Public domain.

almost certainly made in Northern Europe, decorated in the Islamic world and sold in Europe. In Renaissance Italy, the admiration for Islamic artefacts was such that imitations were produced, sometimes almost indistinguishable from the originals.[95] In Venetian households, there were also plenty of representations of Turkish men and women, especially after the Venetian painter Gentile Bellini's portrayal of Muhammad II.[96]

Textiles: the material web of cultural exchanges and conflicts

Textiles significantly contributed to the changes in the material cultures of living. Well-equipped beds, with mattresses, sheets, blankets and, often, curtains, added to people's comfort, while changing sleeping cultures increasingly transformed beds from 'collective' places into places for single individuals or couples.[97] Underwear played an important role in changing ideas and practices of cleanliness (during the early modern age, to keep clean, people changed their clothes rather than wash, if they could afford more than one set). Clothes, besides protecting people from the cold and/or the heat, were crucial – because of cultural norms and often also laws – in distinguishing men and women, adults and children, laymen and the clergy, rich and poor, nobles and not nobles, Christians, Jews, Muslims, etc. Over time, the average number of items of clothing owned increased, fashion made ever more frequent changes to shapes and colours and Europeans experienced a growing freedom in clothing. Nevertheless, clothes remained important to distinguish people. The culture of appearance made appropriate clothes decisive for one's respectability. At the same time, even political choices could be expressed through clothes. During the French Revolution (that on 29 October 1793 affirmed the right to clothing freedom), the *sanculottes* showed their refusal of aristocracy and the Old Regime by refusing the *culotte*, men's knee-length trousers mainly used by the upper classes.[98]

Silk fabrics were particularly appreciated, especially to produce luxury goods. The spreading of European silk production from Italy and Southern Europe to Lyon, London and Paris contributed to the expansion of textile consumption in early modern times.[99] For a long time, however, silk had been mainly imported from Asia: Chinese silk had already been imported to the Roman Empire as a luxury.[100] While, in ancient times, in the Aegean Islands a kind of silk was produced from the cocoon of a local moth,[101] silkworms were introduced to Constantinople from the East around the mid-sixth century. The Arab conquest of Spain and Sicily contributed to introducing silk production to Southern Europe, whereas from Constantinople it spread to Western Europe, especially after the Catholic conquest of the city in 1204.[102] If imported *panni tartarici* (Tatar fabrics) made with silk and gold were appreciated by the elite, the Italian flourishing silk manufacture also produced Italian-made *panni tartarici*.[103] Italians sold their products even in the Middle East and Egypt, followed by the Flemish, thus contributing to the crisis of the Egyptian Mameluke manufactures. Silk production, however, remained multi-centred, and Western worldwide supremacy dates as late as the end of the nineteenth century[104] (today silk is again a mainly Asian product[105]).

On the other hand, in the sixteenth century, when contacts between Europe and India increased thanks to new routes, Europeans 'were astonished by the variety and quality of cotton textiles for sale'[106] and started to export them to Europe. In the first

Figure 12.6 *Palampore* (hanging or bed cover), late eighteenth century. New York, Metropolitan Museum, 25.166.1. Public domain.

half of the seventeenth century, after the first cargoes arrived in Lisbon, thanks to
the Dutch and English East India companies the trade of cotton to Europe reached
a large scale.[107] Customers liked the light and colourful cotton textiles that could be
washed easily. These fabrics were initially used as wall hangings, curtains and bed-
covers (*palampores*), and were perceived as exotic, certainly arriving from far away
(Figure 12.6). Yet they were often expressly produced for Europeans.[108] From the
second half of the seventeenth century, Indian cottons were also used for clothing.[109]
They became so popular that they were perceived as a threat to local textiles production, and were banned throughout Europe from 1686 to 1774. The bans were rather
ineffectual but stimulated the local production of cotton textiles.[110] As discussed in
the English House of Lords, 'the statutory prohibition to prevent the sale in England
of painted calicoes from India' was not 'successful in protecting the wool trade – the
object for which it had been designed'.

> For whereas, then the calicoes painted in India were most used by the better sort
> of people, whilst the poor continued to wear and use our woollen goods, the

calicoes now painted in England are so very cheap and so much in fashion that persons of all qualities and degrees cloth them.[111]

In fact, as early as the sixteenth century, to supply their manufactures with cheap raw material, Europeans had set up cotton plantations worked by African slaves in their American colonies. At first cotton cultivation was limited, competing with sugar, which was more remunerative; it spread only in the eighteenth century, when demand for raw materials grew dramatically. Cotton was crucial during the Industrial Revolution: it 'was the pacemaker of industrial change'.[112] In Britain, between 1785 and 1830, cotton textile production expanded thirtyfold, employing ever-increasing numbers of factory workers (800,000 in 1806). Cotton accounted for just 2.6% of value added in British industry in 1770; by 1831 it reached 22.4%.[113]

When European traders had started to export large quantities of Indian cottons, India was the major worldwide producer of cotton and cotton fabrics, marketed across the Indian Ocean and beyond. In the following centuries, Indian cottons were increasingly exported by Europeans not only to Europe but also to the Americas and Africa, changing the consumer habits of people worldwide, the elites as well as the poor. The European Industrial Revolution changed the cotton import/export trajectory: the European industries increasingly relied on cheap raw cotton produced by slaves in America, and exported cotton fabrics worldwide, thanks to a new, modern, transcontinental 'commodity chain'.[114] Thanks to European traders, cotton textiles reshaped 'not just people's consuming habits but also the economies and societies of Europe, Africa and the Americas'; '[i]n the space of a few decades, India went from exporting large quantities of cloth to losing markets around the world, then importing cheap cotton yarn, and finally importing the cloth itself'.[115] In a sense, Indians were the victims of their own success, since the fascination for Indian cotton had led textile workers around the world to replicate them or to create their own, with the English being especially effective.[116]

Conclusion

The texture of fabrics may be seen as a symbol of the creation of a worldwide web of commercial and cultural exchanges. The growth of exchanges during the early modern era represented an unprecedented phase in human history because of the speed and breadth in the creation of worldwide connections and movements of people, animals, plants, minerals, diseases, things, ideas, languages and faiths. Yet movements and connections had been present since the beginning of humankind and certainly before Columbus travelled to America, as shown here by several cases (wine, olive oil, sugar, carpets, silk, etc.).

The East – the 'real' one and the alleged, American one – has often been assumed to be the mirrored 'other' against which European identity was constructed. However, both Europe and 'European' culture can be seen as a particularly dense crossroads of innumerable fluxes, from and to different parts of the worlds, creating fluid and continuously changing, but peculiar, constellations, which were not the same in different places, periods, social classes, genders, etc. In this chapter, I have tried to illustrate different attitudes towards novelties: curiosity and rapacity, desire and suspicion, attachment to tradition and openness to innovation, radical deforming adoption and imitation, transfer to Europe and/or the colonies, etc. While imports of goods from the unknown New World often implied suspicion and usage differing from the American Indians', imports from the long-known East was generally due to a fascination for exotic civilizations, and often implied an effort to imitate their expertise and customs, even though to some degree adoption always implied adaptation.

Over time, consumption by average Europeans (even at times of falling wages) grew.[117] Yet the quality of their lives did not necessarily improve, but rather the opposite happened: English workers who survived thanks to bread and tea with sugar and Italian peasants who only ate maize polenta were less well nourished than their ancestors. Not by chance, between the eighteenth and nineteenth centuries the average European's height decreased.[118]

Trade, implying people meeting, bargaining and exchanging, is different from war and pillage, yet the growing exchanges that characterized world history in early modern times developed within, and contributed to, harsh competitions and violent conflicts. Nonetheless, thanks to those wider networks, humans today share a largely common culture, which allows them to communicate and sometimes avoid forms of extreme violence. Yet the distance between the richest top of mankind and the poorest bottom is now wider than ever. Furthermore, the exploitation of natural resources and the impact of human activities are threatening our survival. State and over-state policies should find more effective solutions to such problems. At the same time, grassroots movements favourable to fair trade, 'zero-mile' products, environmental sustainability and aware consumption are struggling to save the planet, reduce poverty and shrink differences between rich and poor. Knowing the past is important for all of them in order to build the future.

Notes

1 English revision by C. Boscolo, University of Birmingham. Abbreviations: *EaH* = R. Sarti, *Europe at Home. Family and Material Culture*, trans. A. Cameron, New Haven, CT, London: Yale University Press, 2002 (original edn 1999; 'Cmc' = R. Sarti, 'Cultura materiale e consumi in Europa e nel Mediterraneo', in A. Barbero (ed.), *Storia d'Europa e del Mediterraneo*, vol. 10, R. Bizzocchi (ed.), *Ambiente, popolazione e società*, Rome: Salerno, 2009, 353–416. Bibliographical references are few because of the word limit. As for recent introductions, handbooks, collections and review articles on material culture and consumption in early modern times see K. Harvey (ed.), *History and Material Culture: A Student's Guide to Approaching Alternative Sources*, Abingdon, New York: Routledge, 2018 (first edn 2009); C. Richardson, T. Hamling and D. Gaimster (eds), *The Routledge Handbook of Material Culture in Early Modern Europe*, Abingdon, New York: Routledge, 2017; J. Maegraith and C. Muldrew, 'Consumption and Material Life', in H. Scott (ed.), *The Oxford Handbook of Early Modern European History, 1350–1750*, vol. 1, *Peoples and Place*, Oxford: Oxford University Press, 2015, 369–97; M. Füssel, 'Die Materialität der Frühen Neuzeit. Neuere Forschungen zur Geschichte der materiellen Kultur', *Zeitschrift für Historische Forschung* 42, 2015, 433–63; R. Maruri Villanueva, 'La historia social del consumo en la España moderna: un estado de la cuestión', *Estudis. Revista de Historia Moderna* 42, 2016, 267–301. Recent collections focusing on, or including also, the early modern period are T. Hamling and

C. Richardson (eds), *Everyday Objects: Medieval and Early Modern Material Culture and Its Meanings*, Surrey, Burlington, VT: Ashgate, 2010; I. dos Guimarães Sá and M. García Fernández, *Portas adentro: comer, vestir e habitar na Península Ibérica (ss. XVI–XIX)*, Valladolid, Coimbra: Universidad de Valladolid, Universidade de Coimbra, 2010; P. Findlen, *Early Modern Things: Objects and Their Histories, 1500–1800*, London, New York: Routledge, 2013; P.N. Miller (ed.), *Cultural Histories of the Material World*, Ann Arbor, MI: University of Michigan Press, 2013; D. Rogobete, J.P. Sell and A. Munton (eds), *The Silent Life of Things: Reading and Representing Commodified Objecthood*, Newcastle upon Tyne: Cambridge Scholars Publishing, 2015; G. Franco Rubio (ed.), *Condiciones materiales y vida cotidiana en el Antiguo Régimen*, Madrid: Publicaciones de la Universidad Complutense de Madrid, 2015; A. Gerritsen and G. Riello (eds), *The Global Lives of Things: the Material Culture of Connections in the Early Modern World*, London, New York: Routledge, 2016; S. Cavazza and E. Scarpellini (eds), *Storia d'Italia. Annali*, vol. 27, *I consumi*, Turin: Einaudi, 2018.

2 Cultural history cannot be easily defined; see P. Burke, *What Is Cultural History?*, Cambridge: Polity Press, 2008 (first edn 2004); A. Arcangeli, *Cultural History: A Concise Introduction*, Abingdon, New York: Routledge, 2012 (or 2007 edn). P.N. Miller, 'Introduction, the Culture of the Hand', in Miller (ed.), *Cultural Histories*, 1–29 (2), considers the 'Culture of the Hand' – i.e. a way of 'defining human activity: training the hand, the works of the hand, the world made by many hands' – as the subject of his edited book. As for me, I will focus on the meanings and value attributed to goods.

3 P. Joyce and T. Bennett, 'Material Powers: Introduction', in T. Bennett and P. Joyce (eds), *Material Powers: Cultural Studies, History and the Material Turn*, Abingdon: Routledge, 2013, 4; B. Latour, *Reassembling the Social: An introduction to Actor-Network-Theory*, Oxford: Oxford University Press, 2005.

4 R. Sarti, 'Material Conditions of Family Life', in M. Barbagli and D.I. Kertzer (eds), *Family Life in Early Modern Times 1500–1789*, New Haven, CT, London: Yale University Press, 2001, 3–23 and 288–93; *EaH*.

5 F. Braudel, *Civilization and Capitalism, 15th–18th Century*, vol. 1, *The Structures of Everyday Life: The Limits of the Possible*, trans. S. Reynolds, London: William Collins, 1981 (original edn 1979, 1967).

6 D. Roche, *The People of Paris: An Essay in Popular Culture in the 18th Century*, trans. M. Evans and G. Lewis, Berkeley, Los Angeles, CA: University of California Press, 1987 (original edn 1981); D. Roche, *A History of Everyday Things: The Birth of Consumption in France, 1600–1800*, transl. B. Pearce, Cambridge: Cambridge University Press, 2000 (original edn 1997). Roche, as many other scholars, largely relied on inventories: see I. Palumbo Fossati, 'L'interno della casa dell'artigiano e dell'artista nella Venezia del Cinquecento', *Studi Veneziani* n.s., 8, 1984, 109–53; A. Pardailhé-Galabrun, *La naissance de l'intime. 3000 foyers parisiens XVIIe–XVIIIe siècles*, Paris: P.U.F., 1988; L. Weatherill, *Consumer Behaviour & Material Culture in Britain 1660–1760*, London, New York: Routledge, 1988; P. Malanima, *Il lusso dei contadini. Consumi e industrie nelle campagne toscane del Sei e Settecento*, Bologna: Il Mulino, 1990; D. Quataert (ed.), *Consumption Studies in the History of the Ottoman Empire, 1550–1922: An Introduction*, New York: State University of New York Press, 2000; S. Faroqhi, C.K. Neumann (eds), *The Illuminated Table, the Prosperous Household: Food and Shelter in Ottoman Material Culture*, Würzburg: Ergon Verlag, 2003; R. Ago, *Gusto for Things: A History of Objects in Seventeenth-Century Rome*, trans. B. Bouley and C. Tazzara with P. Findlen, Chicago, IL: University of Chicago Press, 2013 (original edn 2006); I. Palumbo Fossati, *Dentro le case: abitare a Venezia nel Cinquecento*, Venice: Gambier&Keller, 2013.

7 A. Appadurai (ed.), *The Social Life of Things*, Cambridge: Cambridge University Press, 1986.

8 N. McKendrick, J. Brewer and J.H. Plumb, *The Birth of a Consumer Society: The Commercialization of Eighteenth-Century England*, Bloomington, IN: Indiana University Press, 1982.

9 See the chapters by J. de Vries, J. Styles and C. Fairchilds in J. Brewer and R. Porter (eds), *Consumption and the World of Goods*, London, New York: Routledge, 1993; D. Quataert, 'Introduction', in Quataert (ed.), *Consumption Studies*, 1–13; EaH, 4–5. Connections and continuities are also stressed, although without rejecting the category of 'consumer revolution', by B. Blondé and W. Ryckbosch, 'In "Splendid Isolation": A Comparative Perspective on the Historiographies of the "Material Renaissance" and the "Consumer Revolution"', *History of Retailing and Consumption* 1, 2015, 105–24.

10 R. Goldthwaite, *Wealth and the Demand for Art in Italy 1300–1600*, Baltimore, MD, London: Johns Hopkins University Press, 1993.

11 C. Mukerji, *From Graven Images: Patterns of Modern Materialism*, New York: Columbia University Press, 1983 and L. Jardine, *Worldly Goods: A New History of the Renaissance*, London: Macmillan, 1996.

12 S. Schama, *The Embarrassment of Riches: An Interpretation of Dutch Culture in the Golden Age,* New York: Knopf, 1987.

13 J. de Vries, *The Industrious Revolution: Consumer Behavior and the Household Economy, 1650 to the Present,* Cambridge: Cambridge University Press, 2008.

14 J. Thirsk, *Economic Policy and Projects: The Development of a Consumer Society in Early Modern England*, Oxford: Clarendon Press, 1978.

15 de Vries, *The Industrious Revolution*, 82–7; P. Malanima and V. Pinchera, 'A Puzzling Relationship: Consumptions and Incomes in Early Modern Europe', *Histoire & Mesure* 17, 2012, 197–222.

16 Quataert, 'Introduction', 3.

17 F. Braudel, *Civilization and Capitalism*, vols 2, *The Wheels of Commerce* and 3, *The Perspective of the World*, both trans. London: Collins, 1982 (original edn 1979).

18 I. Wallerstein, *The Modern World System*, San Diego, CA: Academic Press, 1974–85.

19 P.N. Stearns, *Consumerism in the World History: The Global Transformation of Desire*, London: Routledge, 2001; M. Berg, 'In Pursuit of Luxury: Global History and British Consumer Goods in the 18th Century', *Past & Present* 182, 2004, 85–142; F. Trentmann, *Empire of Things: How We Became a World of Consumers, from the 15th Century to the Twenty-First*, London: Allen Lane/Penguin, 2016.

20 Gerritsen and Riello (eds), *The Global Lives of Things*.

21 W. Steffen, J. Grinevald, P. Crutzen and J. Mcneill, 'The Anthropocene: Conceptual and Historical Perspectives', *Philosophical Transactions of the Royal Society of London A: Mathematical, Physical and Engineering Sciences* 369.1938, 2011, 842–67 (842).

22 A. Capatti and M. Montanari, *Italian Cuisine. A Cultural History*, trans. A. O'Healy, New York: Columbia University Press, 2003 (original edition 1999).

23 M. Montanari, *Food Is Culture*, trans. A. Sonnenfeld, New York: Columbia University Press, 2006 (original edn 2004), XI–XII.

24 [A. Brillat-Savarin], *Physiologie du Goût, ou Méditations de Gastronomie Transcendante*, Paris: A. Sautelet et Cⁱᵉ Libraires, 1826, viii.

25 S. Gottschalk, 'All You Can Eat: Sociological Reflections on Food in the Hypermodern Era', in L.C. Rubin (ed.), *Food for Thought: Essays on Eating and Culture*, Jefferson, NC: McFarland, 2008, 49.

26 J. Bruinsma (ed.), *World Agriculture: Toward 2105/2030*, FAO – London: Earthscan, 2003, 266.

27 See www.worldometers.info/world-population; www.worldometers.info/undernour-ishment (last accessed 31 July 2018).

28 www.fao.org/edible-insects/en (last accessed 31 July 2018).

29 C. Petrini and G. Padovani, *Slow Food Revolution: da Arcigola a Terra Madre*, Milan: Rizzoli, 2005, 150.

30 https://en.wikipedia.org/wiki/List_of_countries_by_meat_consumption (last accessed 31 July 2018).

31 J. Diamond, *Guns, Germs and Steel: A Short History of Everybody for the Last 13,000 years*, New York: W.W. Norton, 1997.

32 M. Montanari, *The Culture of Food*, trans. C. Ipsen, Oxford: Blackwell, 1994 (original edn 1993); *EaH*, 172–3.

33 V. Tanara, *L'economia del cittadino in villa*, Bologna: Eredi del Dozza, 1651 (first edn 1644), 32.

34 Tanara, *L'economia*, 29.

35 R.W. [R. Wolley], *Galliæ Notitia: or, the Present State of France, Containing a General Description of that Kingdom*, London: J. Taylor, 1691, 16.

36 *EaH*, 171.

37 Ibid., 173.

38 B. Scappi, *The Opera of Bartolomeo Scappi (1570): L'arte et prudenza d'un maestro Cuoco (The Art and Craft of a Master Cook)*, trans. with commentary by T. Scully, Toronto: University of Toronto Press, 2008, 412ff.

39 'Cmc', 401.

40 T. Stuart, *The Bloodless Revolution: A Cultural History of Vegetarianism from 1600 to Modern Times*, New York, London: Norton & Company, 2007, quotation xix.

41 Ibid., *passim*; E. Joy Mannucci, *La cena di Pitagora. Storia del vegetarianismo dall'antica Grecia a Internet*, Rome: Carocci, 2008.

42 M. Montanari, *Mangiare da cristiani. Diete, digiuni, banchetti*, Milan: Rizzoli, 2015.

43 Ibid.; *EaH*, 173–5.

44 L. Rostagno, *Mi faccio turco. Esperienze e immagini dell'Islam nell'Italia moderna*, Rome: Istituto per l'Oriente C.A. Nallino, 1983, 70.

45 B. Rosenberger, 'Arab Cuisine and Its Contribution to European Culture', in J.-L. Flandrin and M. Montanari (eds), *Food: A Culinary History*, trans. A. Sonnenfeld, New York: Columbia University Press, 1999 (original edn 1997), 207–23.

46 J. Soler, 'Biblical Reasons: The Dietary Rules of the Ancient Hebrews', ibid., 46–54; A. Toaff, *Mangiare alla giudia. La cucina ebraica in Italia dal Rinascimento all'età moderna*, Bologna: Il Mulino, 2000.

47 C. Balzaretti, *Il Papa, Nietzsche e la cioccolata: saggio di morale gastronomica*, Bologna: Edb, 2009.

48 *EaH*, 179.

49 D. Gentilcore, *Pomodoro! A History of the Tomato in Italy*, New York: Columbia University Press, 2010.

50 G. Donzelli, *Teatro farmaceutico, dogmatico e spargirico* [Naples]: G.F. Paci, G. Fasulo and M. Monaco, 1675 (first edn 1667), Parte Seconda, 279. The same words were used by C. Durante in 1585; see Gentilcore, *Pomodoro!*

51 *EaH*, 183; Gentilcore, *Pomodoro!*, Ch. 4.

52 J.-L. Flandrin, 'The Early-Modern Period', in Flandrin and Montanari (eds), *Food*, 357.

53 Gentilcore, *Pomodoro!*

54 R.N. Salaman, *The History and Social Influence of the Potato*, Cambridge: Cambridge University Press, 1985 (first edn 1949), 85.

55 A.J. Grieco, 'Food and Social Classes in Late Medieval and Renaissance Italy', in Flandrin and Montanari (eds), *Food*, 302–12.

56 *EaH*, 181.

57 Montanari, *The Culture of Food*.

58 A.A. Parmentier, *Traité sur la culture et les usages des pommes de terre, de la patate et des topinambours*, Paris: Barrois, 1789, iii, 7–8, 384–5.

59 Andrew F. Smith, *Potato: A Global History*, London: Reaktion Books, 2012, 13.

60 *EaH*, 181–3.

61 Montanari, *The Culture of Food*.

62 'Cmc', 403.

63 P. Camporesi, *Il brodo indiano. Edonismo ed esotismo nel Settecento*, Milan: Il Saggiatore, 2017 (first edn 1989); T. Morton, *The Poetics of Spices: Romantic Consumerism and the Exotic,* Cambridge: Cambridge University Press, 2000, 44.

64 G. Fernández de Oviedo y Valdés, *Historia general y natural de las Indias*, Primera parte (1535), Madrid: Imprenta de la Real Academia de la Historia, 1851, 266.

65 *EaH*, 179–81; 'Cmc', 404.

66 M. Berg et al. (eds), *Goods from the East, 1600–1800: Trading Eurasia*, Basingstoke: Palgrave Macmillan, 2015.

67 B.A. Weinberg and B.K. Bealer, *The World of Caffeine: The Science and Culture of the World's Most Popular Drug*, New York: Routledge, 2001, 6.

68 A.M. Fisker and A.E.U. Heilmann, 'East Meets West in Venice; Coffee – the Wine of Islam' (forthcoming).

69 G.B. de Burgo, *Viaggio di cinque anni In Asia, Africa, & Europa del Turco*, Milan: Stampe dell'Agnelli, [1686], 455.

70 W. Clarence-Smith and S. Topik (eds), *The Global Coffee Economy in Africa, Asia, and Latin America, 1500–1989*, Cambridge: Cambridge University Press, 2003.

71 A. Huetz de Lemps, 'Colonial Beverages and the Consumption of Sugar', in Flandrin and Montanari (eds), *Food*, 383–93; 'Cmc', 407–8.

72 Weinberg, Bealer, *The World of Caffeine*, passim.

73 P. Della Valle, *Viaggi di Pietro della Valle il pellegrino descritti da lui medesimo*, vol. 1, Brighton: G. Cangia, 1843 (original edn 1650–63), 76, my translation.

74 For instance D. Magri, *Virtu del Kafe*, Rome: M. Ercole, 1671 (2nd edn).

75 Stearns, *Consumerism in the World History*.

76 Huetz de Lemps, 'Colonial Beverages', 391.

77 S. Mintz, *Sweetness and Power: The Place of Sugar in Modern History*, New York: Viking, 1985.

78 Huetz de Lemps, 'Colonial Beverages'.

79 Voltaire, *Candide* (1759), New York: Boni & Liveright, 1918, 166 (The Project Gutenberg EBook).

80 Weatherill, *Consumer Behaviour*, 26.

81 I. Hoyt Reed, 'The European Hard-Paste Porcelain Manufacture of the 18th Century', *The Journal of Modern History* 8, no. 3, 1936, 273–96.

82 *EaH*, 126–8.

83 C. Fairchilds, 'The Production and Marketing of Populuxe Goods in 18th Century Paris', in Brewer and Porter (eds), *Consumption*, 228–48.

84 P. Marchese, *L'invenzione della forchetta*, Soveria Mannelli: Rubbettino 1989; *EaH*, 151–2; Weatherill, *Consumer Behaviour*, 26.

85 *EaH*, 95, 162–3.

86 M. Calaresu and D. van den Heuvel, 'Introduction: Food Hawkers from Representation to Reality', in M. Calaresu and D. van den Heuvel (eds), *Food Hawkers:*

Selling in the Streets from Antiquity to the Present, London, New York: Routledge, 2016.

87 *EaH*, 133.

88 *Ibid.*, 86–147; R. Sarti, *Ländliche Hauslandschaften in Europa in einer Langzeitperspektive*, in J. Eibach and I. Schmidt-Voges et al. (eds), *Das Haus in der Geschichte Europas. Ein Handbuch*, Berlin, Boston, MA: De Gruyter Oldenbourg, 2015, 175–94.

89 De Burgo, *Viaggio*, 449 (translation by Clelia Boscolo).

90 *EaH*, 103–6; 'Cmc', 366–75.

91 A. Contadini, *Middle–Eastern Objects*, in M. Ajmar-Wollheim and F. Dennis (eds), *At Home in Renaissance Italy*, London: Victoria and Albert Museum, 2006, 308–21 (315).

92 To see the painting seehttps://en.wikipedia.org/wiki/Madonna_with_Sts_John_the_Baptist_and_Donatus_(Verrocchio)#/media/File:Andrea_del_Verrocchio_-_Madonna_with_Sts_John_the_Baptist_and_Donatus_-_WGA24995.jpg (last accessed 11 February 2019).

93 Contadini, *Middle-Eastern Objects*, 315–19.

94 H. Croker, T. Williams, S. Clark et al., *The Complete Dictionary of Arts and Sciences* …, London: printed for the authors …, 1766, vol. I, entry 'Carpet'. The production in Paris started in 1608; see www.toutsurlestapis.fr/styles-et-origines/tapis-europeens (last accessed 16 February 2019).

95 Contadini, *Middle-Eastern Objects*, 306–15. These objects' style is called 'Venetian-Saracen'.

96 Palumbo Fossati, 'L'interno', 132. For the portrait of Mehmet II (1480, London, National Gallery), see https://it.wikipedia.org/wiki/File:Gentile_Bellini_003.jpg (last accessed 11 February 2019).

97 *EaH*, 119–23.

98 Ibid., 195–213.

99 Istituto di storia economica 'Francesco Datini' – Prato, *La seta in Europa. Secc. XIII–XX, Prato, 4–9 maggio 1992*, ed. S. Cavaciocchi, Florence: Le Monnier, 1993.

100 V. Hansen, *The Silk Road: A New History*, Oxford: Oxford University Press, 2012.

101 D. della Torre Arrigoni, 'La seta prima del baco della seta', *La seta* 61, 009, 38–42, www.genm.it/associazione/files/12_670awnu8.pdf (last accessed 12 February 2019).

102 T. Ertl, 'Silkworms, Capital and Merchant Ships: European Silk Industry in the Medieval World Economy,' *The Medieval History Journal* 9, 2006, 243–70.

103 M.L. Rosati, 'Migrazioni tecnologiche e interazioni culturali. La diffusione dei tessuti orientali nell'Europa del XIII e del XIV secolo', *Oadi. Rivista dell'Osservatorio per le arti decorative in Italia* 1, 2010, www1.unipa.it/oadi/oadiriv/?page_id=111 (last accessed 12 February 2019).

104 Ertl, 'Silkworms'; Claudio Zanier, 'La sericoltura dell'Europa mediterranea dalla supremazia mondiale al tracollo: un capitolo della competizione economica tra Asia orientale ed Europa', *Quaderni storici* 25, no. 73, 1990, 7–53.

105 www.statista.com/statistics/263055/cotton-production-worldwide-by-top-countries (last accessed 12 February 2019).

106 G. Riello, 'Cotton: The Making of a Modern Commodity', *East Asian Journal of British History* 5, 2016, 135–49 (136).

107 Ibid., 137–8; G. Riello, *Cotton: The Fabric That Made the Modern World*, Cambridge: Cambridge University Press, 2013, 89–92.

108 Ibid., 100.

109 Ibid., 110–25.

110 Riello, *Cotton*, 121–3; Riello, 'Cotton: The Making', 138.

111 *The Manuscripts of the House of Lords*, vol. V, Great Britain. Parliament. House of Lords, H.M. Stationery Office, 1702, xxi–xxii.

112 E. Hobsbawm, *Industry and Empire: From 1750 to the Present Day*, London: Penguin, 1999 (first edn 1968), 35.

113 Riello, *Cotton*, 240; Riello, 'Cotton: The Making', 238.

114 Ibid., 136; Riello, *Cotton*, 197.

115 Riello, 'Cotton: The Making', 240.

116 P. Parthasarathi and I. Wend, 'Decline in Three Keys: Indian Cotton Manufacturing from the Late 18th Century', in G. Riello and P. Parthasarathi (eds), *The Spinning World: A Global History of Cotton Textiles, 1200–1850*, Oxford: Oxford University Press, 2011, 397–407 (397).

117 Malanima and Pinchera, 'A Puzzling Relationship'.

118 J. Komlos, 'Shrinking in a Growing Economy? The Mystery of Physical Stature', *Journal of Economic History* 58, 1998, 779–802.

13

REVERENCE, SHAME AND GUILT IN EARLY MODERN EUROPEAN CULTURES

Jonas Liliequist

This essay deals with emotional aspects of three of the most prominent themes in the socio-political and cultural history of the early modern period – state building, confessionalization and social disciplining.[1] In the legitimization of state power, a father's household rule over his wife, children and dependants represented the most elementary order of society. *Reverence*, a nearly forgotten concept today, appears as a key emotional concept in the prescribed attitudes and behaviour. State building also implied bureaucratization and the emergence of new groups of civil servants and sol-diery who, not fitting into the pre-existing estate hierarchy, required new and more specific orders of precedence based on rank and office. Accordingly, keeping track of whom, when and how to express social reverence and respect multiplied. Compared to reverence, *shame* is a far more complex emotion felt and assessed in different ways depending on the cultural context. To feel shame in early modern culture was not necessarily shameful. On the contrary, while shame could be considered both an edifying and degrading emotion, shamelessness, the absence of a sense of shame, was unambiguously negative, associated with the brute beasts. *Guilt*, on the other hand, has often been contrasted with shame. Sociologists and anthropologists in particular have made a sharp difference between shame-cultures and guilt-cultures, with guilt characteristic of modern and more sophisticated societies.[2] Cultural historians have generally been more cautious. It will be argued in the following that guilt was as much a key emotion as shame in the processes of confessionalization and social dis-ciplining. The bulk of empirical examples are taken from Sweden-Finland, but the ambition is to say something about England and the German Empire as well.

Honour thy father and thy mother

In May 1712, Master Augustin Renfeld, a sword cutler, appeared before the Stock-holm Chapter of the ecclesiastic court complaining that his son Augustin Renfeld Jr had without his knowledge become engaged to a woman who was a complete stranger to him.[3] He could not possibly give his consent to a marriage between his son and this 'woman folk'. Even less so, since his son had given him a written promise to remain in the trade and show him the obedience that was his due. Augustin Jr replied that he could not see in what way he had been disobedient. He had no inclination whatsoever to continue in his father's trade. His wish was instead to find another means of support and had it not been for his father's interference, he would have secured for himself a good position long ago. As for his betrothed, his conscience would never allow him to abandon her. Not even his father's threat to disinherit him could change his mind. Admonishing him to obey his father, the clergymen hearing the case referred to the Fourth Commandment and the misfortune that would be caused if he failed to show him proper reverence. The younger Renfeld argued, on the contrary, that neither his wish to leave his father's trade to earn his living in other ways, nor his contracting of a Christian marriage, was a breach of the commandment, adding that he had always shown his father all possible honour and reverence. The main task before the clergymen was to achieve reconciliation. Despite the written promise – an obvious attempt by the father to extend his authority and keep his son in the workshop even after he had reached the age of majority – the Chapter told the father not to press his son as long as he had no inclination to ply the trade. It was furthermore remarked that if the son's betrothed was a woman of good reputation, that ought to make it possible for the father to give his consent. Augustin Sr, however, held his ground. Turning to the son, the presiding clergyman read aloud a passage from the Church Law stating the son's duty to ask for his parents' advice and consent when intending to marry. Once again, Augustin Jr was admonished to obey his father and break the engagement, and once again he refused. With that, the Chapter capitulated, and it was decided that the case should be referred to secular court.

Two months later, however, father and son reappeared before the Chapter in a rather different mood. To begin with, the father declared that he still could not give his consent since his son had not asked for his advice at the appropriate time, and since the woman was unknown to him. Because of this, he would no longer provide for his son as a father if he still insisted on wedlock. The Chapter turned to the son and reproached him for his bad behaviour. By failing to seek his father's advice, he had not paid him the honour he deserved, according to the laws of God and Nature. Admonished to apologize and ask his father to forgive him, the son immediately complied. The apology was accepted, and Augustin Sr declared that he was no longer opposed to the marriage. Stretching out his hand, he wished his son all luck and gave him his blessing. In the final moment, settling the dispute was a matter of restoring reverence and honour.

The case illustrates the general trend of a strengthening patriarchal power in Reformation and Post-Reformation Europe across confessional lines. According to medieval Swedish law, a son who had reached the legal age of consent (fifteen) could contract a marriage without asking his parents in advance. This unrestrained freedom had become increasingly restricted during the sixteenth and seventeenth centuries. The Church Law of 1686 not only established the son's duty to ask for consent beforehand, but should his parents resist, and a reconciliation not be reached in the Chapter, the case should be tried in secular court. If it turned out that the parents had good reason to object, their son had no choice but to obey them. If not, they had the right to disinherit him. Daughters did not reach majority until widowhood but could be disinherited as well if they accepted a marriage contract without parental consent.[4]

This more restrictive attitude reflects a further aspect of the general trend towards enhanced patriarchal power – the increasing importance of the household and household authority as the basic model and metaphor for social order and governance. The Fourth Commandment – 'Honour your father and your mother, that you may live long in the land the Lord your God is giving you' (Exodus 20:12) – played a crucial role in this development.[5] In Luther's exegetical comment it appears as the very foundation stone of all social and political commitment among Christians. 'God separates and distinguishes father and mother above all other persons upon earth, and places them at His side'.[6] Thus, God not only commands us to love our parents but also to honour them. Honour is far greater than love, Luther explains. It entails not only love, but modesty, humility and deference together with the duties to obey and revere as well as to serve, help and provide for one's parents when they are old, sick, infirm or poor. Children should thus be understood as a generational category and not only in terms of minority. The parent–child relationship is at the same time extended metaphorically to other issues of authority and subordination in society, 'for all authority flows and is propagated from the authority of parents'. In the household, male and female servants alike should honour their master and mistress as they would their own father and mother. In society, civil government represents fatherhood in relation to all of us as subjects. The duty to honour is thus extended from fathers by blood to fathers of households and fathers of the nation. There are also spiritual fathers governing and guiding us by the word of God who we are obliged to honour, deal well with and provide for. *Reverence* is the overall key concept that best captures the whole range of non-reciprocal emotions subordinates are obliged to express towards persons of parental authority, not only outwardly but 'from the heart', as Luther writes.

Luther's comment in the Large Catechism was boiled down and developed further in the Shorter Catechism structured in question and answer form for explicitly didactic purposes. It comprises three sections beginning with the Ten Commandments followed by the Creed and Lord's Prayer.[7] In a following section, the extended parenthood of the Fourth Commandment is exemplified in a list of duties and responsibilities for the members of the three Christian Estates outlined in the Large Catechism as three kinds of fatherhood, representing the church, the civil government and the household, respectively (biological fatherhood is included in the household estate). This so-called Household Table (*Haustafel*) ordered the population into hierarchies of authority and reverence. One and the same person had a position in each of these three hierarchies.

Luther's Small Catechism became an immediate success.[8] By the time the dispute between Augustin Renfeld and his son arose, catechizing in Sweden had developed into a well-established system of teaching, visitation and examination. Augustin Jr was obviously not unacquainted with the rules of reverence stated in the Fourth Commandment, but he preferred to interpret them in his own way. Disobedience was clearly stated in the questions and answers as a breach of the commandment. But the obligation to obey was not unconditional. As to the question, 'Are children obliged to obey their parents in everything?' the reply is, 'Yes, as long as it is not contrary to God's word and our conscience, for we must obey God over humans'.[9] Augustin Jr took this as his defence. He could not abandon his betrothed because of his conscience, and a Christian marriage could not possibly be against the word of God, implying that it was not for his father to forbid.

What sanctions were at hand to enforce implementation of the commandments? Parents were obliged to raise their children in the courage and admonition of the Lord as stated in the Household Table. Discipline and correction were considered necessary for instilling respect and submission in children. This is treated at length in the extensive treatises on the Household Table and conduct books for housefathers that emerged in the sixteenth and seventeenth centuries. To love one's children is naturally instilled in the hearts of human beings, writes German theologian Aegidus Hunnius (1550–1603). However, just as one can show too little love towards one's children, one can also show too much love for them. The latter is as bad as the former and even worse when a child is permitted to follow its own will.[10] Swedish priest and author Zacharias Brockenius (1645–1713) reminds the reader that children are born in sin and thus immediate prey for vice if not corrected and disciplined in their early years.[11] Still, some parents think that small children are too tiny and too young to be chastised. Instead of using the rod, they just want to take joy in them. Such children, however, bring great sorrow and pain to their parents when they grow older, warns German pedagogue Christoph Fischer (1519–1597).[12] Bow his neck when he is still young; beat his back when he is still small that he will not grow obstinate and disobedient. Correction must at the same time be timely and moderate so as not to evoke fear and bitterness, which will only turn the child against the parent. The tone is somewhat less harsh and reservations more numerous in the comprehensive conduct book for housefathers by English clergyman William Gouge (1575–1653). Nevertheless, he also states that 'a little correction' is often more efficient than the inculcation of admonitions by frequent repetition, since children are 'much more sensible of smart than of words'.[13]

Such attitudes were not something new brought on by the Reformation. What was new, however, was a much stricter attitude to even the slightest disrespectful behaviour in an adult child towards his or her parents. Had there been witnesses testifying that Augustin Jr had lost his temper and uttered a curse or pushed his father aside, he would have been in serious trouble. The condemnation of children who defy their parents in word and deed, while not mentioned in the Catechism, is iterated in House Table literature. Children, writes Hunnius with reference to the Decalogue, who beat or curse their father or mother shall be put to death. This sanction was incorporated in the national law of states including Scotland and the Scandinavian countries.[14] Few such malefactors were, however, executed in Sweden; some were flogged but most were sentenced to jail terms on bread and water or ordered to pay heavy fines. These trials concerned adult children, often the middle-aged sons and daughters of elderly parents. Minor children were to be chastised by their parents.

What about the gendered aspects of reverence? Luther is in fact inconsistent in representing parental authority as paternal in terms of the household. While church and civil government are unambiguously represented as fathers, household authority includes obedience to father *and* mother, master *and* mistress. The married couple was the hub of the household, both as parents and domestic sovereigns. Breaking with a tradition that disparaged women as 'necessary evils' was part of Luther's argument for a reform of marriage, allowing for a new respect for women as *companions*.[15] The images of marriage and parenthood presented in Luther's treatise on *The Estate of Marriage* (1522) do indeed come close to a companionate relationship. Parental authority is characterized as the noblest and greatest thing on earth, without gender distinction. Notable is his reproach of those who poke fun at a father who goes ahead to wash diapers or perform some other menial task to the benefit of his child.[16] Still, the patriarchal nature of household authority and the husband–wife relationship is present, even in this text. To help and *obey* her husband in the daily business of the household is a truly golden and noble calling, writes Luther. The apocryphal story of Tobias was modelled into a guideline for this double role of deferential wife and able housemother.[17] In the play *Tobie Comedia* by Swedish reformist Olaus Petri (1493–1552), Sara, the wife of Tobias, is instructed to always honour her husband, revere his parents and friends and learn how to properly command her domestics.[18] In the Catechism, the relationship between spouses is treated in the household table section without reference to the Fourth Commandment. Addressing women, it states, 'Let wives be subjected to their husbands as to their Lord, as Sarah obeyed Abraham and called him Lord' (1 Peter 3:1, 6). The corresponding address to men reads, 'Husbands, live reasonable with your wives' (1 Peter 3:7), 'and do not be harsh with them' (Colossians 3:19).

Thus, wives had dual status in Lutheran household ideology. A common metaphor of the time was the sun and moon.[19] The moon receives its light from the sun and rules the night but not the day, as it is with the household government of the wife: conditional and restricted to its own circles – a deputy position with special responsibility for housework. In relation to children and servants, however, as mother and mistress the wife could demand reverence and obedience from her charges. By tradition and variously sanctioned by the law, a husband had the right to castigate his wife. In Sweden this had already been modified in the medieval code, but the husband still had the right to castigate his wife *with moderation* for misdemeanours.[20] Relations between child and parent, and husband and wife, were thus both *reciprocal* in their obligation to love, while at the same time *asymmetric* in terms of reverence and the exercise of authority. This latter asymmetry held true for the relationship between master/mistress and servant as well. The House Table states that servants should be 'obedient to their bodily lords with fear and trembling', while the master and mistress are admonished not to abuse them.

When the Fourth Commandment was put into judicial practice, as it was in Sweden, household disputes became more complex and the consequences more dire. In one illustrative case, a farmer named Lars Truedsson became angry with his wife for having decided a household matter without his permission. When his wife asked for a silver coin to pay required expenses, it looked like Lars was going to strike her. His wife took refuge behind her mother-in-law who tried to stop her son, but Lars grabbed his mother's arm and angrily shoved her down onto a bench. No doubt Lars thought he had the right to castigate his wife, and his mother may well have agreed, though she obviously did not sanction his motives and immoderate response. Lars's mother in her turn could refer to her parental authority when she tried to stop him by physical means. As a response to his mother's defensive violence, grabbing and pushing one's biological mother was a capital crime. Lars, however, escaped with twenty days in jail on bread and water and offering a public apology to his mother before the court.[21]

Reverence, rank and precedence

Aside from being inculcated by Catechism and the Ten Commandments, reverence was also claimed according to rank and status. In England, the division into estates had lost its significance and been replaced by a lone, tripartite hierarchy of degrees – the better, the common and the middling sort of people. Apart from the highest levels of society, the social assessment of relative status had become largely informal and open to career advancement based on wealth and lifestyle.[22] A similar process of stratification took place in Sweden. The limited number of domestic aristocrats could not meet the increasing demand for qualified functionaries from the expanding state apparatus and military sector. The solution was to recruit and ennoble individuals based on merit rather than birth. Virtue in the sense of personal merit, benefit to society and Christian morality became key to claiming status in the battles over rank and precedence that followed.[23]

The German Empire has in turn been characterized as a society 'where the rank and status of "high" persons had to be continually asserted before the eyes of all and acknowledged by others through finely graded forms of deference' and where performance and discord over rank imbued every reach.[24] The following example sets a typical scene. In October 1713, a Master of Philosophy from the Electorate of Saxony filed a complaint before the Sovereign Consistory against the Royal Official Advocate. In the words of the plaintiff, during a baptism last Sunday at the local church, the advocate had 'without hesitation and acknowledgement walked right past me' – 'a degreed person and Master, with a Doctorate in Philosophy' – and occupied 'my due rank and honoured place'. Demonstrably summoning all the scholarship available to him, the plaintiff states that the most prominent position at the baptismal font belongs to no one but himself, 'as was conceded and communicated by His Imperial Majesty … with public approval and applause from an entire world-famous university and issued by an honoured Faculty of Philosophy'. He now felt himself obliged to denounce the advocate to the Honourable Consistory with a most humble request to emphatically punish him for this excess and advise the advocate to abstain from this presumptuous behaviour and pretended rank in the future.[25]

The case is representative in two ways. First and most specifically, the claim for precedence was based on academic merits. With more than thirty universities, the German Empire hosted the largest academic community in early modern Europe. Like Swedish state offices, German universities offered great opportunities for upward social mobility. The ideal of *nobilitas literata* was taken most literally as a claim to nobility on the grounds of a doctoral degree. Debate about the social rank of scholars and the battle over precedence between 'the feather' and 'the sword' stamps a particular imprint on German rank conflict.[26] In a more general sense, the case is also characteristic in its allocation. Whether claimed based on wealth, virtue or academic merit, churches offered an important arena for the continuous display of rank and status in early modern society.[27] Such disputes could become both noisy and physical, as happened in the castle chapel of the Swedish town of Kalmar in 1672. The seating plan was strictly gendered, with women sitting to the left on the north side and men to the right on the south side of the central aisle.[28] Tardy to services, the wife of a bookkeeper found that the wife of the treasurer had already occupied the most prestigious seat, closest to the aisle. When the latter rose to let her pass, she exclaimed, 'Move, *thou* woman!' and began jostling her. 'Am I not as good as you?' the treasurer's wife demanded. 'I will never sit below you as if I were your maidservant, you pert girl'. Eventually, the bookkeeper's wife had to accept a less lofty seat, but the quarrel loudly continued. 'You damned bitch, who do you think your father was? Mine was a circuit judge. Only God knows what kind of man your father was, and your husband is no more than a lewd knave'.[29]

The antagonists in these disputes were most typically wives of men of roughly equal relative status from the middle and upper social levels of the congregation illustrating the principle that rivalry and conflicts thrive the most between individuals who are equal or differ little in social standing.[30] The references to fathers and husbands reflect women's lack of formal status independent of male relatives. Thus, status and rank, like household order, was fundamentally patriarchal. The gendered seating order did at the same time provide one of the few public arenas for women to claim, compete for and demonstrate their relative status. Issuing updated seating plans on a regular basis and enacting ordinances punishing disturbances in church curbed the disputes in Sweden. In Germany, as indicated above, conflicts over precedence and rank in general and at church in particular were divided into the independent judicial discourses *ius precedentiae* and *ius subselliorum templorem*, respectively, giving rise to a vast literature on the subject.[31]

From the sixteenth century onwards, detailed lists of rank were issued by most European states, laying down the principal rules of precedence in public ceremonies and gatherings.[32] Honorary titles constituted another mark of rank and precedence. Royalty, aristocrats and commissioned officers in Sweden were titled Highborn, Wellborn, Noble and Manly; the clergy Most Reverend, Very Reverend, Venerated and Highly Learned; civil servants Noble and Highly Esteemed, Well-Trusted and Well-Esteemed; while common burgers and peasants were designated Honest and Sensible. Women were in contrast addressed by civil status as maids, wives and widows.[33] The pronouns of address *thou* and *you* also indicated a hierarchal relationship. *Thou* was used to address someone in a subordinate position, while the more formal *you* was appropriate for equals and superiors.[34] Besides the rules of spatial precedence, rank was also made visible in dress regulated by sumptuary laws, whose main purpose was to ensure recognizability by forbidding people to dress up above their station.[35] Last but not least, status, reverence and authority were communicated in social practice through gesture, posture and facial display.[36] Already illustrated is the advocate's arrogance in the German case. Swedish author Samuel Columbus (1642–1679) provides a further glimpse of salutation etiquette in a note on poet Lasse Johansson (1638–1674), known for his wilfulness. When Count Per Brahe passed in his equipage, Columbus immediately doffed his hat and bowed. 'Why did you do that?' Johansson asked. 'Because the Lord High Steward of the Realm passed us and as the rule says: honour when honour is due. Besides, he is a Gentleman of high age and merits, and merits should be revered and honoured'. 'Count Per travels his ways and I travel mine', Johansson replied. 'If I have some matter to ask him then I will bow and bend but not else'. 'You should take better care of your poetic gifts and seek favours from the highborn, from that you could gain both food and honour', Columbus objected. 'That would be an awkward thing, to sell one's freedom for an annual sum of money', Johansson exclaimed.[37]

As implied by Columbus, navigating the rules of status and precedence could result in personal benefits. In conduct books like the *Book of Compliment* an ideal of sociability was taught as a means of making a social career. A compliment, the author explains, is a polite expression of reverence well adapted to the situation and the individuals with whom one is socializing, whether of equal or higher status. Polite gestures and postures should be discreet and not give the impression of theatricality. To bow constantly, avert one's gaze, stand with arms hanging down to the side or walk too fast or too slow is not fitting for an honest man who has nothing to fear in consort with a superior or a stranger of equal status. Relaxed and easy behaviour is always preferable. Contentiousness, pounding the table with a clenched fist and wild gesticulation is indecent. A contemptuous attitude will only bring shame.[38]

Different shades of shame

Shame played a central role in the early modern social fabric. 'What affects me most', writes the Complainant in the German case above, was that the advocate ignored him 'in front of the assembled Body of the Church'. Honour and reputation were his prime motivation, but shame operated in other ways as well. In a letter to his 'dear Father dear', Swedish courtier Johan Ekeblad (1629–1696) writes that his wife was in great distress because 'she had not called my dear Father dear, *Father* in her recent letter despite the great honour his dear Father dear had shown *her* by calling her 'my daughter'. The letter was written on her behalf and posted without her correction, Ekeblad explains, 'and now she is all in tears over her shameful negligence'.[39] In this instance, feelings of shame were an appropriate sign of reverence and respect in a hierarchal relationship focusing on the deed, not the person. Ekeblad adds that he is convinced that his Father will not think the worst of his daughter-in-law.

Following Australian criminologist Johan Braithwaite, a distinction can be made between *reintegrative* and *stigmatizing shame* of which the latter's purpose is to degrade its subject.[40] Reintegrative shame was most typically connected with public confession and redemption. After executed punishment, a courtroom apology before the violated parent(s) and assembled congregation was the standard in cases of verbal and violent abuse of parents in Swedish judicial practice. Reconciliation was the goal, and the demonstrably humble, submissive demeanour of the perpetrator considered 'good' and 'edifying shame'.[41] Elderly abused parents were usually still dependent on their children for their livelihood and often pleaded for mercy on behalf of their sons and daughters. These circumstances were taken into consideration in penal practice as well. The above-mentioned Lars Truedsson had to endure twenty days in jail on bread and water, a considerable corporal punishment indeed, but without any serious damage to his honour compared to whipping. He could still return to his farm and continue to run the household. During the period of 'God's law', however, public confession was required in church as well, according to the ritual of the so-called 'church duty'.[42] The sinner was required to stand or kneel on a special stool in front of the congregation during morning services and confess his or her sin before being absolved. The repentant sinner was thereby formally reconciled with the congregation, but the public exposure was an obvious source of disgrace.[43] This was in fact acknowledged at the end of the ceremony, when the priest turned to the assembly with a warning that anyone who dared reproach a repentant and absolved sinner, who had humiliated him/herself before God and the congregation, would be castigated and punished. Women were especially vulnerable; in cases of adultery and fornication, both parties were to undergo the ritual, but men often swore to their innocence and when not, the double standard diminished the shaming effect. This gender bias was also reflected in verbal abuse. While whore was the most typical invective against women, men were called rogues and knaves.[44]

Outright shaming like sitting in the stocks in front of the church door was part of ecclesiastical judicial practice as well. In Sweden the stocks were prescribed as a general penalty in the first of a series of state ordinances against swearing, breaches of the Sabbath and disturbances in the church, but only as a last resort when admonishment and escalating warnings had failed. In this hierarchy of moral regulation, parental authority in the extended sense of the house table was given a decisive role. In chastisement, physical means could be used for moral improvement since parental correction was not conceived as degrading and shameful. Negligent parents, masters and mistresses, and persons of parental authority could be held responsible as well and subject to the same system of admonishment, warnings and time in the shameful stocks.[45]

That shame casts its shadow upward in hierarchal relationships is further demonstrated in the shaming rituals of henpecked husbands and disobedient wives. 'Those wives who are not submissive to their husbands and do not prove obedient but oppose them with a stubborn and angry demeanour, bitterness, and obstinacy wear a mark of shame around their necks', writes Aegidius Hunnius in his *Christian Table of Duties*. The husband of such a woman feels not only ashamed but will eventually be brought to ridicule and ruin.[46] Women were thus both shamed and the very cause of male shame. The house table and advice literature in general warns the husband to abstain from violence as being both rash and counterproductive since 'when you beat out one devil, you beat in ten more'.[47] 'No fault should be so great, as to compel a husband to beat his wife', writes William Gouge in *Of Domesticall Duties*. Only if a husband 'is set upon by his wife, it is lawful and expedient that he defends himself, and if he can do it no other ways but striking her, that is not to be reckoned an unlawful beating her'.[48]

The tone is much harsher in the German and English street literature of the sixteenth and seventeenth centuries. Readers are invited to laugh at both the shame of henpecked husbands and the brutal beatings of insubordinate wives.[49] In these fictional battles, the wife's sharp tongue is regularly set against the husband's beating. The notion of the female tongue as a sword was a common stereotype, and 'scold' the archetype of a disobedient wife. Scolding was established as an independent crime category in English judicial practice as early as the late Middle Ages. Over the course of the sixteenth and early seventeenth centuries drastic shaming rituals evolved. Convicted scolds were sat down on a stool and ducked 'over head and ears' in a pond in the presence of a multitude of onlookers.[50] Shame was also inscribed on the body by mutilation and branding, still practised in Europe during the sixteenth and early seventeenth centuries. By the seventeenth century, however, the most common shaming penalty was being pilloried, often accompanied by whipping. While the aim of the pillory was to expose the delinquent to public disgrace, the purpose of a public whipping was to cause both shame and pain. In a century labelled the 'great flogging age' by Lawrence Stone, whipping was by far the most widely employed corporal penalty.[51]

Emerging as the prescribed punitive alternative for those who could not afford to pay fines, the pain and shame of a public whipping bore the definitive imprint of class. Common and poor people had to pay with their bodies and loss of honour to a wider extent than ever before. This coincided with the emergence of what has been described by Norbert Elias and others as a civilizing process among the upper classes based on rising internalized thresholds of shame.[52] Politeness and the disciplining of farting and spitting were contrasted with the humiliation and bloodletting of delinquents at pillories and whipping posts, but the eighteenth century also saw the emergence of a long-term decrease in interpersonal deadly violence.[53]

In time, the efficacy of shame and public exposure began to be questioned. During the first half of the eighteenth century, church repentance rituals were criticized for being a major cause of young, unwed women hiding their pregnancies and committing infanticide. Consequently, Swedish public church duty was abolished for fornication and first-time adultery in 1741.[54] Even more problematic were the numerous cases of self-reported child murder. An illustrative case is that of Catharina Andersdotter. In 1716 she reported herself for having drowned a small girl by pushing her into the water from a bridge in Stockholm. She told the court that she had done this horrible deed out of sadness and great anxiety, after having been badly beaten and universally condemned because she had once been subject to a dishonourable penalty. When temporarily employed in the house of a weaver, she was recognized as having stood at the pillory. Summarily dismissed from work and lodging, she was caught in the street by a soldier who called her a common thief and beat her with a rod. Despite the very public setting, she was lying badly hurt in front of a door in the street the whole day until the wife of a jailer eventually took pity on her. After some days of recovery, she met the small girl in the street and led her to the bridge.[55] Catharina's deed was far from unique. Snatching away small children to drown or cut them to death and thereafter reporting oneself became a recurrent phenomenon in seventeenth- and early eighteenth-century Stockholm.[56] The perpetrators were nearly always women. Often, they had suffered shameful penalties like being flogged, pilloried and being banished from town. Stigmatized and marginalized, they were easy victims of despair and willing confessors of self-reported guilt.

Guilt between absolution and despair

The framing of conscience and the sense of guilt were crucial to the process of confessionalization and enforcement of stricter morals. Within the hegemony of the Ten Commandments the focus in penance shifted from social relationships to concern with personal guilt and direct reconciliation with God.[57] Communal reconciliation still had a strong hold on people, as shown by David Sabean in his study of the refusal to attend the Lord's Supper because of unsettled matters of enmity in local society.[58] Disputes between grown children and parents were similarly problematic. Like conflicts between spouses and neighbours, they were about social relationships, but unlike these, a shove or defamatory word could transform the conflict into a breach of the Fourth Commandment, requiring reconciliation directly with God. The task of catechetical teaching was to explain the seriousness of the deed and instil a sense of guilt. It is, however, doubtful if this was very successful. What seems to have mattered most was the testimony of victims or witnesses, not self-reported confession. In the numerous trials for bestiality – another Nordic or more precisely Swedish peculiarity – the opposite was true.[59] In the course of the seventeenth and eighteenth centuries, an increasing percentage of the cases were brought before the court via self-denunciation.[60] At first, confessing to a serious sin and capital crime like bestiality was considered the highest proof of godly and sincere repentance, accepted as full proof by the legal doctrine as well. Confessions were, however, recanted; others delivered by clearly unstable individuals. The initial enthusiasm for self-incrimination was soon replaced by an increasing scepticism towards all confessions made without the confirmatory proof of witnesses and probable circumstances. For women, self-reported confessions of infanticide committed long ago raised similar doubts.

The great bulk of self-denunciations were, however, not withdrawn. Usually self-denunciators displayed all the expected signs of anxiety and fear stemming from a bad conscience. Agony and sorrow over committed sins was a necessary first step on the road to confession and absolution, but this 'godly sorrow' could also be carried to extremes and lead to despair and suicidal thoughts.[61] Godly sorrow and spiritual despair from bad conscience could, however, be difficult to distinguish from weariness of living due to melancholic thoughts and the hardships of life. Temptations to commit suicide were a recurrent motive for confessions. In comparison, capital punishment appeared as a safe way to die. After witnessing a man attempting to drown himself, a farmer immediately denounced himself for bestiality. His troubled conscience did not permit him to make a private confession before a priest. He would rather undergo worldly punishment because 'then he would have a more blissful death, of which he was fully assured from attending the execution of another man condemned for bestiality, undergoing the death penalty well prepared'.[62] Whether his confession was true or not was impossible to prove.

This willingness to be executed must be seen in the light of a sacralization of the ritual of capital punishment. Parallel and in contrast to the extended employment of deterrent corporal punishments like flogging, the symbolic motive of the convict's reconciliation with God was emphasized.[63] With the enforcement of God's law and a more inquisitorial judicial process, confession became of central importance. Priests were given a more active role both in admonishing the accused to confess and in preparing the convict for death in capital cases. Up to the first half of the seventeenth century, those convicted of bestiality and infanticide could, however, still be burnt alive in the name of deterrence. When this was succeeded by decapitation before burning the corpse, the sacral aspects became more salient. Instantaneous death without a prolonged and painful struggle limited the risk of despair in the dying moment and increased the motivation to confess and prepare oneself as a mandatory part of the process of carrying out capital punishment.

Preparation began in custody with prayers, confession and communion. At the place of execution, the priest, according to his manual, should give a short speech with an exhortation to the convict to show penitence and faith in God. Thereafter he should turn in joint prayer with the assembly for the convict to stand firm in his/

her faith and die a blissful death. At last, up on the scaffold, the convict should be comforted by the priest with the following words: 'Dear brother/sister, do not think of anything but Jesus Christ who has died for you, doubt not, he is certainly with you and will come to your aid'. And finally, 'I say to you, on behalf of Jesus Christ, today your soul shall enter Paradise'.[64] The convict's soul was thus not only assured salvation but also immediate transfer to heaven. The sacral aspects were further reinforced by convicts dressing up in white or black mourning attire festooned with ribbons and other adornments and being carted to the place of execution in the company of not one but several clergymen.[65]

Deeply affected by the sight of an execution, Christina Johansdotter decided to end her life by committing a murderous deed. She had first thought about suicide, but the fate of eternal damnation had discouraged her. Better, then, to die on the scaffold for a foul deed and be assured of salvation. Seeing a woman being executed for infanticide, she wished for nothing more than to be in her place. She had always thought that no one could possibly be better prepared for the afterlife than those who were to be executed.[66] There are some hints of a similar logic in the trials of bestiality as well. A man found in a cowshed declared that his many misfortunes and contentious relationship with his wife had caused him to commit bestiality 'in purpose of getting rid of all his sufferings'.[67] Thus, unproven or false self-denunciations and the committing of capital crimes for the sake of being executed were the unintended consequences of the sacralization of capital punishment. The extensive use of corporal punishment contributed to the situation in a similar way as well. Confessions made just before the execution of flogging or running the gauntlet were often recanted later as desperate attempts to delay or avoid the imminent pain of the punishment.

Concluding remarks

In the course of early modern state building and confessionalization, reverence – the duty to honour and respect not only God but also parents, teachers, monarchs and all figures of parental authority – was prescribed as a key emotion in the legitimization of political and confessional power. Extended to the new emerging social hierarchies as a system of rank and precedence, traditional concepts of honour were undermined and gave way to more individual forms of status and prestige based on wealth, merit and sociability. Alongside the catechetical inculcation of religious doctrine, the instilling of shame and guilt played a crucial role in the efforts of social disciplining. As to whether early modern society was a shame or a guilt culture, the answer has to be both. Though analytically distinct, in practice shame and sin were often intertwined. Public confession of sin produced shame, while stigmatizing shame and the hardships of life produced confessions of guilt, not always earnest and sometimes for the sake of being executed. This was taken one step further in suicidal murder. Suicidal murder and dubious and recanted confessions of capital crimes represented the ultimate challenge to this shame and guilt policy. It was, however, not until the second half of the eighteenth century that the social disciplinary efficacy of shaming and capital punishment was seriously challenged. In terms of gender, application of reverence, shame and guilt as means for social disciplining and legitimation of power reinforced traditional patriarchal structures in household and society. As a mistress and mother, a woman could demand reverence and obedience, but as a wife she still had to honour and submit to her husband. While the relative status of women was derived from the rank of husbands and fathers, women were not only shamed but could also be the cause of male shame and ridicule when not conforming to the patriarchal household order. Public apologies were considered equally edifying for both men and women, but confessions of fornication and adultery had more serious consequences for women than for men according to the double standard.

Notes

1 R. Po-Chia Hsia, *Social Discipline in the Reformation: Central Europe 1550–1750*, London, New York: Routledge, 1989; H. Schilling, 'Confessionalization: Historical and Scholarly Perspectives of a Comparative and Interdisciplinary Paradigm', in J. Headley, H. Hillerbrand and A. Papas (eds), *Confessionalization in Europe, 1555–1700*, London, New York: Routledge, 2016, 21–35.

2 R. Benedict, *The Chrysanthemum and the Sword: Patterns of Japanese Culture*, Boston, MA: Houghton Mifflin, 1946, 223.

3 Stockholm, City Archives, Stockholms Domkapitel, Protokoll AI:64, 1712 7/5, 14/5, 9/7.

4 M. Korpiola, 'Marrying Off Sons and Daughters', in G. Jacobsen et al. (eds), *Less Favored – More Favored* Copenhagen: Royal Library, 2004, 1–30; J. Harrington, *Reordering Marriage and Society in Reformation Germany*, Cambridge: Cambridge University Press, 1995, 197–8.

5 J. Bossy, *Christianity in the West 1400–1700*, Oxford, New York: Oxford University Press, 1985; R. Bast, *Honor Your Fathers: Catechisms and the Emergence of a Patriarchal Ideology in Germany, 1400–1600*, Leiden: Brill, 1997.

6 M. Luther, 'The Large Catechism', in R. Kolb and T. Wengert (eds), *The Book of Concord: The Confessions of the Evangelical Lutheran Church*, Minneapolis, MN: Fortress Press, 2000 ('The Fourth Commandment', 410–11).

7 M. Luther, 'The Small Catechism', in Kolb and Wengert, *The Book of Concord*, 347–75.

8 G. Strauss, *Luther's House of Learning. Indoctrination of the Young in the German Reformation*, Baltimore, MD, London: Johns Hopkins University Press, 1978, 155–61.

9 O. Svebilius, *Enfaldig förklaring öfwer Lutheri lilla catechismum, stält genom spörsmåhl och swar*, Uppsala: Henrich Keijser, 1689, 16, Question 41.

10 A. Hunnius, *The Christian Table of Duties* (1588), trans. P. Rydecki, Malone: Repristination Press, 2013 (Sixth Sermon: Parents, Fathers and Mothers, 80–1).

11 Z. Brockenius, *Huus-taflan eller en christelig, kort och enfaldig förklarning, om the tre hufwud-stånden*, Stockholm: Henrich Keijser, 1696, 'Siette Predijkan Om Föräldrar och Barn', 137.

12 C. Fischer, *Huus Tafla*, trans. Andreas Laurentii, Stockholm: Ignatius Meurer, 1618 ('Trettonde Predikan', 293, 299).

13 W. Gouge, *Of Domesticall Duties* (1622), Pensacola: Chapel Library, 2006 (The sixth treatise: The Duties of Parents, 46 Of Correcting Children).

14 Sweden-Finland: J. Liliequist, '"The child who strikes his own father or mother shall be put to death": Assault and Verbal Abuse of Parents in Swedish and Finnish Counties 1745–1754', in S. Lidman and O. Matikainen (eds), *Morality, Crime and Social Control in Europe 1500–1900*, Helsinki: Finnish Literature Society, 2014, 19–42; Denmark-Norway: J. Koefoed, 'The Lutheran Household as Part of Danish Confessional Culture', in B. Holm and N. Koefoed (eds), *Lutheran Theology and the Shaping of Society: The Danish*

Monarchy as Example, Göttingen: Vandenhoeck & Ruprecht, 2018, 334–5; Scotland: K. Barclay, 'From Confession to Declaration. Changing Narratives of Parricide in Eighteenth-Century Scotland', in M. Muravyeva and R. Toivo (eds), *Parricide and Violence Against Parents throughout History: (De)Constructing Family and Authority?*, London: Palgrave Macmillan, 2018, 101–3.

15 S. Hendrix, 'Luther on Marriage', *Lutheran Quaterly* X IV, 2000, 335–50.

16 Luther, 'The Estate of Marriage', in W.I. Brandt (ed.), *Luther's Works 45: The Christian in Society 2*, Philadelphia, PA: Fortress, 1962, Part Three.

17 G. Strauss, *Luther's House of Learning*, 137–8; R. Bast, *Honor Your Fathers*, 68.

18 O. Petri, 'Tobie Comedia (1550)', in B. Hesselman (ed.), *Samlade skrifter af Olaus Petri, Fjärde bandet*, Uppsala: Almqvist & Wicksell, 1917, 424–5.

19 O. Insulaeo, *Speculum domesticum*, Strängnäs: Barkenio, 1636; H. Wunder, *He Is the Sun, She Is the Moon: Women in Early Modern Germany*, Cambridge, MA: Harvard University Press, 1998.

20 J. Liliequist, 'Changing Discourses of Marital Violence in Sweden from the Age of Reformation to the Late Nineteenth Century', *Gender & History* 23:1, 2011, 1–25.

21 Vadstena, Swedish National Archives, Göta hovrätt, Brottmålsutslag BIIa:54, 1750 22/8.

22 K. Wrightson, 'Estates, Degrees and Sorts: Changing Perceptions of Society in Tudor and Stuart England', in P. Corfield (ed.), *Language, History and Class*, Oxford: Basil Blackwell, 1991, 30–52.

23 J. Liliequist, 'From Honor to Virtue: The Shifting Social Logics of Masculinity and Honour, in Early Modern Sweden', in C. Strange, R. Cribb and C.E. Forth (eds), *Honour, Violence and Emotions in History*, London, New York: Bloomsbury Academic, 52–3.

24 B. Stollberg-Rilinger, *The Emperor's Old Clothes: Constitutional History and the Symbolic Language of the Holy Roman Empire*, New York and Oxford: Berghahn, 2015 (quotation at 271); T. Weller, *Theatrum Praecedentiae: zeremonieller Rang und gesellschaftliche Ordnung in der frühneuzeitlichen Stadt Leipzig 1500–1800*, Darmstadt: Wissenschaftliche Buchgesellschaft, 2006.

25 B. Stollberg-Rilinger, 'Rang vor Gericht. Zur Verrechtlichung sozialer Rangkonflikte in der frühen Neuzeit', *Zeitschrift für Historische Forschung* 28:3, 2001, 385–6.

26 M. Füssel, 'A Struggle for Nobility', in R. Kirwan (ed.), *Scholarly Self-Fashioning and Community in the Early Modern University*, London, New York: Routledge, 2016, 103–20.

27 England: S. Amussen, *An Ordered Society: Gender and Class in Early Modern England*, Oxford: Basil Blackwell, 1988, 134–44; Germany: T. Weller, 'Ius Subselliorum Templorum. Kirchenstuhlstreitigkeiten in der früneuzeitlichen Stadt zwichen symbolisher Praxis und Recht', in C. Dartmann, M. Füssel and S. Rüther (eds), *Raum und Konflikt. Zur symbolischen Konstituierung gesellschaftlicher Ordnung in Mittelalter und Früher Neuzeit*, Münster: Rhema, 2004, 199–224.

28 G. Malmstedt, *Bondetro och kyrkoro. Religiös mentalitet i stormaktstidens Sverige*, Lund: Nordic Academic Press, 2002, 39–42.

29 Vadstena, Swedish National Archives, Kalmar Domkapitel, Protokoll AI:4, 1672 16/8, 21/8.

30 A. Blok, 'The Narcissism of Minor Differences', *European Journal of Social Theory* 1:1, 1998, 33–56.

31 Stollberg-Rilinger, 'Rang vor Gericht'; Weller, 'Ius Subselliorum Templorum'.

32 A. Gestrich, 'The Social Order', in H. Scott (ed.), *The Oxford Handbook of Early Modern European History 1350–1750*, vol. I: Peoples and Place, Oxford: Oxford University Press, 2015, 303–4.

33 H. Ågren, 'Status, Estate, or Profession? Social Stratification via Titles in 1730s Sweden', *Scandinavian Journal of History* 42:2, 2017, 166–92.

34 T. Walker, *Thou and You in Early Modern English Dialogues: Trials, Depositions, and Drama Comedy*, Amsterdam: John Benjamins, 2007, 287–92.

35 A. Hunt, *Governance of the Consuming Passions: History of Sumptuary Law*, Basingstoke: Macmillan, 1996, 118–36.

36 A. Bryson, 'The Rhetoric of Status: Gesture, Demeanour and the Image of the Gentleman in Sixteenth- and Seventeenth-Century England', in L. Gent and N. Llewellyn (eds), *Renaissance Bodies: The Human Figure in English Culture c. 1540–1660*, London: Reaktion, 1990, 136–53.

37 S. Columbus, *MÅL-ROO eller ROO-MÅL*, C. Eichorn (ed.), Uppsala: Sundvallson, 1856, 22.

38 J. Ehrenström (trans.), *Compliment-bok*, Stockholm: Horrn, 1741, 4–6.

39 N. Sjöberg (ed.), *Johan Ekeblads bref 2*, Stockholm: Norstedts Förlag, 1915, 349–50.

40 R. Braithwaite, *Crime, Shame, and Reintegration*, Cambridge: Cambridge University Press, 1989.

41 M. Ingram, *Carnal Knowledge: Regulating Sex in England, 1470–1600*, Cambridge: Cambridge University Press, 2017, 76.

42 *Kyrkio Lag och Ordning*, Stockholm: J. G. Eberdt, 1687, Ch. XI.

43 P. Kenicius, *Handbok huruledes gudztiensten, med christelige ceremonier och kyrckioseder, vti wåra swenska församlingar skal blifwa hållen och förhandlad*, Stockholm: Buckardi, 1693, Ch. VI. For similar rituals see M. Ingram, *Church Courts, Sex and Marriage in England, 1570–1640*, Cambridge: Cambridge University Press, 1987, 53–4, 334–6; R. van Dülmen, *Theatre of Horror: Crime and Punishment in Early Modern Germany*, Oxford: Polity, 1990, 54–5.

44 For different aspects of the double standard, see K. Thomas, 'The Double Standard', *Journal of the History of Ideas* 20:2, 1959, 195–216; L. Gowing, *Domestic Dangers: Women, Words, and Sex in Early Modern England 1500–1800*, Oxford: Clarendon Press, 1996, Chs 2–4; B. Capp, 'The Double Standard Revisited: Plebeian Women and Male Sexual Reputation in Early Modern England', *Past & Present* 162, 1999, 70–100; J. Liliequist, 'Between Passion and Lust: Framing Male Desire in Early Modern Sweden', in S. Lidman et al. (eds), *Framing Premodern Desires: Sexual Ideas, Attitudes and Practices in Europe*, Amsterdam: Amsterdam University Press, 2017, 211–32.

45 A. Thomson, *I stocken: studier i stockstraffets historia*, Lund: Gleerup, 1972, 239–49.

46 Hunnius, *Christian Table of Duties*, 76–7.

47 Fischer, *Huustafla*, 237; Liliequist, 'Changing Discourses', 5–6.

48 Gouge, *Of Domesticall Duties*, The Fourth Treatise: Husbands Particular Duties, 46: Of husbands beating their wives.

49 J. Wiltenburg, *Disorderly Women and Female Power in the Street Literature of Early Modern England and Germany*, Charlottesville, VA: University Press of Virginia, 1992, 107–8.

50 M. Ingram, '"Scolding women cucked or washed": A Crisis in Gender Relations in Early Modern England?', in J. I. Kermode and G. Walker (eds), *Women, Crime and the Courts in Early Modern England*, London: UCL Press, 1994, 51–61.

51 M. Ingram, 'Shame and Pain: Themes and Variations in Tudor Punishments', in S. Devereaux and P. Griffiths (eds), *Penal Practice and Culture, 1500–1900: Punishing the English*, Basingstoke: Palgrave Macmillan, 2004, 58; van Dülmen, *Theatre of Horror*, 50–2; L. Stone, *Family, Sex and Marriage in England 1500–1800*, London: Weidenfeld & Nicolson, 1977, 171.

52 P. Stearns, *Shame: A Brief History*, Urbana, IL: University of Illinois Press, 2017, 42–3; P. Spierenburg, *Violence and Punishment: Civilizing the Body Through Time*, Cambridge: Polity, 2013, 129–50.

53 D. Lindström, 'Homicide in Scandinavia. Long-Term Trends and Their Interpretations', in S. Body-Gendrot and P. Spierenburg (eds), *Violence in Europe: Historical and Contemporary Perspectives*, New York: Springer, 2008, 43–64.

54 J. Liliequist and M. Almbjär, 'Early Modern Court Records and Supplications in Sweden (c. 1400–1809) – Overview and Research Trends', *Frühneuzeit-Info* 2012, 13.

55 Stockholm, City Archives, Stockholms Magistrat och rådhusrätt, Kriminalmålsprotokoll A2A:45, 1716 26/9.

56 A. Jansson, 'Suicidal Murders in Stockholm', in J. Watt (ed.), *From Sin to Insanity: Suicide in Early Modern Europe*, Ithaca, NY: Cornell University Press, 2004, 81–98. For Denmark and Germany, see T. Krogh, *A Lutheran Plague: Murdering to Die in the Eighteenth Century*, Leiden: Brill, 2012; K. Stuart, 'Suicide by Proxy: The Unintended Consequences of Public Executions in Eighteenth-Century Germany', *Central European History* 41:3, 2008, 413–45.

57 J. Bossy, *Christianity in the West*, 35–8.

58 D. Sabean, *Power in the Blood: Popular Culture and Village Discourse in Early Modern Germany*, Cambridge: Cambridge University Press, 1984, 37–60.

59 J. Liliequist, 'Peasants Against Nature. Crossing the Boundaries between Man and Animal in Seventeenth- and Eighteenth-Century Sweden', *Journal of the History of Sexuality* 1:3, 1991, 393–423.

60 For references in the following to legal doctrine and practice, see J. Liliequist, *Brott, synd och straff. Tidelagsbrottet i Sverige under 1600- och 1700-talet*, Umeå: Historiska institutionen, Umeå universitet, 1992, with an English summary, available at http://urn.kb.se/resolve?urn=urn:nbn:se:umu:diva-62940.

61 E. Sullivan, *Beyond Melancholy: Sadness and Selfhood in Renaissance England*, Oxford: Oxford University Press, 2016, Ch. IX, 164–71.

62 Uppsala, Swedish National Archives, Skinnskattebergs häradsrätt, AI:8b, 1749 14/6.

63 Cf. Denmark: Krogh, *A Lutheran Plague*, 115–34; Germany: van Dülmen, *Theatre of Horror*, 119–32. In England, however, executions seem to have been less well staged: T. Laqueur, 'Crowds, Carnival and the State in English Executions, 1604–1868', in A. Beier et al. (eds), *The First Modern Society: Essays in English History in Honour of Lawrence Stone*, Cambridge: Cambridge University Press, 1989, 305–55.

64 Kenicius, *Handbok*, Ch. 9, 182–93.

65 *Kongl. maj:ts Förordning, Angående Dödsfångars och andre Miszgierningsmäns klädebonad wid theras afstraffande.* Gifwen Stockholm i Råd-Cammaren then 12. decembris 1741, Stockholm: Kongl. tryckeriet hos directeuren Pet. Momma, 1741.

66 Stockholm, City Archives, Södra förstadens kämnärsrätt, Protokoll och domar i kriminalmål, A3A:9, 1740 21/12.

67 Vadstena, Swedish National Archives, Åkerbo häradsrätt, AI:12, 1733 2/6.

14

MAKING SENSE OF THE WORLD

The creation and transfer of knowledge

Hjalmar Fors[1]

When discussing early modern European conceptions of the world, there are some features that stand out. The first is that religion was the dominant organizational scheme. From the point of view of most early modern Europeans, the world that really mattered was *The Christian World*, often, but not always, conceived of as a motley collection of European realms. This religious background is essential for any understanding of how global interactions that involved Europeans interplayed with the making of knowledge. Of equal importance is the fact that the early modern period was an era of European innovation, which was tightly connected to imperial and mercantile expansion. During this period a succession of European realms, the Portuguese and Spanish, the Dutch, British and French, as well as additional minor powers, gained the means to project power globally. Europeans established a large number of trading-posts and colonies all over the world during this period, but it remains a topic of hot debate exactly what kind of competitive advantages permitted them to do this.[2] Expansion was underpinned by ideology. When most Christian Europeans encountered the world, it was from a position of confidence in the essential righteousness of their ways, and superiority of their beliefs. This was, of course, an attitude that facilitated exploitation. But from the point of view of the history of knowledge, it is even more important that it interconnected with the well-attested for tendency to perceive the world through a lens heavily coloured by classical and Christian authorities. According to this position, there truly was little new in the world that could not be learnt from or interpreted through the lens of the Classics, and Christian religious teachings. Just as the Jesuit chronicler Fernão de Queirós described Buddhism as a diabolical imitation of Christianity, other non-European customs and religious practices, too, were routinely reduced to foreign examples of European magic, divination and superstition, or European conceptions of Devil worship. Although these interpretations may seem primitive and reductionist to contemporary eyes, there is really no reason to be surprised that it took some time for Europeans to develop an appreciation of the sheer otherness of encountered spaces, objects, peoples and practices.[3]

As their world grew, Europeans fought an increasingly uphill battle to preserve their inherited cultural categories and interpretations of phenomena. Indeed, from the point of view of the history of knowledge, the period was very much characterized by a build-up of tension between, on the one hand, inherited models and explanations, and on the other a massive influx of knowledge, people, natural and manufactured objects that formed a constant assault on early modern European senses and sensibilities.

How, then, did early moderns categorize, systematize and order this massive influx of unsorted information? The early modern period was the age of printing, and travel narratives, along with books on geography, botany, zoology and descriptions of the world's human inhabitants and their customs, were consigned to print along with a great number of texts on all kinds of topics.[4] This development occurred in parallel with and was a part of broader intellectual currents. Reevaluation and reinterpretation of classical knowledge was at the heart of early modern learned culture. At the beginning of the period, scholars had already been long engaged in the translation and writing of commentaries to ancient Greek and Latin manuscripts. By the early sixteenth century, authors and printers had begun to turn increasingly to practical fields, and to supplementing, criticizing and enlarging the knowledge provided in the classical texts. The paradigmatic examples of this are of course the works on astronomy and physics of Nicolaus Copernicus, Galileo Galilei, Johannes Kepler and Isaac Newton, as well as Andreas Vesalius' great anatomical work *De humani corporis fabrica* (1543). Such famous works were no more than the tip of the iceberg. In a great number of areas oral and manuscript knowledge was committed to and expanded upon in print. To give one example among many, the craft of mining saw the publication of Vanoccio Biringuccio's *De la pirotechnia*, (1540) and Georgius Agricola's *De re metallica* (1556); the first comprehensive exposés of the knowledge and practices of miners, smelters and metalworkers. As a body, the literature on practical knowledge of the world was diverse and overwhelming, and above all it was a literature that engendered a greedy curiosity for more knowledge.

Returning now to the world outside of Europe, increasingly reliable accounts and detailed descriptions of geographies, peoples and customs, and objects of trade were published from the mid-seventeenth century and onwards. Simultaneously, there emerged a tendency towards scholarly specialization, and appreciation of cultural differences. At the face of this wealth of information, non-European phenomena and cultural expressions could no longer be reduced to mere examples of the already known, and were assigned categories of their own. Along with this came an increased interest in the knowledge production taking place in non-European spaces. Scholarly specialist fields such as sinology can trace their origins to this time. Thus, the early modern period was a period during which the peoples of the small European sub-continent encountered the non-European world head on and on a large scale. But this was, most definitely, not a linear process of Europe taking and reshaping raw materials provided by the rest of the world in its own image. As Kapil Raj puts it, Europeans depended on 'the active participation of, and negotiation with, local populations and their knowledges, skills, practices, and symbolic and material culture'.[5] As they assimilated and appropriated as much as they could they were, subsequently, transformed. However, it must be noted that the early modern Europeans themselves did not regard their meeting with the world of non-Europeans in terms of transformative cultural encounters. They were mostly concerned with the world in terms of trade and conquest, and sometimes, admittedly, as an unknown place that it could be desirable to understand and relate to.

However, for the vast majority who were neither scholars nor world travellers, the world outside of Europe was first and foremost a place that produced curious and unusual objects and images that were consumed *at home*. Tangible goods offered Europeans a way to relate to faraway places, and fixated meaning that otherwise would be unstable and fleeting.[6] This explains why many early moderns could make do with surprisingly imprecise distinctions between the residents of and goods from the Americas, Asia and Africa. For example, most early modern Europeans would not have cared much whether the word *Indian* referred to a resident of India proper, a Native American or someone from the Dutch East Indies. The main thing was that the Indian was a curiosity. Or to use the words of William Shakespeare, commenting on the fad for exotic curiosities among his contemporaries:

> What have we here? A man or a fish? Dead or alive? A fish. He smells like a fish, a very ancient and fish-like smell … A strange fish! Were I in England now, as once I was, and had but this fish painted, not a holiday fool there but would give a piece of silver. … When they will not give a doit to relieve a lame beggar, they will lay out ten to see a dead Indian.
>
> William Shakespeare, *The Tempest*, Act 2, Scene 2, p. 2

What interested Europeans the most about the non-European world was the *objects* that came out of it. 'Indians', whether dead or alive, were objectified, and considered interesting first and foremost as foreign curiosities to be gawked over. As such, they tended to be reduced to objects of consumption. Objects that could be monetized, not concepts, were at the centre of European discourse about the world. An enormous intellectual labour was devoted to understanding, and putting to systematic order, import goods and foreign curiosities. As we have seen, there was curiosity and interest in foreign customs and geography, philosophies and religion, but its cultural impact should not be overestimated. Most Europeans would have had very vague ideas about what was going on in faraway places and what could be found there. Simultaneously they would have had rather precise knowledge about the spices they consumed and the silks they wore (or longed to wear), and vivid memories of any parrots or monkeys, or indeed *dead Indians* they might have encountered, or paid to gawk over. Perhaps it was even the case that places were not primarily represented in European minds as geographical locations far away, but as objects and images present in the here and now.

The present chapter discusses the interrelations of the expansion of global trade with the acquisition of knowledge and formulations thereof into systems and conceptions. In order to do this and to present a point of view that is early modern (to the extent that any narrative can make such claims), it focuses on a specific class of trading goods which was of tremendous importance to early modern culture: *exotic botanicals*. Trade in cardamom, pepper, dragon's blood, guaiac wood, tobacco, chocolate, coffee, tea and so forth constituted the backbone of early modern intercontinental commerce. As we will see, these substances were also important objects of knowledge. They were subject to drawn-out processes of negotiation, renegotiation and interpretation. Many groups participated in renegotiating foreign curiosities into stable objects of consumption, botanical specimens and (in some cases) bulk commodities. Negotiations were conducted in networks composed of traders, vendors, physicians, apothecaries, learned botanists, global travellers and university scholars, not to mention among groups of consumers. In this way these substances found – and in some cases lost – the more or less stable places in European culture as spice, medicines, luxury goods and objects of everyday consumption that they occupy today.

In the following, I will show primarily how knowledge exchange among the learned depended on knowledge gathered by travellers, and how both piggybacked on early modern trade. The narrative also introduces the wealth and diversity of European knowledge of plant substances and botanical trading goods, before Carl Linnaeus' great synthesis of botanical knowledge in the mid-eighteenth century.

The importance of exotic botanicals to medieval and early modern Europeans was due to their position in the intersection of a triad of deepest cultural significance: sanctitude, health and wealth. Fragrant spices were carriers of religious meanings, part of liturgy, and were of course mentioned in several places in the Bible. Their medicinal qualities were similarly held in the highest of regards. As key ingredients in medieval and early modern fine cuisine, imported spices were items for conspicuous consumption among the rich and culturally influential. Indeed, spices united and intertwined the cultural spheres of cookery and medicine, of health and luxury consumption. Both spheres were grounded in theories of humoral pathology, according to which disease and health in the human body depended on maintaining the correct balance of four factors: moistness should be balanced against dryness, and heat should be balanced against cold. To give an example of this: according to humoral pathology, meats such as eel or pork should be made safe for consumption by frying them to counteract their innate cold and moistness, and then further balanced by serving them with sauces prepared with hot and dry spices. Hence a spicy sauce prepared by a professional chef (sometimes overseen by a physician) for a king or nobleman was seen as serving medical purposes. Similarly, the sugary electuaries prepared by apothecaries for the same clientele blurred present-day distinctions between medicines, desserts and candies.[7]

It must be noted that far from all medicines were ingested because they tasted good or gave rise to other types of sensory gratification. But just as a primary function of physicians was to serve as advisors on dietetics, apothecaries derived much of their income from the preparation of candy, confectionaries and spiced wines. When distilled alcohol gained in popularity in the sixteenth century, spices easily transferred into the new medium, as distillers and apothecaries created an array of heavily spiced distillates and elixirs.

The spice trade experienced continued stable growth throughout the early modern period. The opening up of new trade routes to the Americas and around the Horn of Africa to the Indian Ocean meant that Atlantic ports superseded Venice and Cairo as key depots. Prices also plummeted. However, the cultural and overall economic importance of the traditional spices that had been used for food and medicine since at least Roman antiquity gradually decreased. During the modern era, a succession of substances with more powerful and obvious physiological and neurological effects made their entrance and established themselves on European markets. These substances may collectively be called *intoxicants* and emerged as a new fulcrum of both economic and cultural activity. Soft intoxicants like tobacco, coffee, tea, chocolate and sugar were followed, in the nineteenth and twentieth centuries, by opium, cocaine and heroin. Colonial produce was only part of this growing market for intoxicants. There was also an increased commercialization of domestic production of wine, beer and distilled liquors. Furthermore, all these substances were important for state formation and empire building. To this day states rely on taxes, licences and monopolies on intoxicants for a solid part of their income and derive legitimacy through the policing of consumption.[8]

Here, exotic spices, as well as import medicines and intoxicants, are treated as part of a continuum discussed under the general heading exotic botanicals. Indeed, almost invariably, all botanicals that eventually would find favour with European consumers moved through a similar cycle. Beginning as curiosities, they would find their first applications as medicines, then become objects of luxury consumption among the elite, and finally move on to become bulk commodities. Although this process may seem linear, it was not. An overwhelming number of non-European plants never gained popularity in Europe at all, while some, such as cubeb pepper and guaiac wood, would fade into commercial and/or medical insignificance after an initial period of enthusiasm.

Late Renaissance botanical scholarship

In the medieval period, legends and tall tales shrouded the original plant, growth and harvest of even common spices such as pepper in mystery. Indeed, spice and import medicines were situated in a set of associations which attributed fantastic and exotic qualities to both spices and foreign lands. The origin of most spices was situated in faraway 'India', conceived of as situated somewhere in the proximity of the Earthly Paradise. But a trickle of travel narratives – the most famous being Marco Polo's – slowly expanded European knowledge. Towards the end of the Middle Ages Europeans had begun to get a grasp of the enormous size and wealth of Cathay (China) as well as where it was situated in relationship to India. There was also an awareness that India proper was not the sole source of spice, but that several of the most coveted spices came from islands located to the south of Cathay and east of India.[9]

The pinnacle of ancient learning about medicinal substances, and their uses, was considered Pedanius Dioscorides' five books on *Materia Medica*, written in the first century AD. Copies had been available to Western Europeans throughout the Middle Ages. In the mid-sixteenth century Moses Hamon, a resident of Istanbul and Chief Jewish Physician to Suleiman the Magnificent, offered for sale a manuscript from c. 512 AD. It was subsequently bought by the ambassador Ogier Ghislain de Busbecq on behalf of his employer Ferdinand I.[10] The edition and publication of this text, known as the *Vienna Dioscorides*, became the life-work of Pietro Andrea Mattioli. He published the first edition (in Greek) in Venice in 1544. It was followed by a Latin edition in 1554, now illustrated with 562 small woodcuts of plants. It was a stunning publishing success. Georg Handsch, Mattioli's German translator, claimed in the preface of the 1563 edition that a total of 32,000 copies had already been sold. The staggering numbers testify to the great interest in botanical and pharmaceutical matters among sixteenth-century

Europeans. But Mattioli's shrewd handling of the text also played a part. The great value assigned to it by sixteenth-century Europeans derived from his extensive commentaries. He would become the centre of an extensive network of scholars, and his book the focal point of a generation's botanical efforts. Mattioli produced one expanded and enlarged edition after another. His many correspondents contributed botanical and pharmaceutical knowledge to be included in the *Commentaries*, enemies and competitors were ignored, and former friends turned competitors could see their contributions removed from editions produced after their fall-out with the master. There were many difficult issues at hand. First, the identity of the plants presented in Dioscorides. For a great number of plants, it was not immediately obvious which plants the Greek names, descriptions and images signified. Each plant description and image needed to be compared against actual specimens and previous literature, and contemporary Latin and vernacular names needed to be supplied. This was a substantial task that needed both philological and botanical skills. In an important sense this was a philological enterprise, concerned with precise identification and description of plants known to the ancients. But already in Mattioli we can see an interesting mixture of the old and the new. In one sense, his and other contemporary botanists' work relied on a well-established modus operandi: it referred to and relied on the classical authors, complemented by knowledge gathered from domestic artisanal traditions.[11]

Mattioli's work relied also, as we have seen, on Moses Hamon, a knowledgeable intermediary based in the Ottoman Empire. The agency of Hamon should not be ignored. Indeed, we should pay attention not only to the chain of transactions between Hamon, Busbecq and Mattioli, but also to the learned context of the exchange. Born in Spain, Moses Hamon (c. 1490 to c. 1554) was part of a group of Sephardic Jews who acted as intermediaries between the West and the Ottoman Empire. A prominent member of the Sultan's court, Hamon's political and business networks extended to both Europe and India.[12] Hamon was a patron of learning and a scholar in his own right. The Dioscorides manuscript was a part of his extensive personal collection of ancient manuscripts, of which he seems to have been very proud. Although Moses had offered it on sale, it appears it was sold by his son Joseph after the death of the father. Joseph too was a court physician, and hence neither of them can be described as subservient intermediaries, but rather as fully fledged participants in a Mediterranean network of learned exchanges, comprising Jewish, Muslim and Christian actors.[13] By choosing to part with the manuscript, the Hamons, just as many other Byzantine and Ottoman scholars, facilitated the publication effort of Italian Renaissance scholarship, an effort from which they, too, could benefit. Studies that give these actors their due present a much fuller and truthful picture of early modern knowledge exchanges than those that focus exclusively on the more or less stationary European scholars, who published, organized and systematized knowledge, while simultaneously establishing themselves and their works as obligatory points of passage, and arbiters of truth.[14]

Exotic botanicals in the age of exploration

When the struggling ships of Vasco da Gama arrived in Calicut in 1498 after circumnavigating Africa, Da Gama managed, with some difficulty because of the paucity of the goods he brought to trade, to secure a cargo of spices which more than well compensated for expenses. Indeed, the main motivation of Portuguese oceanic exploration was to take a cut of the lucrative spice trade dominated by the city-state of Venice, which in turn depended on Muslim traders.[15] Da Gama was quickly followed by further, larger, expeditions. Aggressive opportunism paired with naval and military technical advantage subsequently allowed the Portuguese to establish a string of fortified strongholds along Asian coastlines. An important early victory was the conquest of the city of Malacca in 1511 that allowed control of the narrow Malacca strait between Sumatra and Malaya. A few decades into the sixteenth century the Portuguese had, more or less, charted the seas, coastlines and major islands of Southeast Asia.

Available knowledge about the goods that were traded from the East and West Indies would increase rapidly in the seventeenth century. Generally speaking, early modern Europeans experienced an exponential growth in their botanical knowledge, which closely traced naval and territorial expansion. Of importance was the scholarship of the Jesuit order. The order established religious centres and missions throughout the Portuguese and Spanish empires. Because of its influence at the Imperial Chinese Court, it also held a virtual European monopoly on knowledge about China. Thus, Matteo Ricci, in his account of the Jesuit mission to China (published 1615), could write about his first-hand experience of the wealth of medical herbs available to the Chinese.[16] Later, Ricci's successor Michal Boym would become the first Westerner known to have gained a measure of insight into Chinese medical theory and materia medica.[17] Another famous Jesuit scholar, Athanasius Kircher (1602–1680), was conveniently located at the centre of Church power in Rome, and channelled information provided by the vast international network of Jesuits into a magisterial publishing effort. Thus again we can see how transmission of botanical and medical knowledge depended on the interaction of local intermediaries helping travelling Europeans, who in turn, through meetings, letters and through the printed medium, transmitted what they learnt to centrally placed, European actors.

As one would expect, this process involved a gradual invisibilization of the original holders of the knowledge in question. Such invisibilization was not limited to native knowledge-holders, but also to the travelling Europeans, as well as European authors, or whole European knowledge-traditions. The Portuguese physician Garcia da Orta's (1500–1569) *Coloquios dos simples e drogas he cousas mediçinais da India* is usually considered the first account of tropical medicine published for a European audience.[18] However, da Orta's book never achieved wide European circulation. As Harold Cook remarks:

> While few copies of da Orta's book appear to have made it back to Europe, a young Flemish naturalist picked one up during his travels in Portugal and in 1567 brought out a heavily edited and annotated edition in Latin. This edition by Carolus Clusius … made Clusius's reputation as a botanist and remained the standard work on Asian botany for several generations.[19]

The work of Clusius was instrumental in creating a new network, and centre, of knowledge of exotic botanicals. This network would prove to be extraordinary durable, and had its main focal point in the Netherlands, the newly emerging superpower of global trade. Dutch scholars and savants would publish a vast amount of botanical works, also establishing botanical gardens featuring – and commercializing upon – exotic plants previously unheard of in Europe. Thus, early Portuguese scholarship was superseded, and swiftly overshadowed by the emerging Dutch. Later, in the mid-eighteenth century, the great botanical and zoological synthesis of Carl Linnaeus would have similar effects. The clarity, order and all-embracing ambition of the new system was such that its great dependency on previous Dutch scholarship and collections quickly became obscured and mostly forgotten.

But how, then, was knowledge about exotic botanicals articulated and expanded upon in writing? Let us take medical rhubarb as an example. This pungent-smelling root – not to be confused with the pontic, or food rhubarb, found in many gardens today – seems to have been imported in dry or semi-dry form to Europe since antiquity. During the Middle Ages its medical use had been contested. Roger Bacon (thirteenth century) noted that Avicenna claimed that it purged inflamed humours; Aristotle that it purged phlegm; and others that it purged melancholy.[20] Marco Polo reported seeing medicinal rhubarb in situ in China.[21] However, from which plant the root came, and that this plant grew exclusively in certain regions of China and Tibet, was unknown to Europeans. But it was of course not a secret to Muslim rhubarb traders. Around 1550, the Venetian Giovanni Battista Ramusio had a conversation with a Persian trader, Chaggi Memet. He was told that rhubarb grows in abundance in the Chinese region of Campion (Ganzhou/Zhangye).[22] Memet then went on to describe the low esteem that the Chinese had for this drug, instead describing their appreciation of what possibly was ginseng and certainly tea, and explained that 'those people would gladly give (as he expressed it) a sack of rhubarb for an ounce of Chiai Catai'.[23] Mattioli wrote extensively on medical rhubarb, noting (in a 1570 edition) that it came from Cathay, the realm of the Great Khan.[24] His source for this information was Memet, as narrated by Ramusio.[25] In his *Kreutterbuch*, an expanded German edition of Mattioli (1600), Joachim Camerarius the Younger discussed recent works by Portuguese authors Nicolas Monardes and Garcia da Orta, and substantiated Mattioli's claim that rhubarb grew in China and was brought by 'the tartars' to Alexandria, from whence it was traded with Venice.[26] Matteo Ricci, in his posthumously published account of the Jesuit mission to China (1615), stated that there 'you can buy a pound of rhubarb for ten cents, which in Europe would cost six or seven times as many gold pieces'.[27] European knowledge of rhubarb increased radically with the publications of Michael Boym, a Jesuit missionary in China from 1643 to 1659. An excellent botanist, Boym described the plant in situ, as well as how it was grown and harvested. His account became a standard reference in later accounts of the plant.[28] And so it continued. Knowledge of rhubarb among European botanists and other cognoscenti increased slowly but steadily, as various pieces of the complex puzzle of botanical and medical knowledge were joined together and published.

Thus we can see how the thoroughly edited and critically annotated medical herbal, as championed by Mattioli, provided a format through which new botanical knowledge could be integrated into a corpus, the foundation of which was a classical herbal expanded by Renaissance translators and philologists. In illustrated herbals, empirical observation and description paired with philological precision and artful illustration permitted European botanical scholars to describe an ever-increasing number of foreign plants and plant substances.[29] Older accounts were gradually complemented by novel knowledge of exotic plants and substances. This knowledge was garnered from travellers' reports and from botanists and physicians spread throughout the expanding overseas empires. Simultaneously overseas empires and mission- and trading-posts made possible direct study of many of the plants from which traditionally used spices and drugs derived.

Even when this knowledge was published, this did not mean that it was generally available, or even of interest to Europeans at large. Printing revolutionized the circulation of knowledge in early modern Europe, but not all books were available to all kinds of people. The lavishly illustrated herbals were often published in folio format and were objects of conspicuous consumption, reserved for the rich. Furthermore, the introduction of new knowledge, substances and practices is not something that happens automatically. It requires work, and the work was conducted not only in the area of scholarly publication, but also in the spheres of advertising and consumption.

Consuming exotic botanicals

The consumption of exotic medicines was most widespread among Europe's affluent elites. Purgatives such as senna and rhubarb were particularly popular. These were administered both orally and rectally. Samuel Pepys' diary of the years 1660–1669 reveals that this comparably healthy young man took clysters (rectally administered medicaments) quite often to counter various disorders such as constipation, earache, itching and eye strain.[30] According to one source, Louis XIII received 312 clysters within a year.[31] Undoubtedly, such regimes had a strong bodily impact, but also a cultural and economic one. As the English poet Robert Greene concluded the description of a spending spree: 'My purse began with so many purging glisters [clysters] to waxe not only laxitiue, but quite emptie' (Mourning Garment [London, 1590], 52).

Greene's poetic identification of purging with expenses highlights that early moderns, too, were aware of the role medicines and spices filled for those interested in showing off their wealth. The issue was extensively discussed in the many pharmacopeia for the poor (*pharmacopoeia pauperum*) that presented alternative, locally sourced remedies for those who could not afford what the apothecaries had on offer. But for those who could afford it, consumption of goods provided an opening into new and exciting worlds and experiences connected to luxury and high-status knowledge. This contributed to making exotic botanicals – and especially the ones with pleasantly intoxicating properties – into ways of manifesting and distinguishing oneself before others. European consumption of exotic import goods and luxury products surged during the seventeenth century. According to one estimate, by mid-century every European consumed, on average, half a kilo of imported spice a year. And to give a small example of just one medicine and region, in the late sixteenth century, British imports of senna, a commonly used drug with laxative properties, only sufficed to treat a few thousand people. By the 1660s, 'senna imports might equate to between thirty thousand and three-quarters of a million purges for a population of around 5.2 million'.[32]

As observed by Emma Spary. 'The history of knowledge ... can look very different when scientific activity is envisaged from the standpoint of a world of consumers, merchants, and artisans'.[33] This is true also if one considers the history of medicine and botany not from the point of view of textual description and debate, but from the usage of medicine. Enjoyable and addictive commercial successes, tobacco, chocolate, coffee and tea, took the markets by storm with blatant disregard of the views of medical professionals. However, most exotic botanicals continued to be negotiated and interpreted primarily as medicines. This made medical expertise, and interpretation, a key area of contention and opportunity. Medicine was still conceived of widely as advice on dietetics and digestion, and the prize sought by many practitioners was the position of personal advisor to the powerful: in the capacity of personal physician if possible, and if not then at least as the author of tracts on medical advice. As we have seen, the market for publishing lavish folio herbals and descriptions of exotic places and objects tended to be dominated by stationary actors with access to powerful European networks. Travellers, on the other hand, possessed first-hand knowledge of valuable exotic goods, knew how they were used in foreign lands and were furthermore living curiosities in their own right: adding to the lustre of courts in similar ways as giraffes or live pineapple plants.

Similarly, before objects of trade could become objects of general consumption, they had to be objects of consumption among the rich and culturally influential. As most exotic botanicals began their European career as oddities with purported medical effects that were housed in natural cabinets, various interpreters played an important role in bringing them to public attention. Emma Spary traces the beginnings of the French coffee-house to the Orientalist fashion in the decades around 1680. Thus, to drink coffee in Paris between 1670 and 1700 was, 'first and foremost, a way of displaying a fashionable familiarity with the cutting edge of academic scholarship, of marking out one's credentials'. Those who consumed coffee were in the know about the latest fashions; those who did not were old-fashioned and scorned. In the ways exemplified above, the introduction of consumer novelties could have their beginnings not only in the consumption of the rich, but also in the networks of those who were poor but ambitious. By travelling, communicating and seeking patronage, such individuals could introduce novel consumption patterns that soon were emulated in wider circles.[34]

Conclusion

The early modern period has often been characterized as an era of profound intellectual upheaval connected to the scientific revolution in astronomy and physics. Indeed, this 'revolution' has been considered of such importance that it has often lent its name to the entire historical period between the fifteenth and the eighteenth century. Nevertheless, the scientific revolution in astronomy and physics had little influence on the lives of the vast majority of early modern Europeans. From an early modern point of view the upheavals of the times concerned other things.

The opening up of regular contacts between faraway continents was what truly exposed Europeans to the notion that they did not occupy the centre of the world. The European discovery of the Americas arguably changed Europeans' world-views to a much greater extent than Copernicus', Kepler's and Newton's cosmological innovations. Together with the massively increased trade with the East Indies, due to

Portuguese establishment of direct sea routes from Europe to East Asia, new western empires and eastern trade routes gave access to vastly greater amounts of traded consumables, many of which were made available for the first time, or in vastly greater quantities than before. The handling of the influx of exotic objects into Europe and the integration of this inflow of objects into natural history and medicine was the early modern period's equivalent of our present-day digitalization of the world. Of all early modern enterprises concerned with knowledge, bar perhaps only alchemy, it consumed the most resources, and was the subject of the most sustained and intense interest.

The transformation and expansion of Dioscorides' five books on materia medica, and their continued publication well into the seventeenth century, provides us with an example of how Renaissance scholarship could be adapted to changing circumstances, and how it was transformed by the pressures applied to it by the widened horizons gained through European expansion. Later in the seventeenth century in particular Dutch scholars would become the first line of re-interpreters and expounders on knowledge about the world.[35] Men like Carolus Clusius (1526–1609) built their careers and reputations on the interpretation and presentation of the facts and objects that entered Europe through the Dutch trading empire.[36] The tradition was still alive and well during the first half of the eighteenth century. From this point of view, the great systematizing labour of Carl Linnaeus was no more than the setting in place of a capstone on an impressive building that had been long in the making. And indeed, the Linnean project made use of several of the devices and methodologies that have been discussed in this chapter. Not unlike Mattioli, Kircher, Clusius and others before him, Linnaeus set himself up as an obligatory point of passage for knowledge of plants and animals, which partly through his efforts were redefined as belonging to the domains of botany and zoology. He was connected to the learned world through an extensive and well-managed network of correspondents and travellers, who provided him with both information about foreign lands and specimens. Linnaeus was sometimes called 'the second Adam'. An important appeal of his system to early moderns was that he, in a sense, Christianized the living world by presenting a model for how it could have been created, one species after another, at the beginning of time, by a divine Maker. After Linnaeus, the plants and animals of the world were no longer wild and overwhelming but reduced to their proper places in an ordered system which conceivably could be expanded to include every living object, becoming a finite set: the Creation. In this way Linnaeus also contributed to making the world outside of Europe less overwhelming. Bewildering diversity was reduced to an ordered whole.

The present essay has attempted to give an insight into how early modern Europeans 'made sense of the world', but it is far from complete. In fact, the story is not even complete with regards to how they made sense of the plant world. I have not, for example, discussed cabinets of curiosities, or the many attempts to move plants and animals from one location on the globe to another. What I have done is outlined an assemblage consisting of scholarly botany (and natural history more generally) and its relationship to medicine, travel and the consumption of exotic botanicals. I have situated this complex in the context of transcontinental trade and imperial expansion, and pointed to how interpretations of this complex relied on classical and biblical tropes and authority. In doing so I believe that I have focused on the part of the wider story that had the most impact on the lives of early modern people. For them, the trader's booth and the pharmacy were the primary places at which they interacted with the world – and when they tried to make sense of it, it was primarily what they could view, buy and consume that interested them.

Notes

1 I wish to thank Michael Sappol, Karin Sennefelt and Raphael Uchoa for their comments on early drafts of this essay.

2 Useful overviews of this vast topic are given in Joseph M. Bryant, 'The West and the Rest Revisited: Debating Capitalist Origins, European Colonialism, and the Advent of Modernity', *The Canadian Journal of Sociology/Cahiers canadiens de sociologie* 31:4 (2006), 403–44; T. Andrade, 'Beyond Guns, Germs and Steel: European Expansion and Maritime Asia, 1400–1750', *Journal of Early Modern History* 14 (2010), 165–86; H.F. Cohen, 'From West to East, from East to West?: Early Science between Civilizations', *Early Science and Medicine* 17 (2012), 339–50.

3 European appreciation of China is illuminating in this regard. See J. Spence, *The Chan's Great Continent: China in Western Minds*, London: Penguin, 1998; Q. Zhang, 'About God, Demons, and Miracles: The Jesuit Discourse on the Supernatural in Late Ming China', *Early Science and Medicine* 4:1 (1999), 1–36; T. Fuchs, 'The European China: Receptions from Leibnitz to Kant', trans. M. Schönfeld, *Journal of Chinese Philosophy* (2006), 35–49. On Buddhism, S.C. Berkwitz, 'The Portuguese Discovery of Buddhism: Locating Religion in Early Modern Asia', in R.F. Glei and N. Jaspert (eds), *Locating Religions: Contact, Diversity and Translocality*, Leiden: Brill, 2017, 37–63: 42.

4 B. Schmidt, 'Inventing Exoticism: The Project of Dutch Geography and the Marketing of the World, Circa 1700', in P.H. Smith and P. Findlen (eds), *Merchants and Marvels: Commerce, Science, and Art in Early Modern Europe*, New York and London: Routledge, 2002, 347–69.

5 K. Raj, 'Networks of Knowledge, or Spaces of Circulation? The Birth of British Cartography in Colonial South Asia in the Late Eighteenth Century', *Global Intellectual History* 2:1 (2017), 49–66. Quotation on 59.

6 R. Ago, *Gusto for Things: A History of Objects in Seventeenth-Century Rome*, trans. B. Bouely and C. Tazzara, Chicago, IL: University of Chicago Press, 2013 (orig. 2006), 3; A. Cooper, *Inventing the Indigenous: Local Knowledge and Natural History in Early Modern Europe*, Cambridge: Cambridge University Press, 2007, 3–7.

7 P. Freedman, *Out of the East: Spices and the Medieval Imagination*, New Haven, CT and London: Yale University Press, 2008, 52–8; R. Schmitz (with F.-J. Kuhlen), *Geschichte der Pharmazie 1: Von den Anfängen bis zum Ausgang der Mittelalters*, Echborn: Govi, 1998, 556.

8 P. Withington, 'Introduction: Cultures of Intoxication', *Past and Present Supplements 9: Cultures of Intoxication* (2014), Phil Withington and Angela McShane eds, 9–33: 15, 17, 21, 27–8.

9 S. Halikowski Smith, 'The Mystification of Spices in the Western Tradition', *European Review of History: Revue europeenne d'histoire* 8:2 (2001), 119–36; Freedman, *Out of the East,* 95–8, 105, 108, 169–78.

10 U. Heyd, 'Moses Hamon, Chief Jewish Physician to Sultan Süleymān the Magnificent', *Oriens* 16 (1963), 152–70: 166–8.

11 R. Palmer, 'Medical Botany in Northern Italy in the Renaissance', *Journal of the Royal Society of Medicine* 78 (1985), 149–57: 154–5.

12 J.A. Rodrigues da Silva Tavim, 'Sephardic Intermediaries in the Ottoman Empire', *Oriente Moderno, Nuova Serie* 93:2 (2013), 454–76: 462, 466.

13 Heyd, 'Moses Hamon', 152, 166–70.

14 K. Raj, 'Beyond Postcolonialism … and Postpositivism: Circulation and the Global History of science', *Isis* 104:2 (2013), 344; Idem, *Relocating Modern Science: Circulation and the Construction of Knowledge in South Asia and Europe, 1650–1900*, Basingstoke: Palgrave Macmillan, 2007.

15 Freedman, *Out of the East*, 164, 194, 197. For an overview of Ottoman spice trade in the sixteenth century, G. Casale, 'The Ottoman Administration of the Spice Trade in the Sixteenth-Century Red Sea and Persian Gulf', *Journal of the Economic and Social History of the Orient* 49:2 (2006), 170–98.

16 M. Ricci, *China in the Sixteenth Century: The Journals of Matthew Ricci: 1583–1610*, trans. L.J. Gallagher, New York: Random House, 1953 (orig. 1942), 16.

17 H.J. Cook, *Matters of Exchange: Commerce, Medicine, and Science in the Dutch Golden Age*, New Haven, CT and London: Yale University Press, 2007, 365.

18 C. Swan, 'Collecting Naturalia in the Shadow of Early Modern Dutch Trade', in L. Schiebinger and C. Swan (eds), *Colonial Botany: Science, Commerce, and Politics in the Early Modern World*, Philadelphia, PA: University of Pennsylvania Press, 2005, 223–36: 224, 233.

19 H.J. Cook, 'Global Economies and Local Knowledge in the East Indies: Jacobus Bontius Learns the Facts of Nature', in L. Schiebinger and C. Swan (eds), *Colonial Botany: Science, Commerce, and Politics in the Early Modern World*, Philadelphia, PA: University of Pennsylvania Press, 2005, 100–18: 104.

20 R. Bacon, 'The Errors of the Doctors According to Friar Roger Bacon of the Minor Order', ed. and trans. by M.C. Welborn, *Isis*, 18:1 (1932), 26–62: 27.

21 S.G. Haw, *Marco Polo's China: A Venetian in the Realm of Khubilai Khan*, London and New York: Routledge, 2006, 89–90.

22 'Note XVIII Hajji Mahomed's account of Cathay, as delivered to Messer Giov. Battista Ramusio (Circa 1550)' in H. Yule (ed.), *Cathay and the Way Thither: Being a Collection of Medieval Notices of China translated and edited by Colonel Sir Henry Yule*, vol. 1, London: Hakluyt Society, 1915, 290–6: 291. The passage concerns the land of Campion and the city of Succuir. According to Haw, *Marco Polo's China*, 89–90, Succuir is Suzhou, now Jiuquan and Kampion is Ganzhou, now Zhangye.

23 'Note XVIII Hajji Mahomed's account of Cathay', 292–3.

24 P.A. Mathioli, *Commentarii in sex libros Pedacii Dioscoridis Anazarbei de Medicina materia*, Venice: Valgrisi, 1570, 437.

25 'Note XVIII Hajji Mahomed's account of Cathay', 290–6.

26 P.A. Mathioli, *Kreuterbuch dess Hochgelehrten unnd weitberühmten Herrn D. Petri Andreae Matthioli …*, ed. and trans. by J. Camerarius the Younger, Frankfurt am Main: Palthenius, 1600. First ed. of the translation appeared 1586.

27 M. Ricci, *China in the Sixteenth Century: The Journals of Matthew Ricci: 1583–1610*, trans. from the Latin by L.J. Gallagher, New York: Random House: 1953 (orig. 1942), 16.

28 C.M. Foust, *Rhubarb: The Wondrous Drug*, Princeton, NJ: Princeton University Press, 1992, 23.

29 Palmer, 'Medical Botany', 149.

30 Foust, *Rhubarb*, 43.

31 E. Kremers and G. Urdang, *History of Pharmacy: A Guide and a Survey*, Philadelphia, PA, London and Montreal: Lippincott, 1951 (first edition 1940), 84.

32 P. Wallis, 'Exotic Drugs and English Medicine: England's Drug Trade, c. 1550–c. 1800', *Social History of Medicine* 25:1 (2011), 20–46: 34.

33 E.C. Spary, *Eating the Enlightenment: Food and the Sciences in Paris, 1670–1760*, Chicago, IL: University of Chicago Press, 2012, 7.

34 Spary, *Eating the Enlightenment*, 61–2, 68, 75–7, 93–6, 99, 147–8. Quotation on 68.

35 P. Baas, 'De VOC in Flora's Lusthoven', in Leonard Bussé and Ilonka Ooms (eds), *Kennis en Compagnie: De Verenigde Oost-Indische Compagnie en de moderne Wetenschap*, Amsterdam: Uitgeverij Balans, 2002, 124–37: 124.

36 Swan, 'Collecting Naturalia', 224, 234.

15

THE SELF

Representations and practices

James R. Farr

The nature of the self and of the individual have been subjects of debate in the Western world at least since the Renaissance, and have remained a central question to this day. Much attention has been focused on determining just what modern selfhood is and when it appeared on the historical stage, and Dror Wahrman speaks for many when he writes that '"the [modern] self" stands for a very particular understanding of personal identity, one that presupposes an essential core of selfhood characterized by psychological depth, or interiority, which is the bedrock of unique, expressive individual identity.'[1] Jerrold Seigel largely concurs, adding that a wide range of thinkers and writers from a variety of disciplines assume that 'modernity introduced a particular kind of self into the world,' one whose chief attributes are 'an abstract mode of individual self-sufficiency' and 'rational calculation.'[2]

This modern notion of a wilful, unfettered and self-consciously unique individual protagonist strutting across the historical stage is central to Jacob Burckhardt's analysis of the Renaissance in Italy, and he saw its emergence in the years after 1300. Most scholars of the Renaissance today would agree that the individual assumed unprecedented importance then, but few would define the individual in the stark Burckhardtian terms of autonomy, and all reject the teleological implication that the Renaissance individual was the 'first-born among the sons of modern Europe.'[3] Indeed, many scholars now argue that the Renaissance individual must be understood as a product of his or her social and cultural context, and that somehow societies fashion the selves that populate them. Most scholars in one form or another now accept the post-modern argument that the individual and the self are cultural artefacts, with identities that are complex, contingent and fragmented.[4] Some, like Stephen Greenblatt, seek a historicized production of identities and Greenblatt himself perceives in the sixteenth century 'an increased self-consciousness about the fashioning of human identity as a manipulable, artful process.' Indeed, Greenblatt discovered that at this time the new verb 'to fashion' came into widespread use 'as a way of designating the forming of a self.'[5]

More problematic is the post-modern assertion launched by Michel Foucault and others that challenges the very idea of a core inner personal identity, and that contends that selves are 'but the bearers of discourses written upon' them.[6] Most scholars have, in one form or another, accepted the notion of self-fashioning, but few are prepared to abandon the notion that some sort of interior awareness of discrete identity in some way contributes to individuality, whatever its shifting historical form. The challenge, then, has been to reconcile a certain ineffable inwardness prominent in historical sources with an exterior context, and in so doing arrive at a non-teleological historical understanding of the self and the individual.

This essay explores the modalities of the self from the fifteenth to the eighteenth century, and illustrates them from portraiture (including self-portraiture) and autobiography. Both genres witnessed an exploding popularity during these three hundred years.

Modalities of the self

Most scholars would agree with Greenblatt that in history 'there are always selves – a sense of personal order, a characteristic mode of address to the world, a structure of bounded desires – and always some elements of deliberate shaping in the formation and expression of identity.'[7] How and why the individual self and identity take the historical shapes they do, however, is the crux of historical analysis. One approach, and the one adopted in this essay, is to consider the self in three inter-relational dimensions, or modalities. There is, first, a bodily dimension, the physical existence of a discrete organism. And there is a social dimension, the world within which these organisms interact. The interior or reflective dimension to the self, the third modality, interacts with the external world in a social and cultural relationship that gives the individual identity but one that springs from orientations and values shared with others, what Guido Ruggiero has perceptively and concisely termed 'consensus realities.' Interiority is guided and expressed in a specific language or idiom, whether visual as in portraits or written as in autobiographies.[8]

The self, then, might be conceived as a relation, and identities as different ways in which people think about the relations between inwardness or reflectivity, the body and the world outside. Identities can then be grasped as historical products, inextricably situated in a particular world, not in a teleological anticipation of modern or post-modern forms of selfhood.[9]

Renaissance identities illustrate this relationship clearly, as those identities were varied and dynamic. John Jeffries Martin suggests that men and women at that time were anxious and uncertain about the boundaries between the inner self and the outer world, and this drove them to think of and present the self in a variety of ways.[10] Among them are the 'social or conforming self,' an identity largely determined by social location and characterized by a deep concern for social, political and familial status. It is closely related to the 'prudential' and 'performative' selves in that roles were self-consciously assumed to be played by individuals at the appropriate time and in certain places. Strategies of self-presentation, what Greenblatt called self-fashioning, reached a new level of intensity in the sixteenth century, particularly evident in the flourishing literature on civility, such as Baldassarre Castiglione's *Book of the Courtier* (1528), Desiderius Erasmus's *On the Civility of Children* (1530), Giovanni della Casa's *Galateo, or the Rules of Polite Behavior* (1555) and Stefano Guazzo's *Civil Conversation* (1574).[11]

A clear corollary to these modalities of the self is a pronounced emphasis on the individual and his or her distinctive and even singular manifestations. In the fifteenth and even more so in the sixteenth century, especially among the aristocracy, the individual became a more and more carefully considered and significant cultural construct, but one that was distinguished from others by attributes of its own.[12] Ruggiero describes this as an inversion of the Burckhardtian formula that the state emerged as a 'work of art' by suggesting that it makes more sense to see the *individual* as a work of art, presented socially in a series of complex negotiations among the various groups among which an individual lived and interacted. Renaissance men and women were fascinated with articulating notions of what constituted the individual, representing him or her in writings and in a wide range of artefacts – coins, medals, sculpture and, as we will see, paintings.[13] Unfortunately, most of our evidence comes from the writings and visual works produced by and for the male elite (and those aspiring to be part of it).

Such theatrical and plastic presentations of the self and the individual, especially exhibited in the seeming falseness and artificiality of the Renaissance princely courts, however, may have invited a reaction to them. In such a world, it became impossible to distinguish a true self beneath the mask, if one even existed. And at the same time, we find evidence for a self-consciously 'sincere' self with a more pronounced emphasis on inwardness than ever before. For thinkers like the French judge, philosopher and essayist Michel de Montaigne, revealing one's internal beliefs and convictions became an ethical imperative.[14]

The sincere self also prized the particularity and singularity of the individual, especially clear again in Montaigne. Montaigne believed that he could only answer his fundamental question – *que sais-je*? What do I know? – by looking within himself, and that the answer could only be one that applied only to himself as a discrete individual. He was, as he tells us many times in his *Essays* (written between 1570 and 1592 and first published in 1580), irreducibly singular.

The surging of the influence of the ideas of St Augustine in the sixteenth century also played a part in the growing importance of the individual and the inwardness of the self. Augustinianism pointed to the directness and individuality of the self's relation to God. The Protestant and Catholic Reformations of the sixteenth century, despite their theological differences, shared an increasing emphasis on the individual's role in his or her salvation. Martin Luther (formerly a monk in an Augustinian order) and other Protestant reformers famously dispensed with the priest as an intermediary between the individual and God, and although salvation was granted solely by God, the responsibility for salvation rested in the faith of the individual. The Catholic Church retained the centrality of the priest for salvation, but also shifted more responsibility to the individual sinner by emphasizing more frequent (and private) confession as a way not only to atone for past sins but, as a form of self-discipline, to adjust future behaviour as well.[15]

Many sixteenth-century writers, again influenced by Augustine, attached new importance to the heart as the seat of the self and the locus of affections.[16] Montaigne never abandoned his faith in the power of human reason, but he did question its ability to arrive at indisputable truth. In his *Essays* he clearly places a great emphasis on emotions and feelings as true reflections of the self, a departure from the Renaissance ethic of *virtù* which esteemed emotional self-control as essential to effective, performative self-fashioning.[17]

The inward turn of the sixteenth century, so evident in Montaigne, brought to the fore a widespread interest in the passions.[18] Such an interest, however, heightened an anxiety about their potential destructiveness to order, and a concern about how to control them. Neo-stoicism was one response, and this ethic resonated deeply among many Europeans in the sixteenth and seventeenth centuries.[19] Some neo-stoics counselled disciplining the passions by reason, while others sought a natural balance between the passions and the faculty of reason to attain, as Nannerl Keohane put it, 'a good ordering of the soul [that] … provides internal harmony and outward tranquility.'[20] All agreed in one way or another that the self needed to, and could be, shaped, fixed and disciplined in a socially acceptable mode.[21]

Neo-stoicism was resolutely individualistic in its conception of the self, and inherited ideas about self-fashioning from the Renaissance, for it was rooted in the belief that a human agent is able to remake himself by methodical and disciplined thought and action. It was part of a broader cultural emphasis on 'disciplinary practices' evident in, for example, military and governmental organizations, grammar books and dictionaries, treatises and sermons on morality, discourses by jurists and conduct books.[22] Reacting to the perceived chaos of the sixteenth century torn by religious upheaval, economic dislocation, population growth and war, many Europeans of the seventeenth century felt a growing pressure to return to an imagined order, and this yearning entailed among neo-stoics a perceived need to restore an order to the self that the passions threatened to upend.[23]

Conduct books, also called civility manuals, are a reflection of this. They proliferated in the seventeenth century, and like self-fashioning treatises of the sixteenth century, they instructed their readers through advice about appropriate behaviour in particular social situations. More than Castiglione, della Casa and Guazzo (who nonetheless remained widely read), however, the seventeenth-century iterations like Antoine de Courtin's *Rules of Civility* (1672) urged greater self-reflection and emphasized greater self-control, promoting a more conscious refinement based more on inhibition of the bodily functions of the self, of the internal regulation of the self, while still reinforcing through prescribed behaviour accepted social values.[24]

Many scholars have identified a heightened sense of an inward self in the seventeenth century, and point to the French philosopher René Descartes as their star witness. They typically single out his *Discourse on Method* (1637).[25] It is true that in Descartes' well-known formula expressed in this text of *cogito ergo sum* ('I think therefore I am,' or, more accurately, 'I know I exist because I have consciousness of my existence'), he posited a pure reflective self that is distinct and separate from the body within which it resides. In this sense he continued the inward turn of the self towards sincerity so evident in thinkers like Montaigne before him. Descartes was also well aware of the concerns within his culture about the passions and how they pointed to the unwieldy and disorderly carnal and sensual aspects of the human organism. Indeed, he may have devised his dualistic formula in response to this to gain reliable knowledge of the world free of the corrupting and confusing influences of the body.[26] As he wrote in a letter to his friend and fellow philosopher Marin Mersenne, 'this self, that thinks, is an *immaterial substance*, and has nothing bodily to it.'[27]

In the *Discourse* Descartes widened the gap between the self and the world, and he revealed his method in a frankly autobiographical manner told in the first person as the outcome of his personal and singular experiences. In the *Discourse* Descartes openly stated that he was not seeking to instruct the public in 'the method that all should follow to guide their reason, but only to show how I've tried to guide my own.'[28] In fact, despite his earlier writings on the disembodied reflective self, Descartes could not escape a preoccupation with the bodily self. In 1649 he published *The Passions of the Soul* in which he now wrote that self-reflection was somehow linked with the body and was agitated by the passions erupting from it. Tranquility rested upon gaining control over such stirrings through self-discipline derived from both Christian spiritual exercises and neo-stoicism.[29] Descartes, despite his radical separation of cognition and the world in the *Discourse*, wrote in the *Passions* that the soul was 'truly joined to the whole body.'[30]

Close analysis of the nature of the self continued to receive emphasis after Descartes, as the writings of John Locke and David Hume (as well as their many supporters and critics) show. However, whatever the importance of reason and reflection, the interior dimension of the self remained inextricably bound up with the bodily and performative or socially relational modalities of the self. Locke devoted an entire chapter to personal identity in his *Essay Concerning Human Understanding* (1694 edition). Locke's approach to the 'self' starts with his rejection of Descartes' disembodied 'innate ideas' and his insistence on the importance of bodily experience in forming thoughts. Locke's empiricism led him to assert that people were shaped by the world around them. But just what, for Locke, was the relationship between the reflective mind, the body and the outside world in determining personal identity and selfhood?

On the one hand, Locke accepted that 'souls' and bodies are joined organically and the body feels and registers sensations in the mind: 'our very bodies ... whilst vitally united to this same thinking conscious self, so that *we feel* when they are touched ... are part of ourselves; i.e., of our thinking conscious self.' Yet, on the other hand, Locke seems to isolate pure consciousness and locate the self in it: 'By [consciousness] ... every one is to himself that which it calls *self*.'[31] How Locke reconciled these positions goes beyond the focus of this essay, but it rested upon his thinking about the social constitution of the self, for throughout his writings he paid close attention to the relationship between the individual and society, including constituted authorities, that set limits and obligations on the self. Locke's reflective self, whatever the importance of consciousness to his formulation, was still inextricably linked to the body and to the social world.[32]

Locke's writings launched a debate that David Hume engaged in in his *Treatise of Human Nature* (1739, expanded 1748) and that was picked up by a host of others.[33] Hume saw in Locke's theory (arising from the premise of *tabula rasa* that posited the notion of the self constructed through sensory stimuli) a self that was always in formation. Hume wrote that humans are 'nothing but a bundle or collection of different perceptions, which succeed each other with an inconceivable rapidity, and are in perpetual flux and movement.'[34] If we look inward, Hume asked, and discover only perceptions, how is it, then, that we have a sense of continuous identity, for if we lacked this integrative force we would have no stable way to exist in time?[35] What guarantees, Hume and others asked, that I will be the same person tomorrow that I am today? Why does one believe in the continuity of personality?

Hume's answer was that 'identity ... is only ... fictitious'[36] – that is, made or fashioned – and that stability and consistency of the self come from two directions. In part they are related to the reflective dimension of the self, for they come internally from memory that finds connections among the various perceptions.[37] But the self is also constituted outwardly from social relations, specifically in the great force of 'custom and education, which mould the human mind from its infancy, and form it into a fixed and established character.'[38] Indeed, the need for social life was imperative, for the stability of the self depended upon it.

In *The Fable of the Bees* in 1714 Bernard Mandeville joined the fray about the meaning of the self. Here he emphasized individuality and the passions. He asserted that contemporary society is an aggregation of naturally asocial egoists driven by passions for gain. Each individual is a compound of passions which govern him and motivate his actions. Individuals, however, are also socially defined (and here he points towards the performative dimension of the self) for they interact with other individuals in a competitive public market for 'tokens and badges' of social and political esteem.[39]

With such an emphasis once again placed on the performative self, on public presentation that might veil a true inner self, by mid-century a deep concern that being and appearing were not necessarily consonant had become widespread. Philip Stanhope, the Fourth Earl of Chesterfield, stoked this anxiety. Chesterfield's *Letters to His Son on the Art of Becoming a Man of the World and a Gentleman* were first published in 1774, and contain the Earl's correspondence with his son in more than four hundred letters. They begin in 1737 and extend to 1768 when his son died, but the greatest number date from 1746–1754. Chesterfield distinguished between true feelings and appearances, offering concrete advice about outward manners and admonition to never reveal one's innermost thoughts. To its critics like Samuel Johnson, such cynical advice seemed to champion self-interested duplicity and would find a ready audience among unprincipled social climbers eager to ape the manners of the genteel elite. Threatened by such social mobility which accelerated notably in the commercial society of eighteenth-century Britain, the elites of the later eighteenth century were seized by a 'crisis of social confidence,' as they struggled with distinguishing duplicity from sincerity.[40] A widespread 'culture of sensibility' rooted in the sincere self that prized an outward expression revealing rather than hiding one's feelings took hold, the effects of which, at least in part, can be seen in the emergence of Romanticism in the late eighteenth and nineteenth centuries.[41] But that lies beyond the focus of this essay.

Portraits and self-portraits

Scholars exploring the historical dimensions of the self have often scrutinized portraits (and self-portraits) and autobiographies for suggestive evidence. Although some art historians caution against inferring too much about the self from portraits and self-portraits, it is undeniable that artefacts from both genres – portraits and autobiographies – multiplied exponentially in the years after 1500.[42] Some people, like

Montaigne, blended the genres in their minds, Montaigne referring to his writing as 'painting myself for others [in which] I have painted my inward self ....'[43]

Fifteenth- and sixteenth-century Europeans were fascinated with representing the individual in paintings, and the production of portraits all over Europe increased dramatically.[44] For example, Giorgio Vasari, known for his biographies of important Renaissance artists, wrote that it was customary in Venice 'that every man of any note should have his portrait painted,' and that portraits adorned all the houses of Venice.[45] Evidence for portraits further down the social scale is scarce, but in London in 1582 portraits were apparently being sold in the streets, and art theorists frequently scoffed at lowly artisans for having their portraits painted.[46]

The genre of self-portraiture seems to have been invented in the fifteenth century and developed in the sixteenth, reflecting a new self-conscious awareness of the importance of the individual and increasingly that of an inner self.[47] The artificiality of courtly culture and the social self-fashioning it demanded raised questions about the true self, as we have seen, and these doubts were raised about portraits as well. If outward appearance was an uncertain sign of one's true, inner self, might portraits also be simply self-fashioning, the shaping of the self into a role? Or was there a deeper, more sincere self within?[48]

Medieval depictions of people were typically iconic, the purpose of the artwork to evoke deep universal spiritual realities, not to portray a particular individual. Medieval artists were masters of their craft no less than their Renaissance counterparts, but they were relatively uninterested in the physical particularities of persons portrayed. The shift from icon to portrait was gradual, but as the technique of linear perspective was increasingly used in the fourteenth and fifteenth centuries, pictures seemed more like snapshots of moments in a particular world with particular individuals expressing different personal emotions frozen in time in everyday space.

By 1500 the portrait was on its way to replacing the icon in painting.[49] A fascinating depiction of this process is the German Albrecht Dürer's *Self-Portrait* in 1500 (Figure 15.1). Here Dürer appropriates the popular icon of the Holy Face of Christ that was ubiquitous throughout Europe in the late Middle Ages and was especially popular in Germany and the Low Countries in the fifteenth century. But in fashioning his own likeness in the sacred image, he seems to be associating the sacral character of the image of God with the self-portraiture of a particular artist, himself.[50] He thus blends the universal and the particularistic, and highlights the shift in painting from icon to portrait.

Portraits, which were often hung in groups, were renderings of individuals represented to groups of viewers, very public displays of personal or family identity that set themselves apart from others in some significant way.[51] Subjects of portraits and self-portraits were usually deliberately placed in a social framework, and the paintings were loaded with signs that referenced that social self. Paintings were meant to be read as signifiers of status and power. Sandro Botticelli's *Adoration of the Magi*, painted in the 1470s, is one example. As Ruggiero perceptively observes, despite its ostensible religious theme, it doubles as a group portrait of the Medici, the family that dominated Florence politically and culturally for much of the fifteenth century. Cosimo, the family patriarch, is here the lead magus kneeling before the Virgin, while his sons Giuliano and Piero are cast as the other two magi and dressed in such sumptuous and

Figure 15.1   Albrecht Dürer, *Self-Portrait with Fur-Trimmed Robe*, Munich, Alte Pinakothek.
©Bayerische Staatsgemäldesammlungen.

costly clothing that the viewer is almost forced to acknowledge the wealth and status
of this powerful family. This painting is a celebration of Medici piety and power, its
individuals fashioned as works of art.[52]

The notion that the self was mutable was also explored by many artists, like Dürer,
who rendered themselves in self-portraits in multiple, different representations.[53] And
yet, as we have seen, in the sixteenth century some people were becoming more
aware of a divide between an outer, fashioned self and an inner one, and artists increasingly grappled with attempting to depict both in the same painting.[54] Many
of Titian's portraits, like *Portrait of a Man (Ariosto)* (*c.* 1510) (Figure 15.2), invite the
viewer to appreciate the man's social status through the depiction of luxurious clothing, but also to peer into the subject's enigmatic facial features to plumb what's inside.
And Titian was far from alone. Countless subjects of portraits stare directly into the
eyes of the viewer, as if challenging the viewer to determine what might be inside.

Physiognomy was popular among artists in the sixteenth century as a way to penetrate the inner self from external characteristics, and a large literature was summarized
by Pomponius Gauricus in 1504 in a widely read book, *De Sculptura*. He wrote for

Figure 15.2   Titian, *Portrait of a Man (Ariosto)*. National Gallery's title of the work: *Portrait of Gerolamo (?) Barbarigo*. ©National Gallery, London.

many when he described physiognomy as 'a way of observing by which we deduce the qualities of souls from the features of bodies.'[55] The Portuguese painter and theorist of portraiture Francisco de Hollanda and Dürer agreed, as did Leonardo Da Vinci, if the following quote is any indication: 'painting considers the working of the mind as reflected in the movements of the body.'[56] In England portraits themselves were sometimes called physiognomies.[57]

Many sixteenth-century artists accepted the challenge of presenting the outer and inner self in one portrait, reflected in a disparagement among them of simply drawing true to nature (called *vero* in Italy, or simple pictorial likeness). Instead, the most gifted artists were believed to possess a more interpretive capacity to depict the deeper essence of a person (called *verità*).[58]

Portraiture continued in the seventeenth century to be a widely popular genre in Europe, nowhere more evident than in the Netherlands. As Anne Jensen Adams has pointed out, 'in seventeenth-century Holland portraits were everywhere.'[59] There was a steady and increasing demand for them in the marketplace across the century (probably half the urban population could afford at least a modest one) and so a large number of artists specialized in the genre. Individual portraits and group portraits were ubiquitous. In group portraits the subjects who commissioned the paintings were keen on a self-fashioning that projected the status of the particular group, be it family (the number of family portraits burgeoned in the seventeenth century)[60] or as members of important voluntary associations. These paintings typically projected private and public identities and as such were dominated by men of property.[61] Notable among group portraits were those depicting shooting companies, the militias of the civic guard in Dutch cities. One hundred and thirty-five different portraits of shooting companies have been counted for sixteenth- and seventeenth-century Holland, most famously Rembrandt van Rijn's *Company of Captain Frans Banning Cocq and Lieutenant Willem van Ruytenburch*, popularly known as the *Nightwatch* (1642).

Typically, Dutch portraitists employed two different conventions in depicting their subjects, and both reflect preoccupation with the performative self. One captured the figure or figures in an active state of physical movement who were often engaged in exercising judgement or acquiring knowledge. Rembrandt's *The Anatomy Lesson of Doctor Nicolaes Tulp* (1632) is an excellent example of this active ideal (Figure 15.3). It also displays the continued interest evident in many European paintings in depicting explorations of the functioning and inner workings of the bodily self.[62]

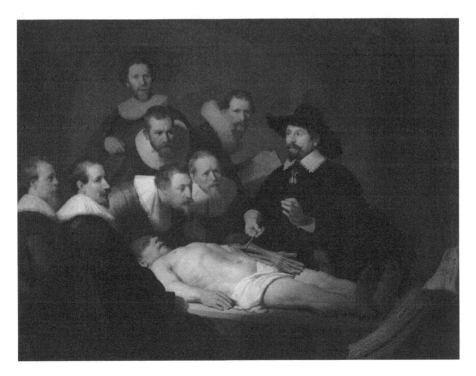

Figure 15.3 Rembrandt van Rijn, *The Anatomy Lesson of Doctor Nicolaes Tulp.* ©Mauritshuis, The Hague.

The other common portrait convention of the performative self embraced a different ideal, the neo-stoic state of tranquility we encountered above. Among many examples one could cite, another well-known and popular Dutch portraitist, Thomas de Keyser, embodied this ideal in a group portrait of another shooting company, the *Officers and Men of the Company of Captain Allaert Cloeck and Lieutenant Lucas Jacobsz Rotgans* (1632) (Figure 15.4). Here the subjects presented themselves in a self-consciously neo-stoic pose, projecting a disciplined group whose members are in complete control of their emotions and are steadfastly loyal to their officers. They had good reason to present themselves this way, for many of the men depicted were Remonstrants or Remonstrant sympathizers. The Remonstrants were at the heart of a theological and political controversy in the 1620s that threatened the very existence of the Dutch Republic, centring on the role of free will in salvation. The Remonstrants favoured it, and so challenged the Calvinist position of predestination that was the official position of the Dutch Republic. The primary function of the shooting companies was to guard the city from external threats and to quell internal disturbances, and so their reliability was essential to the civil magistrates. This neo-stoic representation of discipline and loyalty was, in effect, a statement by the company to the viewers of the painting that the company (despite its Remonstrant members) was trustworthy, credible and dedicated to preserving order in the city.[63]

It is in self-portraiture that the third modality of the self, the inner self, seems most consciously explored by seventeenth-century artists. Rembrandt had a lifelong preoccupation with self-portraiture, but he was not alone, for hardly a Dutch artist existed who did not paint his own likeness. That such paintings were increasingly in

Figure 15.4 Thomas de Keyser, *Officers and other Civic Guardsmen of the IIIrd District of Amsterdam, under the Command of Captain Allaert Cloeck and Lieutenant Lucas Jacobsz Rotgans*, Amsterdam, Rijksmuseum, object number: SK-C-381. Public domain.

demand in the public marketplace suggests that renderings of the performative and the interior self struck a chord in the broader culture. Rembrandt painted, etched and drew his own likeness at least seventy-five times over more than forty years, and between 1627 and 1631 alone he did so at least twenty times. And Rembrandt appears in an astonishing range of roles – beggar, courtier, saint, artist in his studio – and no two are alike. His various poses and costumes show a conception of the mutability and performative nature of the self, and are excellent examples of self-fashioning.[64]

But it is the penetrating self-scrutiny that most captivates the viewer in these self-portraits, and Rembrandt presents himself in a vast array of emotional expressions, as in two works from 1630, *Self-Portrait in a Cap, Open-Mouthed* [Rijksprentenkabinet, Amsterdam] and *Self-Portrait Open-Mouthed, as if Shouting* [Rijksprentenkabinet, Amsterdam] (Figures 15.5 and 15.6). In this sense he is one with his culture, for there are many examples of seventeenth-century Dutch portrait-painting that emphasized dramatic emotional expression and extremes of feeling that were intended to uncover the passions of the soul, to make visible the deepest recesses of the inner self.[65] Like their sixteenth-century forbears, seventeenth-century artists were not seeking simple likeness (and portraits that did only that were criticized), but something more essential.[66] And, again continuing a sixteenth-century emphasis on the sincere self, portrayals of the eyes and facial features, as Rembrandt's two self-portraits depicted here exemplify, were thought to be the window to this inner self. As the

Figure 15.5 Rembrandt van Rijn, *Self-Portrait in a Cap, Open-Mouthed*, Amsterdam, Rijksprentenkabinet, object number: RP-P-OB-697. Public domain.

early seventeenth-century art critic Karel van Mander wrote, the eyes are the 'seat of the passions, mirrors of the soul, messengers of the heart.' The forehead and brows, he continues, 'reveal the thoughts' and in them 'one can read the human mind.'[67]

Portrait-painting had lost none of its popularity in the eighteenth century, for it was arguably the major genre of eighteenth-century painting and portraits and remained in high demand throughout the century, above all in Britain. Portraitists continued the notion that the objective of a portrait was to somehow capture and depict the entire character of the sitter in a single view.[68] But character for British artists need not signify the inner depths of selfhood, and indeed, many portraits seemed to strive for investing their sitters with universal ideals (like chastity, courage or bravery) rather than reaching for some particular, discrete interior quality, as if they were representing a type without losing individuality.[69]

A work of 'characterology' entitled *The English Theophrastus* (1702) echoes these notions. It opened with this: 'The Subject matter of the following sheets is the Grand-Lesson, deliver'd by the Delphian Oracle, know thyself' but by know thyself the author meant knowing the generic type to which one belongs and abstracting oneself into a collective category. As Wahrman sums up, 'its imperative was outward, not inward.'[70] Sir Joshua Reynolds, the premier portraitist of the second half of the eighteenth century, himself advocated raising character to the level of general idea. In one of his annual 'Discourses on Art' delivered before the Royal Academy of Arts, in 1771, he declared 'If a portrait-painter is desirous to raise and improve his subject, he has no other means than by approaching it to a general idea.'[71] His portrait of *Lord*

Figure 15.6 Rembrandt van Rijn, *Self-Portrait Open-Mouthed, as if Shouting,* Amsterdam, Rijksprentenkabinet, object number: RP-P-OB-24. Public domain.

Figure 15.7   Sir Joshua Reynolds, *Lord Heathfield, Governor of Gibraltar.* ©National Gallery, London.

Heathfield, Governor of Gibraltar (1787) well illustrates this objective (Figure 15.7). Although the portrait is clearly invested with individual particularities of the man, Reynolds does not seek to uncover some unique inner character, but rather to portray a bold, triumphant symbol of imperial Britain. Heathfield had defended Gibraltar against a Spanish siege from 1779–1783, and here he resolutely holds a massive key, the emblem of Gibraltar, clutched firmly against those who might wish to take it.[72]

Other artists shared Reynolds' approach. Gainsborough, for example, invested his portrait of *Henry, Third Duke of Buccleuch* in 1770 with the contemporary ideal of the 'man of feeling,' the title of an enormously popular book published by Henry MacKenzie in 1771. Here the Duke is portrayed with soft, inquiring eyes and a faint smile while cuddling his dog in an almost childlike affection for his pet (Figure 15.8).[73]

Even self-portraiture was not always a reflection of an inner self, but rather performed a public function, used to promote the artist's stature and advertise his professional prowess. Reynolds again is a telling example. He produced thirty paintings and drawings of himself over fifty years, but in many of these he was promoting his own image in order to shape his reputation, not to probe the inner depths of selfhood. Already in his *Self-Portrait* of 1747–1748 (Figure 15.9), what Martin Postle hails as 'a

Figure 15.8 Thomas Gainsborough, *Henry, Third Duke of Buccleuch*. ©Collection of the Duke of Buccleuch and Queensberry.

Figure 15.9 Sir Joshua Reynolds, *Self-Portrait* of 1747–1748, Designation: NPG 41. ©National Portrait Gallery, London.

manifesto of the artist's aims and ambitions,' Reynolds seems to cast himself, brush and palette in hand, in the role of a 'man of vision' knowingly peering into a future in which he intends to situate himself prominently.[74] Reynolds seldom dropped the mask of celebrity, as is evident in his *Self-Portrait* of 1779–1780. Now the undisputed leader of the country's artistic community, he exudes an almost arrogant self-confidence, gazing at the viewer as a bust of Michelangelo in the background seems to nod in deference towards him. He depicts himself in a doctoral robe and cap, denoting the honorary degree which gave him great personal satisfaction, something he clearly wanted to impress upon his viewers.[75]

As we have seen repeatedly over the centuries after 1500, the various modalities of the self – bodily, performative, interior – often run in parallel, some artists seeking to probe the interior self, others seeking to represent the outward fashioned self and still others seeking to represent both. For all of Reynolds' outward emphasis, for example, one could counter the self-portraits of another leading portrait painter in the early eighteenth century, Jonathan Richardson. Like Reynolds an influential art theorist, he was also an avid self-portraitist. In 1728, at the age of sixty-one, Richardson began a remarkable series of self-portrait drawings depicting a broad range of moods and expressions that he would continue for ten years. They are all startling in their intensity and were candid explorations of his own character. Never intended for public viewing, each portrait is usually dated precisely, from month to month, and are accompanied by almost daily poems (some penned on the same day as the self-portrait was drawn, and referred to by Richardson as 'a kind of additional life'). In both media Richardson examined his state of mind in a relentless search for his interior self.[76]

Autobiographies

The years between 1500 and 1800 witnessed an enormous increase in the production of what historians now call 'ego-documents' distinguished generally by writing in the first person based on lived experience – diaries, letters, journals, family books, travel-writing and autobiographies.[77] This points to a spreading diffusion of multiple models for the creation of a sense of self. Indeed, as James Amelang cautions us, drawing upon his study of hundreds of autobiographies written by men and women well below elite social status before 1770, one searches in vain for a typical or model one.[78] Still, in all autobiographical writing, he also notes over the course of the early modern centuries 'a radical increase in self-reflection and the expression of personal sentiment.'[79]

Autobiographies more than other ego-documents focused on the writer's retrospective, first-person recordings of the course or significant parts of her or more commonly his life. Within the pages of these diverse documents, however, we can perceive selves that, at times, are performative and, at times, introspective. Autobiographies in the sixteenth century (and among artisans even after that, as Amelang has shown) show a 'relentless focus on externalities' and reveal only the barest traces of the authorial self. The self is less the subject of the writing than the point of view. But by the eighteenth century some autobiographies had moved slowly from a focus on external adventure (although this is never abandoned) towards an emphasis on individual development and internal transformation over the course of the individual's life.[80]

Within the wide array of life-writing practices that became increasingly common after 1500, certain broad generalizations may be offered. For instance, though far from typical, the autobiography of the sixteenth-century Florentine Benvenuto Cellini is consistent with the newly important individual and the performative, fashioned self that were so prominent in his culture.[81] And as such, Cellini's self is inextricably tied to the 'other,' in this case his fellow artists, patrons and, more generally, his readers.[82] Indeed, Cellini, a master goldsmith, silversmith, sculptor and jeweller, defines himself in competition with others, and in daring his readers to disagree with him. He boldly laid claim to the singularity of his own, unique identity, and boastfully asserted that he is not only exemplary, but inimitable and worthy of unparalleled admiration and wonder.

Cellini's telling of his life, however, is notably unreflective. His autobiography is not about self-clarification or self-interpretation, nor is it a confession, but rather a record of how he asserted himself and through that fashioned himself as a work of art.[83] He aggrandizes the representation of himself by his dazzling skills told through a straightforward story of his adventures. As he himself wrote: 'No matter what sort he is, everyone who has to his credit what are or really seem great achievements, if he cares for truth and goodness, ought to write the story of his own life in his own hand.'[84]

Although technically not an autobiography in the sense of telling the story of one's life, Michel de Montaigne's *Essays* stand once again as a turning towards intro-spection (especially in the later essays) in the representation of his self and the grow-ing consciousness of his own individuality. For Montaigne, writing and self-discovery were inseparable, and in the essays we see an author observing himself. In trying to answer his fundamental question, 'What do I know?', he relentlessly committed him-self to sincerity and honesty and consciously sought to tear away masks and condemn the falseness of role-playing.[85]

The turn inward in life-writing can also be seen in the autobiography of St Teresa of Avila (written before 1567). This autobiography in one sense follows the basic Christian pattern, the recounting of a sinful life redeemed by the experi-ence of conversion and a subsequent life devoted to doing God's will. Yet behind this format we see the author wrestle with what is going on within her as she struggles to find the right kind of prayer. She continuously reports on her feel-ings, known by her own individualized experience that, heralding the emphasis on the passions in the seventeenth century, was marked by emotional visions and raptures. She was engaged, like Montaigne but for different reasons, in an intense inward search.[86]

During the early modern period more and more people were keeping written accounts like diaries and daybooks relating to personal experience. Most of these simply recorded external events, and reveal the self only indirectly, if at all, but some show a more inward turn. Indeed, a wide array of autobiographical texts can be located.[87] And it is hardly surprising that, during an age that increasingly valued *individual* faith, spiritual personal writings would proliferate.[88] John Donne's *De-votions Upon Emergent Occasions* (1624) is one illustrative example. Spiritual at base (he believed he was renewed by divine intervention at various junctures in his life), Donne tells the story of his life from his sickbed in a self-analytical meditation on the daily progress of a serious illness he suffered in 1623. It is a probing and startling representation of his bodily self told through the recounting of his bodily history in the grip of disease. Like Rembrandt's *Anatomy Lesson of Doctor Nicolaes Tulp*, Donne's *Devotions* are told through the bodily modality of the self – as he explicitly states, 'I have cut up mine own *Anatomy*, dissected myself.' His body and his illness are texts to be read to gain spiritual insight by discovering the nature and function of the self within.[89]

Puritans and religious sectarians in England in the seventeenth century also were often driven towards inward self-reflection. Often challenged by the question that Calvinist-inspired teachings prompted – am I one of the elect? – many of these individuals sought signs of election by continuous self-examination of the soul.[90] John Bunyan was one of these soul-searchers. *Grace Abounding to the Chief of Sinners* (1666) is a dramatic account told through the story of a private life of an unrelenting inward quest, not for self-understanding, but for the certainty of salvation and a revelation that this particular man is an instrument for the work of God.[91]

Autobiographical writing was fully secularized in the eighteenth century, seen most prominently in the *Confessions* of Jean-Jacques Rousseau but hardly confined to it.[92] Laetitia Pilkington, for example, published her memoirs in the mid-eighteenth century and within them told a story of her life that was intended as a warning, though devoid of Christian intent. As she announced in her preface, she hoped that her memoirs 'may be instructive to the female part of my readers, to teach them that reputation is the immediate jewel of their souls, and that the loss of it will make them poor indeed!' To do this she presents her readers, obeying a 'strict adherence to truth,' 'a lively picture of all my faults, my follies, and the misfortunes, which have been consequential to them.'[93] In writing her memoirs, Pilkington is not seeking some understanding of her inner self, but rather revealing her character to others in the candid, often scandalous, episodes she recounts.

Rousseau's *Confessions* were written between 1764 and 1770 and display a deep urge for self-justification. Rousseau demanded to be understood on his own terms, in his unique individuality. On the very first page he announced that 'I know my own heart … I am made unlike anyone I have ever met … I may be no better, but at least I am different.'[94] Rousseau tells us that from the age of 'five or six' he became aware of the 'unbroken consciousness of my own existence' from when he became 'familiar with every feeling.'[95] Indeed, Rousseau's narrative is a revelation of inner sentiment, and the path to the knowledge of his singular inner state was through the heart and the sentiments that stirred within it.[96]

Rousseau not only stands as an exemplar of the new culture of sensibility that championed sincerity displayed through feelings, but he also was among the first autobiographers to write extensively about childhood and to organize the telling of his life's temporal unfolding in chronological phases.[97] This division and organization of time following life's phases becomes typical of many subsequent autobiographies, as does investing the meaning of one's life as a process of personal development or gaining maturity. Most autobiographers would have agreed with Rousseau's statement in his *Confessions* that 'to know me in my later years it is necessary to have known me in my youth.'[98] The self had become historicized.[99]

Conclusion

Historians of the self often have charted a linear progression towards modernity where the modern individual is autonomous and the core of individual identity is characterized by interiority. This story with the emphasis on the emergence of the reflective individual is not so much wrong, however, as one-dimensional, and as such it can lend itself to a misleading and teleological account. In this essay I have offered a historical understanding of the self by considering the self as consisting of multiple modalities or dimensions – the bodily and the performative in addition to the reflective – and I have explored how these dimensions were culturally expressed in different times and different places. It is not that interiority did not seize the attention of many thinkers, writers and artists – it certainly did – but not in isolation from the other dimensions, especially the performative. Indeed, most of the thinkers discussed here – Montaigne, Descartes, Locke, Hume – certainly were not alone in trying to explain how the interior self was inextricably connected to the body and the world. Portraitists from Titian to Reynolds and autobiographers from Cellini to Rousseau were no less captivated by the self in the world, and yet they expressed the relationship between them in their portrayals of individuals (and individual bodies) in varying degrees of performance and reflectivity. Some may emphasize the former, some the latter. In either case, it is the task of the historian to explain the meaning of the self in strict reference to specific cultural contexts.

Notes

1 D. Wahrman, *The Making of the Modern Self: Identity and Culture in Eighteenth-Century England*, New Haven, CT: Yale University Press, 2004, xi.

2 J. Seigel, *The Idea of the Self: Thought and Experience in Western Europe Since the Seventeenth Century*, Cambridge: Cambridge University Press, 2005, 40–1.

3 J. Burckhardt, *The Civilization of the Renaissance in Italy*, Project Gutenberg Etext, 52:www.paduan.dk/Kunsthistorie%202008/Tekster/The%20Civilization%20of%20the%20Renaissance%20in%20Italy%20-%20Burckhardt.pdf (accessed 18/06/2019).

4 J.J. Martin, *Myths of Renaissance Individualism*, Houndsmills: Palgrave Macmillan, 2004, x.

5 S. Greenblatt, *Renaissance Self-Fashioning From More to Shakespeare*, Chicago, IL: University of Chicago Press, 1980, 2.

6 R. Porter, 'Introduction,' in idem (ed.), *Rewriting the Self: Histories from the Renaissance to the Present*, London: Routledge, 1997, 11.

7 Greenblatt, *Renaissance Self-Fashioning*, 1.

8 G. Ruggiero, *The Renaissance in Italy: A Social and Cultural History*, Cambridge: Cambridge University Press, 2015.

9 Martin, *Myths of Renaissance Individualism*, 14, 132.

10 Martin, *Myths of Renaissance Individualism*, 14; W. Bouwsma, *The Waning of the Renaissance, 1550–1640*, New Haven, CT: Yale University Press, 2002, 135, also identifies a sixteenth-century self whose very plasticity raised troubling doubts about the 'true' self, or even its existence.

11 Martin, *Myths of Renaissance Individualism*, 30, 34.

12 D. Biow, *On the Importance of Being an Individual in Renaissance Italy: Men, Their Professions, and Their Beards*, Philadelphia, PA: University of Pennsylvania Press, 2015, 226.

13 Ruggiero, *The Renaissance in Italy*, 326–7.

14 Martin, *Myths of Renaissance Individualism*, 38; see also C. Brush, *From the Perspective of the Self: Montaigne's Self-Portrait*, New York: Fordham University Press, 1994.

15 J. Bossy, *Christianity in the West, 1400–1700*, Oxford: Oxford University Press, 1985.

16 Bouwsma, *The Waning of the Renaissance*, 21.

17 Ruggiero, *The Renaissance in Italy*, 113.

18 Martin, *Myths of Renaissance Individualism*, 53, 113.

19 G. Oestreich, *Neostoicism and the Early Modern State*, trans. D. McLintock, Cambridge: Cambridge University Press, 1982.

20 N. Keohane, *Philosophy and the State in France*, Princeton, NJ: Princeton University Press, 1980, 151.

21 Bouwsma, *The Waning of the Renaissance*, 136.

22 C. Taylor, *Sources of the Self: The Making of Modern Identity*, Cambridge, MA: Harvard University Press, 1989, 159, 173; M. Foucault, *The Order of Things: An Archeology of the Human Sciences*, trans. A. Sheridan, New York: Vintage, 1973.

23 Bouwsma, *The Waning of the Renaissance*, 165; J.R. Farr, *Authority and Sexuality in Early Modern Burgundy (1550–1730)*, New York: Oxford University Press, 1995, Chapter 1.

24 R. Smith, 'Self-Reflection and the Self,' in Porter, *Rewriting the Self*, 57; Bouwsma, *The Waning of the Renaissance*, 177; N. Elias, *The History of Manners*, vol. 1 of *The Civilizing Process*, trans. E. Jephcott, 2 vols, New York: Pantheon, 1978, 100–1, 114–16.

25 Smith, 'Self-Reflection and the Self,' in Porter, *Rewriting the Self*, 49–50.

26 Seigel, *The Idea of the Self*, 55.

27 Quoted in Seigel, *The Idea of the Self*, 57.

28 Quoted in Seigel, *The Idea of the Self*, 62.

29 Seigel, *The Idea of the Self*, 73.

30 Quoted in Seigel, *The Idea of the Self*, 73.

31 *Essay Concerning Human Understanding* (1694 ed.), I: 448–51.

32 Seigel, *The Idea of the Self*, passim, 88–110. Seigel (174) takes issue with Taylor, Chapter 9, 'Locke's Punctual Self,' in which Taylor emphasizes the capacity of the reflective self to 'radically disengage' from external reality by which 'we turn inward and become aware of our own activity and of the processes which form us.'

33 For example, H. Home, Lord Kames, *Essays on the Principles of Morality and Natural Religion*, 1751; E. Law, *A Defense of Mr. Locke's Opinion Concerning Personal Identity*, 1769; reprinted 1812; anon. *Essay on Personal Identity*, 1770; and J. Priestly, *Disquisition relating Matter and Spirit*, 1771. See C. Fox, *Locke and the Scriblerians: Identity and Consciousness in Early Eighteenth-Century Britain*, Berkeley, CA: University of California Press, 1988, and R. Martin and J. Barresi, *Naturalization of the Soul: Self and Personal Identity in the Eighteenth Century*, London: Routledge, 2000.

34 Quoted in Seigel, *The Idea of the Self*, 126. D. Hume, *A Treatise of Human Nature*, ed. E.G. Mossner, London: 1969, 299–301.

35 P.M. Spacks, *Imagining a Self: Autobiography and Novel in Eighteenth-Century England*, Cambridge, MA: Harvard University Press, 1976, 2; F.A. Nussbaum, *The Autobiographical Subject: Gender and Ideology in Eighteenth-Century England*, Baltimore, MD: Johns Hopkins University Press, 1989, 43.

36 Quoted in Wahrman, *Making of the Modern Self*, 192.

37 Nussbaum, *Autobiographical Subject*, 43.

38 Quoted in Seigel, *The Idea of the Self*, 129.

39 E.J. Hundert, 'The European Enlightenment and the History of the Self,' in Porter, *Rewriting the Self*, 74–6; idem, *The Enlightenment's Fable: Bernard Mandeville and the Discovery of Society*, Cambridge: Cambridge University Press, 1994.

40 M. Morgan, *Manners, Morals and Class in England, 1774–1858*, New York: St Martin's, 1994, 44, 3, 11; G.J. Barker-Benfield, *The Culture of Sensibility*, Chicago, IL: University of Chicago Press, 1992; D. Cannadine, *The Rise and Fall of Class in Britain*, New York: Columbia University Press, 1999, 40, 47.

41 Barker-Benfield, *The Culture of Sensibility*.

42 P. Burke, 'Representations of the Self from Petrarch to Descartes,' in Porter, *Rewriting the Self*, 18.

43 J. Cranston, *The Poetics of Portraiture in the Italian Renaissance*, Cambridge: Cambridge University Press, 2000, 98.

44 L. Syson, 'Witnessing Faces, Remembering Souls,' in L. Campbell et al. (eds), *Renaissance Faces: Van Eyck to Titian*, London: National Gallery, 2008, 14.

45 L. Campbell, *Renaissance Portraits: European Portrait-Painting in the 14th, 15th and 16th Centuries*, New Haven, CT: Yale University Press, 1990, 193.

46 Campbell, *Renaissance Portraits*, 215; and J. Fletcher, 'The Renaissance Portrait: Functions, Uses and Display,' in Campbell et al., *Renaissance Faces*, 51.

47 J. Woods-Marsden, *Renaissance Self-Portraiture: The Visual Construction of Identity and the Social Status of the Artist*, New Haven, CT: Yale University Press, 1998, 1, 16; L. Cummings, *A Face to the World: On Self-Portraits*, Hammersmith: HarperCollins, 2005.

48 Cranston, *Poetics of Portraiture*, 5.

49 Ruggiero, *The Renaissance in Italy*, 328, 329.

50 J.L. Koerner, *The Moment of Self-Portraiture in German Renaissance Art*, Chicago, IL: University of Chicago Press, 1993, 79.

51 Ruggiero, *The Renaissance in Italy*, 367–8.

52 Ibid., 346–7.

53 Cranston, *Poetics of Portraiture*, 14; Koerner, *Moment of Self-Portraiture*, 67.

54 Burke, 'Representations of the Self from Petrarch to Descartes,' 20; Campbell, *Renaissance Portraits*, 24.

55 Campbell, *Renaissance Portraits*, 27.

56 Ibid., 27.

57 Syson, 'Witnessing Faces,' 23.

58 Cranston, *Poetics of Portraiture*, 116.

59 A.J. Adams, *Public Faces and Private Identities in Seventeenth-Century Holland: Portraiture and the Production of Community*, Cambridge: Cambridge University Press, 2009, 1. See also J.M. Montias, *Artists and Artisans in Delft: A Socioeconomic Study of the Seventeenth Century*, Princeton, NJ: Princeton University Press, 1982.

60 Adams, *Public Faces*, 115.

61 Adams, *Public Faces*, 217.

62 Adams, *Public Faces*, 79, 105.

63 Adams, *Public Faces*, 237.

64 H.P. Chapman, *Rembrandt's Self-Portraits: A Study in Seventeenth-Century Identity*, Princeton, NJ: Princeton University Press, 1990, 55.

65 Chapman, *Rembrandt's Self-Portraits*, 11.

66 Ibid., 21, 25.

67 Ibid., 17.

68 M. Pointon, *Hanging the Head: Portraiture and Social Formation in Eighteenth-Century London*, New Haven, CT: Yale University Press, 1993, 36, 95.

69 D. Shawe-Taylor, *The Georgians: Eighteenth-Century Portraiture and Society*, London: Barrie and Jenkins, 1990, 31.

70 Wahrman, *Making of the Modern Self*, 183.

71 Ibid., 300.

72 Shawe-Taylor, *The Georgians*, 49.

73 Ibid., 71.

74 M. Postle (ed.), *Joshua Reynolds: The Creation of Celebrity*, London: Tate Publishing, 2005, 74.

75 Ibid., 82.

76 S. Owens, *Jonathan Richardson: By Himself*, London: Courtauld Gallery, 2015, 10–11; E. Crichton-Miller, 'Review' of *Jonathan Richardson: By Himself*, *Apollo Magazine*, 27 July 2015.

77 J.S. Amelang, *The Flight of Icarus: Artisan Autobiography in Early Modern Europe*, Stanford, CA: Stanford University Press, 1998, 47; Biow, *Importance of Being an Individual*, 42; M. Mascuch, *Origins of the Individualist Self: Autobiography and Self-Identity in England, 1591–1791*, Stanford, CA: Stanford University Press, 1996, Chapter 4.

78 See Amelang, *Flight of Icarus*, 'Appendix: Popular Autobiographical Writing: A Checklist,' 253–350.

79 Amelang, *Flight of Icarus*, 3, 29; Burke, 'Representations of the Self from Petrarch to Descartes,' 22–3.

80 Ibid., 123, 125.

81 Biow, *Importance of Being an Individual*, 5.

82 Mascuch, *Origins of the Individualist Self*, 18.

83 K.J. Weintraub, *The Value of the Individual: Self and Circumstance in Autobiography*, Chicago, IL: University of Chicago Press, 1978, 138.

84 B. Cellini, *The Autobiography of Benvenuto Cellini*, trans. George Bull, New York: Penguin, 1956, 15.

85 Weintraub, *Value of the Individual*, 167, 179, 180.

86 Ibid., 216.

87 Mascuch, *Origins of the Individualist Self*, Chapter 3.

88 Amelang, *Flight of Icarus*, 34–5.

89 H. Wilcox, '"The birth day of my selfe": John Donne, Martha Moulsworth and the Emergence of Individual Identity,' in A.J. Pease (ed.), *Sixteenth-Century Identities*, Manchester: Manchester University Press, 2000, 157–62; quote 159.

90 Mascuch, *Origins of the Individualist Self*, 71.

91 Weintraub, *Value of the Individual*, 234.

92 For England, see Mascuch, *Origins of the Individualist Self*, Chapters 6 and 7. See also G. Vico, *The Autobiography of Giambatista Vico*, trans. M.H. Fisch and T.G. Bergin, Ithaca, NY: Cornell University Press, 1963; E. Gibbon, *Autobiography. Memoirs of Edward Gibbon*, Leopold Classic Library, 2017. On Vico and Gibbon, see Burke, 'Historicizing the Self, 1770–1830,' in A. Baggerman, R. Dekker and M. Mascuch (eds), *Controlling Time and Shaping the Self: Developments in Autobiographical Writing Since the Sixteenth Century*, Leiden: Brill, 2011, 22–5.

93 *Memoirs of Laetitia Pilkington, Written by Herself*, London, 1748, 1759, 1764. For another example of a 'scandalous' memoir by a woman, see C. Charke, *A Narrative of the Life of Charlotte Charke … Written by Herself*, London, 1755, 2nd edn.

94 J.-J. Rousseau, *Confessions*, trans. J.M. Cohen, New York: Penguin, 1953, 17.

95 Ibid., 19, 20.

96 E.J. Hundert, 'The European Enlightenment and the History of the Self,' in Porter, *Rewriting the Self*, 82.

97 Barker-Benfield, *The Culture of Sensibility*.

98 Rousseau, *Confessions*, 169.

99 Peter Burke, 'Historicizing the Self, 1770–1830,' *Controlling Time*, 13–32.

16

THE EXPERIENCE OF TIME

Brendan Dooley

Since a reflection on chronology and change lay at the very heart of Renaissance culture, there is little wonder that the early modern period abounded in discussions about time, often referencing wisdom from classical antiquity if not standard biblical or folkloric sources. When the Spanish humanist pedagogue Antonio de Guevara proclaimed, 'time invents the new and registers the old', he characteristically attributed these sentiments to a philosopher at the court of the emperor Marcus Aurelius. He went on:

> [Time] begins, continues and ends all things, and eventually it ends everything … If time could speak as an eyewitness it would clear up many of our doubts. And among all things that reach perfection and perish, truth alone does not perish or end, bearing this privilege alone, that it triumphs over time and not vice versa.[1]

The playful attribution was plausible enough, in view of the many similar reflections in the emperor's own masterpiece of Stoicism, the *Meditations*. 'Nothing is so whole that it is not diminished by time', de Guevara continued, 'or so healthy that it is not sickened, so safe that it is not corrupted, so fine that it cannot be falsified', until 'finally I say time rules all things except truth which is subject to nothing'.

Such ideas and many more regarding the way humanity was inscribed within a chronological process found expression in myriad poetic and visual representations, often joining a rich medieval tradition to a developing humanist one. The figure of Father Time begins to emerge in the fifteenth century, with standard attributes including advanced age, wings, and occasionally a wheel of fortune, an hourglass, a globe, or accompanying images of the ages of man.[2] By the sixteenth century Cesare Ripa, summarizing iconological developments to date, added a cloak of stars, symbols from the zodiac and the four seasons, a compass for measuring, a balance ('time is what equalizes and adjusts all'), and for scenery, some architectural ruins ('time destroys, spoils, and consumes'). Artists widened the repertory of references by adding interpretations of ancient phrases such as *veritas filia temporis*, in a notable painting by Annibale Carracci with Truth and Time embracing (Hampton Court) or in a sculpture group by Gian Lorenzo Bernini with Time as the revealer (Borghese Gallery), although significantly, only Truth got finished.[3]

The human physique itself stood as a living metaphor for dawn and dusk or for the cycles of birth, death, and decay (i.e. repurposing, in Giordano Bruno's interpretation), just as it stood as a vital archive carrying the traces, the inscriptions, the records of times past – good, bad, indifferent – on skin, bones, brain, and even soul.[4] Moreover, the temporalities of this microcosm were mapped upon those of the macrocosm, especially in those theories, particularly influenced by Platonism and Stoicism, which viewed the heavens as replete with life, and the stars and planets, according to the version of Giovanni Pontano (developed by Bernardino Telesio and Tommaso Campanella), as soul-infused beings coursing through the skies self-propelled 'like fish in the sea'.[5]

But apart from the representations, early modern people experienced time in many different contexts, where the meaning of the concept could vary widely according to the circumstances. There was festival time and normal time, harvest time and planting time, the time it took to get from place to place, time relative to space, the time of certain short-term activities across an hour, a day, and a week, and the time of certain long-term processes like human growth and decay or the decay of structures, built or natural. There was sacred time and the ecclesiastical calendar, and there was secular time ordered by public administration. Then there was historical time: i.e. the time when certain major events (including biblical ones) were believed to have occurred, as well as imaginary time, the time of literature and of storytelling.

All of these underwent profound modification during the course of the period, as a result of interconnected developments in technology, science, communication, transportation, and mentalities; and all will be touched upon in this chapter. Uniformity was mostly neither contemplated nor desired, within what Arjun Appadurai, referring to some remote spots on the modern globe, has called the 'finitude of social experience in traditional societies'.[6] However, this would begin to change in the centres of urban Europe during the course of our period, and developments there would spill out unevenly to adjoining territories. The numerous agents of change operated sometimes sequentially, sometimes in tandem, and various historiographical approaches have assigned priority to one or another. In this chapter we will not privilege a particular interpretation but will attempt to account for as many as practicable.

Also on a prefatory note, we hasten to join with Paul Ricoeur's caution, following Martin Heidegger, against confusing 'time' with the vulgar succession of 'nows', but the discussion does not apply here. We will not be considering the deeper philosophical issues, presciently introduced by St Augustine, regarding how to characterize our subject.[7] However, there is no doubt that then, as now, the fundamental way of conveying experience lived through time was by telling what happened or might have happened, in a sequential order resembling the way the mind arranges memories of events occurring in the past, hence the abundance of literary expressions in all relevant languages and traditions, just as the 'threefold present', including past, present and future, characterized most people's mental grasp on life.

There will also be no attempt here to account in detail for conceptions of time in and about the performing arts, in spite of the interesting possibilities.[8] We only mention the obvious aspect of tempo and rhythm, broadly understood, as intrinsic features of music making and time reckoning. Concerning music as symbolic form with a peculiar relation to time, the mathematician Pietro Mengoli pointed out in 1670 that aural experience existed somewhere between time and timelessness.[9] The theory appears not to have advanced much further until Kant and Hegel, who discussed in contrasting terms the way music served time as a substitute or as an embellishment, or the way it instituted an art of time. At the end of our period, Mozart provided a highly revealing explanation of his own mode of composition, which speaks directly to the issue of time and timelessness. Once the subject of a piece occurred in his imagination, he said he was able to 'survey it, like a fine picture or a beautiful statue, at a glance. Nor do I hear in my imagination the parts successively', he added, 'but I hear them, as it were, all at once'. Of course, he admitted, 'the actual hearing of the tout ensemble is after all the best'.[10] How music was experienced by performers and audiences in the two centuries previous to his, we leave for another inquiry.

The following discussion will be divided according to the three basic chronological worlds where the early moderns lived: namely, local, historical, and cosmic.

Local time

'In the morning I invite all the living to begin the day and in the evening I ring for repose', proclaimed the inscription on the bell atop the cathedral of St Pierre in Geneva, installed in 1609, adding for clarity's sake that 'there is no retiring from life, and happy is death and life for the one who lives well'.[11] Everywhere around Europe the public marking of time was a prominent feature and so were the multiple interests served. In Protestant places the Angelus was no longer rung three times, morning, noon, and evening, because of associations with papism. Often reminders about ecclesiastical celebrations competed for attention with the convening of councils, or meetings partly civic and partly religious, such as the summer fair dedicated to St John in Strasbourg, opened and closed by the specially designated *Messglocke*.

The diffusion of mechanical timepieces refined the available methods for matching human behaviour to the flow of moments, sometimes reaching remarkable complexity already by the fifteenth century, for instance on the public clock in Mantua showing (in the words of Bartolomeo Manfredi) 'the proper time for phlebotomy, for surgery, for making dresses, for tilling the soil, for undertaking journeys, and for other things very useful in this world'.[12] That such mechanisms first emerged more or less with the first firearms in Europe, as Carlo Cipolla remarks, only underlined the growing reliance on devices intended, or at least destined, to increase the potential of human activity. According to Lewis Mumford, 'the clock is not merely a means of keeping track of the hours, but of synchronizing the actions of men'.[13] How this potential would be used, and for whose benefit, depended on the particular social and political arrangements at the local and regional level.

For all the benefits of the medieval public clock mechanism, with its escapement blocking and releasing the motion of the wheels according to a regulated velocity so the indicators could move smoothly with the passing hours or minutes, and for all the progress in creating semi-perpetual motion by the use of weights as a driver, what really opened the door, so to speak, to domestic timekeeping was the early fifteenth-century development of the clock spring.[14] And although Filippo

Brunelleschi, the architect of the Florence Cathedral, may have had a hand in this episode, the process of liberating devices from a heavy encumbrance and offering the possibility of smaller cases is regarded very much as a collective effort. Next came the conquest of greater accuracy, credited to Christian Huygens' invention of the pendulum in the mid-seventeenth century.

For most people, the conceptual revolution from task-time to clock-time (in E.P. Thompson's still-useful formulation) was neither sudden nor complete.[15] Throughout our period, rather than by devices, the day was marked by activities in sequence, of a kind which characterized the specific experiences of individuals and groups in a gender- and status-ordered world. What you did at a certain time of day depended upon who you were, male or female, commoner or lord, clergy or layperson. Tasks lasted as long as they took to complete – the milking, the washing, the food preparation, the hunting, the fishing – and were followed by yet other tasks known more by type than by duration.[16]

Long before the advent of ubiquitous personal timekeeping, certain days and times stood radically apart from the general monotony of ordinary existence, reminding as much about the time of year as about who was in control of the calendar.[17] Particular activities and behaviours marked festive time as distinct from normal time, sometimes involving a figurative stand against normality, in terms acceptable only under the special conditions of festivity. In England schoolboys locked the master out of the classroom on Shrove Tuesday, while women would rebel against men on Hock Monday.[18] Whole communities would playfully overturn ordinary rules during carnival, notably in Venice, where the wearing of masks temporarily removed social identities and allowed gentle expressions of political discontent to go unpunished.[19] Participants in joint performances of ritual acts might experience a reality outside themselves, in which their individuality was enfolded. A fundamental oscillation between individual experience and the group life of celebratory occasions subdivided the day-to-day as much in, say, the sixteenth-century rural France studied by Natalie Davis as it did in the Latin American communities analysed by Émile Durkheim in the early twentieth century.[20] The rhythms of this oscillation were as intrinsic to the social system as the circadian rhythms were to the human organism.

Much has been made of the drive to mechanize time and work in the lead-up to the Industrial Revolution; but in the context of certain working relationships time was a commodity from very early on. Whenever a task was purchased for money, the time to perform it went into the bargain, and wage labour was exchanged like any other goods. Long before the development of the factory system, a day's labour in the field was worth more to the owner than to the worker, in terms of the values potentially in exchange after subtracting overhead costs.[21] The roots of capitalism reached deeply into patterns of subordination and productivity that were as old as the private ownership of land, things, and people.

Access to mechanical timepieces did not bring about any sudden widespread agreement about what time it was, beyond the confines of the community, the region. Variations still occurred from place to place according to prevailing customs and usages. In Italy, a day's hours were counted from a half-hour after sundown on the day before, and the starting point moved forward in the day as spring waned into summer, and backward in the winter.[22] Possibly Islamic in origin, the system seemed to conform to the Christian *habitus* in regard to feast days, and eventually spread to northern Europe. The fixed midnight system, then known as 'ultramontane', could on the other hand claim precedents in ancient Roman jurisprudence. Its obvious appeal due to the promise of greater uniformity and regularity, wherever demanded by the increasing number of widely coordinated tasks and devices, inspired the trend to ever more general adoption.

Differences occurred also in the distribution of weeks and months.[23] In Venice the year began on 1 March (*modus venetus*), a date inherited from the Roman Republic, whereas in Spain it began on 25 December (Nativity style), and so on with local variations from place to place. In Tuscany, England, and Scotland, the Julian new year, 25 March, continued to prevail (also called Annunciation Style), while Russia began the year on the traditional day of the Creation (1 September). Meanwhile, in France as well as in the Low Countries, Germany, and much of the rest of Italy, the observance was on 1 January.

Calendar reform introduced in 1582 by Pope Gregory XIII to bring the beginning of the Easter cycle in line with the astronomical calendar at first deepened rather than eradicating the differences.[24] To be sure, many places with no interest in the *computus* for more accurately identifying the Sunday following the first full moon after the vernal equinox nonetheless appreciated the advantages of correcting the centuries-long slippage caused by an inaccurate calculation of the length of the solar year in the Julian calendar. Those regions that agreed to shave 11 days from the calendar one time only, introducing the leap-year system to avoid future inconsistencies, remained seriously out of sync with those that did not. And in the months after October of the year when the reform went into effect, even those where no confessional differences stood in the way did not all change immediately – creating disagreements between towns in the same general area. Indeed, well into the eighteenth century, travellers had to remember not only that England and Italy were generally many days apart, but that 22 January in, say, the Duchy of Prussia might be 11 January in, say, the Duchy of Westphalia, until 1610, when Prussia changed, with the Principality of Minden remaining behind until 1688.

Gaining a sense of exactly when things were happening was a complex skill that went along with travel practices and every other form of intercity and interstate communication. The same went for the related sense of where things were. For most people local space was probably experienced in terms of directions to the major parts of town; and the nearest approximation of a world picture, at least among most urban dwellers, was probably a series of mental vectors leading out from home towards the major centres, Paris, Rome, London (perhaps Constantinople), where news originated. Only with great difficulty, said Fernand Braudel, can we understand the notion, at the time, of an 'unlimited space' and its effects on daily life – indeed, 'every activity', he says, 'had to overcome the obstacle of distance'.[25] And the lag times he cited (based on Pierre Sardella's survey of manuscript newsletters) are still workable averages for news in the sixteenth and seventeenth centuries travelling to Venice from, say, Alexandria in Egypt (55 days), or from Constantinople (34 days), or from London (43 days), while Milan might be three days or less away, depending on the importance of the message.

That the time of day changed with the position on the globe, from east to west, was known in antiquity, although the importance of this aspect both for accurate navigation beyond the visible coastline and cartographic surveying beyond the outskirts of town took a while to sink in. The problem at sea was to be able to compare the time in two places – current location and point of origin – and from the difference compute the distance travelled. Early attempts were made by Columbus to use shipboard lunar eclipse observations and compare them to shore-based predictions, probably using the calendar of Regiomontanus.[26] Galileo's proposal of reckoning by the highly predictable movements of Jupiter's moons which he had discovered gained some favour for mapmaking applications by the latter half of the seventeenth century, in spite of the disadvantages of exclusive night-time and clear-weather viewing.[27] For gaining greater accuracy at sea, onboard clocks were nearly useless when subject to the vicissitudes of wind and weather, until robust and compact mechanisms could be devised in the eighteenth century.

Weekly, biweekly, and eventually daily news publications, developing out of the requirements of commerce, state administration, and diplomacy, as well as pure curiosity, added yet another marker to characterize the passage of time. Almost contemporary with the printing press, manuscript newsletters began circulating in multiple copies along the public mail routes between the major cities of Europe, of which some of the best known are those eventually collected by the Augsburg-based Fugger family of merchants. Two to six pages in length, usually anonymous and distinguished only by place name and date, appearing at regular weekly or biweekly intervals, they bore multiple stories regarding the economic, political, cultural, and religious news of the day.[28] The first newspapers, printed in Strasbourg by Johannes Carolus from around 1605, simply provided word-for-word transcriptions of newsletter material. By 1650 there was already a daily newspaper in Leipzig, and by 1702, in London too (*The Daily Courant*). Over the course of the seventeenth century in many places newspapers became increasingly differentiated from newsletters in the amount of critical comment they published.[29] How the proliferation of news may have affected the perception of time is a matter of intense conjecture. J. Paul Hunter sees the development of the English novel, in more or less the same period as the periodical press, as one of the ultimate effects of a shift in emphasis and interest to events in the present.[30] For Daniel Woolf, news circulation constructed an extended present waiting to be filled up by newly available happenings regarded as worthy of attention.[31] The increased pace of news reception accompanied a perceived faster rate of change in worldly affairs, noted by Stuart Sherman in the diarists, whose obsession with time-telling, or even of time-appropriation, closely corresponded to the availability of private timepieces.[32]

Hegel, writing in the early nineteenth century, is considered to have been among the first to reflect upon the displacement of religious ritual by a secular habit of news-reading. Benedict Anderson saw here an example illustrating his theory of an 'imagined community'.[33] However, centuries earlier, and in spite of significant limitations imposed by the variety of time systems in use, there was already some potential in the major cities for readers to share a sensation of experiencing events more or less in the same time frame as other readers and actors near and far.[34] A 1690 engraving by Giuseppe Mitelli dedicated to 'those who are passionate about the wars' (Figure 16.1) seems to thematize these issues, where we see, on the left, a group of people in some street or square with Bologna's famed porticoes in the background,

Figure 16.1   Giuseppe Maria Mitelli, *Agli appassionati per le guerre* (1690), etching. Public domain.

gathered about a bespectacled news reader apparently mouthing the words. Around the speaker persons from various professions react to the story by expressing their dismay, or even their disbelief, in reference to what they hear. On the right-hand side we see a Frenchman and a Spaniard in characteristic garb, locked in combat, apparently symbolizing the forces in the War of the League of Augsburg. The story that is transpiring in the space on the right, perhaps many miles from the crowd, seems to reach all members simultaneously, and they may well have the sensation of sharing something not only with each other but with the actors in the conflict. In fact, one of the listeners between the two areas of the page joins the right-hand space to his, declaring 'what folly'. The sharing of a perceived present across small, medium, and large distances, at the various levels of family, neighbourhood, village, and wider world, through new means of communication, we are led to conclude, may have encouraged a critical apprehension of events.

The potentialities of timekeeping, as a way of regulating the self and others, were evident across the period to anyone able to manipulate them. No wonder that, in overturning the French monarchy, the revolutionaries also overturned the calendar. And if total mastery over time may still have seemed elusive, the mastery of humans through the day's divisions, the week's, the month's, seemed within their grasp. The first publication of the revolutionary calendar, with its ten months named after prominent seasonal features (heat, snow, wind, frost), and ten-day weeks, every fifth day named after an animal and every tenth after an agricultural instrument, accordingly announced:

> We thought that the nation, after having ejected this canonized mob from its calendar, must replace it with the objects that make up the true riches of the nation, worthy objects not from a cult, but from agriculture – useful products of the soil,

the tools that we use to cultivate it, and the domesticated animals, our faithful servants in these works; animals much more precious, without doubt, to the eye of reason, than the beatified skeletons pulled from the catacombs of Rome.[35]

Cannon-founding from church bell metal served to complete the process, rendering secular what had been sacred by cancelling an enduring ecclesiastical hold on the tolling of the hours.

Historical time

The Christian notion of human time on earth having a beginning and an end formed the basis of chronological consciousness throughout the middle ages. But the purpose of history, at least as articulated by the twelfth-century theologian John of Salisbury, was so 'the invisible things of God may be seen by the visible things that are done'.[36] For turning the focus instead to human achievement and the ebb and flow of civilization, an awareness was necessary of the vital differences separating the present from the past. The pioneering gaze of Francis Petrarch accompanied an admiration for a lost age that was better than the present, a lost classical past steeped in humanist yearnings.[37]

Already by the fifteenth century the humanist narrative was switching from despair about emulating models of greatness to excitement about creating innovations. Said Leon Battista Alberti, 'I used to marvel and at the same time to grieve that so many excellent and superior arts and sciences from our most vigorous antique past could now seem lacking and almost wholly lost.'[38] However, in the light of accomplishments by Brunelleschi in architecture, Donatello in sculpture, and Masaccio in painting, he had come to believe that 'unheard-of and never-before-seen arts and sciences without teachers or without any model whatsoever' were being perfected in his midst. Other achievements too numerous to name, in his own and later times, seemed to confirm the validity of his observation.

The discovery of previously unknown worlds, around the coast of Africa or across the Atlantic, underscored the profound novelty of the age. Not that the novelty was always necessarily read in terms of the advancement of a human agenda. Christopher Columbus, styling himself 'Christoferens' – Christ-bearer – apparently viewed his activity as the fulfilment of a biblical prophecy, pointing out after his third voyage that

> God made me the messenger of the new heaven and the new earth of which he spoke in the Apocalypse of St John after having spoken of it through the mouth of Isaiah; and he showed me the spot where to find it.[39]

Who the 'new' people were and what they signified in the timeline to salvation was a matter of intense debate. Michel de Montaigne, on the other hand, in an essay 'On Cannibals' (*Essays*, 1:30), viewed the new world savage as a challenge to the concept of civilization itself.

Alternative timekeeping systems in far-off lands offered material for reflection regarding future prospects at home. To be sure, few concluded with such literal consistency as Bishop Diego de Landa, writing of the Mayan calendar in 1566 that the devil's work in this regard must be rooted out. 'They had a high priest whom they called Ah Kin (Daykeeper) Mai … He was very much respected by the lords … and his sons or nearest relatives succeeded him in office. In him was the key of their learning'. De Landa went on:

> They provided priests for the towns when they were needed, examining them in the sciences … and they employed themselves in the duties of the temples and in teaching them their sciences as well as in writing books about them .… The sciences which they taught were the computation of the years, months and days, the festivals and ceremonies, the administration of the sacraments, the fateful days and seasons, their methods of devotion and their prophecies.[40]

The perverse genius of the system only reinforced de Landa's conviction that the Second Coming of Christ was more imminent than was widely believed.

An accurate recovery of past times called for a return to Greek and Roman methodological precepts, including the principles of utility that underlay them. Wrote the early sixteenth-century historian Francesco Guicciardini, echoing Thucydides:

> I have determined to write about those events which have occurred in Italy within our memory … From a knowledge of such occurrences, so varied and so grave, everyone may derive many precedents salutary both for himself and for the public weal.[41]

If early modern historiographical narratives tended at first to focus on recent events not covered by the Greek and Roman precedents, the effort to understand all aspects of antiquity generated an antiquarian trend, which engaged some of the best minds in the areas of archaeology, palaeography, codicology, numismatics, and epigraphy.[42]

In any discussions attempting to take in the longest term and the greatest area, there had to be some way to reconcile pagan and biblical history, and the paucity in the ancient historians of actual references to the earliest Christian events could be no deterrent from this urgent task. If the genealogies of the tribes of Israel yielded a total count of some 4,000 years, as Bede the Venerable had calculated already in the eighth century, everything that ever happened before Christ must be squeezed into that time; and some of the best minds rose to the occasion, including Johannes Kepler and Isaac Newton. Dynasty lists, of Chaldea or Egypt or China, appearing to reach much further back, could only be fictitious. The temptation in those myth-bound societies, according to one interpretation, was to add glory to the present by inventing a long and fanciful past.

Of course, digesting all Olympiads and consul lists and other standards into a single series of conventionally constant numbered years, especially where different systems overlapped, was a challenge of no mean proportions. Dionysius Exiguus, the sixth-century monk who invented AD dating, made no pretence of delving into the time before Christ. Joseph Scaliger, one of the greatest of the early modern chronologists, considered that any simple solution necessarily foundered upon the impossibility of dating the birth of Christ beyond the shadow of a doubt.[43] Undaunted by this difficulty, Domenicus Petavius, in 1623, suggested utilizing an agreed-upon date rather than an actual date as the break between BC and AD.[44] If the new system did not come into widespread use until the following century, it nonetheless testified to an increased concern about the objective reality of the past and the necessity to assert the place of the present observer in relation to it.

For classifying the periods of historical time various schemes emerged. Varro in antiquity held to a three-stage model based on socioeconomic organization, with a state of nature followed in turn by pastoralism and then agriculture. Ovid's more picturesque four-stage approach utilizing metallic metaphors referring to ages of gold, silver, bronze, and iron inspired Renaissance poets and painters from John Gower to Pietro da Cortona. Polybius, drawing on Aristotle, turned instead to the internal organization of states, suggesting a cycle of constitutions, from monarchy to aristocracy to democracy, along with the various degenerate forms in between. Machiavelli and others who later borrowed the scheme showed less confidence than its ancient author regarding the possibility of evading the pernicious force of time by combining virtues from the three pure forms to create some yet untried new structure.[45]

Stage theory developed into nothing less than a New Science at the threshold of the eighteenth century in the hands of Giambattista Vico, who recognized the potential of a systematic approach for understanding the basic dynamics of human society.[46] For him, 'the course the nations run' was marked by divine origins, heroic deeds, and 'human' arrangements, in cyclical progression, each stage attended by the associated life form – mental and material. Reading back into the earliest periods of ancient society, he posited an initial 'poetic' stage of primitive cruelty, without rational thought or articulate speech, in which authority was believed to proceed directly from divine fiat. Next came a 'heroic' stage. And here he defied contemporary admirers of Homer, who associated the first heroic poetry with a lost age of advanced philosophical wisdom. Likewise, he debunked the notion that the Twelve Tables, the oldest record of Roman law, were a product of advanced jurisprudence imported from Greece. Both texts, he argued, were compiled during periods of violence and struggle for domination in their respective countries, periods in which economic and political status were allotted on the basis of the valour of warlike heroes. Finally there came the 'human' stage, which in Greece corresponded to the classical age, and in Rome, to the early Republic. In this stage, the maturation of human reason and the softening of customs permitted the formation of institutions based on equity, impartiality, and utility. Following the decline of ancient civilization, Vico then discerned a repetition of these developmental stages in medieval to modern Europe.

Vico accompanied his reflections on the human past with a doctrine regarding the possibility of verifying knowledge about it. The problem was formidable, also considering the recent onslaught of philosophies inclined to debunk any truth-seeking that involved the weighing of possibly mendacious testimonies, about episodes worthy of recording, by those involved and not. For Descartes and the radical sceptics, unassailable truth was to be found inside and not outside, within the psychological effects of introspection and a method for carefully formulating questions and weighing the sensory experience. Vico refused to concede that such a liberation from dogma might stand at the threshold of a real knowledge of nature, insisting instead that human history was indeed a proper study for humankind. 'The rule and criterion of truth is to have made it', Vico postulated in another work; thus history can be known precisely because the doer, within a reasonable degree of certitude, knows his deeds.[47] Humans, having produced the past, can achieve a greater certainty in this realm than in the realm of nature, made by God, and the pursuit of this knowledge was the fittest object for humankind.

Cosmographical time

'And as they, the ancients (the forefathers) learned. When it appears (rises). According to the sign, in which it (rises). It strikes different classes of people with its rays. Shoots them, casts its light upon them'.

The account of the planet Venus in the *Anales de Quauhtitlan* further specifies, as interpreted by Eduard Seler in 1904:

> When it appears in the (first) sign, '1 alligator'. It shoots the old men and women. Also in the (second) sign, '1 jaguar'. In the (third) sign, '1 stag'. In the (fourth) sign, '1 flower'. It shoots the little children. And in the (fifth) sign, '1 reed'. It shoots the kings. Also in the, (sixth) sign, '1 death'. And in the (seventh) sign, '1 rain'. It shoots the rain. It will not rain. And in the (thirteenth) sign, '1 movement'. It shoots the youths and maidens. And in the (seventeenth) sign, '1 water'. There is universal drought.[48]

What others might have made of the original Aztec document besides Fernando de Alva Cortés Ixtlilxochitl, who translated it into Spanish from the Nahuatl language in the sixteenth century, and Antonio de León y Gama, who in the late eighteenth century made a copy, currently in the Bibliothèque Nationale in Paris, of that now-lost translation is impossible to say. Throughout the early modern period, most Europeans, including a steadily increasing rank of sceptics from Pico della Mirandola to Galileo, believed at least one tenet of astrological doctrine.[49] But if planetary influences were impossible to deny, they were also notoriously tricky to prove. Criticism aimed instead at the techniques employed, skilfully or unskilfully and with more or less sincerity, by researchers and rogues, for determining the significance of the relevant configuration of the heavens at the time of birth, or of any other major event, including coronations and constructions, marriages and massacres.

How individual lives and nations were situated within a mysterious cosmic order only darkly touched upon in the main Christian texts was a matter of intense concern, in spite of ecclesiastical injunctions against carrying such inquiries too far.[50] Physicians cured on the basis of the relation of particular parts of the body or particular humours (i.e., phlegm, bile, atrabile, blood) to particular signs of the zodiac. Similar considerations governed ideas about critical days during the course of any disease from onset through crisis. On important military campaigns major figures such as Albrecht von Wallenstein in the Thirty Years' War brought along their astrologers, in this case Giambattista Zenno, possibly a pupil of the mathematician Andrea Argoli. Artists carried out iconographical programmes and in some cases entire constructions in relation to the stellar configurations of particularly auspicious times – from Baldassare Peruzzi's fresco in the Villa Farnesina in Rome depicting Agostino Chigi's horoscope, to Juan Bautista de Toledo's foundations for the Escorial, laid at an astrologically

favourable moment for Philip II. Astrology, religion, and politics collided spectacu-
larly in the case of a Benedictine monk named Orazio Morandi, who predicted the
death of Pope Urban VIII because of the nefarious influence of a solar eclipse on the
pope's horoscope, and paid for his audacity with his life.[51] A vast literature including
numerous popular genres, from almanacs to brief prognostications, went into print,
beginning in Gutenberg's shop at the same time as the 42-line bible, and informing
about the cosmic risks and the ways to prepare for them, on the assumption that, as
Marsilio Ficino hopefully suggested, 'The good will rule over the stars' – if indeed
the time was right.

The Copernican revolution did little to diminish astrological beliefs, as heliocentrism was simply incorporated into an increasingly complex system regarding the
means and modes whereby the heavens were thought to affect humans. Ptolemy's
geocentric *Tetrabiblos* remained the fundamental text on the subject, Ornella Faracovi has pointed out, also because the obvious movements of the heavenly bodies as
seen from earth were still considered to be relevant, in some cases with the necessary
adjustments in the explanatory schemes to account for changes across the centuries,
due to the precession of equinoxes, in the way the visual aspect lined up with the
calendar.[52] Astronomers such as Kepler breathed new life into the subject by attempting to reconfigure the scheme of influences, even adding new aspects, on the basis
of new hypotheses about the deeper meaning, physical and geometrical, of the latest
astronomical observations.[53]

Until the mid-seventeenth century human history and the history of the earth
were thought to run more or less along the same lines, from Creation to the present,
and within the accepted time frame, give or take a few hundred years. At first, any
evidence of a much older planet was incorporated into existing categories with more
or less success. Fossilized plants and animals, already known and discussed in antiquity,
could now be viewed as jokes of nature, as symbols alluding to occult knowledge, or
as remnants of the biblical flood.[54] Observers who took the fossils as real organic remains, such as Robert Hooke, drew attention to the apparently incongruous absence
of chronicle references to how an obviously tumultuous formation of mountains,
rivers, and valleys scattered these items in the most unlikely places. Others such as
John Ray pointed out the necessity for adding now-extinct species, attested by recent
evidence, to the catalogue of all living things, in spite of any dogmas to the contrary.

Isaac Vossius in his *De vera aetate mundi* (1659) added some 1,400 more years to
the most widely accepted current interpretations of world dating.[55] That was far less
than Isaac La Peyrère's fanciful Preadamite theory, arguing, with little chance of wide
assent, for the earth as a far older planet than ever imagined, and for the Genesis story
as an account of only one people among many who must once have stalked it.[56] Edmund Halley offered astronomical and geometric evidence to support a theory that
came so close to cosmic eternalism as to have confused numerous historians.[57] Meanwhile, an incisive wave of biblical criticism eventually including Spinoza was chipping
away at the foundations of scriptural literalism. More icons would be falling soon.

Georges Buffon is credited with having given authoritative voice, in his *Epochs of
Nature*, to mounting suspicions that the known timeline from the past to the present
was seriously flawed.[58] But we are now in 1778, and his deductions belong to another section, not this, casting geological genesis back not a few thousand but 75,000

years, in a first version, then a hundred thousand more, and in manuscript notes, a half-million more still.

Meanwhile, the emerging concept of infinite space would profoundly affect time-consciousness, but not yet. For theoretical reference points, at least on this question, many Renaissance thinkers looked to Aristotle, who proposed a delimited space, rather than to the atomists and Lucretius, who did not. By the mid-sixteenth century, geographical discoveries had doubled the size of the inhabited globe, but Copernicus still suggested a universe made up of concentric spheres, eight in number and bounded on the outer edge by the divine. Few followed Giordano Bruno, who asked provocatively, 'how could the universe not be infinite?' given the providence of God. Even Galileo, at least in one of his polemics, considered comets to be sublunary phenomena caused by terrestrial exhalations, thus saving sphere theory from excessively erratic orbiters. Although Descartes' vortex approach carried with it the implication of infinite space, the issues were not fully explored until well into the eighteenth century.

Heliocentrism of course opened the door to speculations about cosmic pluralism and the question of how many extra-terrestrial worlds there might be altogether, including those with life upon them. After all, if the earth was a planet, should not others similar exist elsewhere? Apart from the size implications of such insights in regard to the universe, there were interesting possibilities in the realm of time-consciousness in each of these worlds. Christian Huygens, for instance, speculated thus in 1698 regarding the inhabitants of Venus:

> For if Venus shines so gloriously to us when she is new and horned, she must necessarily in opposition to the Sun, when she is full, be at least six or seven times larger, and a great deal nearer to the Inhabitants of Mercury, and afford them light so strong and bright, that they have no reason to complain of their want of a moon. What the length of their days are, or whether they have different seasons in the year, is not yet discovered, because we have not yet been able to observe whether his axis have any inclination to his orbit, or what time he spends in his diurnal revolution about his own axis: And yet seeing Mars, the Earth, Jupiter and Saturn, have certainly such successions, there's no reason to doubt but that he has his days and nights as well as they. But his year is scarce the fourth part so long as ours.[59]

With human history and the history of the earth reduced to mere episodes in the history of a cosmos rolling on from who knew where to who knew when, the implications of infinity began truly to be felt. But was time relative or absolute? The period's cogitation culminated not with Einstein but with Isaac Newton and the foundation of classical physics, such that 'absolute, true, and mathematical time, of itself, and from its own nature, flows equably without relation to anything external'.[60] Thus was confirmed not only the universality but also the value-neutrality of time, a position that, once it gained acceptance during the course of the eighteenth century, would stand unopposed until the twentieth.

Much scholarship has tried to understand how a particular historical sequence in regard to time may have inspired European cultures with a certain dynamism that would have a lasting impact on the structures of global humanity. There are no simple answers. One approach focuses on specific inventions in the realm of chronometry as causing a chain of transformative events in culture (C. Cipolla). Another suggests that a deeply rooted preoccupation with the organization of the day, originating largely in religious institutions, may have generated the need for regular signals, and hence a move to develop mechanical solutions, with consequences that are too well known (D. Landes). Yet another directs attention to a mentality attuned, for whatever reason, to quantification (A.W. Crosby). In any case, the problem remains: modern life around the globe is structured within a shared and calibrated temporality that derives from the historical circumstances we have partially outlined in this chapter. Whether human nature itself has been permanently transformed by the developments analysed here is an issue that perhaps rests outside the remit of this volume.

Notes

1 A. de Guevara, *Reloj de príncipes*, Valladolid, 1529, Argumento.

2 E. Panofsky, 'Father Time', in Idem, *Studies in Iconology*, New York: Harper & Row, 1962, 69–91. But see also S. Macey, 'The Changing Iconography of Father Time', in J.T. Fraser, N. Lawrence, D.A. Park (eds), *The Study of Time III: Proceedings of the Third Conference of the International Society for the Study of Time, Alpbach, Austria*, Berlin: Springer, 1978, 540–77.

3 C. Ripa, *Iconologia overo descrittione dell'imagini universali cavate dall'antichità et da altri luoghi*, Padua: P.P. Tozzi, 1625, 662. On the trope, F. Saxl, 'Veritas Filia Temporis', in R. Klibansky and H.J. Paton (eds), *Philosophy and History: Essays Presented to Ernst Cassirer*, Oxford: Clarendon, 1939, 197–221. Further iconography in L. Albanese, 'I simboli animali del tempo nella cultura Rinascimentale', *Bruniana & Campanelliana* 8/1, 2002, 13–21.

4 On this topic, C. Pancino (ed.), *Corpi. Storia, metafora, rappresentazioni fra Medioevo ed Età Moderna*, Venice: Marsilio, 2000.

5 K. Robinson, 'The Celestial Streams of Giulio Camillo', *History of Science* 43, 2016, 321–41.

6 A. Appadurai, *Modernity at Large: Cultural Dimensions of Globalization*, Minneapolis, MN: University of Minnesota Press, 1996, 53.

7 P. Ricoeur, *Temps et récit*, vol. 3, Paris: Seuil, 1991, 90–146; *Time and Narrative*, vol. 3, trans. K. Blamey and D. Pellauer, Chicago, IL: University of Chicago Press, 1988, 60–96.

8 For instance, P. Alperson, '"Musical Time" and Music as an "Art of Time"', *The Journal of Aesthetics and Art Criticism* 38/4, 1980, 407–17, taking issue with S.K. Langer, *Philosophy in a New Key: A Study in the Symbolism of Reason, Rite, and Art*, Cambridge, MA: Harvard University Press, 1941.

9 *Speculationi di Musica*, Bologna: Benacci, 1670, fol. b2v. In general, O.A.I. Takaharu, 'Pietro Mengoli's Theory of Perception of Musical Intervals: A Mathematical Approach to the Sense of Hearing in the Scientific Revolution', *Aesthetics* 15, 2011, 125.

10 E. Holmes, *Life of Mozart*, London, 1878, 212, where the letter is dated 1789. I owe the reference to Alperson, '"Musical Time"', 415n.

11 J.-D. Blavignac, *La Cloche, études sur son histoire et sur ses rapports avec la société aux différents âges*, Geneva: Grosset, 1877, 56 (quotation), 66.

12 C. Cipolla, *Clocks and Culture, 1300–1700*, New York: W.W. Norton, 1978, 34.

13 L. Mumford, *Technics and Civilization*, Chicago, IL: University of Chicago Press, 2010 [1934], 14.

14 In addition to Cipolla, *Clocks*, 46–8, there is G. Dohrn van Rossum, *History of the Hour: Clocks and Modern Temporal Orders*, trans. T. Dunlap, Chicago, IL: University of Chicago Press, 1996, 120–1.

15 E.P. Thompson, 'Time, Work-Discipline, and Industrial Capitalism', *Past and Present* 38, 1967, 56–97; but see also P. Glennie and N. Thrift, *Shaping the Day: A History of Timekeeping in England and Wales 1300–1800*, Oxford: Oxford University Press, 2009, Chap. 2. Concerning time in traditional societies also N. Elias, *Über die Zeit. Arbeiten zur Wissenssoziologie II*, Frankfurt am Main: Suhrkamp Verlag, 1984.

16 In this regard, Anu Korhonen, '"The Several Hours of the Day Had Variety of Employments Assigned to Them": Women's Timekeeping in Early Modern England', *Journal of Early Modern Studies* 6, 2017, 61–85.

17 D. Cressy, *Bonfires and Bells: National Memory and the Protestant Calendar in Elizabethan and Stuart England*, London: Weidenfeld and Nicolson, 1989. More in general, and taking in the effects of confessional differences, P. Burke, *Popular Culture in Early Modern Europe*, 3rd edn, Farnham: Ashgate, 2009, Chap. 7 ('The World of Carnival') and Chap. 8 ('The Triumph of Lent: The Reform of Popular Culture').

18 P. Womack, *English Renaissance Drama*, Oxford: Blackwell, 2006, 64.

19 P. Lucchi, 'Maniere per vestirsi in maschera: un documento malnoto, e due inediti sul Carnevale veneziano del Settecento', *Bollettino dei Musei Civici Veneziani* 3. Ser. 9/10, 2015, 120–37.

20 N.Z. Davis, *Society and Culture in Early Modern France: Eight Essays*, Stanford, CA: Stanford University Press, 1975, Chap. 4 ('The Reasons of Misrule'); as well as É. Durkheim, *Les formes élémentaires de la vie religieuse*, Paris: Alcan, 1912 (translated by Karen E. Fields as *The Elementary Forms of Religious Life*, New York: Free Press, 1995).

21 G. Clark, 'The Long March of History: Farm Wages, Population, and Economic Growth, England 1209–1869', *Economic History Review*, 2nd ser., 60, 2007, 97–135, and G. Liu, *Agricultural Wage Labour in Fifteenth-Century England*, Durham theses, Durham University 2012, available at Durham E-Theses Online: http://etheses.dur.ac.uk/3353.

22 Dohrn van Rossum, *History of the Hour*, 124.

23 For what follows, F. Bünger, *Geschichte der Neujahrsfeier in der Kirche*, Göttingen, 1911; H. Grotefend, *Zeitrechnung des deutschen Mittelalters und der Neuzeit*, 2 vols in 3 parts, 1891–98, vol. 2 pt 1.

24 G.V. Coyne, M.A. Hoskin, O. Pedersen (eds), *Gregorian Reform of the Calendar: Proceedings of the Vatican Conference to Commemorate Its 400th Anniversary*, Città del Vaticano: Specola Vaticana, 1983, especially the chapters on 'Reception', 243–86, by H.M. Nobis, M.A. Hoskin, O. Gingerich, and K. Fischer.

25 F. Braudel, *The Mediterranean and the Mediterranean World in the Age of Philip II*, trans. S. Reynolds, New York: W. Collins and Sons and Harper and Row, 1972, part 2.1.1, 355–63.

26 D.W. Waters, *The Art of Navigation in England in Elizabethan and Early Stuart Times*, London: Hollis and Carter, 1958, 58.

27 J. Konvitz, *Cartography in France, 1660–1848: Science, Engineering, and Statecraft*, Chicago, IL: University of Chicago Press, 1987, Chap. 1; S.A. Bedini, *The Pulse of Time: Galileo Galilei, the Determination of Longitude, and the Pendulum Clock*, Florence: Olschki, 1991, 10.

28 M. Infelise, *Prima dei giornali. Alle origini della pubblica informazione*, Bari: Laterza, 2005; K. Keller and P. Molino, *Die Fuggerzeitungen im Kontext. Zeitungssammlungen im Alten Reich und in Italien*, Mitteilungen des Instituts für Österreichische Geschichtsforschung, Vienna: Böhlau, 2015.

29 Concerning these developments, V. Bauer and H. Böning (eds), *Die Entstehung des Zeitungswesens im 17. Jahrhundert: Ein neues Medium und seine Folgen für das Kommunikationssystem der Frühen Neuzeit,* Bremen: Edition Lumière, 2011; as well as J. Raymond and N. Moxham (eds), *News Networks in Early Modern Europe,* Leiden: Brill, 2016.

30 J.P. Hunter, *Before Novels: The Cultural Contexts of Eighteenth-Century English Fiction,* New York: Norton, 1992.

31 D.R. Woolf, 'News, History and the Construction of the Present in Early Modern England', in B. Dooley and S. Baron (eds), *The Politics of Information in Early Modern Europe,* London and New York: Routledge, 2001, 80–118.

32 S. Sherman. *Telling Time: Clocks, Diaries, and English Diurnal Form 1660–1785,* Chicago, IL: University of Chicago Press, 1996.

33 B. Anderson, *Imagined Communities: Reflection on the Origin and Spread of Nationalism,* London and New York: Verso, 1981, 35. Hegel's original statement may be found in G.W.F. Hegel, *Dokumente zu Hegels Entwicklung,* Stuttgart-Bad Cannstatt: Frommann, 1974, 360.

34 For what follows, see my 'Introduction', to B. Dooley (ed.), *The Dissemination of News and the Emergence of Contemporaneity in Early Modern Europe,* Farnham: Ashgate, 2010, 1–22.

35 P.F. Fabre d'Églantine, *Rapport fait à la Convention nationale au nom de la Commission chargée de la confection du Calendrier,* Paris: Imprimerie nationale, 1793.

36 G.M. Spiegel, 'Historical Thought in Medieval Europe', in L. Kramer and S. Maza (eds), *A Companion to Western Historical Thought,* Oxford: Oxford University Press, 2002, 79.

37 Relevant passages are in his *Posteritati,* of which the best edition is in his *Prose,* ed. G. Martelotti et al., Milan-Naples: Ricciardi, 1955. A reassessment of Petrarch's novelty is in R.G. Witt, *'In the Footsteps of the Ancients': The Origins of Humanism from Lovato to Bruni,* Leiden: Brill, 2001, Chap. 6.

38 Leon Battista Alberti, *On Painting* [1435–36] trans. with Introduction and Notes by J.R. Spencer, New Haven, CT: Yale University Press, 1970, 'Prologue'. On Alberti, A. Grafton, *Leon Battista Alberti: Master Builder of the Italian Renaissance,* Cambridge, MA: Harvard University Press, 2002.

39 P. Moffitt Watts, 'Prophecy and Discovery: On the Spiritual Origins of Christopher Columbus's Enterprise of the Indies', *The American Historical Review* 90/1, 1985, 73.

40 From A.M. Tozzer (ed. and trans.), *Landa's Relación de las cosas de Yucatan,* vol. 18, Cambridge, MA: Harvard University Press, 1941, 27.

41 F. Guicciardini, *The History of Italy,* trans. S. Alexander, Princeton, NJ: Princeton University Press, 1968, 3. Concerning Italian Renaissance historiography, E. Cochrane, *Historians and Historiography in the Italian Renaissance,* Chicago, IL: University of Chicago Press, 1981. More in general, including the global perspective, J. Rabasa et al. (eds), *The Oxford History of Historical Writing: 1400–1800,* Oxford: Oxford University Press, 2012.

42 W. Stenhouse, 'Antiquarianism', in A. Grafton, G. Most, S. Settis (eds), *The Classical Tradition,* Cambridge, MA, and London: Harvard University Press, 2010; W. Stenhouse, 'The Renaissance Foundations of European Antiquarianism', in A. Schnapp et al. (eds), *World Antiquarianism,* Los Angeles, CA: Getty Publications, 2013, 295–316; and W. Stenhouse, *Reading Inscriptions and Writing Ancient History: Historical Scholarship in the Late Renaissance,* London: Institute of Classical Studies, 2005; H. Wrede, 'Die Entstehung der Archäologie and das Einsetzen der neuzeitlichen Geschichtsbetrachtungen', in W. Küttler, J. Rüsenand, E. Schulin (eds), *Geschichtsdiskurs,* vol. 2: *Anfänge modernen historischen Denkens,* Frankfurt: Fischer Verlag, 1993; as well as biographical studies such

as A. Mazzocco and M. Laureys (eds), *A New Sense of the Past: The Scholarship of Biondo Flavio (1392–1463)*, Louvain: Leuven University Press, 2016, and others below.

43 Concerning Scaliger, A. Grafton, *Joseph Scaliger: A Study in the History of Classical Scholarship*, Vol. 2: *Historical Chronology*, Oxford: Oxford University Press, 1994.

44 In general, D.J. Wilcox, *The Measure of Times Past: Pre-Newtonian Chronologies and the Rhetoric of Relative Time*, Chicago, IL: University of Chicago Press, 1987.

45 D.R. Kelley, 'The Theory of History', in C.B. Schmitt, Q. Skinner, E. Kessler (eds), *The Cambridge History of Renaissance Philosophy*, Cambridge: Cambridge University Press, 1988, 746–61.

46 G. Vico, *Principi di una Scienza nuova intorno alla natura delle Nazioni*, Naples: F. Mosca, 1725, on which, D.P. Verene, *Vico's 'New Science': A Philosophical Commentary*, Ithaca, NY: Cornell University Press, 2015, part 6.

47 G. Vico, *De antiquissima italorum sapientia* (1710) in *Opere*, vol. 1 (Bari: Laterza, 1929), 136. Vico's historiographical ideas are the subject of F. Fellmann, *Das Vico-Axiom, der Mensch macht die Geschichte*, Freiburg: Alber, 1976; L. Pompa, *Human Nature and Historical Knowledge*, Cambridge: Cambridge University Press, 1990, Chap. 3; as well as by D.P. Verene, *Vico's Science of Imagination*, Ithaca, NY: Cornell University Press, 1981. For some of these points I refer to my *The Social History of Skepticism: Experience and Doubt in Early Modern Culture* (Baltimore, MD: Hopkins, 1999), 146–54.

48 E. Seler, 'The Venus Period in Picture Writings of the Borgian Codex Group', *Bulletin of the Bureau of American Ethnology* 28, 1904, 384–5.

49 On this aspect, B. Dooley (ed.), *A Companion to Astrology in the Renaissance,* Leiden: Brill, 2014, 'Introduction', 1–16; and concerning Peruvian astrology, in the same anthology, the chapter by C. Brosseder.

50 For what follows, the chapters in Dooley, *A Companion to Astrology in the Renaissance,* by W. Hübner, W. Eamon, H. Hirai, D. Blume, and relevant bibliography.

51 B. Dooley, *The Last Prophecy of Morandi and the End of Renaissance Politics*, Princeton, NJ: Princeton University Press, 2002, Chaps. 7, 9, 11, 15.

52 O. Faracovi, 'The Return to Ptolemy', in Dooley, *A Companion to Astrology in the Renaissance*, 87–98.

53 B. Dooley, 'Astrology and Science', in ibid., 33–66.

54 For this and the next paragraph, S. Toulmin and J. Goodfield, *The Discovery of Time*, London: Hutchinson, 1965, Chaps. 4–6, updated by R. Rappaport, *When Geologists Were Historians, 1665–1750*, Ithaca, NY: Cornell University Press, 1997, Chaps. 4–7. On jokes of nature, P. Findlen, 'Jokes of Nature and Jokes of Knowledge: The Playfulness of Scientific Discourse in Early Modern Europe', *Renaissance Quarterly* 43, No. 2, 1990, 292–331.

55 E. Jorink, *Reading the Book of Nature in the Dutch Golden Age, 1575–1715*, Leiden: Brill, 2010, 103–5.

56 P. Rossi, *I segni del tempo. Storia della Terra e storia delle nazioni da Hooke a Vico*, Milan: Feltrinelli, 1979, Chap. 1.

57 Concerning the disputes, D. Levitin, 'Halley and the Eternity of the World Revisited', *Notes and Records of the Royal Society* 67/4, 2013, 315–29, taking issue with S. Schaffer, 'Halley's Atheism and the End of the World', *Notes and Records of the Royal Society* 32, 1977, 17–40.

58 J. Roger, *Buffon: A Life in Natural History*, Ithaca, NY: Cornell University Press, 1997, 402–24.

59 C. Huygens, *The Celestial Worlds Discover'd: or, Conjectures Concerning the Inhabitants*, London, James Knapton, 1722, 108. Concerning pluralism, S. Dick, *Plurality of Worlds: The Origins of the Extraterrestrial Life Debate from Democritus to Kant*, Cambridge: Cambridge

University Press, 1982; as well as K.S. Guthke, 'Nightmare and Utopia: Extraterrestrial Worlds from Galileo to Goethe', *Early Science and Medicine* 8, No. 3, 2003, 173–95.

60 Scholium to the Definitions in *Philosophiae Naturalis Principia Mathematica*, Book 1 (1689); trans. A. Motte (1729), ed. F. Cajori, Berkeley, CA: University of California Press, 1934, 6–12.

17

WRITTEN COMMUNICATION IN URBAN SPACES

Publication, textual materiality and appropriations*

Antonio Castillo Gómez

After learning his trade in Cologne and Brugge, William Caxton (*ca.* 1422–1492) headed back to Britain and established himself as a printer in London in 1476. A small typographic poster for advertising books, so far the oldest one preserved, may be dated to this year or the following one. The text announced that the *Ordinale Sarum* (or Sarum Pye), i.e. the directory of the liturgical year as used in Salisbury (and in most of England), which Caxton had just printed, could be purchased at a good price in the store he had set in Westminster Abbey, next to the parish house. At the foot of the poster, the phrase 'supplico stet cedula' asked for the advertisement not to be removed from the wall.[1] Contemporaneously, at the synod held in Alcalá de Henares in 1480, it was agreed that parish priests should direct the dissemination of Christian doctrine using a *board*, 'hung from a nail in an eminent public space where anyone may read it and find out what is contained therein'.[2] A few decades later, on 31 October 1517, it is likely that Luther followed the same procedure for the propagation of his reformist theses, 'since it was common practice at the University of Wittenberg to post disputation theses on the door of the north side of the castle church'.[3]

Although there are medieval precedents about these forms of public lettering, its reiteration is a distinctive feature of the early Modern Age. Since then, the cities of Western Europe were configured as a 'graphosphere', understood as 'the totality of graphic devices used to record, store, display, and disseminate messages and information, and the social and cultural spaces in which they figure'.[4] Solemn inscriptions make power and social stratification visible in public constructions or funeral monuments. The

* This chapter is the result of work done as part of the research project *Vox populi*. Espacios, practicas y estrategias de visibilidad de las escrituras del margen en las épocas Moderna y Contemporánea / Vox Populi. Spaces, Practices and Strategies of Visibility of Marginal Writing in the Early Modern and Modern Periods (PID2019-107881GB-I00), funded by the Ministry of Science and Innovation, and the National Research Agency of Spain. Translation: Enrique Íñiguez Rodríguez.

institutions of power, from the king to the municipality and the ecclesiastical author-ities, appropriated the public space to display their authority or communicate their mandates. Political contestation, religious dissent, social tension or personal confron-tations became visible through libels and pasquinades, which were sometimes fixed on walls and, on other occasions, circulated from hand to hand or sung in the middle of streets and squares. Commercial signs and advertising posters proliferated in these places as a pre-capitalist economic structure gradually became established.

Therefore, while recognizing the significance of the revolutionary invention of Gutenberg's printing press, I consider it unfortunate that many studies on written communication in the cities during the early Modern Age focus almost exclusively on printed texts and marginalize other materialities of writing, even when those texts fulfilled the same functions, as was the case with posters and loose sheets. Instead, the perspective I propose in this essay is addressed through the urban public space as a daily context where communicative acts are exercised through writing, very often in interaction with orality and the visual culture. Consequently, the production that I analysed is the one that was fixed, displayed and occasionally disseminated in squares, streets and other public places.

Communication spaces and rituals

In Paris, an ordinance of 1539 on healthiness indicated how its publication should be done: 'written in parchment in large letters' on some posts distributed around the city. Aware of the fragility of words, the French monarchy began to display the mandates in public places. Nevertheless, the passage from manuscript to print and from parch-ment to paper was a dilemma for the authorities, suspicious of the trivialization and falsification that the mass production of this type of document could involve, against the greater security and control offered by the proclamation by means of royal criers.[5]

Clearly, the publication of mandates and official dispositions could not be done randomly; instead, it was conditioned by certain gestures and procedures, which started by declaiming the proclamation 'out loud, slowly and pronouncing properly'.[6] The pomp of the act depended on the authority or institution that had directed the mandate and its contents. A municipal edict was different from a royal decree, an edict of inquisitorial faith or a papal bull. While there were still many occasions on which the publication of this type of document was limited to the corresponding an-nouncement,[7] as had happened in previous centuries,[8] the novelty in the early Mod-ern Age was the public exposure of the announcement for a specific time, in addition to its proclamation by the criers.[9] This form of publication made the communicative act an event of urban sociability, a reason for public meetings and social exchange.

By fixing the document in public places, the authorities had an opportunity for visibility, and one could even say that this acted as a kind of 'soft conditioning mech-anism', according to the definition of Antonio M. Hespanha,[10] i.e. as a disciplinarian strategy of the powers, even if such documents were also contested. Thus, the writ-ings of the authorities intervened in public life by means of communicating laws and mandates responsible for regulating society according to the political, social and moral system. While the Church published many provisions in Latin, political entities opted for the vernacular. In vast and multi-ethnic empires such as the Spanish and the Portuguese it was common for such mandates to be proclaimed in the native languages. Thus the extensive knowledge of the provisions was assured, as the Council of the Supreme Inquisition considered on 12 June 1688 when it ordered the inquisitors in Sardinia to print an edict on the prohibition of the doctrine of Miguel de Molinos (1628–1696), in sufficient amounts, 'in the language of that kingdom'.[11]

The semantic centrality of the space where the document was exposed can also be applied to the pasquinades and defamatory libels, as was clearly shown by the censorship of this type of writing. The constitutions of the diocese of Braga of 1639 expressly stated that the people involved in fixing and circulating 'defamatory writings, papers and letters' were to be punished with the utmost rigour in case those 'were fixed in the doors or walls of our archiepiscopal palaces or the houses of our judges'.[12] The transgressive effect was made more effective by fixing the documents on buildings linked to the contested power or the defamed person. Thus, in the context of the French religious wars of the late sixteenth century, many libels that harrowingly described the persecutions suffered by Catholics in England were fixed on the walls of the cemetery of Saint-Séverin, in the heart of the Paris of the League.[13] Defamatory posters against individuals were pasted on the door of the defamed person's house, often covered with other elements and symbols that completed the effectiveness of the message.[14] Finally, one paradigmatic case of the significance provided by the place corresponds to the Italian talking statues, the most important being that of Pasquino, which originated the pasquinades. These were of two types: on the one hand, the verses composed by the students on the occasion of the feast of St Mark, on 25 April, which were posted until 1539; and on the other hand, the critical pasquinades against religious and political authorities, which appeared in 1501 and spread throughout the Modern Age.[15]

Just as the statue of Pasquino became the centre of the anti-power protests in Rome, other urban corners played a nuclear role in the dissemination of news and popular prints. In Venice, the Rialto bridge fulfilled this task; in London, Grub Street; in Paris, the Tree of Cracow square; and in the Spain of the sixteenth and seventeenth centuries, the *mentideros* (gossip corners), some as characteristics as the stands of the cathedral of Seville, or the three that existed in Madrid: the Palace Slabs, rather political in nature, where courtiers and public employees used to come; the comedians, on the corner of Santa María and León streets, lively with all kinds of comedians and theatre workers; and the third, the most renowned, located in the stands of the church of San Felipe el Real, at the Puerta del Sol on the corner of the street Mayor, which was especially crowded, boisterous and heterogeneous.[16]

The tracking of the Inquisition and the political authorities on many of the texts disseminated on the streets was constant. In November 1575, when he was stationed at the door of the Doge's Palace in Venice, the Inquisition arrested a street vendor named Battista Furlano to question him about the prayers he was selling against the plague epidemic that was raging in the city at that time. The text was in Latin with a translation into Italian, printed on a loose octavo sheet.[17] Likewise, in 1627 the Spanish king Philip IV approved a pragmatic decree prohibiting all class of popular prints on affairs of State that lacked the compulsory royal licence;[18] despite the promulgation by the English king Charles I of the *Prohibition of corantos* in 1632, 'the streets of London were immediately flooded with news ballads touching by indirection or by metaphor the current events of the day'.[19]

Regardless of the vigilance of political and ecclesiastical authorities, the dissemination and peddling of so-called 'popular literature' was a widespread phenomenon in both Europe and the Americas. Proof that this was the case is the recurrent persecution of those who distributed or sang certain texts, as happened in 1681 with singer John Sequier, of Newcastle, for singing ballads against the Lord Mayor of London and other authorities.[20] No less significant is the testimony regarding the distribution in Mexican towns of a printed prayer of tiny size with a passage in Latin from the Gospel of John where Jesus is described as the Word (1:1–14), sold by a blind man and his Spanish guide in 1621. According to the report sent to the Holy Office, many copies were sold to both Spaniards and natives, as people bought the prayer to carry it with them as an amulet, to protect themselves from fires and storms, or from difficult births in the case of pregnant women.[21]

Street singers, *cantastorie* or the blind were devoted to this market of printed *menudencias*, which was often their main source of subsistence. They sold and sang texts of all kinds, but also their own compositions, improvised on the fly or written shortly before reciting them.[22] To this circumstance the Sevillian printer Francisco de Lira expressly referred in the notice to the reader included in some copies of a list of festivals held in Lisbon in 1609 in honour of Felipe III. There he reiterated that many of those stories were nothing more than 'well or badly composed novels that a blind man devises in the evening, has printed at night and sells in the morning'.[23]

With regard to the news, the burgeoning market of those times – immortalized in some of the works by William Shakespeare (1564–1616) and Ben Jonson (1572–1637) – materialized into a series of editorial products that shared some common features while differing on specific traits. While notices and gazettes included a selection of short news items, the ballads, *occasionnels* or *relaciones de sucesos* focused on the account of a single event, which could be political (entrances, royal weddings, funerals), as well as religious (beatifications, canonisations), military (wars) or extraordinary (miracles, natural catastrophes, personal misfortunes). Specifically, Spanish accounts of events were disseminated both in handwritten and printed form and their extension could range from the loose-sheet flyer and the *cordel* book (chapbooks) for shorter stories to books of larger size.[24] Additionally, the massive character of this type of prints is attested by the 3,000 licences that the Stationer's Register – a court agency that licensed all printed matter – granted between 1577 and 1709 for the printing of ballads, although the real number was greater, since this amount does not include those that, although unauthorized, circulated nonetheless.[25] According to Tessa Watt, with a conservative estimate of 200 copies per edition, we would be talking about a production of 600,000 copies.[26]

Artefacts and meanings

Can we understand this diversity of urban texts regardless of their materiality? As Roger Chartier pointed out, the debate takes up the reflections that Kant raised in the second part of his *Metaphysics of Morals* (1796), i.e. the distinction between the Platonic conception of the text as immaterial and the conception of the text as a reference to the particular object in which we read and apprehend ideas.[27] Although the material forms do not impose an interpretation of each text, it seems indisputable that such interpretation is inseparable from the product where the writing is embodied. There are huge differences between loose-leaf booklets and *in-folios*, as well as between hand-written and typographic posters, or monumental inscriptions as opposed to graffiti. In the words of Donald McKenzie, 'it is in a context like this that texts are perhaps best seen, not as fixed, determined artefacts in a specific medium, but as potential'.[28]

With regard to the urban texts that I am analysing, it must be noted that the public exposure of a part of them was accompanied by certain visibility and readability requirements. To consider how they could be read it is necessary to take into account several circumstances. Firstly, the widespread illiteracy of the time, which is compatible with practices of delegated reading that helped overcome some barriers. Secondly, the fact that the texts, despite their public display, were not always aimed at the whole population, or not in the same way. And thirdly, that their main function was not always focused on alphabetical reading.

In the case of edicts and proclamations, as printed dissemination took precedence, the advantages of typography in order to improve clarity and readability became increasingly visible. These benefits were reflected in the organization of the graphic space, in the distribution of blanks, in the hierarchical use of capital or bigger letters at the beginning of the text and of other relevant sections and in the alternation of typographical round and italic letters, as well as in the insertion of emblems and iconographic motives with enunciative purposes in the heading. The latter is especially evident in the mandates emanating from the pontifical Curia and other ecclesiastical instances,[29] as can be seen in the edict that the Roman Inquisition promulgated on 10 March 1677 against the use of magic. At the bottom of the document it was instructed that the edict should be fixed in the usual places in Rome, read in the churches of the diocese on the first Sundays of Advent and of Lent and displayed at the doors of the churches and sacristies, so that no one may claim ignorance and so 'everything commanded therein would be obeyed' (Figure 17.1).[30]

Similar observations can be made from other types of posters, mainly typographic, which tend to be more elaborated: the ones used to convene literary competitions organized in the framework of Baroque festivals and the announcements of academic dissertations. In the case of literary posters, the upper part was reserved for the title of the contest and the person or saint to be celebrated. There followed a preamble with a broader explanation about the reason for the festival. The central section contained the description of the poetic jousts and the desired characteristics of the poems (language, rhythm and content). The lower part was dedicated to the rules of the contest, the jury, the deadline and the mode of presentation of the poems.[31]

Regarding the academic dissertations, although they were also notified by means of invitations in booklets with four to eight pages,[32] it was characteristic to announce them with posters. At first these were handwritten, but in the second half of the sixteenth century the printed format took precedence, with prior authorization of the rector or another authority: in Germany printed bills are already documented in 1560; in France, the first appeared in the Protestant universities of Orthez and Lescar, between 1585 and 1592, while in the Sorbonne 127 bills were printed between 1588 and 1660; and with regard to the Hispanic universities, the first remaining bill advertising a thesis is the examination that Pedro Balli took on 26 August 1584, 'hora nona antimeridies', to obtain the degree of doctor in Law at the Royal and Pontifical University of Mexico.[33]

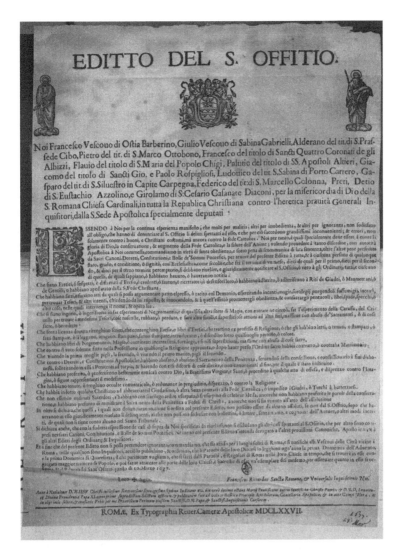

Figure 17.1   Holy Office's edict against magic, necromancy and other condemned practices. Rome: Stamperia Camerale, 1677. By permission of the Biblioteca Casanatense, Rome (PER, est.18.14 58).

The content included the dedication to the sponsor or the principal with all their
honours, represented with a figure in the case of the saints and a coat of arms for
civil and religious figures. There followed the name of the student and the studies,
the degree he aspired to obtain and the conclusion or conclusions that he had to
publicly sustain (one for the minor degree, several for major degrees), the venue of
the discussion, the authority that presided over the ceremony, the time and day. They
stand out because of the use of Latin, in consonance with the public to which they
were dedicated, despite their being fixed in the academic centres and occasionally at
the doors of some churches and other public buildings.

315

In typographic terms, both signposting modalities had a fairly homogeneous layout. The differences affect above all the diversity of typographies in order to distinguish the different sections, decorated capital letters, other typographical ornaments and the insertion of iconographic motifs: the coats of arms and figures representing the convening institution or the person and saint to be celebrated, in the literary posters; and of the sponsor or principal, in the announcements of academic theses. The specimens of the seventeenth century, as well as the edicts, show greater ornamental and graphic richness, thus reflecting the evolution of the engraving technique.

It is evident that, in many of these prints, an eminently visual conception of writing prevailed, as it happened contemporaneously with the mural poetry composed to adorn the ephemeral monuments erected during public displays. Leaving aside strictly alphabetical reading, their main objective was to show 'ostentation and apparatus', as the Spanish rhetorician Juan Díaz Rengifo (1553–1615) wrote in his *Arte poética española* (1592): 'Those sestinas are made for ostentation and apparatus, when they are required for posters, or when during a solemn celebration the poet wants to fill the tapestries with several poems, or in other opportunities that may arise'.[34] This is an exceedingly appropriate observation, since it indicates the key to interpreting these ephemeral writings. Their purpose was linked to their ability to make explicit and visible both power and authority. As a consequence, the care put into the visual aspects of the poems was not so much for readability as for visibility. Beyond text, each poem also had a visual nature, as it was arranged in the form of a hieroglyph, a chain or other creative games. Father Francisco de Rois y Mendoza (1611–1677), archbishop of Granada and author of an account of the funeral that the University of Salamanca organized for the death of King Philip IV (1665), explicitly stated this when he wrote that 'words speak to the ears, paintings to the eyes, and what is seen sets more things in motion that what is heard'.[35]

The main written manifestation where the graphic aspect bestowed on the letter an autonomous significance was in the case of monumental writings. In these, the text may be read in reference to the verbal statement transmitted, but before being read it was certainly perceived as an entirely visual object.[36] This type of inscription conveyed a meaning through its letters, but also through its material form, its relation with other discourses – especially the iconographic discourse – and by its position within the permanent or temporary monumental ensemble. Therefore, limiting its interpretation to alphabetical reading would involve disregarding its symbolic and propagandistic nature.

Moreover, for a large part of the European society of the early Modern Age, alphabet reading was ballasted not only by illiteracy, but in certain cases also by some graphic resources – such as letters inserted within others to save space – and by the frequent use of Latin as an epigraphic language, although the stereotyped character and form of the inscriptions could make up for the inexperience that many had in that language. Therefore, limiting the interpretation of the epigraphic production of the early modern centuries to the occasional alphabetical reading would imply disregarding the symbolic and propagandistic meaning inherent in the showy solemnity of a part of it, both in permanent and festive-ephemeral production, as attested for example by the arches erected in Antwerp to commemorate the triumphal entry of the

Cardinal-Infante Ferdinand of Austria, brother of Philip IV, when he was appointed governor of the Netherlands.[37]

The graphic reform of the humanist movement, which culminated in Italy in the 1460s with the restoration of the Roman square capital led by the Paduan circle of Andrea Mantegna and Felice Feliciano,[38] was the best instrument for popes, kings, nobles and ecclesiastical and town councils to make their authority and prestige visible to their peers and *ad perpetuam memoriam*. This was especially the case in Rome, *caput mundi*, where the monumental inscriptions showed their effectiveness as a visual system of power.[39] A prototypical case of propagandist instrumentation of monumental writing was that carried out in the urban restructuring plan executed in that city between 1585 and 1591 at the initiative of Pope Sixtus V (Figure 17.2). The constructions erected or reformed in that period were finished off with a solemn inscription whose design was the work of Luca Orfei, copyist of the Vatican Library, who created an epigraphic capital of elongated forms modelled on Roman examples of the late fifteenth century, the time of Sixtus IV.[40] At the municipal level, the case of Lyon highlights the politics of epigraphic affirmation of the ruling elite in the seventeenth century, with a total of seventy-three inscriptions mentioned in stories and travel books of the day. The comparison between the text of the epigraphs placed in a piece of black limestone opposite the door of the Basilica d'Ainay (1611) and the fountain of Chana (1670) reflects the rise of city rhetoric as the century progressed.[41]

Figure 17.2   Fontana dell'Acqua Felice (1587). Rome.

At the same time something similar happened with the text of the epitaphs inscribed in the funerary monuments, where graphic innovations were introduced according to the Baroque *pathos*. As stated by Armando Petrucci, these novelties were: rupture with traditional epigraphic formats, simulation of non-stone materials in the cartouches (appearing as wood, rags, sheets, shells, hides, etc.), dislocation of the writing in curved and wavy lines, polychromy of surfaces and letters and decomposition of text into sections.[42] Together with such imposing tombs as those of Lucrezia Tomacelli (1625) in the Roman basilica of St John Lateran, of Pope Urban VIII (1628) in the Vatican (by Bernini) or of George Villiers, Duke of Buckingham (1634) in Westminster Abbey,[43] these features can be seen in many of the 374 tombs of officers and knights of the Order of Malta from the seventeenth and eighteenth centuries arranged on the floor of St John's Co-Cathedral in Valletta (Figure 17.3), which include numerous sentences and allegories alluding to death.[44]

Figure 17.3   Tomb of Brother Thomas de Villages, who died on 29 January 1689. Valletta (Malta), St John's Co-Cathedral. Myriam Thyes, www.thyes.com.

The ramifications of the visual elements extended to ballads, satires and popular prints, in which an iconographic memory became established and then reactivated with each new circumstance. The expansion of the Lutheran reform joined forces with the printing press as a means of propaganda and opinion. One of its fruits was the massive production of prints to hang in the houses and to distribute in the street. Some extolled Luther, while others were very critical of the papacy, such as the famous *Passional Christi und Antichristi* (1521) by Lucas Cranach, where the simple life of Jesus is contrasted with the opulence of his Vicar on earth (Figure 17.4).[45]

Drawing also accompanied other public manifestations of writing in order to clarify its meaning: effigies of the penanced in the inquisitorial *sanbenitos* (penitential robes) and other signs of derision were publicly paraded by criminals and wrongdoers;[46] defamatory paintings with the same purpose were displayed in the republics of central and northern Italy;[47] obscene drawings appeared in defamatory posters for adultery, prostitution or homosexuality;[48] and symbols allusive to the activity of

Figure 17.4   Martin Luther, *Passional Christi und Antichristi*. Strasbourg: Johann Knobloch, 1521. Engravings by Lucas Cranach. By permission of the Biblioteca Nacional de España (U/3139).

each store appeared in commercial signs.[49] In other cases, writing contributed to identifying certain images, as happened in England during the so-called 'Exclusion Crisis' (1679–1681), which sought to exclude Charles II's brother and heir presumptive, James, from the throne. In those years, the Whig party, hostile to the Catholics and eager to limit the powers of the monarch, drafted petitions, published ballads and engravings, and arranged to have effigies of the pope, cardinals, friars, inquisitors and nuns paraded through the streets and identified with labels so that everyone could understand the message.[50]

Readings and other appropriations

The diversity of texts present in the public space is combined with a plurality of appropriations, as many as their functions and uses, combined with the unequal literacy of the public. In the case of monumental inscriptions, the reception was situated halfway between 'the naive reading of the figurative work (*scriptura laicorum*) and the elitist consumption of books'.[51] Regarding public announcements and libels, some testimonies are quite clarifying. At the end of 1574, an ordinary person, Juan Alexandre, owner of a cheese shop in Medina del Campo (Valladolid), read a written paper that was stuck on a wall. He thought it could be an advertisement for rental housing, when in fact it was one of the pasquinades that were published in different Castilian cities against Philip II's fiscal policy.[52] Around the same time, in July 1588, a modest Portuguese *converso* shoemaker named Juan Vicente, of Campomaior, decided to emigrate to Brazil instead of Cape Verde or Angola, as he had planned, attracted by some edicts fixed on the streets of Lisbon, in which the king offered free passage to anyone who wanted to cross the Atlantic with his wife and children.[53]

Along with these scenes of individual reading, sometimes with the help of an intermediary, streets and squares were the space par excellence of community readalouds: literary fiction, recent news, pasquinades and libels.[54] On the latter, one can remember the crowds that, in the Christmas of 1650, gathered in front of the Cathedral of Mexico and in the surrounding streets to read the libels that William Lamport, naturalized in Spanish as Guillén Lombardo, had composed against the Inquisition shortly before he escaped from the prison, where he had been kept since 1642 accused of practising astrology and defending Protestantism:

> that on Monday, the second day of Christmas, between seven and eight in the morning, he was coming down Tacuba street and, at the end of it, he saw many people standing in the corner – where a new house and shop are – reading an oblong paper, written in very small letters, which was fixed and pasted on the wall, in front of the sewer.[55]

The impact of the libels published to criticize the decisions and behaviour of the rulers and ecclesiastical leaders is different from the concurrence of media that intervened in the propagation of the Protestant and Catholic reforms or in any political or religious conflict of the early Modern Age: from the wars of religion in France (1562–1598) to the English Civil War (1642–1651) and the Glorious Revolution of 1688, five to ten million pamphlets circulated in total, without overlooking La

Fronde (1648–1653), with about 5,000 *mazarinades*, or the revolts that arose in different places of the Spanish monarchy during the reign of Felipe IV, as well as the power struggles before Charles II came of age.

In these cases, the combat of opinions used to be transmitted through sermons, theatre, books, libels and pamphlets; the interaction between writing, spoken word and visual culture was very common. Let us take as an example the intense anti-Spanish propaganda deployed in the Netherlands during the Eighty Years' War (1568–1648), i.e. the one held by the United Provinces against their sovereign at that time, the King of Spain, which is considered to be the first 'paper war' at a European level.[56] Many of those prints focused their denunciations on the four fundamental themes of the Dutch black legend: the machinations of the Spanish Inquisition, the cruelty of the Spanish people, the personal vices of Philip II and the plan of universal hegemony of the Spanish monarchy.[57] They presented the king as a tyrant who did not respect the traditional liberties and privileges of the Dutch cities and the Spaniards as descendants of infidel Jews.[58]

The booklets were particularly poignant during the government of the Duke of Alba, Fernando Álvarez de Toledo (1507–1582), governor of the Netherlands in 1567–1573 and responsible for a brutal repression. This can be seen, among other places, in a 1572 issue where the Duke was represented as a grotesque character (Figure 17.5). Sitting on his throne, with the devil behind him insufflating hatred, the Duke is eating a child with his right hand while holding in his left hand a bag filled with coins stolen from Flanders. Beside him, there is a hydra with the heads of the cardinals Granvelle, Guise and Lorraine, and under his feet the decapitated corpses of the Counts of Egmont and Horn, who a few years earlier had led a revolt against the implantation of the Inquisition, precisely at Granvelle's initiative.[59]

In many of those conjunctures, the circulation of papers was of such magnitude that one can speak of actual pamphlet wars. Their effectiveness as instruments of opinion is beyond doubt.[60] On 8 January 1573 the Bishop of Valence, Jean Monluc, wrote a letter to Charles IX of France justifying the use of libels for his duty to defend the reputation of the sovereign, questioned by the intense Protestant propaganda.[61] In this line, the Portuguese Jerónimo Freire Serrão pointed out in his work *Discurso político* (1634) that the *papelinhos* (i.e. the libels) were the 'third way and remedy used by the truth to reach the ears of the King', sermons and books being the other two.[62] Likewise, the English clergyman and pamphleteer John Nalson (1638?–1686) wrote in 1682: 'I know not any one thing that more hurt the late King then the Paper Bullets of the Press'.[63] Finally, in one of the pasquinades that circulated in Barcelona in 1689 against the French King Louis XIV, it was stated that 'interesting papers with few pages are disseminated, read and dispatched much better and more quickly than books'.[64]

With regard to the mandates of power, their public display decisively influenced the plurality of appropriations. In the same way that the Portuguese shoemaker Juan Vicente read or was read the provision contained in an edict because he understood that it could interest him, in other cases these texts triggered acts of contempt and violence. This was the case of the *tablilla* (tablet) – actually a sheet of paper – used in September 1597 by Sebastian de Valderrama, priest and apostolic judge in the town of Colima (Mexico), to notify a mandate of the Vicar-General of the Diocese

Figure 17.5 *The Duke of Alba Killing the Innocent Inhabitants of the Netherlands*, anonymous engraving disseminated in 1572. By permission of the Rijksmuseum, Amsterdam (RP-P-OB-79.012), public domain.

of Valladolid excommunicating some residents that had not paid the ecclesiastical tributes. The mandate was accompanied by the name of the people affected by the excommunication, who, on the same paper, 'at the bottom, between the signature and the letter', insulted Valderrama by calling him 'utter scoundrel, demented, drunkard, thief, who collects what is not owed to him'.[65] Likewise, in the jurisdiction of the Republic of Venice, during the sixteenth and seventeenth centuries, there were various acts of insubordination towards the edicts, which were broken into pieces and 'befouled', amidst public disorder instigated not only by the people, but also by the nobles.[66]

In other circumstances, the conflicts raised by public lettering resulted in acts of *damnatio memoriae*. The destruction or substitution of certain inscriptions, images, statues and symbols, whether in religious conflicts, anti-seignorial revolts or revolutions of greater political significance, was a way of actively intervening in the memory and the re-signification of public spaces, as happened during the Neapolitan revolt against Philip IV in 1647. Initially, as the revolt was a popular reaction against a rise in taxes on consumption, its leader, the fisherman Masaniello, did not suppress the Habsburg arms from the Neapolitan palaces, but ordered that there be placed, next to them, a shield crowned with an uppercase P in the centre of the blazon as an expression of the People. In autumn, after the proclamation for a few months of the Most Serene Republic of Naples, commanded by the Duke of Guise, the arms of the Spanish sovereign were replaced by the symbols of the new republican power: the arms of the Duke, the acronym SPQN (*Senatus Populusque Neapolitanus*) and the word *Libertas*. This dispute of symbols was also manifested in coins, paintings, images and even the representations of the saints.[67] In this light one may also interpret the events that happened at the end of the seventeenth century with the bronze decree that Sofiia Alekseevna, regent of Russia from 1682 to 1689, had placed in the Red Square in Moscow, legitimizing the acts of the nobles who had taken her to power, while Peter I, proclaimed Tsar when he was ten, after the death of his brother Fyodor III, and his mother were removed from the court. At the end of her regency, the decree was destroyed.[68]

In view of these facts, it is evident that the public space was often not an agora of social cohesion, but a place for dispute.[69] The responses provoked by many of the texts displayed on the walls or disseminated throughout the streets appeal directly to their function as 'writing acts' capable of propitiating meaning controversies.[70] From this perspective, one can understand the tensions caused by the concurrence in the public space of legitimated writings, i.e. those promoted by the authorities or consented by them, and other writings that implied an illicit appropriation of those places as areas of communication. This is quite evident in the case of graffiti. In certain contexts and spaces they were not always transgressive writings, but were tolerated, as has been observed in Elizabethan England, in the rich ensemble of the ducal palace of Urbino, in the graffiti made by the faithful in different sanctuaries and churches or in the admirations written on wall paintings in Rome.[71] This type of intervention evidences the same everyday life reflected by Dutch painters such as Pieter Jansz Saenredam (1597–1665), Gerard Houckgeest (*ca.* 1600–1661) and Emanuel de Witte (1615/17–1691/2) when they included graffiti in some of their church interiors (Figure 17.6).[72]

But in other cases graffiti were a persecuted written manifestation, either because they appropriated spaces of communication subject to regulation by different powers (from municipalities to universities), or because the messages inscribed on the walls transgressed the political and moral system. In Lyon, the municipality intervened in 1651 and 1680 against the profusion of unauthorized notices fixed on streets and squares, some even on the door of the City Hall, which in 1682 also had insolent graffiti drawn on its walls with charcoals, and red and black chalk.[73] The same willingness to regulate public spaces as places of writing could be seen in 1683 when the rector of the university of Rome issued an edict threatening to punish anyone who dared

> paint or write with charcoal, pencil, chalk, or any other instrument dishonest sayings or drawings, or any letters, signs, characters, verses, mottoes, lines, arms, or notices upon the walls, doors, columns, capitals, windows, or cornices or in any other way deface them, even if he paints or writes nice things.[74]

Figure 17.6   Pieter Jansz Saenredam, *The interior of the Buurkerk at Utrecht* (1644), oil on oak.
By permission of the National Gallery, London.

We now arrive at the end of this tour. Except for inscriptions in stone, most of the texts that circulated in the public space belong in the category of urban ephemera, some of them handwritten, and many printed. These are usually products whose preservation has been exceptional and quite often the result of factors that are far away from those that led to their writing in the first place. The fact that, for instance, the announcements of theological dissertations mostly came years after the Council of Trent has to do with their use as a repertoire of ideas for the Catholic reform.[75] Edicts and proclamations have been better preserved because they were kept as a testimony of the corresponding mandates and official provisions.[76] Additionally, a large part of the pasquinades and defamatory libels that have arrived to us were kept as evidence of conviction in judicial proceedings, constituting what Laura Antonucci called 'scrittura giudicata'.[77] Regarding propaganda, the most significant pieces usually come from private collectors, e.g. the collection of libels from the wars of religion in France gathered by the Parisian lawyer Pierre de l'Estoile (*ca.* 1546–1611) or the one grouped by the bookseller Georges Thomason (died 1666) with more than 22,000 pamphlets, broadsides, manuscripts, books and news sheets, mostly printed, distributed in London between 1640 and 1661.[78]

Irregular and precarious conservation causes some difficulties in the study of written communication as a global fact. Nevertheless, from this approach one can have a better perception of the plurality of texts destined for permanent or temporary placement on an exposed surface, or their itinerary and performance in the public space. Thus, writing took precedence and reading became essential. Appropriation then appears as a complex fact, provided that messages were plural, materiality varied and the target society was unequal. The reading of many libels was carried out aloud as a group activity, and this also happened with many of the printed ephemera disseminated on the streets. As indicated when discussing ballads, the key in the reception of texts read or recited on the streets was the relationship that the 'presenter' established with the audience, which involved a series of textual strategies: ways of addressing the public, exhortations to promote specific reactions and a colloquial language full of proverbs and sayings.[79]

In contrast, one can think about the complexity of certain iconographic programmes inserted in stone and ephemeral architectures, as well as the inscriptions linked to them. In many of these, Latin was used as an instrument of communication, as well as formulas that were not accessible to the general public. The writer and clergyman Brother Antonio de Guevara made this clear in an epistle to Jerónimo Vique on the subject of a Roman epitaph. There he confessed to be unable to read it despite repeatedly examining it, arguing how incomprehensible the Roman jargon of the epitaph was, concluding that 'to properly understand and read [it], it would be necessary for alive men to conjecture or for the writers to resurrect'.[80]

Overall, no element goes unnoticed when it comes to explaining the communicative fabric made up of all the texts that were fixed on the walls or publicly distributed on the streets. This graphic colonization of the early modern city emphasizes that written communication, then as now, should not be restricted to books or printed products.

Notes

1 L. Hellinga, *William Caxton and Early Printing in England*, London: The British Library, 2010, 54–5. The advertisement is kept in the Bodleian Library of Oxford, Inc. Cat., C-155.
2 Madrid, Biblioteca Nacional de España (BNE), MSS/13021, fol. 97. See also Madrid, National Library of Spain (BNE), MS 13,021, fol. 97. See also A. Castillo Gómez, *Entre la pluma y la pared. Una historia social de la escritura en los Siglos de Oro*, Madrid: Akal, 2006, 215.
3 H. Junghans, 'Luther's Wittenberg', in D.K. McKim (ed.), *The Cambridge Companion to Martin Luther*, New York: Cambridge University Press, 2003, 26.
4 S. Franklin, 'Mapping the Graphosphere: Cultures of Writing in Early 19th-Century Russia (and Before)', *Kritika: Explorations in Russian and Eurasian History* 12, No. 3, 2011, 531; S. Franklin, 'Information in Plain Sight: The Formation of the Public Graphosphere', in S. Franklin and K. Bowers (eds), *Information and Empire: Mechanisms of Communication in Russia, 1600–1854*, Cambridge: Open Books Publishers, 341–68; and S. Franklin, *The Russian Graphosphere, 1450–1850*, Cambridge: Cambridge University Press, 2019, 1–9.
5 M. Fogel, *Les cérémonies de l'information dans la France du XVIe au XVIIIe siècle*, Paris: Fayard, 1989, 105.

6 Madrid, Real Academia de la Historia, 9/3786 (21), fol. 1r.

7 In sixteenth-century France there were even specialized criers such as the 'crieurs des morts', who gradually lost their function as the use of printed 'billets' to announce death became established. Cf. P. Delaunay, *La vie médicale aux XVIe, XVIIe et XVIIIe siècles*, Nice: Éditions Hippocrate, 1935, 156.

8 N. Offenstadt, *En place publique: Jean de Gascogne, crieur au XVe siècle*, Paris: Les Essais, 2013.

9 S.J. Millner, '"… Fanno bandire, notificare et expressamente comandare …". Town Criers and the information economy of Renaissance Florence', *I Tatti Studies in the Italian Renaissance* 16/1–2, 2013, 107–51; I. Castro Rojas, 'Ordenar el universo de los signos. Bandos, pregones y espacio urbano en España y América durante la Edad Moderna', *LaborHistórico* 2/1, 2016, 16–29; C. Judde de Larivière, 'Voicing Popular Politics: The Town Crier of Murano in the Sixteenth Century', in S. Dall'Aglio, B. Richardson and M. Rospocher (eds), *Voices and Texts in Early Modern Italian Society*, London and New York: Routledge, 2017, 37–50; and I. Castro Rojas, *'A noticia de todos'. Bandos, pregones y mandatos del poder en el Madrid de los Austrias (siglos XVI–XVII)*, doctoral thesis, University of Alcalá, 2019.

10 A.M. Hespanha, *La gracia del derecho. Economía de la cultura en la Edad Moderna*, Madrid: Centro de Estudios Constitucionales, 1993, 131.

11 Madrid, Archivo Histórico Nacional, *Inquisición*, Lib. 781, fol. 298v. On the prohibition of Quietism in Sardinia, cf. A. Rundine, *Inquisizione spagnola, censura e libri proibiti in Sardegna nel '500 e '600*, Sassari: Università di Sassari, 1996, 168.

12 *Constituçoens synodaes do arcebispado de Braga, ordenadas no anno de 1639*, Lisbon: M. Deslandes, 1697, 650.

13 C. Jouhaud, 'Lisibilité et persuasion. Les placards politiques', in R. Chartier (ed.), *Les usages del'imprimé (XVᵉ–XIXᵉ siècles)*, Paris: Fayard, 1987, 311–12.

14 C. Evangelisti, 'Libelli famosi: processi per scritte infamanti nella Bologna di fine 500', *Annali della Fondazione Luigi Einaudi* XXVI, 1992, 181–239; and C. Evangelisti, '"Accepto calamo, manu propria scripsit". Prove e perizie grafiche nella Bologna di fine Cinquecento', *Scrittura e Civiltà* 19, 1995, 251–75. Currently in her book, *Parlare, scrivere, vivere nell'Italia di fine Cinquecento. Quattro saggi*, Rome: Carocci, 2018, 13–87.

15 V. Marucci (ed.), *Pasquinate del cinque e seicento*, Rome: Salerno, 1988; C. Lastraioli, *Pasquinate, grillate, pelate e altro Cinquecento librario minore*, Rome: Vecchiarelli, 2012; C. Damianati and A. Romano (eds), *Pasquin, Lord of Satire, and His Disciples in 16th-Century Struggles for Religious and Political Reform/Pasquino, signore della satira, e la lotta dei suoi discepoli per la riforma religiosa e politica nel Cinquecento*, London: The Warburg Institute; Rome: Edizioni di Storia e Letteratura, 2014.

16 F. Nuñez Roldán, *La vida cotidiana en la Sevilla del Siglo de Oro*, Madrid: Silex, 2004, 15–16; J. Deleito y Piñuela, *Sólo Madrid es corte (La capital de dos mundos bajo Felipe IV)*, Madrid: Espasa-Calpe, 1942, 208–23; and C. Moreno Sánchez, 'Los mentideros de Madrid', *Torre de los Lujanes* 18, 1991, 155–72.

17 R. Salzberg, *Ephemeral City: Cheap Print and Urban Culture in Renaissance Venice*, Manchester: Manchester University Press, 2014, 158.

18 F. de los Reyes, *El libro en España y América: legislación y censura: siglos XV–XVIII*, Madrid: Arco/Libros, 2000, vol. II, 846–7.

19 F.S. Sieber, *Freedom of the Press in England, 1476–1776: The Rise and Decline of Government Controls*, Urbana, IL: University of Illinois Press, 1965 (first edition, 1952), 157.

20 D. McKenzie and M. Bell, *A Chronology and Calendar of Documents Relating to the London Book Trade, 1641–1700*, vol. I, *1671–1685*, Oxford: Oxford University Press, 2005, dd. 13-10-1681. Regarding the censorship of ballads, N. Würzbach, *The Rise of the English*

Street Ballad, 1550–1650, Cambridge: Cambridge University Press, 1990 (original German edn, 1981), 23–6.

21 Ciudad de México, Archivo General de la Nación, *Inquisición*, vol. 337, exp. 12, f. 376r.

22 R. Salzberg, L. Degl'Innocenti and M. Rospocher (eds), *The Cantastorie in Renaissance Italy: Street Singers between Oral and Literate Cultures*, Italian Studies 71/2, 2016, 149–258; A. Iglesias Castellano, 'Los ciegos: profesionales de la información. Invención, edición y difusión de la literatura de cordel (siglos XVI–XVIII)', in G. Ciappelli and V. Nider (eds), *La invención de las noticias. Las relaciones de sucesos entre la literatura y la información (siglos XVI–XVIII)*, Trent: Università degli Studi di Trento, 2017, 467–89; and A. Iglesias Castellano, *Entre la voz y el texto. Los ciegos oracioneros y papelistas en la España Moderna (1500–1836)*, doctoral thesis, University of Alcalá, 2019.

23 *Fiestas que la ciudad de Lisboa tiene prevenidas para recibir a la católica Magestad del Rey don Felipe III nuestro señor* [Seville: Francisco de Lyra, 1619]. Cited in N. Pena Sueiro, 'Los autores de las relaciones de sucesos: primeras precisiones', in Ciappelli and Nider, *La invención de las noticias*, 46, note 20, where she points to the fact that the warning is not present in all the copies.

24 Regarding this editorial genre and its news natures, H. Ettinghausen, *How the Press Began: The Pre-Periodical Printed News in Early Modern Europe*, A Coruña: SIELAE, 2015; Ciappelli and Nider, *La invención de las noticias*.

25 R. Perry, 'War and the Media in Border Minstrelsy: The Ballad of Chevy Chase', in P. Fumerton, A. Guerrini and K. McAbee (eds), *Ballads and Broadsides in Britain, 1500–1800*, Burlington, VT: Ashgate, 2010, 253.

26 T. Watt, *Cheap Print and Popular Piety, 1550–1640*, Cambridge: Cambridge University Press, 1991, 141. See also, J. Hyde, *Singing the News: Ballads in Mid-Tudor England*, New York: Routledge, 2018.

27 R. Chartier, *The Author's Hand and the Printer's Mind: Transformations of the Written Word in Early Modern Europe*, Cambridge: Polity Press, 2014, 11–12; and previously R. Chartier and P. Stalybrass, 'What Is a Book?', in N. Fraistat and J. Flander (eds), *The Cambridge Companion to Textual Scholarship*, Cambridge: Cambridge University Press, 2013, 188–204.

28 D.F. McKenzie, *Bibliography and the Sociology of Texts*, Cambridge: Cambridge University Press, 1999, 51.

29 F. Bruni, 'In the Name of God: Governance, Public Order and Theocracy in the Broadsheets of the Stamperia Camerale of Rome', in A. Pettegree (ed.), *Broadsheets: Single-Sheet Publishing in the First Age of Print*, Leiden: Brill, 2017, 139–61.

30 *Editto del S. Offitio*, Rome: Stamperia Camerale, 1677. Rome, Casanatense Library, PER, est.18.14 58.

31 A. Castillo Gómez, '"Salió también, de la parte de la ciudad, un cartel impreso". Usos expuestos del escrito en los certámenes del Siglo de Oro', *TECA. Testimonianze, editoria, cultura, arte* 0 (2011), 11–34.

32 A. Pettegree, 'Broadsheets: Single-Sheet Publishing in the First Age of Print Typology and Typography', in Pettegree, *Broadsheets*, 23.

33 R. Kirwn, 'Function in Form: Single-Sheet Items and the Utility of Cheap Print in the Early Modern German University', in Pettegree, *Broadsheets*, 337–54; M. Walsby, 'Cheap Print and the Academic Market: The Printing of Dissertations in Sixteenth-Century Louvain', in Pettegree, *Broadsheets*, 365–6; and R.M. Fernández de Zamora, *Las tesis universitarias en México. Una tradición y un patrimonio en vilo*, Mexico City: Universidad Autónoma de México, 2015, 21–2.

34 J. Díaz Rengifo, *Arte poética española*, Madrid: Ministerio de Educación y Ciencia, 1977, 83.

35 F. de Rois y Mendoza, *Pyra real que erigió la maior Athenas a la maior Majestad; la Universidad de Salamanca a las inmortales çeniças, a la gloriosa memoria de su Rey y Señor D. Phelipe IV el grande*, Salamanca: Melchor Estévez, 1666, 433.

36 A. Petrucci, 'Escritura como invención, escritura como expresión', in A. Petrucci, *Alfabetismo, escritura, sociedad*, Barcelona: Gedisa, 1999, 171–80.

37 J.G. Gevaerts, *Pompa introitus honori Serenissimi Principis Ferdinandi Austriaci hispaniarum Infantis S. R. E. Card. Belgarum et Burgundionum gubernatoris*, Antwerp: Ioannes Meursius, 1641. See P. Laurens and F. Vuilleumier Laurens, *L'âge de l'inscription*, Paris: Belles Lettres, 2010, 141–55.

38 Petrucci, *Public Lettering: Script, Power, and Culture*, Chicago, IL: University of Chicago Press, 1993 (original Italian edn, 1986), 16–21.

39 A. Paolucci, *Scrittura e simboli del potere pontificio in età moderna. Lapidi e stemmi sui muri di Roma*, Rome: Artemide, 2016, 9. Regarding papal epigraphy, the paradigm of visual value, see also L. Kajanto, *Papal Epigraphy in Renaissance Rome*, Helsinki: Suomalainen Tiedeakatemia Toimituksia, 1982.

40 Petrucci, *Public Lettering*, 36–9.

41 A. Béroujon, *Les écrits à Lyon au XVIIᵉ siècle. Espaces, échanges, identités*, Grenoble: Presses universitaires de Grenoble, 2009, 137–44.

42 A. Petrucci, *Writing the Dead: Death and Writing Strategies in the Western Tradition*, Stanford, CA: Stanford University Press, 1998, 92.

43 P. Sherlock, *Monuments and Memory in Early Modern England*, New York: Routledge, 2016, 161–3.

44 C. de Giorgio, *The Image of Triumph and the Kinghts of Malta*, Malta: privately printed, 2003, 102–30.

45 R.W. Scribner, *For the Sake of Simple Folk: Popular Propaganda for the German Reformation*, Oxford: Clarendon Press, 1994.

46 A. Castillo Gómez, 'Letras de penitencia. Denuncia y castigo públicos en la España altomoderna', *Via Spiritus* 15, 2008, 53–74; M. Peña Díaz, 'Memoria inquisitorial y vida cotidiana en el mundo hispánico', in A. Atienza López (ed.), *Iglesia memorable. Crónicas, historias, escritos … a mayor gloria. Siglos XVI–XVIII*, Madrid: Silex, 2012, 187–203; and L.R. Corteguera, *Death by Effigy: A Case from the Mexican Inquisition*, Philadelphia, PA: University of Pennsylvania Press, 2012, 120–7.

47 G. Ortalli, *La pittura infamante, secoli XIII–XVI*, new edn, Rome: Viella, 2015; G. Bent, *Public Painting and Visual Culture in Early Republican Florence*, Cambridge: Cambridge University Press, 2016, 105–33.

48 A. Petrucci (ed.), *Scrittura e popolo nella Roma Barocca, 1585–1721*, Rome: Edizioni Quasar, 1982, 78–9; Evangelisti, '"Accepto calamo"', fig. 5 and 15.

49 D. Garrioch, 'House Names, Shop Signs and Social Organization in Western European cities, 1500–1900', *Urban History* 21/1, 1994, 20–48; E. Welch, *Shopping in the Renaissance: Consumer Cultures in Italy, 1400–1600*, New York and London: Yale University Press, 2005, 137–9.

50 M. Knights, *Politics and Opinion in Crisis, 1678–81*, Cambridge: Cambridge University Press, 2006 (first edn, 1994), 149.

51 Paolucci, *Scrittura e simboli del potere*, 9.

52 Valladolid, Archivo General de Simancas, *Patronato Real*, leg. 72, doc. 71, f. 1029r.

53 AHN, *Inquisición*, leg. 1647/1, exp. 3, f. 35r.

54 A. Castillo Gómez, *Leer y oír leer. Ensayos sobre la lectura en los Siglos de Oro*, Madrid: Iberoamericana; Frankfurt am Main: Vervuert, 2016, 121–52.

55 AHN, Inquisición, Leg. 1731, exp. 53, num. 24, fol. 149r. About this figure, J. Meza González, *El laberinto de la mentira. Guillén de Lamporte y la Inquisición*, Mexico City:

Universidad Autónoma Metropolitana-Unidad Xochimilco, 2002 (first edn, 1997);
F. Troncarelli, *La spada e la croce. Guillen Lombardo e l'Inquisizione in Messico*, Rome:
Salerno, 1999; N. Silva Prada, 'Orígenes de una leyenda en el siglo XVII: redes irland-
esas de comunicación y propaganda política en los casos inquisitoriales novohispanos
de Guillermo Lombardo y fray Diego de la Cruz', *Signos Históricos* 22, 2009, 8–43;
K. Lynn, *Between Court and Confessional: The Politics of Spanish Inquisitors*, Cambridge:
Cambridge University Press, 2013, 238–93.

56 P.A.M. Geurts, *De Nederlandse Opstand in de Pamfletten, 1566–1584*, Utrecht: HES
Publishers, 1978, 299. Cited in I. Schulze Schneider, *La leyenda negra de España: propaganda en la guerra de Flandes, 1566–1584*, Madrid: Universidad Complutense de Madrid,
2008, 96.

57 Schulze Schneider, *La leyenda negra de España*, 80. Se also H. de Schepper, 'La "guerra
de Flandes". Una sinopsis de su leyenda negra (1550–1650)', in J. Lechner (ed.), *Contactos
entre los Países Bajos y el mundo ibérico*, Amsterdam-Atlanta: Rodopi, 1992, 67–86.

58 R. García Cárcel, *El demonio del sur. La leyenda negra de Felipe II*, Madrid: Cátedra, 2017,
206–22.

59 J. Versele, 'La diffusion et le contrôle des idées associées à la révolte des Pays-Bas', in
A. Hugon and A. Merle (eds), *Soulèvements, révoltes, révolutions dans l'empire des Habsbourg
d'Espagne, XVIᵉ–XVIIᵉ siécle*, Madrid: Casa de Velázquez, 2016, 148–55.

60 J.K. Sawyer, *Printed Poison: Pamphlet Propaganda, Faction Politics, and the Public Sphere in
Early Seventeenth-Century France*, Berkeley, CA: University of California Press, 1990; A.
Halasz, *The Marketplace of Print: Pamphlets and the Public Sphere in Early Modern England*,
Cambridge: Cambridge University Press, 1997; D. Freist, *Governed by Opinion: Politics,
Religion and the Dynamics of Communication in Stuart London, 1637–1645*, London: I.B.
Tauris, 1997; J. Van Horn Melton (ed.), *Cultures of Communication from Reformation to
Enlightenment: Constructing Publics in the Early Modern German Lands*, Aldershot: Ashgate,
2002; S. Landi, *Naissance de l'opinion publique dans l'Italie moderne. Sagesse du people et savoir
de gouvernement de Machiavel aux Lumières*, Rennes: Presses universitaires de Rennes,
2006; and M. Rospocher (ed.), *Beyond the Public Sphere: Opinions, Publics, Spaces in Early
Modern Europe*, Bologna: Il Mulino; Berlin: Duncker & Humblot, 2012.

61 T. Debbagi Baranova, *À coups de libelles. Une culture politique au temps des guerres de religion
(1562–1598)*, Geneva: Droz, 2012, 337.

62 J. Freire Serrão, *Discurso político da excelencia do aborrecimento, perseguição & zelo da verdade*,
Lisbon: Lourenço de Anveres, 1647, 134; and D. Ramada Curto, *O discurso político em
Portugal (1600–1650)*, Lisbon: Centro de Estudos de História e Cultura Portuguesa,
Projecto Universidade Aberta, 1988, 143–55.

63 Cited in J. Raymond, *Pamphlets and Pamphleteering in Early Modern Britain*, Cambridge:
Cambridge University Press, 2003, 161.

64 Cited in A. Espino López, 'Publicística y guerra de opinión. El caso catalán durante la
guerra de los nueve años, 1689–1697', *Studia Historica. Historia Moderna* 14, 1996, 177.

65 Colima (México), Archivo Histórico Municipal, Sección A, caja 26, exp. 84. About
this event, see J.M. Romero de Solís, '"Estos cleriquillos con sus penillas y sus nadas".
Expresiones anticlericales en la Villa de Colima de la Nueva España (siglo XVI)', in F.
Savarino and A. Mutolo (eds), *El anticlericalismo en México*, Mexico City: Instituto Tec-
nológico y de Estudios Superiores de Monterrey-Miguel Ángel Porrúa, 2008, 136–50.

66 F. De Vivo, *Information and Communication in Venice: Rethinking Early Modern Politics*,
Oxford: Oxford University Press, 2007, 132–3.

67 A. Hugon, *Naples insurgée, 1647–1648. De l'événement à la memoire*, Rennes: Presses universitaires de Rennes, 2011, 291–326.

68 Franklin, 'Information in Plain Sight', 348; Franklin, *The Russian Graphosphere*, 148.

69 I. Joseph, *La ville sans qualitès*, Paris: Éditions de l'Aube, 1998, 6.

70 For the concept of 'writing acts', refer to B. Fraenkel, 'Writing Acts: When Writing Is Doing', in D. Barton and U. Papen (eds), *The Anthropology of Writing: Understanding Textually Mediated Words*, London and New York: Continuum, 2010, 33–44.

71 J. Fleming, *Graffiti and the Writing Arts of Early Modern England*, London: Reaktion Books, 2001, 29–72; R. Sarti, 'Renaissance Graffiti: The Case of the Ducal Palace of Urbino', in S. Cavallo and S. Evangelisti (eds), *Domestic Institutional Interiors in Early Modern Europe* (Surrey and Burlington, VT: Ashgate, 2009), 51–81; V. Plesch, 'Using or Abusing? On the Significance of Graffiti on Religious Mural Paintings', in L. Afonso and V. Serrão (eds), *Out of the Stream: New Directions in the Study of Mural Painting*, Newcastle: Cambridge Scholars Press, 2007, 42–68; V. Plesch, 'Come capire i graffiti di Arborio?', in M. Leone (ed.), *Immagini efficaci/Efficacious images*, *Lexia. Rivista di semiotica* 17–18, 2014, 127–47; C. Guichard, *Graffitis. Inscrire son nom à Rome (XVIe–XIXe siècle)*, Paris: Seuil, 2014; R. Sarti (ed.), *La pietra racconta. Un palazzo da leggere*, Urbino: Galleria Nazionale delle Marche – ISIA Urbino – Università degli Studi di Urbino, 2017.

72 The reference about Gerard Houckgeest has been provided to me by Alessandro Arcangeli.

73 Béroujon, *Les écrits à Lyon*, 158–9.

74 Cited in Petrucci, *Public Lettering*, 93.

75 Walsby, 'Cheap Print and the Academic Market', in Pettegree, *Broadsheets*, 367.

76 F. Bruni, 'Early Modern Broadsheets between Archives and Libraries: Toward a Possible Integration', in Pettegree, *Broadsheets*, 33–54.

77 L. Antonucci, 'La scrittura giudicata. Perizie grafiche in processi romani del primo Seicento', *Scrittura e Civiltà* 13, 1989, 489–534.

78 P. de l'Estoile, *Les belles figures et drolleries de la Ligue*, ed. G. Schrenck, Geneva: Droz, 2016; G. Thomason, *Catalogue of the Pamphlets, Books, Newspapers, and Manuscripts Relating to the Civil War, the Commonwealth, and Restoration, collected by George Thomason, 1640–1661*, London: William Cowper and Sons, 1908, 2 vols. It constitutes the Thomason Collection of Civil War Tracts of the British Library.

79 Würzbach, *The Rise of the English Street Ballad*, 54–74.

80 A. de Guevara, *Libro primero de las epístolas familiares*, Valladolid, Juan de Villaquirán, 1541 (first edition 1539), fol. 37r.

18

MOBILITY, GLOBAL INTERACTION AND CULTURAL TRANSFERS IN THE AGE OF EXPLORATION

Giuseppe Marcocci

Introduction: a shared world

A globe displaying the eastern hemisphere is the focal point of the scene. It attracts the eyes and gestures of two groups of men who stand at its sides in the same posture. On the left, there are six Europeans, wearing fine clothes that follow the fashion of their respective countries. On the right, there are six other men whose origins are in Africa, the Americas and Asia, and whose attires correspond to what the Europeans then attributed to the inhabitants of the parts of the world they came from. Realized by the French engraver Jean Picart, this picture (Figure 18.1) stands out in the title page of *Le Monde, ou la Description generale des ses quatre parties*, published in Paris in 1637. A work by Pierre d'Avity, a man of arms and a geographer, who had recently passed away, this five-volume collection of information about empires, kingdoms, states and republics of the world has more than a general resemblance with the *Relationi universali* (1591–96) by the Italian Giovanni Botero. Picart's engraving expresses a clear religious hierarchy. A representation of God as the source of light with the tetragram 'Yahweh' written in Hebrew, dividing the sky into two parts, dominates the globe. The six Europeans are in the sunny part, enlightened by the Christian faith, while the other six men are shrouded in the darkness of error. This asymmetry mirrors the most common opinion among d'Avity's readers, and more in general the mid-seventeenth-century Europeans, about their own superiority. However, it does not annul the overall message of the picture, particularly in its lower section: that is, the consciousness that, by then, the world was a shared object, whose understanding was a matter for all its inhabitants.

The sense of this sharing, which was destined to change deeply over time, emerged during the sixteenth century, a period marked by an increasing global balance fostered by great empires whose rise coincided with an age of exploration and widening of the scope of long-distance trade. From eastern Asia to the Atlantic world, however, each of these empires originated from wars and conquests, a story that reminds us of the grounds of violence of a connecting world. Partly for this reason, the process

Figure 18.1 Jean Picart, *A globe between people from different parts of the world*, engraving.

Detail from the frontispiece of Pierre d'Avity, *Le Monde, ou La description generale des see quatre parties avec tous ses empires, royaumes, estats et republiques. Paris:* Pierre Billaine, 1637, vol. 1.

that some present-day historians call the 'first globalization' was contemplated from different points of view, which encouraged misperception and bias. The distinctive feature of what we may describe more properly as a multiplication of interactions and exchanges among the different parts of the globe, far from being uniform in its spread and linear in its developments, was its polycentric nature. It was the versatile product of impulses with a variety of inspirations and geographical origins, which make this phenomenon especially complex and difficult to study.

All that is even truer in the case of the cultural encounters that resulted from an unprecedented circulation of people across the planet. Behaviours and traditions, languages and writings of any kind came into contact with unexpected outcomes, which we know only in part. Yet, with all the limits and resistance that were associated with the mixing of ideas and knowledge that sprang from contacts and transfers at multiple levels, some cultural commensurability emerged, confirming the possibility of communication between individuals and groups of radically different origins. This new understanding has changed our way of looking at the relationship between culture and mobility. After the enthusiasm of scholars in the period between the 1990s and 2000s for 'brave theories of hybridity, network theory, and the complex flows of people, goods, money, and information across endlessly shifting social landscape', emphasis has been placed on the need to work out 'new ways to understand the vitally important dialectic of cultural persistence and change', though any attempt to project on a given culture 'the assumption that the originary condition was one of fixity and coherence' is now recognized as an illusion.[1] The early modern period was marked by an acceleration of the cultural effects of the mobility of people, objects and ideas. Yet feeling cosmopolitan was an exception in that world. Many travelled with fear and reluctance. Others became 'agents of globalization' against their will, promoting cultural transfers that were an unintentional consequence of other aims, such as the Catholic missionaries often did.[2]

A key distinction that will be considered in greater detail in the final section of this chapter is that between individual and group mobility, something that has enjoyed a renewed interest in recent times for the possibility of keeping together itineraries across the globe and the cultural variety of the localities that were touched. However, any exploration of the consequences of cultural mobility on a global scale from a European perspective should convey a clear sense of the distance that separates the early modern world from the present, rejecting any partition into well-defined areas competing one with another, which has long nourished the master narrative of the so-called 'rise of the West'. Not only did most of the inhabitants of Europe and the Americas have anything but the same culture between the mid-fifteenth and early eighteenth centuries, but they largely took part in, and contributed to, the same process of cultural transformations that women and men from many other parts of the world were experiencing in that period. The examples that follow aim at showing some aspects of this process, which are the more surprising the more they have been forgotten.

Obstacles and encounters when travelling across the globe

Boundless powers in constant communication, early modern empires expanded across the majority of the Eurasian and central and south American continents, vast regions of Africa and increasing spaces along the east coast and the great lakes of north America, as well as controlling more or less successfully the oceanic routes. A variety of people of different cultures and beliefs coexisted within the shifting borders of empires, usually under distinctive legal regimes. The existence of great empires encouraged mobility and exchanges, with obvious cultural effects, through itineraries and port cities which became hubs of commerce on a global scale. However, this should not be exaggerated. Circulation across the early modern world was anything but free, though the lack of a widespread system of personal identification made it easier for people to change identity and move under false pretences.[3]

It was necessary to find such ways even during the union of the crowns of Portugal and Spain (1580–1640), when their respective overseas possessions formed a 'composite empire', whose extent literally encompassed the world, promoting cross-cultural dynamics that have been described as 'Iberian globalization'.[4] A case in point is that of the Florentine merchant Francesco Carletti, who accomplished the first voyage around the globe with no political purpose (1594–1602). His travel account provides a repertoire not only of the obstacles that stood in the way of those who tried to get around the prohibition of passing from one empire to the other, but also of the troubles faced by those who attempted to move across only one, all the more if they were not subjects of the respective crown. The main stops in Carletti's voyage constitute a list of some of the most important crossroads of global interactions.

Setting sail as an agent of a Tuscan merchant's Spanish wife, who was his figure-head in dealings with the *Casa de Contratación*, Carletti travelled from Seville to the Cape Verde islands, where he intended to trade slaves with the New World. His father Antonio stowed away on the same ship. Once they reached America, only a few letters patent written in his favour by Pietro de' Medici, brother of the grand duke of Tuscany, to the governor of Cartagena de Indias allowed Carletti to be released from prison, where he had been sent with the charge of illegal importation of slaves. These letters ensured for him the privilege 'to stay, travel and negotiate in all those west Indies just as though we had been native Spaniards of the kingdoms of Castile'.[5] This did not prevent Carletti from paying the viceroy of Peru a large sum for the licence to move with his goods from Lima to Mexico City. If crossing the Pacific Ocean through the route Acapulco-Manila proved easier, this was not the case with the imaginary border between the Spanish and Portuguese empires in Asia. In order to pass through it, Carletti embarked secretly, by night, without the necessary permission of the governor of the Philippines, navigating to Japan, which was considered outside any Iberian jurisdiction or sphere of influence. However, his plan to enter the Portuguese empire without attracting attention, through the enclave of Macao, in China (where he arrived after a journey tormented by a furious fight between Portuguese merchants and Japanese sailors on a ship commanded by a mestizo pilot), failed. The strategy of hiding in the local college of the Jesuits, where, incidentally, Carletti met the famous missionary Alessandro Valignano, did not suffice to protect him from arrest once again for the rumours about the money he had brought with him and the business deals he wanted to conclude. He defended himself in front of a Portuguese magistrate, declaring that he was travelling 'for our own amusement and curiosity but for no other interests nor for anything that overlooked or contravened the royal orders of either the one crown or the other'. Indeed, since in that situation it was more advisable for Carletti to present himself for what he really was, this time he stressed that he was 'of the Italian nations' and that 'moving about the world was a thing allowed to all the nations'.[6] He was released with the order to reach Goa, the capital city of Portuguese Asia, and present himself to the viceroy who would decide his fate. We do not know if Carletti obeyed, but certainly he continued his itinerary up to that destination. After spending almost two years there, he made an agreement with a Portuguese pilot and bought some space for his merchandise in the ship from imperial officials who had the right to bring a certain amount of goods on their return to the kingdom without inspections at customs. Thus, on Christmas Day 1601 he left Goa for Lisbon together with three servants, a Japanese, a Korean (renamed Antonio, who was living in Rome in the early seventeenth century) and one native of southeast Africa.

Carletti's odyssey required him to resort to cultural practices that were typical of those moving across the early modern world, even closer to home. His case stands out, not only because it includes many different subterfuges in one journey, but also for the discussion of the routes and time to complete a voyage around the world, estimated to be four years – it took Carletti twice as long – except for unexpected obstacles like the decisive event when the Portuguese fleet in which Carletti was travelling was assailed on the high seas and captured by the Dutch. On this occasion, together with his merchandise he claimed to have lost the 'writings and memoranda' that he had written *en route*.[7] Be that a literary device or not, once he was back in Florence in 1606, this supposed loss gave Carletti the justification to send the grand duke of Tuscany a report of his ups and downs, the content of which is clearly fictional in part. There is nothing surprising in this. The increase of mobility on a global scale in the age of exploration was associated with an explosion of travel literature, culminating in great collections like the *Navigationi et Viaggi* (1550–1606), edited by the Venetian Giovanni Battista Ramusio and the *Principall Navigations* (1589), assembled by Richard Hakluyt. Even a history of the world in the form of an account of terrestrial and maritime travels since antiquity saw the light in 1563. It was written by António Galvão, a Portuguese who had served his king in the Moluccas islands. Like many medieval precedents from Marco Polo to Mandeville, these texts did not lack fictional touches, which were designed to make them more engaging, or edifying in the case of missionary reports, especially the Jesuit letters, which became a fundamental source of information about the world in early modern Europe. Hence, the status of travel literature was ambivalent and often uncertain for the readership, as is shown by the trust given to another Portuguese author, Fernão Mendes Pinto, whose *Peregrinação*, published posthumously in 1614, is an account of his stay in south and east Asia (1537–58) that blends together reality and invention in a very particular way.[8]

A great deal of what we know about global mobility in the early modern period, as well as the kind of knowledge that it circulated, comes from this kind of literature. Carletti's report provides a careful description of the natural environment and material culture of the localities he visited, techniques in use among their inhabitants and urban architectural styles. In certain cases, comparisons are developed as in the case of the manners of the Japanese which, as the Jesuit Luís Fróis had done a few years before, Carletti describes as the exact opposite of the Europeans, establishing, however, a connection with the Turks in their way of sitting and in the men's clothes.[9] Moreover, in that global city that Seville was, before his departure Carletti had certainly met *Chinos*, as those coming from the regions between southeast Asia and China were generically called in Spain, being the trace of a diaspora that contributed to giving early modern mobility its global character.[10] Perhaps he thought of them when he encountered the Chinese community of Manila, the *Sangleys*, although he grasped signs of mistrust by the Spaniards that were to result in the massacre of 1603.[11]

Carletti did not limit himself to describing the world he saw, but also took away some valuable fragments of it, such as the seeds of Japanese citrus that he sent to the grand duke of Tuscany and that the wealthy magnate Francesco Capponi tried to grow with meagre results, probably in the garden of his villa at Quinto, where he had a collection of extremely rare flowers and plants. Carletti also brought to Florence a printed Chinese atlas with annotated illustrations, almost certainly bought in Macao, which has been identified with the *Kuang Yü K'ao* by Wang Fêng Yü.[12] A late sixteenth-century result of a number of reworkings of the fourteenth-century map by Chu Ssu-pên (now lost), it made its way to the Medici collection, which already contained a wealth of Asiatic objects and curiosities.[13] Half a century before the difficulty experienced by John Selden at Oxford, when, with the help of a Chinese assistant, he tried to decipher a Chinese map he had come into possession of, Carletti suggested the grand duke have these 'books of the geography of China' interpreted 'when some religious may arrive from those parts and know and understand those hieroglyphic characters'.[14]

The case of Carletti demonstrates the variety of the possible entanglements between mobility and cultural transfer that, despite many obstacles, encounters disclosed to those who travelled across the early modern world. In doing so, it also confirms the brilliant thesis of the key role of trade culture in the exchange of knowledge on a global scale, proposed by Harold J. Cook for the Dutch, which can be extended to earlier merchants from other parts of Europe.[15]

Gifts, clothes and texts out of place

Mobility of people went hand in hand with the mobility of objects, currently a significant field of investigation. In focusing on the criteria for selecting, classifying and displaying that were adopted in early modern public and private collections, historians aim to understand better how the age of exploration contributed to transforming Europeans' knowledge of the world and the ways of organizing it. Moreover, things, too, could have global lives, circulating across the planet and putting its most distant parts into contact.[16] Thus, they often mediated between different cultures, bringing together styles, themes and materials, which lent them a hybrid character. Not always did the journeys of rarities and curiosities end in princely wardrobes or the cabinets of obscure antiquarians and naturalists. Sometimes they set off again, thus gaining new significance and establishing unexpected connections.

This happened to an American feather work depicting an *Ecce Homo*. In the aftermath of the Spanish conquest, a European public quickly emerged for handiwork from the New World that expressed the indigenous artistic and artisanal production.[17] Already after the return of Hernán Cortés from Mexico, it was clear that many of these objects had a mixed nature, because they were made by natives at the request of Spaniards, who commissioned them according to the taste of those to whom they intended to bring them as gifts.[18] In the first half of the sixteenth century, it became usual for those who returned from America to offer monarchs and powerful protectors in Europe works of this kind, which left many traces in inventories and other sources of that period. This is not so in the case of the *Ecce Homo* mentioned above, which was very probably a retable 'having the size of a quarter paper of higher quality, strange shape and material', 'a great gift' which had been sent 'from the west Indies' – almost surely, Mexico – to Queen Catherine of Habsburg, grandmother of the current king of Portugal, Sebastian I.[19] Although many feather works represented sacred scenes, the iconographic theme of Catherine's retable does not seem to have been among the most recurring ones, though other exemplars reproduce it, such as the pendant reliquary from Mexico, today at The Walters Art Museum in Baltimore (Figure 18.2). These devotional objects were usually produced by converted *Indios* under the guidance of missionaries. The *Ecce Homo* was not the first American item to enter Catherine's collection. The queen already had in her chapel another small retable of coloured feathers depicting her brother, Emperor Charles V, in adoration of Christ on the Cross, which was probably made in Mexico, though she owned many more rarities and jewels of Asiatic origin.[20]

Figure 18.2   Pendant in the Shape of a Lantern with Crucifixion and Ecce Homo (side B), Mexico, ca. 1550–1600, boxwood, hummingbird feathers, rock crystal, gold,
enamel, pigments, pearls. Baltimore, The Walters Art Museum.

Catherine might have come into possession of the *Ecce Homo* during her regency
of Portugal (1557–62). Certainly, it is not explicitly recorded in the (incomplete)
inventory of her treasure, prepared in 1558.[21] In March 1569, the retable was in the
queen's *recâmara*, but was removed from it on the occasion of the ruinous expedition for the conquest of the so-called 'Munumutapa Empire', a tributary regime in
southeast Africa headed by the *mwene mutapa* ('ravager of the lands'). We know this
story thanks to the Jesuit Francisco Monclaro, who repeated it in a long report of the
expedition that he wrote a few years later from Goa. Initially against that undertaking,
Catherine had exposed herself to the elements (*muitas chuvas e invernadas*) to reach
the royal court at Almeirim and persuade her grandson Sebastian I to back out of his
proposals, but at last she gave up. Then she put into the hands of Jesuit missionaries
who were to take part in the expedition 'some devotional objects (*algumas peças devo-
tas*)', which may have been displayed until then in her chapel or oratory, to be offered
to the *mwene mutapa* if he converted to Christianity, for which there were high hopes
at the Portuguese court. Father Monclaro describes the *Ecce Homo* as follows: 'It was
made of bird feathers, so delicate as regards their colours and so well arranged that it
reproduced the picture of Christ in that passage with great realism (*muy ao natural*)'.[22]

The choice of entrusting an American object with the task of supporting the possible Catholic faith of an African ruler reveals Catherine's peculiar, if not limited, understanding of cultural difference. But what matters here is the global life that mobility gave to the retable, transforming the significance attributed to it at every stage of its travels from the west Indies to southeast Africa, through the Iberian Peninsula. In this manner, an object could become a material go-between, establishing a sort of changing and itinerant 'middle ground': from the expression of the new mestizo art that was developing in Spanish America as tangible demonstration of the successful conversion of *Indios*, to a devotional curiosity for the overflowing private rooms of a European queen, or assuming the role of a tool for consolidating the conversion of the *mwene mutapa*.[23] If he ever received this gift – we only know that he was visited by the Portuguese ambassador Francisco Rafaxo, who offered him 'valuable objects (*peças ricas*)' – he certainly interpreted its content and origin rather differently from both the missionaries in the New World and Queen Catherine in Portugal.[24] However, we may suppose that at least the *mwene mutapa* would have been able to understand the political context and religious aim of the gift. Meanwhile, in the following decades, travelling through the Pacific Ocean, Mexican feather works also reached Japan and the Chinese court of the Wanli Emperor.[25]

The cultural transfers encouraged by the planetary circulation of these objects were just one of the possible outcomes of the material exchanges that were connected to the practice of offering gifts on the occasion of diplomatic missions and contacts, which has enjoyed increasing attention from historians.[26] The ability to adapt presents to the recipients' expectations had great importance in avoiding unpleasant mistakes and incidents, which not infrequently assumed the form of visual insults at Eurasian courts.[27] In any case, encounters among etiquettes and rituals from culturally different worlds could always produce 'implicit understandings', finding points of intersection.[28] This is shown, for example, by the Jesuit Alessandro Valignano's treatise on the Japanese ceremonies (1582), in which missionaries were carefully taught about the respectful manners to which they had to conform on the most various occasions. This adaptation strategy (*accommodatio*) was probably one of the most sophisticated attempts to negotiate European culture, particularly Catholicism, and included wearing clothes that were in current use in the societies where the missionaries acted, usually among the higher strata. As is demonstrated by the case of the Jesuit Robert Nobili, who dressed as a Brahmin Sannyasin in Madurai, South India, and his coreligionists in China, who went about looking like local high officials, the main goal was to use clothes to convey a message that allowed them to be perceived as important figures, thus gaining enough respect to be listened to and, ultimately, be successful in their work of conversion.

Despite the centrality of religious purpose, we should not forget that effective adaptation required missionaries to cover very long distances, studying with perseverance and difficulty languages, customs and beliefs, about which they ended up producing knowledge that started circulating globally. If dressing up could be of fundamental importance in defining one's own identity in Renaissance Europe, it was even more so, far from the Old World, where mimicry depended on some actual understanding of local cultures, if one hoped to look credible by wearing their clothes.[29] This history also includes the tendency for the diplomatic milieu to follow the fashion of distant lands. This is confirmed by the English adventurer Robert Sherley, who led a mission across Europe between 1608 and 1613 on Shah Abbas I of Persia's behalf, arousing curiosity and surprise in the courts he visited because of his choice to wear Persian clothes, as is also shown by several still existing portraits that represent him in this guise.[30]

The attempt to look like a reliable personality before the most powerful Europeans of the time makes the case of Sherley partly similar to that of the French traveller François Le Gouz, Sieur de la Boullaye, descendant of a family of English origin. After visiting extensively south Asia, the Levant and north Africa around the mid-seventeenth century, chiefly stopping at Isfahan, the capital city of Safavid Persia, Le Gouz de la Boullaye wrote an account of his explorations, which saw the light in Paris under the title of *Les voyages et observations* in 1653. It was published at the request of the young Louis XVI, who had summoned Le Gouz de la Boullaye to appear at court 'with my Persian clothing (*avec mon équippage Persan*)'. The engraving that opens the work depicting Le Gouz de la Boullaye 'in Levantine dress (*en habit Levantin*)' between two globes, one containing the signs of the zodiac and the other displaying a hemisphere, reveals that his decision to present himself with that clothing before the king of France had been well worked out (Figure 18.3). He aimed to be considered so expert in the lands he described as to have gone native. However, this did not entail cutting ties with the world he came from, as is proved by the caption below the engraving which reads: 'known as Ibrahim Beg in Asia and Africa, and as the Catholic Traveller in Europe'. Moreover, several other portraits of Le Gouz de la Boullaye commented on in a variety of languages, including a few pictures included only in a manuscript held in the Biblioteca Corsiniana in Rome, reveal a cultural versatility which was much wider than the dualism reflected by the opening engraving.[31]

The displacement of objects across the early modern globe could have unexpected but meaningful effects. A case in point is that of a successful encyclopaedic collection of customs and manners of the peoples of the world, which became a Renaissance best seller. A German humanist and chaplain of the Teutonic Order, Hans Böhm summarized a huge amount of information in his *Omnium gentium ritus, leges et mores* (1520). This book relied on modern and, above all, ancient authors, providing a comparison among the most diverse cultures, traditions and beliefs without establishing rigid hierarchies, but rather praising the taste for 'variety'.[32] *Omnium gentium* did not even mention the Americas, which had been discovered a quarter of a century earlier, but this did not prevent it from enjoying a revival after the second edition (Lyon, 1535), which was followed by an explosion of reprints, translations and reworkings in the main European languages, typical patterns of cultural mediation from the Renaissance onwards.[33] A few decades later, we find *Omnium gentium* surprisingly cited as the main source of the *Nueva coronica y buen gobierno*.[34] A remarkable cross–cultural object, this peculiar illustrated chronicle by a Quechua intellectual, Guamán Poma de Ayala, offered a reconstruction of the history of the world from a point of view that was at the same time Andean and Spanish. It was probably sent to King Philip III of Spain about 1615 in the (vain) hope of persuading the crown to adopt a policy that was more respectful of the rights of the *Indios*.

The reference to Böhm was meant to reply to the Jesuit José de Acosta, who had been a missionary in Peru for a long time and in the prologue of his *De procuranda*

Portraict du Sieur de la Boullaye-le Gouz en habit Leuantin, connu
en Asie, & Affrique sous le nom d'Ibrahim-Beg, & en Europe
sous celuy de Voyageur Catholique.

Figure 18.3   François Le Gouz, Sieur de la Boullaye, in Levantine dress.

Engraving from François Le Gouz de la Boullaye, *Les voyages et observations* .... Paris: François
Clouzier, 1653.

Indorum salute (1588) had placed the *Indios* in the second and third class of Barbarians, keeping only the Chinese, Japanese and the majority of the Asian populations in the first class. In his hesitant and particular Castilian, Guaman Poma objected that he had also made a 'comparison' among the peoples of the world, arriving at a 'sentence that I write now in favour of the *Indios*, which will look so new to those who are not expert of histories'; that is, that 'the nation of the Peruvian *Indios*, those of Chile, Tucuman, Paraguay, the kingdom of New Granada and Mexico, is one of the noblest, most honoured and pure that exist all over the world'. The list of populations with whom Guaman Poma compared them coincides exactly with that provided by Böhm. However, it is not the one referred to in the Castilian version published in Antwerp (1556) and edited by Francisco de Támara, who had intentionally distorted the work by making it condemn the non-Christian world as a whole, including the humanity encountered by the Europeans in the age of exploration, which was branded as 'barbarian infidels, wicked idolatrous and degenerate men'. Actually, Guaman Poma's quotations derives from the Italian translation of *Omnium gentium* published by Girolamo Giglio in Venice (1558), with a significant addition on the New World. This is the edition that Guaman Poma had in mind when he spoke of Böhm's 'Yndiario'. It is probable that he never had it in his hands. But the journey of Giglio's edition across the Atlantic Ocean aroused the interest of a Franciscan creole with whom Guaman Poma was in close contact, Luis Jerónimo de Oré, a missionary whose position was the reverse of Acosta's. Oré presented his ideas in a peculiar catechism, the *Symbolo Catholico Indiano*, printed for the first time in Lima (1598), which was the very source that Guaman Poma consulted and used.[35] The ability to understand the implications of referring to Böhm's collection for his chronicle demonstrates to what extent the trajectories of cultural transfers were unforeseeable. In that age of global exchanges a European book, originally written in Latin, could convey its deepest message through circulation across languages and cultures, even to those who lived in the Andes, at a huge distance from the place where it had been thought and written, and who apparently did not even read it.

Individuals, communities, forced mobility

The cultural dynamics that have been described so far were the product of a world in motion. However, different forms of mobility fostered an extreme variety of processes, which requires specific analyses. Historians have paid increasing attention to individual itineraries for some years now, believing that the lives of single persons who moved across the world, shifted from one identity to another, changed names and learned to adapt to alien contexts may offer a special thread to follow in order to better understand how cultural encounters and transfers that were connected to long-distance circulation occurred. These investigations are clearly indebted to a scholarly tradition dealing with religious minorities in Europe and the Mediterranean coasts, first of all the Sephardi Jews, whose enigmatic and complex religious and cultural behaviour has often been explored by focusing on individuals.[36] Still more evident is the exchange with microhistory, which has always acknowledged the possibility of shedding light on a general phenomenon through an extremely close analysis of a single case, if chosen with care. So, it is no surprise that, among other scholars, the first steps in this direction were made by the author of a classic in microhistory, *The Return of Martin Guerre* (1983), with a volume on the Moroccan diplomat Hasan al-Wazzan al-Gharnati al-Fasi, known as Leo Africanus in Renaissance Europe, a name he took after being captured in the Mediterranean Sea, offered as a gift to the pope and baptized.[37] Despite Leo Africanus's forced mobility, followed by his flight from Rome once he managed to return to freedom, Natalie Zemon Davis goes so far as to see him as a symbol of an age in which the religious divide was not such a boundary that it prevented cultural transfers. This would be particularly true in the instance of shrewd and astute travellers, able to trick and dissimulate their most secret thoughts, as Leo Africanus did when he quickly identified with his new role as erudite slave of the pope, acting as a broker between the Islamic culture of north Africa and the capital city of the Catholic world.

It is not the anachronistic picture of globe-trotters who easily crossed cultural, religious and linguistic borders in the early modern period that has become popular in historiography. As Sanjay Subrahmanyam remarked, if crossing worlds became a more common experience in an 'age of contained conflict', it was anything but associated with feeling at home everywhere.[38] Quite the opposite: there were recurring cases of those who found themselves travelling, camouflaging, making choices and living far from their houses for decades without any enthusiasm. Their agency suffered the consequences of a cultural experience that was certainly plural but often perceived as a mere accident of life. Thus, they could remain halfway without being able to have a clear sense of belonging, as happened to the Luso-Malay cosmographer Manuel Godinho de Erédia, who lived as a sad and isolated '(trans)cultural impostor' in Portuguese Asia between the sixteenth and seventeenth centuries.[39] His case is a lesson to scholars about the disillusion and frustration that surrounded many individuals who moved across the early modern world. As has been rightly stressed with reference to Ilyās ibn al-Qassīs Ḥannā al-Mawṣilī, an eastern Christian priest from Mosul, better known as Elias of Babylon, whose global mobility never led him to cut ties with his land of origin, 'in our rush to populate global history with human faces, there is a risk of producing a set of caricatures, a chain of global lives whose individual contexts and idiosyncrasies dissolve too easily into the ether of connectedness'.[40] After travelling for a long time across Europe and even the Atlantic Ocean, around 1680 Elias of Babylon started writing the first history of America in Arabic at Magdalena del Mar, a small coastal village near Lima, in Peru. Even in the New World he continued to wear a long black cassock in the Turkish manner and the white collar of a priest, as well as to be proud of his big beard, always thinking of the community he had left behind in Baghdad.

Once we have taken note of their extreme variety and undeniable contribution in terms of cultural contacts and production of literary texts, it is difficult to assess the real effects of these individual experiences, whose allure largely originates from their apparent exceptionality. Global lives, however, gain another significance if we locate them in social landscapes that were marked by a multiplicity of forms of group mobility, as well as by the legacy that the stratification of previous migrations had left in some places. What was new in the early modern world was not so much this kind of mobility as its intensity and spatial dilatation, with deep cultural repercussions deriving from extended contact among fragments of societies that had never had reciprocal relations before, when they were not completely unaware of each other. If the conquest of America was exceptional, for its violence and the rigid hierarchy of the mestizo society that arose from it, Italian merchants who circulated across south Asia were quick to abandon cultural prejudices and recognize the plural character of cities and regions in which people of different customs, languages and beliefs coexisted side by side, though in a fragile balance that was not without tensions.[41] The success of the attempts by European groups to establish themselves far from their lands also depended on their ability to understand, at least in part, compromises and habits which regulated complex social and cultural dynamics on the ground.

Historians are becoming more and more aware that practices of negotiation among groups that followed different behaviour patterns and legal norms were typical of the early modern world. Recent studies on trade and law have demonstrated that it had been so for a long time in the Mediterranean, for instance in the exchanges between Christians and Muslims.[42] But one of the consequences of the rise of global history in the last twenty-five years has been to encourage ever more detailed knowledge of the multiple connections, no matter how empirical, asymmetric and improvised they were, which affected the most distant places. Some authors have identified the key factor for cultural innovation with the so-called 'cross-community migration'; that is, the ability of a group to move across linguistic and cultural borders, becoming part of a new context.[43] Based on a transfer of information, knowledge and expertise related to the arrival of strangers, this process increased tremendously with the first global interactions.

In such a framework, the slow definition of collective identities seems to attract historians less and less. Once inclined to see the early modern period, particularly in Europe, as the initial stage of the making of the future national communities that were destined to bring the formation of the modern states to completion, today they tend to focus on the malleability and adaptability of the communities in motion. This has promoted a new interest in the diasporas of Sephardi Jews and Armenians, with their internal cohesion and the facility to act as intermediaries in long-distance trade spreading through the global networks they created.[44] Fresh attention is also being paid to the emergence of many informal communities of exiles, renegades, fugitives or people who were just seeking their fortune, which arose on the edges of the great empires and gave rise to mixed societies, in which pidgin languages and a combination of cultures emerged.

Not always were these communities open and easy to access, because of the fear of repression, as is particularly clear in those composed of maroons. The slave trade had a global dimension in the early modern world, encompassing all the continents and expanding also to trans-Pacific routes with the import of Asian slaves into America.[45] However, fortified citadels were mainly built by slaves who had been compelled to cross the Atlantic Ocean. In the New World that was so hostile to them, they founded 'maroon states' at a large distance from the colonial cities and settlements and often protected by the forest, where Africans of different origins experienced well-ordered coexistence and the redefinition of their sense of cultural belonging.[46] It was one of the many faces of an immense continent, where the mixed descendants of indigenous people and European settlers could be identified or not as mestizos, depending on the circumstances.[47] Meanwhile, during the second half of the sixteenth century, Spain witnessed many cases of slaves of unclear origin who tried to pass themselves off as *Indios* so as to enjoy the effects of the imperial laws that forbade their enslavement.[48] This, too, was a kind of self-fashioning, which needed to look credible somehow if they wanted to take advantage of their claimed identity. It demonstrates to what extent, in a changing world, belonging to the lowest social strata, and even the lack of corporal freedom, was no obstacle to having agency of one's own before the opportunities provided by the variety of laws and institutions that accompanied the emergence of less and less uniform societies.

The redefinition of the cultural composition of many societies across the early modern world, however, was not the same everywhere. Indeed, historians have learned to single out localities which found themselves at the centre of the flows of global interactions, taking their first steps towards an ideal map of variable degrees of connection and disconnection on a planetary scale. For instance, in port cities, which usually hosted foreign merchant communities, cultural dynamics occurred that were completely absent in other places or regions, which were more isolated and rarely, if ever, had stable relations with groups of very distant origins. This line of inquiry is followed by those who now explore the existence of 'global cities' in early modern Europe. From Lisbon to London, from the sixteenth century the inhabitants of some big cities in Europe had the variety of the world at home, experiencing in their own streets the cultural effects produced by the flow not only of individuals and groups from all over the globe, but also of ideas and objects. It was just one of the possible local consequences of the global interactions that deeply marked that world in motion.[49]

Conclusion

From large cities to the most remote imperial borders, any attempt to understand the nature of the cultural transfers on a global scale that marked the early modern world should come about as a result of detailed analysis of the different kinds of mobility that nourished them. This means, first of all, acknowledging the relevance of the limits to free movement, be they material obstacles or other. If there was no lack of centres where people and objects of the most variegated origins could meet, from the mid-fifteenth to the early eighteenth centuries moving around the planet was a troubled experience, often undertaken reluctantly, if not forcibly. Its effects, however, were felt more and more pervasively, partly because they were anything but the result of an incentive from one single direction.

In this chapter I have most of all considered cases relating to Europeans, but I have tried to restore the context of global balance in which they took place and which was the outcome, among other factors, of the rise of the great Asian empires, the cultural resistance of the indigenous peoples of America before the conquest and the endless number of times an article of merchandise, traded at long distance by dealers and intermediaries, changed hands before reaching its destination. As I have attempted to show, be they the tricks of a Florentine merchant who travelled around the world against his will, the attraction of rare curiosities from all over the globe collected by a queen from one of the most powerful dynasties in Europe or a book whose message was reworked by a Quechua chronicler who had never read it, the inspirations and repercussions of early modern cultural mobility can neither be reduced to one single origin, nor understood as steps along a linear path. The shared awareness of the indissoluble variety of the world, to which the mobility of both individuals and groups, on the one hand, and things, ideas and knowledge, on the other, contributed, was probably the most important cultural process that occurred in that period, the product of myriads of encounters, transfers and (mis)understandings that, with all their asymmetries, modified forever the many different pictures of the world that its inhabitants had.

Notes

1 S. Greenblatt, 'Cultural Mobility: An Introduction', in S. Greenblatt et al., *Cultural Mobility: A Manifesto*, Cambridge; New York: Cambridge University Press, 2009, 1–3.
2 L. Clossey, 'Merchants, Migrants, Missionaries and Globalization in the Early-Modern Pacific', *Journal of Global History* 1.1, 2006, 41–58.

3 M. Eliav-Feldon, *Renaissance Impostors and Proofs of Identity*, London: Palgrave Macmillan, 2012.

4 S. Gruzinski, *Les quatre parties du monde: Histoire d'une mondialisation*, Paris: La Martinière, 2004. The expression 'composite empire' is used by S. Subrahmanyam, 'Holding the World in Balance: The Connected Histories of the Iberian Overseas Empires, 1500–1640', *American Historical Review* 112.5, 2007, 1360.

5 F. Carletti, *My Voyage Around the World*, trans. H. Weinstock, New York: Pantheon Books, 1964, 23.

6 Carletti, *My Voyage*, 142.

7 Carletti, *My Voyage*, 3.

8 F. Mendes Pinto, *The Travels*, ed. and trans. R. Catz, Chicago, IL: University of Chicago Press, 1989.

9 Carletti, *My Voyage*, 123. The reference in the text is to L. Fróis, *The First European Description of Japan, 1585: A Critical English-Language Edition of Striking Contrasts of Customs of Europe and Japan*, trans., ed. and annotated by R.K. Danford, R.D. Gill and D.T. Reff, New York: Routledge, 2014.

10 J. Gil, '*Chinos* in Sixteenth-Century Spain', in C.H. Lee (ed.), *Western Vision of the Far East in a Transpacific Age, 1522–1657*, New York: Routledge, 2012, 139–51.

11 J.E. Borao, 'The Massacre of 1603: Chinese Perception of the Spaniards in the Philippines', *Itinerario* 23.1, 1998, 22–39.

12 M. Muccioli, 'Sull'atlante cinese della Biblioteca Nazionale Centrale di Firenze', *Annali dell'Istituto Universitario Orientale di Napoli* 29, 1969, 397–410, and M. Muccioli, 'Ancora sull'atlante cinese della Biblioteca Nazionale di Firenze', *Annali dell'Istituto Universitario Orientale di Napoli* 30, 1970, 239–48.

13 J. Keating and L. Markey, '"Indian" Objects in Medici and Austrian-Habsburg Inventories: A Case-Study of the Sixteenth-Century Term', *Journal of the History of Collections* 23.2, 2011, 283–300.

14 Carletti, *My Voyage*, 179. See also T. Brook, *Mr Selden's of Map of China: Decoding the Secrets of a Vanished Cartographer*, Toronto: House of Anansi Press, 2013.

15 H.J. Cook, *Matters of Exchange: Commerce, Medicine, and Science in the Dutch Golden Age*, New Haven, CT: Yale University Press, 2007.

16 A. Gerritsen and G. Riello (eds), *The Global Lives of Things: The Material Culture of Connections in the Early Modern World*, London; New York: Routledge, 2016.

17 A. Russo, G. Wolf and D. Fained (eds), *Images Take Flight: Feather Art in Mexico and Europe, 1400–1700*, Munich: Hirmer, 2015.

18 A. Russo, 'Cortés's Objects and the Idea of New Spain: Inventories as Spatial Narratives', *Journal of the History of Collections* 23.2, 2011, 229–52.

19 J. Wicki and J. Gomes (eds), *Documenta Indica*, 18 vols, Rome: Institutum Historicum Societatis Iesu, 1948–88, vol. 8, 685.

20 A. Jordan Gschwend, *Catarina de Áustria: A rainha colecionadora*, Lisbon: Temas e Debates, 2017.

21 A. Jordan Gschwend, 'The Development of Catherine of Austria's Collection in the Queen's Household: Its Character and Cost', Ph.D. dissertation, Brown University, 1994, 378–81.

22 Wicki and Gomes, *Documenta*, vol. 8, 658.

23 R. White, *The Middle Ground: Indians, Empires and Republics in the Great Lakes Regions, 1650–1815*, Cambridge; New York: Cambridge University Press, 1991, 50–93.

24 On Rafaxo's visit see Wicki and Gomes, *Documenta*, vol. 8, 733.

25 S. Gruzinski, 'Mexican Feathers for the Emperor of China: Towards a Global History of the Arts', in Russo, Wolf and Fained (eds), *Images Take Flight*, 190–9.

26 N. Um and L.R. Clark, 'Introduction: The Art of Embassy: Situating Objects and Images in the Early Modern Diplomatic Encounter', *Journal of Early Modern History* 20.1, 2016, 3–18. See also Z. Biedermann, A. Gerritsen and G. Riello (eds), *Global Gifts: The Material Culture of Diplomacy in Early Modern Eurasia*, Cambridge; New York: Cambridge University Press, 2018.

27 S. Subrahmanyam, *Courtly Encounters: Translating Courtliness and Violence in Early Modern Eurasia*, Cambridge, MA: Harvard University Press, 2012.

28 S.B. Schwartz (ed.), *Implicit Understandings: Observing, Reporting and Reflecting on the Encounters between Europeans and Other Peoples in the Early Modern Era*, Cambridge; New York: Cambridge University Press, 1994.

29 U. Rublack, *Dressing Up: Cultural Identity in Renaissance Europe*, Oxford; New York: Oxford University Press, 2010.

30 R. Stevens, 'Robert Sherley: The Unanswered Questions', *Iran* 17, 1979, 115–25.

31 M. Bernardini, 'The Illustrations of a Manuscript of the Travel Account of François de la Boullaye le Gouz in the Library of the Accademia Nazionale dei Lincei in Rome', in *Essays in Honor of J. M. Rogers*, D. Behrens-Abouseif and A. Contadini (eds), *Muqarnas: An Annual of the Visual Culture of the Islamic World* 21, 2004, 56–8.

32 K.A. Vogel, 'Cultural Variety in a Renaissance Perspective: Johannes Boemus on "The Manner, Laws and Customs of All People" (1520)', in H. Bugge and J.P. Rubiés (eds), *Shifting Cultures: Interaction and Discourse in the Expansion of Europe*, Münster: Lit, 1995, 17–34.

33 P. Burke, 'The Renaissance Translator as Go-Between', in A. Höfele and W. von Koppenfels (eds), *Renaissance Go-Betweens: Cultural Exchange in Early Modern Europe*, Berlin; New York: W. de Gruyter, 2005, 17–31.

34 Copenhagen, Det Kongelige Bibliotek, Ms. Gammel Kongelig Samling (GSK) 2232, 4°: *El primer nueva corónica i buen gobierno, conpuesto por Don Phelipe Guaman Poma de Aiala, señor i príncipe*, 1088.

35 G. Marcocci, *Writing Histories of the World in Renaissance Europe and the Americas*, Oxford: Oxford University Press, 2020, 80–111.

36 The pioneering study by Y.H. Yerushalmi, *From Spanish Court to Italian Ghetto: Isaac Cardoso: A Study in Seventeenth-Century Marranism and Jewish Apologetics*, New York: Columbia University Press, 1971, is still a fundamental starting point.

37 N.Z. Davis, *Trickster Travels: A Sixteenth-Century Muslim between Worlds*, New York: Hill and Wang, 2006. Among the earliest work in the same field should also be numbered M. García-Arenal and G. Wiegers, *A Man of Three Worlds: Samuel Pallache, a Moroccan Jew in Catholic and Protestant Europe*, Baltimore, MD: Johns Hopkins University Press, 2003 and L. Colley, *The Ordeal of Elizabeth Marsh: A Woman in World History*, London: Harper Press, 2007.

38 S. Subrahmanyam, *Three Ways to Be Alien: Travails and Encounters in the Early Modern World*, Waltham, MA: Brandeis University Press, 2011.

39 J. Flores, 'Between Madrid and Ophir: Erédia, a Deceitful Discoverer?', in M. Eliav-Feldon and T. Herzig (eds), *Dissimulation and Deceit in Early Modern Europe*, London, New York: Palgrave Macmillan, 2015, 184.

40 J.-P. Ghobrial, 'The Secret Life of Elias of Babylon and the Uses of Global Microhistory', *Past and Present* 222.1, 2014, 58–9.

41 G. Marcocci, 'Renaissance Italy Meets South Asia: Florentines and Venetians in a Cosmopolitan World', in I.G. Zupanov, C. Lefèvre and J. Flores (eds), *Cosmopolitismes en Asie du Sud: Sources, itinéraires, langues (XVIᵉ–XVIIIᵉ siècles)*, Paris: Éditions de l'EHESS, 2015, 45–69.

42 F. Apelláníz, 'Judging the Franks: Proof, Justice, and Diversity in Late Medieval Alexandria and Damascus', *Comparative Studies in Society and History* 58.2, 2016, 350–78.

43 P. Manning, 'Cross-Community Migration: A Distinctive Human Pattern', *Social Evolution & History* 5.2, 2006, 24–54.

44 F. Trivellato, *The Familiarity of Strangers: The Sephardic Diaspora, Livorno and Cross-Cultural Trade in the Early Modern Period*, New Haven, CT: Yale University Press, 2009; S. Aslanian, *From the Indian Ocean to the Mediterranean: The Global Trade Networks of Armenian Merchants from New Julfa*, Berkeley, CA: University of California Press, 2011.

45 T. Seijas, *Asian Slaves in Colonial Mexico: From Chinos to Indians*, New York: Cambridge University Press, 2014.

46 R. Anderson, 'The Quilombo of Palmares: A New Overview of a Maroon State in Seventeenth-Century Brazil', *Journal of Latin American Studies* 28.3, 1996, 545–66.

47 J. Rappaport, *The Disappearing Mestizo: Configuring Difference in the Colonial New Kingdom of Granada*, Durham, NC: Duke University Press, 2014.

48 N.E. Van Deusen. *Global Indios: The Indigenous Struggle for Justice in Sixteenth-Century Spain*, Durham, NC; London: Durham University Press, 2015.

49 A. Jordan Gschwend and K.J.P. Lowe (eds), *The Global City: On the Streets of Renaissance Lisbon*, London: Paul Holberton Publishing, 2015; R.K. Batchelor, *London: The Selden Map and the Making of a Global City, 1549–1689*, Chicago, IL: University of Chicago Press, 2014.

19

FACES OF POWER AND CONFLICT

Tomás A. Mantecón[1]

Conflict and power are both part of social and political practice, and war is an extreme expression of conflict and power; every conflict, whatever its size, is the result of a disagreement, which springs from unsolved social, cultural or political contradictions. In early modern Europe, the social and political intensity of conflict depended not just on the issue at stake and the actors taking part, but also on the social implications of the conflict. Obviously, in a scale of conflict, war ranks much higher than riots, brawls, homicides, assaults and individual verbal insults. War was the reverberation, on a grandiose scale, of deep tensions caused by asymmetric relationships and broken pacts in the international arena. At any rate, all kinds of violence, either between individuals, social factions and groups or between countries, resulted in conflict between parties and disruption of their respective social, political and cultural contexts.

Power relationships are part of every conflict and its resolution. In the international arena, economic and political interests underlie diplomatic conflict. This chapter examines this point in order to explain not only war, but also the faces and historical evolution of interpersonal violence and conflict in Western societies. Interpersonal confrontation, passions and interests, as well as social deviance and intolerance, were factors of conflict, which often were deeply rooted in beliefs, religion, ethnic origin, gender, class and socioeconomic status.

Interpretative paradigms

Power and conflict are two faces of the same coin. From a historical perspective, their interaction has played a key role in social change. The emergence of the so-called Western modern family saw progressively more focus placed on paternity and increasing emotional links between the members of the household. This, along with the adoption of new social customs, the decline in the number of homicides and the consolidation of the state, led to a rapidly changing social structure in early modern Europe that needs to be considered in the context of both global explanations and other broad historical processes. Some processes of change operate *from above*, following the leadership of the elite. In the view of Norbert Elias, elite sensibilities – that is, elite notions of when and how to control emotions, and an understanding of how to rule behaviour in order to facilitate frictionless social relationships – played a substantial role in these top-down processes. The dissemination of elite *civility* to other social spheres fits well with the historiography of state-building, which emphasizes the process of institutional and administrative development as well as the progressive professionalization of public service. The aim of these processes was to monopolize the political control of the *res publica* and thus to achieve social order by the monopolistic and legitimate exercise of justice, government and violence.

The historical progression of this process was connected with two interrelated phenomena: early modern *confessionalization* and social disciplining processes (*Sozialdisziplinierung*). These processes are rooted in the dissolution of the unity of medieval Christianity, and the emergence of various Christian Churches. This led to a thorough revision of both dogma and institutional arrangements, a process that continued until the age of the liberal revolutions. The *top-down paradigm* provides an adequate framework with which to analyse the theory and the practice behind *confessionalization, Socialdisziplinierung*, state-building and civilizing projects. It underlines the total, or partial, success of the dissemination of elite ideology as well as of elite attempts to monopolize social control. From this historiographical perspective, other developments have been considered less constructively; although they directly affect the ultimate outcome of historical processes, they are often dismissed as the expression of discrepancy, social resistance, dissent, deviance and rebellion. The *top-down paradigm* tends to underestimate the creativity of the debate between elite projects and the social answers they encounter, as well as the impact of bottom-up trends on historical change.

In the second half of the twentieth century, the debate about whether the changes undergone by Western European societies have resulted in a progressive reduction of violent crime and an increase in patrimonial crime added some additional arguments to the discussion. Some of these arguments were in favour of using the *top-down paradigm* to explain this process of historical change. The decline of violence and the slight increase in patrimonial crime followed the so-called *judicial revolution.*[2] This process involved the progressive improvement of administrative and institutional frameworks, the consolidation of judicial culture, the increasingly clear definition of illegal behaviours – more clearly and precisely quoted than ever before – and the growing professionalization of the legal trade, which had a positive effect on judicial actions.[3] In short, the thesis was: the more the state develops, the less crime there will be, because the state will be able to monopolize, legally and legitimately, the use of violence, and also to define property rights and economic illegal behaviour and crime, more precisely.

Some of these processes are yet to be proven empirically. For instance, as early as the first half of the fourteenth century, two thirds of registered crime in some English districts were to do with theft and robbery, not physical violence.[4] Research has also shown that, in Victorian Britain, trends concerning violent crime and robbery neatly mirrored each other, contrary to the beliefs of many historians.[5] Despite the great efforts invested in analysing the evolution of homicide and other forms of violent conflict in Western Europe, the long-run trends of violence in these societies are still a matter of debate.[6]

The *top-down* paradigm presents historical change as a seamless process of *modernization*, the result of the total or partial crystallization of elite-promoted social, political and cultural projects. This underestimates the constructive power of social *conversations* and negotiations projected *from below*, which sometimes took the shape of conflict. Deviance, dissension, resistance and opposition played a relevant role in the processes of change.

Sometimes scientific faith in what can be quantified and measured leads to a simplification of historical analysis. When studying the history of social deviance, conflict and crime, numbers, proportions and statistics must not be the end but the beginning of the process. Quantitative data provide very valuable information on global and long-term patterns, but we need to look further to explain the meaning of conflict in specific historical contexts. Qualitative analysis also improves our understanding of when and why a criminal category was recognized or, conversely, when it disappeared.

Incidental information contained in political and forensic documents, such as witness statements, depositions submitted by lawyers and judicial sentences, as well as reports and chronicles, helps to explain the social values and attitudes that underlie every conflict and have contributed to our understanding of elite and plebeian attitudes towards law, justice and discipline. Ordinary people approached the judicial system taking into account not only official concepts and principles, but also cultural values. These often had a direct effect on the resolution of conflict.[7] If all these factors are duly considered, it becomes clear that historical social and cultural trends, and their transformation, were not as univocal or unidirectional as some *modernization* perspectives would have us believe.

War

War was an extension of politics, an extreme act of power to force rivals to assume our will and proposals. It was another element of social existence, another means of intercourse between nations, comparable to others such as trade.[8] War also was – and still is – the last step in a bargaining process.[9] In the international arena, conflicts enforced the deployment of diplomatic means, and in extreme cases, this resulted in the collapse of diplomatic options and the beginning of war. The effects of war were multi-layered, beginning with social and economic upheaval for the contenders, which hindered their financial development. War was a major challenge and, inevitably, affected state-building processes[10] and triggered social change.[11]

War was a constant feature of early modern Europe. In the Mediterranean this was largely due to competition between Italian ports, the economic activity of Western Mediterranean harbours, the permanent Turkish threat and tensions in the intense maritime traffic, sometimes made worse by piratical activity. The Atlantic projection of European powers from the fifteenth century onwards also led to European conflicts increasingly being played out in other parts of the world (Africa, America and Asia). The formation of the European empires was an added source of tension and conflict, as European powers struggled to control various overseas territories. Disputes between the Portuguese and the Spanish were constant between the late fifteenth century and the late eighteenth century, despite the agreement reached in the

Treaty of Madrid (1750). Friction and conflict were also common between the Portuguese and the Dutch in Africa and Asia, and between the British and the Spanish, especially in America. Conflict was connatural to the construction and dissolution of European empires, whatever their nature and historical dynamics.

The European continent lived in a permanent state of war during the early modern age. Before and after the treaties of Utrecht-Rastatt, conflict was chiefly driven by territorial disputes and commercial interests, as well as other sovereignty-related questions, but after 1715 these reasons were largely replaced by colonial competition.[12] Sometimes, war only affected specific territories. This was, for instance, the case with the Italian wars; the conflicts that ravaged Central Europe in the wake of the expansion of radical Protestantism; and the war in the Netherlands, all in the sixteenth century. Sometimes war was a domestic affair, for instance the French Wars of Religion, also in the sixteenth century. At any rate, every international struggle created an arena for broader competition and conflicting areas of influence. Whatever the real reasons for conflict, war could always be justified as a reaction against illicit usurpations or a way to preserve social order and political rights. As a consequence, every war set up the conditions for a rebalancing of power and interests.

The dissolution of Christian unity opened a chasm not only between Catholics and Protestants, but also within each of these religious options. Europe was divided and 'disrupted by war', but it was still united by cultural patterns. As John Elliott pointed out, 'violence was no doubt a normal way of life in Early Modern Europe, and war was seen as an accepted institution rather than as an unfortunate aberration from a long cycle of peace'.[13]

The unstable boundaries in the East and political frictions in Western and Central Europe were sources of tension. As Bonney pointed out, 'empires and kingdoms could be divided by rules, while new dynastic states could arise which challenged those already in existence'.[14] Religious tensions not only intensified international conflict, but were also behind a witch-craze with its epicentre in Central Europe.[15] Between the end of the Thirty Years' War and the War of the Spanish Succession and the subsequent treatises of Utrecht-Rastatt, international relationships in Western Europe were determined by a constant struggle for hegemony.[16]

After the Treaty of Westphalia, international conflict was driven by competition for the control of the ocean and the formation of empires, border disputes and the struggle for influence, both in Europe and overseas. These problems underlay international relations up to the unravelling of the *Ancien Régime*, the emancipation of the American colonies, the French Revolution and the dissolution of the Spanish empire. Occasionally, violence started with military levies, which triggered local movements of resistance. In Finland and Sweden, the *Ildelningsverk*, the system that determined the number of men to be supplied by each community and district, met with resistance from local residents.[17] This sort of conflict became common throughout Western Europe.

Before the Thirty Years' War, the formation of military contingents relied heavily on mercenary forces. As a result, armies were often largely constituted by foreign units. The army with which Henry VIII invaded France in 1544 included soldiers from Scotland, Spain, Gascony, Portugal, Italy, Albania, Turkey, Germany, Burgundy and Flanders.[18] Loyalties were, therefore, a flexible matter, and social participation very complex. Armies had their own rationality, which did not have to agree with the internal logic of the powers in conflict and their strategies. In addition, European rulers also had to constantly deal with local customs and historical institutions, created to protect popular privileges and traditional liberties.

Sometimes this plunged major territorial monarchies and empires into conflict. Everyday social and personal relationships were also disfigured by war. Levies, troop movements, billets and the need to provide horses and equipment were typical causes of social unease and conflict.

War created the right setting for social *brutalization*, or the intensification of everyday conflict and crime.[19] Crime was not only defined in terms of social exclusion, but was also framed in legal terms. While crime is clearly outside the boundaries of lawful practice, conflict does not need to involve a breaking of the law to become a threat to social peace. Every historical setting has its own categories of crime, and develops new definitions in order to better restrain conflict.

War-related conflict is not a self-contained phenomenon, but merely the projection of elite-dominated politics, foreign policy and diplomacy. Social groups, individuals and institutions reacted to war in different ways. Local communities resisting new levies, billets or taxes illustrate one social reaction to war; sometimes these movements had a very real effect on military operations. In many German cities, the end of the Thirty Years' War was celebrated with great joy for this signified the release of the troops and a return to peace and normality; the territories of the Holy Roman Empire had lost between 15% and 20% of the population (more than three million people).[20]

Theoretically, war is a relatively simple bilateral or multilateral affair, but if we take into consideration social perceptions and reactions, the analysis becomes a good deal more complex.[21] Therefore, while the Clausewitzian scheme, which defines war as a projection of politics onto the international arena, explains some of the dimensions and manifestations of war in preindustrial Europe, it is overly simplistic; wider social participation and its implications reveal that war is a more dialectical phenomenon than Von Clausewitz believed.

Revolts, riots, dissent

The large number of revolts, riots and examples of social unrest witnessed by the seventeenth century requires explanation. According to Trevor-Roper, this was a period of *general revolution*.[22] European societies were torn by internal tensions and shifting towards new balances, and this led to numerous riots, rebellions and revolts: Catalonia and Portugal (1640), Naples and Palermo (1647), the Fronde in France (1648–1653), the Netherlands (1650) and Ukraine (1649–1654), plus a huge number of lesser peasant risings taking place all across Europe in countless different locations and contexts. Some time ago, John Elliott emphasized the intensity of social dissent during the 1560s, which witnessed such episodes in Scotland (1559–1560 and 1567), Savoy (1560), France (starting in 1562 and triggering civil war), Corsica (1564), the Netherlands (starting in 1566), Granada (1568) and the Northern Rebellion in England (1569).[23] These phenomena were probably the result of the intensification of the structural problems suffered by Western societies.

In addition to these general trends, local factors also put the social order to the test during this period. In specific political constructs, such as the Spanish Monarchy, some periods may also be regarded as *revolutionary ages*, for instance the 1520s, with the revolt of the *Comuneros*, the critical 1640s, particularly in Portugal, Catalonia, Naples and Sicily, and even the 1760s in Castile and the 1780s in Latin America.

All these conflicts can be grouped under different labels. But we must be wary of creating a lexicon that could lead to an empty nominalist discussion about whether or not any of these conflicts fulfil the criteria to be considered a revolution, a revolt or a rebellion; or about the opportunity of using concepts such as class struggle. Words are fickle, and their meaning changes according to territorial, sociological and chronological factors. In many cases, social struggle pursued very precise political aims, including centrifugal forces that opposed globalizing state-building projects.

In the early modern age, the irruption of Protestantism created an additional source of conflict. The Peasant War in Southern Germany and the Black Forest in 1524 and 1525 is an excellent example of this. Dürer's watercolour *Dream vision*, currently in the Kunsthistorisches Museum of Vienna, and painted overnight on 7–8 June 1525 immediately after the defeat and execution of Thomas Müntzer in Frankenhausen, wonderfully illustrates the concerns of such a privileged witness of the religious, social and political events that shocked Europe during this period. Dürer's watercolour is a metaphorical prayer for a better future.[24]

More frequently, collective feeling that led to riots and unorganized social movements focused on specific issues and on negotiating the notions of *common good* and *good government* with the authorities. This sort of movement was generally restricted to specific territories and circumstances. The French Wars of Religion, troop movements and the demands posed by armies in the context of the Thirty Years' War, compounded by the convulsions brought about by the War of the Spanish Succession before the treaties of Utrecht-Rastatt, offered multiple opportunities for the population to express their rejection of war and the social disorder that then went with it. The passive resistance posed by the population to the French occupation of Barcelona, which had the blessing of the Spanish authorities, in the context of the Napoleonic wars illustrates how ordinary people could react, even to apparently amicable situations.[25] Often, however, wars were aggravated by the violent outburst of social passions.[26]

Antagonisms linked to ethnical, gender, estate, class, cultural and confessional divisions were the source of conflict between individuals and groups, between majorities and minorities and, generally, between competing social groups, corporations and communities. Conflict, at any rate, could confront people who belonged to the same social group as much as it separated people from different economic, social, ethnic or religious communities.

Sometimes conflict followed social and political tension between multinational political structures and their constituent parts. The Spanish Monarchy, in the central decades of the seventeenth century, is only the most outstanding example among many.[27] Downscaling the problem to the most basic spheres of power and authority, the household level, we can appreciate that authority was never far from conflict, as demonstrated by the pervasiveness of domestic violence in Europe.[28]

The same type of conflict explains the contradiction between the military duties of obedience and loyalty and desertion, which was not exclusive of national armies, but also affected mercenary forces. Moreover, the disbanding of military units after the end of the campaigns often resulted in waves of banditry and crime.

In addition to the previously noted types of conflict, we also have to consider crime, organized and otherwise, and the social exclusion of migrants and members of cultural, ethnical and religious minorities. These problems affected the whole of Europe, and put the political measures of social control implemented by villages, towns, cities and states to the test. Jews, for instance, were generally not well integrated, and formed their own separated urban communities. As a rule, they did not enjoy full citizenship. Former Muslim groups never really integrated into Spanish society, even before the expulsion decree of 1609, which meant the end of the presence of *Moriscos* in Spain. While protestants were persecuted in Spain, Catholics were victimized in England, especially after the Glorious Revolution, owing to the cultural and political conflation of the notions of Catholicism, absolutism and foreign interference. Similar conflicts related to religious prejudice were common in other European societies. Christians lived in conflict with the Ottoman Empire, but often also with each other. Frequently, transnational governments, both in Europe and in the Ottoman Empire, had to arbitrate disputes arising between different religious groups within their dominions.

There were countless versions of cultural and religious conflict. In this period, religion permeated all spheres of life, and individual religious feelings and popular practices were often at odds with standard orthodox practice and official liturgy. Broad social conflicts also had a reflection on the strictly individual sphere, shaping micro-conflicts of personal discipline and non-compliance. Conflict had a different face for all individuals involved. Microhistory has produced wonderful studies of how people dealt with personal beliefs, life expectations, the building of personal identities, social deviance, domestic violence and their own personal salvation.[29]

Homicide and violence

Concerning the historical evolution of violence in Western Europe, two major questions need to be addressed: whether there has been a decline in interpersonal violence and, should the answer be 'yes', whether this could be considered a consequence of the civilizing process described by Norbert Elias. In the early 1980s Tedd Gurr, followed by Lawrence Stone, focused the discussion on homicide rates in order to compare long-term trends, paying attention to the most extreme version of violence (homicide) that underestimated the slighter under-registered variety of violent crime (non-lethal and verbal violence). Gurr's British data suggest a progressive decline in the number of homicides (calculated in terms of annual rate per 100,000 inhabitants). Afterwards, Stone placed the discussion within the broader framework of interpersonal violence in general.[30]

Manuel Eisner has demonstrated the decline in the homicide rate in Western Europe between the fifteenth and nineteenth centuries (see Figure 19.1). Many factors, such as the progressive disarmament of society, better medical practice, a more developed penal system, the strengthening of the state and social and cultural changes,

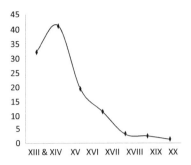

Figure 19.1 Historical evolution of homicide rates in Western Europe. Annual homicides per 100,000 inhabitants.

The graph is based on the quantitative data published by Manuel Eisner.[31]

have been used to explain this historical trend.[32] In some regions such as Britain, Scandinavia, Switzerland and Germany, the annual homicide rate dropped below 5 per 100,000 inhabitants as early as the seventeenth century, but in Belgium and the Netherlands this decrease can only be detected from the eighteenth century onwards, and even later in Italy.[33] It is worth mentioning that the data for southern countries are much less complete than for the rest of Western Europe. Also, Scandinavia[34] and Mediterranean Southern Europe[35] were subject to specific factors.

The data for Stockholm describe a clear downward curve in the number of homicides during the seventeenth century. However, the increasing degree of self-control, which is presumed to have had a positive effect on this statistic, may have, conversely, contributed to the continuous increase in the annual suicide rate. In the early seventeenth century, the number of suicides per 100,000 inhabitants was between 3 and 4 per year, but the figures had more than doubled barely 100 years later. The data presented for the Mediterranean regions to date are inconclusive. The curves are similar to those already detected elsewhere in Western Europe, but the developments that these curves suggest seem to have occurred somewhat later in time in the Mediterranean. At any rate, treating Southern Europe as a single block is certainly problematic.[36]

There is no great difference in the evolution of homicide rates in the largest cities after 1600 (see Figure 19.2). The example posed by the Spanish cities of Madrid and Segovia emphasize some interesting factors, such the relationship between urban violence and social crisis. Social and political crisis seems to have played a significant role in Madrid in the seventeenth and eighteenth centuries, and in Segovia 100 years later. Apart from this, the evolution of homicide in these cities was similar to that attested in other European cities.

Data concerning the number of homicide-related judicial executions in Rome point to a similar trend (see Figure 19.3). The number of executions is lower than that of homicides, but the data can be used to analyse the long-term trends all the same. The sixteenth century and, to a lesser extent, the opening decades of the seventeenth century witnessed the vicious confrontation of Roman aristocratic families, which

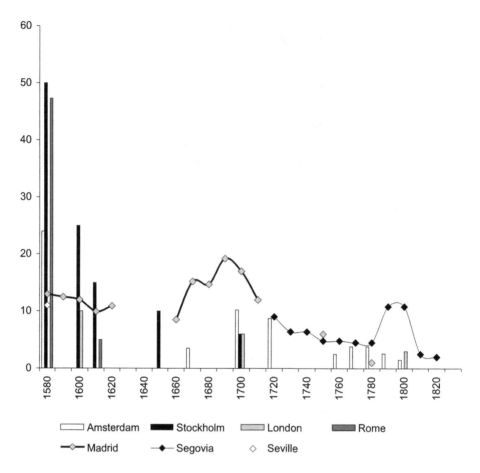

Figure 19.2 Homicide rate trends in Western Europe. Big cities. Annual homicides per 100,000 inhabitants.

AHPS (Provincial Historical Archive of Segovia), box J-1383-1; BUS (University Library of Salamanca), manuscript 573, ff. 247 and following.[37]

were divided into various factions. This led to much violence, mostly conducted by hired hitmen. Some of these are known to have committed several homicides, and, as a result, the number of executed murderers is lower than the number of homicides. Despite this, it is fair to argue that the curve described by convictions responds to the evolution of violent crime. In Rome, homicide rates probably fell below the 10 per 100,000 inhabitants mark in the seventeenth century, and below 5 per 100,000 inhabitants in the eighteenth century.

More data are needed to offer a more precise idea of homicide in Mediterranean societies in the early modern age. Short-term crisis also resulted in brief outbursts of violence. These exceptions apart, Southern and Western European countries seem to have developed along similar lines between the sixteenth and nineteenth centuries.

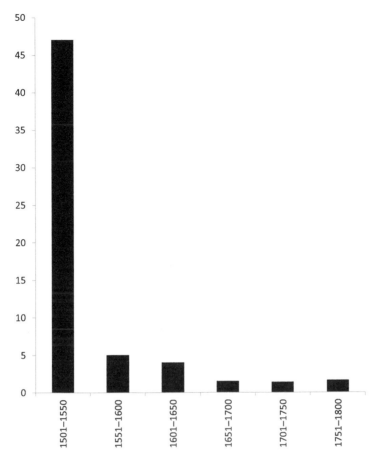

Figure 19.3   Homicide convicts executed in Rome (1500–1800). Annual rate per 100,000
inhabitants.

ASR (Rome State Archive), inventory 285.

Urban and rural interpersonal violence

Concerning violence and homicide, rural and urban societies evolved differently (see
Figure 19.4). In Northern Atlantic Spain, for instance, rural homicide was relatively
rare in the seventeenth and eighteenth centuries. In Cantabria, the annual rate was
between 1 and 2 homicides per 100,000 inhabitants. These figures are low, but essentially consistent with those attested in other rural and poorly urbanized Western
European regions. Recent studies suggest that annual homicide rates in Lorraine,
Anjou, Maine and Normandy ranged from 0.7 to 3.2 per 100,000 inhabitants between 1670 and 1789. Notably, these numbers are significantly lower than in rural
Northern Europe.

Figures for seventeenth-century Surrey are over six times higher than those from
Cantabria, although between 1660 and 1720 the annual homicide rate fell from

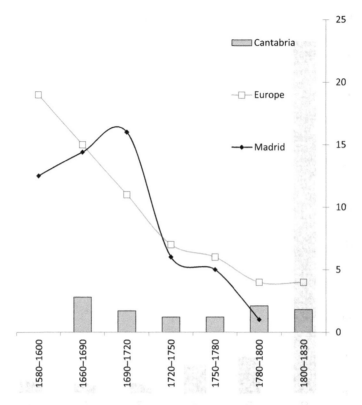

Figure 19.4 Homicide rates in urban (Madrid) and rural (Cantabria) Spain (1580–1800). Annual homicides per 100,000 inhabitants.

AHPC (Provincial Historical Archive of Cantabria), criminal cases series for three rural jurisdictions.[38]

over 6 per 100,000 inhabitants to around 2, and then it fell further to less than 1 in 1780–1802. The figures for Finnish Tavastia were even higher: 25 per 100,000 inhabitants in 1506–1510, before dropping to 2.6 in the second half of the eighteenth century. However, for Ostrobothnia, also in Finland, where a strong kinship structure and robust mechanisms of social control existed, a homicide rate of barely 3 per 100,000 inhabitants is attested as early as the second half of the sixteenth century.[39]

These figures do not mean that interpersonal violence was absent from these societies. In communities where personal relationships were close, other forms of violence were much more common than homicide. In 1534–1543, only 1% of the crimes committed in Swedish Arboga were homicides.[40] In Jääski and Ruokolahti, two Finnish parishes, homicides barely amounted to 0.58% of criminal records in 1549–1598 and 0.97% in 1619–1698;[41] that is, much lower than in Arboga, not to mention Sussex in 1592–1640 (3.92%); Hertfordshire in 1559–1625 (2.24%); Cantabria in 1630–1690 (6.45%); Essex in 1620–1680 (11%); Devon (15%); Cornwall (13%); Norfolk and Suffolk (9%); Lindsey in Lincolnshire (7.31%); Cantabria again just before 1770 (1.96%) and in 1790–1830 (3.6%);[42] and the region of Toulouse

(5%)[43] in the eighteenth century. At the same time, cities such as Stockholm[44] and Arras[45] in the sixteenth century, and Amsterdam and London – including Middlesex – in the eighteenth century, could present percentages of 17.37%, 37%, less than 10% and 13.60%, respectively.[46]

In rural societies, strong family structures, the importance of kinship relations and communalism combined to inhibit homicide. These mechanisms structured social discipline on every level of society, and facilitated public order, social balance and a peaceful coexistence.

Homicide seems to have been more common in urban contexts than in close-knit rural communities, where everyone knew each other and each other's families down the generational line. Urban male youth cultures were environments rife with violence. Homicide could easily be the unexpected outcome of the simplest of tavern brawls. In both rural and urban environments, however, specific historical circumstances could lead to outbursts of violence, for example during war and the subsequent *brutalization* of social relationships. The global trends, on the other hand, were largely independent of these peaks of violence, and were linked to broader social and cultural transformations. Early modern European history is full of events that brought about sudden outbursts of social violence, such as the French Wars of Religion, the Thirty Years' War and the Napoleonic Wars.

In Spain, for instance, the crisis of the *Ancien Régime* created the conditions for an increase in the number of violent episodes, often in connection with robbery, smuggling, banditry and armed resistance to the French invasion troops. War was the final straw after a sequence of bad crops, leading to a severe shortage of basic products and speculative rents. These factors and the ensuing social discontent contributed to an intensification of violent crime which was not to abate until the 1830s, as well as the brutalization of society, including frequent instances of personal vengeance, and the normalization of interpersonal verbal and physical violence.

These phenomena were more intense in rural areas, especially in small communities, than in urban centres. In cities, they were more common in areas where everyday interpersonal contact was closest. In any case, this trend affected all social categories. Statistically, the numbers of court cases involving criminal acts was higher in urban than in rural contexts, owing to the higher population density. In Spain clear differences exist between court cases involving any form of violence – verbal violence, assaults and homicides – in rural and urban contexts (although the previously noted decrease in the number of homicides is attested in both) (see Table 19.1).

Table 19.1 Long-term trends of interpersonal violence in Spain (1660–1830). Percentage of criminal cases of violence in courts of first instance.

	1660–1699	*1700–1769*	*1770–1830*
Urban trends	35.0	47.5	52.8
Rural trends	47.8	43.7	31.7
Average	41.4	45.6	41.2

Data from Cantabria, Montes de Toledo, Galicia, Madrid and Segovia (AHPS, box J-1383-1). The rural trends have been calculated with data from Cantabria, Montes de Toledo, Galicia and La Rioja[47].

Therefore, we can conclude that, if all forms of interpersonal violence are taken into consideration, a slight overall decline can be seen over time. This decline was much sharper in rural societies, probably because traditional informal means of mediation and arbitration were, in these communities, much stronger than in urban contexts, where anonymity also facilitated impersonal forms of violence. The face of violence also changed in both rural and urban contexts; while homicide became rarer, other forms of physical violence became more common, until these were progressively replaced by verbal violence. As such, it seems clear that the most violent forms of expression progressively gave way to more subtle and less physical manifestations. Perhaps this process of historical change may be described as the *civilization of interpersonal violence* or the *progressive moderation of the intensity of violence* in both rural and urban societies.

Conclusions

Our understanding of the evolution of violence and conflict in historical Western European societies rests on a very wide variety of sources, the interpretation of which is by no means simple. Statistical analyses based on historical data, however, can provide a general idea of historical trends over time. For example, homicide rates seem to have steadily declined between the late Middle Ages and the Age of Enlightenment, especially during the eighteenth century. This historical development could be seen as the result of the implementation of improved mechanisms of social control, largely embodied by better judicial and law-enforcement systems, which were part of an elite-driven process to strengthen the state.

As such, it could be said that the more clearly defined the state structure, the more uncontested its monopoly over arbitration and social control mechanisms, including the exclusive right to legitimately use violent means in order to preserve the public peace. An increasingly sophisticated legal apparatus was also part of this process. At any rate, while these arguments might be considered essentially correct, the truth is a little more complex than that. A detailed reading of the sources reveals that this long-term narrative may be subject to a number of caveats.

Power and conflict in early modern Europe were multifaceted phenomena which interacted with one another, sometimes leading to conflict and sometimes to its suppression. Power was present in every sphere of life, and was the source of internal tension as well as of mechanisms of social control and instruments for reconstructing public order, the oft-proclaimed *common good*. War forced dynastic states in the making to look both outwards, to their international rivals, and inwards, to their own internal social problems. Social and cultural prejudice, particular interests and the wish for domination and hegemony (in whatever scale) determined the nature of both conflict and its resolution.

Conflict, at all levels, both in the international arena and in the local context, tested not only conventions and mediation mechanisms, but also the very foundations on which social and political coexistence was built. Conflict and reparation, the construction of public peace at every level, demanded a broad social consensus which reached beyond the social and political elites. In order to fully understand this issue, we must get past historical approaches that argue that change can only come from above, without taking into account other forms of social and cultural dialogue, which sometimes included conflict.

A similar problem ensues when closed categories are imposed. The use of such categories as 'Catholic', 'Protestant', 'Turkish', 'Southern Europe' or 'civilization', which do not reflect the reality of early modern Europe, tends to oversimplify the analysis. In our examination of the evolution of interpersonal violence, the introduction of forms of violence that did not lead to homicide – i.e. physical assaults and verbal violence – as well as the contrast between rural and urban contexts has presented interesting perspectives which provide a better understanding of the implications of the historical decline in the number of homicides. Social struggle, conflict (including violence) and war, cultural change and social participation must not be considered only *from above* but also *from below*. Furthermore, this *from below* must not be related only to resistance and dissidence, but also to active and creative participation in the construction of public peace.

Notes

1 This work has been carried out within the framework of research projects PGC2018-093841-B-C32, sponsored by the Spanish National Research Funds, and RESIS-TANCE-778076-H2020-MSCA-RISE-2017, sponsored by the European Commission.

2 V.A.C. Gatrell, B. Lenman and G. Parker (eds), *Crime and the Law: The Social History of Crime in Western Europe since 1500*, London: Europa Publications, 1980.

3 R.L. Kagan, *Lawsuits and Litigants in Castile, 1500–1700*, Chapel Hill, NC: University of North Carolina Press, 1981; A.M. Hespanha, 'Da iustitia à disciplina, textos poder e politica penal no antigo regime', *Anuario de Historia del Derecho Español* 57, 1987, 493–578.

4 B.A. Hanawalt, 'Economic influences on the pattern of crime in England, 1300–1348', *The American Journal of Legal History* XVIII, 1974, 294–296.

5 V.A.C. Gatrell, 'The decline of theft and violence in Victorian and Edwardian England', in Gatrell, Lenman and Parker (eds), *Crime and the Law*, 238–338.

6 T.A. Mantecón, 'The patterns of violence in Early Modern Spain', *The Journal of the Historical Society* 7.2, 2007, 229–264.

7 T.A. Mantecón, *Conflictividad y disciplinamiento social en la Cantabria rural del Antiguo Régimen*, Santander: University of Cantabria Press, 1997; Idem, *La muerte de Antonia Isabel Sánchez. Tiranía y escándalo en una sociedad rural del Norte de España en el Antiguo Régimen*, Alcalá de Henares: Centro de Estudios Cervantinos, 1998; Idem, 'El peso de la infrajudicialidad en el control del crimen durante la Edad Moderna' *Estudis* 28, 2002, 43–75; B. Garnot, 'Justice, infrajustice, parajustice et extra justice dans la France d'Ancien Régime', *Crime, Histoire & Sociétés/Crime, History & Societies* 4.1, 2000, 103–120.

8 P.R. Moody, 'Clausewitz and the fading dialectic of war', *World Politics* 31.3, 1979, 417–433: 417–418. These features of war have been extracted from the English text of Moody's *On War*, edited in 1943 and compiled several decades ago by V.J. Esposito ('War as a continuation of politics', *Military Affairs* 18.1, 1954, 19–26: 20) as part of his discussion on Von Clausewitz. Esposito stressed the impact of Von Clausewitz on military and strategic decision-making, especially with regard to the need to maintain a large enough military and resource-base in the international context of the Cold War.

9 As R. Powell ('War as a commitment problem', *International Organization* 60.1, 2006, 169–203: 170) has pointed out, 'if the pie to be divided can only be allocated or "cut

up" in a few ways' and 'if none of these allocations simultaneously satisfy all of the belligerents, at least one of the states will prefer fighting to settling and there will be war'. Sometimes this is also the result of imperfect information (asymmetric information leads to different viewpoints that affect mutual relationships) or violation of common agreements. If such lack of commitment ensues, at least one country will prefer war to peace. Knowing whether the information between parties is fair and symmetric or not, or whether all parties are totally committed to previous agreements, poses a substantial methodological challenge. Often, these factors can be explained *ex post* – that is, after the conflict – but not *ex ante*.

10 Despite the multiple works that have dealt with these issues after Von Clausewitz – A. Giddens, *The Nation-State and Violence*, Cambridge: Polity Press, 1988; M. Shaw, *Dialectics of War*, London: Pluto, 1988; C. Tilly, *Capital, Coercion, and European States, AD990–1992*, Oxford: B. Blackwell, 1990; I. Roxborough, 'Clausewitz and the sociology of war', *British Journal of Sociology* 45.4, 1994, 619–636 – more research is needed to analyse the specific effects of war in the local context.

11 Recurrent arguments that see war as a business concern fail to provide a social explanation for war, which is a complex phenomenon. See, for instance, two classic viewpoints on the matter in A. Ireland. 'War as a business problem', *The North American Review* 207:750, 1918, 720–728, and J. Schneider, 'Is war a social problem?', *The Journal of Conflict Resolution* 3.4, 1959, 353–360.

12 Kalevi Holsti (*Peace and War: Armed Conflicts and International Order, 1648–1989*, Cambridge: Cambridge University Press, 1991) has looked at this quantitatively, from a comparative perspective.

13 J.H. Elliott, *Europe Divided, 1559–1598*, London, Glasgow: Collins, 1969, 389–390.

14 R. Bonney, *The European Dynastic States, 1494–1660*, Oxford: Oxford University Press, 1991, 525.

15 Bonney, *The European Dynastic States*, sets the end of confessional conflict in Europe around 1660. R.S. Dunn (*The Age of Religious Wars, 1559–1715*, New York, London: W.W. Norton, 1979 [1st edn 1970]) considered that the effects of religious conflict lasted somewhat longer, until the War of the Spanish Succession.

16 See M.S. Anderson, *Europe in the Eighteenth Century, 1713–1783*, London, Harlow: Longmans, 1968 (1st edn 1961), 217–264. For a recent assessment of the development and global implications of the War of the Spanish Succession see M. Torres and S. Truchuelo (eds), *Europa en torno a Utrecht*, Santander: Editorial Universidad de Cantabria, 2014.

17 G. Parker, *The Thirty Years' War*, London, New York: Routledge, 1987 (1st edn 1984), Chapter VI.

18 L. Horodowich, 'The new cultural history?', *The Sixteenth Century Journal* 40.1 (Special Fortieth Anniversary Issue), 2009, 211.

19 J. Theibault, 'The rhetoric of death and destruction in Thirty Years War', *Journal of Social History* 27.2, 1993, 271–290.

20 Parker, *The Thirty Years' War*.

21 Moody ('Clausewitz and the fading dialectic of war', 433) quotes some eighteenth-century commentators, such as Count Guibert, who stated that 'no people in Europe was prepared to fight for despotism'.

22 R. Mousnier et al., 'Discussion of H.R. Trevor-Roper: The general crisis of the seventeenth century', *Past and Present* 18, 1960, 8–42.

23 J. Elliott, 'Revolution and continuity in early modern Europe', *Past and Present* 42, 1969, 35–56: 38–42.

24 T.A. Mantecón, 'La visión onírica de Durero, a propósito de la Reforma protestante', *Trasdós. Revista del Museo de Bellas Artes de Santander* 11, 2009, 105–120.

25 T.A. Mantecón, 'Ciudad, policía y desobediencia cívica en la España del Antiguo Régimen: experiencias históricas contrastadas', in T.A. Mantecón and O. Rey Castelao (eds), *Identidades urbanas en la Monarquía Hispánica (siglos XVI–XVIII)*, Santiago de Compostela: University of Santiago de Compostela Press, 2015, 237–268. Similar examples of passive resistance are known in other European cities and societies: K. Aalestad, 'Paying for war: Experiences of Napoleonic rule in the hanseatic cities', *Central European History* 39.4, 2006, 641–675.

26 A.N. Gilbert, 'Sexual deviance and disaster during the Napoleonic Wars', *Albion: A Quarterly Journal Concerned with British Studies* 9.1, 1977, 98–113.

27 C.S.R. Russell, 'Wars, and estates in England, France, and Spain c. 1580–c. 1640', *Legislative Studies Quarterly* 7.2, 1982, 205–220.

28 O. Hufton, *The Prospect before Her: A History of Women in Western Europe, Vol. 1. 1500–1800*, London: Fontana Press, 1997, 134–172, 251–298.

29 Some classic studies include those by C. Ginzburg (*I formaggio e i vermi*, Turin: Einaudi, 1976), G. Levi (*L'eredità immateriale. Carriera di un esorcista nel Piemonte del Seicento*, Turin: Einaudi, 1985) and N. Davis (*Women on the Margins: Three Seventeenth-Century Lives*, Cambridge, MA: Harvard University Press, 1995). More recently, other authors have presented different perspectives on these issues. See J. Spohnholz and G.K. Waite (eds), *The Experience of Exile and the Consolidation of Religious Identities*, London: Pickering & Chatto, 2014.

30 J. Sharpe ('The history of violence in England: Some observations', *Past and Present* 108, 1986, 206–215) gave a qualified response to Stone's contribution.

31 M. Eisner, 'Long-term historical trends in violent crime', *Crime and Justice: A Review of Research* 30, 2003, 83–142.

32 E. Monkkonen, 'New standards for historical homicide research', *Crime, History & Societies* 5.2, 2001, 5–26.

33 Eisner, 'Long-term historical trends in violent crime', 83–142; Idem, 'Modernization, self-control and lethal violence: The long-term dynamics of European homicide rates in theoretical perspective', *British Journal of Criminology* 41, 2001, 618–638: 621–627.

34 Nowadays wider analysed information useful for historical approaches can be found in H. von Hofer, 'Homicide in Swedish statistics, 1750–1988', in A. Snare (ed.), *Criminal Violence in Scandinavia: Selected Topics*, Oslo: Norwegian University Press, 1990, 29–45; H. Ylikangas, 'A historical review of violent crime in Finland', ibid., 45–64; P. Spierenburg, 'Long term-trends in homicide: Theoretical reflections and Dutch evidence, fifteenth to twentieth centuries', in E.A. Johnson and E.H. Monkkonen (eds), *The Civilization of Crime: Violence in Town and Country since the Middle Ages*, Urbana, IL: University of Illinois Press, 1994, 63–107; and M. Lappalainen and P. Hirvonen (eds), *Crime and Control in Europe from the Past to the Present*, Helsinki: Academy of Finland, 1999.

35 See some of my previous works: T.A. Mantecón, 'El poder de la violencia en el Norte de España', in *Encuentro de Historia de Cantabria*, Vol. II, Santander: University of Cantabria Press, 1999, 785–813; Idem, 'The patterns of violence'; Idem, 'La violencia en la Castilla urbana del Antiguo Régimen', in J.I. Fortea and J.E. Gelabert (eds), *Ciudades en conflicto (siglos XVI–XVIII)*, Madrid: Marcial Pons, 2008, 307–334; Idem, 'Civilización y brutalización del crimen en una España de Ilustración', in M.R. García-Hurtado (ed.), *La vida cotidiana en la España del siglo XVIII*, Madrid: Silex, 2009; Idem, *España en tiempos de Ilustración*, Madrid: Alianza, 2013; Idem, 'Los impactos de la criminalidad en

sociedades del Antiguo Régimen: España en sus contextos europeos', *Vínculos de Historia* 3, 2014, 54–74.

36 T.A. Mantecón, 'Homicide et violence dans l'Espagne de l'Ancien Régime', in L. Muc-chielli and P. Spierenburg (eds), *Histoire de l'homicide en Europe. De la fin du Moyen Âge à nos jours*, Paris: Editions La Découverte, 2009.

37 Rome figures refer to 1560–1580 averages, calculated by P. Blastenbrei, *Kriminalität in Rom, 1560–1585*, Tübingen: Niemeyer, 1995, 71 and 57–68. T. R. Gurr, 'Historical trends in violent crime: a critical review of the evidence', *Crime and Justice* 3, 1981, 295–353; J.M. Beattie, *Crime and the Court in England, 1660–1800*, Oxford: Clarendon Press, 1986, 77–124; Hofer, 'Homicide in Swedish statistics, 1750–1988', 29–45; J. Liliequist, 'Violence, honour and manliness in early modern Sweden', in M. Lappalainen and P. Hirvonen (eds), *Crime and Control in Europe from the Past to the Present*, Helsinki: Academy of Finland, 1999; P. Karonen, 'In search of peace and harmony: Capital crime in late medieval and early modern Swedish real (1450–1700)', in M. Lappalainen and P. Hirvonen (eds), *Crime and Control in Europe from the Past to the Present*, Helsinki: Academy of Finland, 1999, 208; A. Alloza, *La vara quebrada de la justicia. Un estudio histórico sobre la delincuencia madrileña entre los siglos xvi y xviii*, Madrid: Catarata, 2000, 129–132; B. Llanes, 'Las formas de la violencia interpersonal y su impacto en el Madrid de los Austrias', Master Thesis, University of Cantabria, 2006; A. Jansson, *From Swords to Sorrow: Homicide and Suicide in Early Modern Stockholm*, Stockholm: Almqvist and Wiksell, 1998; Spierenburg, 'Long term-trends in homicide', 63–107.

38 A. Alloza, 'Delincuencia y sociedad en Madrid, siglos XVI–XIX', in V. Pinto and S. Madrazo (eds), *Madrid. Atlas histórico de la ciudad. Siglo IX–XIX*, Madrid: Lunwerg, 1995, 291; Idem, *La vara quebrada de la justicia*, 130–131; Llanes, 'Las formas de la violencia interpersonal'; European data after Eisner, 'Long-term historical trends'.

39 M. Nassiet, *La violence, une histoire sociale. France, XVIe–XVIIIe siècles*, Seyssel: Champ Vallon, 2012, 298–299; Ylikangas, 'A historical review', 49.

40 E. Österberg and D. Lindström, *Crime and Social Control in Medieval and Early Modern Swedish Towns*, Uppsala: Academia Upsaliensis, 1988, 43–44. Annual homicide rates in districts such as Gästrikland, Hälsingland, Medelpad and Ångerman never rose above 4 per 100,000 inhabitants in the sixteenth century. These numbers are far below those attested in cities such as Stockholm (rates around 50 homicides per 100,000 inhabitants in the late sixteenth century) and other Swedish cities: Liliequist, 'Violence, honour and manliness in early modern Sweden', 180.

41 O. Matikainen, *Verenperijät. Väkivalta ja yhteisön murros itäisessä Suomessa 1500–1600-luvulla*, Helsinki: Seura, 2002, 38.

42 For British examples see J. Sharpe, *Crime in Seventeenth-Century England: A County Study*, Cambridge: Cambridge University Press, 1983, 58; C. Emsley, *Crime and Society in England, 1750–1900*, London: Longman, 1993 (1st edn 1987), 209–212; C.B. Herrup, *The Common Peace: Participation and the Criminal Law in Seventeenth-Century England*, Cambridge: Cambridge University Press, 1987, 27–28; B.J. Davey, *Rural Crime in the Eighteenth Century*, Hull: The University of Hull University Press, 1994, 10. On Cantabria see Mantecón, *Conflictividad y disciplinamiento social*, 273.

43 Y. Castan, *Honnêteté et relations sociales en Languedoc, 1715–1780*, Paris: Plon, 1974, 541.

44 Österberg and Lindström, *Crime and Social Control*, 43–44.

45 R. Muchembled, 'Crime et société urbaine: Arras au temps de Charles Quint (1528–1549)', in *La France d'Ancien Régime. Études réunies en l'honneur de Pierre Goubert. Société de Démographie Historique*, Paris: Société de Démographie Historique, 1984, 483.

46 Emsley, *Crime and Society*, 209–212; S. Faber, *Strafrechtspleging en criminaliteit te Amsterdam, 1680–1811*, Arnhem: Gouda Quint, 1983, 78; Spierenburg, 'Long-term trends', 701–716.

47 Mantecón, *Conflictividad y disciplinamiento social*; M.R. Weisser, *The Peasants of the Montes: The Roots of Rural Rebellion in Spain*, Chicago, IL: The University of Chicago Press, 1976; R. Iglesias, *Crimen, criminales y reos: la delincuencia y su represión en la antigua provincia de Santiago entre 1700 y 1834*, Santiago de Compostela: University of Santiago de Compostela Press, 2007; Alloza, 'Delincuencia y sociedad en Madrid'; Idem, *La vara quebrada de la justicia*; Llanes, 'Las formas de la violencia interpersonal'.

PART 3

The Western world and the global challenge, from 1750 to the present

INTRODUCTION

Hannu Salmi

The period from the 1750s to the present has been an era of not only profound and continuous changes but also many contradictions and tensions: an era of modernization and its discontents. It witnessed the Great Revolution of France and many other revolutions thereafter. The nineteenth century transitioned from the optimism of rising nationalism to the pessimistic views of the *fin de siècle*, from grey industrial cities with their forest of factory pipes to the idle calmness of bourgeois life. The twentieth century began with pessimistic visions of the future that seemed likely given the horrors of the trenches during the Great War, but as soon became obvious, these were only a prelude to even more sinister catastrophes. At the same time, however, the twentieth century was an era of popular culture and consumerism as well as the rapid development of technological novelties and many new avenues for individual expression, from home-made films to social media. Some historians have interpreted the nineteenth and twentieth centuries as an era of ever-accelerating history: events not only happen at an exhaustive pace, but the future also seems to escape even more rapidly.[1]

The forthcoming chapters put forward an experiential perspective on the history of these past few centuries: how people have perceived the world around them and how they have communicated and interacted with their environment. In his autobiography, *Mémoires d'outre-Tombe*, French author François-René de Chateaubriand famously expresses his melancholia in the face of inevitable changes: for him, the French Revolution confirmed the irreversibility of history. The new era that was to come seemed to destroy the old order of time.[2] Asko Nivala discusses this sense of time: contemporaries recognized the transient nature of history, which was at the heart of modern sensibility. At the same time, it is necessary to pay attention to how the notion of the self and the idea of an individual have changed. Peter N. Stearns creates an overarching synthesis of individualism and brings forward a whole research agenda on how to study the history of individualism in relation to the changing standards of emotion. Willemijn Ruberg, in turn, explores the modern conception of the self by focusing both on the medical understanding of the gendered body and on the emerging practices of psychiatry.

This *Routledge Companion* has been divided into three parts, and the forthcoming last part deals with cultural history after the 1750s. Obviously, this periodization is only an agreement, one possible way of conceiving the past. Stearns' and Ruberg's chapters both clearly highlight this by drawing on earlier developments. Ruberg starts with a reference to humoral pathology that goes back to ancient medicine. As will be shown, the traces of 'humours' were still discernible in the nineteenth century. In history, thus, every moment is an heir of its predecessors. Similar continuities are also visible in Kirsi Tuohela's analysis of the history of domestic life – of how families developed as child-centred emotional units. To be sure, every century is one of communities, and every era assumes particular social forms. The nineteenth and twentieth centuries were characterized by families and nations, societies and many other kinds of social organizations.[3] The increasing mobility of people and goods enabled new forms of communication and community-building. Dhan Zunino Singh offers a wide view on cultures of mobility – on the multiple ways in which mobile, nomadic, migratory life has intensified, not only for the few but also for the 'masses', who can easily travel or move their material belongings. When the ability to be mobile increased, the expected possibility for movement multiplied accordingly: we are now expected to be able to transgress physical distances.

According to Canadian media theorist Marshall McLuhan, media are 'extensions of man'.[4] That is, media gave people new faculties by helping them, for example, hear sounds that they would have otherwise never heard. Pelle Snickars writes on the changing roles of media, starting with the expansion of newspaper publishing in the nineteenth century and extending his analysis into a myriad of the most imaginative new forms of communication and entertainment, from daguerreotypes to dioramas and from film to television. Contemporary societies are saturated and permeated by media in such a manner that, as Stig Hjarvard argues, they 'may no longer be conceived as being separate from cultural and social institutions'.[5]

Media are an organic part of our sensory environment. Constance Classen and David Howes contextualize this development by offering a comprehensive view on the 'sensory life' of Western modernity since the late eighteenth century. The chapter clearly indicates the growing emphasis on media to disseminate 'the sights, sounds and values of modernity' and, as Classen and Howes argue, encourage 'citizens to speak a common language' and create 'common modes of framing experience'. This can also be seen in Steven Conn's discussion on the culture of the Cold War, which was strongly framed by mediated experiences.

This *Routledge Companion* portrays the 'cultural history of the Western world' while acknowledging the difficulty of defining what that 'Western world' ultimately covers and entails. There is no 'West' as an isolated concept; it is continuously constructed and deconstructed, defined and redefined. This concept is challenged by what it excludes via its very presence. The cultural history of the modern world could not be characterized without paying attention to those internal destructive forces, like violence and war traumas, analysed by Ville Kivimäki as having shaped the Western self-image, to those suppressing actions and processes that Western cultures have exercised upon other cultures, as discussed by Mita Banerjee, or to those economic interests that have had global ramifications, as highlighted by Jared Poley.

During the 2000s, posthumanist theorization challenged the human-centred, or 'anthropocentric', views of traditional humanities scholars, including historians. Kyrre Kverndokk underlines the long presence of catastrophes and natural disasters in human history. Certainly, we must note the inseparability of human and non-human factors in history and recognize that humans both make and do not make history. Still, we hope this book gives food for thought in estimating how human experience has shaped history and also how it has been shaped by a plethora of forces, actions and processes in the past, both human and non-human. This will be discussed in the Epilogue of the volume. Cultural history as an intellectual exercise means looking backwards while simultaneously gazing towards the future.

Notes

1 A. Alecou, Introduction: 'What Accelerates History?', *Acceleration of History: War, Conflict, and Politics*, ed. A. Alecou. Lanham, MD: Lexington Books, 2016, vii–viii. See also F. Hartog, *Regimes of Historicity: Presentism and Experiences of Time*, New York: Columbia University Press, 2015, 123.

2 On Chateaubriand, see Hartog, *Regimes of Historicity*, 123. See also P. Fritzsche, *Stranded in the Present: Modern Time and the Melancholy of History*, Cambridge, MA: Harvard University Press, 2004, 57–58.

3 On the forms of sociability in the nineteenth century, see H. Salmi, *Nineteenth-Century Europe: A Cultural History*, Cambridge: Polity Press, 2008.

4 M. McLuhan, *Understanding Media: Extensions of Man*, London: Routledge, 1964.

5 S. Hjarvard, *The Mediatization of Culture and Society*, London: Routledge, 2013, 2.

20

ENLIGHTENMENT, REVOLUTION, AND MELANCHOLY

Asko Nivala

The eighteenth century has often been depicted as an era of progress, when new scientific inventions were made and disseminated while the middle class gained more economic and political influence. The contemporaries of the century saw the introduction of the steam engine, Mercury thermometer, lightning rod, spinning jenny, and vaccination, to name only a few well-known examples. What is more, a new infrastructure for communication was developed based on the circulation of newspapers and other periodicals. There were postal service and European highway network advancements, which, together with improved reading and writing skills, made private correspondence more common than before. Cafés, salons, and free-mason lodges were new places of gathering for the bourgeoisie, in contrast with the earlier court culture.[1] The stock exchange disclosed many markets for public transactions, especially in the United Kingdom. Finally, the rising middle classes demanded their political rights in the American and French Revolutions.

From this point of view, the eighteenth century appears to be the Golden Age of liberalism. With the Industrial Revolution starting at the end of the eighteenth century and the introduction of the steamship and railway substantially changing the way in which people and commodities moved,[2] it might be justifiable to see a line of progress from the eighteenth to the nineteenth century. The development of science, industrialization, the press, economic trade, and political freedom continued during the next century, despite some occasional obstacles. However, the 1750s can also be seen as a turning point, after which European intellectual history started to show darker shades, and a new sceptical attitude to progress arose. The Lisbon earthquake in 1755 was a setback for the optimist rationalism of the earlier Enlightenment. The American and French Revolutions could be seen as spurring the development of political progress and republicanism, but they also brought a wave of unrest, wars, and, finally, harsh manifestations of political terror in France.

In the field of literature, this change in mentality is reflected in the rise of the Gothic novel in the United Kingdom and the *Sturm und Drang* movement in the German-speaking region. The dark side of political revolutions and industrialism was articulated during the era of Romanticism, which began in the 1790s in England and Germany. This chapter will discuss the European wave of melancholy, which started around the 1750s and culminated in the era of Romanticism (1795–1820), in order to show the complex ways in which the contemporaries related to the inauguration of modernity. It will contextualize the development from the Enlightenment to Romanticism vis-à-vis the Industrial Revolution and French Revolution.

The dark turn of the Enlightenment

In particular, the scholars writing after the Second World War have described the dark turn of the Enlightenment as an irrational 'Counter-Enlightenment', assuming that it was chiefly a German invention and that it teleologically foresaw the horrors of the fascism of the twentieth century. The concept of Counter-Enlightenment was invented by Isaiah Berlin; his interpretation was understandable in the post-war context but now appears to be an anachronistic argument based on too narrow a selection of primary sources.[3] As this chapter will show, the self-critical and sceptical views of the Enlightenment were not irrational reactions to progress. Therefore, the blind spot of Berlin's argument is not only his very schematic understanding of Romanticism as irrationalism but also his monolithic understanding of the Enlightenment as a rationalist movement.[4]

The Enlightenment was a complex, and even contradictory, project from the beginning; it is not accurate to describe it with stereotypes such as the age of rationalism or optimism, for it included many essential figures who vindicated empiricism and sentimentalism (moral sense theory) against earlier seventeenth-century continental rationalism (i.e. René Descartes, Blaise Pascal, and Gottfried Wilhelm Leibniz). Some French *philosophes* – Baron d'Holbach and Julien Offray de La Mettrie, for instance – promoted sceptical, nihilist, and materialist positions that are very difficult to classify under rationalism or idealism, although they promote naturalism and empiricism. According to the Greek historian of ideas Panagiotis Kondylis, the rehabilitation of empiricism, senses, and feelings was in fact the key accomplishment of the eighteenth-century Enlightenment, in contrast to the seventeenth-century rationalism exemplified by Descartes and Leibniz. For example, in Voltaire's *Candide: or, Optimism* (*Candide, ou l'Optimisme*, 1759), Leibnizian professor Pangloss represents the rationalist optimism of the earlier generation, which Voltaire juxtaposed with the real-world terrors of the Seven Years' War and the Lisbon earthquake. There existed a strong empiricist current in the British Enlightenment, which was as significant as the continental Leibnizian wing represented by Christian Wolff and Alexander Gottlieb Baumgarten in Germany.[5]

There are many Enlightenment thinkers – for instance, Johann Gottfried von Herder or Jean-Jacques Rousseau – who do not fit the stereotype of optimist rationalist. However, it would only increase the confusion to consider them teleologically as Counter-Enlightenment or pre-Romantic philosophers – in other words, to see them as predecessors of nineteenth-century Romanticism who simply happen to be living in the wrong century. The nineteenth-century Romantics undeniably criticized the Enlightenment, but one cannot reduce their relationship to simple dualism, such as rationalism–irrationalism, reason–feelings, liberal–conservative, or universal–historical. Sentimentalism, primitivism, or even Medievalism were not nineteenth-century inventions but originated in the latter half of the eighteenth century.[6] The rise of industrialism in England coincided with the increasing interest in picturesque landscape, the ruins of antiquity, and the monuments and documents of the Middle Ages. It was the philosophers of the Enlightenment who invented the ideal of the noble savage, with its primitivist accusations against the overdeveloped luxury of modern culture.

It is probable that no one better represents the contradictions of the eighteenth-century Enlightenment than the Genovese author, composer, and philosopher Jean-Jacques Rousseau. In the second part of his *Discourse on the Arts and Sciences* (*Discours sur les sciences et les arts*, 1750), Rousseau controversially argued that the invention of sciences had contributed to the moral corruption of mankind: 'an ancient tradition passed out of Egypt into Greece, that some god, who was an enemy to the repose of mankind, was the inventor of the sciences'.[7] In a footnote, Rousseau explains that he refers here to the myth of Prometheus, whose torch was chosen as a symbol for the Enlightenment movement. We need to keep in mind that the allegorical interpretation of antiquity was a very common way of referring to contemporary issues. By retelling an ancient myth, Rousseau illustrates the harmful implications of technological progress:

> The Satyr, says an ancient fable, the first time he saw a fire, was going to kiss and embrace it; but Prometheus cried out to him to forbear, or his beard would rue it. It burns, says he, everything that touches it.[8]

Rousseau's reference to the myth of Prometheus is an apt allegory for the Enlightenment movement. As the German philosopher Hans Blumenberg has suggested, the core of the Prometheus myth is the idea of irreversibility. Once fire has been used and given to mankind, there is no going back.[9] Four years later, Rousseau elaborated the same primitivist argument in his *Discourse on the Origin of Inequality* (*Discours sur l'origine et les fondements de l'inégalité parmi les hommes*, 1754). He now argued that it is the very perfectibility of humans that turns against them during the development of society. Civilization and technical progress certainly brought abundance to humankind, but Rousseau maintained that the more advanced the society, the more vulnerable it becomes to disasters and destructive wars.[10]

This ambiguous relationship with the past was also reflected in the Gothic novel, the cult of ruins, and the antiquarian interest in archaeological and historical remains that were developing in the latter half of the eighteenth century.[11] In 1748, Spanish military engineer Rocque Joaquín de Alcubierre (1702–1780) accidentally found Pompeii and Herculaneum, which were destroyed in the eruption of Vesuvius. Giovanni Battista Piranesi's drawings and Johann Joachim Winckelmann's art historical studies depicted the lost world of antiquity based on these findings. After the 1755 Lisbon earthquake, aesthetics required a new concept to analyse nature's agency. Edmund Burke used the concept of the 'sublime' to explain the aesthetics of natural disasters, darkness, and even political terror.[12] Some Enlightenment philosophers, such as Immanuel Kant in Germany, argued idealistically that the sublime was in fact an effect of the human mind and thereby provided indirect proof of our noumenal nature, which implied that there was no teleological agent working behind natural forces. Kant also emphasized that a person must be himself or herself in safety in order to judge a catastrophic event sublime.[13]

However, despite Kant's critical efforts, there developed a new taste that celebrated the non-human agency of nature: the hostile surroundings of the Alps, ancient cities destroyed in earthquakes, and churning seas and shipwrecks were now admired as aesthetic spectacles. Moreover, Gothic fiction charted the unconsciousness, sexual drives, and evil inside the human mind. Horace Walpole's *The Castle of Otranto* (1764) is often considered the first Gothic novel, while Ann Radcliffe's *The Mysteries of Udolpho* (1794) and Matthew Gregory Lewis's *The Monk* (1796) were the bestsellers of the genre and attracted wide attention. Similarly, Friedrich Schiller's *The Ghost-Seer* (*Der Geisterseher*, 1787–1789) was one of his most-read publications in his lifetime, although he is now much better known for his classical plays and poetry.

Obviously, not everyone was enthusiastic about the Gothic: Kant called the medieval Gothic taste of Nordic people perverted and grotesque.[14] Magnificent, obscure, and potentially dangerous objects evoked the sublime experience typical of Gothic horror. In contrast with the harmonious beauty fitting rational limits, the sublime was a sign of excess that escaped the rational capacity of the human mind.[15] Some nihilist Enlightenment philosophers, such as the Marquis de Sade, were interested in the presentation of the dark side of humanity in Gothic fiction. Strikingly, de Sade explains the birth of the Gothic novel as a fruit of revolutionary terror: terror and violence were an understandable reaction to the most grotesque events of contemporary history.[16] At the turn of the nineteenth century, Robertson's (Étienne-Gaspard Robert, 1763–1837) *Fantasmagoria* illustrated the horrible events of the Revolution by using a Fantoscope (a magic lantern on wheels) to project 'wavering images of ghosts and deceased tyrants'.[17] Again, the audience of the spectacle could experience the sublime events of contemporary history from a safe distance. As mentioned at the start of this chapter, the present scholarship no longer interprets these developments as a teleological sign of pre-Romanticism but, rather, as aspects of the Enlightenment. This is not to say that Gothic horror did not influence Romanticism, because it obviously did, but that its origin is in the contradictions present in eighteenth-century culture.[18]

As the case of the sublime exemplifies, the key problem of the Enlightenment was the tension between naturalism and human freedom. The scientific revolution led to the naturalist conclusion that everything in nature was causally determined: there had to be a sufficient reason for all things. Conversely, the Enlightenment emphasized human agency and its political implications. As illustrated by Kant's problems with regard to adapting together the first and second critiques, the causal necessity and the freedom of will were difficult to combine without returning to Cartesian dualism. In Germany, this contradiction of the Enlightenment escalated in the pantheism controversy of the 1780s. Consequent monism and naturalism threatened freedom, whereas the noumenal essence of man appeared supernatural for some philosophers.[19] Kant's solution was to advocate transcendental idealism, whereby naturalism and morality could be seen as two different perspectives of the same world. The Romantic generation used these arguments against Kant's intentions to conclude that there was no pre-given reality, because all human experience was necessarily filtered through space and time, the categories of understanding, and linguistic discourses. Furthermore, the Romantic generation temporalized this contradiction by arguing that the French Revolution and industrialism caused a rupture between the lost premodernity and the alienated present.

Industrial and political revolution

The latter part of the eighteenth century was an era of revolutions in science, politics, and technology. The subject for the French Academy's annual competition in 1737 was the nature of fire. Although combustion belongs among the oldest inventions of mankind, what fire was and how it spread was still a mystery for natural scientists. Voltaire and Émilie du Châtelet (1706–1749) investigated this using experiments and proved that fire had weight.[20] A modern-day Prometheus, Antoine-Laurent de Lavoisier replaced the old phlogiston theory with oxygen, a chemical element that explained the chemical process behind combustion. Lavoisier recognized and named oxygen in 1778. This was among the crucial steps in the early modern natural philosophy that studied the qualities of the quantitative paradigm of modern science: fire was no longer seen as a basic element but, rather, as a chemical reaction between oxygen and a fuel. Despite his scientific success, Lavoisier's situation became problematic after the French Revolution: he belonged to various aristocratic councils of the *ancien régime*, including the notorious tax office *Ferme générale*, because of which he became a victim of the revolutionary terror and was guillotined in 1794. German Romantic author Friedrich Schlegel probably had similar events in mind when he characterized the French Revolution 'as the most frightful grotesque of the age, where the most profound prejudices and their most brutal punishments are mixed up in a fearful chaos and woven as bizarrely as possible into a monstrous human tragicomedy'.[21] This led Schlegel to describe the age of the French Revolution as a chemical era of violent and surprising reactions in *Athenäum* magazine in 1798.[22]

The invention of chemistry through the understanding of combustion occurred in connection with the Industrial Revolution. The burning of fossil fuels was the necessary condition of the steam engine that led to the beginning of the Industrial Revolution in England. This is another process that was impossible to reverse, although the contemporaries, such as British Romantic poet and artist William Blake, were already aware of the potentially dire effects of 'these dark Satanic mills' on the environment.[23] In *Frankenstein; or, The Modern Prometheus* (1818), Mary Shelley associated Victor Frankenstein, an ambitious scientist producing a technological invention that breaks loose to destroy humanity, with the figure of Prometheus, referring to Rousseau's allegory 70 years before. Moreover, the sentimental descriptions of Victor's happy childhood in Geneva paraphrase sections of Rousseau's nostalgic description of the pristine Alpine nature in *Julie, or the New Heloise* (*Julie, ou la nouvelle Héloïse*, 1761), showing continuity from the sentimentalism of the Enlightenment to nineteenth-century Romanticism.

Considering that the Romantic cult of nature is often associated with the history of ecocriticism and the conservation of nature, it is an interesting fact that many German Romantic authors were either educated in geology or even worked in the service of the mining industry. The actual Industrial Revolution happened relatively late in Germany, although the German mining industry had medieval roots. For example, the Romantic poet Novalis (Friedrich von Hardenberg) worked as a mining engineer, and geological motifs are typical in his works, especially in the posthumously published *Heinrich von Ofterdingen* (1802). Novalis's novel clearly idealizes the medieval practice of mining in Germany.[24] In contrast, E.T.A. Hoffmann's *The Mines of Falun* (*Die Bergwerke zu Falun*, 1819) described the harsh reality of the mining shaft, comparing it with Hell on Earth.[25]

Rousseau had warned about the double-edged nature of Promethean technology, but ironically, his own political philosophy contributed to the political emancipation project of the late eighteenth century. This development culminated in the French Revolution in 1789, which certainly brought with it as much terror as deliverance. In addition to technology, the image of Prometheus referred to the idea of rebellion against authorities and religion in the late eighteenth century. Johann Wolfgang von Goethe, one of the key authors of *Sturm und Drang*, wrote the poem 'Prometheus' (1774), which describes a rebellion against religion and Zeus, the leader of Olympian deities.[26] The origin of this reference was Shaftesbury's (Anthony Ashley Cooper, the Third Earl of Shaftesbury) *Soliloquy or Advice to an Author* (1710), in which Promethean poets are called the second maker after God.[27] Yet, the idea of rebellious genius is not a sign of pre-Romantic protest, but it is clearly related to the criticism of authority that is typical of the Enlightenment.[28] In addition to technological progress and the aesthetic rebellion of *Sturm und Drang*, the character of Prometheus was associated with the abolition of slavery. Treated badly by his Dutch owner, a black slave in Voltaire's *Candide* refers to Prometheus, who was chained to Mount Caucasus.[29]

It should be noted that the German reception of the French Revolution was ambivalent and often more cultural than properly political. From a political perspective, German states still formed only an aggregate consisting of a network of small principalities and cities that shared the same culture and language. They had no parliamentary system, political parties, or even a strict separation between political, theological, and moral discourses.[30] Fifteen years before the French Revolution, German cultural life had already seen the wave of youthful rebellion that was called *Sturm und Drang*. Among its most famous works is Goethe's *The Sorrows of Young Werther* (*Die Leiden des jungen Werthers*, 1774). In one of the key scenes in the novel, Werther visits a friend but encounters a gathering of aristocrats at his house. Because Werther is not a nobleman, he is asked to leave. The novel shows the hidden tension in German society, where the rising middle classes had gained economic influence, but not the same social recognition as the nobility.

Especially after the start of the French Revolution, printing activity in Germany was regulated, but in spite of this, references to the French events were very common in literary and cultural magazines. The early Romantic author Friedrich Schlegel was first excited about the political possibilities of the French events. He worked in close co-operation with Caroline Böhmer (later the spouse of his brother, August Wilhelm), who was influential in the short-lived Republic of Mainz. As Friedrich Schlegel's 'Essay on the Concept of Republicanism' ('Versuch über den Begriff des Republikanismus', 1796) shows, Schlegel even considered as a relevant option the possibility of violent insurrection against political tyranny.[31] The text was printed in the radical *Deutschland* magazine, edited by Johann Friedrich Reichardt, who was a known supporter of the French Revolution and the democratic constitution. Reichardt's magazine had constant difficulties with censorship and was suspended by the authorities, but Reichardt founded a new literary magazine called *Lyceum der schönen Künste*, in which Friedrich Schlegel published his first Romantic collection of fragments. Only a year later, Friedrich founded his own Romantic magazine, *Athenäum* (1798–1800), together with his brother August Wilhelm. This shows the way in which the Romantic generation embraced periodicals, the media of the Enlightenment, as the channel of their literary views and social opinions.

However, Schlegel's relationship to the actual events of the Revolution became more moderate than before when he started to pay more attention to the political terror connected with it. In 1800, Schlegel moved to Paris, which made him even more conscious of the everyday effects of the Revolution. Travelling to Paris to witness the new situation after the Revolution was a typical topos among the Romantic generation in general. In addition to Schlegel, William Wordsworth and Swedish-Finnish Frans Michael Franzén (1772–1847) were disappointed after seeing the harsh reality of post-revolutionary France.[32] This led to a conservative turn among many Romantics, although some – for example, P. B. Shelley – remained loyal to the republican cause even in the first decades of the nineteenth century.

The rise of Romanticism at the turn of the nineteenth century becomes understandable in the context of the industrial and political revolutions. In particular, High Romanticism often celebrated the ideas of naturality and national originality, and in a sense, this could be seen as a critical answer to the industrial utilization of nature and 'artificially' made state borders during the Napoleonic Wars (1803–1815). Among the key ideas of the early Romantic cultural theory was that there were two kinds of poetry: artificial and natural. The former was based on classical rules of the learned elite, whereas the latter was an expression of unconscious nature and folk. In *Dialogue on Poetry* (*Gespräch über die Poesie*, 1800), Friedrich Schlegel argues that nature can produce poetry too:

> And what are they [poems], compared with the unformed and unconscious poetry which stirs in the plants and shines in the light, smiles in a child, gleams in the flower of youth, and glows in the loving bosom of woman? This, however, is the primeval poetry without which there would be no poetry of words. Indeed, there is and never has been for us humans any other object or source of activity and joy but that one poem of the godhead the earth of which we, too, are part and flower.[33]

Schlegel's theoretical framework is based on the pantheist idea that humans are part of nature too, and, hence, the original creative activity is based on the realization of nature's creative potential. The creative powers of nature are unconscious, naïve, and feminine, in contrast to the artificial poetry of masculine authors. Later in the *Dialogue on Poetry*, Schlegel explicitly connects his metaphysics of poetry to Baruch Spinoza's monism, according to which creative human activity originates in nature's productive powers. The Greek etymology of poetry is *poiesis*, which means production and creation.

The Romantic oxymoron 'natural culture' was widespread during European Romanticism, and it had connections with the Herderian criticism of colonialism and artificially created empires that consisted of smaller nations. For example, the Swedish-Finnish Romantic critic Fredrik Cygnaeus (1807–1881) argued that Franzén's poetry is a product of nature. In Franzén's works, the Herderian argument about the originality of indigenous peoples and their poetry was used for anticolonial purposes. Franzén's *Emili eller en afton i Lapland* (*Emili, or an Evening in Lapland*, 1802) is set in Lapland, an area of indigenous Sami people that is scattered across the northern parts of Norway, Sweden, Finland, and Russia. In Franzén's *Emili*, Thor and Assa, both of whom are Sami, are kidnapped by a European circus group that travels to Germany and exhibits them with their reindeers as if they are exotic animals. Thor manages to escape over the border to the French Republic, where he fights for the revolutionary cause.[34] Franzén's discussion of the noble savage myth is similar to *Atala, ou Les Amours de deux sauvages dans le desert* (1801) by François-René de Chateaubriand. In Romanticism, the local culture of peripheries was seen as an intrinsic value, in contrast to the universalism of empires and the globalism of the market centres. However, one must keep in mind that the noble savage figure was already widespread in the literature of the Enlightenment, as exemplified by Denis Diderot's *Supplément au voyage de Bougainville* (*Addendum to the Journey of Bougainville*, 1796).[35]

Although Romanticism in general was related to the rehabilitation of nature and ethnic originality, the early theoretical framework of German Romanticism in particular was more complex than simply the fetishism of authenticity. For example, in Schlegel's *Dialogue on Poetry*, the Romantic understanding of poetry as the Orphic original language of nature is soon complicated by his interest in Promethean artificial poetry – the idea of the poet as a conscious creator of artificial inventions.[36] When introducing his project on new mythology, Schlegel now emphasizes that the artificiality of poetry will be necessary in modernity. The ancient mythology of the Greeks was produced unconsciously, but the modern Romantic mythology must be a conscious project from the beginning:

> For it [mythology] will come to us by an entirely opposite way from that of previous ages, which was everywhere the first flower of youthful imagination, directly joining and imitating what was most immediate and vital in the sensuous world. The new mythology, in contrast, must be forged from the deepest depths of the spirit; it must be the most artful [*künstlichste aller Kunstwerke*] of all works of art[.][37]

Schlegel's characterization is based on German author Friedrich Schiller's distinction between naïve (objective) and sentimental (subjective) poetry. The ancients had been naïve, but the moderns could only be sentimental, because one could never return to the past stage of naïveté after it was lost. The ancient poetry was objective in the sense that the ancients simply imitated nature, but it was also naïve because the ancients were not conscious of the agency of the subject. The modern poetry, in contrast, is sentimental, because its key theme is longing for the lost unity with nature. Conversely, sentimental poetry is more reflective, because it assumes that the subject constructs an image of the lost harmony in nature.[38] The sentimental attitude is, thus, typical of the modern era, which understood itself as alienated from the assumed past harmony. Schiller refers to the industrial mentality and distribution of work as a source of modern alienation, resembling Rousseau's primitivism.[39]

Nevertheless, the melancholy became deeper during the first decades of the nineteenth century, and Late Romanticism brought about a conservative turn, especially after the Napoleonic Wars. Many contemporaries already considered the French Revolution as the border that separated the past from the present. The French Revolution, and the wars following it, meant such a fundamental change in political conditions and state borders that Europe was never the same after its occurrence. As Schlegel argued, 'The historian is a prophet facing backwards'.[40] That is to say, history can be written only after the events have unfolded, but historical time itself is irreversible, which is the explanation for the European-wide wave of Romantic melancholy that was felt after the changes of the French Revolution.

The ambiguities of Romantic melancholy

The final section of this chapter will discuss the rise of Romanticism from the point of view of melancholy. The idea of 'melancholy' has a long history prior to Romanticism. Originally, *melancholia* (μέλαινα χολή) was one of the four temperaments matching the four humours of ancient humoralism. Exemplified by Albrecht Dürer's famous engraving *Melencolia I* (1514), it was a popular belief system in the early modern period. Robert Burton's *The Anatomy of Melancholy* (1621) analysed the subject from both a literary and a medical point of view. In the nineteenth century, *melancholia* still had a medical meaning, referring to both a mental and a physical state of depression, but it also became a literary fashion after Edward Young's poem *Night Thoughts* (1742–1745). Young's influence was significant for German *Sturm und Drang* and is visible in Goethe's *The Sorrows of Young Werther*. The echoes of Young's influence were heard in Finland, as exemplified by Frans Michael Franzén's remark during his tour of Western Europe from 1795 to 1796. Franzén describes deep nocturnal melancholy inspired by Young: seeing the sublime ruins of Falkenburg Castle in the darkness of night even led him to play with the idea of committing suicide there someday.[41] Furthermore, William Shakespeare's plays provided another impetus for the Romantic melancholy. August Wilhelm Schlegel had been working with a new translation of *Hamlet* (1602) since the 1790s, and his brother, Friedrich Schlegel, analysed melancholic Prince Hamlet as a picture of the modern man who was incapable of making decisions.[42] Finally, the Romantic cult of night and death culminated in *Hymns to the Night* (*Hymnen an die Nacht*, 1800) by Novalis, which was inspired by the early death of his tubercular fiancée, Sophie, and presented the afterlife as a way in which the lovers could be reunited. In 1801, 29-year-old Novalis died from the same disease and consolidated the Romantic myth of a poet sacrificing himself.

Despite these dark tones, early German Romanticism was often optimistic about the future. For example, 'On Incomprehensibility' ('Über die Unverständlichkeit',

1800), an essay by Friedrich Schlegel that concluded the final number of *Athenäum*, declares the following:

> The new age is heralding itself as fleet of foot and winged of sole; the dawn has put on seven-league boots. For a long time now a storm has been brewing on the horizon of poesy. … Soon, however, one will no longer be able to speak of a single storm. Instead, the entire sky will burn in one flame, and then all of your little lightning rods won't help you. The nineteenth century will indeed begin, and then every little mystery regarding the unintelligibility of the *Athenäum* will be solved.[43]

Admittedly, Friedrich Schlegel's description of a utopian future has ironic tones: he uses the metaphor of the 'storm' and the metonym of the 'lightning rod' to depict the rise of new Romantic poetry as an upheaval of German cultural life whose sparkle has such a high voltage that the Enlightenment's 'lightning rod' cannot handle its energy. After the storm of the Romantic literature, the beginning of the next century is 'dawn', a new morning of humanity, argues Schlegel. The irreversibility of time slowly replaced the cyclical notion of history as an organic development whereby the Golden Age returns periodically. Voltaire had still maintained that although science could progress endlessly, poetry always encountered a certain limit, after which it degenerated.[44] Schlegel's famous definition of Romantic literature as 'progressive universal poetry' should be seen as a polemical argument against this earlier cyclical understanding of history.[45] However, the linear understanding of history also implied that the primal Golden Age could no longer return, because this would again imply cyclicity.

Despite Friedrich Schlegel's utopian optimism, Romanticism often had darker shades, and they became deeper, especially after the Napoleonic Wars raged in Europe. The Romantic elegiac notion of history was based on the conviction that the past could never return. Although many Romantics advocated republican politics, especially in the 1790s, High Romanticism is characterized by the longing for the lost national past. Friedrich Schlegel also contributed to the nostalgic melancholy triggered by the ruins of the past after the Revolution. He described the Rhenish landscape filled with the ruins of medieval castles, feeling deep melancholy for the remains of a bygone past. Schlegel, who had been a revolutionary republican in his youth, represented a typical experience of the time: after the Napoleonic Wars, he became a political conservative, cherishing the remains of the German past. When visiting Paris in 1804, Schlegel described with horror the destruction of the Basilica of Saint Denis in the aftermath of the Great Revolution:

> [T]he deep silent melancholy it inspires becomes stronger and more profound in approaching this ancient and now ruined cathedral. Every part that could be destroyed without too much labour and difficulty has been thrown down; the naked walls alone are left standing, with the massy pillars and the arches that rest upon them. As the doors were opened, a host of jackdaws and rooks, the sole inhabitants of the desecrated sanctuary, took flight, and when the dust they raised in their departure had subsided, we saw the uptorn graves of the sovereigns of France[.][46]

His disappointment with the results of the Revolution explains Schlegel's sudden political turn from radicalism to restoration.

As Peter Fritzsche maintains in *Stranded in the Present: Modern Time and the Melancholy of History* (2004), the contemporaries of the French Revolution understood themselves as the heirs of a completely new period of history. The Romantic melancholy was based on the experience of disconnectedness from the irretrievably lost past and worries related to the unknown future.[47] In addition to the Middle Ages, ancient Greece was an important setting for Romantic poetry. *Ode on Melancholy* (1819) by John Keats associated melancholy with lost Greece and the oblivion of modernity. The poem's first stanza refers to the myth of Lethe, a river in Hades; those who drink from Lethe experience complete forgetfulness. Keats's *Ode on a Grecian Urn* (1820) elaborates the theme in relation to the lost world of antiquity, which can still be remembered in the silence of the material remains that have survived.[48]

The French Romantic author François-René de Chateaubriand compared the French Revolution with 'the river of blood which separates forever the old world, which you are leaving, from the new world'.[49] In Chateaubriand's view, revolution was a rupture that separated the past from the present.[50] His loosely autobiographical novella *René* (1802) was a bestseller about an aristocrat who is not satisfied with modernity and feels melancholy for the lost world. René's travels in Europe both followed and established the itineraries of Romantic melancholy that authors such as Lord Byron followed after him. Because Romanticism celebrated the local identity of places, I will focus on the typical sites of Romantic melancholy using *René* as an example.[51]

Figure 20.1 presents a reconstruction of the map implied in the text of *René*. The place names are embedded with their textual contexts to show Chateaubriand's interpretations of the places. The toponym 'Europe' is located around the Netherlands, because, as a region, it cannot be represented with a point, while the American places are on the smaller map. The map shows the way in which the sites of Romantic melancholy are often located on the periphery. René visits the northern parts of Scotland, the location of *Ossian* (1760), while also climbing Mount Etna in Sicily, combining peripheral places in both the north and south. Rome is also a very typical destination of Romantic narratives, combined with a tour of the Greek ruins. Although Rome can be considered an urban centre, René sees it through its art and history. It is remarkable that in many Romantic narratives, both Italy and Greece are represented as ancient places without any references to their contemporary histories, although Italy was an important battle scene in the Napoleonic Wars and Greece was still part of the Ottoman Empire. *René* also moves on an exceptionally wide horizontal axis, because its frame narrative is located in the remoteness of Louisiana.

The feeling of melancholy presupposes an experience of distance and loss. As these Romantic examples have shown, this distance can be either temporal or spatial. The French Revolution, scientific development, and the beginning of industrialization were a point of rupture, after which history was never the same. Moreover, economic progress increased the division of regions into core and periphery. According to the eighteenth-century colonial attitude, the periphery was often seen only as a source of raw materials, which were then transported to core cities for refinement and sale.[52] Although Romanticism has sometimes been confused with a naïve nostalgia for the past, the Romantic melancholy aroused a new interest in nature, historical

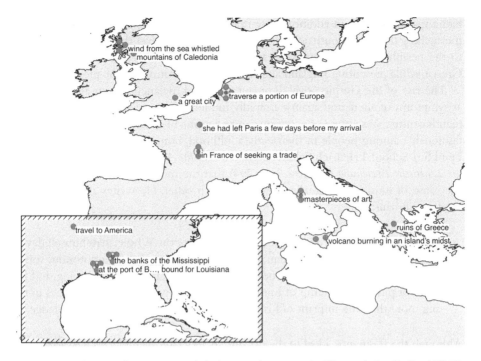

Figure 20.1   A map of toponyms and their textual contexts in Chateaubriand's *René* (1802).
Asko Nivala.

environments, and the original cultures of economically underdeveloped regions. As
has been said, many of these sceptical features were already present during the Enlightenment, which was not ignorant of the complexities of progress.

Conclusion

The dark turn of the Enlightenment in the second part of the eighteenth century
elucidates why there are good reasons to conclude that the age of the Enlightenment
was too complex an era to be reduced to any single idea, be it rationalism or a belief
in progress. In contrast to seventeenth-century rationalism, many key thinkers of the
Enlightenment were empiricists and were sceptical of the ideas of theodicy or optimism. The aesthetic fashion of the sublime and Gothic fiction were in fact integral
parts of the age of the Enlightenment, although nineteenth-century Romanticism
might sometimes have radicalized these developments.

The beginning of the Industrial Revolution in the United Kingdom and the political revolution in France provided the historical contexts in which nineteenth-century
Romanticism developed. The European-wide wave of melancholy was related to these
political, social, and ecological issues. Although especially early Romanticism was often
progressive, optimist, and republican, the Napoleonic Wars were the point after which
the interest of many Romantics turned towards the lost national past. However, like
Rousseau before them, the Romantics were conscious of the impossibility of regaining
the past Golden Age (if there ever even was one). Moreover, the Romantic nostalgia

had a spatial element in addition to temporal references: there were specific sites of melancholy that were constructed in the Romantic narratives that spatialized the past to the peripheries of Europe, such as Scotland or the ruins of ancient Rome and Greece, while presenting England and France as the locations of the present misery.

The rise of the Gothic novel, Romanticism, and melancholy can all be regarded as symptoms of alienation against a rapidly modernizing society. Although the eighteenth century was a time of economic and scientific breakthroughs, melancholy was fashionable among people in their early adulthood. Long before Karl Marx and the Frankfurt School, Friedrich Schiller argued in *On the Aesthetic Education of Man* (*Über die ästhetische Erziehung des Menschen*, 1794) that the modern division of labour was the cause of human beings' alienation from each other. He writes about the lot of modern humans:

> Everlastingly chained to a single little fragment of the Whole, man himself develops into nothing but a fragment; everlastingly in his ear the monotonous sound of the wheel that he turns, he never develops the harmony of his being, and instead of putting the stamp of humanity upon his own nature, he becomes nothing more than the imprint of his occupation or of his specialized knowledge.[53]

Although the Romantic ideal of the organic society later gained a conservative stain, it was originally developed as a critical alternative to the modern specialization of work, which had resulted in the disintegration of knowledge and the mechanization of human relationships. Because of these political implications, early Romanticism in particular shared many critical postulates with the Promethean rebel of *Sturm und Drang* and the Enlightenment. It was not until Late Romanticism that the conservative trend became dominant, which designated a transition whereby the Romantic counterculture slowly transformed from a youthful mutiny to a conservative ideology that supported the status quo and was written by officially appointed national poets.

Notes

1 See the classical studies on the bourgeois public sphere: J. Habermas, *The Structural Transformation of the Public Sphere: An Inquiry into a Category of Bourgeois Society*, trans. T. Burger and F. Lawrence, Cambridge, MA: MIT Press, 1989; R. Koselleck, *Critique and Crisis: Enlightenment and the Pathogenesis of Modern Society*, Cambridge, MA: MIT Press, 1988.

2 See J. Osterhammel, *The Transformation of the World: A Global History of the Nineteenth Century*, trans. P. Camiller, Princeton, NJ: Princeton University Press, 2014.

3 See I. Berlin, *The Roots of Romanticism*, Princeton, NJ: Princeton University Press, 1999, 46–47 and passim. Robert E. Norton has shown the problems of Berlin's reading. R.E. Norton, 'The Myth of the Counter-Enlightenment', *Journal of the History of Ideas* 68, 2007, 635–658.

4 See A. Nivala, 'Critique and Naturalism: Friedrich Schlegel and the Principles of the Enlightenment', in C. Wolff, T. Kaitaro, and M. Ahokas (eds), *The Enlightenment: Critique, Myth, Utopia: Proceedings of Symposium Arranged by the Finnish Society for Eighteenth-Century Studies in Helsinki, 17–18 October 2008*, Frankfurt a. M.: Peter Lang, 2011, 203–219.

5 P. Kondylis, *Die Aufklärung im Rahmen des neuzeitlichen Rationalismus*, Hamburg: Meiner, 2002, 20–21.

6 Kondylis, *Die Aufklärung im Rahmen des neuzeitlichen Rationalismus*, 21; H.R. Jauß, *Literaturgeschichte als Provokation der Literaturwissenschaft*, Frankfurt a. M.: Suhrkamp, 1967, 40–42, 69.

7 J.-J. Rousseau, *The Social Contract and Discourses*, trans. G.D.H. Cole, London and Toronto: J.M. Dent and Sons, 1923, http://oll.libertyfund.org/titles/638.

8 Rousseau, *The Social Contract and Discourses*.

9 H. Blumenberg, *Work on Myth*, trans. R.M. Wallace, Cambridge, MA: MIT Press, 1985, 223, 301.

10 J.-J. Rousseau, *Discourse on the Origin of Inequality*, trans. D.A. Cress, Indianapolis, IN: Hackett Publishing Company, 1992, 78. In the supplements for the second edition of *Discourse on the Origin of Inequality*, Rousseau moderated his primitivist criticism of modernity and reminded the reader that it would be impossible to leave modern civilization behind and 'return to live in the forest to live with bears'. Ibid., 80.

11 W.D. Robson-Scott, *The Literary Background of the Gothic Revival in Germany: A Chapter in the History of Taste*, Oxford: Clarendon Press, 1965.

12 A. Nivala, 'Catastrophic Revolution and the Rise of Bildung', in H. Salmi, A. Nivala, and J. Sarjala (eds), *Travelling Notions of Culture in Early Nineteenth-Century Europe*, New York: Routledge, 2016, 19–37.

13 I. Kant, *Critique of Judgment*, trans. W.S. Pluhar, Indianapolis, IN: Hackett, 1987, 121–123.

14 Robson-Scott, *The Literary Background of the Gothic Revival in Germany*, 11.

15 F. Botting, *Gothic*, London: Routledge, 1996, 38–43.

16 A. Wright, *Gothic Fiction*, New York: Palgrave Macmillan, 2007, 64. On de Sade's place in the Enlightenment, see P. Kondylis, *Die Aufklärung im Rahmen des neuzeitlichen Rationalismus*, 509–518.

17 J. Tresch, *The Romantic Machine: Utopian Science and Technology after Napoleon*, Chicago, IL: University of Chicago Press, Kindle Edition, Ch. 5.

18 On the complex relationship between Gothic fiction and British Romanticism, see especially M. Gamer, *Romanticism and the Gothic: Genre, Reception, and Canon Formation*, Cambridge [England]: Cambridge University Press, 2006. Cf. Robson-Scott, *The Literary Background of the Gothic Revival in Germany*, 34–35.

19 Kondylis, *Die Aufklärung im Rahmen des neuzeitlichen Rationalismus*; F. Beiser, *The Fate of Reason: German Philosophy from Kant to Fichte*, Cambridge, MA: Harvard University Press, 1987.

20 R. Pearson, *Voltaire Almighty: A Life in Pursuit of Freedom*, London: Bloomsbury, 2006, 128, 138–139.

21 F. Schlegel, *Friedrich Schlegel's Lucinde and the Fragments*, trans. P. Firchow, Minneapolis, MN: University of Minnesota Press, 1971, 88 (*Athenäum-Fragment* No. 424).

22 See A. Nivala, 'Chemical Age: Presenting History with Metaphors', in B. Johnson and H. Kiiskinen (eds), *They Do Things Differently There: Essays on Cultural History*, Turku: k & h, 2011, 81–108.

23 Blake, *Milton*, A:1/i in W. Blake, *Blake's Poetry and Designs*, eds M.L. Johnson and J.E. Grant, New York: Norton, 2008.

24 K. Rigby, *Topographies of the Sacred: The Poetics of Place in European Romanticism*, Charlottesville, VA: University of Virginia Press, 2004; T. Ziolkowski, *German Romanticism and Its Institutions*, Princeton, NJ: Princeton University Press, 1992.

25 H.I. Sullivan, 'Dirty Nature: Ecocriticism and Tales of Extraction-Mining and Solar Power in Goethe, Hoffmann, Verne, and Eschbach', *Colloquia Germanica* 44, 2011, 111–131.

26 Goethe wrote 'Prometheus' between the years 1772 and 1774, but it was published anonymously by Friedrich Heinrich Jacobi in 1785. Lessing's reading of the poem started the famous *Pantheismstreit* (Pantheism Controversy). See Beiser, *The Fate of Reason*, 65.

27 See O. Walzel, *Das Prometheussymbol von Shaftesbury zu Goethe*, München: Max Hueber Verlag, 1932; M.-G. Dehrmann, *Das 'Orakel der Deisten': Shaftesbury und die deutsche Aufklärung*, Göttingen: Wallstein, 2008.

28 Jauß, *Literaturgeschichte als Provokation der Literaturwissenschaft*, 69.

29 E. Hall, *Ancient Slavery and Abolition: From Hobbes to Hollywood*, Oxford: Oxford University Press, 2011, 213; J. Hickman, *Black Prometheus: Race and Radicalism in the Age of Atlantic Slavery*, Oxford: Oxford University Press, 2017, 90.

30 See Koselleck, *Critique and Crisis*.

31 See F. Schlegel, *Kritische Friedrich-Schlegel-Ausgabe Bd. 7*, ed. Ernst Behler et al., Paderborn: Schöningh, 1966, 11–25.

32 Nivala, 'Catastrophic Revolution and the Rise of Bildung', 28; H. Rantala, 'Nordic Travellers between the Centres and Peripheries of Civilisation', in H. Salmi, A. Nivala, and J. Sarjala (eds), *Travelling Notions of Culture in Early Nineteenth-Century Europe*, New York: Routledge, 2016, 96–112.

33 F. Schlegel, *Dialogue on Poetry and Literary Aphorisms*, trans. E. Behler and R. Struc, University Park, PA: Pennsylvania State University Press, 1968, 54.

34 P. Lassila, *Runoilija ja rumpali: Luonnon, ihmisen ja isänmaan suhteista suomalaisen kirjallisuuden romanttisessa perinteessä*, Helsinki: Suomalaisen Kirjallisuuden Seura, 2000, 22–26.

35 See T. Kaitaro, 'Nature and Morality in Eighteenth-Century French Materialism', in C. Wolff, T. Kaitaro, and M. Ahokas (eds), *The Enlightenment: Critique, Myth, Utopia: Proceedings of Symposium Arranged by the Finnish Society for Eighteenth-Century Studies in Helsinki, 17–18 October 2008*, Frankfurt a. M.: Peter Lang, 2011, 203–219.

36 On the distinction between Orphic and Promethean Romanticism, see A. Nivala, *The Romantic Idea of the Golden Age in Friedrich Schlegel's Philosophy of History*, New York: Routledge, 2017, Ch. 2; P. Hadot, *The Veil of Isis: An Essay on the History of the Idea of Nature*, trans. M. Chase, Cambridge, MA: Harvard University Press, 2006, 91–100.

37 Schlegel, *Dialogue on Poetry and Literary Aphorisms*, 81–82.

38 Nivala, *The Romantic Idea of the Golden Age in Friedrich Schlegel's Philosophy of History*, Ch. 4, Section 'Tragedy as play'.

39 F. Schiller, *On the Aesthetic Education of Man: In a Series of Letters*, trans. E.M. Wilkinson and L.A. Willoughby, Oxford: Clarendon, 1968.

40 Schlegel, *Friedrich Schlegel's Lucinde and the Fragments*, 170 (*Athenäum-Fragment* no. 80).

41 G. Castrén, *Frans Michael Franzén i Finland*, Helsingfors: Aktiebolaget handelstryckeriet, 1902, 132–133; R. Koskimies, *Porthanin aika. Tutkielmia ja kuvauksia*, Helsinki: Otava, 1958, 274–276.

42 F. Schlegel, *On the Study of Greek Poetry*, trans. S. Barnett, New York: State University of New York Press, 2001, 33, 39, 115.

43 F. Schlegel, 'On Incomprehensibility', *Theory as Practice: A Critical Anthology of Early German Romantic Writings*, trans. J. Schulte-Sasse et al., Minneapolis, MN: University of Minnesota Press, 1997, 126.

44 Nivala, *The Romantic Idea of the Golden Age in Friedrich Schlegel's Philosophy of History*, Ch. 6.

55 Schlegel, *Friedrich Schlegel's Lucinde and the Fragments*, 175 (*Athenäum-Fragment* no. 116).

46 F. Schlegel, *The Aesthetic and Miscellaneous Works of Frederick von Schlegel*, trans. E.J. Millington, London: H. G. Bohn, 1849, 151–152.

47 P. Fritzsche, *Stranded in the Present: Modern Time and the Melancholy of History*, Cambridge, MA: Harvard University Press, 2004.

48 J. Keats, *Keats's Poetry and Prose*, ed. Jeffrey N. Cox, New York: Norton, 461, 473–474.

49 F. de Chateaubriand, *Mémoires d'outre-tombe*, trans. A.S. Kline, Book V, Ch. 7, www. poetryintranslation.com/PITBR/Chateaubriand/ChateaubriandMemoirsBookV.htm.

50 F. Hartog, *Regimes of Historicity: Presentism and Experiences of Time*, trans. Saskia Brown, New York: Columbia University Press, 2015, Ch. 3.

51 On the early nineteenth-century cultural itineraries and the theoretical discussion of the spatial turn, see A. Nivala, H. Salmi, and J. Sarjala, 'Introduction', in H. Salmi, A. Nivala, and J. Sarjala (eds), *Travelling Notions of Culture in Early Nineteenth-Century Europe*, New York: Routledge, 2016, 1–15.

52 See F. Moretti, *Distant Reading*, London: Verso, 2013.

53 F. Schiller, *On the Aesthetic Education of Man: In a Series of Letters* (*Über die ästhetische Erziehung des Menschen*), trans. E.M. Wilkinson and L.A. Willoughby, Oxford: Clarendon, 1968 (1794), 35.

21

INDIVIDUALISM AND EMOTION IN MODERN WESTERN CULTURE

Peter N. Stearns

The individualism of Western culture is probably more often noted than examined with much care. This essay evaluates one strand of Western individualism: the relationship to changing standards for emotion, in order both to move past mere generalization and to link the wider cultural history to the growing field of inquiry around emotional norms and experience. The result, admittedly, is partly an invitation to further work, for several potentially relevant aspects of emotions history have yet to be fully explored. But there are some intriguing connections around individualism, which help link otherwise disparate developments while also suggesting how cultural change can be translated into personal realities for substantial populations.

The chronological framework centres on the emotional implications of that odd combination of forces in the eighteenth century that highlighted Enlightenment rationalism, with its own individualistic implications, with the pre-Romantic culture which targeted individual experience from a somewhat different direction. The individualism that resulted showed up rather quickly in some emotional domains, but worked through more gradually in other areas, through the nineteenth century and into the twentieth. Other factors entered in, of course: relevant emotional changes would reflect new demographic realities, for example, as well as individualism. But comparative analysis, though still limited, suggests that cultural individualism distinctively coloured Western response to these wider factors, ultimately differentiating Western emotional experience from that of other modernizing societies at least to a significant extent.

Elements of Western individualism predate the eighteenth century, of course – but it is not clear that they carried significant emotional overtones. Renaissance individualism was doubtless a real phenomenon for some members of the cultural and social elite, but it did not seem to penetrate widely.[1] Norbert Elias has argued that the Renaissance launched a new campaign to tame Western manners and emotions, subjecting individual impulse to new if informal regulations including heightened shaming – hardly a movement towards greater individualism overall.[2] More widely still, from the later Middle Ages and into the eighteenth century, many forms of shaming actually increased, including the introduction of the charivari as an additional method of community control particularly over sexuality – again, not a trend that suggested greater valuation of individual emotional autonomy.[3] And while the Reformation in principle heightened attention to the individual's relationship to God, and unquestionably loosened some previous controls over individual religious experience, the movement in practice was subjected to deliberate efforts to assure community orthodoxy, including long, didactic sermons designed to counter the potentially subversive effects of rising literacy. Again, evidence of an individualizing impact on emotional experience is decidedly limited.

This is not the case, however, with the innovations of the eighteenth century. Without always focusing on individualism per se, a variety of historians have emphasized the contributions of this new cultural period to a heightened appreciation of individualism. The Lockean attack on original sin and its implication of rational improvability placed new emphasis on the validity and importance of the individual child, a theme that would be carried farther by the educational theorists of the Enlightenment. Colin Campbell has emphasized the impact of early popular Romanticism on individual patterns of courtship and emerging mass consumerism, the latter for example with particular attention to individualizing styles in colourful clothing.[4] Ideas of tolerance shifted increasingly from the more traditional interest in protecting groups – a theme carried on in arrangements like the Treaty of Westphalia – to a new concern for individual rights to religious liberty and freedom of expression, and this shift would be carried further by the declarations of rights of the end-of-century revolutions.[5] In constitutional law, in growing consumerism and in educational theory (though not yet, it must be admitted, wider educational practice, where older habits of rote learning long predominated), the individual was increasingly the measure of social progress.

Recent historical work, both on Britain and on colonial North America, has highlighted the new climate of cultural and emotional individualism, and its contribution to developments such as the American revolution. Thus Dror Wahrman's major study stresses the growing concerns about personal identity that began to permeate aspects of British culture, particularly towards the end of the eighteenth century. Increasingly, by the same token, people began to see personal development as inherent to character, rather than shaped by external forces – a quiet 'cultural revolution' that revised a number of basic assumptions. Novelists like Walter Scott bemoaned the lack of personal features in earlier fiction, in contrast to his own efforts to depict each case as 'an original, discriminated and individual person.' Economists chimed in: Jeremy Bentham recognized some common influences over groups of people but stressed the differences that marked each separate individual. The same thinking began to be applied to children: as against Locke's blank slate, the child was seen as a distinct creature, with his or her own qualities that should be brought out in a sensitive education. New fascination developed for individual faces, and at the same time new anxieties about the dangers of masquerade and disguise that could exploit the new awareness of the individual. And, of course, all this played into the more obvious, though deeply significant, political concerns with individual rights.[6]

For the North American side of things Nicole Eustace has painted a similar picture of growing emphasis on the individual and the validity of individual political passions, ultimately building into the American revolutionary movement. Credit for individualism spread beyond the genteel ranks of society, into the ranks of more ordinary folk, in their private and public dealings alike.[7]

The new individualism was not a matter of ideas and artistic forms alone. It related – though in ways that have yet to be fully charted – to a number of daily behaviours. Increasingly, for example, the popularity of swaddling declined in Western Europe and North America, despite the fact that an unswaddled infant required more attention from the parent (mother) than had been the case when, as in the seventeenth century, many infants were wrapped and hung on pegs so that mothers could continue their work. Increasingly the idea of restricting the individual ran against the growing beliefs in the importance of expression and individual development – as indeed may well have been the case. On another front: parental naming practices began to change, particularly by the later eighteenth century. Instead of relying primarily on biblical or family names (the latter sometimes designed to curry favour with the wealthy relative), parents increasingly opted for names that would seem more original, more appropriate to a child now seen as an independent being. Particularly revealing was the new disinclination against reusing the name of a dead sibling: a name was born, but also died, with the individual, and should not be carried over to complicate the identity of a newcomer. New behaviours of this sort obviously reflected a greater individualism, even in realms of behaviour distant from formal culture or politics, and they could stimulate greater individualism in turn.[8]

While the surge of individualism signalled a marked change in Western culture, it would translate into emotional standards only gradually, sometimes, again, in combination with other factors. Older conventions retained considerable potency, maintaining the importance of community controls over some emotional expression. Continued social and gender divisions long complicated the translation of individualism into more personal domains. Individualism would spur considerable adjustment, but only over time.

But an individualism–emotion linkage does begin to emerge quite clearly, with some foretaste even in the seventeenth century. One intriguing product was a growing, if admittedly not universal, impulse to keep a diary – an emblem that an individual's thoughts were worth recording – and to use the diary in part to chronicle and evaluate emotion. Early diaries – as in seventeenth-century Britain – were often a bit tongue-tied when it came to emotion, displaying little interest in the individual inner life or simply a lack of relevant emotional vocabulary. But connections expanded quickly, expressing but also furthering the idea that one's experience as an individual was closely linked to an array of emotion and, frequently, that the validity of an individual depended on personal emotional control.[9]

Several more specific connections between individual and emotion began to emerge during the eighteenth century itself, though they would become more elaborate, and probably more widely accepted, over time. Enlightenment ideas encouraged a new level of attention to earthly happiness, as a key measure of progress – an idea enshrined by 1776 in the notion of a 'right to happiness' pursuit. And while this notion might seem rather abstract, it actually began to connect to emotional standards through a new and probably unprecedented interest in personal cheerfulness. A second linkage, suggested directly by early Romanticism, involved a new valuation of love, initially particularly as an aspect of courtship or partner choice but ultimately more widely. Both these developments must be traced more fully, and their relationship to individualism more clearly established, but they directly illustrate the power of cultural innovation in the West to affect emotional formulations. Both, finally, had additional ramifications – for example, in extensions of happiness expectations to new identifications of boredom; and shifts in grief rituals to respond to the new emphasis on individualism and love.

Happiness and cheer

The connection between individualism and cheerfulness is, it must be admitted at the outset, clearer in historical correlation than, perhaps, in principle – a conundrum to be explored after the initial pattern is clarified.

Enlightenment emphasis on happiness in this world followed fairly directly from the familiar beliefs that, armed with greater rationality and freed from some of the retrograde forces like religious excess, human beings could improve the world around them. Progress – whether through greater political freedom, new knowledge brought by science, greater longevity thanks to improvements in medicine or simply heightened prosperity – would measurably ameliorate the human condition and generate greater happiness into the bargain. The new enthusiasm has been amply charted by Darrin McMahon and others, and it added up to a significant shift in Western intellectual history.[10]

What is less well known, though not uncharted, is the linkage between the new happiness expectations and a growing insistence that people themselves should become more cheerful, as a basic part of successful, socially responsible self-presentation; and further, how in context this fascination with cheerfulness tied back to the larger theme of individualism.

The backdrop, most pronounced in Protestant regions, had been a certain delight in melancholy that persisted into the early eighteenth century. Humankind could best reflect the pervasiveness of sin and the transcendent majesty of God by adopting a somewhat downcast air, reflecting an appropriate sense of humility – what one observer called 'a kind of melancholic demeanor and austerity.' Overt happiness or a burst of good cheer often provoked a need to apologize. Thus Ebenezer Parkman, a New England minister, 'grievously and sadly reflected' in his diary on a moment of laughter: 'I think I might have spent more time with graver people.'[11]

This was the tone that began to shift as the implications of Enlightenment ideas began to take hold. Alexander Pope declaimed, 'Oh happiness, our being's end and aim!' Or John Byrom, in 1828: 'It was the best thing one could do to be always cheerful … and not suffer any sullenness … a cheerful disposition and frame of mind being the best way of showing our thankfulness to God.' A new breed of mainstream Protestant ministers began urging their charges to think well of themselves, as a means of promoting the 'Happiness of the World.' Their approach was disputed, of course, by the evangelical strand, still attached to brooding over human corruption and original sin, but the division itself was revealing.[12]

The growing embrace of cheerfulness (probably particularly for men, at least initially) spread across social classes in principle. A Boston writer in 1758 described how the 'cheerful laborer shall sing over his daily task … a general Satisfaction shall run through the ranks of men.' Increasingly, a cheerful countenance was taken as a sign of an active, competent personality, capable of solving problems and moving on with life. The previous, widespread acceptance of a degree of sadness had been closely tied to a sense that emotions were forces that assailed the individual, over which he had little control. Now, individualism reversed the equation: emotions were there to be mastered, and a demonstration through cheerfulness was one way to show that the proper controls were in place. Submission was replaced by the new sense of self.

And this, in turn, was the link with the more general promotion of individualism. In principle, after all, the growing insistence on a cheerful disposition was not inherently connected to the new valuation of the individual: it could, as we will see, actually constrain individual emotional choice, by reducing the acceptability of less enthusiastic options. The modern duty to be cheerful can be burdensome. But in the eighteenth-century context, cheerfulness was a demonstration that the individual was not being trapped by earlier insistence on humility before God: if still religious, the individual was adopting a different, more independent approach to the divinity. More important still, the cheerful individual was clearly able to shape the environment around him, rather than being trapped by it. He had control over his emotions, rather than being engulfed by conditions beyond his control. The defiance of earlier standards of melancholy was, in this framework, an advancement of individualism.

Established on this basis, the promotion of cheerfulness would continue to advance, as an ongoing linkage between individualism and emotional presentation. Foreign travellers found American frontiersmen, by the early nineteenth century, 'always ready to encounter dangers and hardships with a degree of cheerfulness, which is easily perceived as the effect of moral courage and consciousness of power.' Children, on both sides of the Atlantic, were increasingly urged to combine obedience – a traditional value – with cheerfulness, a new combination that, during the course of the nineteenth century, placed growing weight on the cheerful side of the equation. By the twentieth century, if not before, successful commercial behaviour was linked with the new demeanour as well. Sales personnel, in particular, were urged to smile over any provocation from a potential customer, for conveying happiness would do wonders in persuading people to buy additional goods or services. Thanks in part to improvements in photography (which reduced the time required to pose), more and more people chose to present themselves to the camera with a wide smile – in contrast even to nineteenth-century options, where a serious demeanour still seemed most appropriate to this venue. Parenting literature was filled with chapters or even whole books on how to create a happy child, while from the 1920s onward industrial psychologists worked to promote an active sense of happiness at work. The theme became ubiquitous. Bookstores between the world wars swelled with titles like *One Thousand Paths to Happiness* or *Happiness Is Within You*, and then after mid-century a similar basic emphasis would anchor the new and varied promotions of the new fashion of 'positivity'.[13]

By this point, of course, the steady crescendo had also revealed some tensions with individualism. Expectations that the individual should present a smiling demeanour easily spilled over into efforts to insist that others, surrounding the individual, should do the same. In the eighteenth century a new word was introduced into the English language (from a German root): 'sulky' became a term designed to designate, and reprove, people who were not measuring up to the happiness requirement. It was initially aimed at servants, now expected not only to wait on their masters and mistresses but also to smile in the process. But by the nineteenth century, as the popularity of the term continued to gain ground, it envisioned children, including the newly invented category of adolescents, particularly. It became hard for individuals to dissent from the emphasis on cheerfulness, lest they be found emotionally wanting, even (another new term, by the 1920s) 'depressed' and in need of psychological support.

While granting this dilemma, where happiness could constrain rather than liberate, the ongoing Western commitment to a measurable degree of cheerfulness in most interactions still retained important elements of its eighteenth-century origins: a belief that the conveyance of happiness was also a conveyance of individual self-control and mastery – and that the individual (even, now, the child) who could not meet this standard was correspondingly a bit diminished, needing some remedial effort to re-establish proper individual capacity.

Extending the cheerful individual: introducing the idea of boredom

The emerging emphasis on the happy individual, from the eighteenth century, generated an even clearer emotional innovation in the concept of boredom, as a means of expressing a sense that the individual was, at least for the moment, not being adequately served by his environment or his companions, or more properly was not adequately utilizing same. The newly articulated individual, in other words, deserved to have an active sense of involvement and/or needed to demonstrate another aspect of individual capacity, through the ability to rise above boredom by means of a positive effort at fulfilment.

Words for boring and boredom originated, in English, in the eighteenth and nineteenth centuries respectively. Various scholars have tried to speculate about relevant emotional experience before the idea of being bored or boring existed. There are descriptions of boring situations – for example, in a poem by the Latin writer Horace – but no word attached, so it is hard to figure out what the components of the individual reaction were. The French word ennui is older, but it does not really describe the same condition. Possibly, many individuals before the eighteenth to nineteenth centuries had a greater capacity simply to turn off the sense, to endure passively, without the need for a term that suggested a more explicit concern. Among theologians, there was certainly a sense that an individual in appropriate relationship to God would not know the kind of emotional slippage that boredom suggests, but this attitude precluded more precise labelling. Obviously, one can only conjecture about individuals before boredom.[14]

As boring and then boredom entered the language, it certainly could suggest the absence of adequate entertainment. Without yet using the word, for example, Charles Dickens attacked a proposal to ban reactions on Sunday with the argument that working people, lacking other recreation, would be listless. Others equated boredom, similarly, with a lack of adequate sources of diversion. Thomas Gray, writing in the later eighteenth century, thus bemoaned his life at the University of Cambridge: 'every thing is so tediously regular, so samish, that I expire for want of variety.' A more individualized life, fairly clearly, should be a life full of interest and activity.[15]

But boredom initially had two other meanings – besides an expectation of entertainment – that ties the concept to Western individualism in additional ways. Most obviously, at least into the nineteenth century, boredom more commonly suggested a moral flaw in the individual than a deficiency on the part of the wider society. Just as individuals should be cheerful, so they should have the ability to avoid boredom or chase it quickly. This emphasis had some links with older moral concepts – being right with God, for instance – but it also suited the new emphasis on individual capacity to shape the environment.

And second, the concept of boredom placed a premium, on proper individuals, not to be boring themselves. This is how boredom translated into manners books in the later nineteenth century, for example. Proper individual character included the capacity to be interesting, to be aware of audience – not, in sum, to bore others. In this sense, too, the links between boredom and the growing interest in happiness and cheerfulness, on the one hand, and between all this and the idea of individual capacity and evaluation, on the other, become clear – and contribute to the wider pattern of emotional innovation associated with Western individualism. Boredom suggested a new kind of awareness of the relationship between individual and context, but also a heightened sense of internal self-reflection.[16]

Love

There is no question about the chronological overlap between the emergence of greater individualism in Western culture, and a new emphasis on the importance of love. The eighteenth century saw a growing interest in the lovability of young children, and the central importance of maternal affection in response. At the same time, the validity of individual emotion in courtship gained new currency, suggesting the centrality of love in family formation as well.

Love was not, of course, an entirely new entrant in Western emotional culture, even aside from the longstanding recognition of the importance of divine love, and human echo, in religious passion. Chivalric love, most notably, provided some interesting precedents for the kind of emotional culture that began to develop in the eighteenth century. As many historians have noted, Protestantism itself, in attacking the spiritual privilege of celibacy, ultimately promoted greater attention to emotional relations between husband and wife.

Further, there were a number of causes for the new attention to love, quite apart from greater individualism – though the factors could overlap. Colin Campbell has stressed the relationship between new forms of consumerism, particularly in more stylish clothing, and changes in the emotional assumptions of courtship.[17] Love for children was certainly facilitated by attacks on the idea of original sin, though here too a link with incipient individualism is fairly clear as well. Growing interest in the new genre of romantic novels highlighted the joys and sorrows of romantic love, in ways that could affect real-life expectations as well. In the long run, the declining economic importance of the family – as work moved outside the home, with industrialization – made it virtually imperative to highlight new emotional sinews, and this would affect the valuation of emotion in courtship and parenting alike.

Direct connections with individualism were involved as well. The redefinition of early childhood, towards greater lovability, was central to the whole notion of seeing childhood as the first stage of individual development. As recently as the late seventeenth century, infants had been viewed with a certain degree of apprehension, even aside from the idea of original sin. Considerable literature stressed their animal-like qualities, for example in tearing at the mother's breasts as they nursed. Crawling was suspiciously animal-like as well, one of the reasons many parents long preferred to swaddle their offspring until they could learn to walk directly. The lovable infant, in contrast, was a more cherished emotional object, and the insistence on the importance of corresponding maternal affection linked love directly to the project of individuality in childhood.[18]

Heightened evaluation of love in courtship had two direct connections with growing individualism. In the first place, emphasis on love placed a premium on the role of individual young people in mate selection, reducing the involvement of parents or other family members. This was, in turn, the arena in which some of the first signs of emotional change emerged. A growing number of European courts, by the middle of the eighteenth century, began to avoid parentally arranged matches where one of the individual parties – male but most strikingly female as well – contended that they would never be able to love their proposed mate. Verdicts from several Swiss cantons, for example, made the new priorities clear. And, in fact, growing economic change – and particularly the opportunity for some young people to earn wages independently, in the expanding reach of domestic manufacturing – loosened parents' economic hold on some of their offspring, setting up a new balance in courtship in fact as well as in principle.[19] The decline of arranged marriage in Western society would accelerate further through the nineteenth century, a vital connection between cultural changes and actual practice.

The second connection with individualism was less concrete, but ultimately more important. As more and more young people were raised with some expectation of individuality and individual opportunity, they would need a strong emotional spur to induce them to modify individualism by accepting ties – in most cases, marital ties – with another party. Similarly, romantic love might be a key ingredient in the emotional transition from being a much-loved child to replacing parental affection with the affection of another adult, or young adult.

Once launched, emphasis on love as a bond between individuals – mother and child, courting couples – amplified fairly steadily through the nineteenth century, leading to some further emotional modifications as well.

Childrearing manuals by the 1820s clarified the central emotional role of the mother. As Catharine Beecher put it, 'the mother holds, as it were, the hearts of her children in her hand.' Happily, according to current thinking, mother love was absolutely natural, 'ready to sacrifice anything at the altar of affection.' From mothers, in turn, individual children, lovable innocents, absorbed the lessons of love and learned to respond in kind.[20]

But a loving environment required more than maternal affection. Other emotions, that might jar the centrality of love, had to be reassessed. Advice literature increasingly argued against the use of fear or anger in childrearing, lest childish innocence be troubled. Discipline might still be strict, but it should be presented as gently as possible, with positive incentives based on the centrality of love. Arguably this larger formula, with parents urged to reevaluate older disciplinary methods that might undermine a child's individual confidence through some kind of physical or emotional browbeating, linked to the growing emphasis on individualism in fact as well as in theory. As many historians have noted, traditional habits bent on 'breaking the will' of a recalcitrant child were now called into question – as they had to be, if greater individualism was to be linked to childrearing.[21]

Emphasis on love carried through to young adulthood, again in part because a strong emotional spur was essential to help guide greater separation from parental or maternal intensity. Same-sex friendships themselves were infused with new passion, for men and women alike, as effusive letters among friends abundantly testify. Here were ways that emotionally intense young adults could bridge between family of origin and courtship, though in the case of middle-class women the friendships involved were often carried lifelong.[22]

It was courtship, however, that drew the greater attention, spurred by the growing emphasis on individual choice and the need for emotional motivation in family formation. For many in the nineteenth-century middle class as well, a clear tension arose between the emphasis on intensity in courtship and the concomitant need to restrain outright sexuality, given the importance of respectability and the larger needs for family birth control. The idea of a deep but ethereal passion, again frequently expressed not only in family advice manuals but also in letters exchanged by courting couples, responded to this tension as well.[23]

Thus Eliza Duffey proclaimed, in *The Relations of the Sexes*:

> Is it not possible that there may be a love strong enough and abiding enough, untinged by sexual passion, to hold a husband and wife firm and fast in its bonds, and leave them little to desire? I believe it; I know it.

But the main point was love itself, as the key link between individuals. 'When there is great love, and it is shared by two … every difficulty is cleared away, and concord ends by hoisting its banner over the house'; 'love is the strength of strengths.'[24]

None of this is to claim, of course, that the new emotional standards around love were somehow automatically translated into actual emotional life in any full sense. Parents might absorb the new emphasis on the importance of a loving approach, and still struggle with anger in discipline. Courting couples might widely hope for love, but it was still noteworthy that – as sociologists have pointed out – they usually managed to select partners in their own social and economic group; emotional criteria were adjusted in practice. But the growing importance of love did spill beyond mere aspiration. It was actively sought and in many cases, as collections of letters abundantly expressed, sometimes clearly discovered. Love and individualism remained closely linked in middle-class life and expectation through the nineteenth century and into the twentieth.

And of course the new relationship between individualism and love, both in principle and in actual family fact, had less comfortable ramifications as well. If love was expected to draw individuals together, it could also be individually reconsidered. Individualism clearly supported movements to facilitate divorce – a key issue in the

French revolution, and then a clear element in legal evolutions in many Western countries during the nineteenth century. The same late-nineteenth-century decades that saw the most fervent declarations of love by many courting middle-class couples in the United States also saw the nation's first divorce 'crisis' – a crisis prompted by many factors, of course, but including the potential tensions between individualism and lasting affection. Even aside from divorce, a growing rash of legal cases involving 'breach of promise,' where pledges of love were withdrawn in courtship, shows the same tension from yet another standpoint in practice.[25]

Grief

Growing individualism and the accompanying emphasis on love inevitably challenged traditional ideas about grief – making grief arguably more poignant and prominent for over a century. Some caution is essential here. Historians of the family several decades ago made the mistake of assuming that premodern Western families were immune to grief, at least around such common occurrences as the deaths of children; but subsequent research has substantially modified that claim, noting that the loss of a child could be a major emotional marker for a family despite its frequency.

Nevertheless, new ideas about the importance of individuals could easily translate into more intense efforts to mark their passing. A greater sense of sorrow was particularly noteworthy in marking the deaths of children. The new genre of the romantic novel featured countless scenes of poignant grief, as did many of the diaries kept by middle-class women – including lamentations over the deaths of young children.

In this case, however, rituals and memorials, more than mere words, most clearly conveyed the new sense of grief's intensity and its links to the valuation of individuals and individualism. Cemeteries famously changed. Instead of modest, fairly uniform grave markers – save for a privileged few – gravestones now became more elaborate and clearly individualized, with distinctive phrases and decorative motifs. Deaths of children were more clearly memorialized, and given individual headstones or at least explicit mention in a family plot – a significant contrast with more traditional practices that have often seen them buried at home, with no marker at all.

Later in the nineteenth century funeral practices took a further step, as the renewed popularity of embalming allowed the novel profession of undertaker to prepare bodies for family viewing, taking pride in making them as lifelike – and in the process, as individual – as possible. As one professional noted, 'when I come for the last time to look upon my dead, they will look to me as natural as though they were alive.' Casket design changed, and became more expensive, mainly with an eye to assuring a grieving family that decay of the individual body would be prevented at least for a time; that some sense of individual comfort could persist even in death.[26]

Grief, in these formulations, merged with love and even a bittersweet cheerfulness in complex ways. The individual would be remembered, made distinctive, even after life had passed. Love for the departed would show through clearly, and nineteenth-century commentators were articulate about the deep if somewhat sorrowful connections between intense affection and grief, as part of the common family emotional experience. But lifelike representations, reductions of the gloominess of cemeteries in favour of more parklike settings, and even new ideas about a loving family later reuniting in heaven were designed to reduce unhappiness at least to some extent. Finally, the ceremonies attached to respectable funerals, complete with mourning clothes and draperies, once again called attention to the significance of an individual passing. The Victorian grief apparatus clearly sought to reconcile love and individual distinctiveness, on one hand, with the continued high rates of mortality, on the other.

Shame

Along with cheerfulness and love, and their several ramifications, the traditional emotional category that was most explicitly challenged by growing individualism was shame. As noted, shame had continued to express considerable power in Western life and culture into the eighteenth century. Historians have debated whether, before modern times, Western shame was already altered by the Christian fascination with guilt. Unquestionably, Augustine and some other theologians did make a distinction (interestingly, in classical Greek there were not even separate words for the two emotions), and Augustine was capable of noting that the good Christian should be able to endure shame, which was merely the judgement of peers, in order to avoid guilt, which defined a far more important relationship with God. But for the most part Christianity in practice, in the West, continued to place primary reliance on shame, even in enforcing religious morality. And in public practice, and as far as we know in family discipline as well, shame, and with it even more the fear of shame, played a vital role. John Locke himself, a hero of early individualism, cavalierly accepted the shaming of schoolboys as the 'greatest part' of desirable discipline. The English language even had a word, *shamefast*, that applied to the transcendent importance of avoiding shame – the importance for the individual, in other words, of conforming to group conventions. Revealingly, the word would gradually disappear in the nineteenth century as traditional reliance on shaming came under attack.[27]

For shame and shaming were incompatible with the new ideals of individualism and individual dignity, precisely because they put group norms first and forced individuals to sacrifice their pride to the imperatives of getting along with others. The conventional set of assumptions and practices now fell under the individualistically inspired category of cruel and unusual punishments. As Benjamin Rush put it in 1787, voicing a sentiment increasingly articulated on both sides of the Atlantic: shaming is 'universally acknowledged to be a worse punishment than death,' because it crushed the individual spirit. The emotion was so degrading that it could not fail 'to make bad men worse.'[28]

The striking about-face on shaming showed in several ways. In the first place, in both American and British English, references to shame began to decline precipitously from the 1820s and 1830s on to the 1960s: the word was becoming unfashionable – according to some social scientists (who exaggerate a bit), one of the modern taboos. Second, public shaming practices were increasingly outlawed. The state of Massachusetts banned the public stocks as early as 1804, and other states, and Great Britain, were not far behind. Somewhat more gradually, a similar concern about the coercive aspects of shame helped lead to a decline and then disappearance of the practice of duelling.[29] The same trends affected advice about family discipline – along with the love-related injunctions concerning limits on fear and anger.

Catharine Beecher, writing in 1841, wanted strict decorum in the household, but through gentle and affectionate guidance. There should be no open criticism, nothing to 'embarrass, vex or mortify': no hint of 'ridicule or rebuke' – because otherwise the 'temper of children would be injured,' and they would become miserable as individuals. Lydia Child was even more explicit in insisting that punishments that 'make the child feel ashamed should be avoided. A sense of degradation is not healthy for character.' A further childrearing manual, from 1856, pushed the sense of individualism still further in urging that parents and adults dealing with children make every effort to bolster self-esteem – one of the first times that this now-familiar term came into currency in relationship to the promotion of individual capacity.[30]

Shame did not disappear, of course. As with other changes in emotional standards, actual practice varied more than the recommendations did; individual families and institutions might well disagree. Shaming in the schools, and in school-related activities like organized sports, maintained considerable and explicit reliance on shaming, regarded as essential for discipline as corporal punishments receded and as more and more female teachers tried to maintain order in often unruly classrooms. Even the fabled dunce cap, that emblem of school shaming, would clearly recede only after the first decades of the twentieth century. Overall, however, shaming did come under new review. By the twentieth century, and to the present day, this review was furthered by the conclusions of most Western psychologists that shaming was damaging and counterproductive because it called the individual, rather than specific actions, into question – more likely to produce more bad behaviour than remediation.[31]

Interim review: individualism and emotion

The impact of the individualistic strand in modern Western culture on a variety of emotions is considerable. Indeed, the vantage point is productive precisely because it helps us see relationships among various seemingly discrete changes in emotional standards.

Some caveats predictably apply. More individualistic emotional standards did not produce uniform results on actual emotional experience. Some linkages are clear – for example, in the elaboration of new grief rituals, or the abolition of public stocks. And certainly there was widespread cultural support for other changes, such as the greater emphasis on love or cheerfulness. Shifts in the frequency in the usage of certain emotion words are another strong indicator of outcomes. But it remains important not to exaggerate.

Social class divisions, and in some cases gender patterns, need more attention. The results of individualism bore more clearly on middle-class norms than on those of working classes or rural groups. In a few cases class differences were even codified: American courts in the later nineteenth century accepted the charge of mental cruelty in divorce cases involving the middle class, presumed to have great sensitivities in matters of the heart and familial affection, but not members of the lower classes, who lacked these qualities. Figuring out how workers responded to new norms of love, or grief, or shame remains largely a task for the future, and an important one – recognizing that individualism might well emerge in these domains as well.

Finally, the assessment of individualism, even amid the middle classes, does not clearly apply to the whole emotional arsenal. Important changes in nostalgia, for example, do not clearly relate to the rise of greater cultural individualism.[32] Discussions of anger and fear may have been affected – new concerns about their role with children have been mentioned – but individualism may not be a clear influence overall, as opposed to other kinds of concerns. A number of new movements – most obviously, the rise of nationalism – generated intense emotional focus but on a collective, rather than individualistic basis – here is another set of complexities to explore. Further analysis may uncover additional relationships – even negative ones, to the extent, for example, that nationalism gained ground in part to compensate for emotional individualism in other domains; but they seem at the least less apparent than with the emotions we have already highlighted.

The comparative challenge

Another analytical vantage point also requires further consideration, but here it is possible to advance at least a few hypotheses. Western individualism, famously, did not inspire widespread acceptance in many other world cultures, during the past two centuries. The Japanese, for example, clearly considered individualism in shaping their new educational system after 1872, but decided against it by the 1880s, opting for more group orientation.

The differentiation clearly sets up some potential comparisons in emotional culture. We would thus expect somewhat different formulations concerning love or grief, despite some ultimately shared experiences in modernization and a good bit of mutual cultural influence under the banners of increasing globalization.

And in two cases, some results are in fact available. East Asian cultures have not, as part of successful industrializations, placed the same kind of premium on happiness that has come to be standard in the West (including, in this case, many parts of Latin America). Polls indicate some systematic differences in expectations in this domain.[33] Differentiation also applies to shame: the emotion is still strongly emphasized in East Asian cultures, despite some common changes in public enforcement. Thus a recent poll found a near-majority of Taiwanese accepting the proposition that serious shame was essential and appropriate in disciplining the young – whereas literally no Chicago respondent agreed at all.[34]

The emotional effects of individualism, in other words, provide a basis for a badly needed comparative approach in emotions history, and probably predict at least some of the resulting outcomes.

The past century

Finally, the impacts of Western individualism require some commentary that extends more clearly beyond the nineteenth century than this essay's previous sections have ventured. There is little reason to doubt the basic persistence of individualism in the more recent extensions of Western culture: the comparisons with other regions still register. Lower birth rates, more attention to individual children – even the increasing provision of rigorously private separate rooms – provide conditions for even further emphasis on this cultural tendency.[35] But other elements in the environment change, creating some adjustments in the individualism–emotions equation. For example, what one Dutch sociologist has called the 'informalization' of manners, reducing stiff Victorian conventions in favour of looser conventions, may have given some new space for individual emotional expression.[36] The same might result from the growing popularity of psychology, with its general support for greater emotional openness. Shifts of this sort at the least required some adjustments, without necessarily reversing some of the earlier connections. A brief assessment may suggest some of the results.

In several cases, emotional trends set in motion from the eighteenth century on-ward largely persist, adding at most some further targets. Thus the expectation of cheerfulness and its association with individual competence continue to play well. The rise of certain branches of psychology support the emphases, often applying them more explicitly to work situations – with further promptings of positive atti-tudes amid co-workers and customers – than had been the case in the nineteenth century. Growing concerns about psychological depression – first identified clearly in the 1920s – suggest some of the complexities of the contemporary Western mood, but the assumption that depression should be treated and combatted maintains the core criteria. Individuals, though possibly with some assistance, should be able to rise above their dark side.[37]

Within this framework boredom continues to win considerable attention – here, too, basic connections developed in the eighteenth century persist. But contempo-rary boredom comes with a slight twist. The original emphasis on boredom as a chal-lenge to the individual – not to be boring, but also to be capable of personal mastery of boredom – tends to diminish, leaving an arguably shallower residue. Increasingly the statement 'I'm bored' was simply a lament about the failure of the environment to provide the individual with adequate diversion – an individual complaint, rather than a more complex challenge to individual capacity. This element had been present in the modern idea of boredom all along, but with the intensification of the consumer society it became undeniably more prominent. So: continuity in this case, but also some adjustment in the theme.[38]

By the twentieth century also, the combination of individualism and consumer-ism was generating a further emotional redefinition, around the subject of envy. To be sure, liberal economists from Adam Smith onward had emphasized the validity of individual economic motivations in spurring social progress. But envy had been left largely untouched, with commentary still guided by older Christian disapproval of the emotion's link to selfish materialism and greed. Children should be urged to avoid selfishness and cultivate contentment with what they had. By the early twenti-eth century, however, a number of studies showed how widely envious children had in fact become: G. Stanley Hall, in the United States, showed the pervasiveness of the emotion as children encountered peers who had consumer goods they wanted as well. Advice also changed, as moralism gave way to new kinds of expertise. Envy itself was still reproved, but now the recommendations shifted from denial and self-control, to suggestions that parents owed their children consumer abundance, so that envy would decline simply because of satisfaction. The emotion was natural, even desirable – one childrearing manual urged that children become more widely aware of better clothing and other amenities: 'Immediately discontent will set in, and striving for higher and better things may follow.' This additional emotion, in other words, now deserved positive attention and fulfilment, as another way of linking the individual child to the world taking shape around it.[39]

As with happiness and related emotions, shame formed another category where the implications of individualism continued to predominate through the past century, with innovations mainly in terms of expanding the scope of earlier formulations. In addition to continuing urgent recommendations that shame be cut back in punishments and family discipline, a variety of groups now explicitly fought shame in other venues: people should work hard to rise above shame in cases of disability or disease or sexual abuse. A variety of experts, particularly by the later twentieth and early twenty-first centuries, urged programmes designed to 'shame the shamers', who were simply trying to bring the individual down. School shaming was more explicitly attacked, and while elements persisted, a growing emphasis on the importance of student self-esteem, as a positive motivator, did provide some alternatives. Appeals to individual pride – for example, by awarding higher grades or by finding additional achievement categories where students could be positively singled out – measurably affected the atmosphere in the more progressive schools, from the 1960s onward. In the United States, to be sure, shame revived in some quarters by 2000, and the rise of social media provided new opportunities for often vicious, anonymous shaming in many parts of the world. On the whole, however, the old formula, which sought to attack shame in the name of individual dignity, continued to predominate in Western emotional advice and in many institutional settings.[40]

Grief, on the other hand, was substantially redefined – without losing the link to individualism that had emerged in the eighteenth and nineteenth centuries. With the rapid decline of infant death rates throughout the Western world in the decades after 1880, elaborate, Victorian-style mourning became less necessary, and decidedly unfashionable. New norms by the 1920s urged that a competent individual should be able to get over grief rather quickly, seeking therapeutic help if the emotion was prolonged. Characteristic nineteenth-century death ceremonies were steadily cut back. However, intense emotion still responded to the deaths of individuals before old age – including children, whose deaths became far more painful as they became less common. Fighting individual death, including the application of heroic medical measures, seized centre stage, particularly as hospitals now became the most common location for death; not only potential grief but also guilt could be minimized by supporting every possible means of keeping individuals alive. At the same time, undue grief now seemed burdensome to other individuals – pressed into providing emotional service that should no longer be necessary. Emotions around death became in many ways more complicated, as rituals changed and the actual incidence of death shifted; but attention to individual survival and, now, some protection from intrusive emotions of others maintained some older connections in new ways.[41]

Finally, the link between individuals and a new valuation of love maintained considerable validity, but amid some new complications of a different sort. The theme persisted, as a major element, for example, in the burgeoning entertainment fare delivered not only in novels but also in films and later television. A variety of studies into the later twentieth century showed continued high individual expectations around love, though more pervasively among women than among men.[42] There were, however, some new elements. Most obviously, changing sexual patterns, emerging in the early part of the twentieth century but expanding more rapidly after 1960 and its 'sexual revolution,' dramatically reduced the age for initial sexual activity, throughout the Western world.[43] The Victorian valuation of an intense but pure love, separate from and ideally prior to sexual encounters, clearly faded. Marriage experts, for their part, warned against too much reliance on fervent love, which could complicate sensible partner selection and lead to unrealistic standards for marriage itself; and in many countries the rising divorce rate might generate some new constraints on romantic expectations as well. Finally, other interests, both for individuals and partners, might compete with the love theme: attachments to consumer goods and entertainments provided new outlets for family emotions.[44] Love persisted, in other words, as a key emotional expression for individuals and a means of linking with others; but its intensity was reshaped. With this, some new questions emerged as well about the compatibility of contemporary individualism with stable family formation.[45]

There was one further angle that had not emerged clearly before the twentieth century. Jealousy was now increasingly reproved, both in children (siblings) and adults. The emotion might reflect individual love, but it also involved a level of possessiveness that was now unacceptable – as social conventions became less formal, and mixing of genders more extensive. The goal, in fact, was a new protection of individual emotional autonomy – though at the expense of a new challenge to self-control.[46]

★ ★ ★

The impact of Western individualism on emotional standards and evaluations provides a vigorous entrée into modern emotional history in this culture and into comparisons with other regional cultural systems. Further assessments remain desirable, to see if the fundamental theme embraces additional emotions and above all to test the continuity of initial connections into the past century. The intensification of consumer values, new management styles and psychological techniques, changes in demography and further secularization (though less pronounced in the United States) are among the themes that complicate the emotional results of individualism after the end of the nineteenth century. The results, however, in all likelihood adjust the results of individualism, even providing new outlets as in less formal manners, rather than introducing an alternative framework. The relationships remain lively.

Notes

1 But see books by A. Gurevich, *The Origins of European Individualism*, New York: Wiley, 1995 and L. Siedentop, *Inventing the Individual: The Origins of Western Liberalism*, Cambridge, MA: Belknap Press of Harvard University Press, 2014, which argue for earlier origins.
2 N. Elias, *The Civilizing Process*, New York: Pantheon Books, 1982.
3 D. Nash and A.-M. Kilday, *Cultures of Shame: Exploring Crime and Morality in Britain, 1600–1900*, Basingstoke: Palgrave Macmillan, 2010; J. Braithwaite, *Crime, Shame, and Reintegration*, Cambridge: Cambridge University Press, 1989.
4 C. Campbell, *The Romantic Ethic and the Spirit of Modern Consumerism*, Oxford: Basil Blackwell, 1989.

5 M. Walzer, *On Toleration*, New Haven, CT: Yale University Press, 1997.

6 D. Wahrman, *The Making of the Modern Self Identity and Culture in Eighteenth-Century England*, New Haven, CT: Yale University Press, 2004.

7 N. Eustace, *Passion Is the Gale: Emotion, Power, and the Coming of the American Revolution*, Chapel Hill, NC: University of North Carolina Press, 2008.

8 E. Shorter, *The Making of the Modern Family*, New York: Basic Books, 1975; D. Hunt, *Parents and Children in History: The Psychology of Family Life in Early Modern France*, New York: Basic Books, 1970.

9 C. Stearns, '"Lord Help Me Walk Humbly": Anger and Sadness in England and America, 1570–1750', in C.Z. Stearns and P.N. Stearns (eds), *Emotion and Social Change: Toward A New Psychohistory*, New York: Holmes and Meier, 1988, 39–68.

10 D.M. McMahon, *Happiness: A History*, New York: Atlantic Monthly Press, 2006.

11 Stearns, '"Lord Help Me Walk Humbly": Anger and Sadness in England and America, 1570–1750', 39–68.

12 C. Kotchemidova, 'From Good Cheer to "Drive-by Smiling": A Social History of Cheerfulness', *Journal of Social History* 39, 1, 2005, 5–37.

13 P.N. Stearns, *Satisfaction Not Guaranteed: Dilemmas of Progress in Modern Society*, New York: New York University Press, 2012; P.N. Stearns, 'Defining Happy Childhoods: Assessing a Recent Change', *The Journal of the History of Childhood and Youth* 3, 2, 2010, 165–86.

14 P.A. Meyer, *Boredom: The Literary History of a State of Mind*, Chicago, IL: University of Chicago Press, 1995.

15 Meyer, *Boredom*, 31–60.

16 P.N. Stearns, *Anxious Parents: A History of Modern Childrearing in America*, New York: New York University Press, 2003.

17 Campbell, *The Romantic Ethic and the Spirit of Modern Consumerism*.

18 Hunt, *Parents and Children in History*.

19 J.R. Gillis, *For Better, For Worse: British Marriages, 1600 to the Present*, New York: Oxford University Press, 1985.

20 C.E. Beecher, *Treatise on Domestic Economy*, 1841; repr., New York, 1970, 134, 122, 139–40.

21 P.N. Stearns, *American Cool: Reconstructing a Twentieth-Century Emotional Style*, New York: New York University Press, 1994, 16–94.

22 E.A. Rotundo, *American Manhood: Transformations in Masculinity from the Revolution to the Modern Era*, New York: Basic Books, 1993; C. Smith-Rosenberg, 'The Female World of Love and Ritual: Relations Between Women in Nineteenth-Century America', *Signs* 1, 1975, 1–29.

23 K. Lystra, *Searching the Heart: Women, Men, and Romantic Love in Nineteenth-Century America*, New York: Oxford University Press, 1989.

24 E. Bisbee Duffey, *The Relations of the Sexes*, New York: Arno, 1974.

25 R. Phillips, *Family Breakdown in Late Eighteenth-Century France: Divorces in Rouen, 1792–1803*, New York: Oxford University Press, 1980; Norma Basch, *Framing American Divorce: From the Revolutionary Generation to the Victorians*, Berkeley, CA: University of California Press, 1999.

26 P. Rosenblatt, *Bitter, Bitter Tears: Nineteenth-Century Diarists and Twentieth-Century Grief Theories*, Minneapolis, MN: University of Minnesota Press, 1983; P.N. Stearns, *Revolutions in Sorrow: The American Experience of Death in Global Perspective*, Boulder, CO: Paradigm Publishers, 2007.

27 V. Burrus, *Saving Shame: Martyrs, Saints, and Other Abject Subjects*, Philadelphia, PA: University of Pennsylvania Press, 2007.

28 P.N. Stearns, *A History of Shame*, Champaign, IL: University of Illinois Press, 2018.

29 U. Frevert, *Men of Honour: A Social and Cultural History of the Duel*, Cambridge: Polity Press, 1995.

30 Beecher, *Treatise on Domestic Economy*; L. Child, *The Moral, Intellectual and Physical Training of the Young Explained*, Glasgow: W. R. M'Phun, 1856, 28.

31 J. Tangney et al., 'Assessing Jail Inmates' Proneness to Shame and Guilt: Feeling Bad about the Behavior or the Self?' *Criminal Justice and Behavior* 38, 7, 2011, 710–34.

32 S.J. Matt, *Homesickness: An American History*, New York: Oxford University Press, 2011; Joanna Bourke, *Fear: A Cultural History*, Emeryville, CA: Shoemaker Hoard, 2006.

33 J. Poushter, 'Measuring the "Good" Life Around the World', Pew Research Center, 2017, www.pewresearch.org/fact-tank/2015/10/29/measuring-the-good-life-around-the-world (accessed 5 January 2019); K. Simmons, 'When it Comes to Happiness, Money Matters', Pew Research Center, 2017, www.pewresearch.org/fact-tank/2014/10/30/when-it-comes-to-happiness-money-matters (accessed 5 January 2019).

34 H. Fung, 'Becoming a Moral Child: The Socialization of Shame among Young Chinese Children', *Ethos* 27, 2, 1999, 180–209; S. Yang and P. C. Rosenblatt, 'Shame in Korean Families', *Journal of Contemporary Family Studies* 32, 3, 2001, 361–75.

35 V.A. Zelizer, *Pricing the Priceless Child: The Changing Social Value of Children*, New York: Basic Books, 1985; J. Reid, *Get Out of My Room! A History of Teen Bedrooms in America*, Chicago, IL: University of Chicago Press, 2017.

36 C. Wouters, *Sex and Manners: Female Emancipation in the West, 1890–2000*, Thousand Oaks, CA: SAGE, 2004; Ibid., *Informalization: Manners and Emotions Since 1890*, Thousand Oaks, CA: SAGE, 2007.

37 *Culture and Depression: Studies in the Anthropology and Cross-Cultural Psychiatry of Affect and Disorder*, eds A. Kleinman and B. J. Good, Berkeley, CA: University of California Press, 1986; Stearns, *Satisfaction Not Guaranteed*.

38 P. Toohey, *Boredom: A Lively History*, New Haven, CT: Yale University Press, 2011; Meyer, *Boredom*.

39 S.J. Matt, *Keeping Up with the Joneses: Envy in American Consumer Society, 1890–1930*, Philadelphia, PA: University of Pennsylvania Press, 2003.

40 B. Brown, *Listening to Shame*, TED, 2012, 20:38, filmed in March 2012,www.ted.com/talks/brene_brown_listening_to_shame?language=en (accessed 20 January 2016); B. Brown, *I Thought It Was Just Me: Women Reclaiming Power and Courage in a Culture of Shame*, New York:Gotham, 2007; B. Brown, 'Shame Perfectionism and Embracing Wholehearted Living', *Iris* 61, 2011, 12–16; P.N. Stearns, *A History of Shame*, 153–200.

41 P.N. Stearns, *Revolutions in Sorrow*.

42 M. Segalen, *Love and Power in the Peasant Family: Rural France in the Nineteenth Century*, Chicago, IL: University of Chicago Press, 1983.

43 B.L. Bailey, *From Front Porch to Back Seat: Courtship in Twentieth-Century America*, Baltimore, MD: Johns Hopkins University Press, 1988.

44 M. Dunlop Young and P. Willmott, *The Symmetrical Family*, New York: Pantheon Books, 1973.

45 See also, particularly for the United States, the tensions that emerged by the later twentieth century between individualism and previous forms of voluntary association: R.D. Putnam, *Bowling Alone: The Collapse and Revival of American Community*, New York: Simon and Schuster, 2000.

46 P. Salovey (ed.), *The Psychology of Jealousy and Envy*, New York: Guilford Press, 1991.

22

HEALTH AND ILLNESS, THE SELF AND THE BODY

Willemijn Ruberg

The modern period is generally seen to have witnessed the rise of a new conception of the self and the separation of body and mind. This chapter will scrutinize
the entanglements of body, mind and self and the most important theories about
their historical development. It will start by discussing the relationship between these
three elements in humoral theory and its medical successors. Then it will turn to the
'modern self', its definitions and historical debates about its existence. Particularly,
this chapter will discuss Michel Foucault's notion of 'technologies of the self', which
constituted a shift towards historicizing the concept of the self, and the way cultural
historians have elaborated on this theme, connecting it with material practices that
shaped the self in daily life.

Body, mind and self from humoral theory to psychiatry

For a long time, the writing of medical history was dominated by the theme of
great doctors and their discoveries. These so-called 'progressivist' histories have been
replaced by social and cultural histories, which emphasize the making of meaning in
regard to the body and disease (and hence also include vernacular beliefs) as well as
the role of the patient him/herself.[1] These social and cultural histories have helped us
to embed developments in medicine within broader cultural developments.

The modern period witnessed major shifts in medical theory and practice. First, the
place and way of treatment changed. Until the eighteenth and nineteenth centuries,
doctors mostly confined their physical examination of patients to hands, pulse, face
or to body fluids like urine. This so-called 'bedside medicine' resulted in doctor and
patient often agreeing on the diagnosis and treatment.[2] In the second half of the nineteenth century, beginning in France, a shift from 'bedside medicine' to 'hospital medicine' took place: medicine became based on pathology and patients were treated in
(teaching) hospitals.[3] The patient now submitted to the physician's authority, based on
reading signs off the body by auscultation or percussion, rather than on the agreement
between doctor and patient in regard to bodily symptoms and their treatment. Instead
of prognosis and treatment, diagnosis occupied central stage and the patient became

subject to the hospital regime. In the clinic, autopsies also helped to gain knowledge of the body. Pain and symptoms were no longer solely pointers to the classification of diseases, but clues directing the doctor to the underlying organs and tissues where the illness was located, a mere guide to the underlying pathology, which provided the only reliable basis of diagnosing disease.[4] Whereas in early eighteenth-century bedside medicine the illness was the same as the pain or symptom reported by the patient (for instance, headache), under the regime of hospital medicine it was ultimately the examining gaze of the physician that penetrated the body to locate the disease in particular sites of the body. As Foucault writes, the question asked of the sick patient was no longer 'what is the matter with you?', but 'where does it hurt?'.[5]

Second, the main conception of the body was transformed: humoral theory, which revolved around the corporeal balance between the four humours (black bile, yellow bile, phlegm and blood), was definitively replaced by other paradigms, such as cellular pathology and laboratory medicine in the mid-nineteenth century, even though it remained vital to lay thought about bodies and character until the early twentieth century. All disease concepts became increasingly anatomical in the nineteenth century. An example of these changes can be seen in the ideas on menstruation. Whereas in the early modern humoral paradigm, health had meant moving fluids and a blocking of the menses was seen as a sign of disease,[6] from the nineteenth and early twentieth centuries, menstruation came to be seen both as a sign of female infirmity and later as the main indicator of fertility: only by 1930 had physicians ascertained the relationship between ovulation and menstruation with the help of the discovery of hormones.[7]

Third, in the nineteenth century psychiatry grew to be a separate and new discipline. Until the mid-nineteenth century, medicine was 'psychosomatic'; boundaries between doctors of the body and the mind were lacking. The 'alienists' – as the early psychiatrists were called, referring to diseases that alienated patients from reality – were primarily preoccupied with the definition and classification of neurosis, forging links between physical changes in the nervous system and behavioural disorders. In the mid-nineteenth century the main category for complete disorientation became 'psychosis'. The new branch of psychiatry was optimistic in regard to the future cure of mental patients, also testified by newly built asylums. Psychiatric disorders were increasingly perceived as disorders of the brain, rather than of the soul, justifying physical treatments.[8]

To demonstrate the complicated relationships between body and mind against the background of the rising discipline of psychiatry, take the involvement of doctors in two nineteenth-century Norwegian court cases, as presented by historian Svein Atle Skålevåg. In 1819 a worker at the ironworks at Nes in southern Norway was charged with the murder of an eleven-year-old beggar: he had thrown the boy into a smelting oven. The murderer was prosecuted before a local court, at which a number of neighbours and colleagues gave testimonies of the deranged mind of the perpetrator. The court then called in two experts: a local physician, who was instructed to search only for the physical signs of a weak mind, and a priest, who had to focus on the criminal's mind and morality. So body and mind were separated, in the sense that morals were seen as belonging to religion. Neither the doctor nor the priest found signs of dementia, so the murderer was held accountable for his crime.

A second court case, from 1888, when a man from Stavanger in south-eastern Norway was imprisoned for life for the murder of an officer of the poor board, shows a different picture. The murderer was examined by a prison physician (who found him mentally 'deranged') and two alienists who had experience working in asylums and subscribed to the prison physician's conclusion. The alienists examined the prisoner by interrogation and by studying the trial documents, concluding that he had been 'physically abnormal' since childhood and could not be held accountable for his deeds. Not only were specialists on the mind now called in as experts; they also studied the relationship between the psychic and somatic aspects of man. The physical (doctor) and the moral (priest) were no longer separated. Skålevåg argues that the early modern medical anthropology depicted man as a dualistic being of mind and body, in which the moral and the physical constituted the self, and madness was composed of both aspects. But this image gave way to a later nineteenth-century stricter separation of body and mind, in which the moral was disconnected from the physical. General physicians no longer had authority over the mind; this expertise was taken up by the new psychiatrists.[9]

The new psychiatric authority in regard to matters of the mind also comes to the fore in the modern notion of (psychic) 'trauma', coined in the 1870s by psychiatrists who applied it to the psychic consequences of railway accidents and connecting physical hurt with recurring mental effects. The construction of railways in the mid-nineteenth century was accompanied by new physical and mental problems. After major train accidents, some passengers, even if they had not suffered bodily injuries, showed symptoms of mental and physical deterioration, frequently resulting in disability. Symptoms, which only appeared after a few days, could include 'fatigue, headaches, difficulty in concentration, digestive problems, forgetfulness, stammering, reduction of sexual potency, cold sweats, states of anxiety'.[10] Physicians had difficulty diagnosing these symptoms and until the early 1880s they concluded that 'railway spine' had a purely pathological cause: it was seen as a microscopic deterioration of the spinal cord due to mechanical shock caused by the accident. From the early 1880s on, however, this purely pathological view was superseded by a new psychopathological view (referring to 'traumatic neurosis'), which forwarded that the shock had affected the victim psychically, rather than physically. Fright and the accompanying mental blow were now regarded to have caused the traumatization of railroad accident victims. Later, the similar concept of 'shell shock' was coined for the traumatic experiences of soldiers during the First World War. And just like doctors had to determine whether railway accident victims were really suffering from a trauma or solely simulating, when they claimed damages in court, during the First World War they were asked to examine the traumatized soldiers, to distinguish between malingerers and real patients and to decide who should be sent back to the front line.[11]

The new concept of trauma can also be traced in the medical discussion on the effects of sexual violence. In the early modern vocabulary of humours, the mind was inextricably connected to the body. In early modern rape cases, for instance, no one spoke of the traumatic experience of victims: attention was mostly directed to traces of violence on the body. Doctors noted the impact of rape on morals, especially the loss of virginity or the risk of corruption, but never referred to structural mental effects. Those effects were not completely denied, but rather described in terms of 'fright'. For example, it was very common for girls and women to claim their menstruation as suddenly having stopped after a shocking sight or experience. Mind and body were aligned in this perspective.[12] And although the French forensic doctor Ambroise Tardieu (1818–1879) had already noted the psychological damage caused by rape to children in 1857, it is especially from psychiatrist Sigmund Freud's (1856–1939) work that we know the notion of trauma as a result of sexual violation (even though Freud notoriously withdrew his so-called seduction theory later, substituting fantasy for real childhood abuse). The idea of mental trauma as an effect of previous sexual abuse would only become widespread much later in the twentieth century.[13]

A Freudian vocabulary now permeates our discussion of mental health, emotion and trauma. Historian Jan Goldstein demonstrates how in the early nineteenth century, this discourse was not yet available. Goldstein found the extraordinary medical case of Nanette Leroux in the archives of the Institut de France in Paris. The eighteen-year-old Nanette Leroux, a servant girl from rural Savoy, fell ill in 1822 with diverse nervous symptoms, such as convulsions, lethargy, loss of speech, suicidal thoughts, sleepwalking and catalepsy, a muscular contraction that, statue-like, fixed her limbs and other body parts in the position they occupied when the symptom took hold. One of the most conspicuous nervous symptoms was the *transport de sens*, a migration of sensory capability from the organs in which it belonged to other parts of the body. For instance, her ability to hear moved from her ears to her elbows, breasts, abdomen and fingertips. At one stage, a doctor talked to Nanette through the nape of her neck and she replied in sign language. Nanette's doctors believed the girl to be suffering from 'hysteria complicated by ecstasy', instigated by the 'frights' resulting from an 'attack on her modesty' by a rural policeman. She was treated by two French physicians, the local Alexandre Bertrand and Parisian Charles-Humbert-Antoine Despine. The latter physician recommended her taking therapies such as baths, showers and electro-magnetism in the cosmopolitan spa of Aix-les-Bains. Medical treatments and experiments took place in the company of many lay spectators, testifying to the public and spectacular character of medicine and science at the time. Both doctors shared an interest in animal magnetism, a precursor to hypnosis, but they favoured different explanations for it: Despine subscribed to the late eighteenth-century tradition of Mesmer, believing that the cure was physical, while Bertrand preferred a mentalist view of magnetism and ecstasy, regarding Nanette's illness as stemming from the imagination.

Today's readers, versed in Freudian language, would interpret Nanette Leroux's case in terms of repression and recognize her illness as a trauma resulting from a sexual assault. Nanette's physicians, however, did not note the sexual nature of the case. Indeed, hysteria as such was not so much gendered and eroticized in the 1820s. Goldstein resorts to two present-day theoretical frames to explain this: a Foucauldian and a Freudian. A Foucauldian interpretation would emphasize that sexuality only became an object of scientific knowledge in the 1830s. Therefore the medical notion of hysteria was not immediately connected to sexuality. Trying to conceptualize Nanette's subjective understanding of her situation and the causes of her illness, Goldstein uses a Freudian perspective: the psychoanalytic assumption that Nanette possessed an unconscious mind that enabled her to manipulate the available cultural symbols for her own means. In this reading, Nanette's illness becomes an expression of an unconscious psychic conflict that centred on questions of rebellion, autonomy and traditional patterns of behaviour and dependence for a woman in her era. Like other historians of hysteria have noted, women could take refuge in illness when alternative opportunities for self-expression had been closed down. In the case of Nanette Leroux, Goldstein points to the historical change of the post-revolutionary era that exposed the French girl to modern, more egalitarian, visions of the future. Nanette may have felt the contradictions between traditional and novel ways of life and may have been frustrated in her quest for emancipation. More importantly, a psychoanalytical reading of this case defines her illness as a sexual trauma that brought on hysterical symptoms, whereas contemporaries only noticed her ailments as a result of the fright due to the encounter with the rural policeman. Eventually, Goldstein argues that Nanette's illness was a 'strategy for self-making'.[14]

Goldstein's analysis of the case of Nanette Leroux from 1822 thus underlines cultural historians' interest in human agency and the patient's point of view. In addition, it demonstrates how medicine and the socio-cultural context are inextricably connected and it unveils the vast shifts in thinking on the relationship between body, mind and sexuality in the nineteenth century, including the slow disappearance of humoral medicine, the rise of the discipline of psychiatry and a stronger emphasis on the mind as a separate entity.

The rise of the modern self

Psychiatry's interest in the human mind involved not only questioning traditional conceptions of the relationship between body and mind, but also thinking about the way mental characteristics were bound to personal identity, or 'the self'. The topic of 'the self' has long been of interest to philosophers and intellectual historians, who have traced a progression from conventional, collective societies to modern ideas of the autonomous, whole and authentic individual, in texts from famous philosophers and authors.[15] As historian Roy Porter aptly puts it:

> the secret of selfhood is commonly seen to lie in authenticity and individuality, and its history is presented as a biography of progress towards that goal. Achieving autonomy implies inner character-building, typically through emancipation from external constraints like religious and political persecution, or the fetters of hidebound convention.[16]

Hallmarks of this route of the rise of the self include the first stirrings of real individual consciousness in ancient Greece, St Augustine's *Confessions* (397–401), that provided the first introspection into the guilty sinner's soul, and Renaissance humanism's shaking off the constraining chains of religious custom, leading to the devotion of individual man in the self-portrait, the diary and the autobiography. Historians have especially emphasized the importance of individual consciousness and self-aware thinking as forwarded in the seventeenth century by the French philosopher René Descartes (1594–1650). Other important founding fathers of individualism include John Locke's philosophy on human understanding (1690), which defines the self as a product of experience and education, and especially the Swiss-born author

410

Jean-Jacques Rousseau (1712–1778), who bared his inner, authentic self in his frank *Confessions* (1782) and despised all social conventions. Both romantics like Rousseau, but also Enlightenment authors, underlined individuality. A final highlight on this path towards the modern self is of course the work of Sigmund Freud (1856–1939), who excavated the hidden desires of the self via the notion of the unconscious, which he also divided into different parts (*superego, ego, id*).[17]

Cultural historians have continued to research the self as a topic, but are more critical of these progressivist intellectual and philosophical histories. Roy Porter, for one, pointed out that it is a linear myth flattering to ourselves, but also an inaccurate story: 'The notion of an ascent from some primordial collective psychological soup to a sharply defined individual identity now seems a question-begging and self-serving leftover of Victorian fanfares of progress'.[18] Cultural historians, moreover, are increasingly sketching the historical and cultural contexts of the development of the self as well as shifting the emphasis towards daily social practices instead of prescriptive or philosophical texts.

One important contribution to the historiography of the self is historian Dror Wahrman's *The Making of the Modern Self: Identity and Culture in Eighteenth-Century England* (2004). Based on a vast array of English sources, Wahrman argues that around 1780 a modern regime of selfhood took root. No longer was identity seen as a group membership, which could easily be exchanged for another, but the individual modern self becomes characterized by 'psychological depth, or interiority' and as innate, natural and unchanging. Whereas, for example, women could easily dress up in men's clothes in the eighteenth century, and vice versa, in the nineteenth century male and female dress were strictly separated. Gender, moreover, came to refer to a natural, fixed identity. The same applied to identity categories like race. Wahrman posits that in the eighteenth century, people thought a racial identity depended on the country one lived in, and hence could be changed by travelling. A black African would grow to be white once he lived in England. But in the nineteenth century, race and skin colour received their naturalistic and innate connotations that have become so familiar from histories of racism. A last example concerns portrait painting, which in the middle of the eighteenth century aimed at revealing the sitter as a general 'type' of character, rather than at capturing the individual likeness and personality, by focusing on their dress and accessories. These indicated surface appearance and cultural references, not the inner, unique self as evidenced by individual facial features. Many sitters also dressed up in masquerade, whose identity-bending options enjoyed wide popularity, until it fell into disrepute by around 1800, which for Wahrman is evidence for the rise of the modern regime of the self.

The shift from the *ancien* to the modern regime of identity was triggered, in Wahrman's view, by the American Revolution (1775–1783), during which the English started to wonder what precisely distinguished them from their American brethren, who had seemed so similar.[19] Wahrman's prizewinning book received much acclaim, but also some critique. His pinpointing the American Revolution as a cause of the shifting ideas on identity, particularly, was singled out as unconvincing.[20] But generally, there seems to be a consensus amongst historians about the novelty of modern selfhood. However, exactly when, where and how this development can be situated is still an open question. The last section of this chapter will therefore focus on *specific practices* of the self in modern Europe.

Technologies of the self

One of the most important theoretical concepts we can use when we study practices of the self is that of 'technologies of the self' of Michel Foucault. Before this particular concept will be explained and applied, we need to situate it in Foucault's body of work.

The French philosopher Michel Foucault (1926–1984) was, especially in his earlier work, preoccupied with questions of power. Not the common type of power historians are interested in, such as kings and parliaments. For Foucault, power was something more complicated, multifarious and omnipresent. His book *Discipline and Punish: The Birth of the Prison* (1975) analyses the shift from early modern practices of punishment, such as the public execution of murderers or the use of torture to extract confessions, to a modern penitentiary practice, which revolved around discipline. Foucault described the modern prison as a Panopticon, a model coined by the English philosopher, jurist and social reformer Jeremy Bentham (1748–1832), in which guards in watchtowers had the opportunity to look down into the separated prison cells, where prisoners felt they could be watched and therefore controlled all the time. This prison system resulted in self-discipline since the prisoners would internalize behavioural norms. Modern power, more generally, was disciplinary in nature. Foucault questioned modern notions of power, which were often seen as enlightened since capital punishment and torture had been abolished. For Foucault, this development was not self-evidently progress: he underlined the fact that modern, disciplinary power, which was not only a feature of the modern prison, but also of daily life, and in which people automatically adapted to social norms, was not as progressive as its proponents such as prison reformers had claimed. Foucault also critically interrogated the increasing role of experts such as psychologists, psychiatrists and social workers in the administration of justice. Their 'normalizing discourses', indicating who could be considered normal and who insane, also seemed a measure of modern progress, but Foucault wondered if people were now being punished for being who they are, rather than for what crimes they had committed.[21] He traced the rise of normalizing, disciplinary power beyond the administration of justice. In his book *The Will to Knowledge* (1976), the first volume of his series *The History of Sexuality*, he referred to the new, nineteenth-century academic disciplines of sexology and psychiatry, which coined the concepts of 'homosexual' and 'heterosexual', thereby forwarding a normalizing discourse.

Foucault's books all revolve around the same themes: the rise of modern power, connected to scientific notions of normality and abnormality, and the accompanying shaping of the modern subject as an object of study. In his earlier work, human subjects did not seem to have any agency, for which Foucault was critiqued by other scholars, but in his later work he grew more interested in the participation of the individual in the processes of modern discipline and knowledge. He first articulated the concept of the technology of the self in a lecture series on 'Subjectivity and the Truth', in 1980–1981. This course would form the basis for the second and third volumes of his *History of Sexuality* (both published in 1984). In his lectures and these two volumes, the French philosopher lay bare the entanglements between truth, power and the self. He saw 'technologies of the self' as permitting individuals to effect by their own means or with the help of others a certain number of operations on their own bodies and souls, thoughts, conduct, and way of being, so as to transform themselves in order to attain a certain state of happiness, purity, wisdom, perfection, or immorality.[22]

Foucault took subjectivity as something that is historically constituted and ontologically distinct from the body; moreover, he presumed the subject constitutes itself, and that subjectivity is a form that is shaped through practices, for which culturally available models are used. For instance, the ancients used a technique of the self Foucault calls 'ethical', i.e. 'the care of the self'. In the ancient world, the care of the self changed from a civic to a personal activity. With the arrival of Christianity, the care of the self was suppressed. Another technology is that of self-knowledge, which has continued to be influential since ancient times and which implies changing and producing our own subjectivity.[23]

The advantage of using Foucault's notion of 'technology of the self' is his explicit historicizing of the idea of the subject, and his idea that it is something that needs to be constructed with the help of social norms, not merely an individual, conscious doer. It contradicts the traditional philosophical notion of subjectivity as universal and transcendent. Even though Foucault never explicitly related his ideas on regimens of power/knowledge to the historical experiences of subjectivity, Jan Goldstein argues that the two are necessarily linked; subjectivation is a result of values disseminated by the power/knowledge mechanisms.[24] Goldstein provides an example of a technology of the self from nineteenth-century France: the philosophical psychology of Victor Cousin (1792–1867). His ideas about an a priori, active, volitional and holistic self were integrated into the school system: introspection to attain self-knowledge by the use of autobiography became a part of the school curriculum. In typical Foucauldian fashion, Goldstein argues, Cousinian pedagogy 'both constrained its recipients and created them' since instruction in psychology became a marker of class and gender: bourgeois males received this education; women and workers did not. It thus helped form a bourgeois identity in France.[25]

Several cultural historians have applied Foucault's notion of 'technologies of the self' to diverse cultural and material practices, for instance the writing of letters and autobiographies. Finnish historian Kaisa Vehkalahti studied the archives of Vuorela State Reform School, which was established for delinquent girls in 1893. As a public reform school Vuorela was designated for under-aged law-breakers: seven- to fifteen-year-old girls who were placed in reform school by public courts of justice and mostly sentenced because of thefts or petty larceny. From 1902 onwards Vuorela housed sixty pupils. The inmates were usually not released until they were eighteen years old and in some cases the placement could be prolonged until the age of twenty. The archives of this Finnish reform school contained notebooks, in which letters written by the inmates were copied by the school's personnel, who in this way checked the girls' letters. This systematic examination of the girls' correspondence revolved, as Vehkalahti argues, not only around control, but also around education and observation. The girls' behaviour and their character were being inspected. Thus, letters were a technique of observation but also of reform: the personal letters were assumed to reveal something about the inmates' inner character and feelings and thus used to track their progress in the institution and reform their personality. This urge to see inside the 'souls' of the pupils and to know them better provided the motivation for investigating the correspondence. Vehkalahti regards the systematic letter surveillance that was developed in Vuorela as one more implementation of the idea of the Panopticon that was so widespread in nineteenth-century prison and reformatory policy. This pedagogic and disciplinary practice moreover dovetails with Foucault's emphasis on self-examination, on the production of the truth about oneself with the help of an expert: in reformatory pedagogy with its emphasis on revealing one's self and soul, the confession of an individual was meant to initiate an inner process of self-scrutiny. Writing thus played a central role in the modern individualized self.[26]

The control of egodocuments as a means to discipline and reform children took place in many other Western European reform institutions and boarding schools. In twentieth-century Dutch reform schools, for instance, girls were forced to write autobiographies to reflect on their sins. Dating boys, going to the cinema and dancing were thought to be especially sinful. Eating sweets would point to a lack of (sexual) self-control and playing in the streets was a road towards prostitution. Seeing how the girl reacted to the practices of assessment was also of central importance in the technique of autobiography writing as implemented in the first half of the twentieth century. The girl was placed in an isolation room with a locked door and given a list of topics to discuss (like 'boys I have had contact with') and paper with a heading that suggested institutional scrutiny. These measures were designed to prompt self-reflection and to instil a sense of guilt and remorse in the girl, urging her towards confession. Saskia Bultman therefore argues that this technique functioned as a tool for re-education, providing psychological and pedagogical experts with a tool to probe the inner depths of the girls. The girls themselves, on the contrary, mostly referred to external causes when explaining their behaviour, instead of laying bare their inner identities. Perhaps this was a form of resistance, a way of consciously protecting their inner selves from the institutional will to know. Rather than a site for self-expression, Bultman suggests, the autobiographical writing of these Dutch delinquent girls was a technique aligned with experts' ideas on identity.[27]

The recent historical focus on techniques and practices, which produce certain selves, bodies or gender, is based on the adoption of the methodology of 'praxeography'. Dutch historian Geertje Mak, for instance, critically analyses medical examinations of hermaphrodites. In her book *Doubting Sex: Inscriptions, Bodies and Selves in Nineteenth-Century Hermaphrodite Case Histories* (2012), Mak shows how different techniques and practices of examining bodies led to different rationales on bodily sex. Using the 1200 – mostly French and German – cases of hermaphroditism collected by the Polish doctor Franz Ludwig von Neugebauer in *Hermaphroditismus beim Menschen* (1908), Mak argues that until 1870, bodily sex was considered as a social position rather than as an inner identity. Clothes, profession and appearance determined what bodily sex meant in public. In villages, people with ambivalent genders were part of the local community and this personal acquaintance made sure they were no threat. Only when they were about to overstep legal boundaries, like marrying a person of the same sex, was a medical examination of the body ordered. In the first part of the nineteenth century, this examination entailed inspection of the genitalia and the appearance of the hermaphrodite and hearing the patient's own description of the functioning of the reproductive organs. Criteria for establishing bodily sex were physical lust and the ability to procreate. In the second half of the nineteenth century, hermaphrodites were examined by physicians in the clinic, where the opportunities for operations expanded because of anaesthesia and antiseptics. Gonadal tissue could now be studied with the help of a microscope. Increasingly, cases of hermaphroditism were discovered by accident during operations for other purposes. Thus, Mak argues, the person of the hermaphrodite was disconnected from his/her body. These new techniques led to a reconceptualization of the relationship between body and self: from the beginning of the twentieth century, gonadal tissue needed to be aligned with inner identity. The 'true' sex was now considered to be a reflection of the inner self, also leading to problems such as the difficulty of deciding what the true sex was when the gonadal sex did not match the self-image of the patient. And should the doctor or the patient have the final say?[28]

Mak follows Foucault by historicizing the (sexual) self and pointing to the way science can make this category. But she emphasizes the techniques, practices and routines used to produce the self of the hermaphrodite, such as medical examinations but also autobiographical writing. This particular focus (praxeography) leads Mak to the conclusion that norms such as heterosexuality, but also hermaphroditism and sex, are not all-encompassing but could have different meanings in practice. She also includes the role of the patient in her description of medical examinations. Last, she underlines the shift towards the modern self as argued by Wahrman. Mak, too, delineates different regimes of self, changing from exteriority to interiority, from flexibility to fixedness and from identicality to authenticity. But she questions Wahrman's periodization, indicating that these developments took place at different paces depending on (social) location.[29] The rise of the modern, inner self, as traced by Wahrman in the late eighteenth century, only occurred in the early twentieth century when medical examinations of hermaphrodites are taken into account.

Cultural historians, therefore, are increasingly studying the diverse local practices in which the self was made, thereby going beyond a discourse analysis and paying attention to individual agency. Some of these studies have repaired problems with earlier histories of the self, such as the focus on influential philosophers rather than ordinary men and women, their teleological bases and the chasm between ideas and experiences of the self.[30] More attention can still be paid to the embodied self, rather than cultural discourses on the self.[31] As a last example, we will therefore turn to the theme of beauty and hygiene. How can we qualify these embodied practices as 'technologies of the self'?

One of the main practices of getting to know oneself must be looking in a mirror. Convex glass mirrors could be found in Northern Europe by the late fourteenth century. At the end of the seventeenth century two thirds of Parisian households owned a mirror. In the eighteenth century the mirror invaded household décor. The psyche, or free-standing, full-length mirror on a pivoting frame, became popular in the early nineteenth century, a period that later witnessed the success of the mirrored armoire. The mirror itself is ambivalent, as Sabine Melchior-Bonnet explains. On the one hand, the mirror offered an untainted image of divinity. On the other hand, the mirror's lure was not to be trusted. It was a dangerous and deceptive tool and particularly ambiguous for women. Whereas medieval thinkers had feared the mirror's power to distort and to provoke pride and vanity, later the looking glass was considered an aid for reaching self-knowledge.[32]

For a long time, however, mirrors were not used on a grand scale in the countryside and popular superstition mentioned that putting a mirror in front of a child would slow its growth, just as neglecting to cover a mirror after a death would lead to disaster. At the end of the nineteenth century, as French historian Alain Corbin posits, the mirror had become so familiar in the cities that it stimulated new beauty ideals. The bourgeois lifestyle included self-reflection; via the mirror one could observe one's own body and appearance as through the eyes of others. The dissemination of the big standing-mirror, in which people could see their entire figures, might even have led to increasing narcissism.[33]

The use of the mirror is only one aspect of modern beauty ideals and practices. More important was the new 'science' of hygiene. During the Enlightenment a bourgeois, 'natural' beauty ideal became popular, which was opposed to the 'artificial', perfumed and painted nobility. Natural looks would reflect a decent and rational character. Whereas the early modern theory of humours had prescribed that the body be dried with dry towels before it was covered in powder, makeup and perfume, the early nineteenth-century hygiene theory presented new demands for taking care of the body, including bathing, walking, healthy food and skin cream. Instead of cementing the skin with oil, wax, paint and powder, the pores were now cleaned with water so the skin could breathe and sweat. Hygiene and cosmetics had been influenced by scientific developments in pharmacology and physiology since the late eighteenth century, and later by radiology, bacteriology, surgery and psychology. Modern pharmacology, for instance, warned against the poisonous ingredients of makeup, like mercury.[34]

Historians have debated whether new beauty and health norms contributed to the modern disciplining of the body. Especially historians of disability regard these norms as hurtful, discriminating against people with different or 'abnormal' bodies. They also point out that what is considered 'normal' or 'abnormal' – these terms themselves being typically modern notions – is historically and culturally variable.[35] Other scholars, however, underline that modern discipline and self-fashioning of the body went together. Hygienic care can thus be regarded as 'technology of the self'.[36] For instance, from the first decades of the twentieth century beauty came to refer to the use of makeup to improve oneself in order to attain a job. The image of youthfulness and aesthetic surgery helped to 'normalize' the body, but at the same time cosmetics offered individuals the opportunity to shape their faces according to their own desires. Already in the first decades of the nineteenth century, for example, German plastic surgeons reconstructed the noses of people who had lost a nose from syphilis or a duel. The patients themselves determined that the social stigma of living without the vital part of the face was too great, and therefore requested the surgery. The same applied to the many men whose faces were maimed in the First World War. The patient was therefore not a victim of normalizing medical practice, but had the power to determine the shape of his or her own body.[37]

This trend towards self-creation when it came to beauty and the body would grow stronger throughout the twentieth century. The use of cosmetics, the focus on slimness and healthy living and, most importantly, the vast impact of sports and a muscular body all underlined how modern self-identity, for both men and women, centred on the body.[38] If the kernel of modern technologies of the self can be located in the late eighteenth and nineteenth centuries, when ideas about the self as having a unique, individual inner identity resulted in new practices to get to know and shape this self, in the twentieth century men and women's opportunities for shaping their embodied selves would become more widespread and less inescapable.

Conclusion

This chapter aimed to provide an overview of the most important developments in (medical) thinking about the body and illness and particularly about the relationship between body and mind. We have seen how the nineteenth century witnessed numerous shifts in ideas about medicine and disease: it is regarded as a period of medicalization, with 'hospital medicine' replacing 'bedside medicine'. Slowly, the humoral model disappeared and was, from the mid-nineteenth century, replaced by other models such as cellular pathology, laboratory medicine and a focus on organs. Psychiatry branched off from general medicine and became a separate discipline, emphasizing the study and cure of the mind. The new notion of mental trauma as a psychic response to shocks caused by railway accidents or sexual assault supplanted a pure focus on physical pathology.

Not only in medicine and psychiatry could a new emphasis on the mind be found. Cultural historians such as Wahrman have also tracked the 'rise of the modern self': a novel focus on identity, which from the late eighteenth century came to be associated with interiority, fixedness and authenticity. Foucault's notion of 'technologies of the self' can aid us in understanding how people have shaped their selves, using the available, and sometimes restrictive, cultural discourses. Several historians have applied this concept to, for instance, autobiographical writing in the context of institutions that aspired to discipline adolescents and juvenile delinquents. This notion of technologies of the self, as well as its application by cultural historians, has uncovered the tension between discipline and agency, between the power of cultural ideals and individual ways of appropriating or navigating them. The historical study of modern beauty practices and sports similarly reveals that modern discipline and self-fashioning are inextricably connected.

Notes

1 M.E. Fissell, 'Making Meaning from the Margins: The New Cultural History of Medicine', in F. Huisman and J. Harley Warner (eds), *Locating Medical History*, Baltimore, MD: The Johns Hopkins University Press, 2004, 364–89; R. Porter, 'The Patient's View: Doing Medical History from Below', *Theory and Society* 14, 1985, 175–98.

2 J. Lachmund, *Der abgehorchte Körper: Zur historischen Soziologie der medizinischen Untersuchung*, Opladen: Westdeutscher Verlag, 1997, 52–100.

3 E.H. Ackerknecht, *Medicine at the Paris Hospital 1774–1848*, Baltimore, MD: The Johns Hopkins University Press, 1967.

4 M. Foucault, *The Birth of the Clinic: An Archaeology of Medical Perception*, New York: Vintage Books, 1994 [1973], 124–48.

5 Foucault, *The Birth of the Clinic*, xviii.

6 B. Duden, *The Woman Beneath the Skin: A Doctor's Patients in Eighteenth-Century Germany*, Cambridge, MA: Harvard University Press, 1998.

7 W. Ruberg, 'The Tactics of Menstruation in Dutch Cases of Sexual Assault and Infanticide, 1750–1920', *Journal of Women's History* 25, 2013, 14–37.

8 E. Shorter, *A History of Psychiatry: From the Era of the Asylum to the Age of Prozac*, New York: John Wiley & Sons, Inc., 1997, 69–112.

9 S.A. Skålevåg, 'The Matter of Forensic Psychiatry: A Historical Enquiry', *Medical History* 50, 2006, 49–68.

10 W. Schivelbusch, *The Railway Journey: The Industrialization of Time and Space in the Nineteenth Century*, Leamington Spa, Hamburg, New York: Berg, 1986 [1977], 140.

11 Schivelbusch, *The Railway Journey*, 134–49.

12 W. Ruberg, 'Trauma, Body and Mind: Forensic Medicine in 19th-Century Dutch Rape Cases', *Journal of the History of Sexuality* 22, 2013, 85–104.

13 G. Vigarello, *Rape: A History from 1860 to the Present Day*, London: Virago, 2007, 130, 161, 197.

14 J. Goldstein, *Hysteria Complicated by Ecstasy: The Case of Nanette Leroux*, Princeton, NJ and Oxford, Princeton University Press, 2010, 5.

15 J. Seigel, *The Idea of the Self: Thought and Experience in Western Europe Since the Seventeenth Century*, Cambridge: Cambridge University Press, 2005; C. Taylor, *Sources of the Self: The Making of the Modern Identity*, Cambridge: Cambridge University Press, 1989; R. Martin and J. Barresi, *The Rise and Fall of Soul and Self: An Intellectual History of Personal Identity*, New York: Colombia University Press, 2008; P. Heehs, *Writing the Self: Diaries, Memoirs, and the History of the Self*, London: Bloomsbury Academic, 2013.

16 R. Porter, 'Introduction', in R. Porter (ed.), *Rewriting the Self: Histories from the Renaissance to the Present*, London: Routledge, 1997, 1–14.

17 For an overview see Porter, 'Introduction'.

18 Porter, 'Introduction', 9.

19 D. Wahrman, *The Making of the Modern Self: Identity and Culture in Eighteenth-Century England*, New Haven, CT: Yale University Press, 2004.

20 K. Berger, J. Campbell and D. Herzog, 'Forum: On Dror Wahrman's *The Making of the Modern Self*', *Eighteenth-Century Studies* 40, 2006, 149–56.

21 M. Foucault, *Discipline and Punish: The Birth of the Prison*, reprint, New York: Vintage Books, 1995.

22 Ibid., 'Technologies of the Self', in L. Martin and P. H. Hutton (eds), *Technologies of the Self: A Seminar with Michel Foucault*, Amherst, MA: The University of Massachusetts Press, 1988, 16–49, 18.

23 M.G.E. Kelly, 'Foucault, Subjectivity, and Technologies of the Self', in C. Falzon, T. O'Leary and J. Sawicki (eds), *A Companion to Foucault*, Chichester: John Wiley & Sons, 2013, 510–25.

24 J. Goldstein, 'Foucault's Technologies of the Self and the Cultural History of Identity', in J. Neubauer (ed.), *Cultural History after Foucault*, New York: de Gruyter, 1999, 37–54, 52–3.

25 Goldstein, 'Foucault's Technologies of the Self', 55–7.

26 K. Vehkalahti, *Constructing Reformatory Identity: Girls' Reform School Education in Finland, 1893–1923*, Oxford: Peter Lang Publishing, 2009. K. Vehkalahti, 'The Urge to See Inside and Cure: Letter-Writing as an Educational Tool in Finnish Reform School Education, 1915–1928', *Paedagogica Historica* 44, 2008, 193–205.

27 S. Bultman, *Constructing a Female Delinquent Self: Assessing Pupils in the Dutch State Reform School for Girls, 1905–1975*, PhD dissertation, Enschede: Ipskamp Printing, 2016.

28 G. Mak, *Doubting Sex: Inscriptions, Bodies and Selves in Nineteenth-Century Hermaphrodite Case Histories*, Manchester: Manchester University Press, 2012.

29 Mak, *Doubting Sex*, 45–55.

30 E. Hofman, 'How to Do the History of the Self', *History of the Human Sciences* 29, 2016, 8–24.

31 L. Hunt, 'The Self and Its History', *The American Historical Review* 119, 2014, 1576–86; M. Scheer, 'Are Emotions a Kind of Practice (And Is That What Makes Them Have a History)? A Bourdieuian Approach to Understanding Emotion', *History and Theory* 51, 2012, 193–220.

32 S. Melchior-Bonnet, *The Mirror: A History*, transl. K.H. Jewett, New York, London: Routledge, 2001 [1994].

33 A. Corbin, 'Le secret de l'individu', in M. Perrot (ed.), *Histoire de la vie privée* 4, Paris: Seuil, 1987.

34 A. Ramsbrock, *The Science of Beauty: Culture and Cosmetics in Modern Germany, 1750–1930*, New York: Palgrave Macmillan, 2015.

35 L.J. Davis, 'Constructing Normalcy: The Bell Curve, the Novel and the Invention of the Disabled Body in the Nineteenth Century', in L.J. Davis (ed.), *The Disability Studies Reader*, London: Routledge, 1997, 9–29.

36 P. Sarasin, *Reizbare Maschinen: Eine Geschichte des Körpers 1765–1914*, Frankfurt am Main: Suhrkamp, 2001, 23.

37 Ramsbrock, *The Science of Beauty*.

38 C.E. Forth, 'Beauty and Concepts of the Ideal', in I. Crozier (ed.), *A Cultural History of the Human Body: Vol. 6, In the Modern Age*, Oxford, New York: Berg, 2010, 127–45; C. Macdonald, 'Body and Self: Learning to Be Modern in 1920s–1930s Britain', *Women's History Review* 22, 2013, 267–79.

23

FAMILY, HOME AND VARIATIONS IN DOMESTIC LIFE

Kirsi Tuohela

'So the big thing has happened. The most important change has taken place – Karin is here now!' writes Carl Larsson in his autobiography in Swedish about meeting Karin Bergöö in 1882:

> I was finally in love in the right way. She was the person I wanted to marry, to live with, to make a family with. For the worthless person that I found myself to be, this was a breathtaking thought. But I knew that my life and my art depended on this.[1]

Carl Larsson (1853–1919) is a model progressive father of the late nineteenth century in many ways. He was as ambitious and forward-looking in his work and art as he was romantic in his views on marriage and true love acting as one's guidance and faith. Indeed, meeting Karin Bergöö (1859–1928) was a turning point in his life, and gradually family life with his wife and children started to mean heaven on earth for him.

Coming from a poor, working-class family, Carl Larsson's path to becoming a middle-class artist and father was not an easy or straightforward one. Nevertheless, he eventually became a famous Scandinavian painter of his time and, together with his wife Karin, created a cultural model for a child-centred family life that cherished love and nature. Their artist-family's home, *Lilla Hyttnäs* in Dalarna, Sweden, was depicted as such in a series of idyllic watercolours that Carl Larsson published in the books, *De Mina* (1895, 'The Loved Ones') and *Ett Hem* (1899, 'A Home'). These images were much loved by contemporaries, and in the twentieth century their popularity grew still further – images in which love, marriage, children and a family home thrived. This not only shows how crucial to modernity such a utopian vision of family life was becoming, but also how it was becoming increasingly accessible to more and more people. Indeed, Larsson contributed to a process in which family happiness was becoming increasingly democratized.[2]

This chapter will chart the key features of modern family life from late Enlightenment onwards. It will focus on how the notion of family developed into meaning a child-centred, emotional unit that ultimately desires a private home. Particularly

it will analyse the intersections of family with class and gender in a historical context destined to constantly change. The themes of class and gender will be enriched
by questions of domestication: how making a home and domestic space for family
members became a cornerstone of private life and personal happiness. Methodologically, this chapter aims to put the empirical and concrete in juxtaposition with more
abstract patterns, and to combine a close reading of the source material with a more
distant reading of the structures and processes of change. In terms of cultural history,
I am starting from the assumption that the materiality and practices of everyday life
reveal the importance of certain emotional ties and the best ways of adapting everyday tasks to meet long-term ideals.

Love and marriage

Carl Larsson echoed the attitudes of many when he described finding 'the right one'
in his future wife. The same idea of one day meeting the right person and only marrying for love was important to Karin Bergöö, the future wife in question, too. She
was the daughter of a bourgeois family, and had studied art in France like Carl. She
was keen to improve her skills in art, but was also willing to change the course of her
life if marriage required it. In some ways, she made a conventional choice by priori-
tizing her marriage over her career; but in others, her decision to marry a painter of
humble beginnings with an unstable income was less conventional. It was clearly a
choice of heart over reason – she was choosing to marry a man she loved, and who
had the same love of art as her. Despite the bourgeois gender roles in their family life,
there was also a new ideal of comradeship and equality.

The 'history of romantic love in courtship' has been studied by scholars such as the
Swede, Eva-Lisa Bjurman, and the German, Ulrike Prokop, who both adhere to the
notion that romantic love played a crucial role in the rise of modernity. They argue
that young upper-middle-class women of the late eighteenth century encountered
a new cultural model that held romantic love to be the only acceptable and honest
basis for marriage.[3] This attitude then spread to the rest of the middle class in the
nineteenth century and to the working class, too.

Prevailing attitudes towards marriage, which saw it as an economic arrangement
above all else, were therefore questioned and opposed, with the onset of modernity
in the late eighteenth century. In studying the letters, diaries and memoirs of young
women – like Sophie Zinn (1774–1851), daughter of a tradesman in Denmark, and
Cornelia Goethe (1750–1777), daughter of a jurist and the sister of Johann Wolfgang
von Goethe – Bjurman and Prokop argue that young women now had expectations
of romantic love from marriage. This meant that their education, manners, sensitivity
and the beauty of their gestures all became highly important as key tools to attract
modern men. Gender inequality in education, and especially in self-cultivation, was
part of this new discourse. According to Prokop, it was really only possible for the
sons of families like Goethe to gain such an education, whereas for girls this romantic discourse often caused only disappointment and sadness in the end. Cornelia
Goethe, for instance, married a man that was not her heart's choice, but that of reason and her family, and proceeded to write many melancholic secret letters during
her marriage which testify to such sadness.[4] Similar stories to this can be found all

the way through the nineteenth and twentieth centuries; but it is clear that these stories would also become intertwined with other discourses such as the women's movement for political rights.[5]

Family, household and class in the nineteenth century

The French Revolution had a lasting political effect everywhere in Europe, and social differences now started to be understood in relationship to the concept of class. Moreover, as the nineteenth century wore on, the growing middle class began to establish itself as the driving force in society, and as a key agent in the formation of new citizenship and nations, through industrialization and urbanization. At the same time this powerful bourgeoisie, or middle class, also spread its values, work ethic, patriarchal family model and way of life to classes both above and below.[6]

The fact that the bourgeois concept of family was fairly new might explain why the term 'family' did not have a fixed meaning in the nineteenth century. It was easily confused with the terms such as 'household', or 'domestic group', and the three terms were difficult to differentiate even for bureaucrats. The definition of a household or family in the *State Census* of 1851 in Great Britain reveals this:

> The first, most intimate, and perhaps most important community, is the family, not considered as the children of one parent, but as persons under one head; who is the occupier of the house, the householder, master, husband, or father; while the other members of the family are, the wife, children, servants, relatives, visitors and persons constantly or accidentally in the house.[7]

Family here is both an intimate and emotional unit but also a household with many members and a definite head. Consequently, the traditional extended household seems caught up with the more modern intimate family.[8]

The idea of family that eventually flourished among the middle classes in the nineteenth century certainly did not spring up overnight, and nor was it the same everywhere. Its key aspects were linked to domestic ideology and economic activity. In the nineteenth century, a bourgeois home was seen as a unit that guaranteed not only financial stability, but was 'a bedrock of morality in an unstable and dangerous world'. It was a place where, as Leonore Davidoff and Catherine Hall have written regarding their particular case in England, the middle-class family established itself to 'educate children, provide for dependants and live a religious life'.[9]

Religion therefore played an important role in the nineteenth century. It offered the middle classes a sense of identity and community; as with their religious principles and practices, they could distinguish themselves from the aristocracy when striving for status and power. Indeed, it was an important principle in Christianity that all were equal in the eyes of God and equally worthy of being saved. This meant compassion for the weak and helpless – 'women, children, animals, the insane, the prisoner' – but, at the same time, a religious framework of thought supported rational planning and an ordered society. The burgeoning bourgeoisie therefore based its values and morals on Christian ideals, which in Northern Europe took the form of a Protestant ethos, but combined these values with rational and scientific ideas. This interest in commercial success, new professions and social order was thus not only a moral position but also a very rational and practical one too.[10]

The family was still the basis of economic activity for many in the middle classes. Family enterprise was organized on the basis of making profit, and it brought together property and authority, with the gender relations and division of labour that this implied – the private and public spheres being clearly gendered. This also affected the inheritance mechanisms implicit in simultaneously raising children. As Davidoff and Hall have put it, family enterprises were a gendering mechanism which designated 'men as those with power and agency' and 'women as passive dependants'.[11] Family was, however, always a flexible social constellation which allowed for various active positions for women as well – mostly within the private, domestic or philanthropic field.

When Scandinavia industrialized in the late nineteenth century, some time after England, it was a period of fervent socioeconomic activity.[12] One of the most successful family enterprises in Finland was the Ahlström company, which founded its wealth in the wood industry during the 1870s. It offers a good example of how a bourgeois and farming family came together through marriage and combined their means to go on and create a family fortune during a period of intense industrialization.

The founder of this family enterprise, Antti Ahlström (1827–1896), was born in the small village of Merikarvia near the Bothnian coast in Western Finland. He was the son of a farmer that would sail to nearby cities to sell tobacco, potatoes, ceramics, timber and goods from the countryside. Antti had seven brothers and they all grew up working on the farm from an early age, also helping their parents and their servants when they sailed off to sell goods along the coast. They were taught manners at home and in church, where they went every Sunday well dressed in homemade blue suits made of raw wool. Antti only went to school for a few years as a teenager before he married and became a businessman.[13]

Antti Ahlström's first wife was a widow, Anna Liljebald (1812–1870), who owned a farm with a watermill, a saw mill, a small paper mill and a ceramics factory. By marrying this woman 15 years his senior, the 23-year-old Ahlström acquired the farm, the mills and the factory, plus a family with five children. He built ships and started to export wood to Lybeck, Tallinn, Copenhagen and beyond. On the return trips the ships brought back grain and flour. He managed well, and in the 1870s he expanded his business first into forestry and saw mills, and then into metal by buying iron mills.[14]

Death was common in nineteenth-century families, and Anna and Antti Ahlström's was no exception, as they lost two of their three offspring when they were still children. When Anna herself died suddenly in November 1870, Antti Ahlström's life took a new turn. He married a young, educated, middle-class governess called Eva Holmström in 1871, and his class status grew accordingly. Soon the family moved to a new estate in Noormarkku, and this became the new base for the family business. Six children were born and raised here to inherit and carry on the family legacy. In addition to being in charge of his industrial communities, Ahlström also became a reformer who founded several schools for the lower classes and helped poor people financially. He advocated education for all, and provided financial support for artists as well as philanthropic organizations. He became one of the richest and most respected people in the country and saw himself as part of the Finnish nationalist movement.[15]

The account of Antti Ahlström is a good illustration of how the middle class was gradually growing, with some individuals entering it from more modest farming backgrounds. This would sometimes occur through marriage and bring not only wealth but also intellectual and social status. The Ahlströms were no exception in thinking that their family's economic and personal welfare was the priority, but the middle classes also often felt a duty to strengthen society and the nation, to educate and help the poor, to create safety, stability and standards in society – and they put their money to these purposes.[16]

Wealthy families wanted to be recognized for what they had achieved, and one result of this was that the fathers of these families – like Antti Ahlström – often came across as being purely businessmen, important social and political actors, rather than family men. Their intimate and private life was to be kept away from prying eyes. Nevertheless, individual memoirs give us more of an idea about personal family experiences and other aspects of domestic life.

Family, childhood and domesticity

Another kind of story reflecting the more personal side of family life, this time from a child's perspective, is Leo Tolstoy's first autobiographical novel – *Childhood* (1852). In it we meet a family typical of Eastern Europe, what Michael Mitterauer calls 'the generational family', which would consist of three generations living on the same property owned by a head of the family, usually from the first generation. This sort of traditional family has also been called a 'stem family',[17] and in Russia, they came mostly from the landed gentry.

Tolstoy includes important servants in the family, too, such as the boys' tutor Karl Ivanitch, and the girls' governess Mimi (Maria Ivanovna), as they figure heavily in the lives of the family's children. Ivanitch otherwise has no other family, while Mimi's 11-year-old daughter is as much part of the family as the other children. Both the teachers feature at the start of the novel and are depicted as strict, somewhat idiosyncratic and having strong feelings and opinions about most matters.

Mamma, the mother in the story, is a typical nineteenth-century angelic female – she is gentle, polite and sad; and yet she smiles, remains charming and is greatly loved by her children. Papa, meanwhile, is often in his office and portrayed as hot-tempered, and mostly concerned with the business of running the estate as head of the household. In other words, he is constantly giving orders to his servants and trying to keep track of his family's declining fortunes. Not only do the parents therefore have separate spheres of life, but they also have sharply contrasting emotional roles in the family. Mamma is tender and spiritual and is visited by madmen, holy fools or 'pure souls' that she understands, cares for and feeds. Meanwhile, Papa takes a more rationalist approach and is exasperated at them.

> 'Yes, I am angry, – very angry at seeing supposedly reasonable and educated people let themselves be deceived. [...] And it is a good thing,' Papa continued as he put the hand aside, 'that the police run such vagabonds in. All they are good for is to play upon the nerves of certain people who are already not over-strong in that respect'.[18]

Tolstoy depicts this family as not only being large, but also having a patriarchal structure which extends over all the domestic staff. They are clearly portrayed as being
dependent on the family and, as such, are given somewhat child-like, emotional and
self-sacrificing characters.

Significantly, Tolstoy portrays the family as being child-centred, as he tells the
story from a child's perspective. Indeed, the story played a big part in creating
the paradigm and myth of a happy childhood that was to be popular for the next
80 years or more. This myth of the 'happy, happy, unforgettable times of childhood' meant having a perfect mother and remote father; and involves equating,
as Andrew Wachtel has put it, 'the locus of childhood – the country estate – with
paradise'.[19] But it was not only the Russian writers after Tolstoy that continued
to portray childhood in this fashion. Like many other writers, Tolstoy had read
Charles Dickens and was also a great admirer of the Swiss-born philosopher and
writer, Jean-Jacques Rousseau (1712–1778), who similarly claimed that childhood
was a time of innocence – a paradise that the later world of grown-ups corrupt.[20]
This loss of innocence is still an essential part of modernity and its relationship
with childhood.[21]

From Tolstoy's *Childhood*, it is apparent that the nineteenth century was a time
when one's family became a viable frame for memory and identity. Historian Peter
Fritzsche writes that the past became more than just that of kings and kingdoms – by
the nineteenth century it was also one of individuals and families. People began to see
themselves as genuinely worthy of history and thus in historical terms as developing,
changing and declining. As their value seemed to increase, the number of autobiographies, memoirs and scrapbooks being written also grew. People started to think of
themselves as individuals with 'broken selves' – a story of ruptures – but often within
the framework of family and household. Fritzsche writes that 'the historicization of
private life went hand-in-hand with the celebration of home and the cultivation of
domesticity'.[22]

Sheltered stability and gender in the family

The concept of family has many roots, including sentimental, moral and religious
ones; but by the nineteenth century, many of the more powerful in the middle class
were being persuaded by social reformers of the time to see the patriarchal family
as the key social unit to ensure a stable society. According to French social reformer,
Frédéric Le Play (1806–1882), this was the kind of family that brought the most
stability. 'Patriarchal', in this respect, meant either a family with one male head and
all his married sons living under the same roof, or a stem family where only one of
the married sons lived with the head of the family, and the others were married off
elsewhere. According to Le Play, there were emotional as well as rational reasons for
seeing both these family types as ensuring a continuation of tradition and the family
line. In contrast, the arriviste families from the working class that were a by-product
of industrialization were seen as corrupting this stability, as their 'bad customs and
laws undermined patriarchal authority'.[23] There was no stability beyond them simply
marrying and having children, but once the children left home and the inheritance
was divided up, that family disappeared.

So, the model that most bourgeois families followed had the husband and father as breadwinner, public representative and sovereign ruler of the family. The wife and mother's role was to manage the domestic sphere. For example, in a German manual for educating girls, dating from 1878, the 'highest and most rewarding female profession' is described as being 'wife and mother'. The reason then given frames a woman's education in terms of social stability:

> if it's true that the wellbeing of the state rests on the well-being of the family, and in turn that the center of the family is to be sought in the woman as wife and mother, then this must be the goal of education.[24]

Books like this – in the form of educational fiction, manuals or books on etiquette – were published in large numbers,[25] indicating that the middle classes were eager to ensure that their children developed into 'good girls and boys', capable of raising stable families of their own, thus ensuring the stability of society and the nation as a whole.

Gabriele Reuter (1859–1941) was a German writer who had this kind of middle-class upbringing and wrote about it in her novel, *From a Good Family* (*Aus guter Familie*), which quickly made her one of the best-known women writers in the German language of her time when it was published in 1895. She had already published a series of novels and short stories and, as an avid reader herself, was aware of literary trends of the time like French naturalism. Yet rather than focus on the 'washerwomen, actresses, waitresses and prostitutes' of naturalism, in her 1895 novel she chose to write about a young middle-class woman.[26] The family she describes, from the perspective of a daughter, is a typical middle-class Prussian family with a father working as a bureaucrat for the state, the mother in charge of the household and managing the domestic staff and a son striving for a career as a military officer. Unlike Nora in Henrik Ibsen's play *A Doll's House* (1879) – who becomes a heroine with enough moral strength to leave her husband and child to seek a better life for herself as an individual – Reuter's female protagonist, Agathe Heidling, is a girl that neither gets married nor does anything heroic. By trying to liberate herself and failing, Agathe's story is a study of milieu, and how women of Reuter's time and class interacted with the customs of their cultural environment. As Lynne Tatlock suggests, Agathe is not a story of *Bildung*, but the opposite, in fact – 'a case of stunted growth, of development that fails to take place because the culture around her does not foster it'.[27]

Reuter's novel was discussed widely at the time and sometimes compared to Thomas Mann's *Buddenbrooks* (1901), a family tragedy in which a German merchant family declines because of an inability to cope with ruthless modernity.[28] Reuter's message might certainly be as pessimistic as Mann's, but it can also be read as a cry for change.

Other writers like naturalist Amalie Skram (1846–1905) from Norway, or the Concourt brothers and Émile Zola (1840–1902) from France, were radicals that criticized the bourgeoisie's gender structures, but most 'good' middle-class families of the late nineteenth century usually disliked and overlooked their texts. Similarly, although some people had criticized the bourgeois concept of family and marriage during the long nineteenth century, most did not seem to share this perspective. Feminist organizations continued to stress the importance of family stability and of mother-hood as the highest calling for a woman, and they fought for it to be recognized and valued as such.[29] Swedish feminist Ellen Key (1849–1926), for example, was famous for her texts and for giving talks all over Europe about women's and children's rights. In her most famous book, *The Century of Childhood* (*Barnets århundrade*, 1900), she claimed that the nineteenth century had been the century in which women had gained recognition and made themselves seen and heard. According to her, the pro-gressive twentieth century to come would be the century of childhood – this would mean many old ideas would be swept away. She wrote and lectured that the new cen-tury would usher in a new scientific era, and that new ideas of love and marriage, and of physical, spiritual and erotic life, would be needed to create better human beings. In this respect, she insisted that bringing children into the world and raising them was the most crucial task of all modern societies, and this would require parents of a dif-ferent kind – educated men and women who would understand the 'sanctity of gen-erations' and the real ramifications of evolution. Instead of being seen as inherently 'sinful', humans should be seen as a potential force for good – not only biologically, but also socially and spiritually.[30] Nevertheless, the precious task of raising children was primarily a woman's task, according to Key. This focus on childhood certainly meant that women were valued more than ever, but only in terms of motherhood, as it left the question of women's political and economic rights unresolved – to the dis-appointment of many women who particularly valued these rights. What constitutes a proper balance between these two still features in the debate over maternity and women's rights in the workplace today.

Family in crisis: the working class and the twentieth century

Despite the increasing visibility and power of the middle class, it was of course not the only way of life for families. The experience of both the urban and rural work-ing classes is not to be forgotten in family histories. In spite of the growing number of people working in mills and factories in the latter half of the nineteenth century, most of Europe's population still lived in a rural setting. In France, this proportion was 69% in 1872. As the rural working class usually shared their living space with others, they were often closely supervised, and the farmhouse was as much a workplace as a home.[31] The history of families must therefore take these experiences into account.

Early industrialization, from the late eighteenth century onwards, brought eco-nomic prosperity and a leading international role for Britain, in particular, and its expanding empire. One notorious image of this growing empire is of the sad figure of the child labourer found, for example, in the novels of Charles Dickens and the fairy tales of Hans Christian Andersen.[32] According to the historian Jane Humphries, children under 13 and young people under 18 made up two thirds of all British tex-tile workers in the 1830s and one quarter of all mineworkers in the 1840s. Indeed, the period when child labour was most prevalent in British industry was during the first three decades of the nineteenth century.[33] Elsewhere in Europe, this peak in child labour occurred later. Tampere in Finland, for instance, had the greatest concentration of cotton mills in Scandinavia from as early as the 1820s onwards, and yet the number of child workers did not peak until the 1870s.[34]

In the nineteenth century, as the term 'working-class family' suggests, everybody in such a family worked. It was hard to say whether the parents were allowing their children to be exploited by putting them out to work, or if the children's contribution had an overall positive effect for the family as a whole. At the beginning of the nineteenth century, child labour was generally accepted, but by the end of it, child labour became increasingly regulated and restricted until in the end it was forbidden for under-12s. The experience of working-class families changed as attitudes and laws regarding child labour changed, until eventually children were to be found only in schools and not in the workplace.[35]

Autobiographies that working-class people wrote often reveal that as children they may have worked from an early age, but they did not blame their parents for that. They might help in the household, on the farm or in shops, or were sent away from home on an apprenticeship. The English poet John Clare (1793–1864), for instance, had a typical working-class upbringing and wrote in his autobiography how his parents managed their various hardships. He described how he had a 'tender father' who was nevertheless 'forced by poverty to overrule his wife's desire for John to remain at school and instead set him to work'.[36] As Janet Humphries points out, fathers were usually decent men but because of economic circumstances they remained remote. They worked long hours and spent a lot of time away from the rest of the family, so when they got home they would be exhausted. Industrialization may have made working men 'distant and shadowy figures' in the family, but it also meant that mothers were given the space to be closer to their children, and this comes across in the praise and adoration lavished on them in their children's autobiographies. As Kate Douglas suggests, however, most of these autobiographies are framing childhood in either nostalgic or traumatic terms; and according to her, the dominant mode prior to the late twentieth century was nostalgic.[37]

Wars have also affected family history. Fathers fighting in the Napoleonic Wars in the early nineteenth century, for instance, had to leave their families for a long time. If and when they did return, they were often crippled – both mentally and physically. The same must have been equally true in the context of the twentieth century, an age of extremes that witnessed two world wars that were new in many ways and affected all aspects of life, and especially family life. The traces of bombs may have littered the physical landscape, but as the historian Carolyn Steedman suggests, the scars remained even longer in the memories depicted in personal and family narratives. Growing up in 1950s South London, she writes that

> [t]he war was so palpable a presence in the first five years of my life that I still find it hard to believe that I didn't live through it. There were bomb-sites everywhere, prefabs on waste land, most things still on points, my mother tearing up the ration book when meat came off points […].[38]

Steedman particularly remembers her mother longing for clothing with the 'New Look' – a long skirt that would replace the short one of the 1940s – a new skirt that she could not afford.

Steedman's story of growing up in a working-class family includes the idea that class consciousness is 'a structure of feeling that can be learned in childhood'.[39] She suggests that childhood memories and the emotional legacy that parents pass on to their children are essential elements is this consciousness:

> My mother's longing shaped my own childhood. From a Lancashire mill town and a working-class twenties childhood she came away wanting: fine clothes, glamour, money; to be what she wasn't. However that longing was produced in her distant childhood, what she actually wanted were real things, real entities, things she materially lacked, things that culture and social system withheld from her.[40]

Steedman's mother was 'a good mother' in that she did not drink or neglect her children. She kept the house and children clean, fed them, and yet she could never quite recommend having children to others. 'Never have children dear; they ruin your life' was one warning that she often repeated.[41] According to Steedman, mothers like hers do not fit into the general iconography of mothering and conflict with the idea that a woman's main purpose is to have children. This is a class issue for Steedman; working-class children have a special kind of ambivalence to deal with when growing up – they are often wanted but also resented. Socioeconomic circumstances may make them a burden, and even if children may also be a burden to middle-class families, this is made less apparent to a bourgeois child when growing up.[42]

In Steedman's experience, her father was present yet did not matter very much. Steedman argues that gender roles were different in the working-class household of the 1950s. The position of men at home was not so powerful, and did not have the same impact as the mother-figure. As Steedman phrases it, 'somehow the iron of patriarchy didn't enter into my soul'.[43]

The cultural historian Luisa Passerini also remembers in her autobiography the stories of her working-class family in Italy and the gender roles demonstrated in it:

> In my mother's family – artisans and tradesmen, after the peasant stock of my great-grandparents, from the Langhe on one side and Monferrato on the other – the women did everything, they assumed every responsibility, while men hovered in the background, weaklings or idlers or miscreants. The traditions included a great-grandfather who went out for a drink and never returned; he left his wife and five children in Italy to emigrate to South America, where he was never heard from again.[44]

Family relationships were complex – British family life was certainly different from Italian, and Eastern different from Western European – but interestingly there seem to be some patterns relating to class such as the absent or at least non-patriarchal men in the family.

Family in crisis

Whether it's bourgeois or working-class, the family has been a political issue throughout modernity.[45] And yet it is only relatively recently that family psychology became an issue of public debate. After World War II, with the advent of the welfare state, greater public attention was paid to the psychological health of families and the help they might require.

One of the movements that focused on family was the antipsychiatry movement of the 1960s that was perhaps more powerful in England than elsewhere. Its leading figure, R.D. Laing, blamed family members and especially mothers for driving others in the family crazy. According to him, these people were trapped in a form of misery, usually referred to as schizophrenia, which was a result of unhealthy family dynamics. These spoiled parent–child relations were particularly prevalent, he argued, in middle-class families. This constituted a radical shift in the way the previously sacrosanct bourgeois family was conceived, as it was now a veritable psychological minefield. Historian Roy Porter proposes that this was part of the legacy that Freud left for the twentieth century.[46]

The birth of psychoanalysis spelt trouble for the middle-class family model, argues Porter: 'from then on, there were not just problem families – the family itself was a problem'.[47] In the 1920s, psychiatry started to be used outside the asylum context in Britain to address this issue of family psychodynamics in counselling. Even though a troubled family background had been seen for some time already as a source of psychiatric concern, the new approach now made the family not only 'the prime site', as Porter terms it, but also 'perhaps the prime source, of personal disorder'. The importance of this cultural shift was in the way it changed scientific thinking in the fields of psychology and sociology, with important ramifications for the modern conception of family. It was not that the family as a social unit was no longer relevant; on the contrary, as a source of 'trouble' it made the family unit all the more significant. Indeed, this new approach has provided the impetus for new kinds of therapy and intervention, in what Porter has called 'the rise of the therapeutic society'.[48]

The dysfunctional family has been a common theme in fictional drama, and especially so since World War II. One could take this as evidence for the family being in crisis. However, this sense of crisis could also just be one symptom in the evolution or transformation of the once predominant patriarchal and nuclear families into a plethora of new kinds of family structure: such as couples with children from former relationships, single-parent families, childless couples and families with same-sex parents.

In this chapter I have analysed the family in its historical journey, as an emotional and economic unit, from the birth of modernity to the opening decades of the twenty-first century. I have followed its evolution from an authoritarian structure to one of equal partnership and togetherness. I have contrasted cultural models and norms and the class-specific features of family, with individual experiences. One of the major changes that occurred in the twentieth century, at least in the West, was the rise of individualism, so that today families consist of a group of individuals, and there is an obvious need to balance the equal rights of all their members. On the one hand, the goals, dreams, happiness and well-being of the individual in this 'me-society' come first and can conflict with the family as whole; but on the other it has allowed for another form of love and togetherness to flourish in new forms of the family. Family still remains a utopian life-goal for many, an idea of everlasting happiness that the majority of modern people still strive for. Similarly, on the public level, the family remains politically, socially and economically very important. Indeed, it is as much because (as in spite of) it possibly being a source of trouble that the modern family is today so highly valued – whether we like it or not, it plays an emotional role at key points in all our lives.

The family is an ideological, socioeconomic and emotional concept, and it is evolving all the time. In the era of individualism, one might think it is less important, but instead of being taken as a social norm family has now become linked to personal identity. Similarly, in the age of individualism, there is now a wide range of family structures that exist to cope with the challenges of living together in a self-sufficient atmosphere of love and togetherness, for raising children and for taking care of loved ones. Family has never referred to only one sort of household or network of relationships, and the multitude of family structures that are increasingly recognized in political, socioeconomic and emotional terms since the latter half of the twentieth century is further proof of this.

Notes

1 C. Larsson, *Jag. Carl Larsson självbiografi* (1931), Falun: Brunkman & Bergöö, 2017, 139. Translation by Kirsi Tuohela.
2 The nineteenth century has been called 'the century of the family'. Finnish historian Kai Häggman entitled his research on families of the Finnish educated class in 1820–1900 accordingly *Perheen vuosisata* (*The Century of the Family*). K. Häggman, *Perheen vuosisata: Perheen ihanne ja sivistyneistön elämäntapa 1800-luvun Suomessa*, Helsinki: Finnish Historical Society, 1994.
3 E.L. Bjurman, *Catrines intressanta blekhet. Unga kvinnors möten med de nya kärlekskraven 1750–1830*, Stockholm: Brutus Östlings Bokförlag Symposion, 1998, 5, 18; E.L. Bjurman, 'Sophie, Education and Love: A Young Bourgeois Girl in Denmark in the 1790s', *Ethnologia Scandinavica* 26; U. Prokop, *Die Illusion vom Grossen Paar. Band I: Weibliche Lebensentwürfe im deutschen Bildungsbürgertum 1750–1770*, Frankfurt am Main: Fisher Taschenbuch Verlag, 1991, 29–30.
4 Prokop, *Illsusion vom Grossen Paar*, 23–8.
5 See also M. McKeon, *The Secret History of Domesticity: Public, Private and the Division of Knowledge*, Baltimore: John Hopkins University Press, 2005, 131.
6 C. Hall, *Worlds Between: Historical Perspectives on Gender and Class*, Oxford: Polity Press, 1995, 180; C. Hall, 'The Sweet Delights of Home', *A History of Private Life IV: From the Fires of Revolution to the Great War* (1987), ed. M. Perrot, Cambridge, MA: The Belknap Press of Harvard University Press, 1990, 74–81.
7 Census of Great Britain 1851: Population Tables I P.P. (1852–3) quoted in R. Wall, 'Mean Household Size in England from Printed Sources', in P. Laslett (ed.), *Household and Family in Past Time*, Cambridge: Cambridge University Press, 1972, 160.
8 For more on family as a social structure see Laslett, *Household and Family in Past Time* (1972), and as a sentimental and emotional unit, see P. Ariès, *L'enfant et la vie familiale sous l'Ancien Régime* (1960), translated into English in 1962 as *Centuries of Childhood*; E. Shorter, *The Making of the Modern Family*, New York: Basic Books, 1977. For more on family and domesticity, and the complex interconnectedness of the public and private in modernity, see McKeon, *The Secret History of Domesticity*. See also L. Stone, *The Family, Sex and Marriage in England 1500–1800*, New York: Harper & Row, 1977, 221–3.
9 C. Hall and L. Davidoff, *Family Fortunes: Men and Women of the English Middle Class 1780–1850* (1987), revised ed., London and New York: Routledge, 2002, xiv.
10 Hall and Davidoff, *Family Fortunes*.
11 Ibid., 32, 198.
12 P. Haapala, *Tehtaan valossa: teollistuminen ja työväestön muodostuminen Tampereella 1820–1920*, Tampere: Vastapaino, 1986, 101–2.

13 J. Aho, *Antti Ahlström 1827–1896, I, Muistokirjoitus*, Noormarkku: A Ahlström Osakey-htiö, 1927, 1–18, cit. 19. For more on child labour and education in rural Scandina-via, see P. Markkola, 'Negotiating Family, Education and Labor', in R. Aasgaard, M.J. Bunge and M. Roos (eds), *Nordic Childhoods 1700–1960: From Folk Beliefs to Pippi Long-stocking*, London: Routledge, 2017, 166–7.

14 Aho, *Antti Ahlström*, 27.

15 Ibid., *Antti Ahlström 1827–1896, II, Muistokirjotus*, Noormarkku: A Ahlström Osakey-htiö, 1927, 314–412; *Suomen kuvalehti* 1876.

16 See also Hall and Davidoff, *Family Fortunes*.

17 M. Mitterauer and R. Sieder, *The European Family: Patriarchy to Partnership from the Mid-dle Ages to the Present* (1977), Oxford: Basil Blackwell, 1982, 29, 33.

18 L. Tolstoy, *Childhood, Boyhood and Youth* (1852), New York: Alfred A Knopf, 1912/1991, 14–17.

19 A. Wachlet, 'Tolstoy's Childhood in Russia', *Encyclopedia of Children and Childhood in History and Society* 3, ed. P.S. Fass, New York: Macmillan, 2004, 837.

20 A.N. Wilson, 'Introduction', in Leo Tolstoy, *Childhood, Boyhood and Youth*, v.

21 J. Ahlbeck, P. Lappalainen, K. Launis and K. Tuohela, 'Introduction: Child Figures as Fragile Subjects', in J. Ahlbeck, P. Lappalainen, K. Launis and K. Tuohela (eds), *Child-hood, Literature and Science: Fragile Subjects*, London and New York: Routledge, 2018, 1–20.

22 P. Fritzsche, *Stranded in the Present: Modern Time and the Melancholy of History*, Cam-bridge, MA, London: Harvard University Press, 2004, 160–9, 178. For more on 'do-mesticity' see McKeon, *The Secret History of Domesticity*, xx–xxi.

23 Laslett, 'Introduction: The History of the Family', *Household and Family in the Past Time*, 16–17; Perrot, 'The Family Triumphant', *A History of Private Life IV*, 99–100, 106–8.

24 C.S.J. Milde, 'Der deutschen Jungfrau Wesen und Wirken: Winke für das geistige und praktische Leben' (1878) cited in L. Tatlock, 'Introduction' in G. Reuter, *From a Good Family* (1895), Rochester, NY: Camden House, 1999, 20.

25 Tatlock, 'Introduction', xxi; P. Lappalainen and L. Rojola, 'Introduction', in P. Lappa-lainen and L. Rojola (eds), *Women's Voices: Female Authors and Feminist Criticism in the Finnish Literary Tradition*, Helsinki: Finnish Literature Society, 2007, 7–14.

26 Tatlock, 'Introduction', ix–xiii.

27 Ibid., xxvii.

28 Ibid., xxvi.

29 Hall and Davidoff, *Family Fortunes*, 149; Tatlock, 'Introduction', xxi.

30 E. Key, *Barnets århundrade*, Stockholm: Albert Bonniers Förlag 1911 (1900), 5–7.

31 M. Perrot, 'At Home', *A History of Private Life IV*, 347–9; L. Davidoff, *Worlds Between: Historical Perspective on Gender and Class*, Cambridge: Polity Press, 1995.

32 Markkola, 'Negotiating Family: Education and Labour', 163.

33 J. Humphries, *Childhood and Child Labour in the British Industrial Revolution*, 3rd ed., Cambridge: Cambridge University Press, 2013, 7, 9, 43.

34 Haapala, *Tehtaan valossa*, 49–60.

35 Ibid., 49–60.

36 Cited in Humphries, *Childhood and Child Labour in the British Industrial Revolution*, 129.

37 K. Douglas, *Contesting Childhood: Autobiography, Trauma, and Memory*, New Brunswick, NJ, London: Rutgers University Press, 2010, 84–5.

38 C. Steedman, *Landscape for a Good Woman*, London: Virago Press, 2000, 29.

39 Ibid., 7.

40 Ibid., 6.

41 Ibid., 85.

42 Ibid., 90.

43 Ibid., 19.

44 L. Passerini, *Autobiography of a Generation: Italy, 1968* (1988), Middletown, CT: Wesleyan University Press, 1996, 5.

45 R. Porter, 'Madness and the Family Before Freud: The View of the Mad-Doctors', *Journal of Family History* 23, 1998, 159. National case studies seem to reveal the same phenomenon. One example is the ground-breaking study on the history of the working-class family in Finland by P. Markkola, *Työläiskodin synty: Tamperelaiset työläisperheet ja yhteiskunnallinen kysymys 1870-luvulta 1910-luvulle*, Helsinki: Finnish Historical Society, 1994, 195–8.

46 Porter, 'Madness and the Family', 159–60.

47 Ibid., 160–1.

48 Ibid., 160–1.

24

NATURAL DISASTERS AND MODERNITY

Kyrre Kverndokk

One of the most dramatic incidents in early modern history happened on 1 November 1755. The earthquake that hit Lisbon that day was disastrous. The heavy shaking of the ground was followed by massive fires and a tsunami, and the fourth largest city in Europe was suddenly and completely levelled. Nobody really knows how many people died that day – today it is estimated to be about 30,000; an estimate at the time was 100,000.

In Europe, this devastating earthquake is still remembered: in Lisbon through the ruins of the church of Conventio do Carmo; and elsewhere, first and foremost, through the works of Voltaire. The cultural historian, Jean Paul Poirier, has remarked that if people nowadays are asked if they have heard of the Lisbon earthquake, they will most probably nod their heads and reply: 'Oh, yes, Voltaire'.[1] In his poem 'Poème sur le Désastre de Lisbonne' from 1756, and in the paradigmatic novel *Candide* three years later, Voltaire used the earthquake as an opportunity to argue against the optimism of the mid-eighteenth century. In polemic terms, he argued against the idea that, despite such a dreadful disaster, we still live in the best of all possible worlds, and claimed that no meaning could possibly lie behind such a catastrophe. At the same time, he also argued against an opposite position, what the historian Kevin Rozario has termed a 'pessimistic cosmic fatalism', the widespread idea of calamities as the rightful divine punishment of sinful humans.[2]

The disaster was seemingly meaningless, and put the religious and moral order of the world on trial. It has been argued that the Lisbon earthquake was as important for Western thought as Auschwitz.[3] The reception of the earthquake contributed to the occurrence of a modern concept of evil, separated from Providence. It contributed to the emergence of what Bruno Latour has termed 'the crossed-out God' – a modern spiritual God, separated from the 'distinct ontological zones' of both nature and culture.[4] Thus, in her seminal book, *Evil in Modern Thought: An Alternative History of Philosophy* (2002), the philosopher Susan Neiman claims that 'Since Lisbon, natural evils no longer have any seemly relation to moral evils; hence they no longer have meaning at all. Natural disaster is the object of attempts at prediction and control, not of interpretation'.[5] Following Neiman's argument, disasters belong to the ontological zone of non-human nature. Yet, is it really that simple? If natural disasters really are fundamentally meaningless, and if they are not objects of interpretation, how do we then make them understandable? The main argument in this chapter is that natural disasters have also been objects of interpretation after the Lisbon earthquake.

This chapter will use the Lisbon earthquake as a starting point to discuss what is today termed *natural disasters*. This term implies a modern distinction between *natural* and *man-made* disasters, that evolved in the aftermath of the Lisbon earthquake, and Voltaire's writings on the earthquake. The term *disaster*, though, refers to an unfortunate constellation of stars, and reveals an historical depth of a concept that, until the mid-seventeenth century, described an interrelationship between a tragic and dramatic event, human infortune and divine power. The modern term *catastrophe*, on the other hand, does not reflect such an interrelationship. The term is secular, with an origin far from natural events. It is Greek in origin, and was used by Aristotle as a concept describing the dramatic turn of a tragedy. The term was still used in this sense until the turn of the nineteenth century, when the denotation of the concept eventually changed.[6] Yet, as late as 1922, the Danish-Norwegian encyclopaedia *Salmonsens Konversationsleksikon* defined the term as both a turn in human life and the dramatic turn of a narrative.[7] The close conceptual connection to the drama gives a hint that modern catastrophes are not merely calamitous events – they are also mediated events. The mediation is, so to speak, embedded in the term *catastrophe*.

This chapter will focus on how catastrophes have been represented, told and interpreted. It will examine the long history of mass-mediation of disasters, and will discuss how disasters have been framed and presented to make them relevant for media audiences far away. Deborah Simonton and Hannu Salmi have remarked that the history of disasters is also a history of fear and understandings of evil.[8] Along with Simonton and Salmi, the chapter aims to examine notions of fear and risk, and understandings of the relationships between nature, culture and morals, through an empirical emphasis on narration and media framing of disasters.

The Lisbon earthquake as a European media event of fear and devoutness

Voltaire was undoubtedly important in the intellectual aftermath of the Lisbon earthquake. He was, however, far from the only one who strived to make some sense out of this seemingly meaningless event; clergymen, scientists and philosophers also had their say.[9] Numerous sermons, poems and philosophical inquiries were published around Europe, discussing the cause of the earthquake in light of the moral and religious order of the world. The earthquake was also extensively portrayed in the popular media, such as newspapers, pamphlets, broadside ballads, peep shows and magic lantern shows. Thus, in order to understand the cultural impact of the earthquake across Europe, it is also necessary to take the media distribution of the disaster into account.

The earthquake was one of the very first globally mass-mediated disasters in history. From Lisbon, the news slowly spread around Europe, and eventually to the European colonies. After about a week, it was commonly known in Spain, while it took several more days and weeks for the news to reach the rest of Europe. The Paris newspaper, the *Gazette de France*, published the news on 22 November, and it reached England

and the *London Magazine* on 26 November. The *Graevenhaegse Courant* brought the news to the readers in The Hague on the same day as it was published in London. It took another two weeks for the terrible news to reach Scandinavia. Accounts of the devastation of Lisbon were published in Copenhagen and Stockholm on 8 December, by *Kiøbenhavnske Danske Post-Tidender* and *Stockholms Post-Tidningar*.[10]

The earthquake was discussed as a divine punishment by Catholics as well as Protestants. While the Catholic Church understood the earthquake as a divine punishment for the tolerant attitude towards Protestants and non-converts, Protestant interpreters emphasized the superstition and idolatry of the Catholic Church, and the heretic brutality of the Portuguese Inquisition.[11]

In Great Britain, the founder of English Methodism, John Wesley, was one of a number of theologians and clergymen who wrote and preached about the earthquake. His sermon *Some Serious Thoughts Occasioned by the Late Earthquake at Lisbon* was already published as a pamphlet before the calendar had turned from 1755 to 1756. Wesley explained how God had righteously turned His wrath upon the people of Lisbon. 'What shall we say of the late accounts from Portugal?', he asked. 'Is there indeed a God that judges the world?' He turned to the practice of the Portuguese Inquisition to answer these rhetoric questions. Was it surprising, he asked, that:

> he should begin there [in Lisbon], where so much blood has been poured on the ground like water? Where so many brave men have been murdered, in the most base and cowardly, as well as barbarous manner, almost every day, as well as every night, while none regarded or laid it to heart. [...] How long has their blood been crying from earth? Yea, how long has the bloody house of mercy [the Portuguese Inquisition], the scandal not only of religion, but even of human nature, stood to insult both heaven and earth?[12]

The pamphlet was not about the earthquake as such. Wesley rather used the earthquake to discuss the importance of piety and devotion. 'Why should we now, before London is as Lisbon, Lima or Catania, acknowledge the hand of the Almighty?' he rhetorically asked.[13] He was well aware of the fear that an earthquake generated. About twenty years later, he emphasized the pedagogical importance of earthquakes. In a letter to a friend he wrote that 'there is no divine visitation which is likely to have so general an influence upon sinners as an earthquake'.[14] The literary scholar Susan Bassnett argues that Wesley used the accounts of the disaster in Lisbon to strongly encourage people to recognize the power of God, and to devote their heart to His almightiness. She points out how he productively used the earthquake as an instrument in his evangelizing mission.[15]

The pamphlet was printed in seven editions, and was probably the most sold and read interpretation of the earthquake in Europe. The text had a strong influence on contemporary public understanding of the earthquake, and later worked as an interpretative key to understand new disasters when they occurred. Wesley's sermon was, for instance, again intensely discussed in the aftermath of the 1906 San Francisco earthquake. It played an important role during the so-called Azusa Street Revival in Los Angeles in April 1906, from which the Pentecostal movement developed.

Wesley's pamphlet was just one out of hundreds, maybe thousands of texts on the earthquake, written all over Europe during the months after the disaster. An extensive number of cheap pamphlets were published, containing dramatic and sensational eyewitness reports from the disaster. Lisbon was probably the most important seaport in Europe at that time. Most of the eyewitness accounts were written by French and English merchants, and reflect the international character of the city. An impressive number of the accounts and letters were also translated and printed in newspapers throughout Europe. The readers were obviously fascinated by the earthquake. On 16 January 1756, the *Gazette de Cologne* wrote that 'the earthquake is still on people's lips'.[16] The same must have been the case in Copenhagen. The newspaper, *Kiøbenhavnske Danske Post-Tidender*, published news from Lisbon in every edition for almost two months, from 8 December 1755 until the end of January 1756.

Not only did a range of accounts and personal experience narratives from Lisbon circulate widely across Europe. Narrative motifs also circulated frequently in between texts and genres. The historian Edward Paice writes that a rumour about the palace of the Portuguese Inquisition being the first building to fall was told among the survivors in the English community in Lisbon.[17] From Lisbon, the rumour eventually reached England, and John Wesley referred to it in his pamphlet. The Inquisition was strongly criticized in Protestant Europe, and the motif was obviously connected to a Protestant understanding of the earthquake as a divine punishment over heretic Lisbon. It was modelled after the Book of Numbers 16,30–32 and Psalms 106,17.[18] Both these passages describe how the Lord made a crack in the ground that swallowed those who despised Him. The motif also spread to newspapers such as the Copenhagen newspaper *Copenhagener Deutsche Post-Zeitungen*.[19] From this newspaper, it found its way into Danish poems and broadside ballads. One of the poems even refers to the notice in the newspaper as the source.[20] The circulation of news motifs like this give insight into how news about the earthquake circulated between different media and reached out to a wider audience.

A closer look at the media distribution in Scandinavia might give an idea of the public reach of the news from Lisbon, and what kind of news reached the public. The depictions, accounts and letters from Lisbon that were published in the only Danish-Norwegian newspaper at that time, *Kiøbenhavnske Danske Post-Tidender/ Copenhagener Deutsche Post-Zeitungen*, merely had a few indirect religious references, while the Protestant interpretations of the poems and broadside ballads on the earthquake were far from subtle. As elsewhere in Protestant Europe, the earthquake was regarded as a divine punishment, and an edifying example of how the Lord punished sinners. The earthquake was further presented as an eschatological omen, as a prediction of Judgement Day. As was the case in John Wesley's pamphlet, the moral was not about the victims in Lisbon. The poems and broadside ballads rather converted the disaster into a Dano-Norwegian concern, and used it as a reminder to the readers to fear God, and to obtain strength through faith and piety in anticipation of the Last Day.[21]

The poems, pamphlets, broadsheets and newspaper accounts on the earthquake were generally printed in a limited number of copies. *Kiøbenhavnske Danske Post-Tidender/Copenhagener Deutsche Post-Zeitungen* had 3,000 subscribers throughout Denmark-Norway, while the number of copies of pamphlets and broadsheets was much lower. Yet, the printed accounts and depictions had quite a broad reach.

Newspapers, pamphlets and poems usually circulated among a group of readers, and were also read aloud, while the broadside ballads were performed and sung. The songs would have been shared and transmitted orally, and it is not unlikely that they were remembered long after the event. In Sweden, some of these broadside ballads were reprinted several times during the latter part of the eighteenth and the first part of the nineteenth century.[22] It is likely that this also might have been the case in Denmark-Norway, even though such reprints are not preserved.

The printed depictions of the Lisbon earthquake still did not reach the entire population, but the picture is more overwhelming if we also include the most efficient early modern mass medium, the sermon.[23] The cultural historian, Gunnar Broberg, has studied the Swedish reception of the Lisbon earthquake, and has emphasized the importance of sermons. In the eighteenth century, there were four national days of prayer in the realm of Sweden, with a general obligation to attend. A prayer day declaration, defining the topic for the sermons and the psalms to be sung, was sent out to instruct every vicar in the realm in advance of the days of prayer. In 1756, the topic for all of the four days of prayer was 'the horrendous wrath of God' that had hit Europe.[24] A morning service, a high mass and an evening service were held on each of the four days of prayer in every one of the 3,000 parish churches. As Broberg points out, during the four days in 1756, there were in total 36,000 sermons held in Sweden, communicating a message about divine punishment over a sinful Lisbon, and working as eschatological reminders to fear God and to live in devoutness and piety.[25]

The case was similar in Denmark-Norway, even though the number of days of prayer was limited to once a year. On the so-called Extraordinary General Day of Repentance and Prayer on Friday 14 May 1756, sermons about the Lisbon earthquake as a divine punishment and an apocalyptic prefiguration were held synchronically in every parish church in the double monarchy of Denmark-Norway. Just like in John Wesley's pamphlet, the earthquake worked as an instrument in the service of faith and piety.

Thus, the Lisbon earthquake was undoubtedly an early modern European media event. This media event was not primarily about the terrible incidents in Lisbon and empathy with the thousands of victims and survivors. It was rather a multi-mediated evocation of a state of fear and piety. As a divine example, the disaster in Lisbon concerned everybody, as a reminder to fear God.[26]

The sublime disasters: fear and entertainment

The Flood was, without doubt, considered to be the most significant of all historical disasters in early modern Europe. It worked both as a religious and historical point of reference for contemporary disasters, and as an explanation for geological and topographic formations.[27] However, after the emergence of geological deep timescale in the late eighteenth century, Biblical and historical time separated. Genesis was no longer equivalent to the origin of the Earth. One consequence was that the Flood gradually lost its position as an historical point of reference for narrating and interpreting contemporary disasters. This position was filled by another ancient disaster.

A Pompeii cult emerged in Europe after the excavation of Pompeii and Herculaneum that began in the 1740s. A visit to Pompeii was, for instance, soon incorporated as one of the destinations in the Grand Tour of young men. Johann Wolfgang von Goethe was among the many young men who went to Pompeii. He visited the site on 13 March 1787, and in his diary he wrote: 'There have been many disasters in this world, but few which have given so much delight to posterity, and I have seldom seen anything so interesting'.[28] He described in euphoric terms how he was sitting in the remains of the ancient city, watching the sunset over the ocean. He portrayed it as a glorious spot, worthy of beautiful thoughts. To Goethe and his contemporaries, the eternal beauty of classical antiquity was materialized in the ruins of Pompeii. Yet, the site was not only romanticized as a classical relic; the petrified moment of death in this lost and buried city also fascinated. The eighteenth- and nineteenth-century cult of Pompeii was characterized by necromantic pathos, and both the classical decadence of the city and its apocalyptic ending in the year AD 79 appealed to a romantic audience.[29]

During the nineteenth century, the destruction of Pompeii was portrayed in a significant range of paintings, poems, novels, plays and panoramas. One of these portrayals, the opera *L'ultimo Giorno di Pompei* (The Last Days of Pompeii), by Giovanni Pacini, had its premiere in Naples in 1825. It was also performed soon after in the opera houses of Paris, Lisbon, Venice and Vienna. The opera inspired the artist Karl Bryullov to paint his version of *The Last Days of Pompeii* (1833). This painting inspired the British author Edward Bulwer-Lytton to write an historic novel, also entitled *The Last Days of Pompeii* (1834). The novel was a tremendous success. Ten thousand copies sold out in London on the first day after the second edition was published. The success was not limited to England; the book was almost immediately translated into several European languages.

It reached an even larger audience when it was put on stage as a tragedy. However, it was not until the end of the century that Bulwer-Lytton's story reached its peak of popularity. It was neither as a novel nor a play, but as a gigantic pyrotechnic show. *The Last Days of Pompeii* was staged in 1879 by the British entertainment entrepreneur James Pain, who specialized in pyrotechnics. The reenactment of the catastrophic eruption of Mount Vesuvius gave him the opportunity to reveal his creativity and commercial talent in spectacular ways. Even though the show was based on Bulwer-Lytton's novel, it barely had a plot. The novel was a highly moral story about the decadence of the city, while Pain's pyrodrama was the opposite. It celebrated Roman decadence, and the plot of the novel was replaced by lightly dressed Roman dancing girls, acrobats, gladiator fights and chariot races. The grand finale was an enormous firework display, which gave an apocalyptic illusion of the volcanic eruption in AD 79.[30]

This was not the first spectacular panorama reenacting the fall of Pompeii. It was not even the first firework reenactment of the eruption of Vesuvius. Such firework shows had already been staged during the eighteenth century. The most remarkable one was probably that staged in the garden of Wörlitz. Prince Leopold Friedrich Franz of Anhalt-Dessau constructed a small copy of Vesuvius in this park. 'Der Stein' was completed in 1796, and the visitors to the garden could enjoy the illusion of volcanic eruptions produced by pyrotechnics and water.[31]

What Pain did was to turn the well-established genre of Pompeii reenactments into mass entertainment. The show was originally staged in London, but it soon moved across the Atlantic. It visited thirty-seven American cities, and was performed regularly on Coney Island from 1885 to 1914. Everybody could afford a ticket – it only cost 50 cents. And it achieved a tremendous popularity. Pain did not put on this open-air show unless there was room for at least 10,000 spectators.[32]

This classical catastrophe was one of the most, if not the most, mediated of all disasters in the nineteenth century.[33] According to the cultural historian Anders Ekström, the numerous mediations and reenactments of the eruption of Mount Vesuvius in AD 79 established certain genre conventions and cultural forms for narrating disasters. In this sense, the devastation of Pompeii was a foundational event for the modern Western disaster imaginary.[34]

The fall of Pompeii was far from the only disaster that was turned into a spectacular show at the turn of the century. Visitors to the amusement parks on Coney Island could walk between fires, battles and natural disasters. One of the shows was simply named *Fight the Flames*. A six-storey building was set on fire, and 2,000 men, performing as firemen, fought the fire.[35] An even more impressive show was the staging of the Boer War. Several natural disasters were also displayed in spectacular ways. The Johnstown Flood, that had caused the death of 2,200 people in 1889, and the Galveston hurricane, that caused the death of 6,000 to 12,000 people in 1900, were among the attractions. The most spectacular of the reenactments of contemporary natural disasters was, though, the Mount Pelée exhibit, housed in an auditorium of 1,200 seats.[36] The volcano, Mount Pelée, on the Caribbean island of Martinique, had so to speak exploded on the morning of 8 May 1902. Just like the eruption of Vesuvius more than 1,800 years earlier, a pyroclastic flow had wiped out the life of a whole city. Within a few minutes, 30,000 people, the entire population of the most populated town of Martinique, St Pierre, were killed. The exhibit on Coney Island simulated the eruption and the death of the people of St Pierre. Similar disaster shows were also staged at larger fairs around North America and Europe, such as The World's Columbian Exposition in Chicago in 1893, St Louis World's Fair in 1904 and The Stockholm Exhibition in 1909.[37]

The distinction between natural disasters and man-made disasters as cultural categories was not clear cut in such entertainment. Both natural and man-made disasters triggered the same exhilarating feeling of horror and fear, mixed with fascination. The contemporary horror of World War I eventually put an end to these disaster shows. This kind of spectacular visualization had, in the meantime, facilitated disaster-narratives presented through the new medium of the motion picture. The first film loosely based on Bulwer-Lytton's novel was made in 1900, and nine movies were based on the novel during the first half of the twentieth century. In fact, Pain's show, or at least the background design of it, also found its way into the movies, and was used in a 1907 film adaptation of *Ben Hur*.[38]

Ekström's point, however, is that the devastation of Pompeii not only constituted a frame of reference for disaster shows like this, but around 1900, it also worked as a narrative and interpretative frame for the mass-mediation of contemporary disasters in general. He claims that disasters such as the Mount Pelée eruption and the 1906 San Francisco earthquake were depicted and imagined through cultural forms that had emerged from the popular reception of Pompeii.[39]

A closer look at how the catastrophic eruption of Mount Pelée in 1902 was depicted in the press may illustrate Ekström's point. The news about the destruction of St Pierre crisscrossed the world through the web of telegraph wires, and horrified a transnational media audience for weeks. The disaster was frequently depicted in the press as a catastrophe just like Pompeii.[40] For instance, the local Norwegian newspaper, *Bergens Tidende*, published an article on 24 May 1902 that summed up the situation in the disaster area two weeks after the catastrophic eruption. The last section of the article was, however, not about St Pierre, but about Pompeii. The newspaper suggested that: 'Perhaps it will be interesting for our readers to see a translation of the report of Pliny, so often mentioned these days, about the downfall of Pompeii'.[41] The article ends with a short summary of the two letters Pliny the Younger wrote to Tacitus about the fall of Pompeii. This illustrates how this ancient eyewitness report worked as narrative optics in disaster discourse at the turn of the twentieth century.

In fact, the destruction of Pompeii not only worked as a framework for media representations of the devastation of St Pierre. When the first scientific field expedition to examine the volcano Mount Pelée set out from New York City just six days after the eruption, the members of the expedition spent the time reading, while they were waiting for their ship to reach Martinique. According to expedition member George Kennan, they read 'volcano literature, from "The Last Days of Pompeii" to Brigham's "Text-Book of Geology"'.[42]

Just four years after the destruction of St Pierre, a major American city was devastated by an earthquake. The San Francisco earthquake and its subsequent fires was the most photographed event in the world at the beginning of the twentieth century.[43] The ruins of the city were captured by both professional and amateur photographers and were reproduced as souvenir photos, postcards, stereographs and lantern slides, as well as in illustrated books and magazines. The visual commodification of the earthquake was a massive commercial success. One of the companies producing earthquake photos advertised that they could produce thirty copies a minute, and that their earthquake pictures had been sold to customers on every continent.[44] The cultural historian Susanne Leikam has studied the visualization of this earthquake. Because of the dominance of photographic representations, the pictures of the disaster did not portray the catastrophic moment – the shaking ground – which earlier had been a common way to visually depict earthquakes.[45] The earthquake was instead visualized as what Leikam terms a ruinscape. It was visually represented though cracks in the streets or as aesthetic ruins.[46] The aestheticization of the building fragments drew on a pictorial tradition of 'beautiful ruins'. This was a well-established way to visualize disasters, which Leikam traces back to the Lisbon earthquake.[47] She further argues that the aestheticized urban ruinscapes from Berlin, Dresden and Hiroshima after World War II have visual resonance in the aestheticized San Francisco ruinscape.[48]

Leikam argues that the earthquake was commodified as a spectacle, as 'a forceful, albeit short-lived, fascinating and simultaneously terrifying moment of rapture in the regular normality of "real" life'.[49] In this way, the mass-mediation of the San Francisco earthquake also contributed to the foundation of the twentieth-century culture of disaster, where catastrophes are commodified and turned into cultural products, such as Hollywood blockbusters.

Like Ekström, she shows how the popular disaster discourse that emerged in the late nineteenth century and early twentieth century was characterized by interme-diality and cross-temporality, in the sense that narrative and visual representations of disasters drew on depictions of other disasters across time.[50] Hence, meaning was, so to speak, transferred between disasters by pictorial and narrative motifs, analogies and comparisons. In this way, disasters of different scales, at different times and at different locations, were intermedially linked to each other.[51]

The cultural turn of disaster studies

It is often claimed that contemporary popular disaster discourse is based on plots from Hollywood disaster movies.[52] It has been documented that news media portray the situation in disaster areas almost like movies, with clear-cut protagonists, such as Western relief organizations, the police and armed forces; and antagonists, such as looters and criminals taking advantage of a chaotic situation. Hence, the mediation of disasters turns real-life experiences into classical tragedies. It is, for instance, well known that the massive globalized news coverage of the disaster area of New Orleans in the aftermath of hurricane Katrina in 2005 was portrayed in cinematic ways.[53] Yet, recent cultural historical approaches to natural disasters, such as those presented by Ekström and Leikam, demonstrate how popular disaster discourse has a long for-mative history. In this sense, the study of the cultural history of disasters is a way to deconstruct present disaster imaginaries.

Disaster studies in the social sciences has also undergone a cultural turn during the last decade. It now seems to be generally accepted, within this field, that cul-tural imaginaries shape social responses to disasters.[54] Hence, it is acknowledged that a better understanding of such imaginaries is significant for improving emergency management.[55] One of the leading figures in this process has been the sociologist Kathleen Tierney. Together with two colleagues, she published the ground-breaking article 'Metaphors Matter: Disaster Myths, Media Frames, and Their Consequence' in 2006.[56] Even though their conceptions of myths and metaphors are vague, they make their point crystal clear – our disaster fantasies can be turned into reality. They describe how the often-used metaphor for describing disaster areas – the war zone – became reality in the aftermath of hurricane Katrina, when 69,000 troops from the National Guard arrived in New Orleans. The warzone metaphor refers to the wide-spread idea that post-disaster situations turn into a state of lawlessness and looting.

This idea is by no means new. It appears in the narrations of the Lisbon earthquake, both in popular pamphlets and in Voltaire's novel *Candide* (1759). Stories about looters also circulated widely in post-earthquake San Francisco in 1906, and the mayor, Eugene Schmitz, proclaimed that military troops and the police force would 'KILL any and all persons found engaged in Looting or in the Commission of Any Other Crime'.[57]

Lawlessness, unscrupulous violence and looting seemingly also dominated the city of New Orleans in the days after hurricane Katrina. The National Guard were supposed to put an end to it, and the governor of Louisiana, Kathleen Blanco, de-clared war, so to speak, on the looters. As an echo of Schmitz's words ninety-nine years earlier, she announced: 'These troops know how to shoot and kill, and they are more than willing to do so if necessary, and I expect they will'.[58] Dreadful accounts from New Orleans of shooting, looting, rape and murder circulated frequently in the American and international press. However, unlike situations of civil disorder and riots, large-scale looting does not usually occur in disaster situations.[59] It eventually turned out that such stories were highly exaggerated; in fact they turned out to be urban legends.[60] Tierney's point is not merely that such stories are disaster imaginaries, but that these imaginaries have implications for the post-disaster emergency response. The looting narratives and the war zone metaphors have led to a militarization of American emergency management, she argues.[61]

The cultural turn in disaster studies, which Tierney represents, is also about cultural history, claims the literary scholar Isak Winkel Holm. He argues that the cultural imagination of disasters has been structured after a few, historically quite stable, imaginary framings. *The apocalypse* is one of the most recurrent. As common as the apocalypse is the *theodicy*, which he claims is present 'whenever disasters – at least once in every Hollywood disaster movie – prompt a question about our trust in the basic goodness of the world or that of society'.[62] A third such frame is the *sublime*, or that thin line between fascination and fear. Other such frames are *the state of emergency*, *trauma* and *risk*. And finally, he mentions *imbalance* between society and nature.[63] Most of these interpretative frames or cognitive schemes can be linked to the disasters discussed in this chapter; the receptions of the 1755 Lisbon earthquake, the fall of Pompeii, the destruction of St Pierre in 1902 and the 1906 San Francisco earthquake.

Hybrids of nature and culture

The number of potential natural disasters seems endless. There are about 1,400 earthquakes on the planet every day, and a new volcanic eruption every week. There are about forty tropical hurricanes or typhoons each year, while the number of floods and landslides are so numerous that they are impossible to calculate.[64] Just a few of these incidents are disastrous. Hazards may be natural, but it is social vulnerability that turns the hazards into disasters. An illustrative example is the Haiti earthquake of 2010. The magnitude of the earthquake was 7.0 M_w. This is a severe but not an infrequent magnitude. There are about twenty earthquakes a year of this magnitude around the globe. It was a relatively moderate earthquake compared to the one that caused the Fukushima accident the year after (which had a magnitude of 9.0–9.1 M_w). The enormous catastrophe on Haiti was not a result of the quake alone. It was also due to poverty and the social vulnerability of the Haitian society.

The distinction between hazards and disasters is today fundamental in sociological disaster and emergency studies.[65] However, Winkel Holm argues that the idea of a distinction between natural hazards and social vulnerability is by no means new. He tracks this distinction back to the aftermath of the Lisbon earthquake, when Rousseau and Voltaire disputed the cause of the disaster. While Voltaire criticized the notion of Providence and how it was presumed to work through nature, Rousseau defended it and turned his critique towards society. In a letter to Voltaire, he wrote:

> [I]t was hardly nature that there brought together twenty-thousand houses of six or seven stories. If the residents of this large city had been more evenly dispersed and less densely housed, the losses would have been fewer or perhaps none at all.[66]

In this way, he 'stumbled on the concept of vulnerability', argues Winkel Holm.[67] Kevin Rozario also tracks the notion of vulnerability back to this dispute. He argues that Rousseau, by criticizing the vulnerability of the city and civilization, paradoxically made a substantial contribution to the notion of progress.[68] The idea of vulnerability is embedded in modernity, according to Rozario, in the sense that vulnerability is the opposite of progress. Modernity is constantly producing collapses, conflicts and an accelerating number of environmental hazards. Hence, modernity may be understood as both a process of keeping the powers of nature under societal control and as a constant process of producing potentials for losing control. Modernity is both a notion of anti-disaster and disaster. He terms this duality *the catastrophic logic of modernity*.[69]

It may also be argued that the distinction between natural and technological disasters is artificial. The intertwining of natural and technological hazards and disasters seems instead to characterize late modern disaster discourse. The opening example in Bruno Latour's seminal book *We Have Never Been Modern* is the hole in the ozone layer. Latour uses it as a case to illustrate how the modern ontological zones of nature and culture are intrinsically intertwined.[70] He claims that what he metaphorically terms the modern Constitution – the idea of modernity – is founded on a distinction between these ontological zones. However, we continually produce hybrids of nature and culture, and we continually strive to eliminate these hybrids. By questioning this distinction, he argues that '[t]here has never been a modern world'.[71]

It is today impossible to overlook such hybrids.[72] The severe environmental consequences of hurricane Katrina and the Fukushima accident in 2011 demonstrate how natural and technological disasters are catastrophically entangled. Anthropogenic climate change has even turned weather phenomena such as hurricanes, floods, droughts and heatwaves into complex entanglements of nature and culture. This once again raises the question about the relationship between natural evils and moral evils. In the popular media, the climate-changed future is framed as an apocalyptic catastrophe, caused by an imbalance between nature and culture. Terms such as 'nature strikes back' appear frequently in the press.[73] The historian Garrit Jasper Schenk argues that the agency of nature in popular climate discourse is framed in established semi-religious terms of rightful punishment. He exemplifies his argument by referring to a cover of *Der Spiegel* from 11 August 1986. The cover shows a manipulated picture of the Cologne Cathedral flooded in water. It is only the roof and the spires that are above water. The headline reads: 'Ozone layer, melting poles, greenhouse effect: Scientists are warning: The climate catastrophe'. The biblical allegory is obvious, and Schenk draws a line between the catastrophic framing in late modern popular climate discourse and early modern ideas of disasters as divine punishments.[74] The historian David Larsson Heidenblad argues in line with Schenk. According to Heidenblad, both the early modern and the late modern notions of disasters are based on a 'moral causality' between human action and the catastrophic event.[75]

The Anthropocene

The moral aspect is obvious in the debates on *the Anthropocene*. The Anthropocene concept was launched by the atmospheric chemist Paul Crutzen and the biologist

Eugene Stoermer in 2000. They claimed that the impact of humanity on the Earth's system had become so fundamental that humans could no longer be overlooked as significant geological agents. According to Crutzen and Stoermer, the geological epoch, the Holocene, had come to an end, and they suggested terming the current, human-impacted, geological epoch the Anthropocene.[76] In 2016 an Anthropocene Working Group, appointed by the International Commission on Stratigraphy, recommended the Anthropocene to be formally approved as a geological epoch.[77]

The notion of the Anthropocene had impacted environmental humanities and theoretical debates on historicity even before the working group had concluded their work. One of the first historians to discuss the Anthropocene was Dipesh Chakrabarty. In his now classic article 'The Climate of History: Four Theses' (2009), he points out that the modern distinction between natural history and human history has collapsed. Geological timescales become historical timescales, while historical timescales become geological. Furthermore, the acknowledgement of humans as geophysical agents has implications for how we approach globalization. He argues that we have to acknowledge that humans are global agents, not only through economic, political and cultural action, but also as the collective agent of a species. Hence, human history is also a species history.[78]

The article has been frequently quoted and also heavily criticized to be Eurocentric. Alternative conceptions of the contemporary geological state, which do not imply a notion of mankind as a collective geological force, have been suggested, such as the Capitalocene and the Econocene. These concepts emphasize capitalism as the driving force, not the human species.[79] Chakrabarty has answered the critique, and argued that these concepts imply a narrowing of the complex concern, reflected in the term Anthropocene, to be dependent on 'more immediate factors'.[80] Instead, he argues that it must be possible to systematically study the development and the global environmental impact of capitalism and the global economic system, and still regard the human species as a geological force. It is a question of scale.[81]

Chakrabarty's main contribution to the theorization of the Anthropocene so far seems, however, to be in his discussions of entanglements between geological and historical timescales. In his first article on the topic, he claimed that the notion of the Anthropocene and '[t]he discussion about the crisis of climate change can [...] produce affect and knowledge about collective human pasts and futures that work at the limits of historical understanding'.[82] This includes a challenge in how to imagine the future dimension of the current planetary crisis.

Today's anthropogenic emissions of CO_2 will affect the Earth's system for tens of thousands of years. Yet, the anthropogenic environmental problem that really challenges the ability to imagine the distant future is the problem of nuclear waste disposal. The high-level radioactive waste produced today has the potential to cause catastrophes for the next 100,000 years. Hence, in order to avoid future nuclear disasters, it is crucial to make sure that future humans understand how dangerous such waste is. How is it possible to communicate this to humans or possible post-human creatures of every single generation for the next 100,000 years? The time prospect is titanic, if we keep in mind that the cognitive ability of mankind is only about 50,000 years old. The timescale is, in other words, double the entire history of human communication.[83]

Most of the high-level nuclear waste in the world today is stored in temporary repositories. But a few permanent repositories are constructed, and some are under construction. Very different communicative strategies are chosen to warn future humans or other potential intelligent beings about these repositories. The Waste Isolation Pilot Plant in New Mexico has chosen a multi-semiotic strategy. The repository is marked out with informative texts, warning icons and diagrams. Information about the project is also placed in archives and libraries. In addition, an architect has designed unfriendly landscape constructions that hopefully will appeal intuitively to future visitors as something frightening and dangerous. The archaeologist Tim Flohr Sørensen has remarked that these communicative strategies imply a semiotic and affective continuity from today and into the far future. And even if future generations will be able to understand the warnings, there is no guarantee that they will respect them. The discipline of archaeology is an example of how scholars of today do not respect the warnings or taboos of the past. The opposite is rather the case; archaeologists tend to find such warnings intriguing, claims Flohr Sørensen.[84] A totally different strategy has been picked for the Finnish repository, Onkalo, which is under construction. The intention is to demolish all traces of the site, so that it will be impossible to find. Yet, as Flohr Sørensen remarks, the site may still live on in cultural memory, maybe not for thousands of years, but for hundreds of years. In order for the site to be fully forgotten, the strategy therefore implies a discontinuation in cultural memory. By taking cultural and historical discontinuity into account, the strategy also opens up for future scenarios, where the waste will still be protected after apocalyptic disasters, and even after the end of cognitive life.[85]

A history of cultural experiences of dangers, risks and anxiety

This chapter argues that Western disaster discourse is genuinely cross-temporal. Pictorial and narrative motifs and depictions of disaster scenes move across time and space, and interconnect disasters with each other. The cross-temporal interconnection of disasters is an interpretative practice – it places a current disaster into an intertextual and intermedial web of disaster representations and realms of interpretation. The interpretative framing of disasters is, as Winkel Holm has pointed out, surprisingly stable. Furthermore, the return of an entanglement between natural evils and moral evils in late modern discourses on climate change and the Anthropocene illustrates that the cultural history of natural disasters is not linear. It also illustrates that attempts to predict and control disasters go hand in hand with interpretations and cultural imaginaries of disasters.

Notions of risk and fear are intertwined with mediations, interpretations and narrations of disasters. Ekström states that the study of historical disaster discourse gives insight into what he terms a risk heritage, in the sense that it offers an historical background for what the sociologist Ulrich Beck has termed the 'risk society'.[86] The risk society is, according to Beck, characterized by hazards and risks that are uncalculable, uncontrollable and global, such as the risks of global terror, pandemics, nuclear disasters and climate change effects. Beck argues that the presence of such risks generates a globalized *commonality of anxiety*. The risk society's 'normative counter-project, which is its basis and motive force, is *safety*', writes Beck.[87] It may very well be that everyday life is now catastrophized, in the sense that the state of anxiety for imminent, unexpected and uncontrollable disasters has turned a safe-ty-desiring state of emergency into being the state of normality.[88] It may certainly be that today's media flow of extreme and spectacular disastrous events transforms such events into media routines, and that such mass-mediation contributes to obtaining an impression of disasters as a state of normality.[89] Yet, the cultural history of natural disasters demonstrates that mass-mediation of spectacular calamities is far from a new phenomenon. Notions of risk and anxiety have a cultural history, which cannot be disconnected from the history of the transnationality of disaster discourse and inter-pretative framing of disasters. The cultural history of disasters is a history of cultural experiences of dangers, risks and anxiety.

Notes

1 J.P. Poirier, *Le Tremblement de terre de Lisbonne*, Paris: Odile Jacob, 2005, 7.

2 K. Rozario, *The Culture of Calamity: Disaster and the Making of Modern America*, Chicago, IL: University of Chicago Press, 2007, 15.

3 U. Löffler, *Lissabons Fall – Europas Schrecken: Die Deutung des Erdbebens von Lissabon im deutschsprachigen Protestantismus des 18. Jahrhunderts*, Berlin: De Gruyter, 1999, 14.

4 B. Latour, *We Have Never Been Modern*, Cambridge, MA: Harvard University Press, 1991, 32–35.

5 S. Neiman, *Evil in Modern Thought: An Alternative History of Philosophy*, Princeton, NJ: Princeton University Press, 2002, 250.

6 D. Simonton and H. Salmi, 'Introduction: Catastrophe, Gender and Urban Experi-ence', in D. Simonton and H. Salmi (eds), *Catastrophe, Gender and Urban Experience, 1648–1920*, New York and London: Routledge, 2017, 5–6; G. Broberg, *Tsunamin i Lissabon: Jordbävningen den 1 November 1755, i epicentrum och i svensk periferi*, Stockholm: Atlantis, 2005, 85–86.

7 K. Kverndokk, *Naturkatastrofer: En kulturhistorie*, Oslo: Scandinavian Academic Press, 2015, 23–24.

8 Simonton and Salmi, 'Introduction: Catastrophe, Gender and Urban Experience', 4.

9 Broberg, *Tsunamin i Lissabon*, 36.

10 Broberg, *Tsunamin i Lissabon*, 33; T. D'Haen, 'On How Not to Be Lisbon if You Want to Be Modern: Dutch Reactions to the Lisbon Earthquake', *European Review* 14, 3, 2006; T.D. Kendrick, *The Lisbon Earthquake*, Philadelphia, PA: J. B. Lippincott Com-pany, 1956, 213–14; *Kiøbenhavnske Danske Post-Tidender*, 8 December 1755, 1.

11 S. Bassnett, 'Faith, Doubt, Aid and Prayer: The Lisbon Earthquake of 1755 Revisited', *European Review* 14, 3, 2006, 323; H. Murteira, 'Between Despair and Hope: The 1755 Earthquake in Lisbon', *Catastrophe, Gender and Urban Experience, 1648–1920*, 50.

12 J. Wesley, 'Serious Thoughts Occasioned by the Late Earthquake at Lisbon', *The Works of the Rev. John Wesley in Ten Volumes*, Vol. 8, New York, 1828, 165.

13 Wesley, 'Serious Thoughts Occasioned by the Late Earthquake at Lisbon', 169.

14 Quoted in Kendrick, *The Lisbon Earthquake*, 11.

15 Bassnett, 'Faith, Doubt, Aid and Prayer: The Lisbon Earthquake of 1755 Revisited', 325.

16 Quoted in A.C. Araujo, 'European Public Opinion and the Lisbon Earthquake', *Euro-pean Review* 14, 3, 2006, 313.

17 E. Paice, *Wrath of God: The Great Lisbon Earthquake of 1755*, London: Quercus, 2008, 118.

18 M. Georgi, 'The Lisbon Earthquake and Scientific Knowledge in the British Public Sphere', in T.E.D. Braun and J.B. Radner (eds), *The Lisbon Earthquake of 1755: Representations and Reactions*, Oxford: Voltaire Foundation, 2005, 87.

19 *Copenhagener Deutsche Post-Zeitungen*, 15 December 1755. This was the German edrition of *Kiøbenhavnske Danske Post-Tidender*.

20 H.A. Brorson, 'Lissabons ynkelige undergang', *Samlede skrifter* Vol. 3, København: O. Lohses Forlag eftf., 1956, 193.

21 Kverndokk, *Naturkatastrofer: En kulturhistorie*, 59–88.

22 Broberg, *Tsunamin i Lissabon*, 45.

23 Cf. B. Widén, *Predikstolen som massmedium i det svenska riket från medeltiden till stormaktstidens slut*, Åbo: Åbo Akademi, 2002.

24 Quoted in Broberg, *Tsunamin i Lissabon*, 39.

25 Broberg, *Tsunamin i Lissabon*, 39–41.

26 Kverndokk, *Naturkatastrofer: En kulturhistorie*, 84–88.

27 N. Cohn, *Noah's Flood: The Genesis Story in Western Thought*, New Haven, CT: Yale University Press, 1999.

28 J.W. v. Goethe, *Italian Journey*, London: Penguin Books, 1992, 203.

29 V.C.G. Coates, K. Lapatin and J.L. Seydl, *The Last Days of Pompeii: Decadence, Apocalypse, Resurrection*, Los Angeles, CA: The J. Paul Getty Museum, 2012; M.D. Bridges, 'Objects of Affection: Necromantic Pathos in Bulwer-Lytton's City of Dead', in S. Hales and J. Paul (eds), *Pompeii in the Public Imagination from Its Rediscovery to Today*, Oxford: Oxford University Press, 2011, 95.

30 Bridges, 'Objects of Affection: Necromantic Pathos in Bulwer-Lytton's City of Dead', 91.

31 K. Salantino, *Incendiary Art: The Representation of Fireworks in Early Modern Europe*, Los Angeles, CA: Bibliographies & Dossier, 1997, 58.

32 Coates et al., *The Last Days of Pompeii: Decadence, Apocalypse, Resurrection*, 277; A. Ekström, 'Remediation, Time and Disaster', *Theory, Culture & Society* 33, 5, 2016, 117–38; N. Yablon, "A Picture Painted in Fire': Pain's Reenactment of The Last Days of Pompeii, 1879–1914', in V.C.G. Coates, K. Lapatin and J.L. Seydl (eds), *Antiquity Recovered: The Legacy of Pompeii and Herculaneu*, Los Angeles, CA: The J. Paul Getty Museum, 2007.

33 A. Ekström, 'Exhibiting Disasters: Mediation, Historicity, and Spectatorship', *Media, Culture & Society* 34, 4, 2012, 477.

34 Ekström, 'Remediation, Time and Disaster', 117–38.

35 Ekström, 'Exhibiting Disasters: Mediation, Historicity, and Spectatorship', 476.

36 T. Steinberg, *Acts of God: The Unnatural History of Natural Disasters in America*, New York: Oxford University Press, 2000, 3.

37 Ekström, 'Exhibiting Disasters: Mediation, Historicity, and Spectatorship', 478–81.

38 Ekström, 'Remediation, Time and Disaster', 125.

39 Ibid., 120.

40 Kverndokk, *Naturkatastrofer: En kulturhistorie*, 152.

41 Quoted in ibid., 153.

42 G. Kennan, *The Tragedy of Pelée: A Narrative of Personal Experience and Observation in Martinique*, New York: The Outlook Company, 1902, 8.

43 Rozario, *The Culture of Calamity: Disaster and the Making of Modern America*, 122.

44 S. Leikam, *Framing Spaces in Motion: Tracing, Visualizations of Earthquakes into Twentieth-Century San Francisco*, American Studies, Vol. 255, Heidelberg: Universitätsverlag Winter Heidelberg, 2015, 220.

45 Leikam, *Framing Spaces in Motion*, 328.

46 Ibid., 278.

47 Ibid., 279.

48 Ibid., 293.

49 Ibid., 319.

50 Ekström, 'Remediation, Time and Disaster', 11.

51 A. Ekström and K. Kverndokk, 'Introduction: Cultures of Disaster', *Culture Unbound: Journal of Current Cultural Research* 7, 2015, 357.

52 See for instance K. Tierney, C. Bevc and E. Kuligowski, 'Metaphors Matter: Disaster Myths, Media Frames, and Their Consequences in Hurricane Katrina', *The Annals of the American Academy of Political and Social Science* 604, 2006, 57–81; G. Webb, 'The Popular Culture of Disaster: Exploring a New Dimension of Disaster Research', in R. Dynes et al. (eds), *Handbook of Disaster Research*, New York: Springer, 2007, 430–40; S. Žižek, 'Some Politically Incorrect Reflections on Violence in France and Related Matters. 3. Escape from New Orleans', 2005, www.lacan.com/zizfrance2.htm (accessed 20 August 2017).

53 D. Alexander, 'Symbolic and Practical Interpretations of the Hurricane Katrina Disaster in New Orleans', 2006, http://understandingkatrina.ssrc.org/Alexander (accessed 27 July 2014). R. Dynes and H. Rodríguez, 'Finding and Framing Katrina: The Social Construction of Disaster', in D. L Brunsma, D. Overfelt and J.S. Picou (eds), *The Sociology of Katrina: Perspectives on a Modern Catastrophe*, Lanham, MD: Rowman & Littlefield, 2007.

54 Webb, 'The Popular Culture of Disaster: Exploring a New Dimension of Disaster Research', 435.

55 K. Tierney, *The Social Roots of Risk: Producing Disaster, Promoting Resilience*, Stanford Business Books: Stanford, CA, 2014; C. Webersik et al., 'Towards an Integrated Approach to Emergency Management: Interdisciplinary Challenges for Research and Practice', *Culture Unbound: Journal of Current Cultural Research* 7, 2015, 529–35.

56 Tierney et al., 'Metaphors Matter: Disaster Myths, Media Frames, and Their Consequences in Hurricane Katrina'.

57 Quoted in R. Solnit, *A Paradise Built in Hell: The Extraordinary Communities that Arise in Disaster*, Viking: New York, 2009, 36.

58 Quoted in K. Kverndokk, 'Mediating the Morals of Disasters: Hurricane Katrina in Norwegian News Media', *Nordic Journal of Science and Technology Studies* 2, 1, 2014, 82.

59 Tierney et al., 'Metaphors Matter: Disaster Myths, Media Frames, and Their Consequences in Hurricane Katrina', 64–65.

60 Cf. C. Lindahl, 'Legends of Hurricane Katrina: The Right to Be Wrong, Survivor-to-Survivor Storytelling, and Healing', *Journal of American Folklore* 125, 2012.

61 Tierney et al., 'Metaphors Matter: Disaster Myths, Media Frames, and Their Consequences in Hurricane Katrina', 76–78.

62 I.W. Holm, 'The Cultural Analysis of Disasters', in C. Meiner and K. Veel (eds), *The Cultural Life of Catastrophes and Crises*, Berlin: De Gruyter, 2012, 26.

63 Holm, 'The Cultural Analysis of Disasters', 24–26.

64 B. McGuire, *Global Catastrophes: A Very Short Introduction*, Oxford: Oxford University Press, 2005, 9.

65 K. Hewitt, *Regions of Risk: A Geographical Introduction to Disasters*, Harrow: Longman, 1997.

66 Quoted in I.W. Holm, 'Earthquake in Haiti: Kleist and the Birth of Modern Disaster Discourse', *New German Critique* 39, 1, 2012, 55.

67 Ibid.

68 Rozario, *The Culture of Calamity: Disaster and the Making of Modern America*, 19.

69 Ibid., 10.

70 Latour, *We Have Never Been Modern*, 1.

71 Ibid., 47.

72 Cf. B. Latour, *Facing Gaia: Eight Lectures on the New Climatic Regime*, Cambridge: Polity, 2017, 119.

73 Kverndokk, *Naturkatastrofer: En kulturhistorie*, 240–47; cf. D.L. Heidenblad, *Vårt eget fel: Moralisk kausalitet som tankefigur från 00-tallets klimalarm till förmoderna syndastraffsföreställningar*, Höör: Agerings bokförlag, 2012.

74 G.J. Schenk, *Katastrophen vom Untergang Pompejis bis zum Klimawandel*, Ostfildern: Thorbecke, 2009, 12–13, 219.

75 Heidenblad, *Vårt eget fel.*

76 P. Crutzen, and E. Stoermer, 'The "Anthropocene"', *Global Change Newsletter* 41, 2000.

77 J. Zalasiewicz et al., 'When Did the Anthropocene Begin? A Mid-Twentieth Century Boundary Level Is Stratigraphically Optimal', *Quaternary International* 383, 2015; J. Zalasiewicz et al. 'The Working Group on the Anthropocene: Summary of Evidence and Interim Recommendations', *Anthropocene* 19, 2017.

78 D. Chakrabarty, 'The Climate of History: Four Theses', *Critical Inquiry* 35, 2, 2009.

79 A. Malm and A. Hornborg, 'The Geology of Mankind? A Critique of the Anthropocene Narrative', *The Anthropocene Review* 1, 2014; *Anthropocene or Capitalocene? Nature, History and the Crisis of Capitalism*, ed. J.W. Moore, Oakland, CA: Kairos, 2016.

80 D. Chakrabarty, 'Anthropocene Time', *History and Theory* 57, 1, 2018, 11.

81 D. Chakrabarty, 'The Politics of Climate Change Is More Than the Politics of Capitalism', *Theory, Culture and Society* 34, 2–3, 2017.

82 Chakrabarty, 'The Climate of History: Four Theses', 221.

83 T. F. Sørensen, 'Dyp fremtid. Atomaffald og fremtiden efter mennesket', *Kollaps: På randen av fremtiden*, eds P. Bjerregaard and K. Kverndokk, Oslo: Dreyers forlag, 2018.

84 Ibid.

85 Ibid.

86 Ekström, 'Exhibiting Disasters: Mediation, Historicity, and Spectatorship'.

87 U. Beck, *The Risk Society: Towards a New Modernity*, London: Sage, 1992, 49, italic in the original text.

88 A. Ophir, 'The Politics of Catastrophization: Emergency and Exception', in D. Fassin and M. Pandolfi (eds), *Contemporary States of Emergency: The Politics of Military and Humanitarian Interventions*, New York: Zone Books, 2010.

89 C. Calhoun, 'Humanitarian Action and Global (Dis)Order'.

25

CULTURES OF MOBILITY

Dhan Zunino Singh

Mobilities refer to both the movement and the immobility of people, things, images, ideas, information, water, disease, rubbish, capital and so on, and has been examined by migration, tourism, communication, transport, urban and cultural studies. In the last three decades, a great diversity of works which can be considered cultural histories of mobilities has proliferated. This is the result, on the one hand, of the influence of the cultural turn in transport history, and, on the other, of the importance of culture in the so-called mobility turn in the social sciences. But it is also a consequence of the variety of phenomena that can be considered cultural as well as the subjects that can be considered mobility phenomena.

This chapter focuses on practices and representations of people in motion to reveal the principal transformations in the forms of practising and representing mobilities during the nineteenth and early twentieth centuries, based on the changes in transport technologies. Introducing some key aspects of mobilities studies and some debates among historians in order to help us understand the state of the art of the field, it is organized through topics related to artefacts and metaphors, the effects of speed, bodily affects and emotions, social interaction and performance, emerging from the railway journey, commercial aviation, cycling, automobility, transatlantic ship journeys and public transport in large cities. Finally, it focuses on the experience of walking in the context of such transformations.

It is important to note that culture or the cultural is not only an aspect or approach, but is central to the definition of mobility since the latter is understood as an embodied social practice shaping and being shaped by meanings.[1] The simple practice of walking, for example, has several meanings depending on geographical and historical contexts. It was considered dangerous when undertaken by the vagabond, or could be aristocratic when involving walking in a promenade. John Urry, one of the main exponents of the mobility turn, points out that moving is dwelling-in-motion, boosting the study of mobility as a meaningful practice – as meaningful as the experience of dwelling.[2] This definition contrasts with the idea that mobility spaces are 'non-places' (Marc Augé) or that mobility experiences erode social ties, and encourages the investigation of the ideas, feelings, sociabilities, identities and subjectivity attached to the experience of being in motion.[3]

Transport historians, although still using a modal view of transport, have also sought to overcome political, economic and technological views of mobility, introducing a cultural perspective that stretches from the metaphors associated with transport technology to people's experiences.[4] The cultural approach has been influenced mainly by the mobility turn but there are important precedents which can be considered cultural histories of transport, such as Wolfgang Schivelbusch's railway history or American historians who have studied automobility.[5] Another important contribution is made by cultural and social historians who are no experts in mobilities but deal with problems and themes associated with mobility, such as national identity and imperialism, gender and race relations, leisure and travel, arts, heritage and museum, circulation and congestion, slavery, pilgrimage and so on.

Finally, the cultural history of mobilities is characterized not only by cultural aspects or themes but also by the types of sources and methods. The use of visual sources, such as photos, films, comics, art, maps and texts, is typical as are personal diaries, miscellanea and advertising. The 'view from below', meaning the experience of travelling, has been one of the main contributions of the cultural perspective, although the 'view from above' has also been well explored by cultural historians, linking transport technology or infrastructure with ideas of flows, speed, modernity, nation, empire and so forth. Most recently, historians have begun to focus on performance, affect and emotion.[6]

Given the influence of post-humanist theories in cultural studies and, particularly, in mobilities studies, it is important to discuss the status of arts, literature, music, films and other forms of representations, because, when applied in the contemporary studies on mobilities, these theories created problems for historians who cannot do direct observation or ethnography of the past as sociologists, geographers or anthropologists do. Going beyond images and discourses, being in motion with the subject capturing moments when language cannot represent experience (performance, bodily emotions, etc.) sounds attractive and puts into question our understanding of culture. However, historians' access to the past is through testimonies which are mainly textual or visual representations of past experiences (except for oral history in which experiences are reconstructed through interviews). Nonetheless, historians can access the materialities of mobilities – from vehicles to tickets, from customs to devices or gadgets – which the material turn or reflections from archaeology can help us to conceptualize as more than representations. While admitting that representations never represent the totality of experience, however, we must recognize that, as Cresswell states, they act in our presentations, being embedded in our experiences.[7]

A recognized landmark in the cultural history of transport is Wolfgang Schivelbusch's *The Railway Journey* ([1977] 1986). This independent German researcher has, from a heterodox approach, enquired wisely into social, spatial, temporal and cultural transformations shaped by the railway in the nineteenth century. He also pays attention to the materiality of technology in analysing practices and social interactions during travel. George Revill has revisited Schivelbusch's work to conceptualize critically his influence on transport historians, focusing on how the author deals with perception ('panoramic view') and the 'machine ensemble'. Revill claims a post-phenomenological approach that problematizes the idea of perception, specifically historical constructivism, in order to include contested and more varied views on railway journeys – for example, the workers' view – as well as concepts of reception and representation. While Schivelbusch concludes that the railway caused an experience of detachment, Revill points out that new attachments also took place.[8]

Modernity: ideas about social and material progress

Rudyard Kipling's well-known phrase 'transportation is Civilisation' synthesizes the way in which vehicles embodied material modernization while also mobilizing modern ideas and values of newness, freedom, progress and future. The discourses about transport show technological innovation as a natural evolution in which every new form supersedes and replaces the old one. The mechanization of transport, from animal to steam traction, occurred with the invention of railways in 1804. The electrification of railways and tramways by the 1890s was combined with the autonomy of some vehicles, such as bicycles, and then cars and aeroplanes appeared in the narratives as autonomous processes expressing a 'technological determinism'.[9] Every new invention seemed to signal a moment of history: the nineteenth century as the 'railway era' or the twentieth as the 'automobile era'. Although such narratives have been questioned from a social constructivist perspective or economic history, which shows the power relations underlying the replacement of one technology by another – such as, most notably, trams by cars – it is important to note what kinds of ideas, values and emotions transport technologies mobilized. Transport, like many other technologies, triggered ambivalent reactions, a mix of fascination and fear that David Nye called 'sublime'.[10] As Freeman shows, the British railways during the Victoria era reinforced optimism about science and technology, although it was also lived or experienced with anxiety and doubt, as shown by John Martin's *The Last Judgement* (1853), a painting in which the railway is depicted 'tumbling into Chaos'.[11]

Inventions had advocates and detractors. Machines were diverse, and evolved and adapted to different needs, claims and complaints. The turn from the steam locomotive to electric traction on the railways had a huge effect on perceptions of this technology, while the transformation undergone by the bicycle between 1817 and 1885, making it safer, signified a popularization of this human-traction based vehicle. Enormous and noisy machines like a locomotive, of course, triggered different impressions from vehicles like the bike. If the former could be associated with the monstrous or infernal – called *Wilfire*, *Dragon* or *Centaur* – the latter could be associated with a toy. Initially, the bicycle was perceived as a mechanical horse but because of its shape was also represented as wings, associating 'the winged figure of the bicyclist with the divine, as a "scientific angel" leading the way for the righteous towards heaven'.[12]

While there was a fascination with novelty, new technologies wore old dresses too, something revealed in their naming and conception: the bike was described as a horse with wheels or mechanical horse and the power of the car engine in terms of horse power, while even the material shape of rail coaches or automobiles was initially similar to that of the carriage. Transport infrastructure, like the underground railway, could even trigger atavistic representations related to the place of Death, the Hell, underworld. The first underground in the world, London (1863), reinforced this representation since the steam locomotive generated a toxic atmosphere. Although from the 1890s electric subways improved the experience of travelling, the perception of inhabiting Hell or a place unsuitable for humans persisted in other cities such as Boston (1897), Paris (1900) and Buenos Aires (1913). The art nouveau design of the édicules, by Hector Guimard, for the entrances of the Paris Metro reinforced the idea that it was the gate to a necropolis, for example.[13]

Along with fear, fascination and anxieties, transport embodied the project of modernity in a technological progress which appeared as a precondition for social progress, within capitalist, nationalist or socialist ideologies. In the early nineteenth century, canals were at the core of Saint Simonian' imaginary; railways in the nineteenth century and road networks in the first half of the twentieth embodied ideas of the modern nation under different political regimes. Infrastructure could show the economic power or level of modernization of a nation, but most important was its capacity to materialize the national identity: the Interstate Highway in the United States (1956), as the materialization of a *longue durée* automobile culture expressing the values of American individualism, or Tito's project of a national road (*Brotherhood and Unity Highway*) during the 1940s–1950s in Yugoslavia, expressing a 'trans-ethnic collective socialist' identity based on equality.[14]

Transport technologies not only allowed the territorialization of different nation identities but also the global market, empires or regions. Plans for Pan-American railways or the non-finished and controversial highway connecting North and South America show how transport could make possible political and cultural ideas of integration in the early twentieth century.[15] Aviation, like maritime mobility previously, was closely related to imperial expansion and networks. For the British Empire, for example, civil aviation between the wars sought to recreate and maintain maritime power. Although in practice it was more difficult, the British conquest of the seas worked out as an allegory for the conquest of the air, with adventurous pilots feeling like older sailors. More notably, the image of the Empire was shaped by the aerial view through a strong visual culture that included exhibitions, maps and painted panoramas.[16]

At an urban scale, plans for mass transportation at the turn of the twentieth century, such as railways, subways and tramways, were associated with progressive ideas: the promise of a better life in the suburbs, well connected with the city centre through a rapid mass transit system. Although the mobility infrastructure was sometimes an instrument of urban renewal that destroyed slums, removing poor people from the city centre as in the case of the London Underground in the 1860s, it was also envisaged within reformist ideas in which railways contributed to improving the quality of working-class life.[17] Similar cases can be found in Stockholm in the early twentieth century where the underground system was implemented 'to create opportunities to build good houses for the masses' following Swedish social-democrat ideology of *folkhem*.[18] In concordance with these political ideas, mostly shaped by hygienist and urbanist discourses, there were plans for the municipalization of mass transport guided by the idea that it was a public service, not a business. To make transport accessible for the masses was understood as a form of democratization.[19]

This relationship between transport and the politics of national identity or social progress highlights that the strong association between mobility and individual freedom was not the only one. If individual mobility was associated with freedom, that occurred in the context of political and economic ideologies of the nineteenth century in the Western world, where the free movement of commodities and individuals was at the core of capitalism and liberalism. If modern mobility, in general, was experienced as liberation from spatial constriction, contributing to the expansion of the world capitalist market, at the same time, particular mobility technologies such as the bicycle and then the car embodied individual freedom as a liberation from social constraints. It is well known that early feminists found in the bike and the car instruments of liberation. While industry was quick to see women as potential consumers of bikes and cars, in accordance with social changes which were taking place in politics, fashions and daily life, women were not passive consumers but used those vehicles as means for socialization and political participation.

Although the car became the epitome of individual freedom and territories tended to adapt to automobile infrastructure, from the 1920s it was subjected to control by traffic regulations and safety norms. At the same time, as mobility scholars point out, while the automobile promised more freedom, it generated more car-dependency, creating subjection.[20] Moreover, the hegemony that the car achieved was always resisted, and this became more visible by the end of the 1960s when urban planners, civil associations of pedestrians and cyclists and other agencies started questioning car-dependency, looking for alternative mobilities, bringing back cycling and walking as modes of sustainable mobilities.

The tautological relationship between transport and modernity has often been overlooked, forgetting the social construction of those technologies and how cultural representations expressed different emotions, ideas, values and meanings attached to transport technologies. Moreover, the relationship between transport and modernity has been ambivalent, as modernization was uneven and history was not linear: vehicles that seemed old-fashioned, such as the bike or the electric car, are today recovered as the future of sustainable mobility. Yet, an idea still survives that sustainability can be achieved through technological innovation and such innovation will bring social welfare as well as the ideas of freedom that certain vehicles offer, showing the strong relations between mobilities and politics and transport technologies as cultural artefacts.

Time-space compression: circulation, speed, stillness

The impression that 'all that is solid melts into air' seems a sign of modernity. Marshall Berman's quotation from Karl Marx epitomizes the latter's observation of the annihilation of space by time, a time that started to be valued by economics.[21] This process, which David Harvey calls space-time compression, was based on the effects of mechanization of transport (steam engines), such as ships and railways in the first decades of the nineteenth century and the automobile and the aeroplane in the twentieth.[22] The acceleration of circulation of people, things and information (images and ideas), and also the pace of life, has been strongly related to material transformations in the forms of mobility. In turn, mobilities were part of processes such as industrialization, urbanization and capitalist expansion around the globe. Speed entails a space-shrinking perception which was accompanied by a sense of fragmentation – becoming both the transient, fleeting feeling of a modern experience – and individual freedom or a world less constrained.[23] Acceleration of movement represented a 'key theme in modern imagination', where the mechanization of speed ('from a velocity of "nature" to one of machinery') sought to close gaps, promising 'to overcome the material realities of space, distance and separation'.[24] Motifs in the *avant garde* poetry and art like Futurism are recurrent examples of this fascination. Yet, impressions of acceleration were rather ambivalent, as we will see with the experience of walking.

A new space-time perception emerged with railways, and was then reinforced and re-signified by the bicycle in the late nineteenth century, and later by the car and the aeroplane. By the 1850s there were railways on almost every continent, accelerating the transportation of freight and passengers. Initially, speed was about 40 mph; not a big change relative to the horse. But what caused a reduction of time and distance was the constant speed of the train. In fact, through the reduction of journey-time, space was both diminished and expanded. On the one hand, distant places became part of regional, national and international markets. The movement of commodities and people brings places closer: either through tourism or consumption. On the other hand, cities expanded through this kind of infrastructure.[25]

A first cultural effect of the mechanization of transport was the 'loss of aura' of places insofar as they were now part of a trans-local system. Standardization was the enemy of the singularity of place and time. Local time was now measured according to new national and international agreements, like the worldwide time zone in 1884, needed to coordinate transport movements. For travellers, used to the coach journey, rail speed signified detachment from the places they traversed. The intensity of traversing places, the attachment to landscape, that a poet like Goethe could depict in his travel diaries during the eighteenth century would be 'destroyed' by the railway, according to Schivelbusch. The train as a 'projectile', a metaphor of its speed, signified 'being shot through landscape' rather than traversing it and this affected the senses, creating a new vista: the 'panoramic view'. As the train's motion shrank space, it 'displayed in immediate succession objects and pieces of scenery that in their original spatiality belonged to separated realms', says Schivelbusch. The panoramic view shapes a global sense of place – 'in a few hours, it [the railway] shows you all of France, and before your eyes it unrolls in infinite panorama', a Parisian journalist claimed in 1865.[26] What could be experienced as a novelty, a loss, an evanescent sense of panorama in the 1840s became in a few decades the normal experience of travelling.

Although propelled by human effort, the bicycle was also a mechanized mobility that triggered representations of a 'kinetic modernity'.[27] Velocity was modelled by modern artists through a sense of lightness. The 'gravity-defying lightness of being suggested by the cyclist's near-flight over the ground' represented the 'motion of the machine and its rider through static art forms', making 'the bicycle's minimal contact with the ground especially resonant'.[28] In the 1890s, with the cycling boom in the Western world, the bike became not only a symbol of speed but freedom or free individual movement. This feeling and cultural value would be embodied by the car a few decades later. Unlike the guided and standardized movement of railways, the sense of autonomy, along with the versatility that these machines offered, were in fact relative since both cars and bikes needed suitable roads and streets and new norms would emerge to control mobility. Nonetheless, the possibility of exploring territories beyond the city and reaching high speeds reinforced an idea of freedom, escaping from the constrictions and routine of an industrialized and urbanized world. Country tours were organized to promote this new mobility culture, but speed was strongly boosted by competition. Race and speed records accompanied and fed the new cultures of bikes and cars; even pedestrianism was popularized by competition, creating spaces such as velodromes and racetracks.

Velocity was also shaped by gender. With the car, for example, speed, freedom and adventure were associated early on with masculine violence as shown by Marcel Proust's automobility experience, metaphorically associated with rape. 'The city-scape becomes a mobile prey' for him and he had 'an insane urge to rape the little sleeping cities' with the car.[29] Car speed became a fascination, or rather a 'modern pleasure', as Duffy Enda states.[30] 'Speed, it seems to me, provides the one genuinely modern pleasure', said Aldous Huxley in *Wanted, a New Pleasure* (1931). As the car is small and near the ground like the horse, both offer an 'inebriating speed-purveyor': the horse at 20 mph and the car about 60 mph. Yet, 'when the car has passed seventy-two, or thereabouts, one begins to feel an unprecedented sensation'.[31]

The linking of adrenaline and vertigo to speed as emotions was based on the experience of the user. For non-users, the speed of the car in the city or even that of the bike became problematic. While cycling clubs sought to cover cycling 'in a gentlemanly and disciplined (neo-militaristic) veneer', young men or '"bicycle cads" subverted the fashioned decorum of bourgeois society with their reckless speed'.[32] If the city accommodated itself to the automobile, the latter was also modified by noise reduction, and safer technologies.[33] Increasing controls over speed underlie a modern notion of safety: road safety. If racing could boost the capacity of vehicles to beat speed records, at the same time a culture of safety emerged since accidents were an aftermath of speed.

Accidents could be experienced ambivalently, generating fear (in the streets, for example) and excitement (in races and exhibitions), but in urban contexts, congestion was the real enemy for modern mobility. It was the expression of the malfunctioning of the city: chaos, lack of planning, wasting of time and money. The idea of freedom of movement was accompanied by the idea of a new spatial order guaranteeing circulation. Flows without friction were only possible if conducted through the material organization of space such as canals, rails, roads, cables, tunnels and so on. These infrastructures of flows became the ideal of modern space. Like the capitalist market, cities and larger territories became organized by a modern notion of circulation. Integration, connectivity and fundamentally frictionless motion was shaped by biological ideas of the body. In modern urban planning, for example, the bodily metaphor of the city as an organism and, thus, circulation as a healthy and vital function was borrowed from discoveries about the circulation of blood within the body (Harvey's *De motu cordis*, 1628). From the eighteenth century 'the words, veins and arteries, applied to the city's streets sought to model traffic system on the blood system of the body'.[34] Hence, 'if motion through the city becomes blocked anywhere, the collective body suffers a crisis of circulation like the individual body suffers during a stroke when an artery becomes blocked'.[35] Hygienists and reformists played a key role in transferring these metaphors from biology and medicine to urban space discourses.

Circulation, however, does not necessarily imply acceleration. But insofar as the car became massive and embodied the symbol of future transport, displacing other

modes of transport such as railways and tramways, a new infrastructure and organization of space was needed. But, first, segregation appeared through traffic norms,
restricting the movement of non-motorized mobilities like pedestrians, and the renewal of streets, through paving and widening them or opening new avenues. Then,
exclusive spaces like highways tended to destroy the built environment, privileging
automobile speed. As mentioned above, the road not only supported automobility in
material terms but also symbolically contributed to the building of national identities
which boosted the construction of automobile infrastructure. Some nations were
identified with this infrastructure: the German Autobahn, the Italian Autostrade, the
American Highway. Automobile infrastructure also created a new urban imaginary.
Ideas and imagines of future cities were probably best expressed by Norman Geddes'
Futurama. Sponsored by General Motors, Futurama was an exhibition of the future
city designed for the 1939 New York World's Fair: urban space was adapted to the
automobile with automated highways, an expanded city with suburbs, concentrating
business, administration and entertainment in a centre with high buildings; and most
important, with segregated ways in which pedestrian and cars did not cross each
other. This idea of segregated mobility, in order to guarantee car speed, persists today.

The aeroplane, in the early twentieth century, contributed to shaping a new representation of a frictionless motion, expressing the real annihilation of physical (terrestrial) space. After a first period of testing, exhibition, expedition and even aerial war
(epitomized by the aviator as a hero), commercial aviation offered a new experience
of mobility to a broader public. From the 1920s the experience of flying was organized through aerial routes and timetables and terrestrial infrastructure: the airport,
which became a space for the spectacle of aviation, was epitomized by the terraces
from which people could watch aeroplanes taking off and landing.

Although the aeroplane, because of its speed, could have been the major symbol
of time-space compression, its effects on perception (for pilots and passengers) were
more related to a 'sublime dislocation' or disorientation, a new point of view (to see
territory as a lived map), rather than acceleration.[36] We can find the effects of aviation
in culture as well as in how art or science has represented the experience of flying.
As Gert Simonsen shows for Le Corbusier's urbanism and the Italian Futurists, the
speed of this modern transport machine has changed our perception of space-time,
creating a new structure of feeling, whose connotations vary and then shape different
representations. Both had similar views on the aeroplane as a revolutionary machine
but their idea of timing was different: 'The timing of Futurism is embedded in historicity, while Le Corbusier's is of straight and progressive history'. Regarding the
compression of space created by the aeroplane, the Futurists found there 'multiple
perspectives of the world, generating new simultaneity', 'dynamism' and 'plasticity',
'fragmentation and destabilised reality', while the functionalist view of Le Corbusier
saw 'precision and order'.[37]

Embodied and social practices

If modern transport mobilized ideas related to modernity that triggered fascination and fear, and modified our time-space perception, it also affected our bodies,
practices and social interactions. Modern mobilities involved new performance and

choreographies: waiting, queuing up, boarding and alighting, keeping balance, driving, keeping quiet. Each mode of transport brought new forms of seeing, such as the panoramic railway view or the aerial view, and also of hearing, touching, smelling: some of them exciting, others disgusting like travel sickness. From railways to aeroplanes, the narratives and medical reports relating to early travel experiences give accounts of the troubles that the machine and movement caused the body.

In the mid-nineteenth century the steam locomotive and the continuous vibration of the train affected the bodies of firemen and workers, causing 'engineer's malady', pseudo-rheumatic pains, but also passengers who travelled with a seating in a more comfortable space: the rapid succession of jolts and the noise provoked discomfort but also fatigue. Boredom and idleness also accompanied the experience of travelling in the rail compartment in Europe.[38] Machine noise could affect conversation between passengers in a railway journey in 1840 as well as in a subway in the 1940s as the Argentinean writer, Julio Cortázar, highlights in a short story entitled *Divertimento* (1949). He said that talking in a coach of the Buenos Aires Underground was 'a task that demands anthropophagical skills', hence it was better to keep silent. Air-trips involved not only disorientation but bodily effects like vomiting. While promoted as pleasant and invigorating, and initially also as a luxurious and exclusive experience, air travel – although varying with the type of aircraft – was deafening, bumpy and nauseating. The 'aerial ideal subject' had to learn 'to deal with nausea, temperature, food, air quality' as much as overcome fear to fly as early rail passengers had to deal with the fear of derailment.[39]

Mobilities involved different forms of sociability. Driving a car or riding a bike or a motorbike could be an individual mobility experience but was also collectively experienced through clubs. Like the bicycle industry in the 1890s, two decades later car culture was boosted by marketing or the industry and also by social groups of enthusiasts who diffused the use of these vehicles. Bikers' clubs or motor-clubs shaped a culture based on leisure and the pleasure of escaping from the city through tours, tourism, picnics or weekend travel. Not only enjoyment but also social awareness could be promoted through this shared experience of mobility, such as socialism or women's rights, although these vehicles also were strongly associated with individual freedom.[40]

Many modes of transport were initially restricted to small social groups; particularly, upper-middle classes who could buy a train or flight ticket or acquire a vehicle. The bike or the car were 'toys' for the aristocracy, the aeroplane journey a luxury and the railway in Europe expressed social stratification through the different classes of ticket. But gradually all these means of transport became a mass and an ordinary experience for a larger public, appropriated in different forms according to gender, class or racial groups. This process of democratization or massification of transport technologies as social progress was, as mentioned, in the imaginary of reformists but also in the minds of transport businessmen. The symbol of this was Henry Ford's project of making the car accessible to everyone through his Ford model T in the early twentieth century.[41] The railway industry saw the emergence of automobility as a threat and, in the UK during the interwar period, for example, sought to attract middle- and upper-class men who were becoming car drivers. Not speed but a 'civilised speed' offered by a safe rail travel – in contrast to the increasing risk of automobile accidents – along with comfort and luxury given by amenities, modern design and 'domesticity' of compartments were used by a 'commercial culture' to make rail travel more attractive.[42]

Neither these forms of sociability nor mass industry eroded the meaning of individual freedom but, on the contrary, could exalt it. In fact, free car motion was questioned mainly in the city. Gijs Mom points out, while individuality and automobility, stressed by the fascination with speed and adventures beyond the city, continued to be associated, by 1930 the early noisy and monstrous car, mainly targeted at men, was domesticated within the city. The design, the norms that regulated it and its imagery shaped the car as a vehicle for the family and it was this model of car that was more diffused.[43]

In fact, individuality was promoted as much as hacked by the modern mobilities. Particularly, urban public transport was the scenario for encountering (completely unknown) others. The experience of commuting became mass in early nineteenth-century Paris, where the omnibus emerged as public transport. Although the fare was still restrictive for the lower classes, the horse-drawn vehicle carrying a dozen passengers became the main transport for multitudes of workers. In Europe and the Americas, tramways, which had been electrified by the 1890s, omnibuses and underground railways (1890s–1920s) were destined to move masses of people and, therefore, the fare became more accessible. These means of transport changed travel experience and subjectivity as well as social relations, as people had to learn new forms of sociability to deal with bodily proximity in confined spaces: for example, before the appearance of public transport, people 'were not in a situation where, for minutes or hours at a time, they could or must look at one another without talking to one another'.[44]

The isolation and boredom that, for example, the railway journey involved was counteracted with reading – a practice that also contributed to avoiding eye contact. This tension between intimacy and the multitude, brought by a crowded train, tram or bus, became a trope of modern social theory and of literature and cinema. Sociological concepts like Georg Simmel's blasé attitude, referring to the conservation of individuality against external stimuli, or anthropological ones, like Edward Hall's proxemics, give accounts of this tension between bodily proximity and social distance. Passengers reading, doing nothing but looking through a window and keeping silent triggered representations of mobility as alienation. The Argentinean writer, Ezequiel Martínez Estrada, said in the 1930s that subway passengers were automatons because they were not engaged in travel because travelling involves individuals' intentions and wishes. Rather, the subway journey was just an unthinking displacement.[45] This perception, that the passenger is not a human but a thing, can be tracked back to the early rail journey where passengers felt that they were like parcels.[46]

Anonymous encounters on public transport could involve voyeurism, the chance to meet another person or even initiate a love story. Literature shows the latter as particularly a male wish. With the increasing use of the metro in Tokyo during the 1920s, the schoolgirl emerged as trope of erotic male fantasies in Japanese literature.[47] The Argentinean writer Julio Cortázar, in the short story *Gatito de cuello negro* (1974), represents this anonymous encounter where a male and female passenger start to touch with their hands and to flirt in the Paris Metro. Yet, even when male imaginary represents the experience as exciting or romantic, female passengers became objects of gazes and also sexual harassment.

If modern transport promised speed, safety and comfort, the latter was questioned by the crowd and the struggle for space. Moreover, delays and interruptions could make the daily experience of travel annoying. Transport companies, political authorities and the press tried to impose norms, not only to teach passengers how to use particular modes of transport but also to regulate social behaviour. The former implied a new material culture of maps, timetables, brochures and magazines that orientated and taught people about travelling, these being also discourses shaping idealized passengers. The latter sought to civilize the crowd through codes of urbanity. In short, travelling needed a new disciplined subject.

Modern walking

Despite the intrinsic relationship between modern mobility and mechanized speed, it would be a mistake to overlook the fact that acceleration was also rejected, contested and criticized.[48] The recent ideas of slow-motion cities, human-scale urbanism or sustainable mobility, which promote cycling and walking in the city, have a long history. Emblematic discourses and practices, such as Jane Jacobs' urbanism or the hippie movement, emerged during the 1960s, rooted in a *longue durée* process of contestation of speed as well as its infrastructure and way of life. This section will approach modern walking, as an example of that contrast, starting with the nineteenth and early twentieth centuries.

Walking is the most natural and primitive way of mobility, but the meanings attached to this practice are social, cultural and historical.[49] Ideas of walking as healthy and sustainable, for example, are recent. Walking was associated with vagabonds in the Middle Age, or related to pilgrimage, but by the 1840s some social groups started walking for pleasure. The leisurely walk in the British countryside can be tracked from the eighteenth century as a contestation (a right to walking) by middle classes to the lack of land access imposed by landlords, but the mechanization of mobility emerging later with the railway allowed a comparison between mechanical and 'natural' mobility.[50] Although for many, particularly the lower classes, walking was still a practice of commuting, even the only one possible since public transport was not affordable, culturally it was extended to a romantic walking. In the promenade or as the activity of a flâneur in the city, and especially in going to the countryside, walking not only contested speed but also reinforced contact with nature. It is a claim not only for a more relaxed space-time but also for a corporeal relationship with the (natural) environment, even when accessing the countryside meant travelling by railways. In fact, the tourism industry would promote walking in different destinations as a part of the tour offer, with long-distance trips mediated by mechanized mobilities such as buses, railways or aeroplanes.

The positive appreciation or romantic view that walking obtained in modernity was, hence, *vis-à-vis* industrialization, urbanization and the acceleration of the pace of life that modern transport boosted.[51] The pleasure of walking was exclusive to the upper class in the context of private gardens or museums, while the promenade appeared later as another exclusive space for a bourgeois walking, and display, where moving on foot became performed and stylized with specific accessories like the walking stick.[52] With the creation of parks in large European and American cities during the nineteenth century, walking was still a bourgeois practice but expanded to the working class. Circulation within the park was seen as a space and a moment of civilized sociability. In the 1860s, Central Park in New York City became a great example of this social reformist apparatus, an 'educator of people', as its creator, Frederick Olmsted, called it, that sought to shape social behaviours through spatial order. In this apparatus, mobilities played a central role since they were planned to be segregated for the orderly management of flows. The walking, but also the circulation of carriages and equestrian practices, worked out as modes of seeing and being seen.[53] The park became a control mechanism, bearing in mind the political potentiality of walking in mass as a form of protest. People, or the 'mob', marching as a mass demonstration was always a constant peril after the revolts in Paris occasioned by food price increases in the late eighteenth century.[54]

With the urban transformations of the mid-nineteenth century, like the Parisian boulevard, the daily movement of people on foot also changed. Portrayed by the practice of flâneurie, wandering or strolling within the crowd in the street became a trope in modern literature, epitomized by Baudelaire's figure of the flâneur, but was also a way of scrutinizing social conditions as Friedrich Engels did in his writing on British cities in the mid-nineteenth century. Engels walked London's streets, highlighting the difference between the large commercial avenues, the showcase of capitalism, and the poor dwelling conditions in the alleys.[55] For Baudelaire, by contrast, according to Walter Benjamin, the street became a 'botanic garden' of social characters and shops a place of phantasmagoria.[56] The crowd moving on foot for commuting or shopping was part of the scenario in which a slow walker (and observer), either a man or a woman, could lose him/herself and develop his/her poetry.[57] Not only the reflectivity and mobility of the individual within the crowd but also the movement of the latter could be a spectacle of mass mobility: as Edgar Allen Poe wrote from a London café in 1845, 'a tumultuous sea of human heads' filled the pavements as 'tides of human population rushed past the door'.[58] In the 1950s, to get lost in the city by drifting became an aesthetic as much as political performance with the Situationist movement in Europe. Walking without a rational purpose but following emotions and discovering new forms of viewing the city contested urban capitalism.

But walking in the city suffered other, more traumatic or less romantic transformations. Daily movement on foot in the city was represented by the pedestrian who, within the context of motorization, tended to be regulated and controlled. The streets belonged less and less to walkers as the car became dominant by the 1930s, changing the meaning of street use. In the US, organized automotive interest groups began calling themselves 'motordom'; they were also called 'joy riders', 'road hogs' and 'speed demons' and their vehicles 'juggernauts', 'death cars' or 'the modern Moloch', and the pedestrian was pejoratively called 'jaywalker'.[59] Pedestrian mobility appeared as an impediment to the automotive city. Traffic safety controlled not only the car but also walkers. As in the US, in Santiago de Chile, for example, in 'the first three decades of the twentieth century, the nature of pedestrianism was deliberately steered away from a natural and unquestionable right of city inhabitants to a position of pedestrian responsibility and conscientiousness', both through motor-orientated traffic norms and public opinion: if pedestrians were at the beginning of motorization represented in the press and cartoons as victims, they were 'increasingly associated with irrationality, insurgency, unpredictability and temerity'.[60]

Conclusion

A cultural history of mobilities allows us to consider the interaction between practices, representations, materialities and social relations to understand the transformations which took place during the nineteenth and twentieth centuries in the Western world, in the ways in which people and things move. We have focused on early changes, particularly when a new mode of transport emerged. However, this genealogy avoided a global and exhaustive account of all those transformations. We have highlighted aspects such as space-time perception, ideas and values with respect to modernity like individual freedom, uses and meanings of mobility technology or walking according to different social groups.

In terms of experience, acceleration and increasing hybridization seem to have marked the period, with the result that both contemporary observers and historians have tended to see transport innovation as the motor of history or to see it in an evolutionary way. The hegemony achieved by the automobile by the 1930s, although questioned today, reinforces the evolutionist view, yet the history was a struggle, characterized by multiple and contradictory meanings. Acceleration and hybridization were questioned by walking and a reencounter with nature. At the same time, while mobility can reinforce the meaning of freedom, it has tended to be controlled by traffic norms, conducted by infrastructures, such that the bodies were disciplined. From the long journeys that allowed contact with the 'exotic' to public transport, which placed strangers in a closed and intimate space, to altered ways of perceiving the world and also the other, mobilities contributed to the expansion of both science and empires; they were at the core of capitalism as a global market altering boundaries but, at the same time, infrastructures for mobility helped to build up national territories and identities.

In social terms, mobility technologies tended to be democratized by the industry and also by the political meanings attached to them. Particularly the transport modes used for public service, such as railways, buses and tramways, sought to move masses; but individual transport which could have had an initial adventurous or playful meaning, such as the bicycle, the car or the aeroplane, then also became mass. At the same time, these individual transports which promised freedom or unfettered movement became more and more regulated, conducted through specific infrastructures. Although free individual movement and the free circulation of people and things persisted as modern conquests or ideals, cultural history has shown that mobilities are more uneven, contradictory and full of friction.

Notes

1 O. Jensen, 'Flows of Meaning, Cultures of Movements – Urban Mobility as Meaningful Everyday Life Practice', *Mobilities* 4, 1, 2009, 139–58; T. Cresswell, 'Towards a Politics of Mobility', *Environment and Planning D: Society and Space* 28, 1, 2010, 17–31.
2 J. Urry, *Mobilities*, Cambridge: Polity, 2007.

3 M. Augé, *Los no lugares*, Barcelona: Gedisa, 2000.

4 M. Gijs, C. Divall and P. Lyth, 'Towards a Paradigm Shift? A Decade of Transport and Mobility History', *Mobility in History* 1, 2009, 13–40.

5 W. Schivelbusch, *The Railway Journey: The Industrialization of Time and Space in the Nineteenth Century*, Leamington Spa, UK; New York; Hamburg: Berg, 1986. For car history see for example C. McShane, *Down the Asphalt Path: The Automobile and the American City*, New York: Columbia University Press, 1994.

6 See for example S. Stalter-Pace, 'Underground Theater', *Transfers* 5, 3, 2015, 4–22.

7 See interview with T. Cresswell in 'Mobilities and Representations: A Conversation with Peter Merriman, Colin Divall, Sunny Stalter-Pace, and Tim Cresswell', *Mobility in History* 8, 2017, 7–8.

8 G. Revill, 'Perception, Reception and Representation: Wolfgang Schivelbusch and the Cultural History of Travel and Transport', *Mobility in History* 4, 2012, 31–48.

9 'Technological determinism' refers to the idea of technology as an independent entity and autonomous agent of change, as a driving force of history. See R. Smith and L. Marx, *Does Technology Drive History: The Dilemma of Technological Determinism*, Cambridge, MA: MIT Press, 1994.

10 D. Nye, *American Technological Sublime*, Cambridge, MA: MIT Press, 1994.

11 M. Freeman, 'The Railway as Cultural Metaphor. "What Kind of Railway History?" Revisited', *Journal of Transport History* 20, 2, 1999, 160–67, 163.

12 P. Smethurst, *The Bicycle – Towards a Global History*, Basingstoke: Palgrave Macmillan, 2015, 70.

13 D. Zunino Singh, 'Towards a Cultural History of Underground Railways', *Mobility in History* 4, 2012, 103–12.

14 C. Seiler, *Republic of Drivers: A Cultural History of Automobility in America*, Chicago, IL: The Chicago University Press, 2008. L. Pozharliev, 'Collectivity vs. Connectivity: Highway Peripheralization in Former Yugoslavia (1940s–1980s)', *Journal of Transport History* 32, 2, 2016, 194–213.

15 R. Ficek, 'Imperial Routes, National Networks and Regional Projects in the Pan-American Highway, 1884–1977', *Journal of Transport History* 37, 2, 2016, 129–54.

16 G. Pirie, *Cultures and Caricatures of British Imperial Aviation: Passengers, Pilots, Publicity*, Manchester: Manchester University Press, 2012.

17 See Charles Pearson's plans for London and de Kérizouet's for Paris in C. Lopez Galviz, 'The Futures that Never Were. Railway Infrastructure and Housing in Mid-Nineteenth-Century London and Paris' in A. Marklund and M. Rüdiger (eds), *Historicizing Infrastructure*, Aalborg: Aalborg University Press, 2017, 115–36.

18 T. Ekman, 'Vision in Solid Form: A Comparison Between Two Solutions to the Traffic Problem in Stockholm, 1941 and 1992', in C. Divall and W. Bond (eds), *Suburbanizing the Masses: Public Transport and Urban Development in Historical Perspective*, Aldershot: Ashgate, 2003, 171–86.

19 See the case of Buenos Aires Underground. D. Zunino Singh, 'The Circulation and Reception of Mobility Technologies: The Construction of Buenos Aires's Underground Railways' in S. Fari and M. Moraglio (eds), *Peripheral Flows: A Historical Perspective on Mobilities between Cores and Fringes*, Cambridge: Cambridge Scholars Publishing, 128–53.

20 M. Sheller and J. Urry, 'The City and the Car', *International Journal of Urban and Regional Research* 24, 4, 2000, 737–57.

21 M. Berman, *Todo lo sólido se desvanece en el aire*, Buenos Aires: Siglo XXI, 1989.

22 D. Harvey, *The Condition of Postmodernity: An Enquiry into the Origins of Cultural Change*, Oxford: Basil Blackwell, 1990.

23 D. Frisby, *Cityscapes of Modernity: Critical Explorations*, Cambridge: Polity Press, 2001.

24 J. Tomlinson, *The Culture of Speed: The Coming of Immediacy*, London: SAGE, 2007, 20.

25 Schivelbusch, *The Railway Journey*, 33–35.

26 Ibid., 61.

27 Giucci uses this term for his cultural history of the car. Guillermo Giucci, *La Vida Cultural del Automóvil. Rutas de la Modernidad Cinética*, Buenos Aires: Universidad Nacional de Quilmes, 2007.

28 Smethurst, *The Bicycle*, 97.

29 William Carter quoted by G. Mom, *Atlantic Automobilism: Emergence and Persistence of the Car, 1895–1940*, New York: Berghahn Books, 2015, 163.

30 E. Duffy, *Speed Handbook: Velocity, Pleasure, Modernism*, Durham, NC: Duke University Press, 2009.

31 Quoted by Duffy, *Speed Handbook*, 28.

32 Smethurst, *Bicycle*, 89.

33 C. Divall, 'Civilising Velocity: Masculinity and the Marketing of Britain's Passenger Trains, 1921–39', *Journal of Transport History*, 32, 2, 2011, 164–91, 166.

34 R. Sennett, *Flesh and Stone*, London: Faber, 1994, 256.

35 Ibid.

36 L. Millward, 'The Embodied Aerial Subject: Gendered Mobility in British Inter-War Air Tours', *Journal of Transport History* 29, 1, 2008, 5–22.

37 G. Simonsen, 'Accelerating Modernity: Time–Space Compression in the Wake of the Aeroplane', *Journal of Transport History* 26, 2, 2005, 98–117, 114.

38 Schivelbusch, *The Railway Journey*, 113–18.

39 Millward, 'The Embodied Aerial Subject', 8.

40 Smethurst, *The Bicycle*.

41 Giucci, *La Vida Cultural del Automóvil*.

42 Divall, 'Civilising Velocity'.

43 G. Mom, *Atlantic Automobilism*.

44 Georg Simmel quoted by W. Benjamin, *The Arcade Projects*, Cambridge, MA; London, Belknap Press, 1999, 433.

45 E. Martínez Estrada, *La Cabeza de Goliath Microscopía de Buenos Aires*, Madrid: Revista de Occidente, 1970.

46 Schivelbusch, *The Railway Journey*.

47 A. Freedman, 'Commuting Gazes: Schoolgirls, Salarymen, and Electric Trains in Tokyo', *Journal of Transport History* 23, 1, 2002, 23–36.

48 Tomlinson, *The Culture of Speed*.

49 G. Giucci, 'Caminar', in D. Zunino Singh et al. (eds), *Términos clave para los estudios de la movilidad en América Latina*, Buenos Aires: Biblios, 2018, 49–56.

50 Urry, *Mobilities*, 77–87.

51 C. Bryant, A. Burns, P. Readman (eds), *Walking Histories 1800–1914*, London: Palgrave Macmillan, 2016.

52 P. Andersson, 'The Walking Stick in the Nineteenth-Century City: Conflicting Ideals of Urban Walking', *Journal of Transport History* 39, 3, 2018, 275–91.

53 A. Sevilla-Buitrago, 'Central Park y la producción del espacio público: el uso de la ciudad y la regulación del comportamiento urbano en la historia', *Eure* 40, 121, 2014, 55–74.

54 Sennett, *Flesh and Stone*, 275–81.

55 F. Engels, *Condition of the Working Class in England*, Panther Edition, 2010 [1845].

56 Benjamin, *The Arcade Projects*.

57 For flâneuse see D. Parsons, *Streetwalking the Metropolis: Women, the City, and Modernity*, Oxford: Oxford University Press, 2000.

58 Bryant, Burns, Readman, *Walking Histories*, 6.

59 P. Norton, *Fighting Traffic: The Dawn of the Motor Age in the American City*, Cambridge, MA: MIT Press, 2008.

60 T. Errázuriz, 'When Walking Became Serious: Reshaping the Role of Pedestrians in Santiago, 1900–1931', *Journal of Transport History* 32, 1, 2011, 39–65, 40.

26

THE CULTURAL LIFE OF THE SENSES IN MODERNITY

Constance Classen and David Howes

The cultural history of the senses treats sensory experience as an historical formation.[1] Recognizing the senses to be constructed by culture, as well as given by physiology, it seeks to discover the ways in which particular historical institutions, practices and developments shaped and were shaped by the sensory life of the time.[2] This chapter takes a history-of-the-senses approach to the modern period in order to explore the sensory features of the age and bring out the developments that played a fundamental role in transforming popular perceptions.

The nineteenth century

The reek of class

The contrasts between the living conditions of the rich and poor were extreme in the nineteenth century and constituted one of the most notable sensory distinctions of the age. Queen Victoria's bedroom at Windsor Castle, for example, was a haven of sensory refinement:

> Elegant lounges were arranged around the apartment, covered with damask satin. A faint and delicious odor filled the room, and I seemed to sink in the soft and luxuriant carpets. Mystery, silence and enchantment prevailed … I walked to the bed and I found that there was an odor of cologne, attar of roses, and musk, proceeding from the counterpane, which was bordered with purple velvet and gold lace.[3]

The rubbish- and sewage-strewn slums of London provided a very different sensory atmosphere. There some fifty men, women and children might sleep together in a room like the one described below:

> All the beds in the apartment were placed upon the bare floor, and the mattresses were filled with dirty straw, which bulged out of their sides, or rugs, and gave

the room a close, fetid odor. For covering, there were dirty canvas quilts, made of the same stuff from which sails or potato sacks are fashioned ... By reposing on the bare, cold floor, the lodger saved a penny and got his bed for three-pence instead of four-pence.[4]

In contrast to the enchanted silence of the Queen's chamber, this bedroom of the poor was filled with 'a torrent of obscenity'. Instead of the fragrance of cologne, roses and musk which permeated the former, there rose up a 'hellish incense' from the filthy bodies massed together there.

However, such sensory differences were not just thought to be due to disparities in income; they were often considered to be innate in some mysterious way. Hence, the working-classes were not only considered to live in coarse, smelly environments, they were also thought to *be* coarse and smelly by the more privileged classes.[5] By shrinking in disgust from such 'dirty' and 'uncouth' people, the bourgeoisie expressed its fear of the sensory and social chaos they represented, and at the same time asserted its own supposedly superior refinement.[6]

Sensory stereotyping occurred not only with class, but also with race and gender. For example, white bodies (with class differences overlooked for the purpose of asserting a general racial typology) were said to have fine skins and mild odours, while black bodies were associated with coarse skins and pungent odours.[7] Given that coarse bodies were assumed to go with coarse minds, such perceptual paradigms helped to support social hierarchies based on race.[8]

As regards women, their social status as the 'lower' sex associated them with the 'lower' senses of touch, taste and smell. 'Women's work' consisted of homey tasks centred on those senses: cooking, cleaning, sewing and family care. Men, by contrast, were conceptualized as masters of sight and hearing: while women stayed at home, they went out to see and oversee the world and take part in public discourse. Women were further typed as soft and weak in comparison to 'hard', 'strong' men. Hence the two main arguments against women's suffrage were that women's duties were restricted to the home and that this was because they were too physically weak.[9] Incorporating such sensory symbolism lent power and seeming veracity to social and physical classifications. Such sensory profiling played a key role in shaping interactions among social groups, and determining their respective roles and supposed intellectual and physical capacities.

The smells, sounds and sights of the nineteenth-century city

The nineteenth-century city was notoriously malodorous. This was true not only of the working-places and homes of the poor, but also of many urban sites. Offices, for instance, smelled of mouldy walls and musty parchment, while courtrooms reeked of unwashed prisoners and decaying judicial wigs. The streets and waterways which traversed cities, in turn, often stank of refuse and waste.[10]

There was some respite for suffering noses. In malodorous Lisbon a traveller noted that 'the inhabitants scent their apartments by fumigating them with lavender and sugar ... and you can hardly pass through a street without crossing a current of this agreeable fragrance'.[11] In Madrid, aromas of cinnamon and chocolate from the abundant chocolate shops perfumed the air.[12] In general, however, such agreeable odours were but pockets of fragrance in the urban miasma. It was not until the Great Stinks of the latter half of the century, when hot, dry summers intensified urban stench in Europe and concerns rose over its potential danger to public health, that campaigns for more sanitary living conditions began to take effect. The result was the building of sewers and the institution of municipal garbage collection.[13]

The nineteenth century was also a noisy time. The rattling of carriages, the cries of vendors, the shouts of children, the bellowing of street organs and the barking of dogs penetrated deep into people's homes.[14] A muffling of the usual noises carried a special significance. Straw laid in the street to dull the sound of passing carriages meant that someone nearby was ill or dying.

> Straw in the street where I pass to-day
> Dulls the sound of the wheels and feet.
> 'Tis for a failing life they lay
> Straw in the street.[15]

Muffled bells were a sign of mourning, or a way of making public discontent heard. Antagonism to the War of 1812 in New England led to 'muffled bells, flags at half-mast, and public fasting'.[16] In Maria Edgeworth's novel *Patronage* muffled bells are used by villagers to express their disapproval of a change in landlords.[17]

The pealing of bells and the firing of guns and cannons, by contrast, were used to mark public celebrations. These sounds might also be employed to dissipate miasmas and malodours linked to disease – a variation of an old belief that the ringing of church bells would drive away demons.[18] While ceremonial bell-pealing and cannon-firing would continue to provide sonic expressions of public rejoicing in the twentieth century, their purificatory use declined in the latter nineteenth century with the rise of new theories of contagion.

The nineteenth-century city of smells and sounds was also, and increasingly, a city of sights. Viewing the city from above, often from a church tower, was popular with tourists and locals alike. Such a perspective expanded the power of vision over the city while decreasing the potency of smells and noises.[19] Painted panoramas provided another mode of surveying the world.[20] These painted scenarios complemented the other new visual offerings of the mid-nineteenth century, which included the unparalleled wealth of images produced by the photographic camera. Added to these new ways of imaging the world were the visual displays provided by newly established museums and world's fairs. Britain's Great Exhibition of 1851 astounded the visiting public with its sumptuous displays of mechanical inventions, artworks and products from around the empire and the world. Just as astounding, however, was the building in which the exhibition was housed, a glass edifice of unprecedented size which proclaimed the triumph of the unfettered eye.

An important technological development which added to the growing visualism of modern life was the invention of gaslight, followed at the end of the century by that of electric light. Installed on city streets and within buildings and homes, gaslight blurred the age-old sensory divide between the visuality of daytime and the tactility of night time. Previously, the sense of touch had furnished an essential means for orienting and occupying oneself in the dark of night. Darkness, in turn, had provided a cover for deviant tactilities, the work of the criminal and the prostitute. With gaslight the realm of touch shrank, as that of sight grew.

Rather than illuminating the city evenly, as was the case with sunlight, however, gaslight gave the city glowing highlights. It reversed the relative visibility of inside and outside, as the illuminated interiors of shops, cafés and houses came into bright prominence with nightfall. It also provided a new vision of the city as an immense tapestry of lights, a sight as fascinating as the panorama of the city during the day. 'It is especially at night that London should be seen'.[21]

Industrial perceptions

The technological and industrial developments of the century brought a mechanical dimension to life at the same time as they created new sensory worlds. For the working-classes, the most dramatic way in which this transition was experienced was within the machine-driven factory. The following fictional description of a cotton mill by Frances Trollope conveys the painful intensity of factory life where all sensations jar and child workers are slaves to the machine:

> The ceaseless whirring of a million hissing wheels, seizes on the tortured ear … The scents that reek around, from oil, tainted water, and human filth … render the act of breathing a process of difficulty, disgust, and pain. All this is terrible. But what the eye brings home to the heart of those, who look round upon the horrid earthly hell, is enough to make it all forgotten … the dirty, ragged, miserable crew … the overlookers, strap in hand, on the alert; the whirling spindles urging the little slaves who waited on them, to movements as unceasing as their own.[22]

The experiential antithesis to the factory was provided by the department store, a commercial cornucopia of plenty which appeared on the scene in the latter half of the century. The factory was a site of mass production, the department store of mass consumption, and if the former was a hell for the senses, the latter was described as a paradise. It was not only the profusion of merchandise within the store that dazzled – the cascades of silk, the rainbows of ribbons – but also the amenities – restaurants, concert halls, reading rooms – together with the palatial architecture. Climbing the great curving staircase in the skylighted atrium of the Bon Marché in Paris, late nineteenth-century shoppers could feel as though they were ascending the rings of a consumer heaven (see Figures 26.1 and 26.2). The fantasy worlds of sensory plenty depicted in earlier visions of paradise or in tales of the imaginary land of Cockaigne seemed to take form and substance in the department store.

Arguably, however, the department store, like the factory, was dominated by a mechanical sensibility, in which clerks and customers functioned as cogs for moving merchandise. 'They were all nothing but the wheels, turned round by the immense machine', wrote Zola of the people working in his fictional department store *Au Bonheur des Dames*.[23] Whether this analogy was valid or not, the fact that many perceived it to be so testifies to the power of the assembly-line as a new model for framing the sensations of modern life.

Figure 26.1   The Heaven of the Fixed Stars. Wood engraving after Gustave Doré.

Granger/Bridgeman Images.

Another way in which perception was mechanized was through the railway experience. Railway travel created a new sense of visual detachment, for scenes whirled
by without travellers having any possibility of interacting with them. In the train,
as in the factory, one subjected oneself to mechanical rhythms and requirements –
there was no stopping until the machine stopped. However, railway travel also helped
stimulate concerns over the living conditions of the poor as previously little-seen
working-class districts came under the view of passengers.

Trains provided an overland means for the rapid, mass transportation of products.
This brought a greater variety of goods and sensations into local stores and markets. It further enabled certain industries, such as dairies and slaughterhouses, which
had previously often been located within cities, to be removed to the outskirts and
thereby erased from urban experience. Milk and meat now seemed to many to simply
arrive by train, rather than by means of animal bodies. Like the products of the factory, and like water, piped into modern homes, they became the stuff of technology.

Figure 26.2   The New Consumer Heaven: Le Bon Marché by Fréderic Lix, from *Le Monde Illustre,* c.1875 (engraving).

Private Collection/Bridgeman Images.

The machine carried, the machine clothed and the machine fed. It was inhuman yet strangely maternal. In the late nineteenth century, the mechanical model would even come to be applied to child-rearing, with mothers advised to keep their children to strict schedules and to avoid any non-functional touching.[24]

Time itself became one more natural material, an almost tactile substance, to be subjected to mechanical control. Standardized 'railway time', required for train schedules, replaced local times based on the rising and setting of the sun. Gaslight turned night into an artificial day. Photography gave permanence to ephemeral perceptions. Museums transformed distant times and places into artefactual exhibits. Assembly-lines demonstrated that the same product could be endlessly reproduced and hence exist in many places at once. In *The Communist Manifesto*, Marx and Engels claimed that capitalism caused 'all that was solid to melt into air' by transforming labour and goods into the irreality of 'capital'.[25] With their new sense of power over time (and space), however, the masters of industrial technologies might also be said to have busied themselves with the reverse accomplishment: solidifying perceptions that had previously seemed as elusive as air.

The civil senses

The mechanization of sensation in modernity was central to the conceptualization of the state system. If the state was to operate as a manageable and productive machine, then a certain social and physical standardization of the population was required. Efficient machines need made-to-measure parts. In the army this was promoted through the practice of the drill, which took individuals with disparate corporeal practices and trained them to perform the same actions at the same time on command. Drilling attained such widespread popularity in the nineteenth century that it came to form part of the routine of many social institutions, from schools to churches and from workers' organizations to prisons. Surrendering one's desire for independent movement to participate in the power of a co-ordinated social machine held great appeal in an age awed by mechanical might and precision, and also increasingly unnerved by a sense of fragmented individualism.[26]

Not only the drill, but also many aspects of life in state institutions fostered a sense of mechanical regularity and order: the production lines of factories, the rows of desks in classrooms, of benches in prison workrooms, or even of displays in museums, the meticulous ordering of time and the repetitious monotony of labour – whether assembling products in the factory, tracing letters at school or peeling apart tarry strands of oakum in prison. As such institutions encompassed ever greater numbers of citizens in the nineteenth century, particularly after schooling became compulsory, virtually no one remained untouched by the new social ordering.

As regards the senses, in the army and the factory, as in the school, the prison and the museum, the sense of touch was disciplined, the sense of smell suppressed, the sense of taste controlled, the sense of hearing attuned to directives and the sense of sight habituated to perceiving the world as an assemblage of units. Perhaps the most important of these labours as regards sight was the process of becoming literate. The printed page (along with the press that produced it) has been seen by Marshall Mc-Luhan and others as offering a formative model for the modern state. In print the fluidity of speech – and by analogy of social life – was broken down into discrete units – typed letters – which were than regrouped in neat, silent and static rows.[27] The comparison with the discrete but uniform bodies of children sitting in rows in classrooms or the uniformed bodies of prisoners in silent rows on work benches – all legible, as it were, to the watching eyes of their supervisors – is striking. Mastering the printed page required intensive visual training – 'eye drill', as it might be called – and, like state institutions themselves, fostered a gaze that dissected and reassembled. Instruction in mathematics, also fundamental to the educational system, would have similarly supported a vision of the world as an assemblage of units rather than a seamless whole.

Through the influence of modernizing elites, as well as that of transnational commerce, conquest and colonization, these new social and sensory models and the institutions and industrial systems that supported them spread throughout the globe.

This led to a certain homogenization of perception across cultures. Every modern nation, it seemed, required factories, railways, armies, schools, prisons and museums, along with standardized modes for demarcating time and space. Every modern nation also needed mass media – first print, then radio and film – to disseminate the sights, sounds and values of modernity, to encourage citizens to speak a common language and to create common modes of framing experience. The European hierarchy of the senses, with sight and hearing associated with cognition and placed above and apart from the so-called lower senses, was likewise exported abroad where it contributed to marginalizing divergent local sensory practices and values.

The homogenization of sensory worlds was further assisted by a certain blurring of social categories. This process, which likewise came to be associated with modernization and progress, helped to create one social body – 'the people' – out of many heterogeneous groups. Slavery was abolished in most countries over the course of the century. The working-class gained improved wages and working conditions. Women were gradually and grudgingly accepted in a number of previously exclusively male spheres. Though marked social and sensory differences still existed, the result of these various developments would be more of a shared perceptual life.

The twentieth century

The senses at war

The twentieth century began with a sense of a growing global culture; new modes of communication and transportation were bringing nations closer and transnational migration was spreading family ties across countries and giving an international flavour to many cities. Although global unity might have seemed to shimmer on the horizon, however, the second decade of the century instead saw the Western world plunged into a global war: World War I. Like all wars, this war was an assault on the senses; the difference was that new technologies and techniques of warfare employed during the First World War resulted in a barrage of new sensory experiences.

The crucial role of modern technology in the warfare of the period, and the salience of machine and factory metaphors for combat, meant that war became an *industrial* experience. As in the factory, the emphasis was on co-ordinated movement and functionality. Wristwatches were issued to officers in order to ensure that the war ran like clockwork. Drab, practical uniforms replaced the colourful dress of nineteenth-century soldiers. Machine-guns automated the killing process and drove soldiers from the battlefield into trenches.

In fact, it was trench warfare in particular that dominated soldiers' sensory impressions of the First World War. The trenches inverted the traditions and practices of ordinary life. They replaced living above ground with living underground – making the modern warrior the lowly antithesis to the high-riding knight of old. They replaced being active during the day with being active at night. The senses themselves changed their relative positions of importance, as attending to sights was replaced by attending to sounds. One French combatant noted in this regard: 'The darkness is a huge mass: you seem to be moving through a yielding substance; sight is a superfluous sense. Your whole being is concentrated on the faculty of hearing'.[28] Whatever views might be had from the trenches were circumscribed views through loopholes or periscopes, or else cautious glances over the top.

Smell, which was often relegated to the background of consciousness during peacetime, shot to the fore in the trenches, with their sickening odours of decaying corpses and ill and unwashed bodies. In his novel *Verdun* Jules Romains described this malodour as almost tangible: 'Every kind of foul vapour, everything least acceptable to nose and lungs, seemed to have been rolled and churned together into a substance just not heavy enough to clutch with [one's] hands'.[29]

The experience from below with its circumscribed sights and its intense sounds, smells and tactile sensations contrasted with the aerial vista of the fighter pilot, which turned battlefields and cities into inaudible, inodorate and intangible panoramas. The German pilot, Ernst Boehme, noted how unreal it seemed to look down on soundless explosions when flying over the front.[30] Rather than attending to sounds, the fighter pilot needed to keep his target in view at all times.

The taste of the war, in turn, was the novel one of tinned food. At first this inno-vation was resisted by many soldiers because of its metallic flavour and its apparent transformation of food into an industrial product. However, eventually soldiers grew accustomed to dining out of a tin and even enjoyed the novelty of eating fruits and vegetables out of season. When the war was over and they returned home such sol-diers helped to stimulate a civilian demand for tinned foods.[31]

The sensory effects of the war, in fact, reverberated throughout society in ways too numerous to discuss here. However, one widespread sensation produced by the conflict was that of repulsion towards warfare. In 1820, when warring was often at-tributed positive virtues, Hegel wrote: 'Just as the blowing of the winds preserves the sea from the foulness which would result from a continual calm, so also corruption would result for peoples under continual or indeed "perpetual" peace'.[32] Even after all the devastating wars of the nineteenth century, the English poet Rupert Brooke could enthusiastically describe soldiers going to war in 1914 as 'swimmers into clean-ness leaping'.[33] In the trenches, however, the 'fresh wind' of war turned out to be a fetid swamp and leaping into 'cleanness' was transformed into wallowing in mud. After the First World War, in the minds of many, war became sensorially and socially foul. Though such feelings may have been pushed aside during the Second World War, war nonetheless became something to be looked on with dread, rather than anticipated with enthusiasm.

The automobile and the airplane

The twentieth century was quickly identified as an age of speed by modernist writers and artists, and at the centre of this whirlwind age was the automobile.[34] The sensory impact of the automobile was not limited to the exhilarating sensation of velocity, however, but included a full range of perceptions. As the Dadaist Guillermo de Torre exclaimed in his poem 'At the Steering Wheel' (*Al Volante*), 'the car is a convex bow that shoots insatiable trajectories … the windshield multiplies our eyes … and the wind liquefies sounds'.[35]

The automobile not only transformed twentieth-century perceptions, it also fos-tered new ways of life and new material worlds. With the increase in car ownership, city streets became more places of passage for automobiles than paths for pedestrians. Highways cut through or bypassed old towns and neighbourhoods, spawning their own network of gas stations, diners, motels and strip malls. Suburbs sprang up in locations once deemed too distant for commuting to urban centres but now seen as only a short drive away. Attached or underground garages enabled drivers to move from car interior to house or building interior without ever stepping outside. As a result, the outdoor world became increasingly foreign to city dwellers – either something one avoided by being in a car or a place one went to occasionally for a change of scene by travelling in a car.

Coupled with the automobile as a marvel of modern transportation, the airplane also transformed people's ways of sensing. Its direct sensory and social impact was not as widespread as that of the automobile. Very few people had private airplanes and, until the latter part of the century, the high cost of flying made it an elite mode of transportation, the prerogative of businessmen, government officials and the vagabond socialites who came to be known as 'the jet set'. However, the airplane's impact on the imagination was enormous. 'Of all the agencies … that made the average man of 1925 intellectually different from [one] of 1900, by far the greatest was the sight of a human being in an airplane', wrote the American journalist Mark Sullivan in 1935.[36]

The airplane freed the human sensorium from earthbound sensations. Blue became the dominant colour, the coldness of high altitude the dominant feeling and the roar of the engine the dominant sound (the onomatopoeic word 'zoom' was coined to express the sound and speed of an airplane as it soared into the sky). Flight provided astounding bird's-eye – or God's-eye – views of the world. Looking down on earth from a plane made the geographic borders dividing countries seem insignificant – there were no borders in the sky. It was, indeed, hoped by many that 'with the new aerial age will come a new internationalism' as people flew from one country to another, dissolving physical and cultural barriers.[37]

It was not only the ability of planes to leave the earth that riveted the twentieth-century imagination, but also their ability to drop things on earth – in particular, explosives. Many parts of the world, beginning with Spain during the civil war, experienced the devastation produced by aerial bombing during this century. The atomic bomb, developed in the United States during World War II and 'harnessing the basic power of the universe', as President Truman put it,[38] vastly intensified the destructive power of aerial bombing. The sudden transformation of the city of Hiroshima into a pile of rubble after an atomic bomb had been dropped on it by one single airplane made it clear that the god-like power of modern technology could destroy, as well as enhance, life. The picture of the giant mushroom cloud produced by the detonation of an atomic bomb became one of the most powerful and disturbing images of the latter part of the century. The purely visual nature of the picture made it all the eerier because its silence seemed to convey a silencing of voices and an annihilation of listeners.

The military use of the airplane tarnished its image as an agent for social transformation. The final blow to the notion of the airplane elevating its passengers above worldly cares and conflicts came not in the twentieth century, however, but in 2001, when four American passenger planes were hijacked by terrorists and used as weapons of mass destruction. The era of the airplane as otherworldly was over.

The skyscraper and the bungalow

The desire to rise above the ground which produced the airplane manifested itself architecturally in the skyscraper. Made possible by advances in engineering and the invention of the elevator, skyscrapers were erected in major cities around the world from the 1930s on. In city centres where land was limited and expensive, it made sense to build upwards rather than outwards, to house people in the sky, rather than on the ground. However, skyscrapers were not only monuments to efficiency, they were also emblems of corporate and urban might and even sublimity – for their great height aroused the feelings of awe evoked in previous centuries by soaring cathedral spires. The majesty of the skyscraper did not point to the power of God, however, but rather to human ingenuity.[39] Standing up straight and tall like giants, skyscrapers were themselves figurative humans, proudly displaying themselves as conquerors of the landscape.

The sensory impact of skyscrapers was experienced corporeally through their looming presence on city streets and the upward movement of their elevators, but it was their visual effects, the views of and from skyscrapers, that had the most impact. Seen from a distance, a skyline of skyscrapers presented the city as a site of power and wonder. And while 'close up there are things that are not very comforting: littered streets, corner drug deals, broken down tenements', by keeping eyes trained upwards, skyscrapers diverted the senses from the often far-less attractive scenario of the ground environment.[40] The view *from* the skyscraper, in turn, minimized the significance of the sensory experiences of life on the ground as it maximized the power of sight to encompass and survey.

It was not just its height that gave the skyscraper its particular visual potency, but also its lack of ornamentation. The sleek, often reflective, facade of the skyscraper seemed to transform the building into pure presence. The skyscraper's lack of ornamentation also suggested that the work undertaken in such a building would be highly functional, and even ruthless, with no deviations from the prescribed course. The main use of the skyscraper was as a corporate office building and therefore its design mimicked the supposedly no-nonsense office work that took place inside, and that ideally resulted in a commercial dominance equivalent to the architectural dominance of the building. Furthermore, just as the skyscraper's facade lacked distinguishing features, so, one might assume, did the lives of workers toiling inside: each individual simply contributed to the monumental effect of the whole. As skyscrapers were the most prominent buildings in the big city, the big city itself became a symbol of faceless corporate power and functionalism.

The counterpart to the urban skyscraper in many countries was the suburban bungalow. Imported from India and redesigned by the British in the early century, the low-profile, open-layout bungalow went on to gain popularity around the world.[41] The bungalow captured the spirit of the time by offering a more informal space for family living that was suggestive of the easier-going social relations of the new century. The lawn that stretched out in front of the house and the roomy yard behind added a relaxing, natural aspect, along with the possibility of outdoor cooking – even swimming in a pool if the budget allowed – which contributed to the bungalow's 'vacation home' atmosphere and its cultural value as an antidote to the pressures and formalities of city life.

Figure 26.3   The sensory regularity of suburbia: Levittown, USA. Public domain.

However, some viewed the expanding tracts of bungalows with dismay (see Figure 26.3). The social historian Lewis Mumford condemned such suburbs as

> a multitude of uniform, unidentifiable houses, lined up inflexibly, at uniform distances, on uniform roads, in a treeless communal waste, inhabited by people of the same class, the same income, the same age group, witnessing the same television programs, eating the same tasteless pre-fabricated foods, from the same freezers, conforming in every outward and inward respect to a common mold.[42]

As the century progressed, women, in their role as housewives, especially came to be seen as the 'victims' of suburban monotony. While suburban men drove off every weekday to their jobs in the city, women remained ensconced in the family bungalow. New labour-saving devices such as vacuum cleaners and washing machines meant that the women left at home had more free time but, stuck in the suburbs as they were, relatively few possibilities for creative action or mental stimulation. In 1963, Betty Friedan's *The Feminine Mystique* detailed the plight of the 'trapped' housewife by depicting her supposedly dull sensory life:

> Each suburban wife struggled with her [dissatisfaction] alone. As she made the beds, shopped for groceries, made slipcover material, ate peanut butter sandwiches with her children, chauffeured Cub Scouts and Brownies, lay beside her husband at night – she was afraid to ask even of herself the silent question – 'Is this all?'[43]

The bungalow, which had once represented freedom, now seemed to be a prison. The time, it seemed, had come for women's liberation.

The camera and the screen

In the twentieth century, photography, previously the domain of professionals, became a hobby that anyone could practise with the aid of an inexpensive compact camera and a photo-developing service. Every middle-class family could have albums filled with snapshots (first black-and-white and then colour) of family celebrations and vacations. As a key means of embodying personal history, the family photo album transformed the past into a series of visual snapshots.

Home photography supplemented the multiplicity of photographs in magazines, newspapers and books. The realistic quality of these images added to their impact. Unlike illustrations, they appeared to offer unmediated visual access to the people and scenes they represented and thus transform their viewers into eyewitnesses. By the end of the century, the photograph had in some ways become more 'real' than the real thing, as photographs and films posted on the Internet began to acquire a life and value of their own.[44]

The function of the camera in modern society, however, was not only to record significant people and places, to capture 'slice-of-life' moments or to showcase desirable merchandise. It was also to survey. Already in World War I cameras, carried aloft on airplanes, were put to the service of military reconnaissance. Over the course of the century the camera became essential to peacetime surveillance as well. Introduced in the 1970s, video surveillance of public spaces as a form of social control was widespread by the century's close:

> Today, the ubiquitous video 'security' camera stares blankly at us in apartment buildings, department and convenience stores, gas stations, libraries, parking garages, automated banking outlets, buses, and elevators. No matter where you live you are likely to encounter cameras; some places simply bristle with them.[45]

Even in the sky, cameras mounted on satellites circled the Earth, capturing images which were viewed down on the ground. The world had never been so watched. 'Has the camera replaced the eye of God?' asked John Berger in 1978.[46]

Turning from the camera to the screen, cinema, the most popular form of entertainment in the first half of the century, further contributed to the optical orientation of the age. Cinema seemingly magnified the power of sight by presenting larger-than-life images. At the same time, techniques of filming and editing – close-ups, slow motion, camera angles, abrupt changes of scene – trained movie audiences in radically new ways of seeing and gave a whole new interest to being a spectator. The fact that movies were shown in a dark theatre – or 'picture palace' – in which people sat motionless and (ideally) silent enhanced their sensorial power. While the fantasy fare of cinema provided an 'escape' from the tedium and restrictions of everyday life, it also taught people to seek release only though their eyes, ears and imaginations, while not moving an inch. The cinema audience seemed like a collection of eyes all fixed on one point.

With the invention of television in the mid-twentieth century, however, a new form of leisure viewing emerged. Television shows had many of the same traits as the movies shown at the cinema, but they appeared on a small screen and were intended for private viewing in the home. Watching television was not something one went out to do, but something one stayed in to do. In 1938 the British novelist Elizabeth Bowen gave as one of her reasons for enjoying the cinema: 'I like sitting in a packed crowd in the dark, among hundreds riveted on the same thing'.[47] Millions of television viewers might all be 'riveted on the same thing' but they were no longer sitting together in a packed crowd. Twentieth-century spectatorship changed from being communal to being largely familial or individualist.

This emphasis on seeing at the expense of other, more traditional, forms of sensory engagement was disturbing to many. Parents worried that their children were spending too much time watching television and not enough playing outside. Social critics feared that the twentieth century's obsession with visual surfaces signalled an ailing and alienated society. 'From television to newspapers, from advertising to all sorts of mercantile epiphanies, our society is characterized by a cancerous growth of vision, measuring everything by its ability to show or be shown, and transmuting communication into a visual journey', proclaimed the French philosopher Michel de Certeau.[48] And then came the personal computer and the Internet, which turned even greater numbers of people into 'hypervisualists', constantly scanning images and texts on a screen. However, the fact that images and texts could be created and transmitted, as well as viewed, on the Internet meant that the new medium of the computer did not simply continue the sensory trajectory of the cinema and television, but rather fostered a new sensory dynamic which would await the next century to disclose its social effects.

Plastic and pollution

The substance that characterized the physical world of the twentieth century and provided a material base for much of its cultural expression was plastic. The term plastic, in fact, covers a variety of synthetic or semi-synthetic substances, from the celluloid used in film and cheap jewellery to the vinyls employed in records, raincoats and exterior siding. However, plastic became the umbrella term for all these creations of the chemical industry. Technical advances resulted in plastics that were amazingly durable, as well as low cost. 'Plastic is forever', touted one industry pioneer, 'and a lot cheaper than diamonds'.[49]

Over the course of the century the material became a familiar component of ordinary life. A family celebrating Christmas in the United States in the 1970s, for example, might have a plastic Christmas tree decorated with plastic ornaments and featuring plastic Barbie dolls and Lego blocks as presents. In a famous line from the 1967 movie *The Graduate*, a recent college graduate who is uncertain about his future is told by his businessman father: 'I want to say one word to you. Just one word … There's a great future in plastics. Think about it'.[50]

Like its material uses, the sensory properties of plastic were multiple. Easy to shape, colour and texture, plastic might approximate anything. Because of its mutability, plastic engendered a notion of the malleability of the material world. The French philosopher Roland Barthes wrote of plastic in the 1960s that it embodied 'the very idea of … infinite transformation'.[51] Plastic's mutability coincided with twentieth-century desires to reshape not only the physical environment, but also society and even the human body through cosmetic and surgical procedures. Limits set by nature or by custom no longer seemed to hold in a plastic world. Anything could take on a new form.

While plastic was embraced by the twentieth century for its malleability and low cost, it was despised (at least by the educated classes) for its 'inauthenticity'. Over the course of the century, in fact, the word plastic came to be a synonym for fake. Social critics saw plastic as a sign and symptom of a society in which simulations had a greater appeal than reality.

Within the context of a material culture that seemed increasingly artificial, the natural world acquired a new value as a place and source of authenticity, where one could experience the 'real' thing. The sights and sounds and scents of nature were extolled as both physically and spiritually refreshing. This desire for natural experiences was bolstered by the dramatic growth in urban populations during the century. Trips to the countryside and camping became popular ways for urbanites to replenish their senses and spirits through immersion in natural settings, especially after workers won the right to paid vacation time in many countries.[52]

At the same time as the pure air and green vistas of the wilderness were acquiring a new value for city dwellers, however, an awareness developed of how the natural world was being depleted and polluted by industrialization and technological development.[53] The lumber industry was devastating forests, factory smoke and automobile exhaust were poisoning the air, chemical waste was contaminating rivers, nuclear power created radioactive by-products and mass production was resulting in mass garbage. All the wondrous inventions and sensations of modernity, it seemed, had negative counterparts in environmental degradation and sensory malaise. In return for the thrill of speeding in an automobile, one breathed air tainted with smog. One 'paid' for the spectacle of electric light by giving up the view of the night sky. That plastic lasted 'forever' no longer seemed such a good thing when that plastic was piling up in landfills and creating vast 'garbage patches' in the ocean.

The natural world had once been conceptualized as immensely powerful with limitless resources, but by the last decades of the century this view was seriously challenged. It was not only accounts and experiences of the proliferation of garbage, smog, oil-spills and deforestation that led to a change in attitude, however. The view from above provided by airplanes and, more dramatically, space ships contributed greatly to the perception of the Earth as bounded and frail. Astronaut Russell Schweickhart, who spent ten days in orbit in 1969, observed that from space the Earth appeared 'so small and so fragile and such a precious little spot in the universe'.[54] These words captured the sentiments of many who saw, or saw a picture of, the Earth looking like a lone, blue balloon floating in a vast dark sky. The new conceptualization of the natural world as vulnerable and requiring human protection, therefore, was partly grounded in an actual view of the world.

The counterculture

The environmental movement that flourished in the second half of the twentieth century was part of a larger complex of social and political developments which challenged conventional modes of thinking about and interacting with the world. These included decolonization, feminism, civil rights movements and anti-war protests. For the older generation, born in the early decades of the century, it often seemed as though society was being turned on its head, with those who were previously 'invisible', 'silent' and subordinate now insisting on being seen and heard and treated as equals.

'Counterculture' was the term often used to refer to the broad, youth-centred movement in the 1960s and 70s which supported new social values, while at the same time rejecting the conventional, middle-class way of life, summarized by one activist, Robert Alter, in 1972 as 'a fresh-frozen life in some prepackaged suburb, Howard Johnson's on Sundays, Disneyland vacations, the cut-rate American dream of happiness out of an aerosol can'.[55] In opposition to this 'synthetic substitute for reality', people were urged to 'reach out to each other with noises/gestures/visions to create a new and common reality', as a flier distributed by one countercultural group put it.[56]

The sensory manifestations of this quest for an alternative way of life were numerous. One of the most visible everyday signs of countercultural trends concerned changes in hairstyles and dress. Long, loose hair, t-shirts, jeans, mini-skirts and bright 'psychedelic' colours all signalled a rebellion against the more controlled and formal modes of self-presentation of previous decades and, more broadly, a rejection of conventional social roles and values. Unisex clothing and hairstyles were often taken by the mainstream to represent an unsettling loss of gender distinctions: women apparently wanted to look and act 'like men', and men apparently wanted to look and act 'like women'. Bare feet, in turn, expressed a desire for a greater closeness with nature.

This brings us to the issue of tactile values. The counterculture asserted that the social role of the police and the military was not only to protect and defend, but also to coerce and suppress. 'Police brutality' became a widely discussed public issue. The pacifist approach adopted by many social reformers and widely associated with the counterculture, by contrast, implied an unwillingness to employ aggressive forms of touch to dominate others. One popular form of social protest of the time, the sit-in, involved the physical occupation of a site. This tactic would result in the protest's opponents taking on the role of aggressors when they resorted to tactile force to clear the site. The sit-in also had the attraction of simplicity – to protest, all one needed to do was to sit. Civil rights marches, in turn, made visible and audible the presence of supressed groups within society, at the same time as they fostered tactile, hand-in-hand solidarity among those marginalized (see Figure 26.4).

Non-violent actions such as sit-ins and marches were not the only form in which the desire for social change found expression, however. In the United States the 1960s were marked by race riots in major cities. Mass riots by protesting students and workers, notably the 1968 riots in France, shook many other countries. A number of countercultural groups began with non-violent protests but, inspired by Marxist ideology and fired by youthful energy and idealism, ended up espousing armed revolution as the only means of overthrowing the political, business and military alliances which maintained the status quo. The social turmoil of the time – and its extensive media reporting – hence brought the politics of touch to the fore of public consciousness.

The counterculture's questioning of the social institutions of marriage and the nuclear family and its experimentation with communal living and 'free love' (facilitated

Figure 26.4   Walking hand in hand: the Civil Rights March on Washington. U.S. National
Archives and Records Administration/Wikimedia Commons.

by the invention of the birth-control pill) brought touch to the fore of public consciousness in another way. At the time, such practices were often seen as evidence
of the moral and corporeal laxity of contemporary youth. Blame was frequently
placed on the mid-century shift in child-rearing practices which had replaced the
strict, no-cuddling, techniques advocated in the early decades of the century with
an approach mandating tender, hands-on care. The child-rearing 'bible' by Benjamin
Spock, *Baby and Child Care*, had helped revolutionize child-rearing by urging parents
to hug their children, feed them when they were hungry and refrain from corporal
punishment.[57] The result, some said, was a generation of soft, self-indulgent 'flower
children' who could not be counted on to discipline their bodies, uphold social values
or defend their country. The debate over tough or tender touch in child-rearing
continued to the end of the century. However, generally the tender approach won
out, with the age-old tradition of corporal punishment in schools, for example, being
banned in many countries in the last decades of the century. And while communal living did not catch on, the 'sexual revolution' supported by the counterculture
ultimately led to widespread changes in public attitudes towards sexuality.

Turning to the sense of taste, this was primarily affected by the counterculture's
desire for a more 'spiritual', 'natural', 'environmentally sound' and 'ethical' diet. Synthetic, industrially produced foods were rejected (at least in theory) in favour of
natural or organic foods, which were touted as both healthier and more flavourful.
Perhaps the defining taste of the movement was that of granola, a mixture of oats,
nuts and dried fruit, which made for a nutritious and 'natural' snack.

During this period vegetarianism, which challenged the values of the 'establishment' at the basic level of food production and consumption, emerged as a popular countercultural diet. Francis Moore Lappé's *Diet for a Small Planet* (1971) argued convincingly that meat-eating supported a wasteful use of natural resources. Others saw clear parallels between the exploitation of women and workers and the exploitation of animals for food. Feminist vegetarian groups were founded. Struck by the miserable conditions of farm animals, the prominent advocate for farmworkers' rights, Cesar Chavez, became a vegetarian. In a few decades vegetarianism went from being regarded as a bizarre fad or cult practice with dangerous health consequences to being tenuously accepted as a healthy and morally defensible alternative to a meat-based diet. Tellingly, when the 1998 edition of *Baby and Child Care* advocated a vegan diet for children, it raised some eyebrows but did not cause much of a stir.[58]

The sensory heart of the counterculture was music. The song 'We Shall Overcome' was sung by civil rights marchers, anti-war protesters and striking farmworkers, with the line, 'We'll walk hand in hand' expressing the sense of solidarity experienced by agitators for reform. While protest songs and folk music played an important role in giving a musical voice to the counterculture, it was rock music that had the most impact. This was not only, or even primarily, because many rock musicians addressed social issues or made countercultural statements in their songs. It was, rather, the music itself which in multifold ways appeared to subvert conventional social mores. Its strong beat gave momentum to desires for social change or, at least, for excitement. Its loudness provided an immersive environment and also expressed the demand of dissatisfied youth to be heard. The simple structure of most pieces, their frequent authorship by members of the band performing them, as well as the fact that many performers were not trained musicians or singers gave rock music the aura of authenticity that the counterculture demanded. Rock musicians were no slick, 'synthetic' crooners performing cover songs. And although rock musicians were overwhelmingly white, by fusing elements from African American and European musical traditions, their music served as a model for a racially integrated society.

Eventually, in the 1980s, the counterculture lost momentum. On the one hand, mainstream society eventually incorporated many of the changes advocated by the movement (particularly as the youth of the 1960s and 70s grew older and acquired positions of authority). On the other hand, most supporters of the counterculture turned out to be not all that radical in their aspirations. Some of the sensory signs and practices of the counterculture, such as psychedelic art, walking barefoot and the scent of patchouli, became dated. Others, such as meditation and alternative medicines – crystal therapy, therapeutic touch, aromatherapy – became part of the New Age movement. Yet others, such as yoga and vegetarianism, acquired increasing mainstream recognition.

Rock music continued to be popular to the end of the century. However, music television transformed it into a media spectacle, with a new emphasis on accompanying visuals. The Walkman, a portable audio cassette player with headphones, privatized the experience of music, with users listening to their personal favourites rather than tuning in to the mass broadcasts of a radio station.[59]

Unlike the popular music of the 1960s and 70s, which was closely associated with dance, the new music, heard through a portable Walkman, accompanied ordinary, everyday movement – walking, shopping, riding a bus. Dance itself declined as a recreational activity and mode of self-expression in the 1990s. In the early 70s Susan Sontag wrote that photography had become almost as popular a pastime as dancing.[60] With the spread of digital cameras and the salience of Internet imagery, by the end of the twentieth century it had become far more popular. Collective culture itself was in the process of becoming digital, as computer networks made new, long-distance and disembodied modes of connectedness possible. As for the senses, their ultimate destination, a destination for which they had been prepared by modernity's succession of technological 'wonders', seemed to be the glowing virtual reality of cyberspace.

Notes

1 This chapter is derived from the introduction to *A Cultural History of the Senses in the Age of Empire* by Constance Classen (2014) and the introduction to *A Cultural History of the Senses in the Modern Age* by David Howes (2014).
2 See C. Classen, 'The Senses', in P. Stearns (ed.), *Encyclopedia of European Social History*, vol. IV, New York: Charles Scribner's Sons, 2001; D. Howes and C. Classen, *Ways of Sensing: Understanding the Senses in Society*, London: Routledge, 2013.
3 D.J. Kirwan, *Palace and Hovel: Or, Phases of London Life*, Hartford, CT: Belknap & Bliss, 563–4.
4 Kirwan, *Palace and Hovel*, 621.
5 C. Classen, D. Howes and A. Synnott, *Aroma: The Cultural History of Smell*, London: Routledge, 1994, 82.
6 See P. Stallybrassr and A. White, *The Politics and Poetics of Transgression*, London: Methuen & Co., 1986, 139.
7 J.L. Stewart, *History and Philosophy of Creation and the Human Race*, Cincinnati, OH: Applegate & Company, 1866, 120–1.
8 M.M. Smith, *How Race Is Made: Slavery, Segregation, and the Senses*, Chapel Hill, NC: University of North Carolina Press, 2009.
9 Howes and Classen, *Ways of Sensing*, 76–7.
10 A. Corbin, *The Foul and the Fragrant: Odor and the French Social Imagination*, trans. M.L. Kochan, Roy Porter, Christopher Prendergast, Cambridge, MA: Harvard University Press, 1986; C. Classen, 'The Deodorized City: Battling Urban Stench in the Nineteenth Century', in M. Zardini (ed.), *Sense of the City: An Alternate Approach to Urbanism*, Montreal, QC: Canadian Centre for Architecture and Lars Müller Publishers, 2005.
11 'Lisbon in the Years 1821, 1822, and 1823', *Quarterly Review* Vol. XXXI, 1825, 381.
12 H.D. Inglis, *Spain in 1830*, Volume I. London: Whittaker, Treacher, and Co., 1831, 74.
13 See D. Barnes, *The Great Stink of Paris and the Nineteenth-Century Struggle Against Filth and Germs*, Baltimore, MD: The Johns Hopkins University Press, 2006.
14 J. Picker, *Victorian Soundscapes*, Oxford: Oxford University Press, 2003.
15 A. Levy, *A London Plane Tree and Other Verse*, London: T. Fisher Unwin, 1889, 25.
16 D.M. Kennedy and L. Cohen, *The American Pageant*, Volume 1, Boston, MA: Wadsworth, 2012, 221.
17 M. Edgeworth, *Patronage*, London: Dent, 1893, 155.
18 A. Corbin, *Village Bells: Sound and Meaning in the Nineteenth-Century French Countryside*, trans. M. Thom, New York: Colombia University Press, 1998, 101.
19 C.J. Ferguson, 'Inventing the Modern City: Urban Culture and Ideas in Britain, 1780–1980', Ph.D. Dissertation, Indiana University, 2008, ch. 4.

20 See A. Griffiths, *Shivers Down Your Spine: Cinema. Museums, and the Immersive View*, New York: Columbia University Press, 2008, ch. 2.

21 Cited in L. Nead, *Victorian Babylon: People, Streets and Images in Nineteenth-Century London*, London: Yale University Press, 2005, 88.

22 Cited in J.R. Simmons Jr. (ed.), *Factory Lives: Four Nineteenth-Century Working Class Autobiographies*, Peterborough, ON: Broadview Press, 2007, 423.

23 E. Zola, *The Ladies' Paradise*, London: Vizetelly & Co, 1886, 119; see, however, M. Nava, *Visceral Cosmopolitanism: Gender, Culture and the Normalisation of Difference*, Oxford: Berg,2007, ch. 3.

24 C. Classen, *The Deepest Sense: A Cultural History of Touch*, Champaign, IL: University of Illinois Press, 2012, 190–1.

25 K. Marx, *Economic and Philosophic Manuscripts of 1844*, trans. Michael Milligan. Buffalo, NY: Prometheus Books, 1987, 212.

26 Classen, *The Deepest Sense*, ch. 8.

27 See, for example, M. McLuhan, *The Gutenberg Galaxy: The Making of Typographic Man*, Toronto: University of Toronto Press, 1962.

28 Cited in E.J. Leed, *No Man's Land: Combat and Identity in World War I*, Cambridge: Cambridge University Press, 1979, 144.

29 J. Romains, *Verdun*, tr. Gerard Hopkins. New York: Alfred A. Knopf, 1939, 88.

30 Y. Jean, 'The Sonic Mindedness of the Great War: Viewing History through Auditory Lenses', in F. Feiereisen and A.M. Hill (eds), *Germany in the Loud Twentieth Century: An Introduction*, Oxford: Oxford University Press, 2011, 58.

31 M. Bruegel, 'How the French Learned to Eat Canned Food', in W.J. Belasco and P. Scranton (eds), *Food Nations: Selling Taste in Consumer Societies*, London: Routledge, 2002.

32 G.W.F. Hegel, *Natural Law*, Philadelphia, PA: University of Pennsylvania Press, 2012, 93.

33 R. Brooke, *Rupert Brooke: The Collected Poems*, Edward Marsh, ed. London: Sidgwick & Jackson, 1942, 146.

34 F.T. Marinetti, *Critical Writings: New Edition*, edited by Günter Berghaus. New York: Farrar, Straus and Giroux, 2006, ch. 2.

35 Cited by G. Giucci, *The Cultural Life of the Automobile: Roads to Modernity*, trans. Anne Mayagoitia and Debra Nagao, Austin, TX: University of Texas Press, 2012, 129–30.

36 Cited in R. Bilstein, 'The Airplane and the American Experience', in D. Pisano (ed.), *The Airplane in American Culture*, Ann Arbor, MI: University of Michigan Press, 2003, 16.

37 Cited in R. Bilstein, 'The Airplane and the American Experience', 20.

38 Cited by L. Hein and M. Selden, 'Commemoration and Silence: Fifty Years of Remembering the Bomb in America and Japan', in L. Hein and M. Selden (eds), *Living with the Bomb: American and Japanese Cultural Conflicts in the Nuclear Age*, New York: East Gate, 1997, 4.

39 This is reflected in a poem by Carl Sandburg; see C. Sandburg, *The Complete Poems of Carl Sandburg*, New York: Harcourt, Brace, Jovanovich, 1970, 320.

40 G. Douglas, *Skyscrapers: A Social History of the Very Tall Building in America*, Jefferson, NC: McFarland & Company, 1996, 2.

41 A.D. King, *The Bungalow: The Production of a Global Culture*, London: Routledge and Kegan Paul, 1984.

42 Cited in C.E. Clark, *The American Family Home: 1800–1960*, Durham, NC: University of North Carolina Press, 1986, 227.

43 B. Friedan, *The Feminine Mystique*, New York: Norton, 1963, 15.

44 See Howes and Classen, *Ways of Sensing*, 89–92.

45 W.G. Staples, *Everyday Surveillance: Vigilance and Visible in Postmodern Life*, Lanham, MD: Rowman & Littlefield, 2000, 59.

46 J. Berger, *About Looking*, Toronto: Random House, 1991, 57.

47 Cited by J. Richards, *The Age of the Dream Palace: Cinema and Society in 1930s Britain*, London: L.B. Tauris & Co, 2010, 23.

48 M. de Certeau, 'The Madness of Vision', *Enclitic* 7, 1, 1983, 18.

49 Cited in J.L. Miekle, *American Plastic: A Cultural History*, New Brunswick. NJ: Rutgers University Press, 1993, 9.

50 Cited in Miekle, *American Plastic*, 3.

51 R. Barthes, *Mythologies*, trans. Annette Lavers, London: Paladin, 1972, 97.

52 C.S. Aron, *Working at Play: A History of Vacations in the United States*, New York: Oxford University Press, 1999.

53 J. Barr, *The Assaults on Our Senses*, London: Methuen and Co., 1970; J. Parr, *Sensing Changes: Technologies, Environments, and the Everyday, 1953–2003*, Vancouver: University of British Columbia Press, 2010.

54 Cited in F. White, *The Overview Effect: Space Exploration and Human Evolution*, Reston, VA: American Institute of Aeronautics and Astronautics, 1998, 38.

55 Robert Alter 1971, cited in W.J. Belasco, *Appetite for Change: How the Counterculture Took on the Food Industry*, Ithaca, NY: Cornell University Press, 2007, 62.

56 Cited by M.J. Kramer, *The Republic of Rock: Music and Citizenship in the Sixties Counterculture*, Oxford: Oxford University Press, 2013, lix.

57 See A. Synnott, 'Handling Children', in C. Classen (ed.), *The Book of Touch*, Oxford: Berg, 2005.

58 B. Spock and S. Parker, *Dr Spock's Baby and Child Care*, New York: Pocket Books, 1998.

59 See M. Bull, *Sounding Out the City: Personal Stereos and the Management of Everyday Life*, Oxford: Berg, 2000.

60 S. Sontag, *On Photography*, New York: Picador, 1973, 8.

27

MEDIA AND MEDIATIZATION

Pelle Snickars

'There are no realities any more, there is only apparatus', lamented the Austrian cultural historian Egon Friedell in the late 1920s. Working during the interwar period with his three-volume cultural history, 'from the Black Death to the World War', media modernity finally seemed to have caught up with him. The spiritual and religious spell of previous ages appeared as disenchanted – the *Entzauberung der Welt*, as famously diagnosed by sociologist Max Weber – where rural society and culture were replaced by urban secularization, cultural rationalization and modernized bureaucracy.[1] For Friedell, however, even reality gave the impression of disintegrating into a mediated dimness, with film and radio as the main perpetrators for blurring cultural hierarchies between high and low.

> As long as the cinema was numb, it had other ... possibilities: namely, spiritual ones. But the sound-film has unmasked it, and the fact is patent to all eyes and ears that we are dealing with a brutish dead machine. The bioscope kills the human gesture only, but the sound-film the human voice as well. Radio does the same. At the same time it frees us from the obligation to concentrate, and it is now possible to enjoy Mozart and sauerkraut, the Sunday sermon and bridge.[2]

This dreadful and mediated 'world of automata' appeared in the epilogue – ultimately entitled 'the collapse of reality' – at the very end of Friedell's majestic *Cultural History of the Modern Age* (1927–31). It was a publication that became a huge commercial success, especially in the German-speaking world, and was also subsequently translated into numerous other languages. Spanning some 1,500 pages covering 600 years, and with the main focus put firmly on 'great men' and their achievements in art, science and culture, Friedell's book was a classic cultural history; a portrait of different ages, with a personal and even anecdotal touch. Friedell's broad historical panorama was colourful, lively and witty – ironically he described himself as a 'dilettante', and it is not surprising that a present blogger designates the book as 'obscenely readable'.[3] With his somewhat odd background as a cabaret performer and actor, at least for a cultural historian, Friedell simply knew how to please an audience.

488

Yet, given his personal experience of 'low' culture and the ways in which various forms of mass media increasingly seemed to alter reality at the time of his writing, it remains surprising how murky Friedell's account of popular media appeared in his cultural historical overview – that is to say, if media were mentioned at all. In passing, Friedell noted that the first newspapers for decades had to fight censorship, and hinted towards the link between printed communication and the rise of nine-teenth-century nationalism. On another occasion, Friedell associated media with a 'particular utensil' symbolizing a given 'culture-period'. The man of the dawning Modern Age, for example, 'might be represented with a compass, Baroque man with a microscope, nineteenth-century man with a newspaper, the man of today with a telephone'.[4] Furthermore, he briefly stated that the 'high-speed printing press' was the most important machine introduced during the 1830s, and his account of the 1840s firmly described the 'characteristic inventions of the age' as being 'telegraphy and photography'.[5] But apart from such quite condensed notations, Friedell was not particularly interested in historical media accounts or descriptions, and consequently left them out, until the epilogue.

Media-historiographically this is odd, since Egon Friedell had previously pub-lished on, for example, the ways in which perception and representation around 1900 had been transformed via the medium of film. In 1912 he wrote that films are 'short, quick, at the same time coded, and [the medium] does not stop for anything. … This is quite fitting for our time, which is a time of extracts'.[6] Taken from his essay, 'Prolog vor dem Film', these remarks and others in many ways forebode cultural critic Walter Benjamin's canonized account of the artwork in the age of mechanical reproduction written during the 1930s.[7] But if Benjamin took a positive stance towards mass me-dia, and especially film, Friedell's characterization was much more gloomy. 'Both cin-ema and radio eliminate that mysterious fluid which emanates from artist and public alike … We already have nightingale concerts and Papal speeches transmitted to us by wireless'. For Friedell this amounted to the real decline of the West: 'Der Untergang des Abendlandes'.[8] However, given the epilogue of *Cultural History of the Modern Age*, Friedell realized and to some extent even anticipated notions of mediatization – that is, mass media's increased importance for ordinary people and society at large. His final remarks were contemporary, but they could also have been historicized if he had paid more attention to the cultural history of media.

Cultural historical media research

Departing from Friedell's paradoxical acknowledgement of both a 'world of autom-ata' and his apparent lack of interest in situating media within cultural history, this chapter will provide an overview of the cultural impact of media forms and formats, technologies and practices from the early nineteenth century until the advent of sound-film and radio; that is, approximately at the time when Friedell was complet-ing his cultural history. The period essentially corresponds with 'the long nineteenth century', lasting from the French Revolution to the First World War.

'If we wish to understand the cultural transformations associated with the rise of modern societies', the sociologist John B. Thompson argued in his book, *The Media and Modernity*, 'then we must give a central role to the development of communication media and their impact'. In a similar manner, this chapter seeks to trace the roots of media modernity within nineteenth- and early twentieth-century culture. Social theorists such as Thompson, however, have usually mounted a top-down approach towards media history, and made sweeping theoretical claims about the ways in which the use of often unspecific 'communication media' transformed the 'spatial and temporal organization of social life' by transmitting 'information and symbolic content'.[9] I am less interested in such non-empirical generalizations about hovering and non-specific 'communication media'. Contrary to media sociologists like Thompson, this chapter will rather take a 'bottom-up' approach towards nineteenth-century media culture.

Taking my cue from novel ways to perform cultural historical media research and equipped with a media archaeological perspective[10] – which seeks to perform media-specific readings of technologies and uncover forgotten media layers in the past, without falling into teleological linearities of mono-media histories from past to present – I will consider both new media and residual media forms, all the while trying to pin down how these were publicly perceived. In general the chapter will focus on broader, yet empirically situated media systems – rather than particular media forms, as the dominant daily press. In addition, the chapter will especially pay attention to hybrid forms of media culture and exchanges of intermediality. Like contemporary digital media, 'old' media during the nineteenth century were highly transnational, entangled and dependent on each other.[11] Media did not exist in isolation. Linked to the rise of consumer capitalism, popular media forms rapidly disseminated, first in Western Europe and North America, then globally. Importantly, both content and form migrated; *The Illustrated London News* first appeared in 1842, the Swedish *Ny Illustrerad Tidning* started in 1865 and the German *Berliner Illustrirte Zeitung* began in 1891. Cultural globalization is hence not a recent phenomenon. By 1910, the same French Pathé Frères films, the leading film company at the time, could be seen in such major cities as Paris and London, Moscow or Tokyo – but basically also in any small town in the European and American countryside that had a permanent cinema.[12] If the technical reproduction of texts and images, sounds and films via fast printing presses, photographic techniques such as daguerreotypes or calotypes and phonographic and cinematographic recordings was almost unimaginable in the early 1800s, a hundred years later these media formed a natural part of everyday life. As can be expected, this had tremendous consequences for how ordinary people perceived both themselves and their world. Hence, towards the end of the chapter, I will conclude with a discussion of how to understand transformations of media within cultural history, particularly with a focus on theories of mediatization.

A popular and entangled media landscape

The most important aspect of the development of various media from the early nineteenth century and onwards – whether in the modality of text, image, sound or film – was arguably their *mass appeal*. The term 'media' is an evasive concept and was not a particularly frequent notion used during the nineteenth century. Yet, it is useful as a term joining different communication forms, as well as stressing how attractions and technologies became increasingly intertwined and hard to separate from the rise of a common popular culture, and to some extent even traditional folk culture. It is during the nineteenth century that notions of 'communication' and 'media' appear, and develop within various parts of Western culture and society. Communication, however, also had a clear linkage to infrastructure and geography. 'In the nineteenth century the movement of goods or people and the movement of information were seen as essentially identical processes and both were described by the common noun "communication"'.[13] A media history of the nineteenth century might thus include looking at infrastructural technologies – or even the usage of media within warfare. It might also incorporate medical media technologies – from refinements of micro- scopic lenses in the 1850s to electromagnetic radiation known as X-rays in the 1890s – or the rise of bureaucratic media formats such as office paper.

This chapter focuses on popular media, even if some cultural historians have ar- gued that it is difficult to label objects or cultural practices as 'popular'. 'People with high status, great wealth or a substantial amount of power are not necessarily different in their culture from ordinary people', as cultural historian Peter Burke has stated.[14] From a media-historical perspective, however, popular culture during the nineteenth century was increasingly interlinked and bound together with media. Popular culture, in short, became ever more *media saturated* as a consequence of media-technological developments combined with consumer capitalism.

In the following, however, media is of primary concern, not popular culture. Ac- cording to media historian Lisa Gitelman, media are 'unique and complicated his- torical subjects. Their histories must be social and cultural, not the stories of how one technology leads to another, or of isolated geniuses working their magic on the world'. Somewhat anachronistically Gitelman uses the digital notion of 'protocols' to describe and define media as 'socially realized structures of communication, where structures include both technological forms and their associated protocols'. The pro- tocols surrounding media comprise a vast 'clutter', which gathers around a media 'technological nucleus', of more or less normative rules and conditions about how and where one used a medium. Looking into a stereoscope during the nineteenth century, for example, involved paying visual attention – since the 3D image would not appear otherwise – but the medium's supporting protocols also involved the actual purchase of the technology, the availability of different images and the regular habit of looking at home. According to Gitelman, media-historically situated 'proto- cols express a huge variety of social, economic, and material relationships'.[15] From a cultural historical perspective, mediated communication can hence be perceived as an evolving cultural practice, where both media and media usage took the form of dynamic sociocultural phenomena which altered over time.

Importantly, the popularity of the flourishing media culture during the nineteenth century made it increasingly different from the realm of art and high culture. As the century progressed, the contrast in scale and scope became ever more staggering. A well-liked painting at an art gallery in 1820, for example, might have been seen by a thousand people, and some 30 years later a reproduction of it featured in an illustrated journal could have reached 100,000 or sometimes even 200,000 potential readers – an impressive number of eyeballs at the time, yet a figure that is completely dwarfed by the 50 million people who saw D. W. Griffith's *The Birth of a Nation* in the five years after its release in 1915. The nineteenth century thus witnessed the increased *spreadability of culture* to 'the masses',[16] often in novel, unexpected and even pirated ways. In 1859, Charles Dickens, for example, published *A Tale of Two Cities* as a 45-chapter novel in 31 weekly instalments in his own literary periodical, and the book thereafter became one of the best-selling novels of all time – with perhaps as many as 200 million copies being sold. At the same time Dickens regularly complained about book piracy and the lack of intellectual property protection (the Berne convention recognizing copyright was signed in 1886).

On the one hand, popular media culture hence democratized access to content for people in general, but on the other hand, selling culture to these 'masses' also made content streamlined, catering to all tastes and thus giving rise to notions of 'low' and later mass culture. Media entrepreneurs, however, usually tried to prevent such denigrating descriptions since they were bad for business. Instead they were keen on promoting their commercial content or popular attractions as instructive entertainment – whether as illustrated journals, stereoscopic peep shows, wax museums or nonfiction film. Occasionally, different media supported and even tried to culturally elevate one another, as when the Parisian wax museum, Musée Grévin, began to screen nonfiction films in 1901, as 'visual corollaries' embedded in 'narratives that occurred off-screen in illustrated newspaper and at the wax museum [itself]', to quote art historian Vanessa R. Schwartz.[17]

In many ways, nineteenth-century popular media culture constantly oscillated between high and low – at least in the eyes of its producers and some audiences, but more seldom among critics of popular culture who usually saw it as coarse or even vulgar. Mass media is a twentieth-century term, but since almost all previous media were commercial by nature and popular in scope, attracting attention from a broad and paying public was essential. The dominant medium during the nineteenth century, the daily press, for example, operated under strict commercial terms. Following historian Benedict Anderson's famous claim, 'print-capitalism' targeting a mass audience created an 'imagined community' – that is, print-capitalism became crucial for the creation of nation states during the nineteenth century.[18] In a more mundane setting, however, news rapidly became a commodity to be reported about, commented upon, sold – and consequently manufactured. From the 1830s onwards, especially the so-called 'penny press' – inexpensive, tabloid-style newspapers mass-produced initially in the United States – achieved previously unheard-of sales figures.

Newspapers and magazines had been widely published in Western Europe already during the eighteenth century. Newspaper readers were predominantly envisioned as male, and according to sociologist Jürgen Habermas, the discussion around such periodicals gave rise to a new public sphere, the *Öffentlichkeit*, where the enlightened (male) bourgeoisie exchanged opinions and debated public matters at coffeehouses and cafés. This type of public interface between sociability and oral and written communication has become essential to our modern understanding of democracy, even if Habermas himself erroneously perceived the press history during the nineteenth century as one of decay and manipulation.[19] Habermas' notion of the public sphere, however, was limited to the educated upper-classes, and in general print culture had during centuries been oriented towards affluent society, since books were expensive. This is essentially why the inexpensive daily press during the nineteenth century became so important; 'not until four centuries after Gutenberg did the printed news media enter the daily lives of more than a tiny educated stratum of society'.[20]

As already noted by Egon Friedell, by the 1830s high-speed presses rapidly printed tens of thousands of newspapers, which started to appear in most major cities throughout the world. During the nineteenth century newspaper production and journalism were both professionalized and industrialized. Advertising revenues gradually increased and made newspapers affordable also for the working class. In short, the daily press was widely read – not least because of improvements in literacy which had taken place across Northwest Europe prior to 1800, and were later reinforced during the century by the introduction of compulsory education in a number of Western countries.[21]

After the different inventions of photography, in the late 1820s, 1830s and 1840s, and ways to reproduce and print images on paper, illustrated journals also began to be published. Popular media culture thus became increasingly visual, and in the mid-1850s *The Illustrated London News* sold as many as 200,000 copies per week. At the time, the press also benefited from another invention, the telegraph, which in its commercial usage permitted overnight news reporting and the ability to communicate globally in real-time – the 'Victorian Internet', as the telegraph has later been dubbed.[22] The electric telegraph made newspapers 'instant', and as media historian James Mussel has shown, they also became 'more explicitly informational' when integrated into broader systems of information technology. 'Telegraphic news' was often labelled as such, 'frequently printed in stacked columns which mimicked its abbreviated forms'.[23] The electric telegraph, which obviously operated with electric signals, had superseded optical semaphore telegraph systems in the 1830s, and in order to work properly telegraphy needed a *media infrastructure* of reliable cables, a task easier said than done. Efforts to lay a stable cable across the floor of the Atlantic, for example, failed on a number of occasions, and the first steadfast transatlantic telegraph cable began operating as late as 1866.[24]

The daily press – as well as the telegraph – were in many ways stable media forms during the nineteenth century. They became widely used and hugely popular: in 1870 a daily total of 2.6 million papers were sold in the United States – and figures kept on rising at an astonishing rate. After the First World War, Sweden had 235 daily newspapers, a total number never surpassed since, while the city of Lemberg where Europe basically 'ended' – today's Lviv in western Ukraine, which during the Habsburg Empire was the fifth largest city in Central Europe – boasted some 200 daily newspapers published in Polish, Ukrainian, Yiddish and Hebrew. Newspapers were text printed on paper, and even if they graphically developed during the long nineteenth century, they basically looked the same.

The development of production of paper, from linen rags to wood-pulp, also made newspapers increasingly inexpensive, as well as precarious and somewhat paradoxically outdated. For nineteenth-century readers, newspaper became a casual media form, almost instantly becoming old – the day after publication – in ardent contrast with the persistent novelty, which was an important trait of the general development of nineteenth-century media culture. 'Newness' can, in fact, be seen as one of the dominant meta-cultural discourses of media modernity. The spread of consumer capitalism is partly to blame since new products needed to be ceaselessly launched, but media history is also often told as a succession of improved technological inventions. It has, for example, often been argued that during the latter half of the nineteenth century, telegraphy and the application of electricity to communication led to the successive and rapid inventions of the telephone (1876), the phonograph (1877), the gramophone (1887) and later (after 1900) wireless transmissions.[25] However, all media were once new media, and the notion of 'new technologies' is always 'a historically relative term', to quote communication scholar Carolyn Marvin's magisterial *When Old Technologies Were New*.[26]

Looking into the novelty years and transitional states of media forms can, as Gitelman has observed, 'tell us much, both about the course of media history and about the broad conditions by which media and communication are and have been shaped'.[27] Then again, novelty and media transitions need not always be in focus, since some media forms kept their popularity among audiences over a very long period of time. Media history tends to privilege the introduction of new technologies – which often occurred at expositions and public exhibitions during the nineteenth century. A history of nineteenth-century world expositions will essentially cover all major media innovations. The cultural impact and extensions of media were occasionally rapid, but often utterly slow.[28] Within nineteenth-century media culture previous and commonly known everyday media were arguably more favoured by general audiences. During the long nineteenth century the stereoscope and panorama buildings are two of the most vivid examples of so-called 'residual media'. The term stems from Raymond Williams' study of culture's dominant, emergent and residual forms, and was later adapted to refer to media that are not new, but are nonetheless prevalent in society and culture.[29] The notion of residual media is hence an attempt to act as a corrective to the idea that when media become old, they always become obsolete.

The stereoscope and the panorama testify that during the nineteenth century this was far from the case. On the contrary; stereo images were as popular in the 1850s when they were introduced as they were half a century later. Stereoscopic images create the illusion of three-dimensional depth from two given two-dimensional images mounted next to each other, and photographed with a slight difference in angle. During the 1850s stereo images became hugely popular; an industry developed with millions of stereo cards and hundreds of thousands of stereoscopes being produced – from the expensive box-like Brewster Stereoscope to the open wooden-stand Holmes Stereoscope, being most favoured during the nineteenth century. Intriguingly, people did not get tired of looking at 3D images; the popularity of the medium lingered, and new attractions were built around stereo images such as the German *Kaiserpanorama*. This was a stereoscopic medium, which strived both to educate and entertain in visual form, with some 50 stereoscopic glass images arranged around a circular, rotating device that audiences peeped into. During the late nineteenth century its inventor August Fuhrmann developed this enterprise into a Central European image empire with some 250 branches. Even more successful was the American firm, Underwood & Underwood, which at the same time became the largest publisher of stereoviews in the world, producing a staggering 10 million images a year. In 1901, the company was said to have published 25,000 stereographs a day.[30]

A similar long-lasting and residual media form during the nineteenth century was the panorama. Even if the media history of the panorama – a visual medium in the form of a 360-degree painting mounted inside a building – stretches back to the late 1790s, a hundred years later it could still be fully praised as a complete novel medium. Among the 'main attractions in cities abroad *now* counts so-called panoramas'[31] (my italics), stated a newspaper article when in 1889 the first panorama building opened in Stockholm, depicting the defeat of the Paris Commune in 1871. The Swedish daily press stressed the splendid illusionary effect and, stepping inside the panorama and immersing himself in the image, one critic stated:

> When you climb up the small spiral staircase, you are unjustly struck by surprise in front of the sight that appears. You are in the middle of Paris. The illusion is complete and has been achieved by seeing only the painting which continues uninterrupted in whatever direction you look. But the reasons for this effect, you do not immediately reflect upon – you have only one impression: you are in the city of the Seine.[32]

The historian Jürgen Osterhammel has argued that nineteenth-century media – like the panorama – 'opened communicative spaces of every conceivable dimension'. Panorama buildings and stereoscopic images literally made it possible for audiences to virtually travel and immerse themselves in a foreign, imagistic space. For nineteenth-century audiences media could hence resemble travelling, but travelling could also resemble media – a kind of 'panoramic travel', which historian Wolfgang Schivelbusch once eloquently described in his classic nineteenth-century study, *The Railway Journey: The Industrialization and Perception of Time and Space*.[33] According to Osterhammel, however, the daily press was particularly important for mediated globalization: newspapers 'from the local sheet to the London *Times*, [were] by the end of the century … bringing news from all around the world while delivering its papers to be read on every continent'.[34]

Another significant spatial question regarding the nineteenth-century communication landscape is where media were actually located. On the one hand, media were individual consumer products to be purchased like any other commodity and disposed of in private. But on the other hand, media were also semi-public attractions (permanent or mobile) as well as infrastructures geared towards the public good, like telegraphy and later telephony. At urban newspaper stands, the daily press and magazines, illustrated press and comics could be bought by anyone who had the means, and in specialized shops visual media like photographs and postcards could be obtained. From the 1840s onwards, daguerreotypes and later *cartes de visite* – small, personal photographs of oneself or family members, patented in Paris by photographer André Adolphe Eugène Disdéri in 1854[35] – were acquired from the local photographer, who could also provide stereo cards or photographic albums. However, nineteenth-century media were also popular entertainment in the form of public attractions. In urban settings, media entrepreneurs tried to lure prospective audiences to splendid and fixed locations – from dance halls and vaudevilles, to wax museums, panoramas or dioramas. In order to get people to return to these entertainment venues, programmes had to be constantly renewed – which was fairly easy regarding vaudeville, but much more difficult and expensive when it came to wax tableaux or panorama paintings. The 1889 Stockholm panorama building, for example, only changed its painting once. Another strategy was to move the medium to prospective onlookers in both different cities and around the countryside; phonography and later cinematography were primarily exhibited in this way during the 1890s. After the Lumière brothers unveiled the Cinématographe at the Grand Café in Paris in 1895, they rapidly opened film theatres in London, Brussels, New York, Stockholm, etc. However, since there were not enough new films to screen, the popularity of the medium soon diminished. The commercial strategy was altered; Lumière cameramen/ projectionists were instead sent out into the world – both to record scenes and produce new films, as well as to showcase the invention at constantly different places.

Hybrid media

Towards the end of the nineteenth century almost all 'new' media were becoming global phenomena. The Lumière cinematographer Gabriel Veyre, for example, toured Mexico, Canada, Japan, China and Indochina during the late 1890s, filming nonfiction actualities and projecting them to amazed local audiences.[36] A key feature of the nineteenth-century press was, arguably, the global character of its leading organizations. 'The major newspapers felt they had a responsibility to print news from all over the world'.[37] Newspapers were thus a global medium, but as the Lumière Cinématographe exemplifies, it is equally true for contemporary audiences that print media formed but a part of a broader media landscape with news and actualities being delivered in a number of different modalities. During the latter half of the nineteenth century, text and images were the most common media that people encountered. Roger Fenton's and Mathew Brady's photographs from the Crimean War and the American Civil War in the 1850s and 1860s, respectively, are canonized examples of visual reports which shocked the general public. But news, events and culture at large also started to reach people in astonishingly different ways; news were hence not only *read* about – they were also *experienced* in a number of other communication formats.

This was especially the case from the 1870s onwards – a period that media philosopher Friedrich Kittler has characterized as a *Mediengründerzeit*, alluding to the contemporary unification of Germany – a founding media age, where new information technologies rivalled and sometimes even dislodged the privileged position of writing with the alluring potential of sound and audiovisual recordings, something that (according to Kittler) fundamentally reconstituted Western culture.[38] One does not, however, need to attribute a significant, and somewhat deterministic, agency of change to the development of particular new media technologies. Suffice to say, towards the end of the nineteenth century, media became intertwined in an ever-expanding *media system* of various communication forms, where similar content reappeared in a range of media. During the 1890s, travelling showmen exhibited thrilling narratives in lantern slides and cinematography; at the same time Swedish audiences could see their king Oscar II portrayed in wax, print media and photography as well as on film, and occasionally hear his voice on phonographic recordings, of which most were fake, however. Similarly, sceneries of beautiful topographies were displayed in both major panorama buildings and minor stereo and postcards, dissolving views or moving pictures. Hybrid media is a digital notion[39] – but late nineteenth-century media culture can also be characterized in terms of increased hybridity. A famous example is the Hungarian *Telefon Hírmondó*, the 'Telephone Herald', a telephone newspaper service in Budapest which from the 1890s to the 1920s provided news and entertainment to subscribers via telephone lines. Another hybrid media format emerging at the same time was the Edison Kinetophone, an attempt to create a sound-film-system. In addition, the actress Sarah Bernhardt (among others) appeared at the Phono-Cinéma-Théatre in so-called 'living visions' at the 1900 Paris Exposition. As these different examples testify, some media forms did indeed technically converge. More importantly for contemporary audiences, however, were the ways in which the protocols – the clutter of rules, conditions and relationship that gathered around media, to use Gitelman's term – generally did merge, and to some extent even converged.

Media scholar Henry Jenkins has argued that media convergence is best understood as a cultural process rather than a technological characteristic. Jenkins' term 'convergence culture' is a digital notion primarily referring to user-generated content and the ways in which contemporary media users become producers,[40] yet hybridity, intermediality and convergence also occurred frequently within the cultural history of media. Arguably, too little scholarly emphasis has been put on stressing the importance of a mixed-media approach towards understanding and describing the media landscape of the past. Even in Asa Brigg's and Peter Burke's great book, *A Social History of the Media*, 'convergence' is a term that appears first towards the very end to describe media convergence within the computer. 'From the 1980s onwards, [convergence was] applied most commonly to the development of digital technology, the integration of text, numbers, images and sounds', Brigg and Burke state, while admitting that these 'different elements in the media' have largely been 'considered separately in the previous periods of history covered in [our] book'. They do admit that convergence involves far more than technology *per se*, yet fail to give specific media-historical examples thereof.[41]

However, one only has to take a closer look at a particular event in media history in order to recognize how mixed media reproductions were. A detailed account of German reports taken from turn-of-the-century Berlin on the devastating Messina earthquake can serve as a case in point on how both entangled *and* differentiated media processes and protocols had become already a hundred years ago – hence, it can be perceived as an example of media convergence in a cultural rather than strict technological sense. The mediation of the catastrophe also points towards the need for a broad media-historical understanding of how news and events were mediated to the public – beyond the daily press.[42] In addition, it is an illustrative example of how an early media event rapidly unfolded and became publicly known to many people.

On 28 December 1908 an earthquake hit southern Italy. A number of cities, especially Messina on Sicily, were almost completely reduced to rubble. Berlin newspapers immediately reported on the event, which was initially believed to have claimed up to 200,000 casualties. During the first week of 1909, the front pages of *Berliner Tageblatt*, *Berliner Lokal-Anzeiger*, *Berliner Morgenpost* and *BZ am Mittag* were all filled with articles on the Messina catastrophe. Besides textual reports, the daily press also printed a number of illustrations. Naturally, the illustrated press like *Die Woche* and *Berliner Illustrierte Zeitung* featured additional images. These publications were both high-circulation illustrated weeklies; each issue of the former was by 1909 printed in approximately 400,000 issues, and the latter in an astonishing 800,000 issues. The visual reports of the Messina earthquake were thus quintessentially mass mediated, but they also drew attention to nuisances in the mediation process. Before the publication of the Messina issue of the *Berliner Illustrierte Zeitung*, for example, the newspaper *BZ am Mittag* featured an article about the photographers depicting Messina. The *BZ* reported that just after the earthquake, a number of Italian photographers had hastily travelled to Sicily, but only a few of them had, actually, managed to reach parts shattered by the earthquake. Thus, according to the *BZ*, a number of the illustrations from the earthquake, which had by then been published, were fake. Some of the published photographs did not at all depict the Messina catastrophe, but instead earlier earthquakes – old photographs had been manipulated.[43]

Somewhat surprisingly, moving pictures from the Messina catastrophe appeared in Berlin even before these illustrations were printed in the daily and illustrated press. Already on 1 January 1909, the *Berliner Lokal-Anzeiger* reported that the cinema at a contemporary film exhibition was to visually report on the earthquake the next day, and that telegraphically ordered films from Messina were projected as soon as they arrived. Finally, the Messina event was visually mediated in Berlin in at least three more ways: in a staged reconstruction, in stereoscopic images and in illustrated lectures. Already by mid-January 1909, the Berlin wax museum, *Passage-Panoptikum*, had put together new visual tableaux displaying the earthquake. The tableaux featured a round trip through the earthquake areas of Messina, reconstructed from authentic images. At the same time, the *Kaiserpanorama* showed stereoscopic images from the event, and during spring 1909 the attraction displayed no fewer than 10 series of images from the earthquake, each one containing 50 stereoscopic photographs. Lastly, illustrated lecturers gave hundreds of slide performances, 'Lichtbilder-Vortrag', focusing on the Messina earthquake at a number of public locations in Berlin.

The different ways in which the Messina catastrophe was represented also raise the tricky media-historical question of whether ordinary people perceived various forms of communication differently; that is, if media representations were understood as distinctly separate and dissimilar from each other. Around 1900, for instance, it can be argued that moving images both referred to cinematography as well as different forms of lantern projections. Prior to 1905 – and the establishment of permanent cinemas, the so-called *nickelodeon boom* (in the U.S.) – audiences often mixed up film and slide projections. Especially so-called *dissolving views*, a popular type of nineteenth-century magic lantern slide that exhibited a gradual transition from one projected image to the next – for example, from day to night – resembled early cinematography. The material technology itself facilitated these transitions, since lantern projectors sometimes had double or triple lenses which made it easy to double-expose and project slides on top of each other.

Then again, dissolving views of landscapes *also* belonged to the painterly tradition of dioramas – a variation of the 360-degree panorama painting. As a theatrical experience, dioramas dated back to the 1820s, and in the diorama building two huge canvases, sometimes featuring real objects, displayed landscapes, battles or earthquakes, usually depicting a 'before' and an 'after'. Importantly, dioramas 'moved' and included revolving seating for the audience, as well as vivid and detailed pictures – which were lit and illuminated from different angles – and thus created visual effects of imagistic transformations. Occasionally sound and living performers were also added. 'In viewing the Diorama', John Timbs stated in his 1855 publication, *Curiosities of London: Exhibiting the most Rare and Remarkable Objects of Interest in the Metropolis*,

> the spectator is placed, as it were, at the extremity of the scene, and thus has a view *across, or through it*. [...] The combination of transparent, semi-transparent, and opaque colouring ... renders the Diorama the most perfect scenic representation of nature; and adapts it peculiarly for moonlight subjects, or for shewing such accidents in landscape as sudden gleams of sunshine or lightning.[44]

Before inventing the daguerreotype process of photography during the 1830s, the painter Louis Daguerre was the owner of the first and most famous diorama in Paris (it opened in 1822). Daguerre's diorama stresses the often intricate interrelations within media culture, and the ways in which boundaries of media became blurred for the public. Even print culture during the early nineteenth century can be seen as involving a number of different media forms which readers did not always perceive as differentiated. Since books, magazines and newspapers were at the time printed sheets of paper, they resemble each other. Processes and methods used for the printing and binding of books were different; bookbinders physically assembled a book from an ordered stack of paper sheets. Hence, the medium of the book and that of the newspaper were not so unalike. In fact, prior to the mass production of inexpensive newspapers, the binding of newspapers into annual volumes was not an uncommon practice and commercial strategy during the early nineteenth century. With indexed categories such as 'foreign news', 'politics', 'war' or 'crime', 'old' newspapers appeared almost as books, with information being recontextualized for potential readers.[45]

One of the historiographical reasons, however, why book history is different from the history of the press, and why mixed or hybrid media forms have often been neglected, has to do with a traditional scholarly understanding of media history as driven by particular media forms. Specific media – or media institutions like the daily press – have usually been perceived as revolutionary for the development of general communication, a view that at the same time has been promoted by the very same media institutions, sometimes with frenetic journalistic excitement. The great relevance of, for example, the daily press for society was not only described in newspapers themselves; statues of newspaper tycoons were erected, journalistic conferences and exhibitions arranged – all with the purpose of underscoring the prominence of the medium. Different audiences were a resource for the nineteenth-century press, according to media historian Patrik Lundell, just as the press was 'a resource for them. Instead of separating proper journalism, the spreading of the self-image [of the press], and the reception of different audiences as clearly defined areas, they must be seen as constituting each other'.[46] It was simply never in the interest of the daily press to promote the film or book publishing industry, for example. As a consequence, the dependence and interaction with other media forms became secondary (at best). Within an academic setting, a similar focus on mono-media studies was later institutionalized; film-historical research was primarily devoted to one medium, media and communications studies initially to the history of the press, etc. Even if an influential media theorist like Marshall McLuhan in the 1960s argued that 'the content of any medium is always another medium', media–historical scholarship for decades by and large disregarded looking at interrelated *media systems* and the ways in which they determined epochs in the past.[47]

A cultural history of the media during the nineteenth as well as the twentieth century, however, needs to stress that 'all media are, from the standpoint of sensory modality, "mixed media"', as art historian W. J. T. Mitchell has argued.[48] A final example can act as a vivid illustration, and at the same time give a detailed impression of the mediated clutter surrounding mid-nineteenth-century popular culture. In 1850, the Swedish 'nightingale' Jenny Lind undertook an extraordinarily popular concert tour in North America. Born in 1820, Lind was considered one of the best soprano opera singers of her time – but since she was a performer just prior to the ability of mechanically capturing sound, there are ironically no recordings of her voice. Responsible, however, for her American tour was none other than the legendary showman P. T. Barnum. He was an early media entrepreneur and booster of popular culture, and is said to have paid Lind an unprecedented amount of money for the almost 100 concerts she gave, riches she mostly donated to charity.

In Barnum's autobiography, published in 1855, he retold the story of how he promoted Lind during her concert tour; the 'Jenny Lind enterprise', as he termed it. Needless to say, Barnum's autobiography was an exaggerated account of both himself and his deeds – *The life of P. T. Barnum,* 'written by himself, including his golden rules for money-making' – yet at the same time it is an exceptional historical source regarding the ways in which popular media culture took form during the mid-nineteenth century. Barnum, for example, described the advertisement strategy for one of his travelling shows as a spectacle in itself: his 'Magnificent Advertising Car' carried

> press agents, the 'paste brigade,' numbering twenty, and tons of immense colored bills, programmes, lithographs, photographs, electrotype cuts, etc., to arouse the entire country for fifty miles around each place of exhibition to the fact that 'P. T. Barnum's New and Greatest Show on Earth' was approaching.[49]

When Barnum reflected on 'Jenny Lind, her musical powers, her character, and wonderful successes', and the way in which she at first was practically 'unknown on this side of the water' – that is, before he brought her to America – he essentially suggested that it was he himself who had made her into a star. Following his own account, he created 'a Jenny Lind mania', invoking a number of subsequent modern media strategies to promote her to stardom. Barnum can thus be seen as an early exponent of the ways in which media and celebrity culture became mutually linked. In short, consumer capitalism promoted, took advantage of and profited from a star to sell commodities or newspaper issues, while Lind herself capitalized on becoming extremely well known through various media accounts. Barnum was in many ways the middle-man who made this symbiosis work. Through his various efforts – at least following his own account – Lind's presence and whereabouts became known and filled newspaper columns day after day. But Barnum also referred to a heterogeneous blend of commodities and newspapers, photographs and illustrated journals, and even riding hats and typical female 'bonnets' that all depicted Lind. In sometimes bizarre ways, merchants tried to profit from and take advantage of Lind's persona – praising her, while at the same time making money from her 'image'. Interestingly, Barnum argued that these manifestations in due time would all give evidence of Lind's fame and 'show that never before had there been such enthusiasm in the city of New York, or indeed in America'.

> For weeks ... the excitement was unabated. ... The carriages of the wealthiest citizens could be seen in front of [Lind's] hotel, at nearly all hours of the day, and it was with some difficulty that I prevented the 'fashionables' from monopolizing her altogether ... Shopkeepers vied with each other in calling her attention to their wares ... Songs, quadrilles and polkas were dedicated to her, and poets sung in her praise. We had Jenny Lind gloves, Jenny Lind bonnets, Jenny Lind riding hats, Jenny Lind shawls, mantillas, robes, chairs, sofas, pianos – in fact, everything was Jenny Lind. Her movements were constantly watched, and the moment her carriage appeared at the door, it was surrounded by multitudes, eager to catch a glimpse of the Swedish Nightingale.[50]

Conclusion: a history of increased mediatization?

During the last decade so-called theories of mediatization have gained academic popularity within media studies as a way to stress the importance of media for culture and society at large, both in a contemporary and historical setting.[51] In many ways, mediatization theory has emerged as a key concept to reconsider old – but still fundamental – questions about the role and effect, influence and impact of media and media culture. Since the concept of mediatization places media at the very centre of culture and society, it has attracted scholarly attention and become fashionable predominantly among media and communications scholars.

Mediatization is generally perceived as an historical metaprocess, a *grand narrative*, in the same manner as globalization, urbanization or modernization. Importantly, mediatization theory stipulates that over time an 'increasing number of technologically mediated forms of communication have become permanently available'.[52] In institutionalist accounts, mediatization is a process in which social actors adapt to media's rules and aims, logics and constraints. In more social constructivist accounts, the mediatization process is driven by media technologies that alter and refine the communicative construction of culture and society. 'Contemporary culture and society are permeated by the media, to the extent that the media may no longer be conceived as being separate from cultural and social institutions', media and communication scholar Stig Hjarvard has argued.[53] In a similar vein, media scholar Andreas Hepp states that media 'have increasingly left their mark on our everyday life'. Through 'the increasing use of media', so-called 'cultures of mediatization' have therefore emerged: 'that is, cultures that are "moulded" by the media'.[54]

Mediatization theory can, on the one hand, describe some of the transformations this chapter has traced that occurred within nineteenth-century media culture, relevant for understanding twentieth-century developments as well. The media landscape did, indeed, develop and grow; more and more people encountered media, hybrid media formats developed and new ways to technologically store and transmit culture were introduced – an extended process in which media increasingly came to constitute the infrastructural basis for human experience and understanding. On the other hand, mediatization theory is not geared towards *really* understanding or explaining media history, since it postulates a continuous and unceasing expansion of communication forms. It is an invalid argument in at least two different ways. Firstly, because some media forms or media usage decreased or even vanished. People went to the cinema more in the 1930s than today, the number of newspapers in Sweden during the 1920s has never been surpassed and in Lviv today there are not 200 daily newspapers. Secondly, as the example of P. T. Barnum displays, popular culture was moulded by the media already 150 years ago. It is not a recent phenomenon. Barnum's account of Jenny Lind might come across as a contemporary Hollywood merchandise campaign, but her concert tour in America took place in 1850. Lind was, no doubt, a great singer, but she is also a vibrant example of the ways in which mediated popular culture already during the mid-nineteenth century *produced* celebrities and stardom. Importantly, Lind was not an exception. Mediated mechanisms of celebrity culture developed in Europe already during the Enlightenment; Voltaire was a veritable celebrity in his time, and Heinrich Heine coined the idea of 'Lisztomania' in the 1840s.[55]

Proponents of mediatization theory usually perceive it as a continuous process which has emerged over a long period of time, but critics of this theoretical fallacy have, in fact, remarked that 'there is little consensus on when it started'. Arguably, there is consequently a need 'for more diachronous research' – that is, studies of media alterations over time, 'demonstrating rather than presuming historical change'. Indeed, 'the diachronous research that has been done seems to show that mediatization may well be an erratic process'.[56] Other scholars have argued that 'mediatization needs to be historicized' since 'too much of existing research has hypostasized the existence of mediatization' and then focused 'the contemporary effects of this taken-for-granted process'.[57] As the many empirical examples in this chapter have shown, however, mediatization theory does not really explain or help us understand the various transformations of media during the long nineteenth century, since it is essentially non-historical in its supposition of a constant increase and accumulation of media and media usage. With its contemporary set-up, the so-called mediatization of culture and society should rather be perceived as a continuation of John B. Thompson's argument in his publication, *The Media and Modernity* – 'a book primarily written as a work of social theory'[58] – with its non-empirical, top-down approach towards media history.

As a classic cultural historian – with an interest in the ways in which contemporary media culture during the interwar period altered reality into a 'world of automata' – Egon Friedell might instead serve as a great reminder that almost all modern epochs have perceived themselves as saturated and moulded by the media. If digital media today increasingly leave 'their mark on our everyday life', following claims made by contemporary mediatization scholars, for Friedell, it was the 1920s bioscope that appeared as 'a brutish dead machine' which presumably made a whole epoch unable to concentrate. Cultural historian Robert Darnton has often reminded us that every age was an age of information. In his presidential address to the American Historical Association at the height of the dotcom boom in the year 2000, Darnton argued that it seemed that society had by now 'entered the information age' with a future 'determined by the media. In fact, some would claim that the modes of communication have replaced the modes of production as the driving force of the modern world'. In his talk, however, Darnton disputed this view, which in many ways can be seen as a variation of mediatization theory. 'Whatever its value as prophecy', he stated,

> it will not work as history, because it conveys a specious sense of a break with the past. I would argue that every age was an age of information, each in its own way, and that communication systems have always shaped events.[59]

As this chapter has shown, a cultural history of media during the long nineteenth century indeed exemplifies Darnton's claim: it was an epoch that historian Eric Hobsbawm once described as the 'age of capital' and the subsequent 'age of empire' – but that could just as easily have been termed the 'age of media'.[60]

Notes

1 The notion of the disenchantment of the world, 'Entzauberung der Welt', appears in Max Weber's classic essay, 'Wissenschaft als Beruf' from 1919 – later translated as 'Science as Vocation' in *From Max Weber: Essays in Sociology*, New York: Oxford University Press, 1946, 129–56.

2 E. Friedell, *A Cultural History of the Modern Age, Volume III*, New York: Alfred A. Knopf, 1932, 475.

3 'What You Absolutely Should Read: Egon Friedell's Cultural History', *Farilian*, 16 January 2013, https://realmsofacademia.wordpress.com/2013/01/16/what-you-absolutely-should-read-egon-friedells (accessed 1 September 2017).

4 E. Friedell, *A Cultural History of the Modern Age, Volume II*, New York: Alfred A. Knopf, 1931, 149.

5 Friedell, *A Cultural History of the Modern Age, Volume III*, 78, 80, 120.

6 E. Friedell, 'Prolog vor dem Film', *Blätter des deutschen Theaters*, no. 2, 1912. Later reprinted in A. Kaes (ed.), *Kino-Debatte. Texte zum Verhältnis von Literatur und Film 1909–1929*, Tübingen: Max Niemayer Verlag, 1978, 42–6.

7 W. Benjamin, 'The Work of Art in the Age of Mechanical Reproduction' (1936), reprinted in M. W. Jennings, B. Doherty and T. Y. Levin (eds), *The Work of Art in the Age of Its Technological Reproducibility, and Other Writings on Media*, Cambridge, MA: Harvard University Press, 2008, 19–55.

8 Friedell, *A Cultural History of the Modern Age, Volume III*, 475. Friedell naturally alluded to Oswald Spengler's *Der Untergang des Abendlandes* (1918–22) – published in English as *The Decline of the West* in 1926 – a cultural pessimistic treatise which predicted the deterioration of 'Faustian' Western culture, a theme enthusiastically picked up by intellectual proponents of German National Socialism. Arguably, Friedell's contemporary dismal was, hence, likely *also* political. Being of Jewish origin, he had witnessed the rise of National Socialism, and later during the 1930s his cultural historical books were all banned by the Nazi regime. Four days after Nazi Germany's *Anschluss* of Austria in March 1938, local SA-men came to arrest Friedell – who committed suicide by jumping out of the window of his apartment on Gentzgasse in Vienna.

9 J. B. Thompson, *The Media and Modernity: A Social Theory of the Media*, London: Polity Press, 1995, 4.

10 For new perspectives on the cultural history of media published after the millennium, see for example L. Gitelman and G. B. Pingree (eds), *New Media 1740–1915*,

Cambridge, MA: MIT Press, 2003; David Thorburn and Henry Jenkins (eds), *Rethinking Media Change: The Aesthetics of Transition*, Cambridge, MA: MIT Press, 2003, and A. Ekström, S. Jülich and P. Snickars (eds), *1897. Mediehistorier kring Stockholmsutställningen*, Stockholm: SLBA, 2006. For an introduction to the field of media archaeology, see W. Ernst, *Digital Memory and the Archive*, Minneapolis, MN: Minnesota University Press, 2012, and J. Parikka, *What Is Media Archaeology?*, London: Polity Press, 2012.

11 'Entanglement is a concept that can be employed in order to problematize the presumed points of departure and the linear understandings of development, production and reception that often characterize media-history scholarship'. M. Cronqvist and C. Hilgert, 'Entangled Media Histories. The Value of Transnational and Transmedial Approaches in Media Historiography', *Media History* 1, 2017, 130–41.

12 R. Abel (ed.), *Encyclopedia of Early Cinema*, London: Routledge, 2005.

13 J. Carey, *Communication as Culture: Essays on Media and Society*, Boston, MA: Unwin Hyman, 1989, 15.

14 P. Burke, *What Is Cultural History?*, London: Polity, 2008, 28.

15 L. Gitelman, *Always Already New. Media, History, and the Data of Culture*, Cambridge, MA: MIT Press, 2008, 7.

16 The term 'masses' can be perceived as problematic – and to some extent the later notion of 'mass culture' as well. The latter term is usually associated with the advent of twentieth-century media (such as film, radio and television), especially in relation to the United States and the rise of Hollywood in the 1920s. Then again, popular media culture during the nineteenth century increasingly catered to the masses. But as Raymond Williams famously put it: 'The masses are always the others, whom we don't know, and can't know. ... Masses are other people. There are in fact no masses, there are only ways of seeing people as masses'. R. Williams, *Culture and Society 1780–1950*, New York: Anchor Books, 1960, 319.

17 V. R. Schwartz, *Spectacular Realities: Early Mass Culture in fin-de-siècle Paris*, Berkeley, CA: University of California Press, 1998, 193. For a further discussion, see also V. R. Schwartz and J. M. Przyblyski (eds), *The Nineteenth-Century Visual Culture Reader*, London: Routledge, 2004.

18 B. Anderson, *Imagined Communities: Reflections on the Origin and Spread of Nationalism*, London: Verso, 1983.

19 J. Habermas, *The Structural Transformation of the Public Sphere* (1962), Cambridge, MA: MIT Press, 1991.

20 J. Osterhammel, *The Transformation of the World: A Global History of the Nineteenth Century*, Princeton, NJ: Princeton University Press, 2014, 38.

21 In Prussia a modern compulsory education system was implemented already in 1763, and later during the modern era Scandinavia followed suit, with for example the establishment of the Swedish elementary school, *folkskola*, in 1842. Levels of literacy were high in Northern Europe; around 1850 almost 80% of Swedes could read, and more than 60% of Germans. France, the United Kingdom and the United States had lower levels of literacy, and were generally slower in introducing compulsory education for children, which happened during the 1870s and 1880s.

22 T. Standage, *The Victorian Internet: The Remarkable Story of the Telegraph and the Nineteenth Century's On-Line Pioneers*, London: Walker & Company, 1998. Within media historiography it is worth noting that the medium of telegraphy has often been ascribed a utopian quality. 'The telegraph freed communication from the constraints of geography. [It] not only altered the relation between communication and transportation; it also changed the fundamental ways in which communication was thought about', to quote communication scholar James W. Carey in his *Communication as Culture*, London:

Routledge, 1992, 157. However, this was not the way in which the telegraph was discussed during the nineteenth century – at least not in the Swedish daily press, *Aftonbladet*. Computationally distant reading some 10,000 pages of *Aftonbladet* between the 1830s and 1860s rather reveals that the most common words associated with the telegraph were profane and precise announcements around the *materiality of the medium* (copper, wire, gutta-percha, etc) as well as the meticulous mentioning of exact distances between telegraphically linked cities – that is, hardly utopian immaterial communication. For a discussion, see J. Jarlbrink, 'Telegrafen på distans: Ett digitalt metodexperiment', *Scandia* 84, 1, 2018, 9–35.

23 J. Mussel, 'Elemental Forms: The Newspaper as Popular Genre in the Nineteenth Century', *Media History* 1, 2014, 4–20.

24 For a discussion on British imperial telecommunications networks between 1850 and 1870, see D. R. Headrick, *The Tentacles of Progress: Technology Transfer in the Age of Imperialism, 1850–1940*, Oxford: Oxford University Press, 1988, 97–101.

25 This is the usual way in which media history is described – i.e. 'the development of print media', 'the development of electronic media', etc. See for example the many editions of James Ross Wilson and Stan Roy Wilson's textbook, *Mass Media, Mass Culture: An Introduction*, New York: McGraw-Hill, 2001.

26 C. Marvin, *When Old Technologies Were New: Thinking About Electric Communication in the Late Nineteenth Century*, New York: Oxford University Press, 1988, 3.

27 Gitelman, *Always Already New*, 1.

28 For a discussion, see H. Salmi, *Nineteenth Century Europe: A Cultural History*, Cambridge: Polity Press, 2008, 3–4.

29 R. Williams, *Marxism and Literature*, Oxford: Oxford University Press, 1977, 121–7. For a further discussion, see also C. R. Acland (ed.), *Residual Media*, Minneapolis, MN: University of Minnesota Press, 2007.

30 W. Uricchio, 'Stereography', in R. Abel (ed.), *Encyclopedia of Early Cinema*, London: Routledge, 2005, 885.

31 'Rundmålningsbyggnaden å Djurgården', not signed, *Stockholms Dagblad*, 27 August 1889.

32 'Rundmålningsbyggnaden', not signed, *Dagens Nyheter*, 28 August 1889.

33 W. Schivelbusch, *The Railway Journey: The Industrialization and Perception of Time and Space* (1977), Oakland, CA: University of California Press, 1986, 123–51.

34 Osterhammel, *The Transformation of the World*, 29.

35 For a discussion, see E. A. McCauley, *A.A.E. Disdéri and the Carte de Visite Portrait Photograph*, New Haven, CT: Yale University Press, 1985.

36 P. Jacquier and M. Pranal, *Gabriel Veyre, opérateur Lumière. Autour du monde avec le cinématographe correspondance (1896–1900)*, Paris: Actes Sud, 1999.

37 Osterhammel, *The Transformation of the World*, 37.

38 F. Kittler, *Discourse Networks 1800/1900*, Stanford, CA: Stanford University Press, 1990.

39 L. Manovich, 'Understanding Hybrid Media' (2009), http://manovich.net/content/04-projects/055-understanding-hybrid-media/52_article_2007.pdf (accessed 1 September 2017).

40 H. Jenkins, *Convergence Culture: Where Old and New Media Collide*, New York: New York University Press, 2006.

41 A. Brigg and P. Burke, *A Social History of the Media: From Gutenberg to the Internet*, Cambridge: Polity Press, 2009, 237, 236.

42 For a further discussion, see J. E. Hill and V. R. Schwartz (eds), *Getting the Picture: The Visual Culture of the News*, London: Bloomsbury, 2015.

43 Exact references to the various Berlin press and media accounts of reports around the Messina earthquake are taken from P. Snickars, 'Reading Berlin 1909:

"Medienöffentlichkeit", Daily Press and Mediated Events', in H. Segeberg and C. Müller (eds), *Kinoöffentlichkeit (1895–1920) Cinema's Public Sphere (1895–1920): Entstehung – Etablierung – Differenzierung, Emergence – Settlement – Differentiation*, Marburg: Schüren, 2008, 44–65.

44 J. Timbs, *Curiosities of London: Exhibiting the most Rare and Remarkable Objects of Interest in the Metropolis*, London: David Bogue, 1855, 252–3.

45 For a discussion, see U. Heyd, *Reading Newspapers: Press and Public in Eighteenth-Century Britain and America*, Oxford: Voltaire Foundation, 2012.

46 P. Lundell, 'The Medium Is the Message: The Media History of the Press', *Media History* 1, 2008, 1–16.

47 M. McLuhan, *Understanding Media: The Extensions of Man*, New York: McGraw-Hill, 1964, 8.

48 W. J. T. Mitchell, 'There Are No Visual Media', *Journal of Visual Culture* 4, 2, 2005, 257–66.

49 T. Barnum, *The Life of P.T. Barnum* (1855), Buffalo, NY: Courier Printers, 1888, 318–19.

50 Ibid., 103, 106. For a further discussion, see A. Nyblom, 'Jennyismen 1845', in T. Forslid et al. (eds), *Celebritetsskapande från Strindberg till Asllani*, Lund: Mediehistoriskt arkiv, 2017, 29–52.

51 For an introduction to mediatization theory, see for example K. Lundby (ed.), *Mediatization: Concept, Changes, Consequences*, New York: Peter Lang, 2009.

52 A. Hepp, *Cultures of Mediatization*, Cambridge: Polity Press, 2013, 53.

53 S. Hjarvard, *The Mediatization of Culture and Society*, London: Routledge, 2013, 2.

54 Hepp, *Cultures of Mediatization*, 1, 2.

55 For a discussion, see A. Lilti, *The Invention of Celebrity*, Cambridge: Polity Press, 2017, and H. Salmi, 'Viral Virtuosity and the Itineraries of Celebrity Culture', in H. Salmi, A. Nivala and J. Sarjala (eds), *Travelling Notions of Culture in Early Nineteenth-Century Europe*, Routledge: New York, 2016, 135–53.

56 D. Deacon and J. Stanyer, 'Mediatization: Key Concept or Conceptual Bandwagon?', *Media, Culture & Society* 7, 2014, 1032–44.

57 M. Ekström et al., 'Three Tasks for Mediatization Research: Contributions to an Open Agenda', *Media, Culture & Society* 7, 2016, 1090–108.

58 Thompson, *The Media and Modernity*, 5.

59 R. Darnton, 'An Early Information Society: News and the Media in Eighteenth-Century Paris', *The American Historical Review* 1, 2000, 1–35.

60 E. Hobsbawm, *The Age of Capital: 1848–1875*, London: Abacus, 1975; E. Hobsbawm, *The Age of Empire: 1875–1914*, London: George Weidenfeld and Nicolson, 1987.

28

INDIGENOUS AND POSTCOLONIAL CULTURES

Mita Banerjee

The cultural history of the Western world from the eighteenth century onwards is inextricably tied to the politics of imperialism and colonial expansion. At the core of European policies of empire building, there were both economic and cultural rationales: the economic benefits of colonial expansion with the emergence of global trade were bolstered, on a cultural level, by the idea of a 'mission civilatrice': the Western values of humanism and the Enlightenment were to be brought to and instilled in the minds of those peoples across the globe who were assumed to inhabit a primitive, pre-Enlightenment state. It is this assumption of pre-civilized peoples that provided a rationale both for colonial annexation and expansion and for the 'internal colonization' of indigenous communities within newly founded Western nation-states.

Colonialism is thus not only a political and economic system, but also a cultural undertaking. It sets up native and indigenous peoples as foils to the concept of Western identity. From the very beginning, the colonization of native and indigenous people was twofold: first, in aimed at instilling Western cultural ideals into peoples to whom such ideas were alien, with the education system as one of the pillars of such 're-education'. Second, it saw especially indigenous peoples as 'primitive' forerunners of Western civilizations. Western scientists hence set out to study their own past in the present: by looking at indigenous groups, it was reasoned, Western culture could travel into its own cultural history. The temporal and psychological move implied here is itself intriguing: Western culture positioned itself as the telos to which all other cultures could aspire; and by looking at these other cultures in their presumably 'primitive' state, Western scientists and historians could reinvestigate their own identity by looking at indigenous cultures as a mirror of their own past. This mirror generated ideas of both nostalgia and cultural superiority: indigenous cultures, it was argued, were trapped in an Edenic state which Western cultures had long since lost. In order to read this narrative of the 'civilizing mission' against the grain and make the voices and lives of native and indigenous peoples visible, then, it is necessary to supplement historical documents through life-writing accounts: through the biographies, autobiographies and testimonies of colonized subjects which are often absent from the records.

Indigeneity and the history of Western science: *Minik, the New York Eskimo*

In his biography of Minik, "the New York Eskimo", historian Kenn Harper charts the journey of a young Inuit boy form Greenland to the New York Museum of Natural History, where he was to be exhibited as a 'specimen' of an indigenous culture which, at the time, was said to be on the verge of extinction. Harper's biography of a virtually forgotten Inuit boy may be exemplary for an understanding of indigenous histories and the histories of Western nations for a number of reasons. First, Kenn Harper, a Canadian historian, married into the Inuit community in Greenland and thus became 'literate' of Inuit signification in both cultural and linguistic terms. As in the case of Eddie Mabo, Sir Edward Durie or Phil Fontaine, the writing of indigenous history is thus characterized by the author's familiarity with two cultural systems, one indigenous and one non-indigenous. It is this twofold literacy, then, which may mark the efficacy of Harper's biography of a young Inuit boy in opening up to the reader an understanding of both Inuit and Western history. Harper's biography also illustrates the fact that both the terms 'Inuit' and 'Western' must be understood as umbrella terms here. Framed in Western discourse as 'Inuit', young Minik comes from a specific indigenous group in Greenland whose cultural specificity Harper's account illustrates; similarly, the biography chronicles Danish and Canadian histories of colonizing indigenous communities living in the territories of these nation-states. Harper's history of the life of a young 'Eskimo' in the early twentieth century is thus truly a transnational one: moving from Greenland to New York and back again, and being written by a Canadian historian living in Denmark as part of the Danish Inuit community. As Harper illustrates in the preface to his biography of Minik, then, his aim in writing this biography expressly was a completion of the archive, the restoring of an indigenous voice virtually forgotten.[1] It is through this indigenous history, then, that Harper retells not only a part of Danish history, but also the history of the New York Museum of Natural History and thus, in part, the history of Western science.

With his voice having been restored by Harper's biography, published decades after Minik's death, Minik asks anthropologists and museum curators a simple question: 'Why am I a scientific experiment?' This seemingly innocent question, it could be argued, rereads the history of the Western world from the perspective of the so-called Fourth World. Implicitly, such a perspective implies that the history of Western humanism and the Enlightenment cannot be read as antithetical to colonial conquest and the colonization of indigenous peoples across the globe, but, rather, as being integral to it.

Moreover, Minik's innocent question, which implicitly captures the entire history of Social Darwinism, points to the fact that the history of the Western world cannot be read independently from the history of science. In virtually all Western nation-states, scientific accounts distinguishing 'higher' from 'lower' races provided the infrastructure on which colonial practices would be based. In many different parts of the Western world, nineteenth-century 'frenology', which ascribed to non-Western peoples an inferior intellectual capacity, became a rational for social stratification.[2] The history of Western colonization of non-Western territories and its inhabitants, then, was undergirded by scientific ideas and the emergence of new fields of science such as anthropology. If the Enlightenment has often been understood as being essential to the birth of modern empirical science, then the history of this science must also be re-read through the inhumane uses to which it was put. It was only through the wedding of scientific and cultural ideas about the 'primitivism' of indigenous cultures, then, that a young Inuit boy could be 'exhibited' as a specimen in New York's Museum of Natural History in the first place.

The 'case' of Minik, the New York Inuit, demonstrates a number of aspects at once. First, the colonization of indigenous groups in Western nation-states, as much as the imperial subjugation of foreign territories in the name of a history of Western progress, relies not only on military force but is also undergirded by a variety of other fields and discourses. Colonization is enabled not only by legal rhetoric, but also by scientific discourse. In order to resist such discourse, moreover, it is necessary to acknowledge alternative forms of evidence. The story of Minik's life may be exemplary because it was through a historian's writing down the story of a young Inuit boy's life that counter-evidence was finally provided against which the scientific discourse of anthropology could be read and critiqued. Harper's biography of Minik was finally successful in eliciting material change: an entire century after the body of Minik's father had unjustly been exhibited in a museum glass case, the body was restored to an Inuit community in Greenland. This process, in turn, was part of a worldwide recognition of the rights of indigenous peoples, and the passing of legal frameworks allowing for the repatriation of indigenous remains which had been kept in museums throughout the Western world. In 1990, the US passed the Native American Grave Protection and Repatriation Act (NAGPRA). The remains of Minik's father were restored to his community in Greenland, then, because rights advocates argued that a law calling for repatriation in a Native American context also had to be extended to an Inuit from Greenland whose body had been kept in an American museum. The remains of Minik's father, Qisuk, finally received an official burial on 4 August 1997, in the presence of the Danish queen. Her presence, as well as the restoring of indigenous rights an entire century after these rights had been breached by the New York Museum of Natural History, marks a turning point in the history of Denmark as a nation. It demonstrates that laws can be recognized as unjust in retrospect, and that rituals and recognition (by governments or royal representatives) can serve as ways of apology and of a long-overdue historic change. The example of Minik hence illustrates the cultural history of the colonizing of indigenous peoples: Western scientists 'study' indigenous culture as a presumed mirror to their own past; and they expose the indigenous subject to a process of 're-education' which would leave indigenous subjects unmoored from their own histories and traditions. Minik's life can hence be situated in a larger context of colonial education systems, the history of Western science and the process of 'reconciliation' which has marked the twenty-first century.

The values of the Enlightenment and the 'civilizing mission'

If the history of the Western world has often been seen as being synonymous with the history of the Enlightenment, then, it would seem that it is essential to re-read this history from the perspective of indigenous and postcolonial histories. It can be argued that the concept of Otherness is built into the dialectic of the Enlightenment: the very metaphor at the core of the Enlightenment necessitates the existence of 'other' cultures, cultures that are deemed pre-rational, instinctual or primitive. Such primitivism had been responsible for bringing Minik to New York in the first place. This assumption of the alleged 'primitivism' of non-Western cultures, however, must be seen as a construction on the part of the Western observer rather than a fact-based description of these cultures as such. From today's perspective, then, the assumption of such primitivism on the part of non-Western cultures would be said to be a practice of 'writing out' the existence of non-Western systems of signification on a cultural, political, legal, social and religious level. The concept of 'writing out' such systems of signification has been used, in the Anglo-American context, to denote not only a denial of other cultures, but also the active practice of trying to erase them. This practice of erasure, as this chapter will demonstrate, has profound consequences not only for the ways in which histories have been written, but also for the archives on which such historiography has been based.

At the same time, in order to understand the practice of 'writing out' alternative histories, it is important to explore the nexus between what postcolonial critic Edward Said, in his later work, has called 'culture and imperialism'.[3] According to Said, the point is not that cultural production constituted a mere supplement to empire building, but rather that the stories told about the Western world and its (prospective) colonies were in fact mutually constitutive. Empire building was made possible, Said claims, because of the innumerable novels, poems and short stories – from Charlotte Brontë's *Jane Eyre* to Rudyard Kipling's *The White Man's Burden* – that depicted the non-Western world as being in need of civilization. In this vein, Said argues that culture was in fact the 'cement' of empire. At the heart of Said's retelling the history of the Western world through its *literary* history is the claim that culture, politics and history cannot be separated from one another. Rather, the Enlightenment philosophy which, on a political and legal level, was used to justify the colonization and annexation of non-Western territories – from Asia to Africa and the Pacific – permeated not only political rhetoric, but cultural production as well. It is this idea that enables Said to argue that in fact the entire canon of Western literature – from Goethe to Flaubert – can be read as a justification for empire building: precisely because, couched in masterful aesthetics and innovative rhetorical techniques, these stories portray a non-Western world as being incapable of self-government,[4] literature served as a rationale for empire building. In order to retell the history of the Western world, and its relationship to its 'others', it is hence essential to conceive of literary and cultural production, on the one hand, and the political, economic, legal and social ramifications of empire in terms of continuity rather than difference on the other.

Said's most daring move, in his earlier study, *Orientalism*, is that he sets out to write nothing short of the literary history of the Western world – a project that would hitherto have been deemed impossible by those critics stressing the national and cultural specificities for canonical writers such as Flaubert, Goethe and Rimbaud.[5] Not only does Said set out to write the literary history of the Western world, then, but he argues that national specificities pale with regard to each of these literature's depictions of the non-Western world. This world, he argues, is portrayed alternatively as primitive, bizarre, perverse, childlike; but the gist of these portrayals is that the 'Orient' (as a catch-all phrase, in Western Enlightenment thought, for the non-Western world) is in need of civilization. In the words of Anglo–Indian poet Rudyard Kipling, then, it was 'the white man's burden' to civilize those who were deemed to be incapable of governing themselves. In nineteenth-century history, this same logic recurs almost verbatim in a number of different contexts. In the history of US empire building, for instance, this vein of thought gave rise to the politics of Manifest Destiny, a term coined by John O'Sullivan in 1845. According to this reasoning, the Anglo-American people as a race of 'yearly multiplying millions' was inherently in need of expanding; such expansion was, if not God-given, nonetheless inevitable and 'manifest' in this people's future. Colonial expansion – both in the conquest of Native American territories within the US and in the annexation of 'foreign' territories such as the Philippines – was hence described as destined by 'nature'. As O'Sullivan put it, territorial expansion was divine providence and hence inherently justified: 'Our Manifest destiny is to overspread the continent allotted by Providence for the free development of our yearly multiplying millions'.[6]

What does it mean, then, to re-read or retell the history of the Enlightenment as this history of empire building? Crucially, such a revisionist practice is not meant as a wholesale dismissal of the humanism and progressive elements of Enlightenment philosophy; rather, it refuses to separate the economic logic of empire building from the philosophy of Enlightenment thought. One of the key questions at the heart of any history of the Western world, then, is the question of whether Enlightenment philosophy, given its implicit distinction between 'enlightened' and 'non-enlightened' societies, was bound to entail an economic practice of empire building. At the same time, as Richard Price has recently noted, there is a paradox at the heart of empire building, which results from the very concept of trying to build a 'liberal empire'.[7] As Price notes, we need to 'address the question of how liberal society attempts to reconcile empire to its values and principles'.[8] At the same time, there was a sense in which different empire-building nations stressed their own liberalism over what they depicted as the inhumane colonial practices of other nations. As Price goes on to observe about the self-perception of the British empire, for instance, 'the culture of British imperialism presented itself both at home and abroad as practicing a liberal imperialism compared to other nations'.[9]

By the same token, Native American historians have argued that the history of the US can in fact be read as a 'history of broken treaties'. Treaties and the signing of treaties with indigenous groups was hence integral to nation building in settler colonies such as New Zealand or the US. In fact, the very practice of treaties is indicative of the attempt on the part of settler groups to build a liberal nation-state. To simply annex these territories would have been seen as being incompatible with the settlers' liberal self-understanding; thus treaties had to be made. These liberal values notwithstanding, however, the settlers would then go on to break the treaties, or the wording of the treaties themselves would be deliberately misleading.

If, according to Said, literature was the cement of empire, then the colonial education system was its backbone. For those at home, the stories they read (as novels, short stories or poem) daily assured them that the childlike inhabitants of the colonies were in need of being civilized; for colonial subjects, on the other hand, empire building meant the attempt, by the colonial power or 'mother country', to deprive them of all means for maintaining their cultural practices. Both the day-to-day operation of colonialism and its long-term stability, then, are inconceivable without an understanding of the role of education in perpetuating both the logic and the practice of colonialism. In India, for instance, this meant that English was to be the language of education; all Indian languages were dismissed as inferior languages or 'vernaculars'. As British historian and politician Thomas Babington Macauley put it in his *Minutes on Indian Educations* (1835), the goal of a colonial education system was nothing short of replicating British culture in India by turning Indians into Englishmen, if not in colour, then at least in character. This civilizing project, systematically instilled in colonial subjects through a colonial education system, has given rise to what critics such as Homi Bhabha and Indian writers such as V.S. Naipaul have termed 'mimic men':[10] colonial subjects were trapped in a vicious cycle of trying to mimic their colonial masters, a goal which, given the fact that these subjects would remain 'Indian in colour', could never quite be achieved. At the same time, it is a key issue here to remember that the history of the education system, the practice of empire building and the perpetuating of the British literary canon through a colonial education system were in close conjunction. For those thus re-educated through a colonial education system which privileged English language and literature over 'indigenous' literary and linguistic traditions, the consequence of such educational practice was devastating both culturally and psychologically. As Algerian psychiatrist Frantz Fanon has observed in his ground-breaking study *Black Skin, White Masks*, the cultural politics of colonialism served to instil an inferiority complex in its colonial subjects, who were forever trapped in striving for a perfection of colonial mimicry they would never quite achieve.[11]

The colonial practice of dismissing or 'writing out' alternative systems of signification links the history of colonialism to what has been termed the 'internal colonization' of indigenous groups within Western nation-states. The history of Western nation building cannot be read without simultaneously bearing in mind that many of these nations were literally built on denying land ownership to the indigenous inhabitants of the territories thus conquered. Here, too, cultural discourse, Enlightenment philosophy and legal conquest are inextricably interwoven.

In the so-called 'settler colonies' of the US, Canada, Australia and New Zealand, the founding of nation-states newly independent from the British crown coincided with the consolidation of conquest: the new nation-states were literally based on the legal, cultural, political and economic disenfranchisement of indigenous communities. In the US, the Declaration of Independence of 1776 marked the beginning of a systematic disenfranchisement of Native American communities; in New Zealand, the Treaty of Waitangi of 1840 officially deprived Maori of their sovereignty.[12]

This 'conquest by law', to use a term coined by Lindsay Robertson, Founding Director of the International Human Rights Law Clinic and a member of the working group which drafted the UN Declaration of the Rights of Indigenous People, held true for all the above-mentioned settler colonies: in all these instances, indigenous peoples were said to hold no right to the territories of which they were the original inhabitants. As the 'terra nullius' doctrine in Australia put it, the territory 'discovered' by European settlers was literally 'nobody's land'.[13] Since, according to the logic of European Enlightenment, indigenous peoples had not cultivated the land they lived on, they held no legal claim to it. It is important to note in this context that the internal colonization of indigenous peoples by no means works through military force alone. Rather, legal discourses are mustered to bolster and perpetuate the newly established ownership of the land. It is this interlocking nature of military conquest and legal rationales which Robertson captures in the metaphor of 'conquest by law'.[14] The colonization of indigenous peoples in settler colonies thus worked in surprisingly similar ways. Even if the legal concept of 'terra nullius' is specific to the Australian context, its underlying logic is not. In the US, too, Puritan settlers argued not only that they were the 'chosen people'[15] who were predestined to take possession of the land, but also that since Native Americans had failed to 'subdue' the land, it had never actually been theirs.

The history of boarding schools and cultural 're-education'

This legal conquest was then followed by the translation of the 'mission civilatrice' into the cultural practice of the New World. There are hence striking similarities between the politics of internal and external colonization. In both contexts, a newly established education system ruled supreme in what was seen as the necessary 'assimilation' of colonized groups. In the US, Canada and Australia in particular, native children were sent to boarding schools often run by missionaries, and were forbidden to practise their cultures or speak their native languages. This politics of re-education would prove traumatic for all the communities afflicted by these colonial policies. In Australia, the term 'stolen generation' has been adopted to convey the idea that colonial policies literally tore Aboriginal children from their families, destroying entire genealogies in the process. Here, too, it is important to note that colonial rhetoric in countries such as Australia held this 'civilizing' of indigenous children through missionary schools to be the colonizer's *humanistic* duty. Humanistic values were thus by no means seen as being incompatible with practices of forced assimilation, but, on the contrary, were thought of as being integral to them. In Australia in particular, this politics of assimilation was both cultural and 'genetic'. In a rhetoric perilously close to the discourse on animal breeding, the aim of the colonial regime was nothing short of 'breeding out' Aboriginal genes in order to generate future generations of white Australians. As historian Henry Reynolds puts it,

> [the] solution was biological assimilation. … Full bloods should only be allowed to marry other full bloods. In fact, they should be 'rigidly excluded from any association likely to lead to any other union'. And eventually they would die out.[16]

The psychological consequences of such policies could not have been more traumatic as Aboriginal children were made to abhor the 'indigeneity' within themselves. They became, as Reynolds phrases it, 'nowhere people', who had literally been made to abhor their own history by the colonial regime. Moreover, this policy drove a rift within Aboriginal communities by 'selecting' or singling out mixed-race children from darker-skinned ones. In a pernicious collapsing of genetic concepts with notions of cultural assimilation, not all children were seen as being worthy of assimilation. In 1996, an inquiry by the Human Rights Commission of Australia found that the policies responsible for creating a 'stolen generation' were nothing short of genocide. The findings of the inquiry were eventually made public in the documentary *Bringing Them Home* (1997).

One of the most striking aspects of dominant discourses on indigeneity in Australia, Canada, New Zealand and the US was the fact that colonialist policies sought to erase, or were simply ignorant of, what were in fact highly complex civilizations. To this day, and despite centuries of forced assimilation, the US recognizes 566 different Native American groups. There may hence be a paradox at the core of Western conceptualizations of nation building. While histories, for instance, about the creation of the US nation-state have focused on concepts of 'Americanization', the idea of the melting pot and hence on the processes through which immigrants from many different European and non-European nations 'amalgamated' into Americans, it was wrongfully assumed that Native American peoples constituted a homogeneous group. In both political and popular rhetoric, the cultural and national diversity of European settlers was hence contrasted with the 'sameness' of indigenous inhabitants. Up until today, however, the term Native American must be seen as an umbrella term under which highly distinct indigenous cultures and traditions have been grouped. In terms of legal definition, moreover, it is more accurate to speak of Indian nations.[17] Indeed, by a bizarre twist of legal rhetoric, colonial law defined Native American 'tribes' as 'nations within the nation':[18] the territories they inhabited (or were forced to inhabit because of subsequent policies of 'relocation' and the reservation system) were legally defined as 'dependent domestic nations': paradoxically, these spaces were extraterritorial to the US, thus turning any negotiation between the US government and Native American communities into foreign relations; and yet, despite their status as 'nations', Native American groups were not granted sovereignty over their lands because they were seen as 'domestic dependent nations' and hence, as in many other colonial contexts, as 'wards' of the US nation-state. It is also important to note in this context that the history of the Western world may be re-read through the history of citizenship of various Western nation-states, particularly with regard to the rights these nations granted to or withheld from indigenous communities. Thus, Native Americans in the US were not given citizenship until 1924, and gained full access to civil rights only through the Indian Civil Rights Act of 1968. In Australia, it would take until 1967 for Aboriginal Australians to gain citizenship.

When the Europeans arrived on their shores, indigenous groups possessed highly complex cultural, linguistic, economic, social, religious and legal systems of signification.[19] Part of the psychological rationale through which internal colonialism operated, then, was to dismiss these highly elaborate systems of signification as 'primitive' or uncultured. As in the case of Meenakshi Mukherjee's concept of the 'perishable empire', however, it would be wrong to assume that colonial policies of 're-educating' indigenous groups were ultimately successful. Despite the traumatic consequences of assimilationist policies, which have left indelible marks on these communities both psychologically and physically, indigenous communities have survived. In order to capture this perseverance even in the face of the most atrocious policies, Native American writer and theorist Gerald Vizenor (Anishinaabe) has coined the neologism of 'survivance':[20] a newly created noun which is meant to form the conceptual opposite to colonial 'dominance', survivance conveys the fact that despite the policies adopted by governments after governments of the colonial regime, indigenous communities found ways to preserve and renew their cultural practices. Paradoxically, the value of these practices was being rediscovered as the twenty-first century opened. In medicine and pharmacology, for instance, the search for alternative medicine has led to the 'discovery', by Western scientists, of indigenous medicines, whose efficacy is now 'proved' through Western laboratory practice. Similarly, in contemporary climate research, indigenous environmental practices are recognized as being sustainable in a way that settler cultures' ways of being in the world have not been.

The twenty-first century as the 'age of apology'?

There is solace in the fact that the late twentieth and early twenty-first centuries have turned out to be an 'age of apology'.[21] This period is marked by a potential about-face in the politics of Western nation-states with regard to their indigenous populations. On a political level, the governments of these states have issued apologies for the disenfranchisement, colonization and traumatization of indigenous peoples. On a cultural and scientific level, recent developments, especially in the arena of medicine and climate research, have led to the above-described re-discovery and re-evaluation of Fourth World knowledge systems. In this recovery of indigenous knowledge, we may in fact have come full circle from the 'mission civilatrice' predicated on Enlightenment values, which had dismissed indigenous cultural and scientific practice as pre-civilized, to a more democratic view of indigenous knowledge as complementary and equal, perhaps even superior, to Western knowledge systems.

The process of reconciliation,[22] which begins with official apologies to indigenous peoples by Western governments, has been framed by the emergence of new forms of jurisdiction on an international level, such as the UN Declaration of the Rights of Indigenous Peoples (UNDRIP, 2007) and the establishing of the UN Permanent Forum on Indigenous Issues (2000).

In this trajectory, national politics have come to be reframed by new, supranational infrastructures such as the United Nations. Crucially, the rights discourse adopted by indigenous communities in the US, Canada, Australia and New Zealand has had profound repercussions on European debates on indigeneity in countries such as Sweden, Finland and Norway. The emergence of Sámi studies in Sweden in the 1990s reminds us that the colonization of indigenous communities was by no means limited to settler societies in the New World, but was also at the core of European nation building.

In order to fully recognize the achievements official apologies constitute, it is important to inquire into the processes, cultural, legal or humanitarian, which have led to these apologies, and to retrace the lives of the agents which were instrumental in bringing them about. In methodological terms, it may thus be useful to link a transnational, comparative indigenous studies to approaches from life-writing research. Such a perspective may enable us to look at these historical developments by analysing historical documents, legal texts and narratives of life writing, especially witness accounts. By adopting a perspective from life-writing research, it becomes possible to reassess historical and legal developments through the accounts of individuals who tried to make sense of them.

While focusing on cultural, legal, political and economic issues in general, the discussion thus also needs to adopt a perspective which focuses on the lives and agency of particular individuals who would prove to be instrumental for the process of reconciliation in the late twentieth and early twenty-first centuries. Thus, a claim filed by an Aboriginal petitioner working for the University of Queensland, Edward Koiki Mabo, succeeded in finally disproving the terra nullius doctrine in 1992. The life and work of 'Eddie' Mabo can be read as a key example of what Gerald Vizenor has termed 'survivance'. First, his life and the ultimate success of his lawsuit illustrate the fact that survival and the maintaining of mental health can be achieved regardless of an individual's level of education. It may be solace to note that the legal doctrine of terra nullius, which made possible and legitimated centuries of internal colonialism, was eventually overturned not by a lawyer, but a man who worked for the University of Queensland as a gardener. Moreover, Mabo succeeded in overturning the law of terra nullius from within its own rationale. The law itself had originally translated cultural assumptions held by the settlers into legal practice: Aboriginal communities, these assumptions held, were nomadic and had hence failed to secure title to the land through which they were said to move, but which they were not seen as inhabiting. It is this claim, then, that Eddie Mabo succeeded in disproving. His tribal community (the Meriam), he was able to prove, had been farmers on Murray Island for many successive generations, and had remained in the same place.[23] Since terra nullius was hence based on an assumption which had falsely homogenized Aboriginal groups by claiming that none of them were farmers, Mabo's retracing of his own cultural lineage and the economic practices of his community dismantled the logic of the doctrine from within. Eddie Mabo himself, however, would not live to see his decade-long lawsuit come to fruition. He passed away in 1992, five months before his lawsuit finally succeeded. In Mabo's case as in many others, it may hence be fruitful to read legal history in conjunction with life-writing doctrines. If history is also understood as a history of ideas, then such ideas can be found not only in official records, in political speeches and legal rulings, but also in the records kept by individuals about their everyday lives, and the ideas which, as in Eddie Mabo's case, enabled them to resist colonial regimes. In this vein, the field of life-writing research sets out to investigate all accounts of individual and collective lives, both published and unpublished, connecting diaries to autobiographies and biographies and, more recently, blogs and websites.

Witnessing the past: the institutionalization of truth and reconciliation commissions

In Australia, then, the turn of the twenty-first century was characterized by an unprecedented change in the relationship between settlers and indigenous groups. In 2008, sixteen years after the overturning of the terra nullius doctrine, Australia's Prime Minister, Kevin Rudd, finally issued an apology to the survivors of the stolen generation.[24] The study of such official apologies is at the core of the newly emergent field of reconciliation studies, which draws attention to the linguistic, cultural, psychological, political, legal and religious underpinnings of reconciliation, from South Africa to Canada, Australia and New Zealand.

The field of reconciliation can also be seen to connect indigenous and postcolonial histories. In many different ways, South Africa has marked what was seen as a model of reconciliation through the institution of the Truth and Reconciliation Commission. As Archbishop Desmond Tutu, the chairman of the Commission, has outlined in his study *No Future without Forgiveness* (2000), South Africa has been understood as having accomplished the miracle of a peaceful transition from colonial rule to post-apartheid democracy. As an institutional framework for attempting to right the wrongs of the past, the Truth and Reconciliation Commission has often been contrasted to the Nuremberg Trials.[25] Unlike in Nuremberg, however, the aim of the Truth and Reconciliation Commission was not to punish the perpetrators of the colonial regime, but rather to enact a process of communal witnessing in which both perpetrators and victims were allowed to tell their story.

Through this process of witnessing, and the opportunity for victims and their relatives to have their stories heard and their suffering recognized, it was hoped that some sort of closure could be achieved. Through this closure, in turn, a new chapter in the history of the South African nation-state could possibly be opened. The South African Truth and Reconciliation Commission has since become a model for other nations trying to reconcile opposing parties in postcolonial regimes. In Canada, a Truth and Reconciliation Commission was set up in 2008 in order to investigate the traumas inflicted on indigenous children through the missionary school system. It can be noted here that structures and processes of reconciliation can be explored on both a national and a transnational level.

In keeping with the idea of transnational processes of reconciliation, it was important to note that after Australia's Prime Minister Kevin Rudd had officially apologized to the survivors of the stolen generation, Canada followed suit the same year. In 2008, the Canadian Prime Minister Stephen Harper apologized to Canadian First Nations for the cultural, physical and psychological injustice inflicted on indigenous children and their parents through the boarding school system. In both the Canadian and the Australian apologies to indigenous communities, the aspect of recognition was central, an aspect that can also be said to lie at the core of the workings of the Truth and Reconciliation Commission in South Africa. In order for the apology to be successful, its wording must prove the awareness, on the part of the colonial regime, of the extent of the trauma that has been inflicted on indigenous communities through colonial policies, also and especially in the field of education.

It is thus important to note that in his apology, Rudd recognizes not only the cultural effects of policies of forced assimilation, but also the extent of the psychological trauma inflicted on indigenous Australians:

> We apologise for the laws and policies of successive Parliaments and governments that have inflicted profound grief, suffering and loss on these our fellow Australians.
>
> We apologise especially for the removal of Aboriginal and Torres Strait Islander children from their families, their communities and their country.
>
> For the pain, suffering and hurt of these Stolen Generations, their descendants and for their families left behind, we say sorry.
>
> To the mothers and the fathers, the brothers and the sisters, for the breaking up of families and communities, we say sorry.[26]

Moreover, Rudd does not refer to the dismal legacies of colonialist policies in the abstract, but explicitly draws on life-writing accounts. Referring to one woman's life in particular, Australia's Prime Minister conjures up for both a national and an international audience which witnesses this televised event of the apology what government policies have meant for those who were made to endure them. In this moment of the about-face of the Australian nation, life writing, legal discourse and political rhetoric converge; each is inseparable from the other. At the same time, Rudd is quick to note in his apology that the concept and political and economic practice of reconciliation must by no means be limited to the discursive act of the apology alone. Unless the repentance by the former colonial regime translates into the improvement of the economic and material situation of those who have suffered from internal colonialism, Rudd acknowledges, any apology risks being mere lip service.

Moreover, it is important to explore the ideas and discursive concepts underlying Rudd's apology. Paradoxically but perhaps not surprisingly, the about-face in the policies of the Australian nation with regard to its indigenous inhabitants is enabled through the logic of human rights. For the full extent of the trauma of the stolen generation had been made visible only through the inquiry of the Australian human rights commission, which was then made public through a documentary film entitled *Bringing Them Home*. Even though it would take another decade for the Australian government to finally acknowledge its breaches of the rights of indigenous Australians, the fact remains that the discourse of human rights, and of indigenous rights specifically, framed the terms in which the apology was finally expressed. The paradox of humanism thus remains: in the logic of empire and the internal colonization of indigenous peoples in settler colonies, humanism was used as a rationale to justify assimilationist policies; yet, it is in the humanistic underpinnings of rights discourse that humanism continues to inform the twenty-first-century logic of apology. Similarly, there may be a cultural and psychological trap in indigenous communities having to adopt a Western discourse of rights in order to make their voices heard in the first place. As Mary Lawlor has argued, the very act of adopting Western rights discourse necessitates a translating of indigenous concepts into a Western logic of rights, thus in a way dismantling a claim before it is even made.[27]

If in Rudd's apology, life-writing narratives, as the lived histories of survivors of the stolen generation, are present in instances such as the Prime Minister's invoking the life and testimony of Nanna Nungala Fejo, an elderly indigenous woman whose narrative was particularly eloquent of the trauma suffered by indigenous Australians, such life-writing accounts are also crucial in understanding Canada's journey to reconciliation. In Canada, Larry Philipp 'Phil' Fontaine, a member of the Sagkeeng Anicinabe Nation and former National Chief of the Assembly of First Nations (1997–2000), was instrumental in bringing about Prime Minister Harper's apology to the survivors of the residential school system.[28] A political scientist and indigenous politician who attended a residential school himself, Fontaine turns the narrative of his own life, and the implicit testimony to the horrors inflicted by colonial education, into a driving force for achieving a national apology. In Fontaine's case, too, resistance is made possible through processes of solidarity which move both beyond national borders and beyond indigeneity. As Fontaine has emphasized in his political speeches, one of the most dismal chapters in Canada's history of colonizing First Nations communities was the physical and sexual abuse which many children had to suffer in residential schools. For the survivors of such abuse, their own life histories were thus marked by shame, preventing them from publicly telling their stories and thus testifying against the colonial regime. As Fontaine notes, it was flying to Ireland and talking to Irish survivors of sexual abuse which finally enabled him to tell his story. His testimony, in turn, made it possible for hundreds of other First Nations survivors of the residential school system to tell their histories. In the face of such testimonies of abuse, then, the act of apology becomes an ethical imperative for the Western nation-state trying to come to terms with its past relationship to its indigenous inhabitants. In the light of the current status of human rights legislation and its relevance for the nation's self-image and self-understanding, then, it becomes almost impossible not to apologize. The link between oral and written history, between life writing and official histories, could not be more crucial in this context. What emerges in the rhetoric of Harper's apology, then, is the superimposing of two mutually incompatible histories of one and the same Western nation-state: the image of a nation which, on account of the injustices it has inflicted on indigenous communities, is now revealed to have been a colonizing nation; and the image or promise of a future nation-state which, on the basis of the long-overdue apology to indigenous groups, will now live up to the promise of its own humanism. It is these two histories, the narratives of both the past and the future Canadian nation, which are present in Harper's apology to Canadian First Nations. Moreover, it is important to note that the force and the sincerity of the apology can by no means be limited to its wording:

> Two primary objectives of the residential schools system were to remove and isolate children from the influence of their homes, families, traditions and cultures, and to assimilate them into the dominant culture.
>
> These objectives were based on the assumption aboriginal cultures and spiritual beliefs were inferior and unequal.
>
> Indeed, some sought, as it was infamously said, 'to kill the Indian in the child'.
>
> Today, we recognize that this policy of assimilation was wrong, has caused great harm, and has no place in our country.[29]

Rather, its material enactment, as both a cultural and political performance, is integral to its working. It matters, in other words, that the Canadian Prime Minister should have delivered his apology at the very site in which the legislation creating the residential school system had once been drawn up. The apology is thus site-specific, and its site-specificity may contribute to the survivors' ability to recover from the traumas of the past. Moreover, Prime Minister Harper's apology is preceded by the testimony of the man who helped bring the apology about. In the full regalia of his indigenous nation, Phil Fontaine provides the cultural and historical context from which the apology ensues and to which it must respond. The fact that, a decade after the closing of the last residential school in 1996, a representative of Canadian First Nations is able to appear in parliament in full tribal regalia testifies to the survival of indigenous cultural traditions against all odds.

Conclusion

What follows from these considerations are a number of aspects, all of which can be said to be interrelated. First and foremost, the history of Western colonialism across the globe as well as the internal colonization of indigenous groups in the so-called settler colonies of the US, Canada, Australia and New Zealand is inseparable from the cultural history of the West. Colonialism was driven not just by economic interest but also by a cultural mission, and the attempt to replicate Western cultural ideals in other parts of the world. Paradoxically, humanism and the cultural values of the Enlightenment have hence undergirded colonial endeavours. Even so, however, and despite its colonial legacy, humanism continues to be central to contemporary movements for both decolonization and reconciliation.

Humanism has thus paradoxically been at the heart of empire building *and* recent strives for reconciliation. In this context, it may be remarkable that the beginning of the twentieth century has shown that Western nation-states can set out to 'right' the wrongs of the past. In this context, the speech act of reconciliation, even as it must then be followed by material forms of compensation and processes of economic restructuring, must not be underestimated. Finally, one of the most central questions in this context is what forms of evidence spark processes of reconciliation on a national level. Here, it can be argued that forms of life writing (diaries, oral narratives, testimonies) may constitute one such form of evidence. One of the most central questions in this context is what frameworks (legal, cultural and political) may be necessary for life narratives to be heard by colonial regimes. Colonial regimes, then, can be said to 'write out' the lives of those they subjugate, relegating them to objects of governance instead. What recent developments at the beginning of the twenty-first century demonstrate is that it is only when these life narratives can finally be heard, enabled in part by the framework of human rights, that reconciliation can be achieved. Yet, the apologies made by the governments of Australia and Canada in 2008, as well as the earlier apology the British queen Elizabeth II had offered to Maori in New Zealand in 1995, show that a complete about-face in the relationship between settler and indigenous populations is in fact possible. In New Zealand, such a rethinking of Pakeha–Maori relations has even led to a referendum aimed at changing the face of the New Zealand flag. Some argued that only a new flag, a new emblem for a nation that has literally gone back to its founding moment (the Waitangi Tribunal) and recognized its founding document as flawed, could aptly represent a truly bicultural future for the nation of New Zealand.[30] What these developments demonstrate, then, is that the histories of Western nation-states are complex especially with regard to settler–indigenous relations; but they also show that Western nation-states, despite their histories of internal and external colonization, are able to reinvent themselves and thus move into a new, more democratic future.

Notes

1 K. Harper, *Give Me My Father's Body: The Life of Minik, the New York Eskimo*, San Val Publishing, 2001 [1986].
2 M.F. Jacobson, *Whiteness of a Different Color: European Immigrants and the Alchemy of Race*, Cambridge, MA: Harvard University Press, 1999.
3 E. Said, *Culture and Imperialism*, New York: Vintage, 1994.
4 Cf. Jacobson, *Whiteness of a Different Color*.
5 E. Said, *Orientalism*, New York: Vintage, 1979.
6 J. O'Sullivan, 'The Philippines Are Ours Forever', *Democratic Review* 1845.

7 R. Price, *Making Empire: Colonial Encounters and the Creation of Imperial Rule in Nineteenth-Century Africa*, Cambridge: Cambridge University Press, 2017.

8 Ibid.

9 Ibid.

10 H. Bhabha, *The Location of Culture*, New York: Routledge, 1994; V.S. Naipaul, *The Mimic Men*, New York: Vintage, 2001 [1967].

11 F. Fanon, *Black Skin, White Masks*, New York: Grove, 2008 [1952].

12 U. Tiemann, *Rechte der Ureinwohner Neuseelands aus dem Vertrag von Waitangi*, Münster: LIT-Verlag, 1999, 29; P. McHugh, *The Maori Magna Charta – New Zealand Law and the Treaty of Waitangi*, Auckland: Oxford University Press, 1991.

13 L.G. Robertson, *Conquest by Law: How the Discovery of America Dispossessed Indigenous Peoples of Their Lands*, New York: Oxford University Press, 2005; D. Dörr, 'The Background of the Theory of Discovery', *American Indian Law Review* XXXIX, 2, 2013, 475–97.

14 Robertson, *Conquest by Law*.

15 S. Bercovitch, *The Puritan Origins of the American Self*, New Haven, CT: Yale University Press, 2011.

16 H. Reynolds, *Nowhere People: How International Race Thinking Shaped Australia's Identity*, Victoria: Viking, 2005, 184.

17 Dörr, *The Background of the Theory of Discovery*, 475.

18 Ibid.

19 C. Allen, 'Earthworks: Native Intellectuals on the Ground', *American Quarterly* 59, 1, 2007, 199–209.

20 G. Vizenor, *Manifest Manners: Narratives on Postindian Survivance*, Lincoln, NE: University of Nebraska Press, 1999.

21 M. Gibney, R.E. Howard-Hassmann, J.-M. Coicaud and N. Steiner (eds), *The Age of Apology: Facing Up to the Past*, Philadelphia, PA: University of Pennsylvania Press, 2008.

22 Cf. B. Bashir and W. Kymlicka, 'Introduction: Struggles for Inclusion and Reconciliation in Modern Democracies', in B. Bashir and W. Kymlicka (eds), *The Politics of Reconciliation in Multicultural Societies*, Oxford: Oxford University Press, 2008, 1–24.

23 N. Loos, 'Preface', in N. Loos and E. Koiki Mabo, *Eddie Koiki Mabo: His Life and Struggle for Land Rights*, Brisbane: University of Queensland Press, 1996; M. Stephenson and S. Ratnapala, 'Introduction', in M. Stephenson and S. Ratnapala (eds), *Mabo: A Judicial Revolution*, Brisbane: University of Queensland Press, 1993.

24 K. Rudd, 'Apology to Australia's Indigenous Peoples', www.australia.gov.au/about-australia/our-country/our-people/apology-to-australias-indigenous-peoples (accessed 27 May 2017).

25 D. Tutu, *No Future without Forgiveness*, New York: Image, 2000; A. Krog, *Country of My Skull: Guilt, Sorrow, and the Limits of Forgiveness in the New South Africa*, New York: Broadway Books, 2000.

26 Rudd, 'Apology to Australia's Indigenous Peoples'.

27 M. Lawlor, *Public Native America: Tribal Self-Representations in Casinos, Museums, and Powwows*, New Brunswick, NJ: Rutgers University Press, 2006.

28 S. McCarthy, 'First Nations Leader Phil Fontaine', *Globe and Mail* 16 May 2014.

29 'Prime Minister Harper's Statement of Apology', *CBC News* 11 June 2008, www.cbc.ca/news/canada/prime-minister-stephen-harper-s-statement-of-apology-1.734250 (accessed 27 May 2017).

30 M. Ehrmann, *The Status and Rights of Indigenous Peoples in New Zealand*, ZaöRV 1999, 463–96.

29

VIOLENCE AND TRAUMA

Experiencing the two World Wars

Ville Kivimäki

In her famous study on pain, Elaine Scarry notes the difficulty of describing pain accurately. Despite its corporeality, the feeling of pain resists objectification in language; and even more, it deconstructs the language that we use to share our experiences socially. Torturous pain remains confined to bodies that suffer it. Yet the pain's 'unmaking of the world' is accompanied by the richness of practices, meanings, rituals and artefacts that surround the experiences of violence – the body in pain is also a source of culture that 'makes the world'. Importantly, Scarry dedicates the second chapter of her book to war, and especially to recognizing war as a fundamentally violent event. This sobering recognition contrasts with vast quantities of military and political history on war, in which the violence at war's root is rarely acknowledged:

> The main purpose and outcome of war is injuring. Though this fact is too self-evident and massive ever to be directly contested, it can be indirectly contested by many means and disappear from view along many separate paths. It may disappear from view simply by being omitted: one can read many pages of a historic or strategic account of a particular military campaign, or listen to many successive installments in a newscast narrative of events in a contemporary war, without encountering the acknowledgment that the purpose of the event described is to alter (to burn, to blast, to shell, to cut) human tissue, as well as to alter the surface, shape, and deep entirety of the objects human beings recognize as extensions of themselves.[1]

These are the simple points of departure for the current chapter: (1) war is violence, (2) violence destroys cultural meanings and (3) violence calls for cultural meanings. Furthermore, I will add a fourth point of departure: unlike individual acts of violence, violence in war is in direct relation to collective identities. In order to sustain the war effort and to cherish a societally cohesive memory of the war, martial violence must be given regenerative meanings; should this fail, the violence of war has the ability to shatter and mould those cultural beliefs and narratives that are crucial for the self-understanding of a given community.[2] Taken together, these four points underline the tension between violence and culture as both a destructive and a productive force – and help to understand why war has such a central place in cultural imagination, even after decades of peace in many Western countries. Against this backdrop, I will discuss the cultural history of martial violence in Europe during the age of the two World Wars.

Cultural means of survival, 1914–18

The average calculation of military deaths during the First World War is around 10 million soldiers. To this we should add several million war-related civilian deaths, the exact number of which is hard to estimate. All this human slaughter was in stark contrast both to the progressive ethos of civilization in the pre-war era and to the popular expectations of a short and glorious war in August 1914. In November 1918, four great empires were in ruins and the victorious nations had suffered such a monstrous death toll that the victory itself was hardly a sufficient compensation. Yet alongside such devastation, many frontline soldiers gave witness to enduring patriotism. As Etienne Derville, a sergeant in the French Army and a student in a Catholic university, wrote in a letter after being wounded twice at the turn of 1914–15:

> In full conscience, I have made the sacrifice of my life, with joy, for the rechristianization of our country, for the greater love of God on the part of my parents and my friends, and I do not feel the least bitterness.[3]

The cultural historiography of 1914–18 could have several first entries, but literary scholar Paul Fussell's *The Great War and Modern Memory* (1975) is a safe classic. Despite its title, the book has relatively little in common with memory studies. As Fussell wrote in his preface, if the study had a subtitle, it would be called 'An Inquiry into the Curious Literariness of Real Life'. The book's central research question rose from the horrors of war: how was it possible to experience all that violence with any meaning? What consequences did this have? To answer these questions, Fussell showed how the British soldiers used 'arcadian resources' and other literary means to survive the war and to preserve some form of agency. Their war experiences were transformed into language and literature and generated the modern era. To Fussell this meant the birth of a fundamentally ironic relation to the world, born out of the discrepancy between the horrors of the trenches and the elegiac language used to describe them.[4] Referring to the curious habit of equating war with theatre in public discourses and literary accounts, Fussell commented thus on the soldiers' own experiences:

> Those who actually fought the war tended to leave the inviting analogy to Greek or any other kind of tragedy to the journalists. On the spot, it looked less like a tragedy than like a melodrama, a farce, or a music-hall turn. Or even a school-pageant played by enthusiastic but unprepared boy actors impersonating soldiers, trying to look like Tennysonian heroes.[5]

In one of the brutal paradoxes of the twentieth century, the war that allegedly gave birth to the modern mentality started as an escape from modernity. Historian Eric J.

Leed captured this paradox in his impressive cultural history of experiencing industrialized violence on the Western Front. In August 1914, men and women celebrated the outbreak of war as a return to heroism, chivalric virtues and national unity. German playwright Carl Zuckmayer, for example, experienced the declaration of war as a liberation from the pettiness of bourgeois family life: the war was a great sport full of Romantic emotions. Entering 'the labyrinth' of the trenches at the turn of 1914–15, the soldiers encountered an altogether different world, characterized by the absurdity and randomness of extreme violence. They tried (and often managed) to survive this world by transforming their identity to match the liminal, subterranean circumstances of their existence and by resorting to various cultural repertoires of myth, ritual and fantasy. Next to death and mutilation, the war neurosis was an attempt to exit the intolerable realities of the front. Similar to Fussell – but drawing rather from cultural anthropology and psychology than from literary studies – to Leed the war was a modernizing experience. It meant disillusionment with traditional ways of thinking and an internalization of war itself as a new mentality.[6]

One of the main endeavours in cultural history that helps explain frontline soldiers' remarkable ability to endure the war's hardships has been the study of masculinities. Advocating emphasis on bodies, historian Joanna Bourke studied the British soldiers' corporeal experiences in 1914–18. Male bodies at war were a site of violence, resistance, comradely bonding, malingering, shock and memory.[7] As historian Jason Crouthamel has shown, the harsh frontline conditions could actually allow for such forms of male intimacy that would have otherwise been considered inappropriate and 'unmanly' – and such outlets of 'divergent' masculinity could foster emotional comfort in the midst of violence. Open homosexuality remained a problematic issue, but the ideal of comradeship and close emotional bonds between men allowed for more freedom to express attraction. 'When we didn't go out of an evening, we dismissed the servants and sat for a long time arm in arm, in close embrace, saying many tender and lovely things to each other, spinning golden for the future and building beautiful castles in the air', wrote a German officer of his love relationship to another officer.[8]

Manliness was a cultural resource at the soldiers' disposal; it included the national ideals and stereotypes of a soldier-hero as well as a multitude of less programmatic male roles from domestic middle-class masculinities to deviant working-class lads. When one reads the soldiers' war narratives, the frontline experience turns more ambivalent than a story of mere terror and disillusionment. Both Leonard V. Smith's study on French soldiers and Jessica Meyer's study on British soldiers came to a similar conclusion: the war changed men, often dramatically and violently, but the soldiers were still able to attach many positive or ambiguous qualities to their experiences as the 'real men of the front'. They were also able to use many traditional narratives of soldiering to experience the war as meaningful.[9] According to Alexander Watson's close comparative analysis of the British and German frontline cultures in 1914–18, 'resilience not collapse was the norm among men on the Western Front'. Even much of the initial patriotism that motivated the soldiers in 1914 actually survived the following four years, albeit in a more down-to-earth style.[10]

Although the homosocial bonds among the soldiers were clearly one of the main sources of their mental endurance, the wartime male–female relations provided further support. Most of the soldiers were very young, and their closest relatives were still their parents. Mothers (and to some extent fathers) took on a role as 'emotional containers', who absorbed the fears and insecurities of their sons at the front and returned them back in a more tolerable form, as Michael Roper's insightful analysis of British soldiers' letter correspondence has shown.[11] Christine E. Hallett's work on nurses of the Great War reveals the same function of female support and encouragement to the wounded and dying men – but also the appallingly traumatic conditions that the nurses themselves had to face in the casualty clearing stations and field hospitals. As Australian nursing sister Elsie May Tranter wrote in her diary on the Western Front in France, May 1917: 'Today I had to assist at ten (10) amputations one after another. It is frightfully nerve-wracking work. I seem to hear that wretched saw at work whenever I try to sleep […] How these boys do suffer!'[12]

The question of surviving violence mentally has remained a key impetus for cultural historical approaches to the Great War. The power of cultural imagination and practices to resist violence and to make it endurable seems to offer a comforting narrative against the backdrop of war's terror. There is, nevertheless, a dark side to this, as Joanna Bourke's cultural history of killing in war underlines. Instead of fear and hate, love of one's fellow soldiers and homefolks was the main motivator that kept the soldiers committing violence, not only surviving it. Human ability to feel attachment and empathy thus made the violence possible. And killing in war was not only a cause for disgust and regret but could also be a matter of indifference and even pleasure. Bourke notes how, during the two World Wars, 'psychiatrists recognized that more men broke down in war because they were *not* allowed to kill than under the strain of killing'.[13]

This remains a controversial issue, and it seems to be an overstatement that acts of violence could actually protect a person mentally.[14] Yet Bourke makes an important contribution by emphasizing the disturbingly positive emotions provoked by the war experience. In addition to survivors and victims, the perpetrators of violence were also using cultural resources to experience their deeds as justifiable and meaningful. One of the main functions of cultural practices was to make the act of killing easier and more tolerable:

> Killing itself could be seen as an act of carnival: combat gear, painted faces, and the endless refrain that men had to turn into 'animals' were the martial equivalent of the carnival mask: they enabled men to invert the moral order while still remaining innocent and committed to that order. Pranks involving enemy bodies were very common in all three conflicts [the First and Second World Wars and Vietnam].[15]

Histories of shell shock and war neurosis

All the studies above also discuss the opposite phenomenon to mental coping: the experience of mental breakdown. Every country that sent soldiers to major combat in 1914–18 had to face the psychological casualties of war. In Great Britain, 'shell shock' had become a catchword for the mental consequences of industrialized massacre already in 1915, and the same happened in France and Germany with their own definitions of war neurosis. Everywhere, both the medical officers and soldiers were puzzled by the emergence of these invisible wounds: some British frontline doctors used the acronym 'GOK' (God Only Knows) for diagnosing their shocked patients.[16] Today, a mentally broken soldier or ex-serviceman is an iconic image of the First World War, inserted in every film or TV series about the war. It is thus surprising to see that the first historical studies specifically on shell shock appeared quite late, at the beginning of the 2000s. But by then the growing interest in shell shock resulted in an avalanche of research, in which cultural history has been the main venue of investigation.

This trend began in 2000 when the *Journal of Contemporary History* published a theme issue on the comparative cultural history of shell shock. Based on a conference in Péronne in 1998, the issue included a keynote by George L. Mosse (1918–99) that turned out to be the last publication of one of the most influential cultural historians of war, masculinity and nationalism. Here, by emphasizing the special relation between soldiers' mental breakdowns and the collective perceptions of manliness, Mosse set the agenda for much of the forthcoming research: 'Shattered nerves and lack of will-power were the enemies of settled society and because men so afflicted were thought to be effeminate, they endangered the clear distinction between genders which was generally regarded as an essential cement of society'.[17] If the image of a soldier-man was fundamental to national self-perception and cultural cohesion in war-waging countries, then the image of a shell-shocked soldier carried with it the stigma of national weakness and degeneration. 'One day the authorities will wake up and realize what a great social danger the war hysterics represent', wrote German military psychiatrist Ernst Rittershaus in 1919, after the German defeat in the First World War.[18]

Both the above-mentioned theme issue and a collected volume entitled *Traumatic Pasts: History, Psychiatry, and Trauma in the Modern Age, 1870–1930* that soon followed it shared a comparative aim: was shell shock really a universal experience of the First World War, or was it rather a particularly British concept? As the contributors to *Traumatic Pasts* showed, there was indeed a general 'Western' genealogy to trauma in the intertwined development of modern psychiatry, the age of industry and new societal policies. In addition, the similarities in war experiences – the violent dominance of artillery fire and the passive trench warfare – created parallel experiences of war neurosis. Yet the medical responses and cultural perceptions of the phenomenon varied from country to country; there was no single 'culture of shell shock' to be found. A crucial contribution by cultural history to the ongoing discussions on mental trauma has been to underline the great varieties of trauma experiences and responses. Historical studies on trauma cannot take the contemporary psychiatric definition of post-traumatic stress disorder (PTSD) for granted. As Paul Lerner and Mark Micale, the editors of *Traumatic Pasts*, wrote in 2001:

> If it proves impossible to write a single, unilinear history of trauma, it is altogether possible to write histories of traumata, or accounts of the multiple contexts of self, science and society that have given meaning to past traumatic experience. We envision writing the 'history of trauma' as the discovery, recovery and reconstruction of these past worlds of meaning.[19]

The first two monographs focusing solely on the cultural history of war neurosis appeared soon afterwards. Peter Leese studied the birth of shell shock as a frontline experience and a medical category as well as its popular understanding and legacy in Great Britain during and after the Great War.[20] Paul Lerner wrote the history of traumatic neurosis in Germany from the end of the nineteenth century to the last years of the Weimar Republic.[21] Both of these works recognized the political aspect of war trauma: as a new and disputed category, war neurosis became an object of conflicting interpretations among psychiatrists, army officers, politicians, journalists and authors. The victory of one interpretation over others came to have very concrete consequences for the victims of war neurosis and their relatives, for instance in the form of psychiatric treatment, pension policy and general attitude towards the traumatized veterans. Thus, although the British military pension system allowed for war-invalid compensations for the 'shell-shocked' soldiers, the 'pensioning officers never relaxed their attempt to prove that mentally ill men were liars and malingerers', as Joanna Bourke has written.[22]

The growing focus on war trauma in research has brought new attention to post-war societies as 'post-traumatic societies'. As the symbols of war's mentally devastating violence, the war neurotics remained a question to be solved after 1918: they required medical care, applied for pensions, needed jobs and sometimes sought to publish their experiences in books and other artworks. Generally speaking, and although there were considerable national differences, the post-war societies replied to this presence of war trauma with silencing, marginalization and sometimes outright violence (most notably in the National Socialist Germany, but also elsewhere). Traumatized ex-servicemen's and their relatives' fight for recognition – and often the vanity of this fight – has produced fine cultural and social historical scholarship.[23]

The keen interest in the traumatic dimension of martial violence over the last two decades may relate to a huge cultural shift in Western societies: for most Europeans and Americans, war has become an anomaly in their everyday life, something belonging to a past world. The contemporary diagnosis of PTSD is an offspring of the anti-Vietnam War movements in the 1960s and 1970s, and thus it includes a moral statement about the fundamentally destructive nature of martial violence – the opposite of the earlier normative ideals of stoic manliness. In the same way, the study of historical war traumas has rejected the idea of war as something natural, rational and heroic. In the next phase of research, the trauma perspective should reach outside the Western (Front) contexts and towards the experiences of war-affected civilians.[24] At the same time, it is important to note that despite the wide societal changes, the experience of mental breakdown is often still considered shameful. 'The John Wayne figure – tough, stoic, brave and seemingly invincible – still constitutes the manly ideal for much of Canadian and North American society, especially in the military', Adam Montgomery summarizes in his history of war trauma in the Canadian military.[25]

Cultures after violence

'Never such innocence again', poet Philip Larkin concluded his 1964 poem *MC-MXIV*, in reference to a photograph of young men lining up in a recruiting station in August 1914.[26] Together with the means of survival and the history of shell shock, the third cultural historical emphasis on the First World War has been to study the war's consequences on the post-war culture. Here we return to Paul Fussell's influential thesis on the Great War as the cradle of modernity. The issue at stake has had two main features. First, did the war experience of 1914–18 produce such a profound breakage that the old pre-1914 world really died in the trenches and a new, distinctly different modern world was born? Second, did the experience directly cause an even more violent apocalypse: the Second World War and the Holocaust?

The idea of fundamental rupture in 1914–18 with the earlier culture and civilization is a dramatic narrative that currently permeates the popular understanding of the Great War. The idea is championed by literary scholar Samuel Hynes, who in 1990 drew on Fussell's thesis in his analysis of post-war British literature. From this perspective, the war experience meant betrayed idealism, bitterness, cynicism and resentment; even the alienated survivors of the war counted as its casualties. At the end of his monumental study Hynes saw the world of 1990 as still the descendant of the First World War:

> In our reality, here at the century's end, the First World War remains a powerful imaginative force, perhaps the most powerful force, in the shaping not only of our conceptions of what war is, but of the world we live in – a world in which that war, and all the wars that have followed it, were possible human acts. Our world begins with that war.[27]

Similar observations on the war's radical consequences have been made in relation to cinema and other arts, in addition to literature.[28] There was no return to the culture and mentality of the pre-war era.

Yet this interpretation of breakage has not gone uncontested. If one lowers one's sight from high culture to the popular imaginations of the First World War, the picture seems to be quite different than that of a profound disillusionment. Jay Winter, one of the most prominent cultural historians of the First World War and its memory, showed how the war made people seek meaning and consolation for their violent losses by returning to religion, tradition and pastoral images. War experience could cause a language shift away from naïve patriotism, but it did not cause a wholesale breakage. In fact, there was a revival and persistence of tradition after the war. People in the aftermath were characterized by their 'backward gaze', not by their radical breakaway with the past. Analysing the war poetry of 1914–18, Winter concluded:

> The soldier-poet was in the end a romantic figure. [...] It was (and remains) his voice which reaffirmed the values of the men who fought, their loyalty to one another, their compassion for those who suffered on both sides, their stoical acceptance of fate. At times, he expressed outrage at the injustice at the young being slaughtered while the old looked on. But most of this body of verse was an affirmation, even when cataloguing the awfulness of war.[29]

It was only after 1945 that the classical, romantic and sacred visions of war vanished. Another question is whether the experience of 1914–18 produced a specifically brutal political culture and mentality that then gave birth to fascism and Nazism. In *Fallen Soldiers: Reshaping the Memory of the World Wars*, George L. Mosse formulated a thesis that the modern warfare, frontline comradeship and massive amount of death

528

on behalf of the nation in the First World War initiated a 'myth of war experience', which cherished a new type of violent, hypermasculine warrior ideal. Taking the German frontline officer and author Ernst Jünger as his paradigmatic example, Mosse described a novel storm trooper of the trenches, who was merciless and tough to the extreme – and ready to annihilate his enemies even after the war. To these men, the war did not end in November 1918 but continued ever on as a state of mind. In defeated Germany, such men sought national and personal regeneration through violence and elimination of inner enemies. This led to the general brutalization of German politics and paved the way for Hitler. For Jünger in 1922, for example, 'poetry is now written out of steel and the struggle for power in battle'.[30]

When the soldiers returned home, the fear of violence and brutalization was quite widespread among the war-waging countries. Moreover, it has been argued that also in Great Britain the collectively traumatic violence of 1914–18 would have led to both real and imagined violence against those perceived as 'un-English' during the post-war years, to a kind of 'fascistic sensibility'.[31] This remains a controversial claim, and in fact there is important evidence quite to the contrary: in Great Britain the war experience led to an unforeseen wave of pacifism and to the cultural model of 'peaceable' and 'tempered' masculinity.[32] The same was true for France, as Antoine Prost has shown: 'However, this conception of politics as the continuation of war was peculiar to Germany. French ex-soldiers, on the contrary, insisted on the duty to make home politics more peaceful'.[33] Accordingly, there was no direct connection between the frontline experience and the brutalization of politics as such; the roots of Nazism had to be in a specifically German combination of cultural and societal traditions, the war experience and the post-war developments.

In any case, the continuation of violence after 1918 was the reality for most Europeans. In Germany and in East and Central Europe the chaotic post-war mayhem gave rise to a new paramilitary culture of violence, perpetrated by armed bands and militias.[34] Klaus Theweleit's psycho-cultural analysis of the German Freikorps officers remains an original classic in the field, although its psychoanalytical orientation and generalized conclusions are open to criticism.[35] Recently, historian Mark Jones has studied the same 'culture of violence' during the German revolution of 1918–19. Although his methodology is completely different from Theweleit's, the conclusions have similarities. Using the Freikorps as its instrument of power, the emerging German state was founded on an unprecedented orgy of violence. This was a full reversal of a long-term reduction of state violence in Germany. For the new state, violence was a means of communicating its power and authority – and even though these practices cannot derive their origin directly from the frontlines of 1914–18, they indeed gave cultural and political legitimacy to the forthcoming Nazi violence at the end of the Weimar Republic. An important notion in Jones's work is that violence is not only an instrument of power with cultural consequences; as a 'culture of violence' it is a cultural phenomenon in itself.[36]

The shattering of earlier state formations and the outbursts of unlimited violence in and after 1918 were naturally linked to military defeats in the First World War. The vacuum of power after all the restraints and sacrifices during the war years tends to bring to the fore a special mode of spontaneity, hedonism and even peculiar euphoria before the harsh new realities make themselves felt, as cultural historian Wolfgang

Schivelbusch has written. In this eschatological 'dreamland' the violence may easily turn against former authorities as the scapegoats for defeat. The long-term impact of defeat is the difficulty to attach sustainable meaning to all the human losses in war, which are in danger of losing their character as beneficial sacrifices on behalf of the nation. In this way, the violence of war haunts the post-war societies and challenges the key cultural meanings of national self-image.[37]

Cultural histories of a genocidal war?

From the 1970s onwards, the First World War has served as a treasury of topics for the new cultural history. The field has flourished with rich cultural interpretations, novel methodologies, fruitful controversies and bold hypotheses. This stems from the profoundly *cultural* aspect of the war's violence either as a cultural rupture or as evidence of cultural tradition's and imagination's ability to survive the violence.

Turning one's attention to the Second World War reveals a remarkable difference. Although the cultural turn in historical scholarship has self-evidently affected also the study of 1939–45, the role of cultural history is by no means as dominant here as in studying the First World War. Political, social, economic and military history are still the mainstream ways of narrating the history of the Second World War. Perhaps symptomatically, Paul Fussell's follow-up book *Wartime*, which extended his analysis of 1914–18 to 1939–45, never gained the same influence as *The Great War and Modern Memory*.[38] A cultural and literary analysis of the Second World War does not seem to have the same scholarly relevance and potential that it had for the previous war.

Why is this so? One essential explanation may be found in the thoroughly ideological nature of the Second World War. This was a war of manipulative top-down propaganda, with less room for individuals and communities to formulate their own understanding of the war. Discussing this issue in their introduction to the third volume of *The Cambridge History of the Second World War* in 2015, Michael Geyer and Adam Tooze gave the following answer:

> war cultures in the Second World War were distinctly more programmatic and were more keenly organized, and more vigorous in their determination to deliver real benefits and results [than in the First World War]. This was as true of Hitler's Germany as it was of the war effort of New Deal America.[39]

The second reason relates to the nature of violence. As horrible as the First World War was, it did not reach the murderous scale and quality of the Holocaust and the war in the east in 1941–45. In relation to the deliberate genocide of European Jews and Romany, cultural explanations may have felt out of place and even inappropriate. As historians from the 1960s onwards wrestled with the Holocaust, it was considered most important to establish the key events of the genocide and the actual decision-making processes that led to it. This was an inquiry into politics, bureaucracy, exploitation and logistics rather than cultural systems of meaning. Furthermore, the relativist standpoint as well as the diversity of interpretations – both hallmarks of cultural history – may have been ill-suited to approach the calculated murder of millions of unarmed civilians. As historian Dan Stone has noted in an important essay on this topic, cultural interpretations of Nazism have been seminal for the understanding of radical anti-Semitism and racial ideology; but regarding the actual murder process, the influence of cultural history is yet to emerge. However, the cultural history of racism and Nazi imagination as a basis for violence is a necessary explanatory addition to Holocaust studies.[40]

The (forthcoming) cultural history of the Holocaust is closely related to the cultural history of violence on the Eastern Front, 1941–45. Just as with the Holocaust, the ideological character of the 'war of annihilation' in the east has required cultural interpretations. Omer Bartov's study on Nazism and the German Army showed how the cultural models of 'Jewish–Bolshevist barbarism' were deeply rooted in the ordinary German soldiers' perceptions of the war in the east – and how these perceptions led to both brutal atrocities and the ideological cohesion of the German Army in the face of towering human losses. 'The Jew is a real master in murdering, burning and massacring […] These bandits deserve the worst and toughest punishment conceivable', wrote a German lance-corporal on the Eastern Front in 1941 – and thus justified the murdering, burning and massacring by the German troops.[41] Thomas Kühne's cultural-ideological analysis of the German concept and experience of soldierly *Kameradschaft* from 1914 onwards came to similar conclusions. Comradeship was not only a safe haven in the midst of violence; especially in the latter years of the Second World War, it was itself the motor of violence:

> Comradeship denoted inclusion, belonging, solidarity, and togetherness, but its reality depended on its opposite, the Other, the foe – exclusion. The Other could be the overwhelming enemy soldier or the denigrated enemy civilian. Terror generated tenderness, destruction enabled cohesion. And vice versa. Producing togetherness, even if only once in a while, enabled the soldiers to cope with the omnipresence of death and devastation they faced in their war of annihilation.[42]

The function and cultural practices of comradeship were similar in the Red Army, too: they enabled the Soviet soldiers to endure and commit violence. And as demonstrated by Catherine Merridale's study, the Communist regime tried to control and define soldiers' social bonds. Both in the Wehrmacht and in the Red Army, the close circle of fellow soldiers could allow a considerable degree of dissidence and resistance against the official ideology. But in the end, these primary groups fought to the extremes for the sake of their totalitarian regimes. Merridale's rich cultural inspection of everyday life in the Red Army returns us to the beginning of this chapter, to the power of cultural practices in coping with the violence of war. The role of religion, for example, was ambiguous: in order to survive the battle and to find consolation, the soldiers of the atheist Soviet state resorted to prayers and carried small crosses, but probably rather out of superstition and ritualistic practice than out of actual Orthodox faith.[43]

Advancing to enemy territory, both the German Army and the Red Army soldiers committed acts of sexual violence. And when the Allied forces liberated the countries occupied by Germany, the local people took revenge by publicly shaming and punishing those women who had had relationships with the Germans. Sexual and gendered violence seems to be connected to the mental and cultural mindscape of war, whereby women are seen simultaneously as 'war bounty', as the warriors' prizes, and as ones to be protected by soldier-men. As Susan Gubar noted in 1987, war promotes misogyny, which is not restricted to the women on the 'enemy side' but tends to sexualize and objectify women at large. The risks and sacrifices of men at the front were juxtaposed with the real or imagined safety and comfort of women at home.[44]

Furthermore, the experience of total war transformed the gender order both concretely and symbolically: women stepped into 'manly' spheres of production and bread-winning, sexual morals loosened and the former masculine soldier-heroes returned home as beaten men. Post-war sexual politics and the restoration of 'normality' after the violence have been important topics for cultural history.[45]

If the emblematic icon of the First World War today is the shell-shocked soldier, for the Second World War the Holocaust retains many of the same ethical judgements about the immorality, destructiveness and vanity of war. Consequently, it seems, the mentally wounded soldier of 1939–45 does not seem to have the same cultural potency to symbolize the war as his peer in 1914–18. For Germany in the 1940s and 1950s, though, the defeated masculinity of the former Wehrmacht and SS soldiers was a powerful cultural image. Returning from foreign captivity, these men epitomized the bankruptcy of the Nazi warrior cult. Disturbing and effeminate as they may have been, the veterans' broken appearances served an important function for the German post-war culture: they turned the Germans from perpetrators to victims of violence. Religious motifs helped to refashion the former soldiers in the war of extermination to Christ-like figures, who – returning from the Soviet prison camps – wore a 'crown of thorns made out of barbed wire'.[46] Yet the ex-soldiers' moral burdens and traumatic experiences continued to haunt their post-war lives, as Svenja Goltermann's reading of the West German psychiatric patient files has shown. The public discourse for these experiences was missing, but the bodies and minds still carried the memory of violence.[47]

In order to fully grasp the massively traumatic legacy of the Second World War, the future focus must shift from soldiers to civilians and from Western to Eastern Europe – and further to Asia. The most murderous violence of the Second World War in Europe took place in the east: in the area from Berlin to Moscow and from Leningrad to the Black Sea, which historian Timothy Snyder has coined with the term 'bloodlands'.[48] Here (as well as globally), the civilian casualties far exceeded the military casualties. It is in fact one of the paradoxes in historical trauma studies that the trauma discourses have developed mostly in those Western countries which have – proportionately speaking – suffered the least of the massive violence of the twentieth century. The first initiatives to expand the cultural history of trauma and violence to civilians and to the east have been taken, and the results are promising.[49] As far as I see, it is here that the history of the Second World War may provide a crucial narrative of its own to supplement and possibly challenge the powerful shell-shock paradigm of 1914–18.

Concluding remarks

Does the cultural history of the two World Wars differ from the cultural history of violence in 1914–45? As we have seen, much of the former has been about the experiences and consequences of violence, although these studies have not been conceptualized as the latter. Yet every now and then, I think an explicit cultural analysis of martial violence is useful in cleansing one's lenses from all the 'fog of war' and in sharpening the focus on the essentials of collective violence and culture. Every war is an assault on human tissue and human minds; every war both destroys and creates culture. In war, the lethal violence that is severely tabooed and sanctioned in inter-personal relations is a legitimate form of inter-state conduct. To make sense of this paradox – to give regenerative meanings to industrialized violence as well as to survive it – has been a major cultural effort which has shaped the conditions of modernity, from gender identities to national sentiments and from state bureaucracies to poetry. It continues to call for critical cultural historical analysis.

Over the nineteenth century – in the aftermath of the Napoleonic Wars – all-male conscript armies were established in most European countries. They turned out to be one of the most destructive inventions of humankind, enabling mobilization and warfare on an unforeseen scale. For the cultural history of violence, the age of World Wars introduced two terrorizing novelties: industrialized genocide and the massive use of indirect fire in warfare. Regarding the latter, the development started with the heavy artillery barrages and gas attacks at the frontlines of the First World War and was then followed by strategic air bombing campaigns in the Second World War. In the form of shells and bombs, death from the skies rained upon soldiers and civilians alike and reduced them to passive objects of violence. The Holocaust and the atomic bombing of Hiroshima and Nagasaki brought the violence of war to such extremes that there seemed to be little room for glorious soldiering. Although the European conscript armies remained in place until the end of the Cold War (and some of them until today), in Western Europe the heyday of heroic citizen-soldier masculinities as well as the culture of martial violence was over in 1945.[50] For the rest of the world, the story is different and does not allow itself to be encompassed only as past history: the violence of war is still unmaking and making the world.

If we look at the first half of the European twentieth century as the age of martial violence, the cultural historical perspective may be best suited to analyse the differences. Just as there was no single 'culture of shell shock' in 1914–18, cultural historians must underline the great variations in the nature of violence, in its cultural framing, and in coming to terms with it. This is a matter not only of separate national histories, but of differences among smaller communities, social groups and individuals. At the same time, cultural historians would do well to look also for similarities and conjunctions in the experiences and cultures of violence. In the spirit of transnational historiography, for example the cultural histories of artillery fire, foreign occupation or war-related nightmares would definitely warrant research: these were fundamental experiences of the twentieth century for tens of millions of people, notwithstanding their nationalities. In fact, and perhaps a bit surprisingly, here the 'traditional' military histories of the Second World War as the first truly global conflict may lead the way for the cultural historians to follow.[51]

Notes

1 E. Scarry, *The Body in Pain: The Making and Unmaking of the World*, Oxford: Oxford University Press, 1985, 3–6, 19–20, cit. 63–4.
2 V. Kivimäki and T. Tepora, 'Meaningless Death or Regenerating Sacrifice? Violence and Social Cohesion in Wartime Finland', in T. Kinnunen and V. Kivimäki (eds), *Finland in World War II: History, Memory, Interpretations*, Leiden: Brill, 2012, 233–75.

3 Cited in L.V. Smith, *The Embattled Self: French Soldiers' Testimony of the Great War*, Ithaca, NY: Cornell University Press, 2007, 65.

4 P. Fussell, *The Great War and Modern Memory*, Oxford: Oxford University Press, 1975, ix.

5 Ibid., 201.

6 E.J. Leed, *No Man's Land: Combat and Identity in World War I*, Cambridge: Cambridge University Press, 1979 (Zuckmayer cited on 58).

7 J. Bourke, *Dismembering the Male: Men's Bodies, Britain and the Great War*, London: Reaktion Books, 1996, 108–9.

8 J. Crouthamel, *An Intimate History of the Front: Masculinity, Sexuality, and German Soldiers in the First World War*, Basingstoke: Palgrave Macmillan, 2014, cit. 117.

9 Smith, *Embattled Self*; J. Meyer, *Men of War: Masculinity and the First World War in Britain*, Basingstoke: Palgrave Macmillan, 2009.

10 A. Watson, *Enduring the Great War: Combat, Morale and Collapse in the German and British Armies, 1914–1918*, Cambridge: Cambridge University Press, 2008, 232.

11 M. Roper, *The Secret Battle: Emotional Survival in the Great War*, Manchester: Manchester University Press, 2009.

12 C.E. Hallett, *Containing Trauma: Nursing Work in the First World War*, Manchester: Manchester University Press, 2009, cit. 209.

13 J. Bourke, *An Intimate History of Killing: Face-to-Face Killing in Twentieth Century Warfare*, London: Granta, 1999, 160–1, 168–70, cit. 248.

14 For criticism, see E. Jones, 'The Psychology of Killing: The Combat Experience of British Soldiers during the First World War', *Journal of Contemporary History* 41, 2, 2006, 229–46.

15 Bourke, *Intimate History of Killing*, 37.

16 B. Shephard, *A War of Nerves: Soldiers and Psychiatrists 1914–1994*, London: Pimlico, 2002, 29.

17 G.L. Mosse, 'Shell-Shock as a Social Disease', *Journal of Contemporary History* 35, 1, 2000, 103.

18 Cited in P. Lerner, *Hysterical Men: War, Psychiatry, and the Politics of Trauma in Germany, 1890–1930*, Ithaca, NY: Cornell University Press, 2003, 193.

19 P. Lerner and M.S. Micale, 'Trauma, Psychiatry, and History: A Conceptual and Historiographical Introduction', in M.S. Micale and P. Lerner (eds), *Traumatic Pasts: History, Psychiatry, and Trauma in the Modern Age, 1870–1930*, Cambridge: Cambridge University Press, 2001, 25.

20 P. Leese, *Shell Shock: Traumatic Neurosis and the British Soldiers of the First World War*, Basingstoke: Palgrave Macmillan, 2002.

21 Lerner, *Hysterical Men*.

22 J. Bourke, 'Effeminacy, Ethnicity and the End of Trauma: The Sufferings of 'Shell-Shocked' Men in Great Britain and Ireland, 1914–39', *Journal of Contemporary History* 35, 1, 2000, 63.

23 See, e.g., P. Barham, *Forgotten Lunatics of the Great War*, New Haven, CT: Yale University Press, 2004; G. M. Thomas, *Treating the Trauma of the Great War: Soldiers, Civilians, and Psychiatry in France, 1914–1940*, Baton Rouge, LA: Louisiana State University Press, 2009; F. Reid, *Broken Men: Shell Shock, Treatment and Recovery in Britain 1914–1930*, London: Continuum, 2010.

24 J. Crouthamel and P. Leese (eds), *Psychological Trauma and the Legacies of the First World War*, Basingstoke: Palgrave Macmillan, 2017.

25 A. Montgomery, *The Invisible Injured: Psychological Trauma in the Canadian Military from the First World War to Afghanistan*, Montreal: McGill-Queen's University Press, 2017, 210.

26 Cited and analysed in Fussell, *Great War and Modern Memory*, 18–19.

27 S. Hynes, *A War Imagined: The First World War and English Culture*, London: Bodley Head, 1990, 439–40, 469.

28 E.g. M. Eksteins, *Rites of Spring: The Great War and the Birth of the Modern Age*, Boston, MA: Houghton Mifflin, 1989; A. Kaes, *Shell Shock Cinema: Weimar Culture and the Wounds of War*, Princeton, NJ: Princeton University Press, 2009.

29 J. Winter, *Sites of Memory, Sites of Mourning: The Great War in European Cultural History*, Cambridge: Cambridge University Press, 1995, 221; see also T. Bogacz, '"A Tyranny of Words": Language, Poetry, and Antimodernism in England in the First World War', *Journal of Modern History* 58, 3, 1986, 643–68.

30 G.L. Mosse, *Fallen Soldiers: Reshaping the Memory of the World Wars*, Oxford: Oxford University Press, 1990, especially Ch. 8, Jünger cited on 101.

31 S. Kingsley Kent, *Aftershocks: Politics and Trauma in Britain, 1918–1931*, Basingstoke: Palgrave Macmillan, 2009, 193.

32 J. Lawrence, 'Forging a Peaceable Kingdom: War, Violence and Fear of Brutalization in Post-First World War Britain', *Journal of Modern History* 75, 3, 2003, 557–89.

33 A. Prost, 'The Impact of War on French and German Political Cultures', *Historical Journal* 37, 1, 1994, 25.

34 R. Gerwarth and J. Horne (eds), *War in Peace: Paramilitary Violence in Europe after the Great War*, Oxford: Oxford University Press, 2012.

35 K. Theweleit, *Male Fantasies 1–2*, Minneapolis, MN: University of Minnesota Press, 1987/1989.

36 M. Jones, *Founding Weimar: Violence and the German Revolution of 1918–1919*, Cambridge: Cambridge University Press, 2016.

37 W. Schivelbusch, *The Culture of Defeat: On National Trauma, Mourning, and Recovery*, trans. J. Chase, German original 2003, London: Granta, 2004; J. Macleod (ed.), *Defeat and Memory: Cultural Histories of Military Defeat in the Modern Era*, Basingstoke: Palgrave Macmillan, 2008.

38 P. Fussell, *Wartime: Understanding and Behavior in the Second World War*, Oxford: Oxford University Press, 1989.

39 M. Geyer and A. Tooze, 'Introduction to Volume III', in M. Geyer and A. Tooze (eds), *The Cambridge History of the Second World War*, Vol. III: *Total War: Economy, Society and Culture*, Cambridge: Cambridge University Press, 2015, 13–14. I am grateful to my colleague Ilari Taskinen for this reference.

40 D. Stone, 'Holocaust Historiography and Cultural History', *Dapim: Studies on the Shoah* 23, 1, 2009, 52–68; as well as the commentaries by Dan Michman, Carolyn J. Dean, Wendy Lower, Federico Finchelstein and Dominick LaCapra in the same issue.

41 O. Bartov, *Hitler's Army: Soldiers, Nazis, and War in the Third Reich*, Oxford: Oxford University Press, 1992, 161.

42 T. Kühne, *The Rise and Fall of Comradeship: Hitler's Soldiers, Male Bonding and Mass Violence in the Twentieth Century*, German original 2006, Cambridge: Cambridge University Press, 2017, 171.

43 C. Merridale, *Ivan's War: The Red Army 1939–45*, London: Faber and Faber, 2005, 168–9.

44 S. Gubar, '"This Is My Rifle, This Is My Gun": World War II and the Blitz on Women', in M.R. Higonnet et al. (eds), *Behind the Lines: Gender and the Two World Wars*, New Haven, CT: Yale University Press, 1987, 249.

45 E.g. D. Herzog, *Sex after Fascism: Memory and Morality in Twentieth-Century Germany*, Princeton, NJ: Princeton University Press, 2005; several chapters in R. Bessel and D. Schumann (eds), *Life after Death: Approaches to a Cultural and Social History of Europe During the 1940s and 1950s*, Cambridge: Cambridge University Press, 2003.

46 F. Biess, *Homecomings: Returning POWs and the Legacies of Defeat in Postwar Germany*, Princeton, NJ: Princeton University Press, 2006, 99.

47 S. Goltermann, *The War in Their Minds: German Soldiers and Their Violent Pasts in West Germany*, German original 2009, Ann Arbor, MI: University of Michigan Press, 2017.

48 T. Snyder, *Bloodlands: Europe between Hitler and Stalin*, New York: Basic Books, 2010.

49 A. Antić, *Therapeutic Fascism: Experiencing the Violence of the Nazi New Order*, Oxford: Oxford University Press, 2017; P. Leese and J. Crouthamel (eds), *Traumatic Memories of the Second World War and After*, Basingstoke: Palgrave Macmillan, 2016.

50 For an overview, see A. Ahlbäck, V. Kivimäki and T. Tepora, 'The Cult of Heroes', in A. Pető (ed.), *Gender: War*, Macmillan Interdisciplinary Handbooks, Farmington Hills, MI: Macmillan Reference, 2017, 303–19.

51 For some examples, see e.g. R. Overy, *The Bombing War: Europe 1939–1945*, London: Allen Lane, 2013; V. Davis Hanson, *The Second World Wars: How the First Global Conflict Was Fought and Won*, New York: Basic Books, 2017.

30

THE COLD WAR CULTURES AND BEYOND

Steven Conn

The Berlin Wall came down in my first year of graduate school. I taught my first class in the year the Soviet Union dissolved. Heady days, as anyone who lived through them will remember, and for those of us who did, it all seemed inconceivable. The Cold War had been woven so completely into the fabric of global affairs and daily life that it seemed impossible to imagine a world without it. Russian anthropologist Alexei Yurchak published his study of the last generation to grow up under Soviet communism in 2006 but its wonderful title captured the sense that many of us surely had in the early 1990s about the vanishing of the Cold War: *Everything Was Forever Until It Was No More.*[1]

Now when I teach the introductory survey course in modern American history, the topic my students struggle with most is the Cold War. The problem is not that the Cold War happened so long ago – it didn't – and my students can fully grasp topics that happened in the more distant past, like the Great Depression or the Progressive Era of reform. The difficulty seems to lie in the fact that the Cold War and the world order that it shaped simply does not resonate in any way for my students today. The Cold War, I try to explain, was both the headline news and the background noise in American life between the late 1940s and the early 1990s. Now, the Cold War seems to have vanished so entirely from the American landscape, both the real and the psychic, that it has left no trace. My students simply cannot understand what a Cold War world looked or felt like, or how it could possibly have occupied so much political, cultural and imaginative space.

What was once ubiquitous has now largely vanished.

The Cold War was a geo-political architecture used by two nations – the United States and the Soviet Union – to structure the rest of the world. It dominated diplomatic discussions and it lay behind and underneath many of the conflicts of the era, from Angola to Zimbabwe, from Guatemala to Vietnam. But the Cold War pervaded and re-shaped American culture profoundly as well.[2] This chapter will examine how the Cold War changed the inflections of four cultural areas, focusing primarily on the United States but taking some detours elsewhere around the world. First, we'll look at cultural production, including music, movies and literature and how these were shaped by Cold War concerns. Second, religion took on a new significance and a new role in the public sphere in the United States during the Cold War. Third, these decades saw a number of social movements, all of which were refracted through the lens of Cold War politics. Finally, I will examine how the understanding of American history changed during the Cold War and, in turn, how the Cold War has been remembered in the post-1991 era.

The Cold War in the arts, high and low

On the outskirts of Memphis, Tennessee, a giant rat perches atop the 'Atomic Pest Control' company building. It is not clear whether the rat symbolizes the strength of the 'atomic' power the company will bring to rid your home of rodents or whether nuclear radiation will someday make the rats grow this large. Either way, it is a wonderful example of the ways in which Americans attempted to domesticate the anxiety of living in the nuclear age during a Cold War arms race that seemed to have no finish line.

Almost immediately after the two atomic bombs detonated over Hiroshima and Nagasaki, American adults were drinking 'atomic'-themed cocktails and American children were pulling out various 'atomic' toys from the boxes of their breakfast cereal. At school, Bert the Turtle, a friendly cartoon creature, taught those children how to 'duck and cover' in the event of nuclear war. Their parents, if they were readers of the decidedly middle-brow weekly *Saturday Evening Post*, could not escape the Cold War and the nuclear age either. The magazine often featured cover illustrations by Norman Rockwell which celebrated a folksy, home-spun Americana. The rest of the cover would carry headlines for stories about the Soviet Union or about the spread of communism around the world. Even Dr Benjamin Spock, whose baby and childcare books helped raise generations of American children, included three paragraphs counselling parents about how to deal with the fear of nuclear war. His advice? 'Parents can give their children partial reassurance if they can say, "Yes, there is a danger but it need not happen if we all work politically for peace."'

Fighting to 'contain' the spread of communism around the world – and rooting out fifth-column communist threats at home – was only half of the work Americans confronted during the Cold War. The other half was learning to live in a near-constant state of fear about the threat of nuclear war and nuclear annihilation. Both aspects of the Cold War world found their way into a variety of cultural forms.

Joseph Conrad may be the first writer of spy fiction in the twentieth century with his novels *The Secret Agent* (1907) and *Under Western Eyes* (1911), but the Cold War caused the genre to explode in the second half of the century and on both sides of the Atlantic. English writers Ian Fleming and John le Carré, both of whom had worked for British intelligence agencies, used their novels as commentary on the place of Great Britain in a post-war, Cold War world. With its empire gone and a navy that no longer ruled the waves, Britain could still participate in the Cold War through superior spy-craft. Fleming's James Bond, first introduced in *Casino Royale* (1953), stood for a Britain as that nation wished it were: suave, sophisticated, cool always and unfailingly effective.[3] Most importantly, he is all those things much more so than his sometimes brutish or stumbling American counterparts.

Le Carré's Cold War, by contrast, is tragedy, not romance. The East vs. West spy game in his novels is filled with intrigue, drama and suspense but little, finally, is heroic, nor does it even mean very much. As Alex Leamas, the protagonist of le Carré's 1963 masterpiece *The Spy Who Came in from the Cold*, summed it up, 'What do you think spies are: priests, saints, martyrs? They're a squalid procession of vain fools, traitors too, yes; pansies, sadists and drunkards, people who play cowboys and Indians to brighten their rotten lives'.[4] The titanic Cold War confrontation reduced to a game of cowboys and Indians.

The Spy Who Came in from the Cold rises to the level of literature in the way that many Cold War spy thrillers don't. But the Cold War provided material for dozens of books both good and not so good. And even those books not directly concerned with Cold War plots can be read as products of a Cold War culture. Jack Kerouac's 1957 book *On the Road* is at one level as an amphetamine-fuelled celebration of anarchic freedom in a stiflingly conformist society. At another level, the characters are reacting to a nuclear-armed world where total destruction has been mutually assured. In a bit of what we might call Cold War post-modernism, Ian McEwan looked back on the Cold War even before it was over in his 1990 novel *The Innocent* which he set in the Berlin of the 1950s.

Likewise, movie-goers found the Cold War portrayed on the big screen in treatments that have been both sublime and ridiculous. Many of the better ones were, in turn, adaptations of books – the Bond books, of course, have become their own movie 'franchise' – and one of the greatest was also one of the first. *The Third Man*, directed by Carol Reed, was adapted from a novella by British writer Graham Greene and released in 1949. Set in post-war Vienna when the city is divided among the Allied powers, the shadows play so thickly in the movie that they created an atmosphere not just for the movie but for the whole of Cold War Europe. John Frankenheimer's *The Manchurian Candidate*, a wonderfully bizarre story of communist infiltration into American politics, was released in 1962 at the height of the Cuban Missile Crisis. It too had been a novel, written by American Richard Condon and published in 1959. Two years after Le Carré published *The Spy Who Came in from the Cold*, Richard Burton played Alex Leamas in the movie version directed by Martin Ritt.

You could laugh at the Cold War at the movies too, most memorably in 1964's *Dr. Strangelove*, directed by Stanley Kubrick. The comedy here is decidedly dark given that the movie chronicles a US nuclear attack on the USSR and the frantic efforts to recall the bombers from their mission. The movie was a tour-de-force for British actor Peter Sellers who played three roles in the film. The idea to have Sellers play multiple roles apparently came after he did the same thing for director Jack Arnold in another Cold War farce, *The Mouse that Roared*. James Cagney did a wonderful comic turn in Billy Wilder's *1, 2, 3*, an antic and racy comedy from 1961, set and shot in Cold War Berlin even as the wall was going up. Filled with heel-clicking Germans and slogan-spouting communists, all Coca-Cola executive Cagney wants to do is sell Coke behind the Iron Curtain. In 1971 the comedic troupe Monty Python satirized Cold War hysteria in a skit featuring an increasingly irate Michael Palin complaining:

'I'd like to say how shocked we are that a pleasant collection of Norwegian folk songs should be turned into an excuse for communist propaganda of the shoddiest kind. What's gone wrong with the world? I can't even take a bath without 6 or 7 communists jumping in with me. They're in my shirt cupboard and Brezhnev and Kosygin are in the kitchen now eating my wife's jam. Oh, they are cutting off my legs! I can see them peeping out of my wife's blouse! Why doesn't Mr. Maudling do something about it before it is too late? Ohhhh … God!!!'[5]

Still, for the most part the Cold War did not play as comedy in popular culture, whether on the page or on screens large and small. Instead, cataclysmic danger seemed imminent and apocalypse nigh. Indeed, Stanley Kramer's movie adaptation of the novel *On the Beach* in 1959 strips away a political cause for World War III and focuses instead on the fate of those few left after nuclear war has destroyed most of the planet. That apocalyptic vision of a world after nuclear war reached a crescendo in the public imagination almost a quarter-century later in November 1983 – at the height of Ronald Reagan's revved-up arms race and Cold War – with the broadcast of the television movie *The Day After*. In the movie, the Soviet Union invades Western Europe, precipitating a nuclear war between the two super-powers. Viewers then watch the effects of nuclear destruction on the central characters, all of whom live in Kansas. *The Day After* was watched by almost 100 million Americans. That year college students knew what the Cold War meant; many watched *The Day After* in groups in their dormitories, sharing their fear and confusion with their peers.

Whatever the particulars of a Cold War plot, the stakes were almost invariably the same: nuclear destruction. And reflecting a sense of a world beyond human control, a number of these scenarios are the result not of ideological conflict but of misunderstanding, miscalculation or simple human mistakes. Rarely did popular culture question the rationales undergirding the Cold War, but novels and movies did sometimes force readers and viewers to ask about the costs of it all. The Cold War was simply taken as a basic fact of life and viewed as the probable cause of our collective death as well.

The Cold War culture of American religion

It has been a well-observed irony that a nation founded by Deists, Enlightenment sceptics and perhaps one or two atheists – a nation founded without a state religion and with what Thomas Jefferson considered to be a 'wall of separation' between church and state – should become the most religiously enthusiastic country in the Western world. But the Cold War, and especially its first decade or so, gave religion a new valence in public life.

America's post-war religiosity was doubtless rooted in the American experience of the Second World War. For Americans, WWII was a triumphal moment and one that came at a comparatively small cost, certainly as compared with the devastation wreaked on other countries. The United States stood stronger, more prosperous and more influential after the war than it had been before it, and for many Americans there was something providential about this fact. Primo Levi, who survived the Holocaust, may have summed up the religious feelings of some number of Europeans when he famously declared, 'There is Auschwitz so there cannot be God', but for many Americans the victories over Germany and Japan could only have come with God's blessing.

This may help explain the distinctly religious cast to America's Cold War posture against the Soviet Union once wartime allies became Cold War antagonists. The United States, after all, had always been hostile to varieties of left-leaning political movements. Between the Bolshevik Revolution and the onset of the Cold War, however, that hostility centred on the threat that communism posed to capitalism and to the American free enterprise system. That threat seemed greatest during the economic collapse of the 1930s when the Soviet Union, at least from a distance, appeared to be the only country still working, and when America's vaunted free enterprise system had to be saved by Franklin Roosevelt's New Deal.

After the war, and with the nation's economic confidence fully restored, America's Cold Warriors increasingly latched on to religion as a key difference between the two societies and cast the Cold War as a struggle between the freedom of worship and the tyranny of state-sponsored secularism. 'Godless' was the adjective that increasingly modified the noun 'communism' in Cold War American discourse.

Dwight Eisenhower would seem an unlikely leader of this quasi-crusade. Raised in a religious household, Eisenhower rejected the pacifism of his parents' Mennonite and Jehovah's Witness faith and joined the army. Though he described himself as a deeply religious man, Eisenhower's religion was private and he was not a member of any religious denomination for most of his life.

That changed on 1 February 1953. On that day, Dwight Eisenhower was baptized very publicly in the Presbyterian Church near the White House in Washington, DC. Eisenhower thus became the first American president to take part in such a religious ceremony while in office, and that act set the tone for Eisenhower's use of religion during his presidency. He frequently opened his cabinet meetings with a prayer, for example.[6]

And Eisenhower presided over the insertion of religion into several American rituals during the 1950s. Beginning in 1892, the American school day (not to mention countless civic meetings and other public events) started with the 'Pledge of Allegiance', and, with hands on hearts, children pledged their allegiance to 'one nation with liberty and justice for all'. This bit of patriotic pablum was written to coincide with the 1893 World's Columbian Exposition in Chicago. Sixty years later, in 1954, Eisenhower urged Congress to add the phrase 'under God' to the pledge. In fact, Eisenhower was simply catching up with a movement that had begun several years earlier as various groups began adding the phrase to the pledge on their own. When he signed the bill into law, Eisenhower made the Cold War implications of the edited version clear. America 'shall constantly strengthen those spiritual weapons which forever will be our country's most powerful resource', by having schoolchildren recite this phrase, 'one nation under God', every morning.

Likewise, Americans have always put their faith in the US dollar, but starting in 1957 Americans have found the phrase 'In God We Trust' on their greenbacks. That came because of two laws passed in 1956, one authorizing 'In God We Trust' to be the 'official' motto of the United States, replacing the more expansive 'e pluribus unum' which had served in that role since 1782. The bill's sponsor, Representative Charles Bennett of Florida, made the Cold War impetus behind the legislation clear: 'In these days when imperialistic and materialistic communism seeks to attack and destroy freedom, we should continually look for ways to strengthen the foundations of our freedom'.[7] For Bennett, as for so many Cold War Americans, freedom and religion were virtually synonymous. That these could be combined on American cash only made the equation better.

But if the Cold War context of American life became more explicitly religious, religion itself paradoxically became less explicit. Fine and often fractious doctrinal differences faded in the Cold War era and Americans began to refer to the 'Judeo-Christian tradition', never mind that the term was somewhat vague and did not have much of a tradition behind it. What mattered most in Cold War America was that one *had* a religion; what mattered less was *what* that religion might be.

In the midst of this Cold War religious revival – as many as 95% of Americans identified themselves as 'religious' according to one poll taken in the 1950s – Will Herberg conducted a study of American religious belief and published it in 1955. The title captures much of the book's argument: *Protestant, Catholic, Jew*.[8] Herberg found that in the post-war period, virtually all Americans belonged to one of these three religious tribes. Gone, Herberg found, were the ethnic – and theological – qualifiers that used to attach to those terms: Italian Catholic, Russian Jew, German Lutheran. The convictions behind these three 'communions', as Herberg also called them, were not particularly deep, nor were they in any way difficult or challenging for adherents. But these watered-down versions of the three faiths allowed Americans to put aside religious differences and worship together the 'common religion' of the 'American way of life'. Thus, Herberg concluded, Americans 'tend to think of their church as a denomination existing side by side with other denominations in a pluralistic harmony that is felt to be somehow the texture of American life'. When candidate Dwight Eisenhower met with his former World War II counterpart Soviet Marshal Grigori Zhukov, he anticipated Herberg's findings by saying: 'Our government has no sense unless it is founded in a deeply felt religious faith, and I don't care what it is'. The Cold War fostered both a new religiosity in American life and a more generous notion of religious tolerance.

No group benefited more from that Cold War culture of religion than American Catholics. From the founding of the United States Catholics had been viewed with uneasiness by some and downright hostility by many Americans, and this anti-Catholicism persisted well into the twentieth century. When Al Smith ran for the presidency in 1928, he was the first Catholic to be nominated by a major party and his candidacy inflamed Protestants, particularly in the American South. The Cold War gave Catholics an opportunity to re-position themselves in American society.

The Vatican itself took sides in the Cold War when Pope Pius XII issued the Decree Against Communism in 1949, but in the United States Bishop Fulton Sheen had been railing against the Soviet Union as the 'most anti-Christian nation on the face of the earth' since the mid-1930s on his nationally syndicated radio show. (In 1938 Sheen also organized a rally in New York's Carnegie Hall to support the fascists in Spain.) With the Cold War underway, a number of the most important American anti-Communists were Catholic, including the aristocratic (William Buckley), the monstrous (Joseph McCarthy) and the hypocritical (Phyllis Schlafly). Indeed, Buckley served as McCarthy's most energetic and pugnacious defender.

Buckley, of course, was also the founding editor of the *National Review*, which became the most important gathering place for conservative writers in the mid-twentieth century. It was Buckley, therefore, who began a rapprochement between conservative Catholics like himself and other conservatives which began with their Cold War anti-communism (and also included a shared hostility to the civil rights movement). For her part, while Phyllis Schlafly is best remembered for her crusades against feminism, she began her political activism as a resolute Cold Warrior and, among other things, actively opposed any arms control negotiations between the United States and the Soviet Union.

Political rapprochement did not precisely bring Catholicism into the mainstream of American life – that was happening already – but more importantly it offered Catholics a way into the national political conversation. The common cause that conservative Protestants, Catholics (and even several Jews) made during the Cold War became the foundation for the New Right politics of the late twentieth century.

Putting God on the American currency, having schoolchildren pledge their allegiance to a nation 'under God' and the public spectacle of Dwight Eisenhower getting baptized were all acts of Cold War religiosity designed to put God on our side (to borrow from a Bob Dylan song from the early 1960s) in the struggle against the Soviet Union. And while the Constitution of the United States explicitly prohibits any religious test for holders of Federal positions, the Cold War effectively created such a test for office-seekers which has lasted well past the Cold War itself.

Social movements in Cold War America

Even when politics was not about the Cold War specifically, it was about the Cold War indirectly.

For advocates of African American civil rights in the 1950s and 1960s, the Cold War offered muscular leverage against the Southern regime of Jim Crow segregation. Victory in a global war to save freedom and democracy from fascism and tyranny only underscored the tyrannical and decidedly un-free conditions under which African Americans continued to live. After the war, and as European colonial empires dissolved, the United States parried with the Soviet Union to win the hearts and minds of those in the decolonizing world. In that competition, the regime of legalized racial segregation in the United States proved an increasing international embarrassment.

For its part, the Soviet Union was only too pleased to distribute stories about racial inequality and racial violence in the United States to news outlets around the world. In 1963 alone, for example, the USSR broadcast over 1,400 commentaries about civil and human rights violations during Martin Luther King, Jr.'s campaign in Birmingham, Alabama. Doubtless they reported on the now-iconic photo of a woman being arrested while carrying a placard reading: 'Khrushchev Can Eat Here, Why Can't We'. The Cold War, therefore, meant that American racial tyranny was no longer a local or even regional problem but an international one as well. And that woman photographed in the back of a police van, like so many civil rights activists, was aware of that fact.

This meant that the White House and the State Department in particular took an interest in civil rights to an extent neither entity had before. When President Eisenhower addressed the nation to announce that he was sending Federal troops to Little Rock, Arkansas to enforce the school desegregation order there, the speech was translated into 43 languages and broadcast by the Voice of America all over the world. The State Department archives are filled with correspondence from these years expressing concern about how segregation made the United States look bad on the international stage. In reply, the State Department began to recruit African Americans to the diplomatic service aggressively and to sponsor lectures and cultural events featuring black Americans in countries around the world.[9]

But the Federal government is a large and unwieldy institution, and even while some parts of it eagerly promoted civil rights (or appeared to), other parts remained deeply suspicious of the movement and worked to undermine it. J. Edgar Hoover, perhaps the most dangerously influential unelected figure in American history, had been watching black leaders since 1919, convinced that they were subversive. Once the Cold War began, he became even more convinced that the entire civil rights movement was nothing more than a front for international communism. Hoover once called Martin Luther King, Jr. 'the most notorious liar in the country'.[10]

In 1956, Hoover secretly opened the FBI's Counter Intelligence Program (COINTELPRO) to keep tabs on communists and others deemed by Hoover to be subversive. Civil rights leaders became the central focus of COINTELPRO almost immediately, and Hoover attempted repeatedly to smear the movement with charges that it had been infiltrated by communists.[11] Billboards popped up around the South claiming that Martin Luther King, Jr. had attended a 'communist training school', while the Southern Baptist preacher – and future advisor to Ronald Reagan – Jerry Falwell opined in 1965, 'I do question the sincerity and non-violent intentions of some civil rights leaders such as Dr. Martin Luther King and others, who are known to have leftwing associations'. The Cold War turned black civil rights in the United States a distinctive shade of red.

Students for a Democratic Society, remembered largely as the vanguard of the student New Left in the 1960s, took its inspiration from the black civil rights movement, and there was a great deal of overlap between the two phenomena. But SDS formed in response to the Cold War arms race and the threat it posed. Their 1962 manifesto, 'The Port Huron Statement', begins by expressing the fear that 'because of our common peril [nuclear weapons], [we] might die at any time'. They imagined a newly invigorated democratic politics as a way out of the political stalemate of Cold War and as an antidote to the sense of helplessness that the Cold War created for so many Americans.

By 1965 SDS had emerged as the driving force behind the opposition to the Vietnam War, itself an outgrowth of America's Cold War foreign and military policies. Vietnam, perhaps more than anything else, forced at least some number of Americans to question the basic architecture of the Cold War – and particularly the policy of containment – and the rationales behind it.

Ironically, as the 1960s rolled forward, and as Hoover's COINTELPRO infiltrated, spied on and otherwise destabilized civil rights and anti-war organizations in the name of protecting the nation from communists, more young people were drawn further to the left. Some left-wing organizations looked to Marxist-style liberation struggles in the developing world for models of what they might do in the United States. Posters of Che Guevara and Chairman Mao popped up on college dormitory walls. This infatuation with third-world revolutionaries and Marxist slogans became pervasive enough that writer Tom Wolfe could deride the alliance of left-wing politics and celebrity culture as 'radical chic' in 1970.[12] No matter the particulars of the issue at hand – urban poverty, Southern segregation or feminism – virtually all domestic politics in the United States got refracted through a Cold War lens during the era.

The confluence of the Cold War and political movements reached a crescendo of sorts on 12 June 1982 when roughly one million Americans gathered in New York's Central Park to demand a freeze on the construction of nuclear weapons and an end to the nuclear arms race between the United States and the Soviet Union. Until 21 January 2017 demonstrations against Donald Trump, the 'freeze rally' in Central Park was the largest demonstration in American history.

In fact, the protest against nuclear weapons and nuclear proliferation began with the dawn of the nuclear age itself and it grew alongside the development and deployment of nuclear weapons themselves. In 1945, a number of physicists, some of whom had worked on the Manhattan Project, began publishing *The Bulletin of Atomic Scientists* to monitor issues of science and world security. In 1947 the *Bulletin* included the 'Doomsday Clock', a clock with its hands approaching midnight, symbolizing how close the scientists feel we are to nuclear destruction. The minute hand on that clock has been moved forward or backward depending on the group's assessment of world events. And in the United Kingdom, the Campaign for Nuclear Disarmament (CND) formed in 1957 and held its first large-scale protest in 1958.[13]

Like those who marched for civil rights or protested the war in Vietnam, those who wanted an end to nuclear weapons were accused repeatedly of being communists or communist dupes. In the minds of conservatives and military hawks, to oppose nuclear weapons was *ipso facto* to support Soviet victory in the Cold War. For them, the choice about nuclear weapons, like the Cold War itself, was that simple and that Manichean.

And like so much else about the Cold War, the concern over nuclear weapons largely evaporated once the Soviet Union ceased to exist. Plenty of Americans and Europeans today worry about the possibility that a terrorist group might acquire a nuclear device, or nuclear material, but few protest the over 4,000 nuclear weapons that remain in the American arsenal. The Doomsday Clock is still set perilously close to midnight.

Missing the Cold War: memory and history

Before it was swept into the dustbin of history, the Cold War profoundly changed the way Americans understood their own past. Mid-twentieth-century historical writing, exemplified by figures like Louis Hartz, Richard Hofstadter, Arthur Schlesinger Jr. and Daniel Boorstin, became dominated by the 'consensus school' which extolled, one way or another, the virtues of centrist liberalism as the best alternative to totalitarianisms right and left – though in the Cold War context, mostly left. When historian Schlesinger published *The Vital Center* in 1949, he argued that an energetic liberalism, exemplified by Franklin Roosevelt's New Deal, was the only way to restore the relationship between individuals and communities that had been eroded by technology and capitalism. Even though the memory of Nazi Germany was still painfully fresh, Schlesinger spent more of his time warning about the 'failure of the Left' and the danger posed by those seduced by Soviet Marxist-Leninism.[14]

For a quick gloss on the nature of the 'consensus school', contrast one of the towering historical works of the Progressive era, Charles Beard's 1913 *An Economic Interpretation of the Constitution*, with Hartz's 1955 book *The Liberal Tradition in America*. The former re-read the nation's founding document and found little but the naked protection of economic self-interest for the class that wrote it. It was entirely of a piece with historians who found American history riven by class conflict. The latter book argued that liberalism, defined loosely, was really the only political ideology Americans had ever had. Or non-ideology, actually. Looking back, Hartz found American politics to be remarkably devoid of ideological conflict, with no real conservative traditions or any socialist ones either.[15]

Americans might have preferred pragmatism over ideology in their politics in the Cold War conception of American history, but religion was seen to have played a much larger role in the founding of the nation. And much like the religion of the American 1950s, the religion that Americans now insisted had always been present in American life was vague, non-denominational and utterly essential. 'Nothing can be more certain', Florida Representative Charles Bennett told his colleagues when he introduced the legislation to put God on the nation's bills, 'than that our country was founded in a spiritual atmosphere and with a firm trust in God'. At Monticello, Thomas Jefferson spun in his grave.

There was never as much consensus, and certainly not as much Whiggishness, among the consensus generation as later critics pretended. Still, in the service of the Cold War and writing in the confident, victorious and prosperous 1950s and early 1960s, historians found the American past looked a lot like the American present. As Henry Steele Commager summed it up in his sweeping study *The American Mind*, another monument of consensus historiography, the American of 1950 'still believed that such words as honor, virtue, courage and purity had meaning … they revered the flag and the Constitution … They still professed faith in democracy, equality, and liberty'. Commager too allowed that living in a nuclear-armed world meant that 'he could not rid himself of the fear that his world might end not with a whimper but with a bang'. But what Commager did not say, because it did not need to be said, was that in their faith and optimism Americans in 1950 stood in stark contrast to jaded Europeans and duped Soviets. Whether all or any of that was really true was not quite the point. Our history (non-ideological, practical and driven by common-sense values), the consensus writers argued, was what allowed us to avoid the cataclysms that had engulfed the rest of the world.

The reaction against the consensus school came in the 1960s. Just as the civil rights movement and the war in Vietnam prompted many Americans to question, and reject, the Cold War political consensus that had emerged after World War II, when historians in the 1960s looked back, they found a very different America. Gabriel Kolko picked up where Charles Beard left off and found collusion between big business and government all at the expense of workers and ordinary people. Conflict was everywhere now in the American past – on slave plantations and factory shop floors, in ethnic urban neighbourhoods and even within individual families – just as conflict seemed everywhere in the American 1960s. In 1959, within just 15 years of the American victory in World War II, William Appleman Williams considered the history of American diplomacy and found it tragic. Historical revisionism came in many flavours and was driven by dynamics internal to the historical profession, but both directly and indirectly American historical writing, and thus our understanding of the American past, bore the stamp of the Cold War. When it was over in 1992, when liberal democracy and free market capitalism seemed poised to take over the world, Francis Fukuyama announced 'the end of history'.[16]

Historical revisionism came much later to those countries on the other side of the Iron Curtain. Soviet history was revised regularly during the Cold War – a Soviet joke featured a dinner toast: 'Comrades! The future is certain. But the past is changing all the time' – and history was used as an adjunct of state propaganda. That joke turned into a kind of collective existential crisis for Russians in the late 1980s. Central to Mikhail Gorbachev's reforms was a rehabilitation of history itself. Archives opened up, censorship eased and Russians began to confront their own past in a way that they had not for over half a century.

On 2 November 1987 Gorbachev, in front of the Soviet Communist Party Congress and surrounded by the leaders of virtually all of the Soviet client states, addressed the nation on the occasion of the 70th anniversary of the Bolshevik Revolution. His subject was history: 'Many thousands of members of the Party and nonmembers were subjected to mass repressions', Gorbachev lectured. 'That is the bitter truth'. He wasn't finished. 'Even now', he continued,

> we still encounter attempts to ignore sensitive questions of our history, to hush them up, to pretend that nothing special happened. We cannot agree with this. It would be a neglect of historical truth, disrespect for the memory of those who found themselves victims of lawlessness and arbitrariness.[17]

Seven months later, the national end-of-year exams in history were cancelled for students aged 6–16 – all 53 million of them. The reason was as straightforward as it was extraordinary. 'Today, we are reaping the bitter fruits of our own moral laxity', *Izvestia* editorialized in announcing the news. 'We are paying for succumbing to conformity and thus to giving silent approval of everything that now brings the blush of shame to our faces and about which we do not know how to answer our children honestly'. *Izvestia* was merciless in describing Soviet crimes against history. 'The guilt of those who deluded one generation after another, poisoning their minds and souls with lies, is immeasurable', the editors thundered. The decision to cancel the exams was 'sober, honest and dignified', the paper concluded. Why, after all, test students on their mastery of lies? In a profound way, the end of the Cold War in the Soviet Union and its satellite states was not the end of history but the beginning of it.[18]

The results were disorienting and vertiginous, especially in the heady, open days of the 1990s. In the former Soviet Union Russians had their entire conception of their past upended and everything, it seemed, was on the table for historical reconsideration: economic history, political history, family history. Even World War II – The Great Patriotic War – which provided the foundational myth of the Soviet state in the Cold War years did not escape historical scrutiny. Writer and veteran Viktor Astafyev created a sensation when he published his semi-autobiographical novel *The Accursed and the Dead*, an unsparing story of what ordinary Soviet soldiers had to endure during the war.[19] Neither glorious nor particularly patriotic, the war experience as told by Astafyev was senseless, often arbitrary and almost without meaning.

In the rest of the eastern bloc, the return of history after the end of the Cold War took a different direction. All along the now-former Iron Curtain, from the Baltics at least to Hungary, the history project in the post-Cold War era has consisted of revealing the crimes of the Communist years, exposing those who collaborated with the discredited regimes and celebrating the stubborn nationalism that finally triumphed after 1992. While they differed in their details, all the historical narratives constructed in most of these countries have been remarkably the same: the story of double victimhood. First, we were victimized by the Nazis and then without reprieve we were victimized by the Soviets.

At one level, of course, there can be no arguing with that story. The space between Berlin and Moscow saw the worst of World War II's suffering and devastation; those bloodlands then became the geo-political plaything of the Soviet Union in its Cold War conflict with the United States. As a Polish joke I heard in Warsaw goes: 'Why does a Polish soldier shoot at Germans first and then at Russians? Duty before pleasure'. Today in Warsaw, schoolchildren troop to the lavish (and loud) Uprising Museum, which celebrates, and that is the only word for it, the doomed (and perhaps quixotic) rebellion against Nazi occupation in 1944 while Soviet troops watched, doing nothing, on the other side of the Vistula River. Across town the Polish government and press work to bring those who collaborated with the communist regime to public scrutiny.

But turning the history of World War II and the Cold War into a story of double victimhood serves to erase as much as illuminate the past that had been buried by and during the Cold War. The Lonsky Prison Museum in L'viv, Ukraine, for example, preserves and interprets the place where Soviet NKVD agents killed hundreds and perhaps thousands of Ukrainian nationalists between 1939 and 1941; then the prison was taken over by Nazi invaders who rounded up Jews in the city and in so doing precipitated a city-wide pogrom. Jews are absent from the museum's interpretation, however, and the message is clear at Lonsky: the Ukrainian nation has been built on the sacrifice of those Ukrainian nationalists imprisoned and executed by the Soviets at Lonsky Prison. Jews need not apply, not even Simon Wiesenthal who lived in L'viv and was arrested, though not shot, along with the city's other Jews in 1941. There is no mention of him at the museum.[20]

Poles have been equally reluctant to acknowledge their own wartime collaborations with the Nazi occupiers. Historian Jan Gross has spent much of his career studying Poland under the occupation and his 2001 book about the destruction of the Jewish community in the town of Jedwabne created a storm of controversy because of his contention that Poles themselves had done much of the killing.[21] The Uprising Museum tells the story of heroic resistance while in 2015 Polish prosecutors opened a libel case against Gross.

However much people were victimized by communist regimes in the Cold War years, the suppression of history during those years meant that those nations – Poland, Hungary, Ukraine and others – never reckoned with their own role during the war or their complicity in its many atrocities. The memory infrastructure being built in those places today suggests that they still have not. Many were the sins committed against Eastern Europeans during the years of communist control, but the Cold War allowed them to hide some of their own sins as well.

Writing in *The Atlantic* in August 1990, political scientist John Mearsheimer predicted that we would all wind up missing the Cold War. After the euphoria had faded, he believed, nations would find themselves adrift, without a stabilizing order in the world, and not sure exactly how to proceed.[22]

When news of the September 11 attacks reached an Air Force base in upstate New York in 2001, planes were scrambled and they headed north towards the North Pole. The response plan still sent them to the Soviet Union, which had not existed for a decade. That minor mistake underscored how difficult it has been at least for some to give up the Cold War. It also highlights, however, a certain continuity between the Cold War world and what has emerged since. Substitute 'terrorism' for 'communism', and Eisenhower's 'military-industrial complex' and its capacity to project American force anywhere around the world can be justified again.

The United States fought the Cold War with the objective of 'containing' the spread of communism – a strategy Walter Lippmann called at its inception a 'monstrosity'. Standing alone as a superpower, the United States pivoted to a policy designed to spread liberal democracy (and laissez-faire capitalism) to all corners of the globe. To the victors, at least in the minds of many in America's foreign policy secretariat, go the spoils. We are an empire now, said Karl Rove infamously in 2003, and we make our own reality.

The facile conclusion drawn by these people about the nation's Cold War 'victory', and about how the world would be ordered, led, of course, to the worst foreign policy disaster in American history: the invasion of Iraq. This is not the place to review that fiasco, as journalist Thomas Ricks called it in the title of his book about it – save to say that it is hard to imagine the United States launching such a reckless, feckless adventure in the geo-political context of the Cold War. And if that is true, then we all miss the Cold War indeed.

In fact, the rest of the world has not wholly cooperated with the American vision of American hegemony. As I write, the inevitable triumph of liberal democracy seems much less inevitable. Francis Fukuyama's announcement that history was over has proved a tad premature. The fact that the world has been more recalcitrant than American leaders have demanded might explain Americans' ineffective (and sometimes dangerous) responses to international situations since the end of the Cold War. It might also explain the politics of angry resentment among conservatives who fulminate that America isn't as great as it once was.

Outside the world of military and foreign policy, however, the disappearance of the Cold War has been met largely with amnesia in the United States and with some nostalgia elsewhere. In Berlin the DDR Museum opened in 2006 to exhibit the now-vanished world of ordinary life in East Germany – from consumer goods to leisure-time activities to a Stasi interrogation cell. Just over two kilometres away, Checkpoint Charlie, that fraught crossing point between East and West at the centre of so many Cold War spy novels and movies, is now a kitschy tourist spot complete with actors dressed as soldiers busking for tips. And let's face it, spy novels themselves have never been the same since the end of the Cold War, which may explain why in 2015

German television began showing 'Deutschland '83', a drama about a rookie East German spy sent to the West. Nothing since has seemed as dramatic or consequential.

The Cold War, I tell my students, was once like God in the Christian catechism: where is the Cold War? The Cold War is everywhere. It still is in so many ways. But while it was once front and centre, now its legacy is hidden and opaque. It may be forgotten, but it is certainly not gone.

Notes

1 A. Yurchak, *Everything Was Forever, Until It Was No More: The Last Soviet Generation*, Princeton, NJ: Princeton University Press, 2006.

2 While the Cold War was indeed a global phenomenon, this chapter will look at its effects on American culture. The writer is not in a position to discuss Cold War culture in other parts of the world.

3 I. Fleming, *Casino Royale*, New York: Macmillan, 1953.

4 J. le Carré, *The Spy Who Came in from the Cold*, New York: Coward-McCann, 1963.

5 Cinema during the Cold War has become a rich area of scholarly discussion. See for example: T. Shaw, *Hollywood's Cold War*, Amherst, MA: University of Massachusetts Press, 2007; J. Hoberman, *An Army of Phantoms: American Movies and the Making of the Cold War*, New York: New Press, 2011; T. Shaw and D. Youngblood, *Cinematic Cold War: The American and Soviet Struggle for Hearts and Minds*, Lawrence, KS: University of Kansas Press, 2010.

6 For more on this subject see D. Holmes, *The Faiths of the Postwar Presidents: From Truman to Obama*, Athens, GA: University of Georgia Press, 2012. See also William Inboden, *Religion and American Foreign Policy, 1945–1960*, Cambridge: Cambridge University Press, 2008.

7 https://history.house.gov/Historical-Highlights/1951-2000/The-legislation-placing-%E2%80%9CIn-God-We-Trust%E2%80%9D-on-national-currency.

8 W. Herberg, *Protestant, Catholic, Jew: An Essay in American Religious Sociology*, Garden City, NY: Doubleday, 1955.

9 For more on this topic see J. Skrentny, 'The Effect of the Cold War on African-American Civil Rights: America and the World Audience, 1945–1968', *Theory and Society* 27, 1998, 237–85.

10 Hoover quoted in John Herbers, 'Dr. King Rebuts Hoover Charges', *New York Times*, 20 November 1964.

11 COINTELPRO was exposed to the American public after a group of Philadelphia-area peace activists broke into a branch office of the FBI and stole files which they then released to the press. Among the first books to come out on the programme was N. Blackstock, *COINTELPRO: The FBI's Secret War on Political Freedom*, New York: Vintage Books, 1975.

12 See T. Wolfe, *Radical Chic and Mau-Mauing the Flak Catchers*, New York: Farrar, Straus & Giroux, 1970.

13 For a history of CND see P. Byrne, *The Campaign for Nuclear Disarmament*, London: Croom Helm, 1998.

14 A. Schlesinger, *The Vital Center: The Politics of Freedom*, Boston, MA: Houghton, Mifflin Co., 1949; D. Boorstin, *The Genius of American Politics*, Chicago, IL: University of Chicago Press, 1953.

15 C. Beard, *An Economic Interpretation of the Constitution of the United States*, New York: The Macmillan Company, 1913; L. Hartz, *The Liberal Tradition in America: An Interpretation of American Political Thought Since the Revolution*, New York: Harcourt, Brace, 1955.

16 G. Kolko, *The Triumph of Conservatism: A Re-Interpretation of American History, 1900–1916*, New York: Free Press, 1963; W. A. Williams, *The Tragedy of American Diplomacy*, Cleveland, OH: World Publishing Co., 1959; F. Fukuyama, *The End of History and the Last Man*, New York: Free Press, 1992. Fukuyama actually first used the phrase in an article in 1989.

17 Quoted in David Remnick, *Lenin's Tomb: The Last Days of the Soviet Empire*, New York: Vintage Books, 1994, 50.

18 Gorbachev quoted in D. Remnick, *Lenin's Tomb: The Last Days of the Soviet Empire*, New York: Vintage Books, 1994, 50. *Izvestia* quoted in *Gorbachev's Glasnost: Red Star Rising*, Fact on File, 1 August 1989, 49.

19 Astafyev's novel has not had an English translation. For more on the book see A. Brintlinger, *Chapaev and His Comrades: War and the Russian Literary Hero Across the Twentieth Century*, Boston, MA: Academic Studies Press, 2012, Chapter 7.

20 For more on the relationship between forgetting and museums in the post-Soviet world see S. Norris (ed.), *Museums of Communism: New Sites of Memory in Central and Eastern Europe*, Bloomington, IN: Indiana University Press, forthcoming.

21 J. Gross, *Neighbors: The Destruction of the Jewish Community in Jedwabne, Poland*, Princeton, NJ: Princeton University Press, 2000.

22 J. Mearsheimer, 'Why We Will Soon Miss the Cold War', *The Atlantic Monthly*, August 1990.

31

THE CULTURE OF COMMERCE AND THE GLOBAL ECONOMY

Jared Poley

In an essay published in 1930, 'Economic Possibilities for our Grandchildren', the economist John Maynard Keynes imagined a future relatively free of toil. Noting the growth of the global economy since the sixteenth century, Keynes foresaw huge economic and cultural changes that would be in place by 2030 – a century after the essay was written. Envisioning a world with three-hour work days and 15-hour work weeks, Keynes turned his analysis to the problem of leisure and the cultural shifts that such freedom would permit. 'When the accumulation of wealth', Keynes writes, 'is no longer of high social importance, there will be great changes in the code of morals'.

> We shall be able to rid ourselves of many of the pseudo-moral principles which have hag-ridden us for two hundred years, by which we have exalted some of the most distasteful of human qualities into the position of the highest virtues. We shall be able to afford to dare to assess the money-motive at its true value. The love of money as a possession – as distinguished from the love of money as a means to the enjoyments and realities of life – will be recognised for which it is, a somewhat disgusting morbidity, one of those semi-criminal, semi-pathological propensities which one hands over with a shudder to the specialists in mental diseases. All kinds of social customs and economic practices, which we now maintain at all costs, however distasteful and unjust they may be in themselves, because they are tremendously useful in promoting the accumulation of capital, we shall then be free, at last, to discard.[1]

In this chapter, we explore the cultural ramifications of the globalization of commerce in the modern period. While that topic is far too vast to take on in its entirety, we can address aspects of the problem by considering the ways the market itself was conceptualized. The market specifically and the economy generally have traditionally been ciphers for larger analyses of human motivations. They are, in other words, heavily enculturated. Never only a mechanism for exchange or a way to distribute resources, the market was also a way to ruminate more broadly on what it meant to be a human and how society was constituted. Only in the twentieth century, and only then by a small segment of economists, was the economy understood to be in some way outside of culture. The market is at once a catch-basin for human desires, a mechanism for satisfying those desires and an expression of social value.

Luxury and desire

In the eighteenth century, debates about the culture of commerce unfolded within the context of decline of the *ancien regime*; the reconstitution of society on the basis of individualism and the elaboration of free-market principles. The conceptual value of categories like luxury, utility and inequality was heightened in the shift from a moral to a political economy. The morality of the marketplace was a key indication of the health of the larger political body, as well as that of the individuals who constituted it. Luxury, beginning in the eighteenth century, was a vexed category. While some imagined that luxury indicated a social effeminization or envisioned it in terms of useless spending, others were sure to emphasize its positive elements. Luxury was a tool of economic development. Its commercial value existed in the way that it defined desires and generated the economic mechanisms necessary to satisfy them. Luxury, a culturally defined good that by definition exceeded its use-value in significant ways, radiated throughout the economic and political worlds. Members of the Scottish Enlightenment were also taken with its ability to produce virtue through a refinement of desire that had valuable economic effects. The markets produced by the desire for luxury were ones that also generated a suite of other positive elements. David Hume, writing in a 1752 essay titled 'On Luxury', noted the social advantages that luxury fostered. 'The encrease and consumption of all the commodities', Hume writes,

> which serve to the ornament and pleasure of life, are advantageous to society; because, at the same time that they multiply those innocent gratifications to individuals, they are a kind of *storehouse* of labour, which, in the exigencies of state, may be turned to the public service.[2]

We see in this passage evidence of the ways that luxury by the mid-eighteenth century was potentially something that could transform the social demeanour and the cultural tastes of people. Luxury tames and civilizes; asceticism, on the other hand, contributes to vice, sadness and disorder. Hume's position on the value of luxury to the cultural status of the nation and its economic vitality is a useful reminder of the ways that culture and economy were joined in the minds of Enlightenment-era thinkers.

Hume's 1752 essay also contained a description of the global nature of these economic transformations. Global trade not only spurs domestic transformation but it also helps transform the wider horizon within which desires unfold. Markets, both domestic and global, do important cultural work by encouraging industry and improvement. The wealth generated by merchants who are able to satisfy desires holds immense potential, and Hume equates the industrial products created domestically with the luxuries provided by the global market. David Hume's celebratory stance on the virtues of luxury provides a helpful indication of the ways that commerce and trade – or more generally stated, the global market – were able to transform the terms of human desire, and were thus intimately bound to the logic of both self-expression and exchange. It is useful to explore these issues in a different dimension by considering how the father of capitalism, Adam Smith, explored the relationships between passions and markets in his work before *The Wealth of Nations* (1776). In his *Theory of Moral Sentiments*, published in 1759, we see evidence of the ways that Smith considered the cultural effects of marketplace interactions. Specifically, we can see how he began to piece together an argument about how commerce – especially in its global dimensions – might be changed or transformed by the cultural and social environments within which people operated.

Smith poses a series of questions to the readers of his book related to his thoughts on the origins of economy, exchange and commerce. Significantly, these origins are found in the innate desires of humans. Smith argues at the outset of a passage related to the question of cultural valuations of avarice and poverty that the 'concern for the sentiments of everyone else is the main reason why we pursue riches and avoid poverty'.[3] The profit motive in this formulation stems from sentiment and sympathy. This insight leads Smith to pose the question: 'what *is* the purpose of all the toil and bustle of this world? What is the purpose of avarice and ambition, of the pursuit of wealth, power and pre-eminence? Is it to supply the necessities of nature?'[4] His answer is a seemingly simple one in which he argues that 'the wages of the poorest labourer' are sufficient to provide for one's basic necessities.[5] The desire that people have to appear wealthy, to live a better life, to experience quality beyond that which might be considered necessity is the key to understanding commercial exchange, the origins of the profit motive and the imbrication of culture and economy. Smith probes what he calls the source of that 'emulation that runs through all the different ranks of men', and he seeks to understand the advantages that may be obtained by attempting to satisfy what he calls 'that great purpose of human life that we call "bettering our condition"'.[6] People, Smith suggests, seek to better their condition not because of the material benefits of doing so but because of the elevated social and cultural status that external displays of wealth bring.

Smith remains suspicious of attempts to gain wealth merely for the social attention and 'emulation' it might bring. In a different passage of the book, Smith laments how the desperate search for new objects that indicate the power and worth of the one possessing them has fundamentally damaging consequences. In a section dedicated to the 'effect of utility', Smith asks, 'How many people ruin themselves by laying out money on trinkets of frivolous utility?'[7] He describes in his answer a loathsome figure, burdened by the material show of wealth that generates its own culture of ostentatious display. Altogether, Smith provides in *Theory of Moral Sentiments* an explanation for how culture and commerce interacted. A desire to be noticed or considered a person of rank generated increasingly ostentatious displays of wealth. In contrast, poverty or conscious asceticism marked a person as beneath consideration. People engage in commerce for two reasons, then. They seek to improve their conditions, but in such a way that the social and cultural prestige associated with certain forms of living or with the acquisition of certain material goods marked them culturally in significant ways.

Adam Smith's *Theory of Moral Sentiments*, of course, is not his most famous work. *The Wealth of Nations* (1776) offered new ways to understand the cultural significance of a market in luxuries. Smith defined luxury in cultural ways, describing the difference between a luxury and necessity as something that would evince shame in a person were they to not have it: items 'but whatever the custom of the country renders it indecent for creditable people, even of the lowest order, to be without'.[8] For example, a linen shirt, which any 'creditable day-labourer would be ashamed to appear in public without … the want of which would be supposed to denote that disgraceful degree of poverty, which, its presumed, no body can well fall into without extreme bad conduct'.[9] Shame then is the element that distinguishes the necessary from the luxurious. Culture, not surprisingly, has 'established rules of decency' and emotional regimes of shame that translate into basic economic considerations of luxury and necessity.[10] *The Wealth of Nations* was an intellectual blockbuster, and it set the stage for larger debates about the role of commerce, the creation of inequality and the value of luxury. In short, *The Wealth of Nations* transformed the terms of the luxury debates, creating a new field within which debates about the connections between commerce and culture unfolded. We can see evidence of this shift in the transformed ways that the political left wrote about the significance of labour, the origins of poverty and the virtues of leisure.

Leisure and work

William Godwin, whose 1797 collection *The Enquirer* delved into these topics, provides an example of how the issues that so animated the eighteenth-century luxury debates were reinterpreted in the new light of capitalist exchange. In his essay 'Riches and Poverty', for instance, Godwin seems to echo aspects of Smith's language on poverty, writing that

> Poverty is an enormous evil. By poverty I understand the state of a man possessing no permanent property, in a country where wealth and luxury have already gained a secure establishment. He then that is born to poverty, may be said, under another name, to be born a slave.[11]

Indeed, wealth held value for Godwin only to the degree that it provides luxury, eases life and produces culture; poverty is bad because it impedes these things. 'As to the abridgment of life we are scarcely competent judges, since wealth, expended in sensuality and indulgence, is scarcely less hostile to the protraction of existence'.[12] Wealth finds resolution most clearly in the freedom of leisure. The luxury of not working is the true benefit of wealth, in part because it allows a greater human capacity for creativity to be unleashed. Without leisure, culture dissolves, and leisure is produced by the time-savings embodied in wealth.

Many of these themes reappeared in other essays by Godwin. 'Avarice and Profusion' (the essay that prompted Thomas Malthus to write *An Essay on the Principle of Population*), for instance, revolves around Godwin's descriptions of the perfect economy. The 'superficial' and 'erroneous' view of a perfect economy privileges luxury as a motor of economic development. This image of luxury's importance culminates in a false view of the economy: 'Industry has been thought a pleasing spectacle. What is more delightful than to see our provinces covered with corn, and our ports crowded with vessels? What more admirable than the products of human ingenuity?'[13] Godwin mercilessly mocks the idea that luxury helps the working poor, writing

> It has been inferred, that the most commendable proceeding in a man of wealth, is to encourage the manufacture of his country, and to spend as large a portion of his property as possible in generating this beautiful spectacle of a multitude of human beings, industriously employed, well fed, warmly clothed, cleanly and contented.[14]

Luxury, for Godwin, was a moral catastrophe, one that distracted from the real purpose of economic exchange.

> Every man who invents a new luxury, adds so much to the quantity of labour entailed on the lower orders of society. The same may be affirmed of every man who adds a new dish to his table, or who imposes a new tax upon the inhabitants of his country. It is a gross and ridiculous error to suppose that the rich pay for any thing.[15]

The implication of Godwin's argument was to craft a positive view of the miser (as opposed to the profligate rich man). Avarice, typically understood as a moral failure, is in Godwin's view positively charged by virtue of the fact that it allows workers a form of leisure. This leisure time is then a more virtuous spur to economic and cultural development than any mere bauble.

Determining the moral nature of the market was one of the major issues animating Godwin's work. He dipped into the topic in the essay 'On Avarice and Profusion' and continued the analysis in sections of the essay 'Trades and Professions'. The topic is significant for this essay because it allows us to see the ways that the market was perceived, even in the late eighteenth century, as something that warped or deformed the personality of the trader. Godwin's opening position was that markets were essentially evil, a position he arrived at by initiating a thought experiment in which he imagined the historical invention of money and trade. 'Barter and sale being once introduced', Godwin explains,

> the invention of a circulating medium in the precious metals gave solidity to the evil, and afforded a field upon which for the rapacity and selfishness of man to develop all their refinements. It is from this point that the inequality of fortunes took their commencement.[16]

Inequality was the evil twin present at the birth of the market. Godwin expands on these arguments by suggesting that traders are little more than parasitic middlemen who exhibit all the femininity of the courtier and the dishonesty of the thief:

> There is one thing that stands out grossly to the eye, and respecting which there can be no dispute: I mean, the servile and contemptible arts which we so frequently see played off by the tradesman. He is so much in the habit of exhibiting a bended body, that he scarcely knows how to stand upright. Every word he utters is graced with a simper or a smile. He exhibits all the arts of the male

coquette; not that he wishes his fair visitor to fall in love with his person, but that he may induce her to take off his goods.[17]

The gender critique of the merchant class continues:

> Yet this being, this supple, fawning, cringing creature, this systematic, cold-hearted liar, this being, every moment of whose existence is centred in the sordid consideration of petty gains, has the audacity to call himself a man. One half of all the human beings we meet, belong, in a higher or lower degree, to the class here delineated. In how perverted a state of society have we been destined to exist?[18]

Merchants, both individually and as a class, are debased through their connection to the market and to commerce. Commercial activities corrode the soul of the merchant, and this corrosion extends to a larger perversion of the entire society. The culture of commerce – in Godwin's vision, at least – deforms and perverts. The luxury debates of the eighteenth century – in which the material wealth of empire, the market for new commodities and the moral languages of luxury and necessity, greed and prodigality circled one another – provided the context for a robust discussion of the ways that commercial changes helped shape a broader discussion of emotional and moral life. In the early nineteenth century, ideas about the cultural effects of marketplace transactions took on renewed significance. That said, we have so far ignored a different set of questions that animated early nineteenth-century discussion of the marketplace that revolved around the basic question: what called the marketplace into being? We have so far examined the issue from the standpoint of desire and how desires shaped the market. We turn now to examine the ways that the market shaped desire and its expression.

Supply and demand

The issue of the origins of the market, and how the market related to or intersected with human desire and culture, was taken up by Jean-Baptiste Say in the first decades of the nineteenth century. Rather than subscribing to the view that desire preceded the market, Say famously flipped that logic upside-down, suggesting instead that the market created desire. Writing in his *Treatise on Political Economy*, published in 1803, Say expounds on the relationships between desire, accumulation and the global economy. Providing evidence of the ways these concepts were related to one another in the minds of early nineteenth-century Europeans, Say argues that

> When the Europeans had recently discovered the passage round the Cape of Good Hope and the continent of America, their world was suddenly expanded to the East and West; and such was the infinity of new objects of desire in two hemispheres, whereof one was not at all, and the other but very imperfectly, known before, that an adventurer had only to make the voyage, and was sure of selling his returns to great advantage.[19]

The commercial logic of mercantilism shaped an emotional context for desire, and then with the invention of capitalism in the eighteenth century that emotional context changed. Say perhaps recognized this shift, and sought to understand the expressions of desire – now shaped through market forces rather than the other way around – as the key to understanding both modern economic and modern emotional relationships.

One of the ways that Say examined the logic of consumption as a means not only to satisfy desire but also to spur economic transformations was to distinguish between various forms of consumption, most significantly for our purposes the differences between productive and unproductive consumption. Say was especially dismissive of 'unproductive consumption', the consuming of food or of fashion. His critique of unproductive consumption focuses on those areas of life that we might consider the most indicative of the cultural realm. He writes that

> In most countries, if a part of what is squandered in frivolous and hazardous amusements, whether in town or country, were spent in the embellishment and convenience of the habitations, in suitable clothing, in neat and useful furniture, or in the instruction of the population, the whole community would soon assume an appearance of improvement, civilization and affluence, infinitely more attractive to strangers, as well as more gratifying to the people themselves.[20]

Say is clearly firing another shot in the luxury wars with this position. Consumption, ideally, would be functional – 'useful', to employ his term – and would thereby contribute to an orderly but affluent society. While 'Say's Law' would later be interpreted as demonstrating the power of the market over the desires of the individual consumer – a type of 'if you build it, they will come' mentality of the early nineteenth century, it is striking to note how resistant Say was to the idea that the market might hold such powerful sway over the desires of consumers.

Say placed an inordinate emphasis on the limited value of luxury, seeing it in ways that highlighted the 'unproductive' nature of finery. 'Misery', he writes, 'is the inseparable companion of luxury'.[21] One consequence of such unproductive consumption was to highlight inequality. Consumption of luxury items that serve merely to oversatisfy desire, or to satisfy it in ways that were beyond the normal use-value of an item, was to be considered a moral blight that promoted a 'squandering' of valuable resources. This marketplace for cultural goods was in fact a danger zone, one that might render the consumer deadened to other sensations. Say's argument contains several important points. We see in his work not only the idea that markets might shape desires (that supply creates demand), but more importantly that the market might heighten desires inappropriately. The concatenation of passions that the market might first generate and then satisfy held dangerous consequences. Consumption was unproductive, meaning that it did not generate a flood of virtuous pathways, and in this respect Say was unlike previous critics who saw luxury and prodigality as economic positives. Say also notes how consumption, luxury and inequality generate socially damaging relationships built more on envy and greed then on generosity and charity. Say also notes the difference between ephemeral 'artificial' wants and those he termed 'real ones'. The explosive market for the former supplanted the latter. From the standpoint of how Say imagines the nexus of commerce and culture, we can see that he remains critical of luxury but also views the marketplace as a forum through which desire was channelled. The market was neutral; consumers and their desires were not, and in fact were predictably tainted by moral failure.

Consumers and capital

Say's ideas indicate some of the ways that the marketplace was understood to function in the early nineteenth century, and his positions certainly set the stage for later critique of consumption, consumerism and the role of luxury in society. By 1847, shifts in the logic of social and economic organization demanded new ways of understanding the relationships between market forces and human culture. The global nature of this social and economic organization was especially significant to Karl Marx, who wrote in the *Communist Manifesto* that he was witnessing a novel type of market, one that had its origin in the Columbian exchanges of the sixteenth century but that was now coming into its own. Marx commented on these issues in a number of areas, but established the world-historical significance of Columbus's voyages by noting the ways in which that event ushered a transformed global market. Famously describing capitalism's corrosive abilities to make sure that 'all that is solid melts into air', Marx explains that the global market has transformed the nature of the bourgeoisie and shaped a new culture at the same time. Marx of course made similar claims about the timing of the creation of the world market in volume one of *Capital*. In the section of that work dedicated to the circular motions of money to commodity to money (and the inverse, commodity to money to commodity), Marx fixates on the transmutative properties of the marketplace in order to distinguish between the origins of use- and exchange-values. Marx's capitalist, the 'rational miser' who achieves a 'ceaseless augmentation of value' by 'throwing his money again and again into circulation', merely confirms the alchemical power of the marketplace, that magical space originating in the sixteenth century in which 'value has acquired the occult ability to add value to itself. It brings forth living offspring or at least lays golden eggs'.[22] If there is a culture to Marx's global market, it is a magical one that allows capitalism – at least in its theoretical form – to achieve continuous and miraculous growth. Yet Marx also hints at the ways that one's relationship to the market, or the ways in which one interacts with or participates in the market, shapes that person in unmistakable ways.

We have to this point used the term 'market' in abstract ways, but it is important to remember that the nineteenth century saw a dramatic material shift in markets. As historian Michael Miller explains, 'The department store was not only the bourgeoisie's world; it was the most visible symbol of how that world was changing'.[23] Department stores like the Bon Marché represented a gesture towards the 'democratization of luxury', but one that still reified status and hierarchy in new ways.[24]

> The department store alone did not lead to the appearance of a consumer society, but it did stand at the centre of this phenomenon. As an economic mechanism it made that society possible, and as an institution with a large provincial trade it made the culture of consumption a national one. Above all, as a business enterprise predicated upon mass retailing, it played an active role in cultivating consumption as a way of life among the French bourgeoisie.[25]

The dramatic creation of new avenues for commerce – the department store perhaps most significant among them – was of course not limited just to France. Across Europe and North America, we see the growth of new retail settings and the creation of the large department store model. Miller explains that the process began in the 1840s but expanded quickly in the next two decades, when a wide variety of retail empires were founded, including Lord & Taylor, Arnold, Constable and Co, Macy's, Marshall Fields and the Bon Marché. It is worth noting that the process did not abate; Gimbels, Harrods, Selfridges and Berlin's *Kaufhaus des Westens* were each launched between 1885 and 1910.

The department store represented a dramatic new way not only of matching supply with demand, but more importantly to manufacture desire itself. Unlike the old luxury debates, which sought to describe desire for material objects as moral failures or as the inability to appropriately assign value to an object, the new venues for commerce raised a different set of debates around the turn of the twentieth century. Georg Simmel, in his great work *The Philosophy of Money* (1900), described the psychic hold that material objects held over consumers. Importantly for Simmel, the logic of the marketplace was one that required a new psychological approach to possession and valuation, one in which a person was required to constantly measure the value of different objects through the lens of fungible money. Simmel explains that

> The value of an object acquires such visibility and tangibility as it possesses through the fact that one object is offered for another. This reciprocal balancing, through which each economic object expresses its value in another object, removes both objects from the sphere of merely subjective significance.[26]

Recognizing that the process of assigning value was a precarious and emotional one, Simmel's work suggests that desire itself underwent important changes around the turn of the twentieth century, when it was suddenly possible to assign a monetary value to an item, thus relating its value to a suite of emotional and psychological processes on the part of the consumer.

Mind and self

One of the worrisome facts of this new market was the recognition that the interaction of supply and demand was never a fully thought-out or rational process on the part of producer or consumer. Indeed, a mark of degeneracy at the time was the inability to set aside one's emotions when one entered the marketplace. Max Nordau, for instance, explains in his 1895 work *Degeneration* that the surfeit of products in the marketplace could induce a failed set of object relations. Examining the figure of the 'oniomaniac', Nordau concluded that unthinking accumulation was a symptom of degeneracy.

> The present rage for collecting, the piling up, in dwellings, of aimless bric-á-brac, which does not become any more useful or beautiful by being fondly called *bibelots*, appears to us in a completely new light when we know that [Valentin] Magnan has established the existence of an irresistible desire among the degenerate

to accumulate useless trifles. It is so firmly imprinted and so peculiar that Mag-
nan declares it to be a stigma of degeneration, and has invented for it the name
'oniomania', or 'buying craze'. This is not to be confounded with the desire for
buying which possesses those who are in the first stage of general paralysis. The
purchases of these persons are due to their delusion as to their own greatness.
They lay in great supplies because they fancy themselves millionaires. The oniomaniac, on the contrary, neither buys enormous quantities of one and the same
thing, nor is the price a matter of indifference to him as with the paralytic. He is
simply unable to pass by any lumber without feeling an impulse to acquire it.[27]

The market, in other words, could overwhelm sensibility, rendering the consumer
unable to function in modern society.

Max Nordau's *Degeneration* was published in 1895; Georg Simmel's *Philosophy of
Money* first appeared in 1900. The previous year saw the publication of Thorstein Veblen's *The Theory of the Leisure Class*, a book that helped shape contemporary understandings of the ways that consumerism, commerce and culture intersected around
the turn of the twentieth century. Veblen viewed the emergence of the 'leisure class'
as a distinct historical phenomenon, one tied inextricably to important shifts in what
he called the 'sequence of cultural evolution'.[28] Most significantly, the origins of the
leisure class could be traced to the 'beginning of ownership'. In this way, Veblen tied
the emergence of a market (and legal norms that protected property rights) with
radical cultural changes. As people responded to the emergence of this new class
of people and perhaps sought to join its ranks, they adopted a range of new cultural practices and social norms. Veblen explains the primary mover of these cultural
transformations was the money economy. He writes in his chapter on 'pecuniary
emulation' that the

> motive that lies at the root of ownership is emulation .... The possession of
> wealth confers honour; it is an invidious distinction. Nothing equally cogent can
> be said for the consumption of goods, nor for any other conceivable incentive to
> acquisition, and especially not for any incentive to the accumulation of wealth.[29]

Wealth, accumulation and consumption could serve as markers of status and distinction. 'Conspicuous consumption of valuable goods is a means of reputability to the
gentleman of leisure. As wealth accumulates on his hands, his own unaided effort
will not avail to sufficiently put his opulence in evidence by this method'.[30] Veblen's
insights, perhaps intuitive today, nonetheless indicate more than just a new front in
the luxury wars. Veblen's identification of the ways that acquisition and leisure had
been weaponized for use in the fashioning of social hierarchies was a novel way of
imagining the power of market forces.

Veblen recognized that consumption was a form of self-fashioning. Accumulation
– now no longer tied specifically to the satisfaction of individual desires – was instead
usefully considered as a tool of social engineering and a factor in class formation and
self-identification. In this way, *fin-de-siècle* social science could observe the ways that
the market had been leveraged into social capital. 'It becomes indispensable', Veblen
explains,

to accumulate, to acquire property, in order to retain one's good name. When accumulated goods have in this way once become the accepted badge of efficiency, the possession of wealth presently assumes the character of an independent and definitive basis of esteem.[31]

In Veblen's estimation, these parallel processes of accumulation and display represented a new formulation and deployment of capital in the service of social mobility and consolidation.

> The possession of goods, whether acquired aggressively by one's own exertion or passively by transmission through inheritance from others, becomes a conventional basis of reputability. The possession of wealth ... becomes, in popular apprehension, itself a meritorious act. Wealth is now itself intrinsically honourable and confers honour on its possessor. By a further refinement, wealth acquired passively by transmission from ancestors or other antecedents presently becomes even more honorific than wealth acquired by the possessor's own effort.[32]

Commerce, in this formulation, was a subset of behaviours that represented a de-escalation of social (and potentially, political) violence in favour of a demilitarized marketplace in which aggressive tendencies could be relegated to the past in favour of competitive forms of acquisition.

Veblen identified certain patterns of consumption that together cohered into a set of cultural attitudes and practices. Such practices were useful as a type of social display, but Veblen did not discount the personal pleasures that accompanied conspicuous consumption and leisure, which he suggested remained 'directed to the comfort of the consumer himself, and is, therefore, a mark of the master'.[33] Even when conspicuous consumption was undertaken simply for the pleasure of the act, it nonetheless continued to function as a vehicle of cultural expression of the most significant values of a social class. A culture of commerce and patterns of leisure might in the end provide the tools of social differentiation. Writing around the turn of the twentieth century, this observation developed in the context of the high inequality characteristic of the *fin-de-siècle* and the gilded age.

Veblen's insights into the cultural meanings of consumption and leisure worked in two ways. Consumption of luxuries and time indicated a certain social status and also produced feelings of pleasure in the conspicuous consumer. Consumption, in other words, was social and individual at once. Researchers in the early twentieth century remained fascinated by the dynamic movement between individual pleasures and larger social structures, and there were significant attempts to unravel the connections between individual lived experience and broader social types. Psychoanalysis provides one example. Sigmund Freud's short essay 'Character and Anal Eroticism', published in March 1908, provided an argument that a person's attitude towards money – and by extension commerce – was driven by one's psychosexual development. The anal personality type, which is found in a person who Freud believed was 'especially orderly, parsimonious and obstinate', was a result of delayed toilet training.[34] Freud's essay was a bombshell. It suggested to other researchers at the time that behaviours that seemed innate were in fact the outer expression of embodied experiences of childhood. The implications of Freud's argument in the essay were dramatic in that he suggested that psychosexual development produced not just certain behaviours in adults, but more importantly, character types that informed the behaviours of entire social classes. Freudian characterology, in other words, could be used to understand the culture of capitalism, economic exchange and the social mores of the bourgeoisie.

Freud's disciple Sándor Ferenczi addressed these issues in a 1914 essay titled the 'The Ontogenesis of the Interest in Money', in which he traced the development of a symbolic chain connecting faeces to money. His conclusions bear on the issue of the culture of commerce in that he suggests that capitalism and market exchange were not rational processes, but ones deeply informed by psychosexual development. 'The character of capitalism', Ferenczi argues, is 'not purely practical and utilitarian, but libidinous and irrational' because the mechanisms of exchange – money – are invested with values derived from psychosexual development.[35] Money is not simply money, but something more deeply connected to psychosexual processes tied to the anal phase of development. The implications of Ferenczi's argument were that capitalism and the market were arenas of human activity with entrenched meanings that then drove human behaviours and their cultural meaning and significance. The culture of capitalism, in Ferenczi's estimation, was an expression of anal eroticism.

Psychoanalytic attempts to understand the character of – and the libidinous energies that drove – capitalism represented a new way to understand the subterranean motivations that propelled the market. These market forces were not just the sum of millions of small interactions but were an intimate part of the structure of global exchange. Ernest Jones, for instance, connected Freudian ideas about the anal character of capitalism to global financial principles founded on the gold standard. As Jones explained in 1916,

> Modern economists know that the idea of wealth means simply 'a lien on future labour', and that any counters on earth could be used as a convenient emblem for it just as well as a 'gold standard'. Metal coins however, and particularly gold, are unconscious symbols of excrement, the material from which most of our sense of possession, in infantile times, was derived.[36]

Prominent economists also adopted the language of psychoanalysis when describing the inner workings of the global economy. John Maynard Keynes, for example, connected the gold standard to the libidinous energies of the anal stage. In his 1930 essay 'Auri Sacra Fames', Keynes invoked Freudian thought on gold and its symbolic meanings when writing on the gold standard and the transfers of wealth among the various central banks that lubricated the global economy.[37] Psychoanalytic theories about psychosexual development, characterology and the libidinous character of capitalism, in other words, were incorporated into the ways the global economy was thought to function.

Uniting psychoanalysis and economics was not just a way to make the global economy comprehensible through an appeal to common human experiences and a culture derived from those experiences. The positions generated by Freud and his followers could also be used to understand larger social structures. Erich Fromm, writing in *Zeitschrift für Sozialforschung* in 1932, used Freudian characterology to produce an analysis of bourgeois society informed not only by Freudian categories but also by Marxist principles. In this way, Fromm suggested that the Freudian character traits of 'orderliness, parsimony and obstinacy' could also be used to understand society as a whole and to examine the traits he considered central to modern mass society. His conclusion was that anality was peculiarly connected to and displayed in bourgeois society. Fromm acknowledges that acquisition is key to understanding capitalism, and in this regard he was not significantly different from previous analysts of the economic order. Looking at the acquisitive personality, its links to anality and the foundations of a modern capitalist economic order, Fromm suggests that bourgeois culture was indebted to those who

> enjoy a possession only if no one else has anything like it. They are inclined to regard everything in life as property and to protect everything that is 'private' from outside invasions. This attitude does not apply to money and possessions only; it also applies to human beings, feelings, memories and experiences.[38]

The spirit of capitalism, and especially the spirit of the bourgeois order within which commerce unfolded, derived from a set of common human experiences. While the bourgeois spirit might help shape the experience of psychosexual development, Fromm was clear in the ways that anal eroticism was a fundamental part of the modern global economy. Fromm approached these issues again later in his career. In an essay titled 'Freud's Model of Man and Its Social Determinants' published in 1969, Fromm equates what he calls 'Freud's homo sexualis' and the 'classic homo economicus'.[39] Indeed, the two types were qualitatively identical. Fromm writes that the

> social determination of Freud's theory by the spirit of the market economy does not mean that the theory is wrong, except in its claim of describing the situation of man as such; as a description of interpersonal relations in bourgeois society, it is valid for the majority of people.[40]

In this way, Fromm's insights into the emotional foundations of capitalism and the culture of commerce developed in relationship with other members of the New Left who offered critiques of the cultural products of capitalism.

Frankfurt School thinkers like Theodor Adorno and Max Horkheimer sought to understand the superstructural products of capitalist exchange. Their model influenced Erich Fromm and Herbert Marcuse, whose influential position within the New Left meant that the culture of commerce and capitalism was a target of critical theory in the 1960s and beyond.

Marcuse's 1964 book *One-Dimensional Man: Studies in the Ideology of Advanced Industrial Society* cemented his fame as a leading critic of the New Left. Marcuse produces an analysis of the social and cultural forms produced by capitalism in the mid-twentieth century. Most significantly, market forces and the logic of capitalist exchange had produced a series of false choices: ideological traps in which people were constrained. The market was key to these processes. 'Independence of thought', Marcuse writes, 'autonomy, and the right to political opposition are being deprived of their basic critical function in a society which seems increasingly capable of satisfying the needs of the individuals through the way in which it is organized'.[41] He continues, suggesting that this withering of critical capability was an outgrowth of advanced industrial capitalism:

> the apparatus imposes its economic and political requirements for defense and expansion in labor time and free time, on the material and intellectual culture … For 'totalitarian' is not only a terroristic political coordination of society, but also a non-terroristic economic-technical coordination which operates through the manipulation of needs by vested interests.[42]

The culminating principle of this system is one that produces conditions of unfreedom. The market – and the society and culture it produces – renders people unable to break free.

The most important section of the book for our purposes is Marcuse's chapter on culture and what he dubs 'repressive desublimation'. For Marcuse, a central problem was the integration of culture into the logic of the marketplace, a trend that neutered high culture and rendered it incapable of functioning as an arena of criticism or resistance. Culture collapses as a realm of criticism or utopianism. Dreams are contaminated with advertisements. Marcuse explains that in the course of this integration, 'higher culture becomes part of the material culture. In this transformation, it loses the greater part of its truth'.[43] The consequence of the expression of culture as just another industry that follows the logic of other productive realms is that the people who do not fit in – either in life or as characters in artistic productions – are also assimilated. 'They are no longer images of another way of life but rather freaks or types of the same life, serving as an affirmation rather than negation of the established order'.[44] Whereas in previous periods, culture remained an area of human life and expression that was capable of advancing a critical position, by the 1960s culture was merely a commodity like any other. Marcuse found the consequences devastating: 'Pleasure', he writes, 'generates submission'.[45] If at one point culture could be said to have stood outside the marketplace and its corrosive powers, by the mid-twentieth century it had been enveloped. The market creates a levelled cultural landscape; anything above or below grade finds itself obliterated.

Fromm and Marcuse represent a perspective on the market coming from the political left. The liberal and conservative centre – represented by the logicians of the Austrian school of economics – envisioned a market that through the profit motive sought to operate in ever more efficient ways, and the market was fundamentally value-neutral. Any attempt to inject notions of morality or ethics – we might call these cultural attitudes – represented an attempt to control or tame an otherwise uncontrollable force. Because the market consisted of millions of small interactions, any attempt to assert some overarching control was a fool's errand. The Uruguayan economist Ramon Diaz, for instance, issued an attack on what he called the 'moralizing of economic life'.[46] His essay titled 'The Political Economy of Nostalgia' was based on the idea that price controls and 'just price doctrine' constituted an inappropriate moralization of the marketplace. Indeed, Diaz suggests that utopian visions of the reintroduction of morality into economic life were nothing less than a nostalgic return to medieval principles. The market, an abstract and swirling chaos, resists attempts at institutional morality: 'There is nothing moral or immoral about the production of so many tons of pig iron or so many barrels of oil more or less'.[47]

★ ★ ★ ★ ★

Thinkers like Fromm and Marcuse envisioned the market and its culture differently than earlier critics. Unlike the concerns that animated the partisans of the eighteenth-century luxury debates, twentieth-century observers suggested that the market was created from common human experiences. While visions of the market prior to Jean-Baptiste Say contemplated it as a mechanism for satisfying human desires, by the nineteenth century the market was assumed to take on a different role, one that could actively shape those desires even as it satisfied them. In neither case, however, was it assumed that the market was somehow neutral or value-free. Even those who analysed the market and related it to emotional life (whether that was constituted socially or psychosexually) never imagined that its culture was value-free or that it was subject to human control. The shifting terrain upon which the market was thought to exist or to function, like the way in which the market was related to aspects of human experience or emotion, has changed dramatically in the modern period. And the ways in which the market itself was imagined – its qualities, its power and even its ability to transform the basic elements of human existence – are deeply reflective of historical changes in the culture of the West.

Notes

1 J.M. Keynes, 'Economic Possibilities for Our Grandchildren', in *Essays in Persuasion*, Harcourt, Brace and Company, 1932, 369–70.
2 M. Berg, *Luxury and Pleasure in Eighteenth-Century Britain*, Oxford: Oxford University Press, 2005, ix; 'Hume, Essays, Moral, Political, and Literary, Part II, Essay II, Of Refinement in the Arts, Library of Economics and Liberty', www.econlib.org/library/LFBooks/Hume/hmMPL25.html (accessed 17 November 2017).
3 A. Smith, *The Theory of Moral Sentiments*, New ed., London: H.G. Bohn, 1853, 70.
4 Ibid.
5 Ibid.
6 Ibid., 70–71.
7 Ibid., 259.
8 A. Smith, *The Wealth of Nations*, New York: Modern Library, 2000, 938–39.
9 Ibid., 939.
10 Ibid., 939.
11 W. Godwin, *The Enquirer: Reflections on Education, Manners, and Literature*, Edinburgh: J. Anderson, 1823, 144.
12 Ibid., 146.
13 Ibid., 153.
14 Ibid., 154.
15 Ibid., 158.
16 Ibid., 195.
17 Ibid., 197.
18 Ibid., 198.

19 J.B. Say, *A Treatise on Political Economy: Or, The Production, Distribution, and Consumption of Wealth*, trans. Clement Cornell Biddle, Grigg & Elliot, 1832, 25.

20 Ibid., 360.

21 Ibid., 369.

22 K. Marx, *Capital: A Critique of Political Economy*, London: Penguin Books in association with New Left Review, 1981, 254–55.

23 M.B. Miller, *The Bon Marché: Bourgeois Culture and the Department Store, 1869–1920*, Princeton, NJ: Princeton University Press, 1981, 4.

24 Ibid., 166.

25 Ibid., 166–67.

26 G. Simmel, *The Philosophy of Money*, 3rd enl. ed., London: Routledge, 2004, 79.

27 M.S. Nordau, *Degeneration*, New York: D. Appleton, 1895, 27.

28 T. Veblen, *The Theory of the Leisure Class: An Economic Study of Institutions*, London: Macmillan and Company, 1912, 22.

29 Ibid., 25–26.

30 Ibid., 75.

31 Ibid., 29.

32 Ibid., 29.

33 Ibid., 72.

34 S. Freud, *The Standard Edition of the Complete Psychological Works of Sigmund Freud*, London: Hogarth Press, 1953, IX:169.

35 S. Ferenczi, *Sex in Psycho-Analysis (Contributions to Psycho-Analysis)*, New York: Dover Publications, 1960, 275.

36 E. Jones, *Papers on Psycho-Analysis*, 5th ed., Boston, MA: Beacon Press, 1961, 129. The essay was first published as 'The Theory of Symbolism' in the *Brit Journal of Psych*, vol IX; 29 January 1916.

37 J.M. Keynes, 'Auri Sacra Fames', in *Essays in Persuasion*, Harcourt, Brace and Company, 1932, 181–85.

38 E. Fromm, *The Crisis of Psychoanalysis*, New York: Holt, Rinehart, Winston, 1970, 143–44.

39 Ibid., 31.

40 Ibid., 31.

41 H. Marcuse, *One-Dimensional Man: Studies in the Ideology of Advanced Industrial Society, 2nd Edition*, Boston, MA: Beacon Press, 1991, 1.

42 Ibid., 2–3.

43 Ibid., 58.

44 Ibid., 59.

45 Ibid., 75.

46 R. Diaz, 'The Political Economy of Nostalgia', in F.A. von Hayek et al. (eds), *Toward Liberty: Essays in Honor of Ludwig von Mises on the Occasion of His 90th Birthday*, vol. II, Menlo Park, CA: Institute for Humane Studies, 1971, 441.

47 Ibid., 451.

32

EPILOGUE

Cultural history in retrospect

Hannu Salmi

In the evening of 15 April 2019, devastating news spread around the world in a few seconds. The medieval cathedral Notre Dame de Paris, a UNESCO World Heritage Site, known so well not only to the locals but to millions of travellers from every continent, had caught fire at 6:18 pm local time. Soon its roof and spire were in flames. The fire fighting continued until the next day, when *BBC News* summarized:

> The fire, declared fully extinguished some 15 hours after it began, ravaged the 850-year-old building's roof and caused its spire to collapse. But firefighters who worked through the night managed to save the Paris landmark's main stone structure, including its two towers.[1]

Considering how many irreplaceable works of arts and relics from the past it housed, the Parisian catastrophe could undoubtedly have been worse, but the destruction was still irreparable, since, as the news coverage noted, Notre Dame is 'deeply rooted in France's cultural history'.[2] The 'main stone structure' of the cathedral was preserved, but much was lost, for example the centuries-old wooden roof structures that had been carved by medieval carpenters. Their cultural legacy, still visible to modern eyes, was destroyed by the embrace of the hungry flames.[3]

The fire at Notre Dame was a disaster that started in the attic beneath the cathedral's roof where renovation work was taking place. This was unintentional, but sometimes the destruction of cultural heritage can be initiated consciously with an intention to cause harm to sites that are valued in order to wound those people who cherish them. In 2015, the ancient city of Palmyra in present-day Syria, a UNESCO World Heritage Site as well, came suddenly into the headlines. ISIS soldiers conquered the city and consciously destroyed the Temple of Baalshamin and many other historic buildings. Only photographs and video recordings, and of course archaeological documentation, of these monuments remain for future generations, but the ancient constructions themselves were eradicated.

Notre Dame de Paris and Palmyra are examples of historical sites that have been valued and were to be preserved for posterity. They represent cultural history in the present turbulent world. UNESCO began its world heritage programme in 1972, and the agreement has been ratified by 193 nations, but not even international treaties can safeguard remains of the past in the middle of crises, particularly in situations where historic sites are seen as cultural symbols, the destruction of which can have grave political consequences.

The question of how the past lives in the present is always relative. History lives, but it is also fragile and transient by nature. Therefore, it is important to identify means through which the past is present and to analyse the different forms of public history and *Geschichtskultur* (historical culture) around us. It is obvious that many phenomena of the past, artefacts, symbols and practices, are not part of the present horizon. Their existence, or memory, can only be restored through careful research. At the same time, what we understand and define as the past is constantly changing. Therefore, cultural history has to be written again and again. In the case of Notre Dame, for example, the stone structures themselves still stand in the very same place as they have stood since the thirteenth century, but the webs of significance that have surrounded the cathedral have been in constant flux and have undergone significant transformations. Let us only think of how Victor Hugo's novel, *Notre Dame de Paris* (1831), shaped our vision of the monument. In the 1820s, there were thoughts of deconstructing the cathedral because of its state of decay. In his preface for the novel, Hugo pointed out the need to renovate the cathedral and this idea was probably one of the leading motives behind the whole literary enterprise by Hugo.[4] But, of course, this example again turns attention to material remains. There have been countless meetings, ceremonies, gatherings and political activities that, in the end, established the cultural significance of this particular site of memory.

This volume, *The Routledge Companion to Cultural History in the Western World*, portrays cultural historical processes and developments from the thirteenth century to the present. Notre Dame, the wooden structures of which were carved from oak during the thirteenth century, could well represent the continuity that still exists between the medieval past and the present day. It has, obviously, also portrayed discontinuities, phenomena that do not exist today but were significant in their own time. And, to complexify this further, the relationship between past and present is always a question of continuities and ruptures. There are many phenomena that are simultaneously similar and dissimilar. For example, urbanization as a process can be identified throughout human history, and it is a process that has not ended but seems to extend to the uncertain future. Urban centres in the Middle Ages were the foundation of later city structures, as exemplified by such landmarks as Notre Dame. However, the cities of the thirteenth century were quite different from the industrial cities that developed in the nineteenth century. Urbanization has had regional variations that have in many ways been the salt of cultural historians' work. These differences mean that urbanization has unique local meanings and cultural ramifications. In Finland, for example, most citizens lived in cities as late as in 1969, while the majority of people in Britain, France and Germany had been urban dwellers since the nineteenth century. Many urban phenomena were only mediated representations for the rural population of Finland in the early twentieth century. Certainly, the same goes for many other regions in the world, since globally the majority of people have lived in cities only after 2008.[5] Urbanization is a story of cultural continuities, but at the same time, it is obviously full of ruptures and multiple temporalities. Currently, many of the largest cities in the world are in Africa, where urbanization can hardly be understood on the basis of nineteenth-century industrialism. In that sense, our knowledge of the Western development of urban centres in the nineteenth and twentieth centuries is not sufficient in itself for understanding the formation of megacities today. One could, therefore, wonder how relevant cultural history, as conceived in this volume, is for the future.

This book describes numerous forms of sociability and community, families and nations, sects and religious orders, local and transregional groups, emotional bonds and standards, and those communities that have been constructed by media and through oral and printed knowledge transmission to the era of digital cultures. The book pays close attention to those transborder flows and forces that, since the Middle Ages, have in various ways not only positioned these communities in relation to each other, but also opened them and set them into new contexts. The book showcases the *situatedness* of cultural history and the need to understand past phenomena in the specific contexts where they appeared. Therefore, urbanization as a global megatrend can also be viewed and analysed in those specific circumstances. In this sense, cultural history has currency as an intellectual enterprise, although there is an increasing need for comparative, transregional and global research settings.

Today, cultural studies and other heirs of the so-called 'cultural turn' are also challenged by the recent theoretical emphasis on non-human agency. In his 1991 compelling book, *We Have Never Been Modern* (*Nous n'avons jamais été modernes*), Bruno Latour began his exploration with the chapter, 'Proliferation of Hybrids', a newspaper description of the world around us. At the turn of the 1980s and 1990s, the world was in turmoil, not only in the aftermath of the Cold War, but particularly because nature and culture seemed to be more deeply intertwined than ever before. In a newspaper, 'The same article ties together chemical reactions and political reactions'.[6] Human and non-human factors seemed inseparable, like in Latour's observations on the threat of the widening hole in the ozone layer. Nature was not something to be externalized outside human behaviour and culture.

Latour's observation decades ago did not actually question or undermine cultural studies as such. It is evident that, in order to understand phenomena like the threat of the increasing hole in the ozone layer in the 1990s, it was necessary to emphasize those cultural practices that, in the end, have contributed to the success of aerosol products. In a similar vein, the present question of microplastics can be historicized by exploring how the consumption of plastics has expanded and how plastics have been woven into the fabric of the modern world. This poses two critical questions for cultural historians. On the one hand, the question is whether cultural historians define and frame their research problems in a way that meets current concerns. On the other hand, it raises the question of whether historians aim to find those kinds of forms of research cooperation where the observations of cultural studies can encounter those of natural sciences or interdisciplinary research in general.

During recent decades, post-humanist theory has presented considerable criticism towards the 'anthropocentrism' of humanities and social sciences. Cultural history can be seen as human-centred by default, the human condition having been its major source of inspiration and renewal. Predominantly, the history of the past has been written in a human-sized manner, from the perspective of individuals and communities, with an emphasis on meaning-making and webs of significance. In his book, *A Thousand Years of Nonlinear History*, Manuel DeLanda stressed the idea that human culture should not be seen as a separate sphere of reality but should be explored as an integral part of non-human flows.[7] Conceptually, DeLanda draws on the ontological ideas of the French philosophers Gilles Deleuze and Félix Guattari, according to whom reality is never stable but always in a constant state of flux. Everything flows – people, populations, genetic material, capital, raw materials, wastes, viruses. Therefore, the perspective on the past cannot derive only from human beings. The philosopher of history Ewa Domanska has answered this post-humanist challenge and emphasized the urgent need for historians to consider the critique of anthropocentrism and pay serious attention to the role of non-human agency in history.[8] In fact, this challenge, often called 'more-than-human history', has already been addressed by historians who work in such areas as animal studies, technology and digital culture.[9]

The critique against the supposed anthropocentrism of cultural studies does not necessarily mean that the concepts of culture and culturality should be abandoned or that these concepts have lost their explanatory power. However, it is reasonable and timely to revisit the basic premises of research and interests of knowledge. There are many possible avenues for fruitful insights for future research. In humanities, the critique of anthropocentrism offers an impetus to consider the boundaries of what is 'human'. The study of human/non-human entanglements is essential for understanding human-ness in the first place. Another intriguing aspect is that 'culture' has often been defined only in terms of human history, but recent scholarship in animal studies points out that non-human animals can also pass their experiences to the next generation and, in that sense, have culture too, which therefore cannot be owned only by us humans.

Despite the discussion above, it is obvious that the need for critically studying human communities, identities, emotions, gender systems and their historical development will be an essential agenda in the future. The cases of Notre Dame and Palmyra illustrate that history has profound weight in the construction of communities. Cultural history is not only retrospective; it is social engagement with issues that continue to be critical. The present prediction of future changes in climate, economy and global sustainability refers to major challenges during the forthcoming decades. For understanding these changes, and for encountering things to come, cultural history offers an approach that continues to be appealing. It remains vital to look back into the past from new perspectives, not only by focusing on things that have been remembered or trying to identify things forgotten, but also by trying to find territories that have not yet even been conceived in historical terms.

Notes

1 'Notre-Dame Fire: Millions Pledged to Rebuild Cathedral', *BBC News*, 16 April 2019, www.bbc.com/news/world-europe-47943705 (accessed 5 July 2019).
2 'Notre Dame Cathedral Is Deeply Rooted in France's Cultural History: Raheem Kassam', *Fox Business*, 17 April 2019, https://video.foxbusiness.com/v/6027304503001/#sp=-show-clips (accessed 5 July 2019).

3 This was pointed out, for example, by the architect and historian Panu Savolainen in the newspaper *Turun Sanomat*, 19 April 2019.

4 For further details, see F. Bandarin and R. van Oers, *The Historic Urban Landscape: Managing Heritage in an Urban Century*, Oxford: Wiley-Blackwell, 2012.

5 'UN Says Half the World's Population Will Live in Urban Areas by End of 2008', *International Herald Tribune*, 26 February 2008.

6 B. Latour, *We Have Never Been Modern*. Trans. Catherine Porter, Cambridge, MA:- Harvard University Press, 1993.

7 M. DeLanda, *A Thousand Years of Nonlinear History*, New York, NY: Zone Books, 1997.

8 E. Domanska, 'Beyond Anthropocentrism in Historical Studies', *Historein: A Review of the Past and Other Stories* 10, 2010, 122.

9 On animal history, see for example É. Baratay, *La Société des animaux de la Révolution à la Libération*, Paris: La Martinière, 2008; É. Baratay, *Le Point de vue animal: Une autre version de l'histoire*, Paris: Éditions du Seuil, 2012; S. Nance (ed.), *The Historical Animal*, Syracuse, NY: Syracuse University Press, 2015; S. Swart, *Riding High: Horses, Humans and History in South Africa*, Johannesburg: Wits University Press, 2010. On technology and digital history, see for example A. Nivala, H. Salmi and J. Sarjala, 'History and Virtual Topology: The Nineteenth-Century Press as Material Flow', *Historein* 17.2, 2018, http://dx.doi.org/10.12681/historein.14612; J. Winters, 'Digital History', in M. Tamm and P. Burke (eds.), *Debating New Approaches to History*, London: Bloomsbury Academic, 2018.

INDEX OF NAMES

NB: references in bold are to authors' contributions within this volume.

9780367530334